The Structure of Financial Regulation

T0304146

How should financial integration be organised in a globalising world? With the rash of financial crises in recent decades there has been a rush to introduce ever more comprehensive and complex regulation.

The Structure of Financial Regulation examines the motivation behind the regulation, who should organise it, whether it should vary according to the sector of activity or the regulatory culture of the country. Individual contributors examine the main regions of the world, with particular emphasis given to Europe and the United States. The book also examines areas where there have been clear failures, such as the scandals in the United States in recent years and the failure to address cross border issues. Attention is also given to the regulation of the core but often overlooked area of the 'plumbing' of the financial system – payments, settlement, securities depositories and custody.

Under the authoritative editorship of Geoffrey Wood and David Mayes, this authoritative volume will be a useful addition to any serious economist's bookshelves.

David G. Mayes is Advisor to the Board at the Bank of Finland, Professor of Economics at London South Bank University, Visiting Professor at the University of Auckland and Adjunct Professor at the University of Canterbury. **Geoffrey E. Wood** is Professor of Economics at Cass Business School in London, Visiting Professor of Monetary Economics at the University of Buckingham, and visiting Professorial Fellow in the Centre for Commercial Law Studies at Queen Mary and Westfield College, University of London.

Routledge international studies in money and banking

The Structure of Financial Regulation

Edited by David G. Mayes and
Geoffrey E. Wood

LONDON AND NEW YORK

First published 2007
by Routledge
2 Park Square, Milton Park, Abingdon, Oxfordshire OX14 4RN

Simultaneously published in the USA and Canada
by Routledge
711 Third Avenue, New York, NY 10017

First issued in paperback 2014

Routledge is an imprint of the Taylor and Francis Group, an informa business

© 2007 Selection and editorial matter, David G. Mayes and Geoffrey
E. Wood; individual chapters, the contributors.

Typeset in Baskerville by Wearset Ltd, Boldon, Tyne and Wear

British Library Cataloguing in Publication Data
A catalogue record for this book is available from the British Library

Library of Congress Cataloging in Publication Data
A catalog record for this book has been requested

ISBN 978-0-415-41380-0 (hbk)
ISBN 978-1-138-80610-8 (pbk)
ISBN 978-0-203-96231-2 (ebk)

To
Matti Vanhala
Governor of the Bank of Finland
who sadly did not see this work completed

Contents

Contributors

David G. Mayes, Bank of Finland.

Geoffrey Wood, Cass Business School and Bank of Finland.

Kern Alexander, University of Cambridge.

Harald Benink, Erasmus University, Rotterdam.

Robert R. Bliss, Wake Forest University and Federal Reserve Bank of Chicago.

Charles Calomiris, Columbia University.

Forrest Capie, Official Historian, Bank of England.

Robert A. Eisenbeis, Federal Reserve Bank of Atlanta.

Charles Goodhart, London School of Economics and Bank of England.

Peik Granlund, Finnish Financial Supervision Authority.

Philipp Hartmann, European Central Bank and CEPR.

Alicia García-Herrero, Bank of Spain.

Stefan Huemer, European Central Bank.

Charles M. Kahn, University of Illinois.

Karlo Kauko, Bank of Finland.

Kari Kemppainen, Bank of Finland.

Evan Kraft, Croatian National Bank.

Harry Leinonen, Bank of Finland.

Donato Masciandaro, Bocconi University.

Alastair Milne, Cass Business School and Bank of Finland.

Thorvald Grung Moe, Norges Bank.

María Nieto, Bank of Spain.

Justin O'Brien, Queen's University, Belfast.

Sander Oosterloo, Ministry of Finance, Netherlands.

João Santos, Federal Reserve Bank of New York.

Elvira Scheben, Bank of England and Deutsche Bundesbank.

Dirk Schoenmaker, Ministry of Finance, Netherlands and Free University Amsterdam.

Anna J. Schwartz, National Bureau of Economic Research.

Tuomas Takalo, Bank of Finland.

Jan Toporowski, School of Oriental and African Studies and Bank of Finland.

Preface

This book is the product of one of the Bank of Finland's two research programmes, that on the future of financial markets. The other programme is on modelling monetary policy. The Bank is concerned under the terms of its charter to ensure that, in the process of development of financial markets, Finnish firms, households and, indeed, the government have access to a financial system that is efficient and effective by international standards and gives access to the full range of financial instruments at competitive prices. It would be easy in a small country on the geographical periphery of Europe to find that innovation, the main markets and the best prices were all somewhere else and hence the economy put at a disadvantage. The Bank's research is therefore focused not merely on trying to assess where the trends in market development are going but in understanding the factors which shape them so that pressures and problems can be anticipated.

Perhaps unusually among central banks, the Bank of Finland has pursued a rather active role in ensuring the efficiency and early adoption and development of financial instruments. This includes involvement in the development of smart cards, venture capital and most recently tools for improving the efficiency of payment systems (see H. Leinonen and K. Soramäki, 'Simulating Interbank Payment and Securities Settlement Mechanisms with the BoF – PSS2 Simulator', Bank of Finland Discussion Paper 23/2003). This pre-emptive approach applies to the question of the structure of financial regulation. Finland had an unpleasant banking crisis at the beginning of the 1990s, when incidentally banking supervision was not a responsibility of the Bank, and is keen to ensure that similar mistakes are not made again. One of the clear messages from that period is that the regulatory framework has to anticipate new risks and not merely add to them. Then, much of the risk came from financial liberalisation. On the whole, specific new risks, whose realisations cause problems, are by definition almost impossible to detect but those which stem from changes in the structure of regulation are. And in this specific case we can identify them clearly from the creation of the single market in financial services in the European Economic Area. The whole point is to break down protective barriers, increase competition and contribute to a more dynamic economy. In other words it is intended to change behaviour. While Basel 2 helps provide an increasing focus on risk management within the financial system, it is not yet clear whether that will increase the volatility of the financial system along with our ability to cope with it or decrease the volatility in the first place.

We therefore organised a conference in September 2004 to complement our own research in this area. By drawing on information from a range of countries and analyses from a variety of perspectives we hoped to throw light on the state of existing knowledge on structures for financial regulation, supervision and systemic stability. We hoped then to use that base to discuss whether there were optimal structures for handling these topics and how they could be achieved. Our own perspective is that we exceeded expectations and attracted a fascinating set of papers and comments.

The conference and this book cover three main facets of the topic. The chapters by Charles Goodhart (Chapter 2) and Forrest Capie (Chapter 3) are primarily historical in character and explain not just what the systems are in the main countries but how these systems arose. There has been a complex interaction between the institutional structures and the environments in which they operate. Thus the success of the 'free banking' period in Scotland reflected not just the inherent prudence of the Calvinist tradition but the very real exposure under unlimited liability.

Anna Schwartz, in the chapter which was given as a luncheon speech at the conference, considers the lapses from regulatory standards and regulatory expectations that have occurred in recent years, sometimes in the US and sometimes elsewhere. From these she draws some implications and questions, most important the old but, as her speech emphasised, the still unsatisfactorily answered question – 'Who will regulate the regulators?'.

As the subsequent chapter, by Justin O'Brien, colourfully illustrates, the modern world lacks the neat cultural and institutional balance which served so well in Scotland's 'free banking' period. He accordingly argues that major changes to corporate governance are needed to overcome the recent scandals. The next four chapters cover the issue of the design and operation of regulatory structures that seek to handle cross-border activities. While this is primarily a European concern, Robert Bliss reveals many of the difficulties experienced in the US system. Although the US system has had around 150 years to adapt to a single market rather than the 15 or so in Europe, it still has a complex network of regulators and supervisors. While there are elements of hierarchy and a clear responsibility at the federal level for handling problems through the FDIC it is much less than ideal, as its success might suggest. If Europe is looking for a model to copy the US is not it. However, as the chapter by Dirk Schoenmaker and Sander Oosterloo reveals, Europe has considerable problems of its own. There is no clear match between supervisory responsibility and the access to resources to maintain systemic stability. This is a recipe for a serious problem. Robert Eisenbeis addresses this by setting out the agency problems and goal conflicts in Europe and suggesting routes through which they might be addressed. Kahn and Santos take the issue rather wider and discuss how countries organise all of the parts of banking system regulation. They explore in some detail how responsibilities overlap and may conflict and explain why many of the models that assume a neat compartmentalisation may be misleading and not reflect the inherent complexity and potential conflicts of interest.

The final section of the book, moves on to the problems of regulating and encouraging the development of the key parts of the financial system itself: payments, clearing and securities settlement. Kari Kemppainen sets the scene by explaining why it seems to be so difficult to develop a European level payment system. Although it may sound a caricature, much of the discussion about banks is concerned with how excessive enthusiasm and risk taking can be dampened, while in the case of payments and, to a lesser extent securities settlement, the problem is to encourage development. This is a classic network industry difficulty. Harry Leinonen goes on to offer technical solutions and ways forward that should improve efficiency while maintaining the pressure of competition. Alistair Milne extends this discussion of the need to rationalise while maintaining competitive pressure to securities clearing and settlement. The difficulties are highlighted in the final chapter by Karlo Kauko that shows how a duopoly can readily lead to a suboptimal outcome from the investors' perspective.

A more detailed guide to the structure and content of the book which resulted from this conference is to be found in the Introduction (ch. 1). We are grateful to Janet Mayes for her help with the editorial work.

1 Introduction

With the advent of Basel 2 the supervision and regulation of banks has probably reached a high water mark. Yet such detailed supervision is a new phenomenon in many countries. Even 30 years ago the controls would have been at arms length. The reform of the system has, to a large extent, been the response to unfortunate experience. While full-blown financial crises have fortunately struck only a few of the main countries all have experienced strains from time to time.

However, there are strong differences in traditions. The United States, for example, has a long history of banking regulation. Many continental European countries also have quite long-standing traditions of regulation and official supervision of financial institutions.

New Zealand is one of few countries that has reacted differently and argued that the solution to improving the prudential behaviour of banks lies not in regulating and supervising them evermore closely but making sure that the stakeholders in banks are aware of and are exposed to the risks they are running. Moreover the stakeholders, both actual and potential, need to be able to act on the information they receive and hence manage their risk exposure as they think fit. It is for the directors and managers of banks to run banks not the supervisors. Their task is to ensure compliance and to ensure that the system is designed in such a way that the sort of shocks that assail the system do not result in generalised problems that harm the economy as a whole and those who have not knowingly taken on risks in particular banks.

Much of the problem relates to bank exit. People not only think that banks are safe but the managers of banks may come to believe that they will be saved if the bank gets into trouble. Indeed the trend has been to try to make banks so large that it is inconceivable that they could be allowed to fail. In smaller economies this results in substantial monopoly. It is highly debatable whether the economies of scale match the losses from limited competition.

The organisation of regulatory and supervisory responsibility within most countries is largely the result of history rather than of optimal design but in recent years several countries have changed the arrangements.

There is no single pattern (Table 1.1). Some such as the UK, Australia and Estonia have separated supervision from the central bank and in the UK, in particular, collected a diverse group of supervisors of different parts of the financial sector under a single grouping. Some like Ireland and the Netherlands have done the exact opposite and collected all the supervisory arrangements under the aegis of the central bank. Others like Finland have set up a financial supervisory agency that is legally separate but closely integrated with the central bank, however, a part of the system (insurance) remains separate because of the compulsory state determined pension system that is administered in the private sector.

What has emerged very clearly in this bout of reorganisation is the recognition of distinct features of the task. Three can readily be identified: prudential regulation and supervision; conduct of business regulation; responsibility for the integrity of the financial system as a whole. In the case of banking and insurance it is possible to treat regulation and supervision of individual entities as a largely separate exercise from concern for the system as a whole. Indeed, there can be conflicts of interest between the two. This can, therefore, enable a helpful division of focus between a central bank charged with ensuring a stable system and a supervisory authority charged with ensuring prudentially managed institutions within it. With some exceptions reality is not that neat. Deposit insurance, for example, can sit uneasily in the middle, being the agent of neither the supervisors nor of the central bank – nor, indeed, of the banks themselves. The incentives for the different organisations may not match, with a central bank being keen to see problems tackled early to avoid threats to the system and supervisors or insurers keen to give problems time to resolve themselves in the hope of avoiding failure or demands on funds. The neatness does not even apply in Finland, as it is the Financial Supervisory Authority that is charged with maintaining the stability of the financial system not the Bank of Finland. Nevertheless, it is the Bank that produces the annual overview of Financial Stability.[1] When it comes to financial markets neat divisions are more difficult as the system and the individual institutions are often effectively the same in smaller countries.

Despite this development in regulation it is clear that the system has not kept pace with the internationalisation of financial markets. This is somewhat ironic in a European context as the driving force behind financial regulation has been the aim of creating a single internal market in financial services. The dichotomy occurs because supervisory powers and regulatory powers are only national in scope. Hence when bank operations run across borders they necessarily run across jurisdictions as well – even if regulations are harmonised to a substantial degree.

Table 1.1 Institutional organisation of central banks and supervisory authorities 2000

Country	Monetary policy	Supervision				Comments
		Banking	Payments system	Insurance	Securities	
Argentina	Banco Central de la República Argentina	Superintendencia de Entidades Financieras y Cambiarias	Banco Central de la República Argentina	Superintendencia de Seguros de la Nación	Comisión Nacional de Valores	Independent CB (currency board) The Superintendencia is subordinated directly to the CB governor (Art. 43 of law 24.144, dated 23.09.1992).
Australia	Reserve Bank of Australia	Australian Prudential Regulation Authority (APRA)	Reserve Bank of Australia	Australian Prudential Regulation Authority (APRA)	APRA and Australian Securities and Investment Commission (ASIC)	Independent CB since 1959 1998 – withdrawal of banking supervision from RBA and merger with insurance and Superannuation Commission
Austria	National Bank of Austria	Ministry of Finance				Independent CB (European CB)
Belgium	National Bank of Belgium	Banking and Finance Commission	National Bank of Belgium		Banking and Finance Commission	Independent CB (European CB)
Bolivia	Banco Central de Bolivia	Superintendencia de Bancos y Entidades Financieras	Regulation by the BCB	Separate	Shared	Independent CB since 1995 1987 – creation of the Superintendéncia de Bancos y Entidades Financieras

continued

Table 1.1 Continued

Country	Monetary policy	Supervision				Comments
		Banking	*Payments system*	*Insurance*	*Securities*	
Canada	Bank of Canada	Office of the Superintendent of Financial Institutions	Bank of Canada	Office of the Superintendent of Financial Institutions	Office of the Superintendent of Financial Institutions	Independent CB 1925 – Creation of the Office of the Inspector General of Banks (OIGB) 1987 – merger of the OIGB with the Department of Insurance
Chile	Banco Central de Chile	Superintendencia de Bancos y Instituciones Financieras	Banco Central de Chile	Superintendencia de Valores y Seguros	Superintendencia de Valores y Seguros	Independent CB since 1989 1925 – Creation of the Superintendência
Colombia	Banco de La Republica de Colombia	Superintendencia Bancaria de Colombia (MF)	Banco de La Republica de Colombia	Superintendencia Bancaria de Colombia	Superintendencia Bancaria de Colombia	BRC is an independent CB since 1991, though the Minister of Finance is the governor of the Junta Monetaria (seven members of which 6 are from the BRC)
Costa Rica	Banco Central de Costa Rica	Superintendencia General de Entidades Financieras		Separate	Superintendencia General de Valores	The CB is not independent The Superintendencia General de Entidades Financieras is a subsidiary of the CB

Denmark	Danmark Nationalbank	Danish Financial Supervisory Authority	Danmarks Nationalbank	Danish Financial Supervisory Authority	Danish Financial Supervisory Authority	Independent CB 1988 – creation of DFSA through merger of the Supervisory Authority for Banks and Saving Banks and the Insurance Supervisory Authority 1980 – merger with the Supervisory Authority for Mortgage Credit Institutions
Ecuador	Banco Central del Ecuador	Superintendencia de Bancos	Banco Central del Ecuador	Superintendencia de Bancos	Superintendencia de Compañías del Ecuador	The CB is not independent 1927 – creation of the Superintendencia following separation from the CB
El Salvador	Banco Central de Reserve de El Salvador	Superintendencia del Sistema Financiero		Superintendencia del Sistema Financiero	Superintendencia de Valores	The CB is not independent
England	Bank of England	Financial Services Authority	Bank of England	Financial Services Authority	Financial Services Authority	Independent CB since 1997 1997 – withdrawal of bank supervision from Bank of England and merger of supervisory agencies
Finland	Bank of Finland	Financial Supervision Authority	Bank of Finland		Financial Supervision Authority	Independent CB (European CB) 1922 – creation of the Bank Inspectorate 1993 – creation of FSA through merger of the bank and securities supervision functions

continued

Table 1.1 Continued

Country	Monetary policy	Supervision		Insurance	Securities	Comments
		Banking	Payments system			
France	Banque de France	Banking and Financial Regulatory Committee/Credit Institutions and Investment Firms Committee/Banking Commission	Banque de France		Banking and Financial Regulatory Committee/Capital Markets Council/Stock Exchange Commission	Independent CB (European CB) 1996 – Independence of the Banque de France
Germany	Deutsche Bundesbank	Federal Banking Supervisory Office			Federal Securities Supervisory Office/Federal Supervisory Office for Securities Trading	Independent CB since its creation in 1957. (European CB)
Greece	Bank of Greece	Bank of Greece	Bank of Greece			Independent CB (European CB)
Guatemala	Banco de Guatemala	Superintendencia de Bancos		Superintendencia de Bancos	Shared	The CB is not independent Banco de Guatemala and Superintendencia de Bancos are subordinated to a Junta Monetaria
Holland	De Nederlandsche Bank	De Nederlandsche Bank	De Nederlandsche Bank		De Nederlandsche Bank	Independent CB (European CB)

Country		Bank Supervisor	Bank Supervisor	Bank Supervisor	See Aguirre (1997)
Honduras	Banca Central de Honduras				
Hong Kong	Hong Kong Monetary Authority	Hong Kong Monetary Authority	Hong Kong Monetary Authority	Hong Kong Securities and Futures Commission	CB Independent (currency board) 1993 – merger of the bank supervision with central bank
Ireland	Central Bank of Ireland	Central Bank of Ireland	Central Bank of Ireland		Independent CB (European CB)
Israel	Bank of Israel	Bank of Israel	Bank of Israel		Independent CB
Italy	Banca d'Italia	Banca d'Italia	Banca d'Italia		Independent CB (European CB)
Japan	Bank of Japan	Financial Supervisory Agency	Financial Supervisory Agency	Financial Supervisory Agency	The CB is not independent
Korea	Bank of Korea	Financial Supervisory Commission	Financial Supervisory Commission	Financial Supervisory Commission	Independent CB 1998 – withdrawal of bank supervision from Bank of Korea and merger of the supervisory agencies (Securities and Exchange Commission and Insurance Supervisory Commission)
Luxembourg	Luxembourg Monetary Institute	Luxembourg Monetary Institute	Luxembourg Monetary Institute		Independent CB (European CB)

continued

Table 1.1 Continued

Country	Monetary policy	Supervision		Payments system	Insurance	Securities	Comments
		Banking					
Mexico	Banco de México	Comisión Nacional Bancaria y de Valores		Banco de México/Comisión Nacional Bancaria y de Valores	Comisión Nacional de Seguros y Fianzas	Comisión Nacional Bancaria y de Valores	Independent CB since 1993 (constitutional reform) 1995 – creation of CNBV, through merger of banking and securities supervision
Nicaragua	Banco Central de Nicaragua	Bank Supervisor			Bank Supervisor	Bank Supervisor	See Aguirre (1997)
New Zealand	Reserve Bank of New Zealand	Reserve Bank of New Zealand		Reserve Bank of New Zealand		Reserve Bank of New Zealand	Independent CB since 1989
Norway	Norges Bank	Banking, Insurance and Securities Commission		Norges Bank	Banking, Insurance and Securities Commission	Banking, Insurance and Securities Commission	Independent CB 1986 – creation of the Banking, Insurance and Securities Commission
Panama	Central Bank	Bank Supervisor			Separate	Separate	See Aguirre (1997)
Paraguay	Central Bank	Central Bank			Separate	Separate	See Aguirre (1997)
Peru	Banco Central de Reserva del Perú	Superintendencia de Banco y Seguros		Banco Central de Reserva del Perú	Superintendencia de Banco y Seguros	Comisión Nacional Supervisora de Empresas y Valores (CONASEV)	The CB is not independent 1931 – creation of the Superintendencia 1979 – administrative and functional independence of the Superintendencia

Portugal	Banco de Portugal	Banco de Portugal	Banco de Portugal			Independent CB (European CB)
Spain	Banco de España	Banco de España	Banco de España	la Dirección General de Seguros	la Comisión Nacional del Mercado de Valores	Independent CB (European CB) 1994 – independence of Banco de España
Sweden	Sveriges Riksbank	Swedish Financial Supervisory Authority	Sveriges Riksbank	Swedish Financial Supervisory Authority	Swedish Financial Supervisory Authority	Independent CB 1991 – merger of the Bank Inspection Board and of the Supervisors of Bank Securities and Insurance Companies
Switzerland	Swiss National Bank	Federal Banking Commission	Swiss National Bank			Independent GB
Uruguay	Central Bank	Central Bank	Central Bank			See Aguirre (1997)
Venezuela	Banco Central de Venezuela	Superintendencia de Banca y Otras Inst. Financieras		Separate	Separate	1993 – creation of the Superintendencia

Source: Lundberg (2000).

Note
CB, Central Bank. All labelling is as in the original, so 'England' applies to GB and Northern Ireland, 'Holland' to Netherlands, for example, some small corrections have been applied.

The extent of financial supervision and regulation

It is easy to adopt the mindset of recent years and assume that extensive regulation of banks is necessary in order to have a prudent and stable system. However, as Charles Goodhart and Forrest Capie point out in Chapters 2 and 3, respectively, extensive regulation is a product only of the last 150 years or so and then only in some countries. In countries such as the UK, Sweden and France, which have the oldest central banks, these banks emerged as a part of the banking system that primarily acted for the government. Because of this role they became more powerful than the other banks and started to play a central role in the banking system, particularly in the settlement of obligations among banks. In particular, such central institutions came to be looked on as suppliers of liquidity – the lender of last resort, in the terms of Bagehot, lending against security at a rate above that prevailing in the market, so they were indeed only the last resort after more favourable borrowing opportunities had been exhausted. The lender of last resort does not have to be the central bank, and in Germany this function is performed by the Liquidity Consortium Bank, but that bank is owned by the central bank and the banking industry and has resort to the central bank in the event of difficulty.[2]

In this sort of framework, the financial system is more of a self-regulating club, where the structure protects it against the unexpected. The structure normally has two elements: constraints on behaviour to limit the risk of problems and a set of procedures to come into play to control the impact if problems are nevertheless realised. The same structure applies to highly regulated systems where there is corporate law, extensive regulation of what banks may and may not do and supervision (monitoring) to check that they comply in the first element and lender of last resort, deposit insurance, implicit guarantees and bankruptcy law in the second. The greater the insurance liability of the other members of the club, whether or not that includes the taxpayer, the more they will want to be convinced of the risk management methods of the other members.

In the period before limited liability, creditors would be paid out in the event of failure up to the point that the last shareholder had been bankrupted. In the case of the City of Glasgow Bank in 1878, for example, it proved to be necessary to bankrupt all but 254 of the 1,819 shareholders to make a full payout. (It is worth noting in our context that some of the residual (solvent) shareholders formed a new company that acquired the assets of the bank, which could be sold off at a favourable juncture, thereby assisting the receivers in the completion of their task.) Given that joint stock banks normally had quite a large number of wealthy individuals as their shareholders this could effectively mean that depositors and creditors were fairly secure even in the absence of any explicit insurance. No bank with more than nine partners failed to pay out in full on failure and total losses to creditors over the entire period of so called free banking in

Scotland, 1716 to 1845, were trivial (White, 1984). Indeed, the shareholders would have every incentive to recapitalise a bank in difficulty rather than let it close because of the crippling nature of their exposure under default. A bank tends to be worth more as a going concern even if its liabilities exceed its assets and recapitalisation saves having to pay the receiver's costs, which can be substantial. In the same way this would encourage prudence. The banks which expected to pick up market share from those who were weaker or failing would need to be strong enough to do so, as some element of new capital would be needed. Not surprisingly the prevailing Scottish banking arrangements were viewed very favourably by Adam Smith (1776) in *The Wealth of Nations*, who argued not simply that the competition involved encouraged prudence ('circumspect in their conduct' (p. 268) to use his more ringing tones) but also innovation.

However, to some extent the way a market operates is the product of its time. For example, in the period of 'free banking' in Scotland, the system could be satisfactorily self-regulating because of the shared Presbyterian codes of conduct among directors and shareholders.[3] Such unwritten codes govern the fair treatment of customers, levels of charges and hence profits as well as the honesty of interbank dealings. Such systems stop working when some of the members no longer share the common ethos, as Goodhart and Bliss point out with respect to the London system as difficulties started to emerge in the 1970s.[4] This idea of mutual obligation seems to extend to the German system (Beck, 2003) even today and was one of the facets of the successful operation of the building society sector in the UK until banks started to enter the private mortgage market on a significant scale. Although the (monthly) fixing of interest rates could be viewed as highly uncompetitive, it was highly predictable (Mayes, 1979). Margins were low, as were the rewards of the managers and directors and the concept of mutuality developed a framework of prudence as long as the industry remained in its traditional business. Strong cash ratios were required. The small number of failures were dealt with by takeover by larger societies as the failures were almost entirely of small societies, hit either by the actions of a single individual or a heavy asymmetric shock that impaired either collateral or regional income (as most societies were regionally concentrated).

If we look to the United States, the position is different. Bank failure has been a more common occurrence, and the interaction between the structure of regulation there and failure has been quite complex. Regulation has responded to weaknesses in a series of steps. Initially banks could only be set up by specific legislation but this was replaced by a period of 'free banking' between 1838 and the passing of the National Bank Act in 1863. The prohibition on interstate banking and in some states, branch banking, was a response to try to ensure that banks were properly licensed, properly managed and that all their operations could be under the control of a single locally knowledgeable authority. However, it has also meant that there could be a greater concentration of risks. Similarly, the prohibition of 'universal banking' under the Glass–Steagall Act of 1932 also affected the risk characteristics of banks. However, the 1933 Banking Act provided the more major response to the wave of failures after the 1929 crash and led to the creation of the FDIC (Federal Deposit Insurance Corporation). The move towards having bank holding companies as a means of having banks in more than one state has looked a benefit in that with concentrated ownership it would be easier to get support for a bank in difficulty from the resources of a much larger group. Indeed this 'source of strength' doctrine has been promoted by the Federal Reserve. Unfortunately, as pointed out by Robert Bliss and by Kern Alexander, this source of strength applies in the initial acquisition and merger discussion and cannot be relied upon in the case of difficulty, i.e. just when it is needed. In turn FDICIA (Federal Deposit Insurance Corporation Improvement Act 1991) has been part of a reaction to the failures and difficulties in the savings and loan industry, which were themselves assisted by deregulation of the sector.

Even so it is easy to confuse the early onset of banking regulation with the involvement of the Federal Reserve, which only acquired the key role in that area when it acquired supervisory competence over bank holding companies under the Bank Holding Company Act of 1956.[5] (It had always been intended to act as lender of last resort – although it sometimes failed to do so – but had no supervisory competence until that date.)

By comparison, the UK (and related Commonwealth countries) stands out as rather an anomaly. Until the early 1970s it had experienced little in the way of banking problems and hence had not felt the need for extensive regulation. The need for regulation seemed to develop largely as a result of the opening up of competition after the introduction of Competition and Credit Control in 1971, and a number of bad experiences, including Johnson-Mathey in 1984, BCCI (Bank of Credit and Commerce International) in 1991 and Barings in 1995. No only was legislation tightened up but in 1997 the whole framework was changed with the creation of a single unified regulator in the FSA (Financial Services Authority) which amalgamated all nine different financial regulators in a single body, separate from the Bank of England.

It is difficult to know how far to go with regulation. Charles Calomiris points out that there is 'an optimal amount of financial crime'. No doubt a similar remark can be made about imprudence. If the system is to be organised such that financial crime is impossible, then it will not operate effectively and will be cumbersome and expensive. For people to have confidence in the system the levels of such crime needs to be sufficiently small and the forms of insurance and redress sufficiently cheap and effective. These will not be hard and fast lines but functions of the desires of society for protection at any particular time and of the degree of criminality that is perceived. Calomiris argues that, despite the notorious examples of recent years in the United States, the system has been operating very well in terms of providing a return to shareholders and fair treatment of customers in the face of strong competition. Hence it has been in need of relatively limited changes.

This stands in contrast to Justin O'Brien's hugely stimulating review of the various examples of unacceptable behaviour in US markets in recent years and the inability of the authorities to secure convictions in many instances. These examples were quite enough to stimulate a vigorous response, not just in terms of the prosecutions but in a rewriting of the accepted behaviour with the Sarbanes–Oxley Act. However, as Stefan Huemer points out in his comments, Europe has not been immune from these scandals, with the Parmalat and Ahold affairs being the most prominent. European regulation in turn has responded, remaining a notch more prescriptive than its US counterpart.[6] There are some ironies in the contrast between the two systems. In accounting standards, for example, despite its name, the Generally Accepted Accounting Principles (GAAP) in the US (generally accepted accounting principles) is in practice a highly rule-based scheme whereas the approach of the International Accounting Standards (IAS), which the EU is hoping to adopt, is more explicitly based on principles (Myddelton, 2004).

Calomiris stresses the importance of reputation in policing a system of self-regulation. If those who break the rules or act against the spirit of them are going to be heavily penalised through loss of jobs, drastic reduction in the profitability of the company and loss of market share, then most examples of rule-breaking will occur when the parties involved are desperate. The Nick Leeson case in Barings is a clear example – there seemed to be no other way of correcting the errors. Sanctions do not have to be imposed by outside authorities. In the case of the coup in euro bond markets perpetrated by Citibank in 2004, they did nothing which was against the rules but it was a clear case of manipulating a market in a way that people felt was inappropriate. As a result Citibank has had to take significant action to try to repair its reputation. Furthermore, others in the industry will not attempt to pull the same stunt, even if the authorities are not completely successful in making the market transparent enough to prevent it.

Retribution by the market can be far more drastic than the sorts of penalties the authorities might impose. Arthur Anderson's actions resulted in their demise as a firm; this occurred before their later acquittal of the charges which brought them down. Shareholders can push out directors for strategies and actions which they feel could cause them loss, as was revealed with first the resignation (in 2005) of the chief executive of Deutsche Börse and then the departure of the chairman. There does not have to be any proof or evaluation in a court. Whether or not the price offered for the London Stock Exchange was appropriate and what the net gains might be was an opinion, which cannot be tested before or after the event. Schwartz cites the case of Riggs Bank that came to an out of court settlement to pay the Office of the Comptroller of the Currency US$25mn (in May 2004) in the face of allegations of insufficient action to avoid money laundering. The Federal Reserve also ordered it to close its Miami subsidiary and to seek approval before it paid any dividends or bought back stock. However, the market impact was that Riggs was bought by PNC Financial Services Group in July and the business with embassies, which was the focus of the allegations, is being picked up by HSBC. Similarly the requirement by the Japanese regulators for Citygroup to close its four private banks in Japan resulted in publicity that was probably more damaging to its reputation than its revenues.

Calomiris argues for more opportunity for the market to act to provide incentives for prudent management.[7] In previous work (Calomiris, 1999) he has emphasised the importance of all banks having subordinated debt, a point repeated here by Benink in his comments on Chapter 6.[8] On this occasion Calomiris cites the issue of not needing to warn shareholders before trying to buy significant holdings in a company. The warning raises the price and hence removes some of the opportunity for such bids. Clearly there are issues involving the fair treatment of small and less informed shareholders but reducing competitive pressure beyond a certain point is unlikely to be in the interests of anyone except the incumbent management.

The problem is to determine the point at which the competition ceases to act as a spur to do better and starts to introduce such panic that prudence is sacrificed and 'excess' risk taking from the point of view of the stakeholders begins. The debate in the banking literature about where this occurs continues. Other features of the regulation of the market can alter its incidence. The greater the degree and rapidity of disclosure then the less the opportunity for inordinate risk taking as stakeholders will be able to respond.

Regulation and the behaviour of the regulated are very much a 'dialectic', as Anna Schwartz puts it in Chapter 4, a description also put forward by Kane (1977). Increasing regulation is a response to behaviour which society finds unacceptable. Avoidance of regulation then occurs where firms feel that their profit opportunities are being unduly inhibited. However, it is not simply a cycle of ever-increasing regulation. There have been periods when good behaviour has been rewarded with an easing, in the 1970s, for example. Schwartz regards this dialectic as being a process by which regulation can be improved but while one may be able to assess whether regulation has been able to achieve its desired objective in terms of limiting the behaviour causing concern to acceptable levels, this says nothing about its cost. Here the FSA in London has gone a long way towards trying make cost–benefit analyses of regulation. However, such studies are strongest on the direct costs to the regulator and the regulated of compliance. Analyses of the wider implications have found quantification much more difficult (NERA, 2004). As Masciandaro points out in his comments, a cost–benefit assessment of the structure of the system as a whole sounds desirable, but it is too complex a suggestion to be practical. Benston (1995) has a much more cynical view of the interaction between regulation and behaviour, arguing that regulation and financial instability are positively correlated rather than part of converging dialectic process.

The dialectic in regulation extends to the organisational structure of the system. The unified and independent Financial Services Authority in the UK is a product of the uneven quality of regulation among its nine predecessor bodies, and the criticism that the Bank of England received for its handling of banking problems and the failure of BCCI and Barings in particular.[9] In the US the creation of the Federal Reserve was a reaction to the problems encountered in the absence of a central bank to act as lender of last resort. The creation of Federal Deposit Insurance was the result of the Fed failing to act in that lender of last resort role. FDICIA and change in institutional balance it involved was a reaction to the savings and loan debacle and the exhaustion of the deposit insurance funds in the industry. Similarly the switch of responsibility for banking regulation and supervision from the Finnish ministry of finance to the Bank of Finland, reflected the horror of the banking crisis at the beginning of the 1990s.

However, a chequered history is not the only explanation. Size of country also matters. Unifying the whole system in the Central Bank and FSA of Ireland in 2003 made eminent sense. It is difficult to put together more than one sufficiently qualified team. Roles are separate and delineated. The Irish Financial Services Regulatory Agency is an autonomous body within the Bank, responsible for regulation and consumer protection in the sector. The set up in Finland is not particularly different. Although the Central Bank and the Financial Supervision Authority (Rahoitustarkastus) have a common administration, they are in separate buildings and have separate boards, that of the FSA being chaired by the Deputy Governor of the Bank. As a result although the tasks are clearly separate there can be a ready exchange of information and ideas (there is only one research department for the two organisations (located in the Bank). The relationship between the Banque de France and the Commission Bancaire in France is somewhat similar (with the Governor of the Banque de France being the Chairman of the Commission). However, there are also anomalies; whereas the Bank of England and the Central Bank of Ireland are charged with maintaining financial stability, this is only explicit for the Finnish FSA and the Bank of Finland's responsibility for the financial system is more generally defined.[10]

The United States offers a completely different paradigm in terms of structure and one which no one starting with a clean slate would think of creating. The US system is a complex network of overlapping regulators, stemming from the days when much of the regulatory responsibility was at the state, or even more local, level. These regulators have been supplemented by country-wide regulators, who are often specific to particular parts of the industry (as set out by Robert Bliss in Chapter 6). As a result financial firms have to deal with many regulators but regulators need to co-operate in order to get the task completed efficiently. (Robert Eisenbeis gives several examples in Chapter 8 of how the US can end up with agency conflict rather than co-operation.) However, as discussed in more detail in the next section, if one wants to put in place a non-overlapping system for a large area, it is difficult to avoid a very centralised system. Because of the size of organisation involved that would then face the opposite problem of size, namely bureaucratic inefficiency. The UK FSA is a large organisation and probably pushing the limits of efficiency. Creating a single agency for Europe would involve an organisation at least five times the size, if we multiply up by the number of significant institutions in the rest of the area, and one where national differences would make it very difficult to achieve synergies. Anything in the short run would necessarily be largely of the form of creating an additional tier at the top.

There are two separate concerns here. One is how far regulation of banks and other financial institutions should be concentrated under a single body in a given jurisdiction.[11] The other is whether that body should be the central bank, particularly in the case of the narrowly defined banking system.

Not surprisingly the authorities tend to find favour in the system that they already have – if there were strong dislikes or problems then it is likely that there would have been pressure for change. There is no obviously superior model of supervision, as Masciandaro puts it. Lundberg (2000) presents a summary of the issues for a country that is trying to weigh up the advantages of a change. The key issue is whether concentrating all activities in the Central Bank provides information that leads to better monetary policy (Peek *et al.*, 1999) or whether it leads to a conflict of interest and hence worse supervision and monetary policy as a result.

Monetary policy might be easier in the face of potential system financial problems and supervision might be more tolerant if it felt that monetary policy was likely to accommodate major problems. Similarly if the Central Bank were provider of various parts of the payment system it might prima facie seem sensible to have another institution regulate it. On the other hand, having supervision in the Central Bank might reduce the chance of regulatory capture (Haubrich, 1996). Furthermore, as we have noted, there is a clear element of reputation risk. Even though monetary policy and supervisory divisions may be very separate, problems affect the reputation of the whole institution. In particular, it may be more difficult for a Central Bank to be equally independent from current political pressure on monetary and on banking issues. Bolstering confidence in the banking system may involve a degree of co-operation with government that would look inappropriate in maintaining the credibility of monetary policy.

However, changing the system has costs – not just in the direct sense of the disruption of those being reorganised and the spillover to those they deal with – but at a more general political level. There has to be a reason for change and while that might be derivable in terms of a simple costs–benefit analysis, it is difficult to avoid the implication that something was 'wrong' with the previous system otherwise it would have been able to reform itself as a part of its normal operation. This may be a signal that a government does not want to give. Indeed it may have the alternative better plan in the drawer, ready to roll out if the need arises but only if there is need from the pressure of events or the revealed (loss of) confidence in the system. The ammunition once used will not be available subsequently.

The information needs are not simply one way from supervisors to the Central Bank. The Central Bank may be able to detect incipient problems, particularly in the last stages before a problem emerges from its monitoring of payment traffic and settlement accounts (Pauli, 2000). However, to some extent, the foregoing very much characterises the position in the more advanced market economies. In other environments it may be very difficult to operate a highly professional and incorruptible system. Central Banks tend to offer the greatest chance of independence from undue political and commercial influence (Goodhart, 2000) and hence in these circumstances concentrating the whole of the supervisory and regulatory system in them may be the best solution, despite its drawbacks. The chances of being able to recruit and fund a satisfactory array of qualified and experienced supervisors may be very limited.

Evidence on the subject is rather mixed. Copelovitch and Singer (2004) suggest that countries where bank lending is a more important route to company finance will tend to opt for locating banking supervision within the Central Bank while those that are more capital market based, are more open to trade and have relatively concentrated banking systems, will opt for separation of supervisory responsibility (a point confirmed by Masciandaro's work). However, with only 21 OECD countries to consider it is difficult to draw strong conclusions. Widening the net to 107 countries, Barth *et al.* (2001) find that only a quarter of countries have banking supervision clearly separated from the central bank compared with the largely equal split in the OECD.[12] Although the trend in the OECD has been towards separation from the central bank (Australia, Canada, Denmark, Japan, Korea, Sweden and the UK have made this move in the last 20 years). Not surprisingly therefore, in a study of the whole dataset, central bank supervision tends to be associated with the characteristics of those non-OECD countries – greater government ownership of banks, less foreign ownership, etc. The nature of the monetary policy regime is also relevant. In currency boards and fixed exchange rate regimes where there is no or little discretion on monetary policy the conflicts of interest are necessarily lower in a direct sense but weak supervision or forbearance could still destroy the monetary policy regime.

As it is becoming progressively more difficult to draw hard and fast lines between financial activities (what Masciandaro describes as 'financial blurring' in his comments[13]), it becomes more difficult to produce arguments for supporting separate regulators of the different institutional classifications. In practice the same activities undertaken by different institutions would be regulated differently. However, this may be no bad thing. Such regulatory competition may both encourage better regulation and help determine which sorts of institution are better placed to undertake the activity. There is no reason to suppose this will be a rush for the bottom, as showing you are regulated in a weaker manner is scarcely going to be a recommendation for those interested in the prudent management of the funds they have lent, whatever their appetite for risk. However, Eisenbeis suggests that such competition in the EU environment is likely to lead to a less regulated environment, limited by the extent of minimum standards laid down at the EU level. Quality of institution as revealed by the regulatory framework is used as a positive feature in prospectuses (see the example of Deutsche Bank explored in Mayes *et al.*, 2001). Competition may also encourage innovation both on the part of regulators and the regulated. Greenspan (1994) described it more starkly: 'a single regulator with a narrow view of safety and soundness and with no responsibility for the macroeconomic implications of its decisions would inevitably have a long-term bias against risk-taking and innovation. It receives no plaudits for contributing to economic growth through prudent risk-taking, but it is severely criticised for too many bank failures. The incentives are clear.'

However, the potential gains are not unidirectional. Eisenbeis suggests a number of adverse incentives that appear in the US because financial institutions try to find the most favourable regulatory climate for particular products. The income of regulatory organisations and hence the jobs of their employees depend upon the size of what they have to regulate, both in terms of the number of institutions and the complexity of the framework of rules. Number of institutions covered and complexity of the system would tend to be inversely related in an environment of regulatory competition.[14] It is possible that in trying to protect their client base, regulators themselves might be tempted to offer lower compliance costs, not so much from efficiency of regulation but simply a reduced level of monitoring. That implies that they themselves are not particularly accountable, which is becoming less and less the case. Furthermore, as Masciandaro points out, a single regulator puts all of the authorities' reputation in one basket. A mistake in one branch harms the reputation of the whole. Given that one would want to recover reputation it is more difficult to suggest what the next step is in the case of a unified regulator; presumably one would return to the beginning of the cycle.

The more separately defined the objectives of a regulator, the less the scope for internal conflict, but it is not clear that inter-organisational interaction is a more effective way of resolving conflicts than internal decision, as Eisenbeis discusses in Chapter 8. In the latter case at least, someone has the power to decide, whereas inter-institutional conflicts may go unrecognised and even when recognised, unresolved. There is something to be said for a comprehensive review along the lines of the Wallis Committee in Australia, to check what the different objectives are and whether the structure of the various parts of the system adds up to a coherent and comprehensive whole. It can provide an opportunity for streamlining and simplification both for the treatment of the financial sector when it is working normally and in the case of difficulty as we discuss at some length in the next section. However, although there are unique opportunities for review, the more normal circumstance is the need for a continuing ability to check that the trade-offs between the various objectives of regulation are being met in a way that maximises society's welfare. Eisenbeis argues that the legislature has to decide how it can delegate that process to the relevant agencies as it can only handle obvious discrepancies. The continuing micro-management of the trade-offs and assessment of the relevant costs and benefits is necessarily administrative or it would be unmanageable and have a rather short-run horizon, given the frequency of the electoral cycle. Any such 'contracts' are inevitably incomplete as neither the legislature nor the agency can foresee all the possible outcomes. Thus the general principles set out will need to be revised from time to time.

Kahn and Santos in Chapter 7 consider a somewhat narrower division into the lender of last resort, deposit insurance and supervisory functions. Even here there are some potential conflicts of interest in addition to the normal moral hazard problem from providing insurance in any form (supplemented by adverse selection if it is voluntary). Having deposit insurance as part of the Central Bank responsibilities is relatively unusual (Ireland, the Netherlands, Spain; shared in Greece and Portugal) and normally it is run by a separate public body, the industry itself or some combination of the two. Under separation of responsibility, the biggest conflict tends to occur between the body responsible for taking decisions on the bank's actions (especially closure), and those who have to bear the costs. Thus the supervisor may be exposed to reputational costs in the event of a problem, the deposit insurance agency may have to pay out and the lender of last resort may be secure through its collateral (see Wood, 2004; Wood and Capie, forthcoming). Nevertheless last resort lending could increase the costs to the deposit insurance agency by allowing losses to mount, as could delays by supervisors hoping to avoid a publicly acknowledged problem.[15] As discussed in the next section there are various ways in which the different authorities can advance themselves on the ladder of priority in the event of failure.

The key issue, also identified in Repullo (2000), is that in addressing the costs to the banking system of different solutions to a problem there, all factors should be taken into account, whereas in collateralised lending to an illiquid bank it is the narrow costs that have to be considered. Because a central bank can take a longer-term view than much of the market it may well price assets differently. In the Kahn and Santos framework this ends up with a clear separation of responsibility, with smaller liquidity issues being the preserve of the Central Bank under the lender of last resort function and bank system consequences being the decision of the deposit insurer. However, this is a very US-centric conclusion as most deposit insurance agencies in the EU do not have the structures that would enable such responsibility to be exercised, as Maria Nieto points out in her comments on the chapter.

In many respects deposit insurance is the weak link in the system of banking regulation in various countries and this is the topic that Eisenbeis focuses on in Chapter 8.[16] The insurer will want a say in the activities of the supervisor, especially in the event of emerging difficulties. If the two are not organised in a coherent package then each will have an incentive to try to shift the burden onto the other to the detriment of the other stakeholders. This can result in increased risk or belt and braces over-regulation, depending upon how the system is structured. Not only does deposit insurance have an element of moral hazard and reduce the extent to which depositors will exercise market discipline and monitor the performance of banks, but it offers rather different guarantees from what many of those insured may expect. As Nieto points out Member States in the EU are not under an obligation to support their deposit insurance funds. If they were to be insufficiently funded in a crisis then depositors might not get paid out to the extent they expect. However, this results in just the same ambiguity as in countries with no deposit insurance. Depositors believe there is some implicit contract with the government that they will be bailed out at least in part, if there were to be a serious crisis. In a major crisis the losses would be electorally significant, and hence action would be taken – either to prop up existing funds, or create new funds or indeed avoid the call on the funds in the first place by supporting the banking system.

Eisenbeis goes to some length to show that the US experience has some very negative lessons for the EU from the behaviour of state level deposit insurers or from sectoral insurers as in the case of the Savings and Loan collapse. The Ohio state fund collapsed in 1985 and Rhode Island in 1991 so these are not examples from distant history. Moreover, it was not simply a question of financial resources – the GDP of Ohio is greater than that of all but the seven largest of the 25 EU members and the total loss was less than 0.1 per cent of GDP. It was more a question of willingness.[17] However, the distinction between US states and the Member States of the EU is important in this regard as their ability to tax and to borrow is considerably greater, both in practice and constitutionally. Whether that should make the taxpayer feel more comfortable with the deposit insurance schemes is a different matter. As is clear from Table 1.2 there is considerable variety

Table 1.2 Deposit protection in the EU (25)

Systems in EU	Supervisor	Deposit insurer	Funded	Fund target	Risk-based	Coverage	Co-insure	Off-set	Timing (months)
Austria	Separate	Private company	Ex post	No	No	€20,000	Yes	Yes	3+
Belgium	Separate	Supervisor	Fund	Yes	No	€20,000	No	Yes	3+
Cyprus	CB	Separate	Mixed	Yes	No	€20,000	Yes	Yes	3+
Czech Republic	CB	Separate at CB	Fund	No	No	Higher	Yes	Yes	3+
Denmark	Separate	Separate at CB	Mixed	Yes	No	Higher	Yes	Yes	3+
Estonia	Separate	Separate	Fund	Yes	No	Lower*	Yes	Yes	<3
Finland	Separate	Supervisor	Mixed	Yes	Yes	Higher	No	Yes	3
France	Separate	Private company	Fund	No	Yes	Higher	No	No	3+
Germany	Separate	Supervisor	Fund	Yes	No	€20,000	Yes	Yes	3+
Germany	Separate	Private company	Ex post	No	Yes	Higher	No	Yes	>21 days
Greece	CB	Separate	Fund	Yes	No	€20,000	No	Yes	3+
Hungary	Separate	Separate	Fund	Yes	Yes	Higher	Yes	Yes	<3
Ireland	CB	CB	Fund	No	No	€20,000	Yes	Yes	3+
Italy	CB	Private company	Ex post	Yes	Yes	Very high	No	Yes	3+
Latvia	CB	MoF/CB	Fund	No	–	Lower*	Yes	No	3+
Lithuania	CB	MoF//Government	Fund	Yes	No	Lower*	Yes	Yes	3+
Luxembourg	Separate	Separate	Ex post	No	No	€20,000	Yes	No	3+
Malta	Separate	Separate	Mixed	Yes	No	€20,000	Yes	Yes	3+
The Netherlands	CB	CB	Ex post	No	No	€20,000	No	Yes	3+
Poland	CB	Separate at MoF	Fund	No	Yes	Higher	Yes	Yes	<3
Portugal	CB	CB	Fund	No	Yes	Higher	No	Yes	3+
Slovakia	CB	Separate	Fund	Yes	No	Lower*	Yes	Yes	3+
Slovenia	CB	CB	Banks make deposit to CB	Yes	No	Higher	No	Yes	<3
Spain	CB	Separate at CB	Fund	Yes	No	€20,000	No	No	3+
Sweden	Separate	Separate	Fund	Yes	Yes	Higher	No	Yes	3+
The UK	Separate	Separate	Fund	Yes	No	Higher	Yes	Yes	3+
Total = 26 includes German public and private systems	Separate = 14, CB = 12	Separate = 13, Private = 4, CB = 4, MoF = 2, Supervisor = 3	Fund = 16, Ex post = 5, Mixed = 4, Other = 1	Y = 16, N = 10	RB = 7, N = 18	Base = 10, H = 12, L = 4	Y = 14, N = 12	Y = 21, N = 5	20 days > 3 months

Source: Garcia and Nieto (2005).

Notes
CB, Central Bank; MoF, Ministry of Finance.
* Transitionally on way up to EU minimum.

among the EU deposit insurance schemes, which is particularly a problem from the point of view of cross-border schemes as noted in the next section.[18] Perhaps the most useful precedent comes from Calomiris (1992) who finds that in the US it was the privately funded deposit insurance schemes that effectively imposed unlimited liability on their members that tended not to fail. There the incentives to encourage prudence in others beforehand, act quickly to limit losses and if necessary apply the least costly approach if resolution of a bank was nevertheless required.

Despite the Deposit Insurance Directive, what people are likely to get according to the rules in the different countries varies considerably. There may be much more convergence in practice, outside asset rich countries like Norway, once the new members have completed their transition period, as those with more generous provision may find they have more of a solvency problem. Indeed, normal regulatory competition, if banks or their customers have a real opportunity for regime shopping as the market integrates, will lead to a greater equalisation of the insurance fund provisions, presumably clustering near the minimum required by the Directive. The biggest difficulties are likely to occur in the unfunded insurance arrangements, as the call on the other banks may come just when they are also pressed, as they would be if it is a macro-economic rather than an idiosyncratic event that causes the problem. As Eisenbeis points out there are many respects in which the incentives of the insurers, the taxpayers and the contributing banks are not aligned. A comprehensive review of the arrangements seems called for, especially if, as in the US, the Deposit Insurance agency is to be given a greater role in deciding when action is to be taken in the face of impending losses as suggested in the next section in order to obtain such an improved alignment.

There has been very little empirical work done on these issues but, in his comments on Kahn and Santos, Masciandaro explains the results of some work he has done on the structure of financial regulation in a sample of countries covering the OECD and non-OECD Europe (Masciandaro, 2005). In line with the foregoing discussion, he emphasises that while it is possible to devise some criteria for deciding what arrangements would be economically efficient, the political economy of the choice seems to be dominant.[19] The expected control variables, the relative importance of equity markets, the smallness of the financial system and having a Nordic/Germanic legal system all increase the probability of having a single financial authority. In this and Barth *et al.*'s (2001) analysis, it is much easier to show what is the case than to explain it. Barth *et al.* (2001) find no significant features that differentiate countries with single regulators from those with several. However, they do find clear differences between those where the Central Bank is the regulator and the rest: government ownership of banks is higher, as is the rate of rejection of applications for bank licences and the level of foreign ownership of banks is lower, the restriction on range and scope of permitted activities for banks is lower as is market discipline, but the incidence of deposit insurance is higher as is a measure of moral hazard. One is not clearly the cause of the other. On the whole they are both a function of the level of development of the economy. So we end up where we started, with only a very limited range of factors, other than history, that help explain why one set of institutional arrangements has been preferred over another.

The same sort of conclusions apply to choice over whether to have deposit insurance (Demirgüç-Kunt *et al.*, 2005), and over the generosity of the systems chosen. Ironically, simple emulation is a major stimulus. Rather like the spread of financial stability reviews, if comparable countries have adopted deposit insurance that prompts others to do so, and not necessarily with features that fit their particular circumstances. A decade ago deposit insurance was primarily a feature of high income countries with well-developed financial markets. As with research on supervision, there is some indication that deposit insurance is more a characteristic of accountable democracies but this may also be simply, a rather better means of specifying income and trend components of the relationship. Because of the element of emulation many of these newer schemes seem to be somewhat over-generous by comparison, with a stronger element of moral hazard as a consequence.

Banking regulation as a whole is in the process of being geared up with the introduction of Basel 2 and the associated Capital Adequacy directive in the EU. While this may not in itself alter the structure of regulation, it alters the relationship between the regulator and the regulated and the relationship between regulators. In this second regard it encourages consolidated supervision and the application of single approaches to risk management and the holding of capital across the group, as is discussed in more detail in the next section. But in the first, pillar 2 requires a closer relationship between the supervisor and the supervised as the supervisory review has to decide not just whether risk management systems are adequate but whether the bank should hold extra capital against risk, over and above that required under pillar 1. This close relationship, as pointed out by Benink in his comments, will inevitably make it more difficult for regulators to impose discipline. Because the bank itself will be the source of information an element of regulatory capture is possible and the degree of implicit responsibility on the part of the regulator, should anything go wrong in the bank, will be increased. It is interesting, as Benink notes, that the Basel Committee has recommended floors for the extent of the reduction in the capital charge that can be made under the advanced approaches, thereby limiting the amount by which the largest banks might hope to see their capital requirement fall. This could imply a certain caution with respect to the pressures involved.

Ideally, pillar 3 would have provided an offsetting balance through the market, so that not only could market pressure be exercised, as a result of the increased information, and not just supervisory pressure, but supervisors could commit to intervene if market information indicates possible problems. Under pillar 2, and the traditional arrangement, much of the relevant information will remain confidential to the supervisor, perpetuating the dilemma about whether to reveal a problem and run the risk of being held responsible and, indeed, of being accused of causing a crisis unnecessarily, or forbearing and thereby increasing the size of any resultant problem. Benink suggests that much of the information to be disclosed will not in itself be particularly valuable and that the key information will continue only to be obtained by the more sophisticated of external watchers.

The organisation of financial supervision in a cross-border world

The increasingly cross-border nature of financial institutions and the development of regulation of banks with Basel 2 are forcing supervisors to work more closely with each other. This has been emphasised in the EU with the rapid implementation of the Financial Services Action Plan (FSAP) (unfortunately having the same abbreviation as the IMF Financial Sector Assessment Programme) under the Lamfalussy process, aided by the two committees of supervisors CEBS and CESR (Committee of European Banking Supervisors and Committee of European Securities Regulators). However, the way they work together and the relative benefits and costs of these different relationships have only been touched on fairly lightly in public discussion. It is therefore one of the foci of this book.

There are some clear factors that are helping determine the structure of this interaction but the picture is far from complete. The main drivers are largely from practical necessity and progress is being made where it can, rather than necessarily, where it is most needed from the point of view of all the stakeholders. The most forms of interaction that are most suitable depend upon whose benefit is being considered:

- supervisors, in conducting a full and efficient job;
- the supervised, in being able to run their businesses in an efficient manner and minimise compliance costs subject to meeting the prudential (risk management) requirements – we can no doubt differentiate between the return to shareholders and the more immediate gains to management from less complexity;
- customers, in being able to have a full range of services, informed choice and maximised benefits from the structure of costs and returns;
- society at large, from having a dynamic but stable financial system in which they can have confidence;
- taxpayers, in their role as underlying insurers of the system;
- Central Banks/supervisory agencies in addressing financial stability and emergency liquidity assistance/lender of last resort.

The full list is longer insofar as counterparties, creditors, employees etc. are not properly included under one of the other headings.

There is no reason why these various stakeholders should receive an equal weight but if the design of the system is to be primarily driven by the immediate practical concerns of the supervisors and those whom they supervise this is not a guarantee that all of the interests will be met in a balanced manner. In a single jurisdiction it is possible to decide upon an appropriate balance but once we cross borders the different parties can only negotiate and their powers of negotiation vary according to the aspect involved. In Chapter 9, Dirk Schoenmaker and Sander Oosterloo consider five dimensions of this problem: effectiveness of supervision, efficiency of supervision, financial stability, competitiveness of financial firms and proximity to financial firms, but this is only part of the problem.

The principal distinction of concern is between the issue of appropriate supervision of cross-border institutions and activities in a framework of normal working and general compliance and one where something starts to go wrong. Once there is a question of actual or potential reallocation of significant losses either across people or across time then the game changes as do the players and their jurisdictional responsibilities. This has long been recognised and was addressed specifically in the European environment by the two Brouwer Reports (EFC, 2000, 2001; Brouwer *et al.*, 2003), the first on the handling of supervision across borders and the second on the handling of crises. However, the two *are* related. Since there is not a one-to-one match, those who are going to have to handle a problem need to be convinced that those who were responsible for prior supervision protected their interests adequately.[20]

There are two obvious routes out of this. One is to try to establish the appropriate means of working together. The other is to try to internationalise the structure so that there is a much closer mapping between the supervisory and problem handling agencies. The latter is already largely the case in the United States, where, despite a strong international role in the banking system, it still retains supervisory control over its systemically important banks and over the outcome of systemic events that impinge on its citizens. As we come down the ladder of economic and financial size, similar conclusions can probably be drawn for Japan, Germany and the UK, but they do not apply even to all of the G10. Belgium, the Netherlands, Sweden and Switzerland, at least, face systemic threats from the activities of cross-border institutions, where either the controllable cause or solution are outside their jurisdiction.

For small countries the problem can be acute, where almost all their banking system is foreign owned. Outside the EU/EEA small countries have somewhat more scope to organise supervision and problem solution on a basis that helps them match powers and responsibility rather better. But inside the EU/EEA, the home country principle, where the supervision of branches and direct cross-border activity are the responsibility of the home country supervisor, makes the mismatch more difficult to solve. This is emphasised by the current lack of appetite for creating new supranational institutions. (In their chapter, Schoenmaker and Oosterloo try to advance the agenda just a little by advocating a European System of Financial Supervisors, which, while driven by the national supervisors, would have some sort of centralised body with a European mandate in some sort of parallel to the European System of Central Banks (ESCB).)

Under Basel 2, the multiple supervisors of a cross-border institution are supposed to act together under a lead supervisor, who will normally be the home country supervisor, where the home country is expected to be the country of the bank's principal operation and incorporation. In the new Capital Adequacy Directive for implementing Basel 2 in the EU, the home country principle of appointing the lead (referred to as the 'consolidating' supervisor in this case) supervisor is even stronger and decisions on the approach to be applied to the bank and the options to be permitted can be made by the lead should the host country supervisors fail to agree.

The FSAP and the working of CEBS is helping regulatory structures in Europe converge but at present the forging of detailed agreements is on a case by case basis relating to individual institutions. Maria Nieto, in her comments, describes this as 'improvised co-operation' (Freixas, 2003). Such improvisation is needed because the strict interpretation of the principle of home country control would not meet the needs of the parties. Greater involvement of host countries facing systemic concerns for the bank in question is required. How such arrangements should be labelled is a sensitive issue. Vesala (2005) has described them as 'collegial' but it is the practice which really matters.[21] Host countries need to be sufficiently involved that they can anticipate problems just as well as if they were the sole supervisor themselves. They also need to be able to convince their governments (on behalf of taxpayers and financial system participants) that the supervisory task is being performed to the same standards they would impose on themselves. Otherwise the whole system would be open to recrimination as soon as anything starts to go wrong.

This process is perhaps most advanced in the Nordic–Baltic region, where the largest bank, Nordea, which is already the most cross-border of all the European banks (see Table 9.3), has announced that it expects to take advantage of the European Company Statute and turn itself into a single entity, based in Sweden but operating branches in Denmark, Estonia, Finland, Norway, Poland and Sweden. (Nordea is also an insurance company group as well as a banking group and has financial activities elsewhere, including New York.) As at March 2004 Nordea had a 40 per cent share of the Finnish banking market, 25 per cent of the Danish, 20 per cent of the Swedish and 15 per cent of the Norwegian. Its share of the insurance markets was somewhat smaller: Finland 35 per cent, Denmark 20 per cent, Norway 9 per cent and Sweden 6 per cent (all data from Rahoitustarkastus).

Such collaboration among supervisors seems elementarily sensible both in easing their co-ordination and in lowering the compliance burden on banks. The more that a single system can be applied to a bank the easier it will be for it to rationalise its operations and cut costs to the benefit of its customers. Many bank operations in managing risk only make sense if the same principles can be applied right across the group, as in many respects capital is held to support activities right across the group. The more the needs for economic and regulatory capital are aligned, subject to their different purposes, then the more efficient the organisation can be. However, this common sense is the driving force only where the home country is dominant compared to the various host countries. In the EU, where a bank operates through branches in other countries the host country does not have powers of prudential supervision (all the conduct of business rules are still applied by the authorities in the country of operation). A strong measure of 'collaboration' is thus enforced.

While in theory the home supervisor could dictate to the host supervisors or indeed simply dispense with their services and recruit staff locally, this is unlikely to be the case. A solution more like that which applies in the US is likely to be arrived at; supervisory activities will be joint under the leadership of the home (consolidating) supervisor. The solution host supervisors are hoping for is some sort of 'college' of supervisors for each major bank where the information is shared among the college and not merely dispensed when the home supervisor deems it appropriate under some extension of the current Memoranda of Understanding.

The reason that such a closer arrangement is necessary is that the host country authorities, whether supervisors or central banks, could not perform their financial stability function properly otherwise. If the host country is to ensure systemic stability it not only has to be informed about the state of the financial group but it has to be clear that its interests are being taken into account in deciding about the actions to be taken. Such actions fall into three groups (Mayes, 2005):

- voluntary actions undertaking by the bank itself or the market in the event of under-performance but regulatory compliance;
- compulsory and voluntary actions taken when regulatory limits are breached but the bank appears solvent;
- actions taken when the point of insolvency or licence withdrawal has been reached.

Each of these areas takes us beyond a narrow definition of supervision yet host supervisors have a view on how they should be handled which needs to be taken into account. There are enormous advantages in the market sorting out problems without recourse to supervisor intervention, or worse still having to address the issue of whether public funds should be used. Hence host supervisors, who fear they will be at a disadvantage in the event of difficulty, will be particularly keen to see effective market discipline, with clear market signals and a strongly functioning market for corporate control that converts these signals into action. Unfortunately, the banks and financial groupings for whom the problem is most acute are among those more immune from external pressure as their takeover or merger would usually involve difficult questions of excess market concentration. The route of effective pressure will therefore have to come more from shareholders within the existing grouping.

The effectiveness of this pressure also depends on whether people believe that, should the bank get into difficulty the authorities will pressure it effectively and ultimately resolve it in a way that would mean that the management loses their jobs and the shareholders get wiped out if the bank appears insolvent. Supervisors all have in place requirements for prompt corrective action (PCA) should regulatory limits be challenged or broken. However, what these imply in practice and what the host supervisors can predict the lead supervisor might wish to do is far from certain. Problems with large institutions are fortunately rare so there is not a clear history of response which would act as guidance. Indeed insofar as there is a history it would tend to lead people to believe that a degree of forbearance is more likely. That is not what the host country supervisors, threatened with systemic problems, want to hear. A home supervisor might very well feel that there is an opportunity for some enforced burden sharing should the forbearance turn out not to work and the difficulties increase.

The largest concern, however, is not the incentives to relatively weak PCA but the realisation that the authorities do not have in place some system for resolution that will involve much other than a somewhat incoherent bailout with the help of taxpayers' money (Mayes, 2005; Mayes and Liuksila, 2003). In other words it is the lack of a believable ex ante agreement on how any such crisis might be addressed that is the issue rather than sorting out how supervision of the institution in normal times might go.[22]

However, the problem is not a straight-forward application of the 'too big to fail' epithet. (In any case what is meant here by too big to fail is 'too important to the financial system for the business to close', or perhaps, in Alan Greenspan's phrase, 'too big to close quickly', not literally that the existing bank must be kept in being. Thus business continuity is required for at least the main operations of the bank even if there is to be a change of ownership and management, say through the formation of a bridge bank (Mayes, 2005). Hüpkes (2004) has an interesting discussion of whether some 'inessential' lines of business can be closed or a least held in suspension while the main operations are maintained and ownership changed.) In a very real sense cross-border banks can be 'too big to save' (Mayes, 2005; Sigurdsson, 2003; Hüpkes, 2003) where they are headquartered in countries that are small compared to size of the possible exposure. Switzerland has explicitly recognised in the case of UBS and Credit

Suisse and has actually capped the payout from its deposit insurance fund. This puts the incentive rather differently, because, then the lead supervisor needs the predictable co-operation of the host authorities if it is to be able to put together a sensible outcome. Thus, if the outcome is going to have systemic consequences in both the home and the host countries unless it is properly managed, rather than just in some host countries, the chance of getting a prior agreement is enhanced. A country cannot provide support just for its part of the troubled institution; its support will go, the institution as a whole, and its creditors and depositors.

Outside the EU, the common response is to find some means of carving up these systemically important banks among the various authorities in the event of failure. This is a form of applying the territoriality principle (Baxter *et al.*, 2004). While inelegant and probably suboptimal for some of the creditors it does enable the institution to be kept going. New Zealand has probably articulated this most clearly, by insisting that foreign-owned systemic banks not merely adopt a corporate form in New Zealand that permits a ready takeover by the New Zealand authorities but that they actually keep all systemically relevant functions inside the New Zealand subsidiary (Bollard, 2005). A really rationalised cross-border bank would concentrate its functions, treasury operations for example, so that the subsidiary does not constitute something that could function on its own. This has already been happening with Nordea and although it is at present operating through subsidiaries rather than branches in most of the Nordic countries (Mayes, 2005), it is not clear how readily the constituent banks could operate on their own, even now, because of the centralisation of functions that has taken place (a point also made by Eisenbeis in his chapter). (It is a separate issue whether territoriality will normally allow the carving out of a sufficiently 'fair' or viable portion of the net worth to avoid the resolution being a systemically harmful event. It can work in the US as the chances are that a disproportionate amount of the net assets will be there and that foreign banks will in any case not be systemic.)

It is worth pursuing the New Zealand example a little further because the proposals there have taken a new turn, one which illustrates very clearly the need to balance the interests of the various stakeholders. The systemic banks in New Zealand are now all Australian owned. These banks have lobbied the Australian government to try to get a single regulatory environment, based on the Australian system. While one could debate whether their motivation was purely to keep the most efficient form and avoid the inefficiencies of facing multiple regulators, and did not involve some element of opting for what appears the more debtor-friendly regime, there is clearly great sense in having a single regulator for a financial system that is in many respects rather more integrated than those in Europe despite the use of separate currencies. While the New Zealand supervisor, the Reserve Bank, has resisted the move it appears that the New Zealand government views the proposal favourably (RBNZ, 2005).

However, the issues that need to be sorted out before both countries could be confident that the systemic issues are addressed are considerable. Australia has domestic depositor preference which would clearly have to be removed or at least extended so that New Zealand depositors are treated equally. Similarly there will need to be a government level agreement on how problems are to be handled as the supervisory authorities do not have access to their own funds but would have to deal either through their respective Central Banks or governments, i.e. exactly the same problem as in Europe. In this instance since all the systemic banks already have APRA (the Australian prudential regulator) as the lead regulator it would be fairly easy to set up a single system, with the Reserve Bank of New Zealand, both as the supervisor and as the lender of last resort charged with ensuring financial stability in New Zealand, included sufficiently inside the framework that it can carry out its task. They have formed a Trans-Tasman Council on Banking Supervision, which will have a monitoring and advisory role. Problems would of course remain with conduct of business supervision unless that were eventually also to be harmonised but that involves different regulators in both countries.

It would at least in principle be easier to leap towards the grand supranational design in the European case as well but, as Table 9.3 indicates, the number of cross-border banks in the EU with systemic implications for host countries is reasonably limited. If we regard being systemic as having a market share of 10 per cent or more, then the number is likely to be clearly below 30 even in the enlarged EU. If we draw the line at 5 per cent the number will be larger but the problem is still countable. Furthermore, this would require agreement not between two authorities but between regulators in the 28 countries of the EU/EEA (soon to be 30) and since not all countries have consolidated regulators this would be an even more complex task. The argument for concluding a limited number of individual collegial agreements among each of supervisors concerned therefore seems more attractive, at least in the short run. However, the longer term is likely to involve an EU-wide agreement as the process of integration continues and the pragmatism is replaced by 'neatness'. Schoenmaker and Oosterloo argue against such interim regional agreements on the grounds that they will need to be changed when the Europewide agreement is negotiated. That of course is correct but since the timing of such an agreement is indefinite and could easily come after the first crisis, this sounds like a cost that the parties and those whom they supervise would be prepared to bear. In any case there is a strong chance that Europe-wide agreement would embrace most of the pre-existing arrangements.

While not identical to the Schoenmaker and Oosterloo proposals in Chapter 9 this discussion comes close to them. They opt for the home supervisor having the task but with what they describe as a European mandate, which would come from the 'European System of Financial Supervisors' they outline. The real issue will be in the detail, as to how the host supervisors and other authorities in the host country are to be sufficiently involved both to tap their local knowledge and to provide enough information and power to exercise their mandate for financial stability. Someone has to have the authority to act in the case of difficulty and the other authorities have to find a way of delegating power to them or being part of the organisation that satisfies their worries of the maintenance of stability.

Nevertheless, such supervisory agreements will not necessarily fully involve the governments. Maria Nieto suggests a different way out, based on the US example (an approach also advocated in Mayes (2005)), namely that the structure should be augmented by a body separate from the supervisors that is responsible for resolution. In the US this is the FDIC.[23] In the EU many deposit insurance companies are in effect pay boxes, which just collect and manage the funds, and pay out on the say so of other authorities. Mayes (2005) only offers the deposit insurance company as an example of a suitable organisation but suggests that some entity with both the power to act across the borders and the necessary resources needs to exist. The advantage of placing a deposit insurance agency in this role is that it has incentives to intervene before losses mount and hence to counter the tendency towards forbearance. Mayes *et al.* (2001) and Mayes and Liuksila (2003) advocate very strongly that there should be intervention before there are any significant losses, so that the scope for cross-border argument among the countries involved is much smaller as they have little at stake, and the resolution can be a technical and not a political matter.[24]

The extent of the problem to be covered is illustrated in Table 1.3, drawn from Nieto's work with Garcia (Garcia and Nieto, 2005). In trying to put together procedures for cross-border banks it is necessary to encompass all of the jurisdictions in which they have significant operations. However, there are wide differences in the legal framework governing how countries operate when a bank needs to be resolved. Not only is there variation in whether banks are treated specially in the event of insolvency, but there is also variation in the application of territoriality as opposed to universality and single versus separate entities. One might have thought that at least there would be substantial similarity of treatment of depositors within the EU, given the existence of the Deposit Insurance Directive.[25] However, this is not the case, some EU/EEA countries offer depositor preference, while most do not. The discrepancies are quite wide ranging, as the degree of harmonisation entailed by the directive is decidedly limited (Garcia and Nieto, 2005). Even the level of protection varies across countries, with some exceeding the minimum prescribed and the new members having derogations permitting lower

Table 1.3 Examples of different resolution practices worldwide: EU and rest of the world

Region	Separate insolvency for banks	Banks subject to general insolvency laws	Universal proceeding	Territorial approach	Single entity	Separate entities	Comity	Depositor preference	No depositor preference	Ring-fencing
EU	Ireland The UK Spain		EU directive for EU banks and branches of EU banks within the EU (with exceptions)	EU directive for non-EU banks	EU directive for EU banks	EU directive for branches of non-EU banks	EU directive within the EU	Austria Italy Norway UK	Belgium Denmark Finland France Germany Ireland The Netherlands Portugal Spain Sweden	Germany Possibly also for branches of foreign banks in the EU
RoW	Japan The US	Hong Kong The US bank holding companies		The US for foreign financial firms with US branches	The US for US banks	The US for non-US banks		Australia Hong Kong The US	New Zealand	Australia The US for branches of foreign banks

Source: Garcia and Nieto, 2005.

levels for a period of adjustment. All this makes the idea of orderly and well co-ordinated action for a cross-border bank where several countries face systemic difficulties somewhat difficult to conceive, without further changes and enhanced co-operation.

The chapters in the book do not develop these ideas. Clearly the details for such ideas to be workable are extensive, such as how a resolution agency separates its judicial decision making function from its implementation function. However, there is a substantial difference between constructing an international deposit insurance agency or empowering existing agencies to act on behalf of all the countries in systemic cases and creating an agency that can act in all cases. The FDIC is a major organisation yet it has not had to cope with the failure of a systemic bank in the US. It has had to deal with a steady flow of smaller failures, it would not make sense to construct an agency facing a small risk of substantial problems on such a scale but attaching it to existing organisations might make more sense. What is really needed is a body of expertise to draw on in an emergency. It is somewhat analogous to the fire brigade in rural areas; although well trained, they are normally employed in other jobs and just drop everything in an emergency. Thus either attaching the function to an organisation in the lead country or creating a contingency organisation in an EU/EEA context might meet the need, rather than expensive institution building that would take a long time to agree. However, it is easy to have sympathy with the pessimists who argue that no action is likely before the first serious problem (Sigurdsson, 2003; Kane, 2005, for example[26]).

Kane (2005) bases his pessimism in part on the experience in the US where there was strong state resistance to having economy-wide solutions. He at least suggests that there may be some routes for making introduction to many of the necessary systems possible without a crisis. One feature is to make the supra-national body trim, as we suggest, likening it to a holding company that is trying to reconcile the behaviour of different subsidiaries operating in different cultures. Such a 'company' might measure, manage and fund cross-country risk, including the risk of cross-country contagion. If it were possible to create a market in deposit insurance derivatives in the Member States then cross-border trade could spread the risk. He likens a deposit insurance guarantee to a credit default swap. The deposit insurer would charge a premium to each bank equivalent to the management cost plus the value of the risk exposure. There could then be a secondary market in these contracts. This in itself might lead to a better valuation of the exposures across the different countries with their different schemes. He suggests that the European Central Bank (ECB) foster the market and the 'holding company' would facilitate the derivation of comparable information.

Regulation and the development of financial markets

While the literature on the regulation of banks is generally concerned about the danger of over-regulation, that on the regulation of financial markets generally has the opposite slant and is looking to intervention to improve what is seen to be a rather poor performance (as explained by Kemppainen, Chapter 10, Leinonen, Chapter 11 and Milne, Chapter 12).

Regulation is normally justified on the grounds of market failure without it. In all but the very largest jurisdictions there tends to be a monopoly in the provision of financial marketplaces and in the payment and settlement systems. In these cases the authorities have two main interests. The first is to ensure, as for the banking system, that market participants and society at large can have confidence in the system and that the risks of systemically damaging consequences from unfortunate events are managed to standards acceptable to the authorities. Many of these risks are operational but others relate to the limiting of exposures, granting of credit in addition to conduct of business concerns to ensure fairness, transparency and quality of reporting standards. It is commonly argued that in some cases the necessary confidence can only be obtained by the authorities participating in the system themselves, typically by the central bank in the payment system, for example. Only central bank money is regarded as providing the necessary certainty for interbank transactions in the framework outlined by Harry Leinonen in Chapter 12. The second, and the one which is the main focus of this book, is that because these marketplaces and systemic services are network industries they have difficulty evolving. As a result participants and society at large may be subject to unnecessary costs and consequent welfare loss.

The losses can be simply because technology is not updated and hence people have to pay more per transaction than is strictly necessary. Transactions may be unduly time consuming to carry out and may also be unnecessarily slow to complete. It is already technologically feasible to run most payment and settlement systems in real time, for example, as Leinonen points out. However, many of the costs are imposed, not within existing markets but because in an integrating world it is proving difficult to link markets. While this problem is highlighted in the EU, which has a positive mission to achieve an integrated financial market, it applies generally as investors wish to diversify risks across markets and assets and firms wish to raise capital in international markets. Progress is proving aggravatingly slow, despite the Lamfalussy process, which is trying to accelerate the implementation of the Financial Services Action Plan, and the continuing efforts to create a Single European Payment Area in which cross-border transactions in euro are no more costly than current within country transactions.

The reasons why the process is slow are obvious. There is first of all a competitive factor. If in the resultant single market there is only to be one or two systems some of the existing providers will either have to exit or combine with others. These changes are happening, albeit slowly, but with the existence of monopolies there is a danger that the price the losers will extract to exit. However the structure of the market makes some forms of amalgamation and competition/co-operation impossible. Deutsche Börse for example has a vertically integrated form whereby it owns the clearing system and securities depository (Clearstream and Eurex clearing) as well as the trading platform. This not only means that Deutsche Börse's customers have no choice but that horizontal linkages that do not involve Deutsche Börse dominating the system (or being taken over) are unlikely.

Leinonen and Milne offer nicely contrasting perspectives. Leinonen shows the facets which the various payment and settlement systems need to harmonise if there can be a single well integrated system. Milne on the other hand offers a rather different solution to this problem by suggesting that to some extent harmonisation issues can be put to one side and that what is necessary is the requirement to allow access and choice to customers. (The means by which they communicate has to be harmonised, which is an aspect of Leinonen's focus.) Thus, Deutsche Börse customers should be entitled to settle elsewhere if they wish and other customers should have access to Clearstream all at non-discriminatory prices. Harmonisation can then follow and will be encouraged. The euro RTGS system TARGET is a good illustration. When it was first set up it was the minimum necessary for the system to function, namely each national RTGS needed to be able to connect to the ECB system and offer sufficient common protocols that payments could be passed through successfully in real time with a minimum of delay. They did not need to link to each other and they could offer a wide range of services domestically. Now with TARGET2 the number of different platforms is being reduced and the degree of interoperability and communality of service level substantially increased. Ultimately it will probably go to a single platform. Of course this system is run by the members of the ESCB, who have an obligation to make some such system work under the terms of the EU treaty, so it is not totally compatible with how private sector monopolies might work together.

There are differences among the securities settlement systems in Europe: technical standards; access; timing; taxation and legal treatment, according to the Giovannini (2003) expert group working on the topic. If all those involved in making transactions have to be able to handle every system then the burden on their costs will be considerable and the incentives will be to concentrate on the national system. In the same way changing all national systems just to assist international transmission is even more burdensome as the majority of transactions are normally within rather than between jurisdictions. According to Milne, the key feature inhibiting development of a much more competitive system is access to the securities themselves in the depository where they are held and it is only the access to this basic book transfer function and its non-discriminatory pricing that needs to be tackled by regulators in order to open the system up. The whole of the rest of the sequence from placing the buy or sell order, finding someone with whom to trade, agreeing the price, down to transferring title against the payment can be accomplished and improved with market pressures.[27] There are different routes to doing this. Large global custodian banks have their own networks through which they can complete much of the process and only need recourse to others when they cannot net transactions, smaller dealers can transact trade through their domestic securities depository that then accesses the other country and in some cases it is possible to deal direct. Similar complexity can exist in other network industries, whether telephony or gas or electricity. The customer knows with whom they placed the order and they eventually get the product but the routing can be various and is not their concern except in as far as it affects the price.

As with the payment system, the issue is how much co-operation is necessary to get a Europe-wide or indeed world-wide system inside which the various suppliers can compete for services. At present we face two forms of competition – competition among suppliers to provide the market system, which Kemppainen labels 'competition for the market' and competition inside the common system 'competition in the market'. At present the payment system is highly differentiated. European countries still use different payment instruments – cheques are the main means of payment in some countries and non-existent in others. Clearly some basic forms of agreement are necessary for a system to function under any protocol; for example, who pays for the costs of the transactions – the payer, the payee or do they share it? To a large extent it is for the industry to come to an agreement, with the European level regulators in the background. Progress by unilateral action of one of the major players is relatively unlikely, because, if the others do not follow by definition in a network it will not function. The person with whom you wish to communicate also has to be connected. The more people join the network the more valuable the network is to each of them but as Kemppainen points out this is a typical chicken and egg problem. If the others are linked then I will join but this argument applies to all participants so the process does not start if the investment is on the major scale involved here.

Taken together this ends up with quite a limited role for regulators:

- trying to see that there are not legal impediments;
- trying to assist in the development of the common standards and infrastructure;
- trying to promote competition, particularly in the downstream services.[28]

In some countries the role may go somewhat further, in trying to encourage innovation and to ensuring new and efficient services.

However, in major parts of the payment system the public sector sees that the only way it can exercise its role is to be a provider. This is less true in the case of retail payments but it is predominantly the case for large value payments (Khiaonarong, 2003). This then adds a major potential conflict of interest to the problem. As a provider the public sector may feel inclined to subsidise in order to ensure as widespread a membership as possible – thereby driving the borderline of what is large value into the territory of the retail systems. As it has a special concern for the safety of the system, it maybe over-engineered and hence expensive, as Leinonen points out.

It is easy to understand what the inhibitions are to development, but as Leinonen also observes, the payment system is far from the real time system that one could initiate from anywhere in reach of a mobile phone or landline that one might reasonably expect. Seeing the payment system operate like the internet sounds a possible ambition. Big steps can be made, as with the setting up of the Continuous Linked Settlement (CLS)[29] to transform the market for trading and settlement in the main currencies round the world. Simply listing the inhibitors and how they might be addressed, as Leinonen does, provides an agenda for progress.

Notes

1 The Preface to the 'Financial Stability' edition of the Bank of Finland *Bulletin* explains that the Bank sees itself as a 'promoter of stability' as a means to achieving the objective of a 'reliable' system and contributing to the ESCB role of 'promoting the smooth operation of payments systems and the stability of the financial system' (Bank of Finland, 2004: 1).
2 There is a debate about whether nowadays one should regard the lender of last resort function as normally providing liquidity to the market as a whole rather than to individual institutions in the traditional Bagehotian manner (see Nieto's comment on Chapter 7 and Goodfriend and King (1988)).
3 However, it is important not to over-emphasise the point. Competition in Scotland was intense and one of the two largest banks, the Royal Bank of Scotland, actually managed to force its rival, the Bank of Scotland, to close its doors for a while, by acquiring so many of its claims that it made it illiquid (but not insolvent). The English lender of last resort arrangements did not apply.
4 The period of 'free banking' was ended by the introduction of regulation with the Scottish Banking Act of 1845, not by any failure in the system.
5 Goodhart (2000) credits George Kaufman with this insight.
6 Cynics might argue that in countries where banks are protected and inefficient, the robbery of customers and shareholders alike through impaired services and returns is more insidious.
7 This theme of finding means of increasing effective market discipline also underpins the approach in Mayes *et al.* (2001). There are many routes to such discipline including both equity and debt markets.
8 Benink criticises pillar 3 of Basel 2 for only introducing an element of disclosure in order to provide market discipline. If banks do not issue much in the way of marketable instruments then the routes for that discipline are limited. Furthermore unless there is a response to the market information then discipline does not work – discipline comes from signal plus action not signal alone. Benink suggests that supervisors should make it clear that they will start an

investigation if at any stage there appears to be an abnormal deterioration in a bank's subordinated debt.

9 Some might argue that it was also partly a quid pro quo for the increased independence given to the Bank in 1997 for the running of monetary policy.

10 Such overlaps can be healthy in that they foster competition. The Bank of England produces a quarterly *Financial Stability Review*, while the UK FSA produces an annual *Financial Risk Outlook*. These reflect their two perspectives, one from the aggregate and the other from the analysis of the individual institutions. Approaching stability from these two directions and overlapping in the middle seems to be a positive outcome. The fact that there can be a contrast of views will encourage the parties to discuss them. This is clearly different from having contradictory regulation from two perspectives or duplicative supervision.

11 Regulators can be divided in more than one dimension. Here we have tended to concentrate on prudential regulation rather than conduct of business, as it is less clear why a central bank should have a great advantage in supervising or regulating conduct of business issues. Indeed one might argue that in conduct of business there is no particular reason why financial services should be treated any differently from the rest of the economy and a unified conduct of business regulator could be economy-wide. Nevertheless many financial regulators cover all aspects of the business and are hence unified in that sense. They are doubly unified if they also cover all parts of the financial sector. The Wallis Report (1997) in Australia provides one of the clearest expositions of the framework for financial regulation and how it might be allocated.

12 Llewellyn (1999) uses a sample of 123 countries and comes up with very similar proportions.

13 Goodhart (2000) also uses this concept as well as the word 'fuzzy'.

14 There are various ways these interactions can work, as in the case of general agreements such as Basel 2, where complexity will be applied by all regulators, increased complexity could be in the interest of larger financial institutions as they can spread the fixed costs over more operations.

15 Kahn and Santos presented a different paper (2004) in the conference, which addressed the potential conflict between a lender of last resort and a deposit insurance agency directly.

16 As part of the general increase in regulation deposit insurance is becoming more widespread. Out of 170 countries in the Demirgüç-Kunt *et al.* (2005) database, 49 had deposit insurance schemes in 1995 and 87 (half) in 2003.

17 Eisenbeis suggests that since banking is more concentrated in the EU the chances are that, should there be a failure, it will be more likely to present solvency problems for the deposit insurance funds.

18 The Table distinguishes the following characteristics of deposit insurance funds in the EU:

- who is the agency responsible for the fund (in the majority of cases it is separate from the central bank or the supervisory authority and four of them are private companies);
- whether they are funded (by the industry) (most are funded in full or in part but some expect to pay out with the use of funds raised from the surviving banks only in the event of the problem);
- whether there is minimum size for the fund compared to the value of the deposits covered (in the main);
- whether contributions are weighted by the risk of the institution (only in a minority of cases);

- coverage of deposits (most are higher than the Directive's minimum but four new members (denoted by *) have transitional arrangements to bring them up to the minimum);
- whether the state provides some element of the insurance (equally split);
- whether claims can be offset;
- how long it is before the fund pays out (in the vast majority, it is over three months for a full pay out so very considerable difficulty may be imposed on some depositors).

19 The introduction of deposit insurance is, in many respects, part of the dialectic we described earlier. Countries that have had unpleasant crises with substantial costs to the taxpayer and society at large will try to limit the costs and chance of any further crises and establishing a deposit insurance fund where the limits of the exposure are delimited and in most cases the primary responsibility for recompense is taken away from the taxpayer. Demirgüç-Kunt *et al.* (2005) find that having a crisis is a major stimulant for the introduction of deposit insurance in their survey.

20 As Garcia and Nieto (2005) point out, the problem of a convincing arrangement in which the supervisory and safety net authorities can trust at the cross-border level is greatly enhanced by the lack of such arrangements at the country level in some of the member states. In any case at least five different structures can be distinguished where the arrangements work differently inside the EU:

- a parent bank authorised in an EU country;
- a subsidiary whose parent bank is authorised in another EU country;
- a subsidiary whose parent bank is authorised in a non-EU country;
- a branch whose parent is bank authorised in another EU country;
- a branch whose parent bank is authorised in a non-EU country.

On top of this we can impose the categorisation of parents, subsidiaries and branches as to whether they are of systemic importance in their respective countries.

21 The European Financial Services Round Table (EFSRT, 2004) has come up with a similar proposal of forming a 'college of supervisors' for each cross-border entity that requires it. The key issue they identify is 'How do you resolve conflicts?' They suggest referring the issue to CEBS or the competent European level committee for a conglomerate. While some sort of reference might work for generalised issues, it would not work in a crisis or where PCA is required, nor would it have a legal basis unless incorporated by the parties involved. The college we envisage has its own clear decision making structure, led by the consolidating supervisor, with clear rules laid down in advance as to how problems, whether PCA or insolvency are to be handled. Least cost resolution needs to be a clear concept. Since the EFR is a grouping of banks and other financial companies it is not surprising that their report does not mention the issues of PCA or actins in the event of failure.

22 Even in the case of supervision there is cause for scepticism, as Eisenbeis (Chapter 8) puts it: 'While the Basel Committee may call for different countries to "cooperate" and "coordinate" their supervisory activities, these pleas are likely to have little effect or substance in actual cases, unless there are specific arrangements and procedures for handling institutions in place ex ante.'

23 In the US there is rather more variety in the treatment of financial institutions than in Europe, for example, so the FDIC only deals with a reasonably narrow definition of what constitutes a bank and separate funds insure thrifts and housing finance. In the present context we are treating it as if it had all embracing coverage as that is a closer description of the position in the EU.

24 Here also the US system has well aligned incentives because the FDIC is required to step in and close the bank if its capital ratio falls below 2 per cent, which limits the likely loss. Being able to invoke an exception because the bank is of systemic importance requires both swift action and explicit acceptance by the Comptroller of the Currency, the Federal Reserve Board and The Secretary of the Treasury (Stern and Feldman, 2004: x).

25 Directive 94/19/EC 30 May 1994, *OJ L* 135, 31 May 1994.

26 '[I]t is hard to resist, at least as a working hypothesis, the proposition that for the foreseeable future only painful crisis experience – and not the logical force of abstract economic argument – could convince national authorities to cede sufficient authority to Brussels to permit the construction of an incentive-compatible PanEuropean crisis-prevention and crisis-management agency' (Kane, 2005: 2).

27 There is one important over-simplification here. All trades do not have to go through the full sequence. In many cases it will be possible to net earlier as traders themselves will have a stream of buy and sell orders for the same securities. Since the securities are largely 'dematerialised' these days, we are not discussing transferring particular certificates but simply making electronic book entries, where the total book is the number of series of a particular sort available. While the basic book will be held in a particular location the book can effectively be spread over a number of custodians if the secondary custodians hold blocks of securities on behalf of specified clients. The secondary custodians can transfer the ownership of the block it controls – and inform the primary depository, if required, of who the beneficial owner is.

28 This list reflects the core principles which have been developed by the Basel Committee on Payment and Settlement Systems.

29 Within the CLS Group, CLS Bank International provides the payment versus payment settlement and CLS Services provides the operational and back-office support.

Bibliography

Aguirre, E. (1997) 'Basic reforms of the banking systems in Latin America: comparative analysis, trends and outlook', Second International Conference on Reforms of the Banking Systems in Latin America, Caracas, Venezuela, 27 October.

Bank of Finland (2004) 'Financial stability', *Bulletin*, Special Issue.

Barth, J.R., Dopico, L.G., Nolle, D.E. and Wilcox, J.A. (2001) 'An international comparison and assessment of the structure of banking supervision', mimeo, Auburn University, Auburn, AL.

Baxter, T.C., Hansen, J. and Sommer, J.H. (2004) 'Two cheers for territoriality: an essay on international bank insolvency law', *American Bankruptcy Law Journal* 78(1), 57–91.

Beck, T. (2003) 'The incentive-compatible design of deposit insurance and bank failure resolution', in Mayes, D.G. and Liuksila, A. (eds) *Who Pays for Bank Insolvency?*, Basingstoke: Palgrave Macmillan, pp. 118–41.

Benston, G.J. (1995). 'Safety nets and moral hazard in banking', in Sawamoto, K., Kakajima, Z. and Taguchi, H. (eds) *Financial Stability in a Changing Environment*, London: Macmillan, pp. 329–77.

Bollard, A. (2005) 'Being a responsible host: supervising foreign owned banks', in Evanoff, D. and Kaufman, G. (eds) *Systemic Bank Crises: Resolving Large Bank Insolvencies*, Singapore: World Scientific Publishing, pp. 321–45.

Brouwer, H., Hebbink, G. and Wesseling, S. (2003) 'A European approach to banking crises', in Mayes, D.G. and Liuksila, A. (eds) *Who Pays for Bank Insolvency?*, Basingstoke: Palgrave Macmillan, pp. 205–21.

Calomiris, C.W. (1999) 'Building an incentive-compatible safety net', *Journal of Banking and Finance* 23: 1499–519.

Copelovitch, M.S. and Singer, D.A. (2004) 'The stability dilemma: the institutional structure of central banks and bank regulation', mimeo, Harvard University, Department of Government, Boston, MA.

Demirgüç-Kunt, A., Kane, E.J. and Laeven, L. (2005) 'Determinants of deposit-insurance adoption and design', mimeo, World Bank, Washington, DC.

EFC (2000) 'Report on financial stability', Economic and Financial Committee Economic Paper, no. 143.

EFC (2001) 'Report on financial crisis management', Economic and Financial Committee Economic Paper, no. 156.

European Financial Services Round Table (EFSRT) (2004) *Towards a Lead Supervisor for Cross Border Financial Institutions in the European Union*, Brussels, EFSRT.

Freixas, X. (2003) 'Crisis management in Europe', in Kremers, J.J.M., Schoenmaker, D. and Wierts, P.J. (eds) *Financial Supervision in Europe*, Cheltenham: Edward Elgar, pp. 109–12,

Garcia, G.H. and Nieto, M.J. (2005) 'Banking crisis management in the European Union: multiple regulators and resolution authorities', *Journal of Banking Regulation*, 6(3): 206–26.

Giovannini, A. (2003) *Second Report on EU Clearing and Settlement Arrangements*, Brussels: European Commission, April.

Goodfriend, M. and King, R.G. (1988) 'Financial deregulation, monetary policy and central banking', *Federal Reserve Bank of Richmond Economic Review* 74: 3–22.

Goodhart, C.A.E. (2000) 'The organisational structure of banking supervision', Financial Stability Institute Occasional Paper, no. 1, Basel: BIS.

Greenspan, A. (1994) Testimony Before the US Senate Committee on Banking, Housing and Urban Affairs, 103–692, US Senate, Washington, DC, pp. 130–2.

Haubrich, J.G. (1996) 'Combining bank supervision and monetary policy', Federal Reserve Bank of Cleveland Economic Commentary, November.

Hüpkes, E (2003). 'Learning lessons and implementing a new approach to banking insolvency in Switzerland', in Mayes, D.G. and Liuksila, A. (eds) *Who Pays for Bankruptcy Insolvency?*, Basingstoke: Palgrave Macmillan, pp. 242–71.

Hüpkes, E. (2004) 'Protect functions not institutions', *The Financial Regulator* 9(3): 43–9.

Kahn, C.M. and Santos, J.A.C. (2004) 'Allocating bank regulatory powers: lender of last resort, deposit insurance and supervision', Bank of Finland Conference on the Structure of Financial Supervision, Helsinki, 2–3 September, forthcoming *European Economic Review*.

Kane, E.J. (1977) 'Good intentions and unintended evil: the case against selective credit allocation', *Journal of Money Credit and Banking* 9(1): 55–69.

Kane, E. (2005) 'Can the European Community afford to neglect the need for more accountable safety net management?', *Atlantic Economic Journal* 34: 127–44.

Leinonen, H. and Soramäki, K. (2003) 'Simulating interbank payment and securities settlement mechanisms with the BoF – PSS2 simulator', Bank of Finland Discussion Paper, 23/2003.

Llewellyn, D. (1999) 'The institutional structure of regulatory agencies', in Courtis, N. (ed.) *How Countries Supervise their Banks, Issuers and Securities Markets*, London: Central Banking Publications.

Lundberg, E. (2000) 'Monetary policy and banking supervision functions of the central bank', Banco Central do Brasil Working Paper, no. 2.

Masciandaro, D. (2005) 'Central banks or single financial authorities? A political economy approach', in Masciandaro, D. (ed.) *Central Banks and Single Financial Authorities*, Cheltenham: Edward Elgar.

Mayes, D.G. (1979) *The Property Boom: The Effects of Building Society Behaviour on House Prices*, Oxford: Martin Robertson.

Mayes, D.G. (2005) 'The role of the safety net in resolving large financial institutions', in Evanoff, D. and Kaufman, G. (eds) *Systemic Financial Crises: Resolving Large Bank Insolvencies*, Singapore, World Scientific Publications, pp. 275–306.

Mayes, D.G. and Liuksila, A. (2003) *Who Pays for Bank Insolvency?*, Basingstoke: Palgrave Macmillan.

Mayes, D.G., Halme, L. and Liuksila, A. (2001) *Improving Banking Supervision*, Basingstoke: Palgrave.

Myddelton, D.R. (2004) *Unshackling Accountants*, London: Institute of Economic Affairs.

National Economic Research Associates (2004) *The FSA's Methodology for Cost–Benefit Analysis*, London: NERA.

Pauli, R (2000) 'Payments remain fundamental for banks and central banks', Bank of Finland Discussion Paper, 6/2000.

Peek, J., Rosengren, E. and Tootell, G. (1999) 'Is bank supervision central to central banking?', *Quarterly Journal of Economics* 114(2): 629–53.

Repullo, R. (2000) 'Who should act as lender of last resort: an incomplete contracts model', *Journal of Money, Credit and Banking* 32(2): 580–605.

Reserve Bank of New Zealand (RBNZ) (2005) 'Review of the regulation and performance of New Zealand's major financial institutions', available online at http://www.rbnz.govt.nz/finstab/banking/supervision/1498932.html.

Sigurdsson, J. (2003) 'Small countries, large multi-country banks: a challenge to supervisors – the example of the Nordic–Baltic area', in Mayes, D.G. and Liuksila, A. (eds) *Who Pays for Bankruptcy Insolvency?*, Basingstoke: Palgrave Macmillan, pp. 142–63.

Smith, A. (1776) *An Inquiry into the Nature and Causes of the Wealth of Nations*, Edinburgh: William Strahan.

Stern, G. and Feldman, R. (2004) *Too Big to Fail*, Washington, DC: Brookings Institution.

Vesala, J. (2005) 'Prudential supervision and deposit insurance issues raised by the European Company Statute', Colloquium on the European Company Statute, ECB, Frankfurt, 23 February.

Wallis Report (1997) *Financial System Inquiry Final Report*, Canberra: Australian Government Printing Service.

White, L.H. (1984) *Free Banking in Britain: Theory, Experience and Debate, 1800–1845*, Cambridge: Cambridge University Press.

Wood, G.E. (2004) 'A skeptical view of bank regulation', *Journal of Financial Regulation and Compliance* 15(3): 1–23.

Wood, G.E. and Capie, F. (forthcoming) *Studies in the Lender of Last Resort*, London: Routledge.

2 Financial supervision from an historical perspective

Was the development of such supervision designed, or largely accidental?

Charles A.E. Goodhart[1]

Introduction

I have approached the history of financial supervision through the lens of a Central Bank (CB) economist, and have focused on two periods of history. The first relates to the period before 1914, working primarily on US banking history (Goodhart, 1969) and UK banking history (Goodhart, 1972) – both primarily relating to the period 1895–1914 – before turning to a more general study of central banking in developed countries in *The Evolution of Central Banks* (Goodhart, 1988), with much of the material for that coming out of the invaluable studies of CB and monetary histories contained in the collected papers of the US National Monetary Commission (1910/1911). The next section of this chapter is essentially a potted version of that collection of work.

The second period of focus covers my continuing work as an economic adviser to the Bank of England (BoE). This is the main subject matter of the fourth section of the chapter.

This leaves some gaps. The first relates to expertise on developments in other developed countries, particularly in Continental Europe and especially between 1914 and 1970. I cover the history between 1914 and 1970 briefly in the third section, but this is far sketchier and less confident than the other two main sections. The second relates to my standpoint as a Central Bank economist. There are multiple other starting points for looking at the past development of financial supervision, e.g. from the viewpoint of a practical commercial banker, as a bank customer, as a professional supervisor or an historian of varying hues.

A brief history, 1800–1914

While it might be possible to establish the need for, and functions of, a CB, from abstract first principles, in practice they have evolved historically over the course of time.[2] Initially CBs were set up by special government charter. The earlier CBs, e.g. BoE, Banque de France, were established to enable the government to raise money (for the purpose of fighting a war). The initial capital, raised from the private sector, was invested in government debt, and the CB usually became the adviser to, and financial operator for, the government in debt management, i.e. arranging new issues and redemptions, keeping the debt register, making the regular interest payments. Naturally the CB also became banker to the government, with tax receipts and public sector expenditures passing through its books. In return for this support for government finance, the government usually provided the CB with certain competitive advantages in its role as an ordinary commercial bank, e.g. a special charter, limited liability, monopoly of joint stock banking in the capital city of the country etc.

These advantages meant that, during their early years, such CBs became by far the predominant, and strongest, commercial bank in the country, particularly so in the central capital city. This was at a time, up till the middle of the nineteenth century, when the banking system in European countries was fragmented into many small, and often unstable, local banks. Such country banks then found it more economical to hold their liquid reserves as deposits with the nascent CBs, than as gold or silver coins in their own vaults. Among other advantages the settlement of interbank payment orders could be done cheaper and better by transfers over the books of the CB than by carting specie, or notes, physically around the country. Moreover, the local small banks were in a standard customer/banker relationship with the CB. When the local bank/customer was short of ready cash, it would seek to borrow directly from the CB. As the acknowledged strongest bank in the system, the CB became, during the course of the nineteenth century, the Lender of Last Resort, when other lenders could, or would, not also lend.

Initially the CB was perceived as just another commercial bank, though the strongest and with certain special attributes, with profits as its main aim. However, the monetary regime of that period was the gold (or silver) standard. For a country to be forced off the gold standard (GS) would have serious adverse consequences for its creditworthiness, and its ability to borrow or make payments abroad (especially important in times of war), and for financial and social stability at home.[3] The GS implied that bank notes and sight deposits could be converted on demand into gold. To meet such demands local banks would draw gold from the CB by running down their deposits there. Consequently the gold reserve in the CB became the effective central reserve of the country as a whole.

This led to a number of problems. First, gold was non-interest bearing. So if the CB were to protect its gold reserves, and hence the functioning of the GS, by holding additional gold, it would damage its short-term profitability. Critics of the Bank of England (the Currency School) argued that profit-seeking expansion by the BoE caused the suspension of the GS (1797–1819), and the ensuing inflation. Their answer was to separate the gold reserve holding function of the BoE (the Issue Department) from its ordinary banking functions (the Banking Department), and leave the latter free to compete as an ordinary commercial bank.

The problem with this solution was that the Banking Department of the BoE was not, and could never now become, just an ordinary commercial bank. In particular the other smaller commercial banks looked to it for the provision of liquidity, notably via lender of last resort (LOLR) in crises. This gave the CBs a real problem. In most financial crises, there would be an external drain of gold from its reserves.[4] To protect its reserves from these crises, the CB would then prefer not to lend at all to additional borrowers, since the proceeds of such loans would also be withdrawn, an internal drain of gold. The resolution of this conundrum was worked out by the great early monetary theorists, Henry Thornton, Joplin and Bagehot; the answer was to lend freely, internally during crises, to borrowers who would be solvent under normal conditions, but at high (N.B. *not* penal) interest rates. In effect, the solution was to vary interest rates in accord with fluctuations in the reserve position, down when reserves were high and rising, up when reserves were low and falling.

Another problem was that the CB could always make its control over interest rates effective when liquidity was low, and all the other banks wanted to borrow from it. But what if liquidity was plentiful? Then market rates could fall well below the Bank rate, and an unsustainable credit expansion set in motion that could trigger the next financial crisis. Here the answer that was found was open market operations (OMO), whereby the CB sold enough debt (sometimes the government's, e.g. Treasury Bills, or the private sector's, e.g. Commercial Paper, or even its own) to make the banking system (net) short of immediate cash reserves, and having to come to the CB to replenish them (see Sayers, 1936 and 1957). This made Bank rate continuously effective. For a variety of reasons the market on which the CB operates via OMO is, almost always, a short-maturity, liquid and broad 'money market', though this is not necessarily so, indeed the BoE did repos in undated Consols as its OMO in the 1890s and 1900s (for more on this, see Goodhart, 2003).

What we have now, by the end of nineteenth century, is a CB who manages the monetary regime (GS); who runs the payment system; who sets interest rates (via OMO); and who decides to whom, and on what basis, e.g. what collateral, to lend in periods of crisis. Two of these functions, i.e. the payment system and LOLR, also make the CB concerned with ascertaining the financial health of the other banks, and of trying to insure that others can also do so by encouraging the publication of relevant bank data, i.e. transparency, and regular audits by accountants, so as to enhance market discipline Meanwhile it remained also a commercial competitor of these other banks; naturally this was resented. In the UK, between 1880 and 1910, the answer to this latter problem, was for the CB to withdraw from all new commercial activity with non-bank entities, and similarly for its finances to be structured so that it had no incentive to be concerned with its own immediate short-term profitability.

In fact, prior to the second half of the twentieth century, most of the regulation of commercial banks, in particular of the backing required for their note issue (before these latter became concentrated and monopolized in the CB), was undertaken by the government, not by the CB. Licensing of commercial banks, capital requirements, minimum backing for note issue, publication of accounts, bank examinations (e.g. by the Comptroller of the Currency in the USA), etc., were governmental responsibilities, not part of the role of the CBs.

To summarize and conclude this sub-section, if the CB is to supervise, regulate and control the commercial banks, it should not also directly compete with them for commercial business.

Some implications of this historical development for CB's current role

The clear implication of this latter argument is that there is a strong presumption that the CB should only act as banker for those entities which its core functions necessitate. These are:

1   the main accounts of the central government;
2   the reserve accounts of commercial banks;

In addition, it will be highly convenient, perhaps even necessary, for the CB to hold,

3   foreign central government and CB accounts.[5]

Otherwise banking functions, e.g. payments, lending, for other non-bank customers *can* be done by commercial banks; and to prevent commercial rivalry between the CB and the commercial banks *should*, in principle, be so done. Note that in October 1987, and 9/11, the Fed lent only to banks, and that there was no direct banking involvement of the Fed with Long-Term Capital Management (LTCM). When a non-bank financial enterprise in the UK/US gets into difficulties, the BoE/Fed calls in its bankers for discussions rather than the enterprise itself.

As already noted, historically the CB lent directly to individual commercial banks, usually but not necessarily collateralized. Nowadays there are arguments that, given the existence of a well-functioning and liquid interbank deposit market (and other money markets), it is more efficient for a CB to inject funds into the market as a whole, and also to be less subject to the moral hazard of appearing ready to rescue failing and insolvent banks, than to lend to individual banks with liquidity problems. This is a contentious issue. It is covered, for example, in many contributions in the book of readings on, *Financial Crises, Contagion, and the Lender of Last Resort*

(Goodhart and Illing, 2002). Be that as it may, there have recently been several examples of operational market failures, (e.g. 9/11, and the Bank of New York computer malfunction in 1985) that make it absolutely clear that any CB *must* retain the right and ability to lend directly to commercial banks, and on any basis that its top management considers appropriate, though when there is any foreseeable concern about possible financial losses to the CB, the Ministry of Finance (MoF) and the politicians responsible should be immediately notified, and give permission, if at all possible to advance disbursement of moneys.

As noted above, interbank payments are finally settled, as a generality, by a transfer of funds between commercial bank reserve deposit accounts held at the CB. This means that the CB will be a party in the settlement process. As a consequence it has often, in many countries, been felt efficient for the CB to also run the payments' clearing system(s) itself, whether electronic or paper based, but this is *not* necessary. The banks may choose to run a payments' system themselves, with settlement effected via transfers of funds held at the CB. In other financial markets, e.g. the foreign exchange (fx) market, equity market, bond market, clearing is usually arranged by a designated body, which is very rarely the CB, and settlement is done most often by transfers of balances on the books of a particular commercial bank(s), though the CB can be asked to act as settlement bank for the clearing house, but should only do so if this is not perceived as unfair competition with commercial banks.

Thus the extent to which a CB may itself operate a clearing system, as contrasted with its more generally passive role of having final settlement go through its books, for payments can vary from country to country, and from case to case. Especially, but not only, in developing countries CBs can frequently play a major role in establishing improved clearing and payments' systems, and this can in some instances involve them in setting the systems up, or even running them (e.g. CREST in UK). Once they are established, and whoever may operate them, the continuing smooth functioning of clearing and settlement systems in financial markets, and of the nationwide general payments system, is a major public good, and crucial to the financial stability of the economy. Ensuring this smooth functioning, e.g. by examining and maintaining appropriate risk (loss) control mechanisms, in such markets is a major objective and pre-occupation for all CBs. Indeed, the original argument for direct supervision of the (main) commercial banks by CBs was to ensure that the main participants in these financial systems, especially the general payments' system, were strong enough to maintain systemic viability. But, even should the supervision of individual banking and other financial *institutions* be transferred to a separate financial services authority, the CB should want and need to concern itself with risk management in all the financial clearing and settlement systems, and require that such systems are properly managed.

Many such payment and settlement systems depend on access to liquid-ity when needed to function efficiently. Where such access involves bor-rowing from the CB, the CB will define the terms, e.g. the collateral, on which such borrowing can be done. As part of its oversight of other finan-cial markets, the CB will want to satisfy itself on similar issues, e.g. accept-able collateral, margining requirements, as part of any official authorization. (N.B. There need be no requirement that all financial clearing and settlement systems *have* to be financially authorized; that would be much too restrictive. But there should be a clear distinction between those that are, and those that are not.)

A CB will often pay closer attention to the operational characteristics of those markets in which it operates itself directly, e.g. the inter-bank market, the money market, the government bond market and, perhaps, the fx market, than those where it does not, e.g. the equity or corporate bond market. In those markets, especially the money market, where it is a major, perhaps the predominant player, it will often shape the operations of that market directly, e.g. by arranging the structure of the auction or market-making systems, in addition to its concern with risk control. As the predominant player in such markets, the CB does not usually require legal powers to do this, since the other players involved have little alternative but to go along with whatever the CB proposes.

Monetary regimes, 1919–73

We left our earlier brief history of CBs in approximately the first decade of the twentieth century (1900–10), managing a GS regime by varying inter-est rates, which in turn were controlled by OMO. The most immediate change thereafter was the breakdown of the GS in the First World War. A combination of public sector deficit finance – to pay for the war, rising domestic inflation and a soaring current account deficit in the European combatant countries led to a massive shift of gold reserves to the USA; European countries ran out of gold, and were forced off the GS, while the USA, naturally enough, sterilized the incoming gold rather than accept European-level inflation. Attempts thereafter in the inter-war period to re-establish the GS failed, for reasons well set out in Eichengreen (1992).

The collapse of the GS left the bank notes of the CB (N.B. the note issues of commercial banks had in most countries been constrained and then gradually eliminated towards the end of the nineteenth century) inconvertible into specie. With no real (or commodity) backing, what gave them value? What did give them value was the fiat of the government, that they were legal tender, especially so for the purpose of tax payments to the government. So the value of the currency rested on the reputation, power and fiscal rectitude of the government. Such reputation was (is) not very high. Legal tender, fiat money (also known as *cours forcé* in French) had generally been issued prior to 1914 only when government finances had gone off the rails, owing to war, revolution and incompetence, and specie fled the inflationary country. Fiat money has had a bad name, deservedly so with most hyperinflations in history due to a combination of public sector deficit finance and the overissue of currency (see Bernholz, 2003).

While the fundamental need is to ensure that government finances remain in a long-run, sustainable condition, there is a concern that governments should not feel that monetary expansion is a cheap and initially popular way of meeting fiscal deficits. To this end the structure of fiat money regimes is usually constructed in such a way as to make it appear that barriers exist preventing the government from directly monetizing a deficit.

In particular the note issue in a fiat money regime usually represents the liability of the CB, not of the central government itself. Notes are issued by the CB to the commercial banks – the latter paying for them by running down their deposits at the CB – when the customers of the CB need them for transactions purposes. The note issue is *not* controlled by the government, and *not* printed to pay for immediate fiscal expenditures. Moreover, in an attempt to bolster the independence of the CB and its control over the money stock, and hence inflation, the CB is generally by statute prevented from lending *directly* to the Central (or Provincial) Government. All this is, perhaps, more for appearance than of much real value since a determined government can always force a CB to buy public sector debt in secondary markets, thereby financing itself and raising monetary growth and inflation. Nevertheless appearances matter, and affect confidence and credibility.

Under the GS, the value of the currency was linked to gold, and interest rates had to be varied in a quasi-automatic manner to maintain note convertibility into gold. With the shift to fiat money, there was no bond to the internal/external value of the currency, and interest rates could be managed in a discretionary fashion. With the government, and other powerful groups in the economy, notably business managers, being endemic debtors, the consistent pressure, both for this and other reasons, especially in the last 60 years, has been for interest rates to be held too low, i.e. below the level that would maintain price stability.

That led, after the break-down of the Bretton Woods system in 1971–3, to a search for alternative, i.e. alternative to the GS, anchors to maintain price stability. Three main such anchors have been tried: (1) intermediate monetary targets, (2) fixing the currency by a peg to some central stable currency, and (3) setting an inflation target. Intermediate monetary targets have been largely abandoned, mostly owing to unpredictable shifts in velocity. This leaves a choice between (2) and (3). In so far as a country maintains comprehensive exchange controls, as in China and India, the above choice is less stark. With exchange controls limiting capital flows, interest rates can be varied to maintain domestic price stability up to a point without endangering the external exchange rate peg.

But this is to run ahead of the historical story. The collapse of the GS in the early 1930s led to a somewhat chaotic period of semi-managed floating (Nurkse, 1944). This was followed by the imposition of tight controls, at the outset of the Second World War, by all the combatant countries (except the USA), with centralized controls over all external flows (trade as well as capital) and on the exchange rate itself. This was accompanied with direct controls on bank lending to the private sector, and requirements that they hold increasing amounts of government debt, so as to pay for the war at relatively low interest rates.

The inter-war experience had led expert opinion to regard the maintenance of a completely fixed commodity standard, i.e. the GS, as excessively and impossibly restrictive, whereas a system of managed floating was seen as having been chaotic, and tending to lead towards international disharmony and autarchy. Consequently a middle way, of pegged but adjustable exchange rates, was adopted at Bretton Woods. So long as exchange controls over capital flows remained in place, and the central country, the USA, maintained reasonable price stability, this international monetary regime worked reasonably well, until the strains began to build in the late 1960s.

There were, nevertheless, several scattered exchange rate crises, often involving developed European countries, e.g. in the UK (depreciation in 1949 and 1967), Germany (appreciation in 1971). On the other hand during these years 1945–73, there were virtually no banking crises, as remarked and demonstrated by Eichengreen and Bordo (2003) and Bordo *et al.* (2001). Table 3.5 from Eichengreen and Bordo is reproduced here as Table 2.1.

In this respect, the absence of banking crises, in this period was unique in the history of commercial banks and of CBs, although there have been examples of some countries who have avoided such crises in other periods as well, for example the UK and Canada managed to avoid banking crises in the inter-war period. We seek to explain how it came about in the following sub-section.

Table 2.1 Crisis frequency

Year	Banking crises	Currency crises	Twin crises	All crises
1880–1913	2.30	1.23	1.38	4.90
1919–39	4.84	4.30	4.03	13.17
1945–71	0.00	6.85	0.19	7.04
1973–97 (21countries)	2.03	5.18	2.48	9.68
1973–97 (56 countries)	2.29	7.48	2.38	12.15

Prudential regimes, 1919–73

The functions of the CB at the end of the First World War did not in most countries involve any formal obligation to supervise and to monitor the main commercial banks. Indeed, in some countries where the CB had recently (or remained as in Australia – see Schedvin (1992), especially Chapter 2) been perceived as a commercial rival, that would have been resented. In the USA and Canada, there were in any case institutions, e.g. the OCC in the USA, that had been set up prior to the institution of the CB to monitor and report upon the condition of the commercial banks. In the UK the monetary system had been organized by the BoE purposefully to place a buffer between themselves and the main commercial banks. The discount market, through which liquidity management was normally arranged, took on this buffering role. It was not until the 1990s that the Bank felt in a position to deal with the main London clearing banks directly, and so also allowed the somewhat archaic discount houses to disappear.

Nevertheless the CBs knew that they had ultimate responsibility for maintaining systemic financial stability in general, and the payment system in particular. That could involve them in lending either to the money market as a whole, or depending on the structure of the system to individual banks. The preferred method of channelling funds to the market and/or to individual banks was, after the First World War, through the discount of commercial bills. This was partly because of the 'real bills' doctrine (see Meltzer, 2003), but also partly because inspection of the quality of bills submitted for discount was taken to be a measure of the quality of the overall loan book (see Hawtrey, 1932). Certainly the BoE paid close attention to the details of the commercial bills submitted to it for discount, and discussed this with the Discount Houses and Accepting Houses.

Relationships between the Bank and the main banks were more distant. There was no question of on, or off, site examinations. The commercial bank accounts were, of course, audited, but not only was window-dressing prevalent but also hidden reserves were allowed, even encouraged. That said, the commercial bank chairmen knew that the Bank not only could influence the authorities' attitudes to certain possible structural openings, e.g. new issues, M&A, company restructuring, but in extremis could provide emergency (liquidity) assistance. So there were fairly close informational relationships established between the Governor of the Bank and chairmen of the main London clearing bankers, with perhaps a matching lower level connection between Chief Cashier and CEO. But the informational inter-change was private and confidential, and its quality and content is difficult to discern.

No doubt there were similar informational links of varying degrees of (in)formality between the CB and the main commercial banks in other countries. As a generality, however, the establishment of a formal structure of banking supervision was not then generally regarded as one of the requisite, or necessary, functions of a CB.

Nor were the banking failures in the 1920s and 1930s blamed on insufficient supervision by the CB. I am not aware of any examples where banking failures were attributed in large part to a lack of sufficient information on the part of the CB; instead, such blame has been attached to misguided macro-monetary actions (Friedman and Schwartz, 1963; Meltzer, 2003) by the monetary authorities, or to an inappropriate structure of banking and the moral hazard incentives that such structures generated for wrongful actions by the bankers themselves.

In particular, the combination of investment and commercial banking functions within a single bank was widely held at the time to have had a major responsibility for banking crises, not only in the USA but also in Germany and Italy. It was argued that such direct links between large companies and their main bank not only limited bank diversification but also put pressure on the banks to extend loans on occasions when such loans would not have been given in an arms-length relationship. While such arguments and analysis have been subject to much revisionist reinterpretation recently, they formed the basis for many of the new laws then passed in the 1930s, e.g. the Glass–Steagall Act, to focus commercial banking, and to separate investment and commercial banking.

With the links between commercial banking and private sector industry coming under pressure in the recession of the 1930s, those between government and banking became much more important. In the depressed years of the 1930s the volume of bank lending to the private sector fell back, especially that undertaken via commercial bills. First the depression, and then quantitatively far more important, the need for war finance brought fiscal deficits, and with that large purchases by banks of Treasury Bills and Government Bonds, with governments increasingly putting pressure on the banks to do so. With both short-term and long-term interest rates being kept low and constant, banks had no liquidity management problems.

Those same conditions, of depression followed by war, led to the adoption of greater government activism, centralized control more generally, and to academic support for such policies. Particularly during the war, credit controls became general, apart from North America. With the belligerent countries, other than the USA, running large external deficits, as and when they could, to finance the war effort, such credit controls not only constrained the quantum of such private sector lending, but also directed it to well-established, tradable-goods, manufacturing companies to help provide exports to pay for war-related imports. Lending to service sector companies was discouraged and lending for consumption or for imports almost prohibited.

Thus the banks came out of the Second World War with an asset portfolio that was massively distorted but extremely safe in relation to credit risk. It consisted of a high proportion of government debt and a relatively low proportion of loans to the private sector. Moreover those latter loans were mostly to the largest, longest established, safest (partly owing to those companies also being too large to fail), industrial companies. The run-off of government debt, and rise in long-term nominal interest rates, in line with *slowly* accelerating inflation only occurred gradually over the decades.

By the same token official direction of bank lending to the private sector continued in many countries into the late 1960s or early 1970s; *Competition and Credit Control*, the UK reform, introduced by the BoE, and intended to get rid of such direct credit controls, occurred in 1971. Until then, the authorities normally determined and constrained both the total and direction of such lending. The commercial banks became in some senses co-opted into the public sector, rather like public utilities. Given that their lending was primarily directed to large industrial companies – with implicit government support – the basic banking skills of risk assessment and risk management atrophied. The main requirement for a bank manager was to learn how to say 'no' gracefully to those from low-priority sectors seeking a bank loan. By the same token there was very little call for any supervisory, or regulatory, activity or skill from CBs. That too largely atrophied.

But the old system of centrally directed, uncompetitive banking was drawing to a close by the end of the 1960s. The removal, or avoidance, of exchange controls was leading to greater global competition in finance, more so in wholesale than in retail markets. Information technology was also spurring competition. Just as important, the academic fashions of the age were changing, with competition becoming seen as preferable to central co-ordination as a spur to efficiency and growth.

Supervision, financial stability and the lender of last resort, 1973–2004

What is surprising in retrospect was how *little* formal responsibility the BoE either took, or was assigned by the government, for oversight of the British banking and financial system prior to the fringe bank crisis which began in December 1973 (Goodhart, 2004). The supervisory role in the Bank was restricted previously to one senior official (the Discount Office principal, at that time J. Keogh), with a handful of supporting officials. The Bank's money-market dealings were with the discount houses, a set of institutions which had been fostered by the Bank to mediate between itself and the much larger London clearing banks. The Discount Houses were highly levered and subject to market-rate risk, and the Bank wanted to be well informed of the positions of its main market counter-parties. Moreover, part of the stock-in-trade of the discount houses continued to be commercial bills, though these had been increasingly dominated in volume by Treasury Bills. Such commercial bills were accepted by the Accepting Houses, i.e. the London merchant banks, becoming two-name bills. As the Bank dealt in such bills with the Discount Houses, it wanted to be sure of the quality of the business and standing of the Accepting Houses whose credit also stood behind such bills.

For the rest, what was remarkable was how sparse were the formal links between the Bank, the commercial banks, and the rest of the financial system. In this respect the Bank had far less intelligence about, and effectively no supervisory control over, the commercial banking system at this time (late 1960s) than was, I believe, the case either in the USA – where the Office of the Comptroller of the Currency, the Federal Reserve System, the Federal Deposit Insurance Corporation and the State authorities all played a much larger role – or in most continental countries. There was a limited provision of monetary data, mostly provided on a voluntary basis by the clearing banks, more so after about 1963, following the Radcliffe Report's (1959) recommendations for improving the availability of monetary data. The Bank did no off or on-site bank inspections, though it did discuss their annual results with most of the banks, with the Clearing Banks not deigning to talk with anyone other than the Governor. The Bank did not generally licence, nor authorize, financial institutions; this was done by government, mostly the Board of Trade, which subsequently metamorphosed into the Department of Trade and Industry.

This lack of formal involvement in the supervisory/stability field was quite largely due to the 'command and control' approach to monetary policy which persisted longer in Britain than in most other countries, and so made the need for such supervision less pressing. This approach, in turn, was partly due to the then daunting size of the British national debt, which led governments to be even more concerned about using interest rates flexibly as a policy instrument. Anyhow, with interest-rate increases used somewhat unwillingly, primarily in response to external weakness in the balance of payments, endemic internal inflationary pressure was (partially) constrained by direct quantitative constraints over bank lending to the private sector. This policy favoured large manufacturing exporters. The banking sector was, in the years immediately after the Second World War, stuffed to the gills with government debt, and its ability to assume risky lending was tightly restricted.

Such a system gave the Bank an informal role as 'go-between' of the government on the one side, and the banks and other financial intermediaries on the other. For its part the government relied on the Bank to introduce, monitor and maintain (if not quite enforce) its commands; while the banks and other intermediaries knew that they had to get the Bank on their side if any special pleadings that they wished to make would be taken seriously by government. This role provided considerable informal leadership of the City for the Bank, and a process of similarly informal gathering of information, e.g. via City lunches.

Insofar as there were any stability-related controls over the banks at this time, they related to liquidity rather than to capital adequacy. In any case outsiders could not assess the capital adequacy of the clearing banks so long as they maintained hidden 'inner reserves'; discussion whether such opacity was a source of strength, or weakness, to the system was common-place in the 1950s and early 1960s. Cash and liquidity required ratios were maintained, though whether their function was related to monetary policy or to financial stability was never very clear; nor was their efficacy, in either guise. Assessment of the role of such ratios was a common academic pastime in the 1960s, as a survey of articles written then would reveal.

Perhaps largely, certainly partly, because of such credit constraints lim-iting innovation and risk-taking, banking was an extremely safe, and boring, occupation between 1945 and 1973. There was little credit risk, though there was considerable interest-rate risk, and there were occasions when financial intermediaries became (temporarily in most cases) burnt by this. Nevertheless there were no publicly-perceived domestic financial crises worthy of the name. Although Britain has been the home of mone-tary experts who have expounded on the theory of lender of last resort (with the 200th anniversary of Thornton's great book having been celeb-rated with a conference in Paris in September 2002), the reality is that the BoE has been involved in the last two centuries in very few episodes of lender of last resort, far fewer than in most European countries, or in the USA.

Those few cases when the Bank was asked to help virtually never involved a pure case of liquidity shortage (money markets could cope with those) but almost always some mixture of liquidity problems and solvency concerns, usually with the latter triggering the former. Sometimes the solution was an arranged merger. When there was a call for the injection of funds, the Bank did not feel capable of putting up more than a small share of the money itself; it had limited capital. In the most serious and dramatic case, at the outbreak of war in August 1914 – a still under-researched episode, though Seabourne (1986) has done an excellent study – the government took on the burden. In the Barings case (1890 version) the Bank co-ordinated a consortium of banks in London to provide guarantees that Baring's debts would be met. The Bank was com-fortable with a role as arbiter of concerted private sector responses to a crisis, much less so to act as an independent, sole rescuer. Moreover the club-like ethos in London fostered such a preference; but in truth lender-of-last-resort operations by the Bank had been largely dormant for decades at the start of the 1970s.

All this was to change in the 1970s, a frightening decade for central bankers. The decade began with a worldwide boom. In Britain this was amplified by an extremely rapid expansion of credit. Among the many problems of a command and control system of direct quantitative con-straints is that 'fringe' organizations develop, whose only rationale is that they are structured so as to avoid those direct controls, an unintended consequence of such direct controls. This had happened in Britain's financial system where various kinds of finance houses and 'fringe banks' had developed in the 1960s to take advantage of such loopholes, and often these were lightly capitalized and highly leveraged. This distortion of the banking system, and the consequent increasing ineffectiveness of the system of credit controls, was the main reason why the Bank lobbied the government to restore a more competitive financial system.

This was achieved by the reform 'Competition and Credit Control' in 1971. Competition was immediately redoubled as the main clearing banks sought to regain market share, though more so through inter-bank loans than by loans directly to the property companies and other customers of the 'fringe banks'.

Meanwhile the boom, especially in the property market, encouraged the fringe banks to expand even faster. Eventually, with the occurrence of the first oil shock, and an upsurge of inflation, the boom ended in a crisis. The property market was struck by a combination of sharp increases in interest rates and additional taxes, and collapsed. This collapse then led to the failure of, first, one fringe bank (London and County Securities Group), and then, partly through a process of reputational contagion, whereby loans to similar institutions were withdrawn, to the closure of a swathe of other fringe banks.

Without any form of direct supervision in place, the Bank was short of basic intelligence. The fringe banks, being initially small upstarts, had to clear their payments through a much larger correspondent clearing bank. The Bank then asked the relevant clearing bank, which had a correspondent relationship, in each arising case to assess whether the associated fringe bank was insolvent or salvageable. When the fringe bank was assessed as salvageable, then the Bank co-ordinated injections of liquidity via a 'life-boat' to which all the major clearing banks and the Bank contributed – together with related interests, e.g. large shareholders of the affected fringe banks – typically (I believe but cannot confirm) with the correspondent taking the major share and others on a pro-rata basis (the Bank of England 10 per cent).

The collapse in asset prices, and in the economy, in 1973–5 was extremely steep, and their life-boat contributions were an unwelcome added burden to the clearing banks. At one stage there were even published rumours about one of the clearers (National Westminster). So the clearing banks in due course informed the Bank that they were no longer willing to contribute new money. The Bank then had to go it alone; it has not been reported whether the Bank received any offers of potential support, or an indemnity from the Treasury (i.e. the government), in this role. By the time this stage had been reached, however, the crisis was on the wane, and relatively little new money from the Bank was in fact required.

What this episode revealed was that there was little, or no, prudential control, or supervision, of the banking, or wider financial, system, and that, in the new competitive, and thereby riskier milieu, such oversight was felt to be necessary, and would need an associated regulatory dimension. The immediate result was a re-organization in the Bank. Initially a nucleus of a new specialized Department was established in the Discount Office, which absorbed staff and resources rapidly. Thereafter this became a separate department, devoted to banking supervision and regulation (initially under George Blunden, who handed it on to Peter Cooke in 1976) culminating in the Banking Act of 1979, which gave formal powers to the Bank to authorize, monitor, supervise, control and, under certain circumstances, to withdraw prior authorization, which was tantamount to closure, for banks. No such powers had been available before that date. Meanwhile other financial intermediaries, such as building societies or insurance companies, remained lightly regulated by various government departments, apart from quite restrictive constraints on the assets that some of these non-bank financial intermediaries could hold and activities in which they could engage.

The fringe bank crisis was almost entirely domestic, i.e. confined to British head-quartered companies. Meanwhile, however, the onwards march of liberalization, involving the removal of direct controls, notably exchange controls in 1979, and of information technology were leading to a growing internationalization of financial business. For a variety of reasons, mostly relating to the innovation of the euro-dollar and euro-markets, London regained its role as an international financial centre in the 1960s, and thus international monetary problems became of particular importance to the Bank, which took a leading role in such issues from the 1970s onwards.

The Herstatt failure in June 1974 was, perhaps, the first with major international implications, though the Franklin National failure in the USA in 1973 was the first to shatter the calm. The German authorities had shut this bank after financial markets had closed in Germany, but before foreign-exchange transactions, in which Herstatt had participated in quite large amounts, had been settled in New York, causing a degree of chaos there. Growing internationalization, in this and many other respects, now led to a need for a common meeting place to discuss such supervisory and regulatory issues. Central bankers had met regularly at the headquarters of the Bank for International Settlements (BIS) in Basel for many years. It was, therefore, a logical step for supervisory officials also to come together in Basel on regular occasions to discuss matters of common interest. Thus, in 1974, was born, as a result of an initiative from Gordon Richardson, the Basel Committee on Banking Regulation and Supervisory Practices. For the first 15 years of its existence, it was chaired by the participant from the BoE and was usually known by his name; thus the Blunden Committee (1974–7) gave way in due course to the Cooke Committee (1977–88). The failures of Franklin National and Herstatt prompted the First Basel Concordat which allocated responsibility for supervising internationally active banks to home and host authorities.

The next important milestone was the collapse of Banco Ambrosiano in 1981, an Italian bank with supposed connections both to the Vatican and to right-wing subversive groups, but the important feature – from a regulatory viewpoint – was its structure, with a holding company in Luxembourg, and two main subsidiaries, one in Italy and one, dealing in international business, headquartered in Panama. It was not supervised in Luxembourg, because it did no banking business there, and supervisors in Rome and in Panama could only see part of the overall picture, a picture that the bank could retouch to taste by transfers of assets/liabilities between its two parts. The need was to establish consolidated supervision at the headquarters of any international banking business. This required international agreement, monitoring and potential sanctions; these latter were that any bank that did not submit to consolidated supervision might be excluded from operation in the main international financial markets, notably New York, London and Tokyo.

This Committee was in no position to pass binding laws. The Basel Concordat and other Basel Committee initiatives were statements of principle to which those participating were prepared to be bound; some countries did pass legislation as the only way to give them effect, notably via EEC directives. But the Basel initiatives had no legal standing in themselves. Indeed there is no real international law in this field. However the Committee can recommend measures, and sanction banks failing to adopt them by excluding them from its members' markets. This amounts to 'soft law'.

So by the mid 1970s, a need was perceived for banking supervision at both the domestic and, via consolidation, at the international level. The purpose of these initiatives was to clarify where responsibility lay for the supervision of international banks, to prevent fragile, and possibly fraudulent, banking leading to avoidable failures and potential systemic crises.

But what was the analytical and conceptual basis on which financial regulation and subsequent supervision was to be applied? Initially there was little, or no, formal analysis. Apart from a concern to mandate sufficient liquidity to deter runs – an approach with its roots in the nineteenth century – the main approach seemed to be to examine the procedures of those banks commonly regarded as following 'best practice', and then encouraging all other banks to do the same.

Some time in the 1970s and early 1980s, however, attention began to swing from liquidity to capital, as being the touchstone for ensuring safe and prudential banking practices. It would be a nice exercise in the history of economic thought to explore that process. In a sense it is obvious that a bank, with limited liability, whose capital, and franchise value, had been eroded to a low level would be much more prepared to gamble for resurrection than a better capitalized bank. Also, the greater the capital, the greater the loss that could be absorbed. On those simple insights a huge regulatory edifice has subsequently been erected.

An initial impetus to the case for strengthening bank capital was the pressure on the balance sheets of 'good' banks – prominently including the major American banks and the British clearers – from the recycling of oil surpluses from the Middle East back to New York and London. This concern, based on the very rapid growth in the dollar liabilities of these banks, surfaced quite strongly, as early as late 1974. Much, perhaps most, of the early concern about capital adequacy occurred in the USA, especially in the Office of the Comptroller of the Currency.

A further spur to that process was provided by the less-developed countries' crisis in 1982. The need to recycle petro-dollars from oil-exporting to oil-importing countries in the 1970s had encouraged a major growth in international bank lending, and successfully so during this inflationary decade, with its associated low, often negative, real interest rates. But when Volcker changed monetary policy in October 1979, real interest rates rose sharply and commodity prices slumped. Mexico, Argentina and Brazil then found themselves unable to refinance their borrowing in 1982. If the loans to these countries had been marked to market, some, perhaps a majority, of the major money-centre international banks in the world, and especially those in New York, would have been, technically, insolvent, and the world's financial system would have faced a major crisis. It was, almost certainly, the most dangerous financial occasion of the second half of the twentieth century, much worse than October 1987 or August to October 1998.

One lesson that the world's central bankers took from that episode was that bank capital ratios had been diminishing, under the pressure of competition, were insufficient and needed to be rebuilt. Competition was now, however, international. In particular, Japanese banks, sitting on large capital gains from their equity portfolios, and state-guaranteed banks (notably in France) could undercut interest rates by trading on the basis of lower basic (tier 1) capital. The need was to get international agreement to establish a common minimum level of capital adequacy ratios. The Basel Committee worked to this end, from 1982 till 1988, under the leadership of Peter Cooke, while Quinn from the BoE, and Taylor and subsequently Corrigan from the New York Federal Reserve Bank maintained close bilateral relationships between the UK and the USA.

The eventual result of the inevitable haggling over detail was the 1988 Basel Accord. One key feature of this was an acceptance of the view that the amount of capital that a bank required should be weighted by the relative riskiness of its assets. While this seems reasonable as a protection against depositors' losses, at the same time the real buffer providing flexibility for the banks is the margin of capital in excess of the required reserves; once 'required' such capital is in some senses no longer freely usable. Moreover, it took the Basel Committee down the complex route (is it a dead-end?) of trying to measure such relative riskiness. The 1988 Accord did so in a broad-brush manner and hence not only laid itself open to arbitrage, but also artificially encouraged some continuing market trends, e.g. securitization. Basel 2 is trying to repair the shortcomings of its predecessor (Basel 1), but many fear that Basel 2 will similarly introduce unfortunate side-effects (e.g. enhanced pro-cyclicality and excessive prescription).

Despite the growing number of bank supervisors, and notable success in reversing prior declines in capital ratios, the history of banking in the subsequent decades in the UK was spotted by occasional bank failures. Unlike the fringe bank crisis none was, or was allowed to become, systemic, nor did individual depositors lose any money, except in the case of Bank of Credit and Commerce International (BCCI), and even in that case the Deposit Protection scheme provided some relief. The Johnson-Matthey failure (in 1984), BCCI (in 1991) and Barings (in 1995) were all isolated cases of bad, in some respects fraudulent, banking. In the adverse macro-economic context of 1990–2, with high interest rates, a weakening economy and a collapsing housing/property market, and in the febrile market conditions of autumn 1998, the British banking and financial system remained robust. In so far as the main purpose of banking supervision is to prevent systemic problems (and/or to protect depositors), then the Bank performed effectively.

Unfortunately the adoption of hands-on supervision will be interpreted by public, politicians and the press as involving a responsibility for preventing *any* failure. It is arguable that the objective of enforcing good behaviour on all individual bank managements, especially when they have consciously decided to behave fraudulently (BCCI), or to fail to apply adequate internal control mechanisms to investigate inexplicably good trading results in distant countries (Barings), could only be prevented by such nannying, invasive supervision that the private banking system would be smothered under public sector intervention. Nevertheless, despite all protestations that supervision neither can, nor should, prevent all bank failures, that was the way that it was publicly perceived.

Meanwhile, the Bank's role as lender of last resort was becoming subject to change, and some further attenuation. In the case of Johnson Matthey Bankers (JMB), a small bank, which failed in 1984 after using up much of its capital in bad loans to two West African traders, the Bank first tried to get the parent conglomerate to rescue it. When that did not work, the Bank turned to its usual stratagem of encouraging the commercial banks in London to 'volunteer' to contribute to support the bank in trouble. But now the large, incoming US banks refused to play, citing legal problems in the USA if they were perceived as using shareholder funds for extraneous purposes. If the US banks would not contribute to the Bank's begging bowl, it was only *amour propre* for the other foreign banks to refuse too. Eventually the British clearing banks acceded to the Bank's requests, but only grudgingly and, it was clear, 'for the last time'.

Moreover, at one juncture in this episode the Bank felt that it needed to go ahead and place a sizeable deposit (£100 million) with JMB, and did so on its own accord, only bringing Lawson, the Chancellor of the Exchequer, and the Treasury into the loop at a later stage, by which time the commitment had been given against the time constraints of the market opening in Asia. Time constraint excuses, or not, the Chancellor was furious. What became obvious, after this event, was that any funds risked by the Bank itself during a rescue were in a very real sense 'public moneys', ultimately owed to the taxpayer. From this date onwards no significant LOLR commitment could be contemplated without the prior consent of the Chancellor (and Treasury), who would in turn have to answer to Parliament. The old image of the Bank able to dispose of unlimited lender of last resort funds, as a *deus ex machina*, always invalid, was now even further from the truth.

Each failure led to recriminations, the establishment (in two cases) of a formal enquiry and, after JMB, a new Banking Supervision Act in 1987. Thus by the mid 1990s the conduct by the Bank of its direct supervisory duties was not assessed by the general public or the politicians as notably successful; what view historians will later take remains to be seen. Meanwhile, the conduct of regulation and supervision for the financial system elsewhere, e.g. in securities' business, by the Securities and Investments Board and its various subsidiary Self Regulatory Organizations (SROs), was assessed as even worse, e.g. for failing to spot and to end the pension mis-selling scandal.

The Labour party in opposition, prior to their election as government in 1997, had made it clear that they would introduce an act to put financial regulation on to a firmer statutory basis and to get rid of both the SROs, and of the associated concept of practitioner-based supervision, amalgamating all the SROs into a single, hopefully more efficient, body; but they had made no mention of incorporating banking supervision into what then became a unified and comprehensive Financial Services Authority (FSA). So when they did so, at the start of their period in office (May 1997), it came as something of a shock.

Since this latter step had not been publicly debated, it not only came as rather a shock, but it is also not yet possible to discern all the arguments that led to this policy decision. Among them, however, were the facts that the demarcation lines between banking, securities business and insurance had become blurred, so that supervisory unification should enhance efficiency and commonality of treatment; and that the conduct of banking supervision had not enhanced the reputation of the Bank. What was less clear was whether removing supervision from the Bank was in some sense a *quid pro quo* for giving it operational independence in setting interest rates; perhaps on the grounds that a Bank with too many functions could be too much of a power centre within the democratic system, or could, in theory, become subject to conflicts of interest.

Be that as it may, the role of lender of last resort could hardly also be transferred to the FSA. Moreover, responsibility for the (smooth) operation of the payments system and the main financial markets remained with the Bank. So it retained responsibility for 'financial stability', though exactly what that meant remains somewhat fuzzy. In practice, it tends to mean that the Bank shares responsibility for regulatory changes, for example through the Basel Committee and the various European fora with the FSA, and still tends to lead on international monetary issues in discussion in the various G groups (for example G7, G20 etc.) and with the International Monetary Fund (IMF) and other international financial institutions. Meanwhile urgent domestic financial issues, for example the prevention and resolution of crises, are to be handled through a tri-partite standing committee, involving the FSA, Bank and Treasury. Moreover, the chairman of the FSA and the Deputy Governor of the Bank responsible for financial stability are members of each other's respective Boards as a further means of getting the exchanges of information channelled efficiently. How well all this will work in a crisis remains to be seen, since the economic and financial conjuncture since 1997 has remained comparatively calm and stable.

Conclusions

What this historical record, I believe, demonstrates, and as every CB practitioner comes to understand, regulation and supervision are primarily reactive. Something goes wrong in the financial system, and some people lose money. Almost by definition the existing system of supervision and regulation is held to be at fault. The Press takes up the cry, 'Heads must roll'. Since the politicians do not want it to be their own heads that become parted from their bodies, they feel the need to be seen to be taking actions to make sure that that particular disaster never happens again.

So financial innovation, and new potential disasters, breed new kinds of regulation and supervision. The key innovation in this respect is, in these last 40 years, been the growing global reach of financial intermediation, via globalization and IT. This causes a real problem because regulation is about laws, and laws are national in character, whereas financial intermediation is now international.

This distinction, between the national characteristics of regulation and supervision and the global nature of the financial system, has been papered over by two developments. The first was the, constitutionally extraordinary, establishment of a private club of CBs at Basel to agree on sets of 'soft laws' in order to co-ordinate a common international approach. The second is that retail financial services, notably retail banking, have been much slower to become international in character. Since it is in retail financial services that crises have been more prevalent, expensive and difficult to handle, this has meant that most financial crises have been primarily national in character, and could still be managed nationally.

It is my expectation that both these developments will come under greater external pressure. If so, the future of banking regulation/supervision may become even more fraught with difficulties over the next 30, or so, years than it has been over the last 30 years.

Notes

1 My thanks are due to Elvira Scheben and Juha Tarkka, my discussants, and to Geoffrey Wood for support, advice and comments on this chapter.
2 For a more extended account see Goodhart (1988).
3 Both the inflation that usually accompanied a suspension of the GS, and the deflation that similarly often attended a return to the GS, would tend to generate economic and social tensions.
4 The initial internal drain, during a crisis, would mostly fall on the various commercial banks, whereas the external drain would be focused on the Bank, because of the latter's responsibility to maintain the GS.
5 Though it is *not* necessary, custom and convention lead most CBs to hold the accounts of their own staff, and a few other special accounts. Note that the Bank of England has finally (July 2004) announced that it will now give up all such retail activity.

Bibliography

Bank of England (1971) 'Competition and credit control', in *Bank of England Quarterly Bulletin* 11(2), June.

Bernholz, P. (2003) *Monetary Regimes and Inflation*, Cheltenham, UK: Edward Elgar.

Bordo, M., Eichengreen, B., Klingebiel, D. and Martinez-Peria, M.S. (2001) 'Is the crisis problem growing more severe?', *Economic Policy* 32: 51–82.

Eichengreen, B. (1992) *Golden Fetters: The Gold Standard and the Great Depression, 1919–1939*, New York City: Oxford University Press.

Eichengreen, B. and Bordo, M. (2003) 'Crises now and then: what lessons from the last era of financial globalisation', in Mizen, P. (ed.) *Monetary History, Exchange Rates and Financial Markets: Essays in honour of Charles Goodhart*, Vol. 2, Cheltenham, UK: Edward Elgar, ch. 3, pp. 52–91.

Friedman, M. and Schwartz, A.J. (1963) *A Monetary History of the United States, 1867–1960*, Princeton, NJ: Princeton University Press.

Goodhart, C.A.E. (1969) *The New York Money Market and the Finance of Trade, 1900–13*, Cambridge, MA: Harvard University Press.

Goodhart, C.A.E. (1972) *The Business of Banking, 1891–1914*, London: Weidenfeld and Nicolson.

Goodhart, C.A.E. (1988) *The Evolution of Central Banks*, Cambridge, MA: MIT Press.

Goodhart, C.A.E. (2003) 'Intervention in asset markets', in Pringle, R. and Carver, N. (eds) *How Countries Manage Reserve Assets*, London: Central Banking Publications, ch. 3.

Goodhart, C.A.E. (2004) 'The Bank of England 1970–2000', in Michie, R. (ed.) *The British Government and the City of London in the Twentieth Century*, Cambridge, UK: Cambridge University, ch. 17.

Goodhart, C.A.E. and Illing, G. (2002) *Financial Crises, Contagion and the Lender of Last Resort: A Reader*, Oxford, UK: Oxford University Press.

Hawtrey, R.G. (1932) *The Art of Central Banking*, London: Longmans, Green & Co.

Meltzer, A.H. (2003) *A History of the Federal Reserve: Volume 1: 1913–1951*, Chicago, IL: University of Chicago Press.

Nurkse, R. (1944) *International Currency Experience*, Geneva: League of Nations.

Radcliffe Report (1959) *The Committee on the Working of the Monetary System: Report*, Cmnd. 827, London: HMSO.

Sayers, R.S. (1936) *Bank of England Operations, 1890–1914*, Oxford, UK: Clarendon Press.

Sayers, R.S. (1957) *Central Banking After Bagehot*, Oxford, UK: Clarendon Press.

Schedvin, C.B. (1992) *In Reserve: Central Banking in Australia, 1945–75*, St Leonards, NSW, Australia: Allen & Unwin.

Seabourne, T. (1986) 'The Summer of 1914', in Capie, F. and Wood, G. (eds) *Financial Crises and the World Banking system*, London: Macmillan, in association with Centre for Banking and International Finance, The City University.

COMMENT

Elvira Scheben

I will take up a few details which are rooted in countries other than the UK, and which resulted in a different course of banking supervision from that discussed in Charles Goodhart's chapter. I will also raise a few issues regarding financial supervision, in the sense of what can we learn from history and what supervision is all about.

From an historical point of view one could argue that the first attempt to supervise banks was the control of bank note issuance (Moeschel, 1991: 575) which became the CBs' monopoly only in the nineteenth or twentieth century, depending on the country. This is no longer the reason for regulation of banks. The states of Massachusetts and New York took a lead, in 1799 and 1804, respectively, by passing a law that obliged note issuing banks to have the legal form of a corporation; this enabled the government to exert control. The US Free Banking Act of 1838 already contained regulation on capital and liquidity.

Agreement that bank business in general requires state control came much later. Sweden was in 1846 the first country to introduce banking supervision aimed at deposit protection. Again in the US, the establishment of the Comptroller of the Currency through the National Banking Act in 1864 not only established control of National Banks but also requirements of licensing, capital and liquidity for banks in general. It is noteworthy how early this was done. This means that apart from Sweden, the US were frontrunners for the establishment of regulation and supervision of banks in the middle of the nineteenth century.

Banking regulation in most continental European countries (e.g. Germany, Italy, Belgium) only became an issue in the aftermath of the international financial crisis of 1931. Countries that were not hit as hard introduced financial supervision even later. And although Britain was hit by the crisis, banking supervision was still not really an issue. It was however the trigger for financial regulation in Germany.

The big banking crisis in 1931 led to the first Banking Law in 1934. Before that banking supervision had been discussed since 1874, but without any result. Only mortgage banks were regulated at an earlier stage, 1899. This is said to be a reaction to a widespread practice of misevaluation of property. In 1934 a law introduced standards for capital, liquidity and licensing, but also regulation of interest rates and also other competition restrictions (the result was similar to what emerged in the UK without regulation).

The 1931 banking crisis has been given many different names: payment crisis, credit crisis, crisis of trust or liquidity crisis, all of which stem from the effects of the Great Depression. While the Great Depression has been analysed exhaustively, the banking crisis seems to have attracted less attention (Cheng, 1986: 13–23). But it has been noted that none of the countries off the GS experienced a financial crisis, whereas *not* all countries in the GS had one (notably Italy and Poland). The question is why. It would be a nice result for regulators if they could claim that it was the result of their banking policies. Unfortunately that was not the case (Temin, 1993: 87). Equally, it has not generally been claimed that the lack of banking supervision was the reason for the crisis.

Can we now draw the conclusion that crises happen with or without regulation/supervisors? As a consequence of the prolonged and severe worldwide recession after 1929, banks' balance sheets were eventually eroded; a result which could not have been avoided by any bank prudence or asset diversification. The prolonged bad economic situation also created an atmosphere of uncertainty. The financial crisis started off in the US with several banks failing, followed by banks (beginning with Kreditanstalt) in Austria, then in Germany and more countries in Europe. The breakdowns did not seem to be interconnected.

In Germany, after the First World War, inflation had eroded the financial assets of the population including bank deposits. The very much needed bank deposits had to be raised abroad and eventually a third of GDP (25.6 billion Reichsmark) was owed to other countries; of that a third was owed by the big German banks. In the course of the world recession, capital flows came to a standstill and when the bad news about the German economy started to spread, foreign deposits were withdrawn at an increasing pace. After one of the biggest banks (Darmstaedter-und-Nationalbank, Danat-Bank, second biggest bank at the time) failed, the run on the banks, not only by foreign investors, but also by domestic depositors, was unstoppable. The Reichsbank felt unable to provide the required liquidity, because of statutory restrictions (40 per cent coverage of notes with gold or foreign exchange reserves; GS). The payment crisis ended after the establishment of the Akzeptbank which enabled the CB (Reichsbank) to buy bills of exchange again and provide liquidity. Also an international agreement was reached in Basel which gave the banks more time to repay their debt.

The BIS had been established in 1930 to facilitate the transfer of war reparations and to promote international co-operation. The development of the crisis had demonstrated how badly informed CBs were and how much co-operation was needed. But it took a few more decades before international co-operation really took off.

The introduction of banking supervision in Germany was controversial; in particular, it was pointed out that existing banking supervision in the US had not prevented bank failures. But the government insisted on the introduction of banking supervision. Interestingly, one argument was that the government wanted to be able to exert influence on the banks after it had helped them in times of crisis (the banks had previously refused to help the government to finance its budget deficit). The purpose was the establishment and maintenance of a well-working financial system, and regulation covered licensing, capital and liquidity requirements. Simultaneously interest rate controls were introduced which meant that banking supervision was fairly unchallenging until these controls were abandoned in 1967. In 1962 the Banking Act came into force and focused not only on the financial system, but also on deposit protection.

The next crisis, triggered by the failure of Herstatt, demonstrated the inadequacies of the existing system, which had not prevented solvent banks getting into problems. As a result the Liquiditaetskonsortialbank, LIKO-Bank (liquidity syndicate bank), was founded by the CB and all banking groups in order to help banks facing a liquidity crisis although solvent. This was aimed at maintaining the smooth functioning of payment system operations (Muehlhaupt, 1982: 435). Furthermore, all three banking sectors, private banks, co-operative banks and public banks, founded their own deposit protection schemes. The LIKO-Bank mainly assumed the role of LOLR.

Conclusion

I agree with Charles Goodhart's argument that regulation, at least from a historic point of view, is reactive. But does it need to be reactive? The recent developments, by which I mean Basel 2, put that very much into question. Whereas past regulatory initiatives were triggered by crises, Basel 2 was not. Basel 2 tries to be proactive.

History shows that regulation does not prevent failures, unless it undermines competition, but it can mitigate crises. Despite the big exposures of the financial industry the Latin American and Asian crisis did not end in worldwide disaster, because since the big crisis, apart from adopting floating exchange rate regimes, all developed countries have introduced financial regulation and international co-operation has improved.

Historically, regulation of banks was not an issue from the beginning of bank business. And the discussions over whether to introduce supervision show that it was regarded as interference with freedom. Nowadays regulation of the financial industry is widely accepted, because failures can affect the whole economy of a country, and possibly, of several countries. Looking at the increasing regulatory requirements, however, I think we should go back and remind ourselves about the reasons for regulation. Limitation of note issuance is not on the agenda anymore; that is the exclusive privilege of the CBs. LOLR requires collateral and is designed to help out in a liquidity crisis. What is today widely regarded as a reason for regulation is the maintenance of the functioning of the financial system, with micro prudential supervision often carried out by an authority separate from the CB and macro prudential supervision left to the CB. Deposit protection is widely provided by deposit protection schemes. Internationalization has increased the complexity of the business and made regulation more difficult. But the issue is still the maintenance of the system. If we were content to accept that failures cannot be avoided, but rather mitigated, does that not mean that a few simple rules could suffice for this purpose?

Internationalization of the financial industry increases the difficulty of monitoring, as Charles Goodhart points out. He was also rather gloomy about future achievements by the Basel Committee. This may suggest that a global regulator is required. But would it help? The scope of such a regulator would have to be agreed in advance, which would make a consultative process no easier than any other Basel agreement.

Bibliography

Cheng, Hang-Sheng (1986) 'International financial crisis, past and present', *Federal Reserve Bank of San Francisco Economic Review* 4: 13–23.

Moeschel, W. (1991) 'Wurzeln der Bankenaufsicht', *Festschrift fuer Theodor Heinsius,* Berlin and New York: de Gruyter, p. 575.

Muehlhaupt, L. (1982) 'Von der Bankenkrise 1931 zur Bankenaufsicht 1981', *Schmalenbachs Zeitschift fuer betriebswirtschaftliche Forschung,* p. 435, available online at www.vhb.de/zfbf/register/abhandlung82.html.

Temin, P. (1993) 'Transmission of the Great Depression', *Journal of Economic Perspectives* 7(2): 87.

3   Some historical perspective on financial regulation[1]

Forrest Capie

This chapter asks the question: What, over the long run – roughly the previous two centuries – have been the principal sources of financial regulation? An examination of British experience reveals an interesting, even peculiar, and possibly exceptional story. There was relatively little statutory legislation for most of the time and very little pressure for any. And for a long time there was none of the reactive behaviour found elsewhere and at other times. On the contrary there was a strong desire to avoid responding to crises. That contrasts with the US where there was a lot of regulation and where bank crises and the role of interest groups dominate the explanation. A cursory review of the secondary literature on other countries points in the main to the role of crises and government responses to them.

It could be argued that England in the eighteenth century was an emerging market economy. And it would be encouraging to believe that the results of the learning process England went through might be applied in current contexts.

The chapter follows the pattern implied. First there is a brief definition of regulation, then a list of policy-making motives. It turns next to the case of England/Britain, then looks at the US and some other countries before some conclusions are drawn.

Financial regulation

Regulation can be defined in different ways. Rule-making is an inevitable feature of an economy, but most of it is voluntary, to allow people to live more ordered lives. When government sets rules for others that can be considered regulation. This is close to the definition given by Stigler: 'any policy which alters market outcomes by the exercise of some coercive government power' (1988: 210). That distinguishes between influences on outcomes either by coercion or by incentive. For example, tax and subsidy policy may well be intended to 'influence market outcomes' but neither constitutes regulation. Also, the definition contains no hint of the direction of influence (towards or away from a competitive structure), or of who its beneficiaries might be.

Among economists there have been two sharply contrasting approaches to regulation. The economist's traditional view of regulation is, 'Competition when possible, regulation where necessary'. Regulation, then, seeks to identify market failures that prevent an industry from functioning competitively, and to correct for such failures. On this view it is a way of reducing market failure. The alternative view sees regulation as in fact producing market failure – of producing monopoly profits. This approach is identified particularly with Stigler. Over a wide range of industries he found that regulation was either totally ineffective or worked to the benefit of existing firms in the industry. It did not eliminate harmful market failures. These results have led to the view that regulation, ostensibly intended for the benefit of the consumer, is often encouraged by producers as a way of restricting competition. If a regulatory regime obstructed new entry into banking this would be the outcome.

But whether regulation is said to correct for market failure, or produces market failure, what are these failures? There are three aspects of market failure that are generally cited as requiring regulation. The first is the possibility of a natural monopoly. The second is that an externality might occur. And the third relates to the nature of information.

The first can be dismissed quite quickly. A natural monopoly – the outcome of particular cost conditions – is unlikely in banking. Indeed, the examples that exist of complete freedom in banking suggest that competition is likely to prevail. There may however, be a potential problem with the clearing house since that can have monopolistic tendencies.

The second possibility is that of an important externality – the failure of one bank can lead to the failure of others, perhaps the collapse of the whole system, and a collapse in the stock of money and hence in real output. Though whether this can or should be achieved by regulation or by means of the lender of last resort is another question.

The third area of concern lies in information problems. Information is essentially what is being bought. In banking it is suggested that there is asymmetric information of a kind that matters more than in other sectors. Borrowers know more about their situation than the lender can. 'Power' therefore rests with the borrower initially and the trick is to resolve this problem for the lender. A variety of means have been found to do this ranging over monitoring, using collateral, and so on. But there are those who argue that the potential for damage is considerable and this therefore provides another case for regulation. Competition and disclosure requirements would be sufficient in most areas of the economy. But are banks different?

Historians and other social scientists take a wider view of policy-making

But on what basis has regulation actually been introduced? Policy-making is obviously a complex activity with many influences at work. But there have been perhaps three main approaches to the analysis of policy-making: the old political economy which had in it the notion of a beneficent state that sought to provide the most appropriate environment; the new political economy (public choice) with its emphasis on private interest; and third there is the part that ideas play. But having said that there is also the role of history, trend and cycle, the part that crises play, the part that general events play, the possibility of path dependency, the working of the bureaucracy, and the possibility of self-perpetuating tendencies. And there is the interaction of some of these elements.

The old political economy was more often than not identified with a wise altruistic/paternalistic government and the public interest. Action was taken to correct for obstructions to the working of the market. The new political economy, sometimes called public choice analysis, is associated more with private interest. The principal competing explanation in policy making is the role that ideas, good or bad, play in the process.

A long line of British writers has stressed the importance of ideas. From David Hume who gave pride of place to the power of ideas, through Adam Smith to A.V. Dicey at the end of the nineteenth century, who might be taken as a central exponent of the view that it was ideas that mattered above all else. And of course in the twentieth century there is Keynes's famous remark, now almost cliche, 'the ideas of economists and political philosophers, both when they are right and when they are wrong, are more powerful than is commonly understood. Indeed the world is ruled by little else.... I am sure that the power of vested interests is vastly exaggerated compared with the gradual encroachment of ideas' (1936: 383).

The American view tends to be different. George Stigler, for example, lies at the other end of this spectrum. 'I have not concealed my deep scepticism of the role of opinion, in bringing about basic changes in the direction of a society.... I would claim that a modest role in the deregulation of the financial markets has been played by the modern theories of efficient markets and of economic regulation' (1971: 9). Stigler contends that politically effective groups have used their power in all periods of history, even if sometimes their scope is limited.

While interest and ideas are clearly powerful factors in the formulation of policies, historians have long been well aware that there have been other forces at work. An obvious one in the field of banking is that of crisis itself. Some business cycle connection may also be made, or there may simply be a coming together of a number of elements to which policy-makers respond.

Whatever the prime mover for introducing new regulations, it is necessary for the establishment of a bureaucracy to implement and administer them. But the bureaucracy once established almost invariably goes beyond its primary task and grows apace. Apart from monitoring and enforcing the regulations it begins to interpret them and explores new applications. It certainly drafts complicated reporting requirements and compliance procedures that in turn require careful scrutiny that of themselves impose a burden on the firm. This is only to be expected, for regardless of the drafting skill of the legislature, statutory regulations and other directives are often open to some interpretation and fastidious and ambitious bureaucrats will frequently find more to do than was originally intended. Additionally, the regulators will be used by producers to extend the rules to cover other 'legitimate' targets. Bureaucracies have an interest in their own preservation, and better still, growth, and will generally find ways of achieving these.

Thus there are likely to be self-perpetuating tendencies at work and that the trend in regulation will continue. Even where the populace desired change and elected governments for that reason, these governments even where they were genuinely determined to effect change, have found it extremely difficult to accomplish in the face of equally determined, or simply cumbersome, bureaucracies. When regulatory creep is under way it is difficult to contain, let alone reverse.

Thus there is a long list of possible sources of regulation. It is tempting to begin to attach weights to these influences, but that is a temptation that should be resisted, introducing as it would a spurious precision to a notoriously difficult area of discussion. In nineteenth-century Britain the main source of new regulatory change was government, but at that time it was deregulating. In the first half of the twentieth century governments were also responsible, but in that period it was for regulating (possibly the result of a bad idea). And then in the latter part of the twentieth century pressure groups were more obviously at work and the bureaucracy had begun to have a dominant influence.

Financial regulation in England, 1700–2000

Table 3.1 tries to bring out the broad pattern of regulation relating to finance across three centuries in Britain.

The Usury Laws had long been in place and were revised from time to time before the start of our period. But for our purposes we can pick up the story with the privilege given to the Bank of England at its foundation in 1694, and renewed with each renewal of its charter for the next 130 years. In 1708 the Bank was given a monopoly of joint stock banking in England and Wales. There were very few joint stock companies at all at the time and each needed the sanction of parliament. When the 'South Sea Bubble' erupted in 1720 it was seen as damaging the reputation of

Table 3.1 Regulatory changes/legislation

Eighteenth century

1708	**Bank of England JSB monopoly – others partnerships**
1720	**Bubble Act – prevented joint stock formation**
1700s	**Hundreds to do with money/financial instruments**

Nineteenth century

1810	Bullion Committee
1814	*Amendments to Statute of Artificers*
1825	*Repeal of Bubble Act*
1826	*Joint Stock Banking Act – JSBs allowed outside London*
1820s	*Relaxing of Usury Laws*
1833	*Bank Charter Act – joint stock banks inside London*
1844	Bank Charter Act – note issue and gold standard
	Joint Stock Banking Act – more restrictive
1857	*Repeal of 1844 Joint Stock Banking Act*
1858–62	*Several pieces enabling limited liability*
1879	Companies Act – annual external audit requirement
1880s	*Easing of bankruptcy laws*
1890s	Disclosure requirements – JSBs to publish accounts
1890s	Building Societies

Twentieth century

1918	Treasury approval for mergers
1940s	**Various wartime agreements and controls – retained after the war**
1946	**Liquidity and cash ratios agreed**
1947	**Exchange Control Act**
1950s	**Special deposits**
1960s	**Special deposits**
1965	**Ceiling on lending**
1969	Disclosure of profits
1971	*Competition and Credit Control*
1979	**Banking Act – restrictive**
	Abolition of Exchange Control
1986	*Big Bang – restrictive devices lifted*
1987	**Banking Act**
1997	Central Bank Independence
	Financial Services Authority

Note
Greater regulation in bold, lighter regulation in italic, related changes in roman.

joint stock companies and resulted in further measures to contain their formation.

Although modern fractional reserve private banking had begun to get established in the closing years of the seventeenth century such banks were thus restricted in their development. They were denied the chance to expand through joint stock formation. But more than that they were confined to being partnerships of no more than six. That greatly limited their activities and they were to remain small and ultimately under-capitalised (and under-diversified) in relation to the growth of the firms in the rest of the economy. Further, as partnerships they were subject to unlimited liability. There can be some merit attaching to unlimited liability, but there are disadvantages. It can produce considerable caution, and while that is no bad thing in banking it is another factor limiting the scale of operations.

Against these restrictions on the operations of banks there was one feature that remained free and that was note issue. Any bank could issue its own notes more or less without constraint. This was commonly regarded as being a key reason for going into banking although in fact most of the London banks in the City did not avail themselves of this freedom. But as the table shows, there were hundreds of pieces of legislation in the eighteenth century relating to financial instruments where the general aim was to make commerce secure.

Although the English financial system grew through the eighteenth century it was characterised by repeated financial distress with consequences for the real economy. Clearly, the constraint placed on the banks prevented them from taking many of the courses they otherwise would, and this contributed to the fragility.

The table shows that for most of the nineteenth century, legislation was of a liberalising kind. In the course of the nineteenth century English/British (the two effectively came together with the legislation of 1844) banking legislation followed a trend of deregulation. This story should not be overdone but that is certainly the general direction. First the Usury Laws went. Then joint stock banking was allowed outside London, and then inside London. The gold standard was more clearly defined and the access of the discount houses to the Bank sorted out. Alongside this a prudent, diversified, and ultimately limited liability banking structure developed.

There was a slight reversal of the deregulatory trend in the 1844 Joint Stock Bank Act which made it more difficult to establish a bank. But that proved short-lived as most of it was repealed in 1857. Stability, while improving, was not completely guaranteed. One possible explanation lay in the fact that the banks were still subject to unlimited liability. So it was that limited liability was permitted in legislation of 1858 and 1862 and many banks, though far from all, took advantage of the opportunity. Initially too, the denomination of share prices acted as a further constraint, for they originally had a minimum value of £100. In time this too was relaxed. Most of the new banks formed after 1833 had shares of £10 and £5.

A move in the more restrictive direction came in 1844 when the Bank of England was given the sole right of note issue. But this was phased in. No new bank established could issue its own notes and where one bank was acquired by another bank, as was increasingly the case, they lost the right of issue. By the 1870s the extent of private issue was extremely small in relation to the total note issue. Thus the 1844 legislation did create a monopoly note-issuer even if it was done with the intention of providing greater monetary stability.

Across the period from 1870 to 1945 there was little new statutory regulation. The system regulated itself. But as the table again shows, moving across the twentieth century it is clear that regulation became more restrictive. This came not just from statutory legislation but from a variety of other sources too.

For the purpose of completing the picture then we note the principal features of the second half of the twentieth century. The picture was to change after 1945. The Labour Government elected in 1945 immediately nationalised the Bank of England. Within the banking sector there were increasing controls. Foreign exchange controls that had been introduced in wartime were consolidated in law in 1947 and tinkered with thereafter.

The Nationalization Act gave the Treasury power to direct the Bank, and the Bank power, with Treasury consent, to give direction to the banks. And yet in practice informality prevailed. It was not easy to change arrangements that had evolved naturally over a long period. Although the world had apparently changed greatly, the Bank and the banks were in effect still to be left largely free to sort out their own affairs. There were instructions to the commercial banks on their reserve and liquid asset ratios. There were also directives from the Bank: on the raising of capital; ceilings on lending; special deposits at the Bank.

Whether the informality that prevailed in the quarter century after the Second World War could have survived after 1970 when there were new entrants who were not always prepared to play by the unwritten rules is moot. This may have been part of the reason for the attempt at introducing some competition in banking in 1971 with 'Competition and Credit Control'. It seems that most pressure for this came from the Bank of England and there was little or no resistance from the banks.

But then banking regulations reached something of a peak in 1979 with a law that among other things specified the limits of lending to any one customer. This legislation seems to have derived directly from the secondary banking crisis of 1973–4. And further restrictions followed in the Banking Act of 1987. Another factor that led to increasing regulation was the bureaucracy. The Financial Services Authority (FSA), established in 1997, became an all-powerful single regulator for the whole of the financial sector. Since that time it has produced tens of thousands of pages of detailed instructions on how to conduct business within any financial firm. Compliance costs have soared as firms have sought to first interpret and then to carry out the instructions. In October 2003 in Britain the Better Regulation Task Force (the regulators' regulator) listed 108 watchdogs of different kinds, though this did not claim to be comprehensive. Most had been created since 1997.

If it were possible to construct an index of regulation it might, at least in very rough terms resemble that charted in Figure 3.1. That figure shows what the likely course of the regulatory burden was across the last three centuries. In the eighteenth century, regulation was high and rising

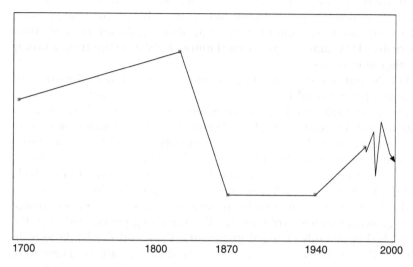

1700   1800   1870   1940   2000

Figure 3.1 The regulatory burden, 1700–2000.

throughout. From the first quarter of the nineteenth century it was falling
and reached a low point around 1870. From the late nineteenth century
through to around the Second World War it remained relatively low but
was undoubtedly on the up. Then from 1939 through to around the 1980s
it was rising. And after that the picture is mixed. There was a desire to lib-
eralise the markets but that went with ever greater concern for their
stability and the belief (misguided or not) that that was best achieved by
intervention. While there have been attempts to free up the markets, the
bureaucracy (in the principal form of the FSA) has behaved like all
bureaucracies and grown apace and justified its growth by increasing the
rules and hence the burden of compliance.

A full explanation of the changes that came about in the early nineteenth century would embrace a number of factors such as property
rights, the nature of the legal system, the basis for trust and the possible
role that religion played. There was a great reaction against the waste and
corruption of large government at the end of the Napoleonic Wars. There
was a desire for small government, sound money and free trade. But there
was a need to build trust and that was done in part through a fiscal constitution that emphasised probity in collection and expenditure with, in
modern parlance, full accountability and transparency. The building of
trust was no doubt facilitated by the particular brand of non-conformist
religion that was growing at the time, and importantly was embraced by
leading policy-makers.

A central aim was to keep interest groups at a distance from the policy-
making business and that allowed deregulation to proceed more rapidly.
Rent-seeking never became established. So it was that stability and deregu-

lation went hand in hand and persisted long after the more general return to mercantilism that took place at the end of the nineteenth century.

But around 100 years after the beginning of good behaviour, government began to renege on the contract and allowed and then encouraged inflation. At the same time the fiscal system became more complex and confusing and burdensome. The beginnings of the breakdown in trust can then be traced to the middle years of the twentieth century. By the third quarter of the century the deterioration in industrial relations and the erosion of standards of public and private honesty were clear, and reflected that declining trust. Regulation began to increase. It is a substitute for trust.

Some other experience

United States

The British experience described this far contrasts greatly with that of the US. The US is clearly a very different country with different history and institutions, and the fact of a written constitution which is said to have encouraged codification. For long periods in the last two centuries the political climate favoured inviting interested parties to express their views and lobby for their own interest. Public choice analysis has been used extensively in the analysis of policy-making.

Political economy in the US means the new political economy. For example, in a recent book on bank regulation in the US the distinguished economist Calomiris writes: 'A central principle of political economy is that concentrated minority interests can be more successful in extracting concessions from the political process than majorities. In a world where forming coalitions is physically costly, concentrated minorities face stronger incentives to lobby (and pay) for their desired outcomes' (2000: 383).

At the end of the eighteenth century Alexander Hamilton (the Secretary to the Treasury) had championed a National Bank to exercise discipline over the practices of the state banks, particularly with respect to over-issue of notes. The founding of the First Bank of the United States in 1791 was not greatly successful in this respect and its charter expired in 1811. In the second quarter of the nineteenth century there was an explosion of new banks and of note issue in the free banking era. According to some accounts there was considerable chaos and malpractice in this period. While this has been overstated it is not surprising that the desire for control over the banking system reappeared. One of the most important pieces of legislation was the National Banking Act (1864) which sought to bring all commercial banks under the control of the Federal government. After some early success in this respect it began to lose control as financial innovation and less demanding state regulation lessened the attractions of belonging to the National Banking system. The states often required lower capital and reserve ratios, and incorporation thus became more profitable under state than under Federal legislation.

Banking then became one of the most regulated industries in the US. One of its leading historians, Eugene White, in an examination of banking regulation from the Civil War to the Great Depression says, 'Changes in banking regulation were the product of protracted political struggles among different interest groups seeking to influence the structure of the industry' (1982: 33). The three interested parties were the banks, the depositors and the regulators, and the outcomes depended on the coalitions that arose. The most effective coalition was that of the small unit banks and they were successful over a long period in maintaining restrictions on branching. Indeed they have retained considerable influence right up to the present day.

Both Federal and state restrictions on branch banking meant the system was vulnerable to panics. There were many bank runs in the second half of the nineteenth century and up to the Second World War. Before 1914 the most serious of these was that of 1907. It was this crisis that led to the establishment of the National Monetary Commission whose investigation and report led on to the founding of the Federal Reserve in 1914. The Federal Reserve Act (1913) had a similar ambition to the National Banking Act in seeking control of the commercial banking system. Like its predecessor it failed in this respect, for the correspondent system rendered it unnecessary for a bank to join the Federal Reserve System. And as with its predecessor there followed some regulatory competition between the states and the centre. That competition led to serious consideration of branching, an issue that has for long occupied American banking historians. Bank failures had been common across the nineteenth century and that pattern persisted long after the Fed was founded. Thousands of small unit banks failed across the 1920s. The 1920s was a decade of booming economic conditions in the US. But banks were generally seen as behaving imprudently and indulging in unacceptable lending practices, on consumer loans, on real estate, various kinds of dubious ventures and at the same time lowering their credit standards. After thousands more failed in the depression years of 1929–32, the Banking Act of 1933 was passed. It introduced severe restrictions on entry, on types of assets held and gave directions on risky activities. The 1935 revision to the Act gave more authority to the Fed.

The many failures discredited the regulatory policies that had long been in place. And then when deposit insurance was proposed in the 1930s small town bankers saw it as a viable alternative that would protect the banking system. Depositors were on the side of the small banks and that proved a powerful coalition.

It is a common response of governments to find the solution to a banking crisis (that was in some instances the result of previous regulation) to be increased regulation. New legislation was introduced but the existing regulation remained on the statute book. This was common in the United States from the second half of the nineteenth century onwards (White, 1982). This was again a typical response in the US in 1931 at the height of a banking crisis.

The branching issue was seldom very far from discussion. It might be wondered how it was that small and, after 1930/32, weakened banks, could hold on to such restrictions. Strong support for removal of the restrictions came from the bigger banks and, led by Giannini of the Bank of America, they lobbied hard for removal. But to illustrate that the interest group story can be more complex Calomiris and Ramirez (2002) have introduced another element into this story. Calomiris (2000) had already demonstrated that branching restrictions were socially costly from the standpoint of macroeconomic growth and stability. Single office banks favoured restrictions that gave them protection from large branched banks. What the more recent paper shows is that there were certain kinds of borrowers who supported the restrictions. Borrower support for restrictions had varied across time and territory. Since entry barriers affected the terms on which borrowers could access credit they could therefore benefit some classes of borrowers. These borrowers turn out to be borrowers of high net worth whom Calomiris and Ramirez (2002) identify as, in the main, large landowners. They develop models to show, 'that barriers to varying the inter-regional allocation of credit by banks, created strategic advantages for borrowers that hold their wealth in the form of immobile factors of production (for example land)' (Calomiris and Ramirez, 2000: 7). (They assume that manufacturing interests owned relatively mobile factors of production and preferred branch banking.) These borrowers then are likely to have supported unit banking laws out of their own self interest, and so another element in the coalition is identified.

The explanation for new regulation in the US has been explained most commonly and in large part as the outcome of interest group pressure. And it is usually claimed that the public interest theory better explains the deregulation. But the world can change and some argue that the case of deregulation in the late twentieth century can be explained in terms of private interest; see for example Kroszner (1997). Kroszner and Strahan (1999) showed how the timing of deregulation on branching was determined by the relative strength of the interest groups involved. From the 1970s onwards the restrictions on bank branching in the US began to be lifted. Kroszner and Strahan (1999) accept that private interest theory had great success in explaining how well organised groups captured rents at the expense of dispersed interest in banking and that, in contrast, public interest theory had been given greater credit in explaining episodes of deregulation. However, unlike most other deregulation that was going on across the US from the 1970s onwards in railroads, airlines, telecommunications, gas and so on, bank branching regulation operated on a state by state basis and deregulation had taken place gradually. This means there are both time series data and cross sectional data available. Using this data and a 'hazard model' these authors show that the private interest theory can account for the pattern of bank branching deregulation that was taking place in the 1970s and 1980s. Thus even in the liberalisation of the late twentieth century, private interest theory is seen to provide most of the explanation. This then provides some challenge to the 'bigger' view that it was ideas or events that were responsible for the changes of the 1980s and beyond.

Banks in other countries

The experience in other major countries was certainly different from that in Britain. The biggest contrast being the one between Britain and the United States. At an early stage in Britain there was a passion for limited interference. The United States's particular history shaped a different approach. A passion for democracy, and a fear of central banking as found in Britain, determined the early shape of the American financial system. Then after the attempts at bringing some central control the pressures were found in the behaviour of interested parties. The role of interest groups was therefore far greater in the US than in Britain. These two countries were among the very earliest with developed financial systems in the modern period.

On turning to other countries what we find is that there were some attempts at replicating, or at least copying some features of the systems in the US and Britain. And then, in the second half of the twentieth century following the Second World War, there were further attempts, in some cases, of adopting practices from these countries. But some practices were effectively imposed on the defeated nations. The countries with strong British (and quite often in the field of money and banking that meant Scottish) influence not surprisingly followed many of the British practices. (Much of the following is drawn from Allen *et al.*, 1938.) What follows simply provides a flavour of the variety of experience across different kinds of countries at different stages of economic development.

In Canada the first chartered bank was the Bank of Montreal founded in 1817. But the striking feature of the system that developed in the nineteenth century was the spread of branching, particularly what took place in the period 1870 to 1910. This was of course in stark contrast to its next door neighbour. In 1879 the number of banks peaked at 49 but they were well-branched. Canada certainly followed British traditions and also suffered fewer fears over the central bank than did its neighbour. It also evolved, much like its British precursor, to a more concentrated system so that by 1928 there were only 28 banks. It was a stable system and while that undoubtedly derived in part from the branching which provided some diversification, that story needs to be tempered. Canada was even by the

1930s still predominantly a primary producing country. Thus the geographic diversification did not bring the same portfolio diversification that was found in the British system. Nevertheless, the relatively light regulatory environment with little regulation of a statutory kind, together with the diversified banking structure helped to avoid crises, and in turn the absence of crises is no doubt partly responsible for the continuing light statutory environment.

Australia and New Zealand were even more closely related to their British parent. In fact most of their systems in the nineteenth century were made up of branches of British banks. Apart, therefore, from those banks carrying with them the well-tried practices of their domestic experience, they also had the implicit support of the parent firm. Regulation then, in the early years, was almost non-existent. And in spite of both these countries being essentially primary producers, and, there therefore, being relatively little opportunity for portfolio diversification, there was little fear of financial distress prior to the Second World War. And while that calm continued after the war there was nevertheless, again like Britain, increasing intervention from the authorities.

Continental Europe provides a much different picture. There, the inclination deriving in part from civil law and the Napoleonic codification, was for much more centralisation, and again that was influenced by the legal system. In France the Bank of France was founded in 1800 and exported its own policies across the country through its extensive branch network. The main credit institutions began to appear in the middle years of the nineteenth century – from the 1830s onwards, but particularly in France in the period 1850 to 1865. The system evolved pragmatically. The European trend was for large universal banks often with closer links to industry than their Anglo-Saxon counterparts. Thus although the Bank of France was seen as being powerful its power was limited by the size of the main banking firms. Interestingly, it was not until 1941 that France had a statute organising the banking system. Then in 1945 the leading financial institutions were nationalised. Then again, after some relaxation, there was another burst of nationalisation under the Mitterand government in the 1980s. In the later twentieth century, regulation was conducted by a profusion of supervisory authorities.

For the nineteenth century, a similar story could be told for Germany. Large universal banks emerged in mid-century with close industry relations. For a long time these were hailed as being superior to British banks and responsible for superior German economic performance. A problem was that banks closely tied to heavy industry ran the risk of liquidity and solvency problems when the industrial sector with which they were involved ran into difficulties. Such difficulties might be either cyclical or secular. And these problems were realised in the summer of 1931 when the system collapsed. After 1945 the Germans adopted many features of the American system and some were imposed by the occupying powers, particularly in the shape of the central bank. Supervision after that was carried out by another agency.

It is not possible to describe in detail the experience of every continental European country but it does not distort the picture too much to say that most of the rest of Europe conformed to the general picture provided by these three large countries. There were differences in timing naturally, depending to some extent on the stage of economic development they had reached.

The Nordic area is slightly different. It should not of course be treated as one entity for while there are some close similarities there are some major differences. Sweden is the biggest and most important economically of the four countries. Its financial development paralleled its economic development from the mid-nineteenth century. There was a strong Scottish influence in these early years, and some desire and achievement of relative freedom in banking. But at the same time there was the continental European tradition of the credit mobilier. As late as 1864 however, there was a freeing-up of entry. There was a financial crisis in 1877 but no apparent knee-jerk reaction. However, in the years following, and up to, the First World War there was increasing supervision and regulation. By 1903 private note issues had disappeared. In 1907 a Bank Inspectorate Board was set up to which banks had to report regularly. The Board was given extensive powers. In 1911 new legislation brought stricter control – on size of lending, capital requirements and cash reserves. Following the First World War there were severe liquidity crises in the years 1920–3. That led to the establishment of a new state-owned bank and to the consolidation of the system. Then, in the quarter century after the Second World War Sweden pursued more vigorously than most a Keynesian policy, and extensive state control. That was accompanied by increasing financial regulation. Then Sweden followed the world fashion for deregulation in the 1980s and beyond. Thus, Sweden presents a mixed picture moving from an open system initially to ever increasing regulation prompted in the first place by crises but after 1945 by the triumph of an idea, and then again by a different idea after 1980.

The Nordic country closest to the Swedish experience was Denmark. Again there was some Scottish influence in the developments that took place from the mid-nineteenth century onwards. But in the period from 1870 to 1914 there were one or two crises of different sorts and these were followed by increasing scrutiny of the banking system and of growing regulation. Following the First World War, an act was passed in 1919 establishing a public inspectorate. Then in the early 1920s there were crises that provoked new legislation restricting lending.

Norway differed from these two in that from the earliest point of financial development in the mid-nineteenth century there was strong public sector involvement, a weak structure of private institutions, and a heavy dependence on foreign capital. The system remained essentially inadequate until the twentieth century. It was only after 1895 that a commercial banking system began to prosper but then it was hit by the crises following the First World War and those of the early 1930s. From 1935 to 1980 it was a heavily regulated system. It then joined in the deregulation that was going on almost everywhere.

Finland's experience was closer to that of Norway than the other two. It had of course been a Swedish province before being annexed to Russia. Nevertheless, from the mid-nineteenth century, although its currency was pegged to the rouble, it had a relatively independent monetary and financial system. But from its beginnings it was strictly regulated. No new bank could open without express permission from the authorities. There were even Usury Laws in place. The Finns too had crises after the First World War and more regulation followed, as it did again after the Second World War.

Japan presents another kind of story. It was a relative late-comer to industrialisation. After the Meiji restoration of 1868 there was greater openness to outside influences. In 1872 a national banking system was established modelled essentially on the American model. Then following a severe burst of inflation in the late 1870s there was a reorganisation and a determination to found a central bank. The Bank of Japan was established in 1882, and in 1890 a banking law permitted the formation of private commercial banks. Something similar to what had evolved in Britain emerged – a largely self-regulated system, and one that had the appearance of being quite highly cartelised. And it operated with government approval. Up until the 1920s there was limited regulation, at least when compared with the late twentieth century. But then in the 1920s there was a banking panic (sometimes traced to the devastating consequences of the 1923 Tokyo earthquake) and the response was a banking law (1928) that greatly extended regulation. It also encouraged further amalgamation. In 1942, a further Bank Act extended the influence of government. And then, after the war the US dissolved the zaibatsu, redefined the relationship between the Bank of Japan and the government, and applied Glass–Steagall type restrictions.

That brief survey suggests that while there was quite different experiences across a range of countries the most common determinant of new regulation was the response to crisis. And there is little in these respective accounts that suggests that lobbying by interested groups was prominent, let alone, the main determinant of the kind of regulation that resulted. Rather it could mostly be seen as the response by government to perceived market failure, usually coming in the shape of a crisis.

Conclusion

In Britain the great reaction against large and wasteful government at the beginning of the nineteenth century resulted in the removal of interest groups from the policy-making process. There followed a long period of financial and macroeconomic stability. It is important to stress that the successful performance of the economy, in this respect, over the next 100 years and more depended first of all on two elements. The first was the Bank of England learning to be a true lender of last resort; and the second was that the banking system was learning prudence. Together the lender of last resort and the prudent banking system produced remarkable financial stability and ensured that there was no financial crisis after 1866. The absence of crises in turn removed an important source of regulation – the response to crises. And the less regulation there is, the less scope there is to interpret legislation or regulatory directives and extend these further, and so the lower is the contribution of the bureaucracy. Thus the period of deregulation (roughly from the 1820s to the 1860s) which helped to produce stability (and was generally accompanied by good behaviour which was a product of trust engendered largely by government) resulted in relatively little further legislation that impinged on the financial sector. That, in its turn, meant that the environment for lobbying was relatively barren and rent-seeking did not become a habit and was certainly not encouraged in British economic life. There was correspondingly little scope for regulatory capture.

These conditions survived/persisted long after the more general return to mercantilism in the late nineteenth century. But when intervention did start to reappear in both world wars and after, it began to grow. Although ideas and good intentions have promoted some deregulation other sources of regulation have prospered and continued well into the period of neo-liberalism at the end of the twentieth century. Across at least two centuries there was a relative absence of lobbying, of rent-seeking, of interest-group influence, and ultimately, there were low levels of regulation.

The British experience has been changing. After governments began to go back on the original contract allowing inflation and raising taxes steeply, trust began to break down. Intervention has produced a huge bureaucracy. And crisis has made some contribution too. In fact earlier this year the head of the FSA asserted that most reform in financial regulation were implemented in the throes of crisis (*Financial Times* 3/2/04, p. 19).

For the United States the story is almost always told in different terms – opposite terms – to the UK. Regulation played its part in producing crises and then crises were important in sparking fresh regulation. But then interest groups played a vital part in shaping regulation and extending it. In other countries a mixed picture emerges but it can nevertheless be simplified by again noting the role that crises played.

Note

1 I thank my two discussants for thoughtful and helpful comments.

Bibliography

Allen, A.M., Cope, S.R., Dark, L.J.H. and Witheridge, H.J. (eds) (1938) *Commercial Banking Legislation and Control*, London: Macmillan.

Calomiris, C.W. (2000) *US Bank Deregulation in Historical Perspective*, New York: Cambridge University Press.

Calomiris, C. and Ramirez, C.D. (2002) 'The political economy of bank entry restrictions: theory and evidence from the US in the 1920s', mimeo, March.

Keynes, J.K. (1936) *The General Theory of Employment, Interest, and Money*, London: Macmillan Press.

Kroszner, R. (1997) 'The political economy of banking and financial regulation in the United States', in von Furstenberg, G.M. (ed.) *Integrating Economies: Banking and Finance in the NAFTA Countries and Chile*, Boston, MA: Kluwer Academic Publishers.

Kroszner, R.S and Strachan, P. (1999) 'What drives regulation? Economics and politics of the relaxation of bank branching restrictions', *Quarterly Journal of Economics* 38: 1437–69.

Stigler, G.J. (1971) 'The theory of economic regulation', *Bell Journal of Economics and Management Science 2* 1: 1–21, reprinted in Stigler (ed.) (1988) *Chicago Studies in Political Economy*, Chicago, IL: University of Chicago Press.

Stigler, G.J. (1988) *The Regularities of Regulation*, David Hume Institute Occasional Paper, no. 3.

White, E.N. (1982) 'The political economy of banking regulation, 1864–1933', *Journal of Economic History* 42(1): 33–41.

White, E.N. (1983) *The Regulation and Reform of the American Banking System, 1900–1929*, Princeton, NJ: Princeton University Press.

COMMENT

Alicia García-Herrero[1]

I drew a number of interesting ideas from Forrest Capie's very illuminating chapter. First, financial regulation is not a clear-cut concept. There
can be many definitions, particularly from an historian's perspective.
Second, Forrest points to a number of determinants of financial regulation, which I also find very relevant. These are vested interest and self-
perpetuating bureaucracies and also the economic ideas of the time.
Finally, Forrest recalls that there are two opposite approaches to understanding financial regulation. One is that regulation reduces market
failure. The mirror one is that it fosters market failure. My main general
comment, as I explain in more detail later, is that Forrest is probably too
close to the latter while I think that there is also evidence supporting a
more favourable view of financial regulation.

Forrest offers an accurate and interesting description of the historical
developments towards financial regulation, with particular attention to
the cases of Britain and the US and a brief account of other major countries. In Britain, the free-market ideas, the economic thought in place at
the beginning of the nineteenth century, limited the power of pressure
groups and was accompanied by a remarkable degree of financial stability.
In the twentieth century, however, when mercantilism was already well
established, there was a surge in interventionism and financial regulation
was introduced. This led to a growing bureaucracy and was accompanied
by a number of financial crises. Britain is thus a clear case of the influence
of the governing economic thought of the time, while bureaucracies and
crises are a consequence of financial regulation. In the US, on the other
hand, vested interests were key in shaping regulation and regulation was a
source of crises. In France, centralisation and intervention were the most
important determinants of financial regulation. In Germany, the emphasis
was more on vested interests and a major banking crisis as a consequence
of the Great Depression, in shaping financial regulation. From these cases,
Forrest concludes that financial stability may be achieved without regulation and, if introduced, it may be for the profit of certain power groups
(vested interests) and/or lead to financial crises. This seems to me a
rather negative picture of financial regulation. I would argue that there
are other aspects – in addition to financial regulation – which explain the
degree of financial stability in a country. A key one is the structure of the
financial system itself. Another important one is the existence – or
absence – of safety-nets, such as the lender of last resort and the deposit
guarantee scheme. Other relevant institutional aspects are the quality of
the rule of law, creditor rights and bankruptcy procedures.

In addition, it should be acknowledged that regulation is not the same
everywhere. There are differences in the mix of discretion versus rules,

the degree of stringency of regulation, the types of enforcement, which can go from positive incentives to moral suasion or punishment. Sanctions can also vary widely. Finally, the institutional setting of financial regulation may be different in terms of the human and technical resources available as well as the degree of independence. All these differences may have a bearing on the quality of financial regulation, as Currie (2003) argues but most probably also on financial stability. In this line, García-Herrero and del Rio (2003) find empirical evidence of the relation between the location of the responsibility of financial regulation, as well as the institutional design of the central bank, on the occurrence of banking crises.

A more specific comment to Forrest's work is that it does not differentiate between regulation and intervention. Regulation can be understood as prudential norms, not necessarily limiting sound business opportunities. Intervention, in turn, is a more stringent concept which fits better with some of the harmful historical developments described in his chapter. Another interesting conceptual difference worth considering is that of self-regulation and deregulation, the former being understood as more extreme than the latter. This is especially the case if deregulation follows from a very regulated system, as has happened in many countries in the last three decades.

Finally, there are historical cases which would lead to a more positive assessment of financial regulation. This is the case of the Great Depression where, according to Mitchener's (2004) empirical evidence, the states with better regulation suffered from less financial instability, as measured by the number of failing banks. In particular, the insulation of supervisors from the industry's influence and higher capital requirements reduced the number of bank failures. Instead, more restrictive branching requirements led to more bank failures.

Finally, I will briefly describe the case of Spain, which also offers a more positive view of the influence of regulation on financial stability.[2] Spain was under a free banking regime between 1869 and the First World War. The only limitation was the monopoly for money issuance, in the hands of Bank of Spain. As in the case of the UK, this was a period of financial stability although there was speculation during and after the war. In fact, many new banks were established, particularly foreign ones, which fostered competition but also vested interests. This period ended up with a number of large bank failures, opening the door to some regulation. In fact, in 1921 a system of self regulation was introduced through the Banking Advisory Body. Minimum capital requirements were introduced for any banks that wanted (voluntarily) to become members of the Banking Advisory Body. This was a relatively stable and positive period although it also led to collusion among banks and to a reduction of competition. After the Spanish Civil War, tight intervention in the whole economy was introduced. In the case of the financial system, the allocation of credit was decided centrally and a number of state-owned development banks were created. While financial stability was ensured, it was at the expense of competition and efficiency. After 1952, a slow but steady liberalisation was introduced although it still aimed at maintaining existing banks. The combination of liberalisation, leading to a dangerous interrelationship between banks and companies and the lack of strict banking supervision, led to a large banking crisis from 1978 until 1985 (110 banks were closed, amounting to 27 per cent of total assets). As a consequence of the crisis, prudential regulation was improved while the liberalisation continued. With Spain's entry into the EU in 1986, financial liberalisation accelerated along with the internationalisation of the Spanish banking system. The Spanish case is an example of what can be lost from state intervention in the financial system but also of what can be gained from sound prudential regulation.

In conclusion, Forrest's chapter is interesting and draws an important conclusion: the economic ideas in place in a certain period are an important determinant of financial regulation. While in agreement with this view, I would argue that they probably matter more for the extreme cases – intervention and self-regulation – than for regulation and de-regulation. For these, other factors are at least as important: the country's financial structure and institutional aspects, such as the safety nets of the banking system. Belonging to a club (such as the EU) is also very relevant. In the same vein, the type of financial regulation may also vary widely across countries and is not easily comparable. Finally, no strict bilateral relation should be inferred between the existence or absence of regulation and the occurrence of financial crises.

Notes

1 The usual disclaimer applies.
2 This is mainly drawn from Faus Monpart (2001).

References

Currie, C.V. (2003) 'Towards a general theory of financial regulation: predicting, measuring, and preventing financial crises', School of Finance and Economics, University of Technology, Sydney, Working Paper, no. 132.

Faus Monpart, E. (2001) 'Regulación y desregulación: notas para la Historia de la Banca Española', editorial *Península*.

García-Herrero, A. and del Rio, P. (2003) 'Financial stability and the design of monetary policy', Banco de España, Working Paper, no. 0315.

Mitchener, K.J. (2004) 'Bank supervision, regulation and financial instability during the Great Depression', National Bureau of Economic Research, NBER Working Paper, no. 10475.

4 Bank regulations and money laundering

Anna J. Schwartz

My remarks will cover three topics. First, I will review developments in government regulation of financial services institutions in the United States since the 1930s. Until the mid-1980s the main objective of regulation was to ensure the safety and soundness of these institutions.

Second, I will discuss the key new regulations that impose anti-money laundering obligations on US financial institutions. These obligations have been superimposed on the performance of normal banking activities. Society has determined that national security requires banks to play a part in responding to this need, much as airlines have been given the responsibility to participate in the screening of passengers and their belongings before permitting them to board. It is useful also to consider the inordinate foreign demand for US banknotes as a source of large cash deposits in US banks that constitute one of the roots of the money laundering problem. In this context I refer to the Federal Reserve's Extended Custodial Inventory Program although it involves only financial institutions that have accepted a contractual agreement to participate in this programme, not the entire class of financial service institutions.

Third, I will describe the dialectical process by which regulated institutions discover loopholes in regulation as originally formulated and regulators' subsequent amendment of the regulations to close the loopholes. The process then repeats. I cite examples of the dialectic based on safety and soundness regulation. Compliance with money laundering regulation has been spotty, but there is no predisposition to change the content of the regulation, so the dialectic is not operative.

Regulations to ensure financial institution safety and soundness

Let me now begin with a brief review of US regulation of financial institutions. The scope of regulation alternated between maximization and minimization. The period of maximization extended from post-1933 to 1970. It was marked by the creation of new institutions like Federal Deposit Insurance, Federal Home Loan Banks to provide credit to banks servicing home owners. The Bank Holding Company Act and its amendment gave the Federal Reserve supervision of bank holding companies. Demand and time deposit rate regulation was an important component of the general belief structure of the period. It is questionable whether all these regulatory initiatives accomplished their objective.

Minimization of regulation thereafter gradually reversed earlier legislation and programmes that were judged to have distorted markets were ended. Minimization began with removal of rate ceilings on large, negotiable CDs and proceeded until all deposit interest rate regulations were eliminated. Some changes had mixed effects, such as enactment of the Depository Institutions Deregulation and Monetary Control Act which imposed reserve requirements for the first time on non-member banks of the Federal Reserve System. The Garn–St Germain Act made the banking system as a whole more competitive. However, repeal of the New Deal Glass–Steagall Act, empowering the financial services industry to engage in securities, real estate, and insurance business and authorization of interstate banking and branch banking were unmixed changes freeing markets. In addition, the FDIC Improvement Act changed the way US deposit insurance is administered, requiring early intervention by regulators, in the case of banks with below average capital ratios. The change was intended to insulate the taxpayer and insurance funds from undue risk, in response to former forbearance by regulators.

One general observation about bank safety and soundness regulation, whether or not the overall results were favourable, is that regulators did not publicize the name of an individual institution whose performance fell short of regulatory standards. Market participants might have had suspicions about the integrity of the institution in such a case but its public reputation would not have been at risk. As we shall see when I now turn to the new regulations to which financial institutions have been subject in the past two decades, loss of reputation is at stake if an institution is singled out for violating these legal requirements.

Anti-money laundering and other new financial institutions regulations

It is not only recent legislation that imposes on US financial services institutions the obligation to fulfil the demands of a broad purpose that society values. The US Community Reinvestment Act, for example, is social engineering, to assure that banks do not discriminate against residents of low-income districts in allotting mortgage loans. Banks may believe that the Act impugns the impartiality of their judgement of the creditworthiness of mortgage applicants, but they nevertheless must comply.

Anti-laundering legislation is of the same genre as the Community Reinvestment Act. It is designed to prevent the movement of illicit cash through US financial institutions. Three laws prescribe their basic anti-money obligations: the Money Laundering Control Act of 1985, the Bank Secrecy Act of 1970 and the USA Patriot Act of 2002, which amended both prior laws.

The Bank Secrecy Act, as amended, requires the institutions to: (1) establish anti-money laundering programmes, an internal audit function, and appoint an employee training officer; (2) verify the identity of persons seeking to open accounts; (3) exercise due diligence when opening and administering accounts for foreign institutions, wealthy foreign individuals including senior foreign political figures. The Treasury Department also is authorized to require institutions and other firms to file reports on large currency transactions.

The Money Laundering Control Act was the first in the world to make money laundering a crime. It prohibits any person from knowingly engaging in a transaction which involves the proceeds of a long list of specified unlawful activity including terrorism, drug trafficking and fraud. The Patriot Act expanded the list to include foreign crimes involving bribery and misappropriation of funds. It is therefore illegal for a US bank knowingly to accept funds that were the proceeds of foreign corruption.

The Secretary of the Treasury is the primary Federal regulator of enforcing anti-money laundering laws, and the Comptroller of the Currency within the Treasury Department is responsible for overseeing banks with a national banking charter. The agency of the Treasury that has primary responsibility for money laundering is FINCEN, the Financial Crimes Enforcement Network. In addition, the Financial Action Task Force represents a group of OECD countries that is trying to coordinate efforts to combat money laundering internationally.

Despite the legislation, a prominent Washington, DC national bank has recently been found guilty of infringement of statutory and regulatory anti-money laundering requirements, and regulators have been charged with disinclination to compel the bank to correct its deficiencies.

Riggs Bank is a well-known long-standing institution incorporated in Delaware, which operates primarily in the Washington, DC metropolitan area but also maintains foreign offices in London, Berlin, the Bahamas, the Isle of Jersey and a subsidiary in Miami. The bank, with over $6 billion in assets as of last year, is the principal operating subsidiary of a holding company, Riggs National Corporation. The bank provides retail, corporate and institutional banking services, and wealth management services to high-income individuals through its domestic and international banking departments. A speciality of Riggs is Embassy Banking, administering accounts at more than 95 per cent of foreign missions and embassies located in Washington.

Riggs has large numbers of foreign clients as well as some from countries with risks of money laundering and foreign corruption. The bank since 1997 has been repeatedly charged with disregard for anti-money laundering requirements and facilitation of suspicious activities, principally on the handling of accounts for Augusto Pinochet, which the bank concealed from the Comptroller of the Currency, as well as of turning a blind eye to evidence of foreign corruption for the government of Equatorial Guinea, its officials and family members. The bank's accounts with Saudi Arabia are still under investigation.

In May 2004 Riggs paid the Office of the Comptroller $25 million to settle allegations that it had failed to report, detect or even look for clearly suspicious transactions in accounts related to foreign embassies. The Federal Reserve Board at the same time ordered the parent company of the bank to take steps to ensure that the bank reports suspicious financial transactions to federal authorities. The Federal Reserve also ordered Riggs to close its Miami subsidiary and to seek Fed approval before it paid any dividends or bought back stock.

With its reputation in tatters, in July 2004 Riggs agreed to be bought by Pittsburgh-based PNC Financial Services Group for about $700 million. Thus a historic name will be gone from Washington banking.[1] Riggs still faces serious legal problems as the investigation of its failure to abide by regulators' strictures continues. This August 2004, Riggs placed its chief risk officer on leave.

The regulators themselves, as has been noted, are under a cloud. The examiners from the Office of the Comptroller identified the deficiencies in the Riggs weak anti-laundering programme, but were slow to use enforcement tools. More disturbing, the Comptroller's Examiner-in-Charge at Riggs until he retired in 2002 then joined Riggs' staff. The former examiner appeared before his former agency in connection with matters relating to Riggs' compliance and attended meetings with the agency for two years without prior approval of the Comptroller's ethics office. The Federal Reserve was also charged with being slow and passive in implementing its overseeing role.

There is no agreement among various Congressional investigating bodies about how to remedy the problem of regulatory agency failure to provide the effective overseeing of bank anti-money laundering performance. The investigators concluded that the scandal is not limited to Riggs, that it is not an isolated case, but symptomatic of a pattern of ineffective enforcement by federal regulators.

There are at least two other banks besides Riggs and UBS that have been in the news recently in connection with money laundering lapses. One is the New York branch of the Dutch banking giant ABN Amro. It is being investigated by regulatory and law enforcement officials for its dealings with foreign financial institutions. FRBNY alleged that the bank was improperly moving funds of questionable origin through the financial system. Dozens of accounts were transferred to ABN Amro in New York from the Bank of New York when it was under investigation in the 1990s.

ABM Amro in July 2004, agreed in a 14-page document to sever relationships with nearly 100 correspondent loosely regulated banks in

Eastern Europe, the Mediterranean, and Caribbean because of questions of compliance with money laundering regulations. The Justice Department is investigating $885,000 in transfers from Latvia through ABN Amro in New York that were allegedly part of a fraudulent deal to avoid Russian taxes. That and similar transactions are part of a broader pattern of fraud, tax and money laundering involving millions of dollars, passed through ABN Amro in New York by banks in Russia and Eastern Europe.

A provision in the Patriot Act put the legal onus on banks to know the identity of their customers and where their money comes from. In the 1990s Bank of New York moved more than $7 billion from Russia, believed to be proceeds of corruption, tax evasion and organized crime through correspondent accounts with Russian banks. Two Bank of New York executives pleaded guilty to money laundering and have not yet been sentenced. The bank was not punished pending full cooperation.

Correspondent accounts allow foreign banks to conduct dollar-denominated transactions and move funds into the US without setting up a US branch, simply by paying fees to a host bank that has a US banking licence. ABN Amro has also cut off its correspondent banks in Cyprus, an offshore banking centre that caters to the Russian market. ABN Amro failed to certify that its customers were not foreign shell banks, entities that exist primarily on paper for the purpose of moving money secretly. It agreed to enhance its filings of Suspicious Activity Reports on unusual transactions.

Another institution that regulators have targeted for lack of compliance is Beacon Hill, a small Manhattan firm not licenced by New York State doing suspicious money transmitting business all over the world. JP Morgan Chase opened 40 accounts with Beacon Hill in 1994. Morgan Chase in New York took on Beacon Hill after its London office shut down Beacon Hill in 1994 for suspicious activities. Between 1997 and 2000 Morgan Chase moved $6.5 billion in wire transfers for Beacon Hill. Its clients included offshore shell corporations and money exchange houses in Brazil and Uruguay. Money was linked to the drug trade, some to official corruption and government fraud in Brazil. Beacon Hill also transmitted $32 million to accounts in Pakistan, Lebanon, Jordan, Dubai, Saudi Arabia and other Middle East countries. Investigators have not discovered the real parties behind the transactions because Beacon Hill record-keeping was sloppy. Its business was run out of a pooled account that served many customers so it was impossible to connect specific deposits to specific transfers out of the account.

In February 2004 Beacon Hill was convicted of operating as a money transmitter without a licence. Morgan Chase was not charged with any crime. The New York State Banking Department and New York Fed were asked in March whether Chase violated the 'Know your clients rule'. Morgan Chase has since stopped dealing with wholesale money transmitters.

Another big US financial institution in trouble for failure to prevent suspected money laundering is Citigroup. Japanese regulators in

September ordered Citigroup to shut down its four private banks in Japan for other violations as well. The publicity has damaged Citigroup's reputation probably more than its revenues.

One of the charges brought against Riggs was that over a two-year period it accepted cash deposits of $1 million or more in bank notes in six separate transactions. It did not treat them as unusual or requiring scrutiny. Cash is a traditional way of hiding the source of income. US banknotes have for many years been a preferred banknote medium for residents of foreign countries the purchasing power of whose domestic currency is unstable and lacks anonymity. Foreigners have no problem obtaining US banknotes. It is estimated that over $400 billion of $680 billion in circulation is held abroad. Of course, not all suspicious money transactions are conducted with cash. It is easy to transfer funds by wire from even the least advanced countries. Riggs was also charged with failure to conduct routine or special monitoring of frequent and sizeable transfers of funds across international lines.

Providing the banknotes that foreigners demand is a financial benefit for US taxpayers, so it makes sense for the Federal Reserve to have introduced the Extended Custodial Inventory Program in 1996 primarily to facilitate the distribution abroad of a new design $100 note. The primary purpose of the programme then shifted to enhance the international banknote distribution system, which began to function in January 1998. The programme maintains an inventory of Federal Reserve notes in strategically located international distribution centres. Currently, a total of eight facilities are operated in five cities by five banks: American Express Bank (London), Bank of America (Hong Kong, Zurich), HSBC (London, Frankfurt, Hong Kong), Royal Bank of Scotland (London) and United Overseas Bank (Singapore). These five cities are now the principal hubs for the distribution of US banknotes. Thirty institutions worldwide participate in wholesale buying and selling of the notes that are exported to international markets by the Federal Reserve Bank of New York.

The Federal Reserve Bank of New York manages the programme, and negotiates an Agreement with each of the five bank operators. The Agreement specifically prohibits operators from engaging in transactions affecting the programme inventories with countries subject to sanctions by the Treasury Department's Office of Foreign Asset Controls. The operators are required to provide the New York Fed with monthly reports of all countries that engaged in US dollar transactions with the operator and the volume of those transactions.

Until late October 2003 one other bank was an operator of the banknote inventory programme. The bank was UBS, which operated a site in Zurich The Federal Reserve Bank of New York terminated its contract with UBS in connection with the investigation of the discovery by US armed forces in Baghdad of $650 million of US currency with a New York Fed wrapping. Serial number records identified a sample of the notes as part of 24 shipments to several operators including UBS. The other operators provided information concerning the counterparties to whom they sold the banknotes in question. UBS eventually revealed that it had sold the notes to Iran, it claimed by mistake, and gave a false explanation for its failure to account for the sale in its monthly report to the New York Fed. The Iranian transaction violated the agreement UBS had signed prohibiting shipment of currency to countries subject to sanctions by the Treasury Department's Office of Foreign Assets Control. UBS was also fined a $100 million civil money penalty for deceptive conduct. Investigation of the trail of the currency to Iraq continues.

The case of UBS differs from that of Riggs. Riggs did not exercise due diligence in performing its anti-money laundering regulatory obligations. UBS violated a commitment it had explicitly agreed to abide by. The test of even well-conceived regulation is whether it works.

The regulatory dialectic

US commercial banks are regulated by many obligations, beginning with obtaining a charter, submitting to periodic examination by its regulatory and deposit insurance supervisor, meeting capital requirements, operating with restrictions on asset holdings, until recently constrained by state branching restrictions. A similar situation applies to other financial institutions, including savings and loan associations, mutual savings banks and credit unions.

Financial regulation imposes costs on the regulated, so regulation fosters incentives to avoid them. Regulators in reaction to avoidance behaviour by the regulated, find ways to tighten the rules they originally imposed. In the following round, the regulated again try avoidance, to which the regulators again respond. This is the dialectic of regulation. It applies, not only to financial regulation but also to regulation in general. Examples of the dialectic are easily found.

Sometimes, however, avoidance is not needed. The market may innovate a new financial instrument that serves the purpose of the regulated and clearly improves the general welfare. Regulators in such a case do not respond by attempting to undo the change. An example of such an innovation is the introduction of the eurodollar market, which served the aim of commercial banks to avoid the opportunity cost of reserve requirements on deposits and the costs of deposit rate ceilings. Eurodollars, US dollars deposited in foreign banks abroad or in foreign branches of US banks, were subject neither to reserve requirements nor to former deposit interest rate ceilings, when US banks borrowed these funds from the foreign bank or their own foreign branch. The same was true of commercial paper issued by the parent bank holding company, which was not treated as deposits. These were permanent changes the regulators simply lived with.

A good illustration of the dialectic was the effect on savings and loan institutions and mutual savings banks when market interest rates rose above deposit rate ceilings. Depositors withdrew their savings from these institutions, thus limiting their ability to issue residential mortgages. Home ownership, however, was a valued social objective. The Federal Reserve responded by raising the ceiling on time deposits in these institutions by one-quarter of 1 per cent higher than commercial banks could pay and extending the higher time deposit ceiling to formerly unregulated credit unions. In addition, to channel the flow of money from small savers to the preferred institutions, small-denomination Treasury Bills were eliminated. As a consequence, low-income households were effectively barred from earning higher market interest rates. Bank holding companies and corporations were encouraged to issue small-denomination debt securities, but these were not a typical investment of such households.

The regulators' strategy to keep low-cost deposits in mortgage-issuing institutions was ultimately foiled by the development of money market mutual funds, which low-income households embraced. The ensuing loss of deposits by the institutions prompted the use of another stopgap measure to help them. They were allowed to issue money market certificates, which paid market interest rates, issued in denominations of $10,000. Low-income households got no benefit from this change and had no alternative but to keep their savings in the mortgage-issuing institutions. Ultimately, the plugging of loopholes was abandoned by legislation allowing the mortgage-issuing institutions broader scope in lending.

To sum up, financial safety and soundness regulation in the US at times has been ill-advised. The regulatory dialectic, however, may serve as a corrective for some misbegotten measures. Even when regulation has been socially beneficial, as in the case of anti-money laundering, some US banks have acted to aid and abet money laundering. The reason is that the international money transmittal business is lucrative. The potential loss of fat fees, earned from that business, if those banks stopped dealing with wholesale money transmitters whose activities are suspicious, accounts for their misbehaviour. There is a corresponding indifference on the part of regulators to the urgency of enforcing compliance. This is a matter that requires the attention of top-level authorities in charge of public safety.

Note

1 In a bid to replace Riggs Bank as Washington's premier diplomatic bank, HSBC Bank, a global institution with headquarters in London, will open a DC branch in November. Riggs, which is winding down its one billion dollars in embassy banking, has agreed to refer its embassy clients to HSBC.

Embassies have established accounts with other banks including Citibank, Wachovia and Bank of America Corp. A small community bank in Potomac has also won a few small embassy clients.

HSBC has affiliates in 76 countries, some of which have strict secrecy laws, US authorities believe secrecy laws impede rules designed to prevent international money laundering. HSBC says it has rigorous controls at its affiliates and will follow regulations closely.

Bibliography

CCH Group (2004) 'Senators criticize Riggs' weak anti-money laundering program: call for Congress to act', July (Catherine Hubbard).

Kane, E.J. (1988) 'How market forces influence the structure of financial regulation', in Haraf, W. and Kushmeider, R.M. (eds) *Restructuring Banking and Financial Services in America*, Washington, DC: American Enterprise Institute for Public Policy Research.

New York Times (2004) 'ABN Amro raises guard on money', 30 September P.W. 1.

OECD Financial Action Task Force, available online at www1.oecd.org/fatf/.

Pratt's Letter 'Money laundering crisis angers Congress', 10 July, 2004.

Reuters (2004) 'Riggs puts chief risk officer on leave – SEC filing', 9 August, 6:36 pm ET.

US Department of the Treasury (2001) 'The 2001 National Money Laundering Strategy', prepared by the Office of Enforcement, in consultation with the Department of Justice, September.

US Senate (2004) 'Testimony of Thomas C. Baxter, Jr before the Committee on Banking, Housing, and Urban Affairs, oversight of the Extended Custodial Inventory Program', Federal Reserve Bank of New York, 20 May.

US Senate Permanent Subcommittee on Investigations, Committee on Governmental Affairs (2004) 'Money laundering and foreign corruption: enforcement and effectiveness of the Patriot Act: case study involving Riggs Bank', report prepared by the Minority Staff, 16 July.

US Treasury, Financial Crimes Enforcement Network.

Wall Street Journal (2004a) 'Morgan and Beacon Hill', editorial, August 18, p. A10.

Wall Street Journal (2004b) 'Amid probe, ABN Amro cuts off nearly 100 banks', 29 September (Glenn R. Simpson).

Wall Street Journal (2004c) 'Banks increase spending to fight money laundering', 20 September (Sarah Spikes).

Wall Street Journal (2004d) 'Congress questions Treasury, Fed on handling of ABN Amro', 1 October (Glenn Simpson).

Washington Post (2004a) 'Fed order puts Riggs under closer oversight', 17 May, P. E01 (Kathleen Day).

Washington Post (2004b) 'HSBC to open D.C. branch pursues embassy clients', 5 October.

5 Governing the corporation

Transcending compliance in an age of scandal[1]

Justin O'Brien

Corporate malfeasance and misfeasance on the scale witnessed in the late 1990s and early part of this century in the United States cannot be reduced to a single factor. Rather a multiplicity of internal and external checks failed simultaneously: within the corporation; the self-regulated professions and exchanges; the research analysts; the rating agencies; and the regulatory agencies and their political masters. Despite having one of the most codified securities markets in the world, with a plethora of inter-locking federal, state and self-policing mechanisms, the regulatory system proved incapable of either insuring against market failure or instilling credible ethical restraint. This has been underlined by a recent address by the Chairman of the Federal Reserve, Alan Greenspan at a meeting of the Federal Reserve of Atlanta in which he warned that 'rules are not a substitute for character' (Greenspan, 2004). It was recognition that ethical shortcomings within the governance of the financial markets play a major contributing role in facilitating scandal. Yet, the United States policy response has been conditioned by the continued power of two interlocking mechanisms: market-based self-regulation, which has demonstrably and repeatedly failed, underpinned by more detailed proscriptive rules, which are mostly tangential to the root causes of scandal.

Lest there be any suggestion that a principles-based alternative, as advocated by the corporate governance regimen in Europe, across equity and bank financed market structures, is any more efficacious in preventing scandal, one only has to point to the degradations evidenced within Parmalat and Royal Ahold and a series of scandals dating back to the 1990s. These include Robert Maxwell's raiding of the Mirror pension fund, the looting of Polly Peck, the failure of Marconi and the fiasco governing Equitable Life. Nor has the introduction of more detailed principles calibrated risk management across regulatory regimes, as evidenced by the rogue trading in Allied Irish Bank's US subsidiary (Promontory Financial Group, 2002; Dunne and Helliar, 2002), or within the principle paradigm itself, as seen most recently in the systemic corruption within National Australia Bank's subsidiary in the Republic of Ireland (ODCE, 2004).

In both rules and principle regimes the primary force governing change – more proscriptive rules or greater granularity in the articulation of principles – has been scandal occasioned by regulatory and self-policing failure. Redressing this imbalance should be a corporate and policy imperative. Instead the business community complains of becoming burdened by red tape with improvements to corporate governance structures reduced to box-ticking. Policymakers remain reticent about revisiting the partial settlement agreed in the aftermath of the collapse of Enron. The new status quo, however, is far from stable.

A retreat to rules will not necessarily guarantee better ethical practice or probity. Indeed, the passage of the rules may itself constitute a serious problem. It serves to obfuscate systemic failure, creating the illusion of change: a spectacle that resonates with the public through the parading in handcuffs of once deified business executives but leaves intact the structural defects (O'Brien, 2004a). Despite the undoubted financial costs to business associated with a greater degree of rule-based compliance, the failure to tackle the situational factors that inculcate within the corporate sector a banal culture of misfeasance represents a missed opportunity. It also preordains further ethical breaches.

It is far from clear that the primary mechanism driving change, what Charles Calomiris has termed the 'new god of independence', can prove to be an effective shield. For Calamoris, as for many economists, the problem to be addressed is a simple agency one (Jensen and Meckling, 1976). Increasing the level of independent directors on corporate boards risks elevating ignorance while failing to rebalance the advantage in corporate knowledge away from the very management that stands charged with the inability or unwillingness to control rapacious instincts. As Galbraith (2004: 74–5) has acidly noted, the 'relationship [between independent directors and management] somewhat resembles that of an honorary degree participant to a member of a university faculty. The soap-operatic scheming for control of the Hollinger media empire reveals the danger of relying on a somnambulant board as a vehicle to stop rapacious management engaging in what the former chairman of the Securities and Exchange Commission referred to as a 'corporate kleptocracy' (Breeden, 2004). It also demonstrates the complicity of fiduciary professionals who facilitated the transfer of 95 per cent of profits to a vehicle controlled by management over a period 1997–2003, a period that includes the post Sarbanes–Oxley era.

For agency theorists the only way to ensure restraint is to elaborate and facilitate more efficient market mechanisms. These mechanisms include the accurate and timely release of corporate information and the facilitation of changes to the market for corporate control that would allow for the sacking of non-performing management (Fama and Jensen, 1980; Learmount, 2002). The entire structure of the markets in the United States is predicated on diffusing ownership to avoid the build up of formidable blocks, thus making institutional investors relatively powerless to change management (Roe, 1994), a point that angers those agency theorists who argue that the legislation presents a missed opportunity to redefine the capacity of the markets to instil credible restraint.

There is considerable merit in the argument that insights derived from agency theory help deal with problems within the firm. It becomes much more problematic, however, when one considers that a primary factor facilitating the cycle which led to systemic failure was the operation of the market itself (O'Brien, 2004b). The gatekeeper failure by the mutual funds, which have traditionally and systematically voted with management, particularly in the expensing of stock options, is a continuing reality. As Bill Stronberg, head of research at T Rowe Price, one of the leading mutual funds in the United States, explained to the *New York Times*, 'we do not feel companies should be forced to expense options when the accounting conventions are otherwise' (Morgenson, 2004).

The manipulation of the Eurobond market by Citigroup in August, now under formal investigation by the Financial Services Authority ('Citigroup faces probe over bonds', *Financial Times*, 19 August 2004), shows that the 'casino capitalism' identified by Susan Strange (1984b) remains open for business. The defining characteristic of a system governed by the doctrine of technical compliance is pathological gaming. In this context, credible enforcement strategies become an imperative. The escalation in both malfeasance and misfeasance in the United States can be traced directly to their absence along with the increased complexity of the financial environment and resultant change in the perception of gatekeepers as to their function, away from professionalism and towards hired guns. The reactive regulatory, judicial and legislative activism generated in response to the consequences of this amoral reality only address it in a tangential and piecemeal manner. This does not necessarily render the reforms unimportant or meaningless: far from it.

Given its liquidity and power, any change in the system of financial governance of Wall Street has profound implications for external national regulatory structures and non-US domiciled corporations. This power is made manifest both through the demonstration effect of changed norms and the capacity of the United States regulatory regime and its associational actors to influence the promulgation of globally applicable accounting and listing standards actively, a process of globalization that 'constitute the corporatization and securitization of the world' (Braithwaite and Drahos, 2000: 143).

It is indeterminate whether this will provide a panacea or lead merely to the global export of precisely the same kinds of systemic gaming, creative compliance and juridical paralysis that informs the contemporary American regulatory arena. If, as argued, the reforms introduced in the United States are designed primarily as a domestic attempt to nullify public anger and present the image of decisive action while leaving unexamined the structural reasons for the inculcation of malfeasance and mis-feasance, rather than a credible attempt to realign the control levers of the market, is a false sense of security created which, in turn, heightens potential future volatility in the equity markets? The changing regulatory framework of the financial markets in the United States necessitates particularly close examination, therefore, for domestic and external reasons.[2]

Setting out the stall: Sarbanes–Oxley in context

The systemic nature of US market failures (O'Brien, 2003a) has prompted what, on paper, represents the most far-reaching changes to American corporate law since the 1930s. Introduced in the immediate aftermath of the collapse of Enron and WorldCom, the two largest single bankruptcies in US corporate history, the Public Company Accounting Reform and Investor Protection Act (2002), more commonly referred to as Sarbanes–Oxley after its co-sponsors in Congress, serves four interlinked purposes. It creates new structures to regulate both the audit process and the profession; increases the responsibilities and criminal liabilities of corporate boards to insure against future malefaction; provides greater protection for 'whistleblowers'; and enhances the authority of the Securities and Exchange Commission to police the market. As such, Sarbanes–Oxley imposes new restrictions on the capacity of corporations seeking to raise finance on US capital markets.

While the legislation targets the accountancy profession, it also provides the mechanism to ensure that only those with accountancy qualifications can chair an audit committee. Business complains that the legislation has dramatically increased the amount of red tape, leading in turn to a form of compliance that is based on crude box-ticking and minimum or creative compliance designed to reduce criminal liability. Despite the early idealism of the governance project, what is particularly striking is the downgrading of the concept within the financial markets that its inculcation can either guarantee improved performance or have wider normative value.

To secure access to the liquidity offered through listing on the primary exchanges, all corporations, irrespective of domicile, must follow the more restrictive provisions of the Act. They must also follow stricter listing requirements mandated under the guidance of a more assertive SEC. The interaction between legislation, forced changes to the self-regulating exchanges and greater federal oversight over the professions creates a powerful dynamic towards a global regime based on US norms. That process, which has been in evidence since the expansion of financial engineering in the 1980s and the resulting increase in securitization (Braithwaite and Drahos, 2000: 154) has been intensifying ever since. The passage of Sarbanes–Oxley and its centrality to the creation of

International Accounting Standards serves to further accelerate the privileging of US approaches (see Figure 5.1).

In this context, it is particularly striking that the debate has moved towards testing the efficacy of the legislative reforms without sufficient analysis of the structural and ethical defects exposed as a consequence of the stock market collapse and subsequent revelation of moral failure. Investors are encouraged to return to the marketplace, with the assurance that the conditions that led to the excesses of the past have been eradicated, that policymakers have dealt with 'the basic fact of the twenty-first century – a corporate system based on the unrestrained power of self-enrichment' (Galbraith, 2004: 44).

Confidence is gradually returning. Contrary to early claims that the legislation would lead to substantial delisting and capital flight, the American securities market netted $75 billion per month from foreign investors in the first seven months of 2004, an increase of 50 per cent on the same period last year (Foreign Investors Boost Purchases of U.S. Securities, *Wall Street Journal*, 17 August 2004). Whether the reforms warrant such confidence is a highly questionable assumption; see O'Brien (2003b); Demirag and O'Brien (2004) and Chandler and Strine (2002). At the heart of the reforms is the charade of the illusion of ownership as an effective restraining mechanism on management. As Galbraith (2004: 41) has pointed out, 'No one should be in doubt: Shareholders-

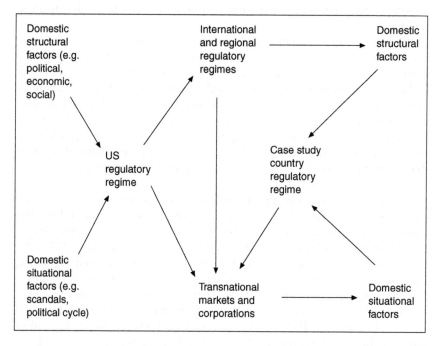

Figure 5.1 Regulatory regime dynamics.

owners – and their alleged directors in any sizable enterprise are fully subordinate to management. Though the impression of owner authority is offered, it does not, in fact, exist. An accepted fraud.' This is a particularly American malaise, where the ownership structure is much more diffuse that in the European Union, particularly outside of the United Kingdom and Ireland. (It is interesting in this regard to note that the Parmalat problems began in the United States and that the financial misreporting in Ahold occurred in its North American subsidiary, where the pressure to meet quarterly earnings targets over-ruled caution (Berenson, 2003).)

The growing international focus and remit of the SEC has already prompted a backlash, with the legal representative of one major transnational corporation complaining publicly of 'US regulatory imperialism' (Schroeder and Ascarelli, 2004). This contingent dynamic raises a profound question of critical importance both to the United States itself and the wider governance of the global financial services industry. Will the reforms make any tangible difference or are they fatally undermined by a continued subservience to the premise, despite the evidence, that self-regulation can deliver effective policing?

In order to explicate these issues, it is necessary to examine how associational actors have framed the range of public policy options in the United States itself. What has been enacted in statute, through Congress, and contract, through the listings requirements of the primary Exchanges, is merely the corporate governance agenda agreed, and largely implemented, in voluntary capacity during the 1990s. As such, they fail to address a primary cause of malefaction, what Lowenstein (2004: 221) has graphically termed 'the cultural debasement of Wall Street'.

The market in harlotry

As we approach the seventy-fifth anniversary of the Great Crash, it is time to take stock of the perennial rationales put forward for market as opposed to individual corporate failure (Kindleberger, 2000). 'Irrational exuberance', derived from Alan Greenspan's evidence to the Senate Banking Committee in July 2002, is a common explanation for the contemporary malaise but fails to place in context the structural factors that enabled the mania of the dot.com boom. The metaphor of a 'perfect storm', a formulation favoured by industry associations (Conference Board, 2002), serves both an economic and a political purpose. It indicates a collective responsibility while absolving any one sector of causal guilt for failing to predict the confluence of events (Coffee, 2003).

The striking image of 'casino capitalism' (Strange, 1986), updated before her death to encompass psychosis (1998) retains its potency. So too does the gastronomic metaphor deployed by one former market participant, who likens the markets to 'a Swiss cheese, with the holes –

the unregulated places – getting bigger every year, as parties transacting around legal rules eat away at the regulatory system from within (Partnoy, 2003: 394). For Partnoy (2003: 2) 'any appearance of control in today's financial markets is only an illusion, not a grounded reality'. Perhaps the most appropriate metaphor dates from the twenty-fifth anniversary of the Great Crash. 'Wall Street', remarked John Kenneth Galbraith (1992: 46), 'is like a lovely and accomplished woman who must wear black cotton stockings, heavy woollen underwear, and parade her knowledge as a cook, because, unhappily, her supreme accomplishment is as a harlot'.

By the end of the twentieth century the financial devices deployed by the tease merchants of Lower Manhattan to lure the greedy and the incautious had become more sophisticated than trading on margin but the basic premise remained substantially unchanged (as did the reliance of the political establishment on vociferous, but empty, exhortations to the brothel providers to deny themselves and their customers).

Galbraith has returned to the fray with the publication of *The Economics of Innocent Fraud* (2004), an elegant and deeply subversive book, the central argument of which is that corporate power has become uncontrollable. For Galbraith, the 'market system' is a deliberate misnomer. 'Sensitive friends and beneficiaries of the system do not wish to assign definitive authority to the corporation. Better the benign reference to the corporation' (Galbraith, 2004: 21). While the primary focus of the Galbraith volume is on corporate power, the role of Wall Street is pithily examined. Tainted research is characterized as 'an intense and ultimately definitive manifestation of fraud ... A blight on professional economics; a fraud close to home (2004: 55)'. It is striking that the range and direction of policy response has been limited by continued acceptance of an existing flawed paradigm that posits malefaction arising as a result of corrupted actors rather than a system that has been rendered susceptible to corruption as a consequence of a flawed system of incentives. The parading of executives in handcuffs is symptomatic of this phenomenon in action. It projects an image of decisive action (Edelman, 1985, 2001) that is in sharp contrast with the reality of corporate power.

The limits of criminal prosecution

Despite the rebarbative testimony on offer in state and federal courts in New York and elsewhere, successful prosecutions after jury trials on *substantive* issues have been elusive. Martha Stewart, the demigod of American design has been in a federal penitentiary for lying to prosecutors, not the more serious charges of securities manipulation (dismissed by the judge) or insider trading (not even on the indictment). Frank Quattrone, one of the most successful investment bankers of the dot.com era, was tried unsuccessfully in October 2003 for impeding a federal investigation, not complicity in the rigging of the lucrative IPO market. A retrial in May provided prosecutors with a unanimous verdict on scaled back charges. His employers, Credit Suisse First Boston, on whose behalf the 'Friends of Frank' programme was initiated, did not feature on the indictment. He was sentenced to 18 months in a federal penitentiary in September (*Financial Times*, 9 September 2004). It was a telling indication that federal guidelines calling on prosecutors to indict corporations for demonstration effect (Thompson, 2003) failed to overcome competing political and economic imperatives.

The difficulties of securing successful substantive prosecutions have been magnified by flawed prosecutorial design. Conflating malfeasance with misfeasance may create a plausible rhetorical strategy. It also carries a substantial risk of 'blowback'. This uncomfortable reality was evidenced by the spectacular collapse of the Kozlowski grand larceny and securities fraud case in early April 2004. Following six months of testimony the judge ruled a mistrial because of fears that a juror had been intimidated.

While significant media coverage concentrated on the perceived intransigence of Juror No. 4, a retired lawyer from the Upper East Side, the case also highlights why adopting the civil route of securing compliance through financial penalties is a preferred strategy for federal corporate lawyers. In a criminal trial, with a higher standard of proof required, defendants are likely to elude conviction unless criminal intent is proved alongside culpability (O'Brien, 2004a). While unedifying, the collapse demonstrates that moral superiority is an insufficient basis on which to build a successful prosecution. The lesson was further underscored by the acquittal of Tyco's General Counsel in a separate trial in July.

Prosecutors in the multi-agency Enron Task Force convened to unravel the complexities of wrong-doing in the Houston conglomerate have been successful in securing guilty verdicts through plea-bargaining against executives up to and including the former Chief Financial Officer, Andrew Fastow. Building incrementally, the unsubtle arm-twisting has now opened the door for charges to be brought against Jeffrey Skilling, the Chief Executive Officer and Ken Lay, the Company Chairman. Similar pressure on Fastow's counterpart at WorldCom has brought about the indictment of its Chief Executive Officer, Bernie Ebbers, for orchestrating an $11 billion deception, the largest securities fraud in American history.

For the prosecutors, the most difficult obstacle is whether a future jury will find the evidence tainted. After being paraded in handcuffs to demonstrate prosecutorial resolve, Ken Lay staged a remarkable press conference on the steps of the federal courthouse in Houston in which he accepted responsibility for Enron's failure, but refused to accept that there was any merit in the indictment. The key issues in both trials will essentially be parsed down to two interlinked basic questions: who was culpable and who had intent. Ebbers' lawyers have indicated that they will play the criminal intent defence, suggesting that the Chief Executive was the unwitting victim of accounting shenanigans, presented as legal by a subordinate now seeking absolution in return for cooperation. Lay has set the ground for a similar defence.

It is an audacious strategy and one that should not necessarily be dismissed. The jury in the Adelphia Communications trial took more than a week before handing out guilty verdicts to the Rigas family, which was accused of the most egregious example to date of the looting of a corporation for private benefit. The Rigas defence was designed specifically to pour scorn on ten former employees who cooperated with investigators in exchange for leniency or immunity.

Taking 'low-to-high' cases to trial in the absence of plea arrangement with cooperating witnesses, however, poses a much more problematic dynamic. Juries may refuse to convict for actions mandated or tacitly accepted as standard corporate practice. This danger was underlined by the unsuccessful prosecution of four executives at Qwest Communications in a trial that was presented as talismanic of enforcement resolve. Civil and criminal charges had been filed against the four executives in February 2003 in a blaze of publicity in both Denver and Washington, DC. The Chairman of the SEC, William Donaldson, and the Secretary of Justice, John Ashcroft, held a joint news conference at which they vowed to 'pursue aggressively anyone and everyone who has participated in an illegal effort to misrepresent a company's financials and mislead the investing public' (O'Brien, 2003a: 60).

According to the SEC's civil indictment, Qwest's business model, formulated by senior management and endorsed by the board, was predicated on earnings management. It 'placed extraordinary pressure on their subordinate executives, managers and employees to meet or exceed those earnings objectives at all costs'. The trial ended in April with two acquittals, a partial acquittal on a third defendant and deadlocked on a fourth accused of manipulating those earnings.

What is at issue therefore is how to deal with an underlying business culture, which retains its hegemonic capacity and visceral faith in the market's ability to police itself. This brings us to the heart of the problem. Much of the excess in the 1990s was legal, if morally dubious. And it did not occur in a vacuum. Significant changes to the regulatory environment resulted in the denigration of effective oversight by either the state or the self-regulatory organizations franchised to act on its behalf, and the elevation of 'chrematistic logic' (Daly and Cobb, 1994) via Wall Street metrics over integrity.

Governance from boom to bust

Given the importance of maintaining the integrity of the structural environment in which corporations operate, there is a need to transcend the operational boundaries of the contemporary debate on the intersection between corporate and political governance. Mapping that process through an examination of the wider political determinants of corporate governance design allows for both a better understanding of the changes that have taken place and the factors that brought them about. These variables include, but are not limited to: degree of interaction between political and economic elite; ideological support for and degree of private-interest government through self-regulation; primary method of raising political and financial capital; and degree of regulatory codification (O'Brien, 2004b).

The crucial point to consider is that the shift to governance does not, necessarily, in itself, lead to a normative improvement in the quality of policymaking. An increase in partnership, cooperation and participation in the development of policy on the grounds of ensuring the development of appropriate rules and regulations for professional groups or industries may, in fact, disguise special interest group pleading. Franchising authority to associations whose primary interest is to define, organize, secure and advance their own self-interest does not necessarily create viable public policy nor protect the public interest (Demirag and O'Brien, 2004; O'Brien, 2004b). Rather, it can exacerbate conflicts of interest by legitimating them (Kaufman, 2003), a fact long acknowledged by the political establishment, particularly those charged with overseeing the securities industry.

Responsibility for negotiating the granularity of the new rules on corporate liability now passes to the very bodies that failed to exercise internal or regulatory oversight: the corporate boards, auditing and legal associations and self-regulatory bodies. As Strange (1998: 20) has noted, 'history, including economic history, is the essential corrective to intellectual hubris'. Legislators would do well to revisit conclusions reached just 31 years ago. In 1973 the Senate Sub-Committee on Securities concluded:

> The inherent limitations in allowing an industry to regulate itself are well known: the natural lack of enthusiasm for regulation on the part of the group to be regulated, the temptation to use a façade of industry regulation as a shield to wield off more meaningful regulation, the tendency for businessmen to use collective action to advance their interests through the imposition of purely anti-competitive restraints as opposed to those justified by regulatory needs, and a resistance to changes in the regulatory pattern because of vested economic interests in its preservation.
>
> (Seligman, 2003b: 439–40)

The partial targeting of only one component of the 'associational matrix' (Schmitter and Streeck, 1985), the accountancy profession, while leaving intact the other key sectoral players indicates the relative subservience of political actors dependent on corporate donations for the financing of electoral contests (O'Brien, 2003a). In this context, a fascinating article appeared in the *New York Times* recently. It detailed how a Republican challenger campaigning against a five times incumbent for a House of Representatives seat in a Democratic stronghold in Texas was receiving enormous corporate donations. The backing was based on a complex calculation, which centred on George Bush retaining the presidency and the proselyte losing her race but gaining a subsequent position on the Federal Communications Commission (Labaton, 2004). This is not to suggest that the challenger is in any way compromised, or, that either she or her corporate benefactors have broken any ethical guidelines. Rather it illustrates just how targeted campaign contributions have become in contemporary American politics (McChesney, 1997; Lewis, 2004).

The historical record demonstrates that scandal and inability to self-police drives regulatory change and judicial activism. Precisely the same irresolution afflicts the New York Stock Exchange, where the exposure of hypocrisy drives reactive reform programmes. This governing dynamic drove the exchange's response to the indictment of Richard Whitney, its Chief Executive on charges of grand larceny in 1937. It also informed the response to the indictment of Dick Grasso in 2004, charged with allegedly hoodwinking his board. In each case reform was ushered in to protect the self-regulating model (Demirag and O'Brien, 2004).

The board of the NYSE contained some of the most influential corporate leaders in America. The failure to reform its practices is not a single actor failure but a collective one, leaving one sceptical of the efficacy of William Donaldson's call for a transfusion of corporate DNA to cleanse the economic body politic of a particularly virulent strain of corporate greed (O'Brien, 2003b: 17; Mr Grasso's Money, *Wall Street Journal*, 14 August 2004). A senior investment banker in New York, speaking on condition of anonymity has argued that tinkering with the governance of the NYSE is a charade: 'The entire system is broken and self-regulation is fatally flawed' (interview, New York City, 25 October 2003).

Contesting the paradigm: self-regulation in an age of scandal

Just as excessive codification leads to creative compliance and juridical paralysis, self-regulation without credible enforcement is doomed to failure. In order to prevent a reoccurrence of the myopia that contributed to the boom, there is a pressing need for sustained research into the design and implementation of effective compliance programmes. Given the complexity of financial instruments, it is necessary to recalibrate the way in which the regulation of the market is governed in a much more fundamental manner.

A brief survey of major corporate governance failures after the passage of Sarbanes–Oxley illustrates the point. Bankruptcies, financial engineering to meet analyst expectations, suspect trading with related parties, the abusive use of tax shelters to game the system, failure of due diligence processes; these are not merely the outplaying of an unethical past. Rather, they represent an unethical present.

Take, for example, the scheming for control of the remainder of the Hollinger media empire following revelations of inappropriate payments made to the Chief Executive, Lord Black. When his former supine board sacked him, Black lodged a defamation suit and tried to convince Leo Strine, a Vice-Chancellor of the Delaware Chancery that he had an untrammelled right to dispose of the company he had founded without reference to his fiduciary or stewardship responsibility.

Strine launched a damning attack, which was unprecedented in its expression of outrage at Black's behaviour (Strine, 2004). That record now belongs to Breeden's report into Hollinger. For the former chairman of the SEC 'to fully gauge the level of Black's and Radler's [Former COO] disregard for shareholders interests, one must step back from individual transactions and note the myriad of schemes, fiduciary abuses and fraudulent acts that were used to transfer essentially the entire earnings output of Hollinger over a seven year period to the controlling shareholders. In this case, more than most, one must not overlook the forest for the trees (Breeden, 2004: 4–5).

A discourse that privileges corrupted actors, however, over a system that had been rendered susceptible to corruption because of legislative manipulation and the deification of misfeasance as a legitimate business practice and source of reward structure, risks distortion. The Delaware ruling raises profound questions over the failure of the corporate governance paradigm to deal with the scale of the crisis befalling global capitalism. Black did not act alone. He required technical, legal and accounting expertise. Why did the firm, its financial advisors, or those facilitating the strategic sell-off to Conrad Black's preferred partners not calibrate reputational risk? Ultimately, why did the legislation introduced to combat this misfeasance not work?

In part, Strine answered the question in his co-authored working paper issued in the aftermath of the passage of Sarbanes–Oxley: it was not its function to deal with the excess. Rather, many of the reforms 'appear to have been taken off the shelf and put into the mix, not so much because they would have helped to prevent the scandals, but because they filled the perceived need for far-reaching reform and were less controversial than other measures more clearly aimed at preventing similar scandals' (Chandler and Strine, 2002: 6).

A similar problem arises through the audacious raid staged by Spiros Skordos, a Eurobond trader working for Citigroup on 2 August 2004. In just two minutes the trader dumped €11 billion ($7.4 billion) split across 100 different bonds in 13 different markets using 13 trading platforms. As much as 70 per cent of the platforms used belonged to MTS, which is owned by a consortium of banks, including Citigroup itself. Fifty-three minutes later the bank bought back €4 billion of the bonds, netting a profit of €15 million. The market manipulation occurred precisely because of the market-making model, which allowed for greater transparency by mandating participating banks to post the value of trades.

While there is no suggestion of illegality, the effect of the trading coup was to undermine the credibility of the market. One trader quoted by the *Sunday Times* noted sardonically, 'It was like stealing a car in the street because its doors are open and the keys are in the ignition' ('Bond Raiders', *Sunday Times*, 15 August 2004). It is perhaps indicative that despite the fallout, the premier business paper in the United States carried only one item on the trading move, and that, simply to report the introduction of temporary trading limits ('MTS to Keep Curbs on Bond Limits', *Wall Street Journal*, 11 August 2004).

In this regard, Citigroup's annual report makes for interesting reading. 'Importantly in 2003 we continued our thorough re-examination of the way we do business, with an eye towards developing standards that are not merely "common industry practice" or "letter of the law" but the best practices in a given area. We need to be clear about this subject; because of our size and scope, because of our position of business leadership, we are held to a higher standard. We accept this responsibility.' ('Is this the rogue elephant of global finance?' *Financial Times*, 16 August 2004). The CEO of Citigroup, Charles Prince appeared to accept that the conglomerate was failing when in an interview with the *Wall Street Journal*, he noted that, 'all the talk about culture and values, I think, is exactly right ... We have to have the right moral compass that steers so down the middle of the road ... You can't think of this in terms of control' (Pacelle, 2004). The Citigroup raid is a talismantic example of imaginative circumvention of legally enforceable rules and regulation.

The costs to bank shareholders from the Enron and Worldcom debacles have been striking with Citigroup agreeing to pay out $2 billion and $2.6 billion and J P Morgan Chase $2.2 billion and $2 billion to settle with major groups of claimants, this in addition to the settlements with regulators and other claims outstanding.

Reintroducing character: enforcing an alternative

The view of the Federal Reserve in this matter was particularly illuminating. I have already quoted Mr Greenspan. Let me now turn to an address given by one of his fellow Governors, Susan Schmidt Bies, to the Bank Administration Institute's Fiduciary Risk Management Conference. The gathering was held, appropriately enough, in Las Vegas in April 2004. Susan Schmidt Bies maintained: 'Senior management must move from thinking about compliance as chiefly a cost centre to considering the benefits of compliance in protecting against legal and reputational risks that can have an impact on the bottom line.'

The concept of 'enforced self-regulation' provides a potential solution to this conundrum. Pioneered by the Australian criminologist, John Braithwaite and his co-author, Ian Ayres (1992), there are two prerequisites: 'First, the firm is required to do the self-regulation. Second, the privately written rules can be publicly enforced' (Ayres and Braithwaite, 1994: 101). These principles underpinned the decision by the Department of Justice to enter into a far-reaching agreement with Merrill Lynch, one of the country's biggest financial houses, over its dealings with Enron, in exchange for the temporary abeyance of criminal charges. Of all the changes set in place since the era of scandal emerged, this represents the most imaginative, intrusive, far-reaching and potentially most effective.

Merrill Lynch has become an unlikely lightning rod for internal governance change. Its tainted analyst research teams were the first to be targeted by the New York Attorney General in his pursuit of wrongdoing on Wall Street. Merrill settled without admitting liability but the malefaction exposed by the publication of private email correspondence guaranteed industry wide investigations. These resulted in fines of $1.3 billion and significant exposure of the structural involvement of Wall Street in corporate scandal. Building on the template forged by Spitzer, the Department of Justice has agreed a settlement with Merrill over its dealings with Enron that has the potential to replicate the same effect.

On 17 September 2003, three of Merrill Lynch's most senior executives were indicted in Houston with knowingly and intentionally engaging in an illegal scheme to defraud by masking a loan to Enron as a transaction sale. They were further charged with obstructing a federal investigation and perjuring themselves before Congress. To avoid a corporate prosecution from the Department of Justice, which, quite clearly distrusts the financial services conglomerate, Merrill agreed to a remarkable degree of external oversight. The corporation has been forced to appoint an external auditing firm to examine all structured finance deals. The auditing work will be overseen in turn by an attorney chosen by the Department of Justice. The company is explicitly precluded from engaging in any form of structured finance deal in which any term of the transaction related to risk transfer (whether or not legally enforceable) is not reflected in the written contractual documentation for the transaction.

The company is also precluded in engaging in or acquiescing with creative accounting unless specifically approved by a newly created Special Structured Products Committee. The committee is to be made up of senior representatives from various disciplines (Head of Group or experienced designee) including Market Risk, Law and Compliance, Accounting, Finance, Tax and Credit. Transactions will require unanimous approval. Each transaction is to be vetted for legal and reputational risk. Furthermore, if a transaction is deemed suspicious, there must be a review of all relationships with that third party.

The work of the committee is to be overseen by independent auditors and a copy of all documentation forwarded to the Department of Justice, which has sole discretion in ascertaining whether the terms of the agreement have been broken. It will stay in place for 18 months, although any future infraction will not preclude the Department of Justice from initiating proceedings from matters covered by the agreement.

The compromise had a number of advantages for both the Department of Justice and the corporation. Merrill Lynch avoided a criminal indictment and therefore an implosion of integrity; for the government enormous leverage has been gained to prosecute the individuals concerned, providing a talismantic political spectacle (Edelman, 1985). Under the terms of the agreement Merrill is obliged to provide full and truthful disclosure about all aspects of the Nigerian barge contract over which the former employees are indicted and to provide the Federal Enron Task Force with professional help to prosecute its case. The trial provides the opening course in the menu of corrupt practices that will see Houston replace New York as the destination of choice for epicures of legal argument throughout the autumn and winter of 2004–5. The deal, which removes, temporarily, Merrill from criminal indictment has caused considerable consternation on Wall Street. One prominent investment banker, who asked the Securities and Exchange Commission if the deal had industry wide implications, was told, rather ambivalently, 'not necessarily' (interview, New York City, 17 November 2003).

Conclusion

What is at issue, therefore, is how to deal with a business culture based on technical compliance with narrowly defined legislation and a working assumption that unless a particular action is explicitly illegal, it is socially and politically acceptable. The absence of an ethical or cultural framework, rooted in personal experience and responsibility, lies at the heart of the crisis of confidence. The unrelenting focus on the punishment of individual malefactors and the creation of new stringent corporate liability legislation, centred on boards but not the wider financial arena in which they operate, risks obscuring fundamental systemic flaws in the corporate governance model. Neither policy approach deals with the problems of perverse incentives. The agency theorists appeal for market restraining mechanism fails to give due cognisance to the problems of the equity markets themselves in helping to design, market and implement the financial engineering schemes that contributed to the myopia. It is for this reason that enforced self-regulation offers perhaps the only credible way forward.

The public lynching of Merrill, which forces responsibility for misfeasance back onto the corporation itself, is an innovative form of forced self-regulation that offers a way out of barren legalism and empty principles.

Certain aspects of the agreement are quite distasteful. The corporation is effectively sacrificing three of its employees on the altar of ritual symbolism. Their defence is predicated on the fact that they are being made scapegoats for the bursting of the bubble. More importantly, the agreement focuses responsibility for limiting future misfeasance back onto the corporation itself. While the heavy hand of the Department of Justice is unlikely to be replicated across all the investment houses on Wall Street, it serves as a timely reminder of the dangers of not calibrating reputational risk. It is a warning that other players in the market ignore at their peril.

Notes

1 I am grateful to the discussants, Charles Calomiris and Stefan Huemer, for their insights, which have served to sharpen the analysis here.
2 A team at Queen's University, Belfast, led by the author has begun a major research project that examines the policy challenges that the American response to corporate malfeasance and misfeasance create in a range of systemically important countries.

Bibliography

Ayres, I. and Braithwaite, J. (1994) *Responsive Regulation*, Oxford: Oxford University Press.
Berenson, A. (2003) *The Number*, New York: Random House.
Braithwaite, J. and Drahos, P. (2000) *Global Business Regulation*, Cambridge: Cambridge University Press.
Breeden, R. (2004) *Report of Special Investigation by the Special Committee of the Board of Directors of Hollinger International*, 30 August.
Chandler, W. and Strine, L. (2002) 'The new federalism of the American corporate governance system: preliminary reflections of two residents of one small state', New York University Center for Law and Business, Working Paper, no. CLB 03-01, available online papers.ssrn.com/abstract=367720.
Coffee, J. (2003) 'What caused Enron', in Cornelius, P. and Kogut, B. (eds) *Corporate Governance and Capital Flows in a Global Economy*, Oxford: Oxford University Press, pp. 29–52.
Conference Board (2002) *Commission on Public Trust and Private Enterprise, Findings and Recommendations*, 17 September, available online at www.conferenceboard.org.
Daly, H. and Cobb, J. (1994) *For the Common Good*, Boston: Beacon Press.
Demirag, I. and O'Brien, J. (2004) 'Conflicting and conflating interests in the regulation and governance of the financial markets in the United States', *Journal of Corporate Citizenship* 15(Autumn): 111–19..
Dunne, T. and Hellier, C. (2002) 'The Ludwig Report: implications for corporate governance', *Corporate Governance* 2(3): 26–31.
Edelman, M. (1960) 'Symbols and political quiescence', *The American Political Science Review* 54(3)(September): 695–704.
Edelman, M. (1964) *The Symbolic Uses of Politics*, Urbana: University of Illinois Press.
Edelman, M. (1985) *The Symbolic Uses of Politics*, Chicago, IL: University of Illinois Press.

Edelman, M. (2001) *The Politics of Misinformation*, New York: Cambridge University Press.

Fama, E. and Jensen, M. (1980) 'Separation of ownership and control', *Journal of Law and Economics* 26: 301–26.

Galbraith, J.K. (1992) *The Great Crash 1929*, London: Penguin Business.

Galbraith, J.K. (2004) *The Economics of Innocent Fraud*, London: Penguin.

Greenspan, A. (2004) 'Capitalizing reputation', Remarks to Financial Markets Conference of Federal Reserve Board of Georgia, 16 April, available online at www.federalreserve.gov/boarddocs/speeches/2004/.

Jensen, M.C. and Meckling, W.H. (1976) 'Theory of the firm: managerial behavior, agency costs and ownership structure', *Journal of Financial Economics* 3: 303–60.

Kaufmann, D. (2003) 'Rethinking governance, empirical lessons challenge orthodoxy', available online at: www.worldbank.org/wbi/governance/wp-governance.html.

Kindleberger, C. (2000) *Manias, Panics and Crashes, A History of Financial Crises*, Hoboken: John Wiley & Sons.

Labaton, S. (2004) 'A Texan's race could lead to the FCC', *New York Times*, 17 August.

Learmount, S. (2002) 'Theorizing corporate governance: new organizational alternatives', Centre for Business Research, University of Cambridge, Working Paper, no. 237.

Lewis, C. (2004) *The Buying of the President 2004*, New York: Perennial.

Lowenstein, R. (2004) *Origins of the Crash*, New York: The Penguin Press.

Marinetto, M. (2003) 'Governing beyond the centre: a critique of the Anglo-Governance School', *Political Studies* 51: 592–608.

McChesney, F. (1997) *Money For Nothing, Politicians, Rent Extraction and Political Extortion*, Cambridge, MA: Harvard University Press.

Moran, M. (2003) *The British Regulatory State*, Oxford: Oxford University Press.

Morgenson, G. (2004) 'A door opens. The view is ugly', *New York Times*, 12 September.

Nadel, M. (1975) 'The hidden dimension of public policy: private governments and the policy-making process', *Journal of Politics* 37(1) (February): 2–34.

O'Brien, J. (2003a) *Wall Street on Trial, A Corrupted State*, Chichester: John Wiley & Sons.

O'Brien, J. (2003b) 'Profits with integrity: the lessons of Enron', XI International Anti-Corruption Conference, Seoul, 26 May 2003, available online at www.11iacc.org/download/pln/11IACC_Plenary_Transcript_26_May_03.doc.

O'Brien, J. (2004a) 'Beyond compliance: towards the criminalization of Wall Street practice, *International Journal of Business Governance and Ethics* (forthcoming).

O'Brien, J. (2004b) 'Ethics, probity and the changing governance of Wall Street: cure or remission', *Public Integrity* 7(1) (Winter 2004–5): 43–56.

Office of the Director of Corporate Enforcement (ODCE) (2004) *Report of the Inspectors into the Affairs of National Irish Bank and National Irish Bank Financial Services Ltd*, 30 July, available online at www.odce.ie/new/article.asp?NID=326&NCID=42.

Pacelle, M. (2004) 'Citigroup CEO makes "values" a key focus', *Wall Street Journal*, 1 October.

Partnoy, F. (2003) *Infectious Greed*, London: Profile Books.

Philips, K. (2002) *Wealth and Democracy, A Political History of the American Rich, Uncertain World*, New York: Thomson Texere.

Promontory Financial Group Inc. and Wachtell, Lipton, Rosen and Katz (2002) *Report to the Boards of Allied Irish Banks plc, Allfirst Financial and AllFirst Bank Concerning Currency Trading Losses*, Allied Irish Banks Plc.

Roe, M.J. (1994) *Strong Managers, Weak Owners*, Princeton, NJ: Princeton University Press.

Schmitter, P. and Streeck, W. (1985) 'Community, market, state and associations?', in Streeck, W. and Schmitter, P. (eds) *Private Interest Government*, London: Sage.

Schroeder, M. and Ascarelli, S. (2004) 'New role for SEC: policing companies beyond U.S. borders', *Wall Street Journal*, 30 July.

Seligman, J. (2003a) 'Cautious evolution or perennial irresolution: self-regulation and market structure during the first seventy years of the Securities and Exchange Commission', paper presented at Global Capital Markets Center – NYSE Conference on Current Issue in Institutional Equities Trading, West Palm Beach, 13 December, available online at: www.fuqua.duke.edu/conference/dei/nyse/.

Seligman, J. (2003b) *The Transformation of Wall Street, A History of the Securities and Exchange Commission and Modern Corporate Finance*, New York: Aspen.

Simpson, S. (2002) *Corporate Crime, Law and Social Control*, Cambridge: Cambridge University Press.

Smith, L. (2003) 'A fresh look at accounting ethics', *Accounting Horizons* 17(1) (March): 47–9.

Strange, S. (1986) *Casino Capitalism*, Oxford: Blackwell.

Strange, S. (1998). *Mad Money*, Manchester: Manchester University Press.

Strine, L. (2004) *Hollinger International Inc vs. Conrad Black, Hollinger Inc*, Case no. 183-N, *Court of Chancery of State of Delaware*, 26 February.

Stiglitz, J. (2002) 'The roaring nineties', *Atlantic Monthly*, October.

Stiglitz, J. (2003) *The Roaring Nineties*, New York: Norton.

Thompson, L. (2003) 'Principles of Federal prosecution of business organizations', *Department of Justice*, 20 January.

Zeff, S. (2003) 'How the US accounting profession got where it is today' *Accounting Horizons* 17(4) (December): 267–86.

COMMENT

Charles W. Calomiris

Justin O'Brien's chapter considers the recent wave of corporate scandals and evaluates the legal and regulatory systems' responses to those scandals. He finds that the 'regulatory system proved incapable of either ensuring against market failure or instilling a credible ethical restraint'. O'Brien argues that malfeasance largely reflects 'systemic flaws' which are not addressed by current regulation. The responses to the scandals have produced a combination of prosecutions, settlements and fines directed against specific individuals and corporations involved in the scandals, and new laws, regulations and policies that address perceived shortcomings of corporate practices (e.g. Sarbanes–Oxley's laws regarding auditing oversight, new SEC rules regarding the separation of research and selling, and new NYSE policies). O'Brien finds these reforms 'highly questionable' as means of addressing the core problems. He points to the need to strengthen enforcement by combining self-regulation with much more intrusive public enforcement of self-regulatory standards (as proposed by Ayres and Braithwaite, 1992), and he views the recent agreement between Merrill Lynch and the Justice Department as the most promising approach undertaken thus far: 'of all the changes set in place since the era of scandal emerged, this represents the most imaginative, intrusive, far-reaching and potentially most effective'.

I agree with O'Brien that the recent scandals must be seen as failures in every component of the ethical infrastructure of oversight of the corporations that suffered these lapses because 'a multiplicity of internal and external checks failed simultaneously: within the corporation; the self-regulated professions and exchanges; the research analysts; the rating agencies; and the regulatory agencies and their political masters'. I also agree that the combination of 'market-based self-regulation' as currently conceived and the sorts of 'proscriptive rules' envisioned by Sarbanes–Oxley and the SEC in response to the scandals will not put an end to scandals in the future.

But I disagree with what I understand to be O'Brien's conception of the core problem that needs to be addressed, and I favour an alternative approach for reforming the system. In his diagnosis of the core problem, O'Brien places too much weight on the views of economists like John K. Galbraith, who offer overbearing prose as a substitute for reasoned analysis. This 'elegant and deeply subversive' style of discourse may sell books, but Galbraith's rants against 'corporate power' do little to advance our understanding of what is wrong or how to fix it.

Galbraith and O'Brien offer too jaundiced a view of our financial and economic system. Does anyone (even Galbraith) really believe that Wall Street's 'supreme accomplishment is as a harlot'? I count our financial system's contributions to the high and persistent real returns generated for stockholders of American corporations for over a century as its greatest accomplishment. Large and increasing numbers of stockholders in American corporations are willing to own minority positions in those corporations because – despite all the weaknesses of our corporate governance system – our system offers substantial and meaningful competitive opportunities and protections for both firms and their investors, which goes a long way to explain the high, persistent stock returns earned by outside investors. The primary protections that matter for investors have little to do with SEC rules, NYSE rules or Sarbanes–Oxley, but much more to do with the extremely competitive market environment in which American corporations and Wall Street firms struggle to survive, and with the crucial supporting role played by an established rule of law, an independent judiciary and our common-law heritage, which protect the rights of corporations to compete and the rights of corporations and individual investors to receive what is owed them according to established principles of fairness.[1] Economic freedom embodied in market competition and the enforcement of contracts under the rule of law has always been, and remains, the key line of defence against all abuses, including those by corporate managers.

Before turning to the weaknesses, it is worth basking in the glow of the historic success of the US's and the UK's financial systems' achievements, at least for a moment – just long enough to recall the key elements of the current state-of-the-art financial and economic system that we should strive to preserve.

Consider America's institutional successes in contrast to the financial 'rules of the game' in most developing economies, where corrupt politicians, crony oligopolistic firms and a non-competitive financial system (either owned by the cronies or controlled by the state to further their interests) conspire to channel much of the public's savings to inefficient, large firms controlled by the elite. Three decades of institutional empiricism suggest that what is most lacking in those systems is competition among financial institutions for savings and competition among corporations for the privilege of using those savings.[2] In contrast, in the United States, the market is unforgiving of inefficiency, either on the part of banks or corporate users of funds. Large and small firms alike face the prospect of failure and disappearance if they are unable to compete, and globalization continues to enhance competition in virtually every industry and product niche.

The malfeasance that produces scandals generally is not part of a successful, competitive corporate strategy. All of the recent scandals making the headlines were cases where managers harmed *shareholders*, not society at large. And when the scandals were uncovered, the corporations whose managers perpetrated them suffered lost business and stock price collapse, as well as substantial legal costs and penalties.

Given that shareholders are the ones who stand to lose from managerial dishonesty, it follows that shareholders should be a strong constituency for honesty. Competition among firms, when combined with effective means for stockholders to control managers, encourages all manner of value-creating improvements, including managerial honesty. Firms run by stockholders have strong incentives to police themselves. O'Brien points to the recent renegade bond trading in Europe by a Citibank team of employees but he fails to appreciate the degree to which those actions harmed Citibank's reputation and destroyed value for its stockholders and the extent to which Citibank now seems determined to prevent similar breaches from occurring in the future. Unethical and illegal acts generally are not part of a positive net present value-creating corporate strategy. They are better seen as acts of desperation or stupidity by corporate management or other employees, often undertaken in extreme circumstances (e.g. frauds tend to occur during recessions, or in the wake of large idiosyncratic losses by particular employees, as in the case of Nicholas Leeson of Barings).

Not only do firms and their funding sources compete; analysts and asset managers also compete, and that competition also encourages honest behaviour. Records of analysts' relative performance are visible for investors to track. Not surprisingly, analysts and fund managers that do relatively well at predicting winners grow and prosper, and those that do poorly fade into obscurity. Of course, there are times when short-sightedness and 'harlotry' can pay. In particular, the dot com bubble was a time when financial gatekeepers apparently faced little incentive to offer critical perspectives on high-tech firms coming to market. But that episode and others like it are the exceptions in financial history, not the rule, as evidenced by the roughly 8 per cent annual real returns earned on stock market investments since 1926.[3] That record indicates that, on average, the gatekeepers of American capitalism have been doing a pretty good job.[4]

O'Brien laments the fragmented structure of ownership of large US and UK corporations: 'At the heart of the reforms is the charade of the illusion of ownership as an effective restraining mechanism on management.' But he fails to recognize that insider ownership concentration adjusts as it needs to in order to ensure adequate protection of owners. The low ownership concentration of American and British firms is an indicator of the success of the Anglo-American corporate governance system.

Empirical studies of ownership concentration across many countries show that the unusually strong legal protections enjoyed by investors in the US and the UK contribute to the low concentration of stock ownership. Insiders own only about 2 per cent of the stock of the largest firms in the US and UK, while in France and Germany, where investor protections are much weaker, insider shares average roughly 60 per cent.[5] If corporate scandals really threatened the average value of investments in US and UK firms, outsider shareholders would be turning away from these markets, as their Gallic and Germanic counterparts have done; but the opposite has been happening – small investors' participation in the US stock market has been increasing, and stock prices have recovered their pre-2000 levels (with the exception of the dot com stocks). O'Brien views the high investor confidence in US corporations today as 'highly questionable'; I view many years of impressive average real returns as an indication that investors may know something that he does not.

Does all this mean that we should regard corporate scandals as the unavoidable cost of running a successful market economy? There is an element of truth to that point of view; I would not want to live in a society completely devoid of crime (including corporate crime), since such a society would also necessarily be devoid of freedom, and the fruits of freedom (including economic progress). But I do not believe that the current level of corporate crime is the optimal level.

In my opinion, the goal that we should focus upon is improving the incentives of managers to act in the interests of stockholders (which generally means acting ethically), and the key means for achieving that goal is improving the ability of stockholders to discipline managers. The 'agency' problem that O'Brien mentions in his reference to my comments refers to any actions by managers that conflict with the interests of stock-holders. If we can agree that dishonest behaviour is not generally in the long-run interest of stockholders, then it follows that managerial dishon-esty is first and foremost an agency problem.

What sorts of regulatory changes would improve market discipline, and thereby mitigate agency problems? First, changes in takeover laws that would make it easier to displace managers are an obvious place to start. For example, eliminating the Williams Act requirement that stockholders announce their intentions to acquire controlling interests in firms before doing so (which produces run ups in stock prices for would-be acquirers) would substantially increase the contestability of corporate control.

Second, there is a host of potential regulatory changes that would enhance the role played by institutional investors in corporate governance (Shadow Financial Regulatory Committee, 2004), including the relaxation of limits on ownership concentration, and the relaxation of trading rules and other rules that would encourage participation by institutions on corporate boards. The relaxation of these rules could create a new class of informed and powerful owners sitting on corporate boards of directors. These sorts of changes would go a long way towards closing the gap between the interests of managers and the interests of stockholders, which would encourage more ethical behaviour by management, especially in those extreme circumstances where undisciplined managers are tempted to behave inappropriately.

The advantages of strengthening market discipline, instead of imposing more proscriptive rules or increasing regulatory enforcement, include greater flexibility, better access to information, and stronger incentives to collect and use information effectively. Owners (unlike courts or the SEC) do not have to provide a legal reason to fire a manager; they can do so if they decide they are better off without him. The flexible 'rules' enforced by owners cannot be gamed. Owners (particularly board members, who have regular access to management and firm performance records) generally have better information than regulators, too, and get that information sooner. And owners have the incentive to collect and use information to further their interests and prevent managers from abusing their discretionary powers.

Contrast my suggested market-strengthening reforms with the reforms undertaken by the SEC and the US Congress. The SEC and the US Congress worship the false god of independence. Politicians and regulators imagine that disinterested third parties (independent directors and auditors) will have sufficient incentives to monitor and constrain managerial behaviour. To my mind, independent directors or auditors who are not significant shareholders have little to lose from failing to uncover and stop abuse, and therefore, have little reason to expend much effort doing so.

Furthermore, a reliance on market discipline not only provides a more effective means of achieving proper regulatory goals, it also avoids a potential downside to government-enforced rules, namely protection against overzealous rulemakers, who sometimes have a hidden agenda, or who serve the dark purposes of some of the regulated. In his chapter for this volume, Forrest Capie reminds us that Tacitus long ago recognized that corrupt governments are the ones most likely to create superfluous rules, which the rule makers use to tighten their grip on economic agents to extort greater rents for themselves or their allies. It is worth bearing in mind that the public enforcement of private regulations (championed by O'Brien) entails that same risk of regulatory abuse as the public enforcement of government regulation. US securities and banking regulations have often been criticized for their tendency to limit entry and effectively promote the special interests of the regulated.

Recent studies of financial regulation by Barth *et al.* (2005) and others find that the extent of government financial regulation is positively correlated with measures of the extent of government corruption, and that more extensive financial regulation promotes neither financial stability nor growth (see also LaPorta *et al.*, 2003). In contrast, Barth *et al.* (2005), along with many others (including Cecchetti and Krause, 2004), find that regulatory regimes that promote market discipline by allowing competition and by limiting government safety nets so as to place bank debtholders at greater risk of financial loss offer the only reliable means of promoting financial stability and growth.

In summary, corporate ethical lapses have principally been lapses of corporate governance in which stockholders have suffered losses due to managers' pursuing unethical conduct that was not in the interest of the stockholders. When considering the failings of our present corporate governance systems, and in particular when lamenting the shortcomings of market discipline and self-regulation, we should bear in mind that market discipline and self-regulation have been hampered by constraining regulations that have limited their effectiveness. Government policies that limit takeovers, that constrain the governance roles of institutional investors, and that otherwise protect corporations or banks from the discipline of the marketplace have limited the potential effectiveness of market discipline and self-regulation. Logic and recent empirical research suggest that relaxing those limits on market discipline could be the most effective means of addressing the corporate governance problems that are at the heart of our corporate ethics problems.

Notes

1 See, e.g. Bekaert *et al.* (2004), LaPorta *et al.* (2002), Berkowitz *et al.* (2003), Pistor *et al.* (2002) and Pistor *et al.* (2000).
2 See, e.g. Morck *et al.* (2004) and Barth *et al.* (2005).
3 Ibbotson Associates (2005: 8) reports that large company stocks earned compounded real returns of 7.4 per cent, and small company stocks earned compounded real returns of 9.7 per cent for the period 26/1/1–31/12/04.
4 O'Brien chides T. Rowe Price for failing to serve as a proper gatekeeper because it opposed the expensing of stock options. It is, of course, possible that, contrary to O'Brien's presumption, expensing stock options is not a good idea. Indeed, I have argued as much (Calomiris, 2004), and other economists share that view (Calomiris *et al.*, 2005).
5 See Himmelberg *et al.*, 2002.

Bibliography

Ayres, I. and Braithwaite, J. (1992) *Responsive Regulation*, Oxford: Oxford University Press.
Barth, J., Caprio Jr, G., and Levine, R. (2005) *Rethinking Bank Regulation and Supervision: Till Angels Govern*, Cambridge University Press, forthcoming.
Bekaert, G., Harvey, C.R., Lundblac, C. and Siegel, S. (2004), NBER Working Paper, no. 10990, December.
Berkowitz, D., Pistor, K. and Richard, J.-F. (2003) 'Economic development, legality, and the transplant effect', *European Economic Review* 47: 165–95.
Calomiris, C.W. (2004) 'What financial economics can tell us about the desirability of expensing employee stock options', Columbia Business School, August.
Calomiris, C.W., Hassett, K., Kroszner, R.S. and Lindsey, L. (2005) 'The technical challenges to accurately valuing employee stock options', February, www.savestockoptions.org/pdf/lindsey_study.pdf.
Ceccetti, S.G. and Krause, S. (2004) 'Deposit insurance and external finance', NBER Working Paper, no. 10908, November.
Himmelberg, C.P., Hubbard, R.G. and Love, I. (2002) 'Investor protection, ownership, and the cost of capital', World Bank Policy Research Working Paper, no. WPS2834, April.

Ibbotson Associates (2005) *Stocks, Bonds, Bills, and Inflation 2004 Yearbook*, Chicago: Ibbotson Associates.

LaPorta, R., Lopez-de-Silanes, F. and Shleifer, A. (2003) 'What works in securities laws?', NBER Working Paper, no. 9882, July.

LaPorta, R., Lopez-de-Silanes, F., Pop-Eleches, C. and Shleifer, A. (2002) 'The guarantees of freedom', NBER Working Paper, no. 8759, February.

Morck, R., Wolfenzon, D. and Yeung, B. (2004) 'Corporate governance, economic entrenchment and growth', NBER Working Paper, no. 10692, August.

Pistor, K., Keinan, Y., Kleinheisterkamp, J. and West, M.D. (2002) 'The evolution of corporate law: a cross-country comparison', *University of Pennsylvania Journal of International Economic Law* 23(4): 791–871.

Pistor, K., Raiser, M. and Gelfer, S. (2000) 'Law and finance in transition economies', *Economics of Transition* 8(2): 325–68.

Shadow Financial Regulatory Committee (2004) 'Enabling institutional investors to play a more effective role in corporate governance', Statement no. 204, February, www.aei.org/publications/pubID.19886/pub_detail.asp.

COMMENT

Stefan Huemer[1]

Justin O'Brien's paper provides a highly interesting and stimulating overview of the recent series of failings in corporate governance, in particular in the US.[2] The following comments provide suggestions for *additional* considerations that seem to be relevant in the context of corporate governance. The comments are in three parts: an explanation of the reasons for failings in corporate governance; an overview on the regulatory approach vis-à-vis corporate failings within the EU; and a comparison of some of the key features in the corporate environment of the US and the EU that could help to explain some of the features in their regulatory approaches.

Explaining the reasons for failings in corporate governance

Principal–agent problems and the problems of information asymmetry are not new to financial markets. Hence, we should ask what explains the concentration of financial irregularities at one particular time (basically around the turn of the decade)? A review of recent literature on the subject suggests that the following aspects are of particular relevance.

First, *changes in the role of 'gatekeepers'*,[3] in particular audit firms, rating agencies and securities analysts. These changes are mainly associated with the following factors:[4]

- The rising importance of non-audit services (in particular consulting) provided by auditors – in 2000, consulting accounted for 50 per cent of revenues of the 'Big Five' accounting firms, whereas it was only 13 per cent in 1980 – provided companies with a tool to exercise some degree of control over their auditors in order to obtain more favourable assessments. While the dismissal of an auditor may become subject to the scrutiny of oversight authorities and may also carry reputational risks, a consultant firm can be dismissed more easily. Similarly, it is argued that there have been incentives for bank analysts to produce favourable analysis on companies in order to attract or maintain business with these companies in other fields.
- As a consequence of regulatory changes and court rulings, a gradual decline of liability costs for auditors could be observed over the 1990s. At the same time, the benefits for auditors from acquiescence with their clients rose steadily (in particular, as indicated above, through the increased provision of services other than auditing).
- Acquiescence between auditors and their clients was further facilitated through the oligopoly situation in the audit sector ('Big Five'), which resulted in a near-total absence of competition among audit firms.[5]

- Another set of explanations relates to the financial market environment. In times of booming financial markets investors tend to rely less on the critical assessment by gatekeepers and frequently align their investment decisions so as to produce herding behaviour.

Second, *increased asymmetry of information:* growing disintermediation in corporate finance, the rising importance of off-balance sheet activities and special purpose entities as well as increased use of derivative instruments by non-financial corporations during the 1990s led to a growing complexity of disclosure of financial information. As a result, it became more difficult for investors to interpret this information in a meaningful manner (Walkner, 2004).

Third, *executive compensation* shifted during the 1990s, from being primarily cash-based to being primarily equity-based (stock options). This development fostered a, sometimes excessive, focus on short-term company developments, with the inherent risk of manipulating company reporting. Another effect was the increased incentive for managers to misreport on the selling of their company shares once the company's outlook started to deteriorate (Bar-Gill and Bebchuck, 2003).

More detailed analysis would be needed to assess whether the Sarbanes–Oxley Act (SOA), which – as pointed out by Justin O'Brien – relies to an important extent on self-regulation by the industry, provides an adequate response to these structural problems in corporate governance. The requirements for a strict separation of audit and consulting activities, for shifting the competence to decide on executive remuneration from executive management to independent audit committees, and for an early disclosure of share sales by managers would seem to address some of the above concerns. At the same time, increasing civil liability for acquiescence in managerial fraud or the reduction of harmful incentives caused by remuneration in stock options are issues that remain to be addressed. Justin O'Brien's chapter highlights the limits of the approach adopted in the SOA.

The regulatory response to corporate failings adopted by the EU

The EU witnessed a similar – albeit much smaller – series of highly publicized corporate scandals (most prominently the cases of Parmalat and Ahold). In response to these events, the EU reviewed its corporate governance regime.

The EU's Financial Services Action Plan (FSAP) of 1999 contains few references to corporate governance and is largely focused on the securities sector. Indeed, harmonization of securities law within the EU is much more advanced than harmonization in the area of company law.

At the time of the launch of the FSAP, the issue of corporate governance was primarily considered in terms of eliminating legal or administrative barriers to allow companies and investors to reap the benefits of the Single Market fully. Strengthening the framework for combating corporate mismanagement or fraud gained importance with Enron, making it an issue on the EU policy agenda. Indeed, at the informal meeting of ECOFIN ministers in Oviedo in 2002, the European Commission presented proposals for an EU regulatory response to policy issues arising in the wake of the Enron collapse (Commission, 2002). Over time, additional measures were added to the FSAP such as the Directive on market abuse and the Regulation on the application of International Accounting Standards (IAS), which will be used as from 2005 (with a transition period in certain cases until 2007) for the preparation of consolidated accounts of companies governed by the law of a EU Member State and listed on a regulated market within the EU.

In May 2003 the Commission issued a Communication on Modernising Company Law and Enhancing Corporate Governance (Commission, 2003), which contains proposals on the following issues:

- Enhancing disclosure requirements, such as the release of an annual statement on corporate governance disclosing the major shareholders and any key agreements or other relationships between them and the company, the disclosure of remuneration of individual company directors in the Annual Reports, and disclosure requirements regarding the company's group structure.
- Strengthening shareholders rights, for instance by measures to facilitate the exercise of voting rights.
- Strengthening the role of non-executive/supervisory directors, who should be in charge of taking all decisions that may cause conflicts of interests to executive directors (such as decisions on executive remuneration and on the audit of the company's accounts).

So far, several steps have been taken, including the adoption of a Directive to clarify Board responsibilities and to improve disclosure of information on financial and corporate governance matters (EU, 2006). Moreover, the Commission issued Recommendations on executive pay and on the role of independent directors (Commission, 2004b and 2005). A legislative proposal to facilitate the cross-border exercise of shareholders' rights is currently under consideration (Commission, 2006).

Another centrepiece in the reform of the EU's corporate governance regime is the Commission's Proposal for a Directive on Reinforcing Statutory Audit (Commission, 2004a). The key features of this proposal are the following:

- A public oversight regime for the audit profession: the Commission does not suggest creating an EU regulatory authority for this purpose. Rather, the draft directive proposes standards for creation of regulatory authorities at the national level which should, inter alia, oversee the process of approving auditors as well as adopt and control the standards of the profession.

- Enhancing auditor independence through enhanced transparency, in particular by requiring companies to state the amounts paid for auditing and possible other services provided by the auditor in their annual reports, and through mandatory rotation of audit firms.
- Requiring 'public interest entities' (a term that includes all listed companies as well as banks and insurance companies) to set up internal audit committees, which are in charge of monitoring the auditor, of reviewing potential weaknesses in internal control structures and of making the proposal for the appointment of an auditor to executive management.
- Opening up of the auditor market by facilitating cross-border activities of audit firms within the EU.

The Directive was adopted in May 2006.

Key differences in the corporate environment in the EU and the US

The EU and the US corporate environments and the regulatory approaches that were adopted vary in a number of features. In the relevant literature several issues are considered to be of major importance.

The US corporate landscape is characterized by a dispersed *structure of company ownership* while in the EU company ownership tends to be more concentrated.[6] The predominance of small shareholders in the US, who may buy and sell shares rapidly, can enhance volatility in the ownership structure. By contrast, the ownership structure in the EU tends to be more stable as large shareholders often take a more long-term view on their investments. Furthermore, in a dispersed shareholder structure shareholders may have less incentive and ability to monitor executive performance and may allot more discretionary power to managers while large shareholders are better able to monitor and sanction managers.

In addition, the *relative importance of financial markets* differs significantly in the US and the EU. Financing in the US economy is predominantly capital market-based, while it is largely bank-based in the EU. Lannoo and Khachaturyan (2003) argue that the latter, albeit less efficient from a corporate finance angle, is easier and less costly to regulate and supervise. The difference in the relative importance of financial markets is also reflected in the field of executive remuneration. In comparison with the US, stock options play a lesser role than in the EU, thus reducing incentive for executive management to take an excessively short-term view on share price developments.

Against this background, Coffee (2003) concluded that, on the whole, the EU is less likely to be affected by corporate scandals than the US as fewer incentives to manipulate short-term share prices appear to exist. However, these considerations do not take account of the possibility that the company's controlling shareholders may be involved in fraud, which is one of the chief incriminations put forward by prosecutors in the Parmalat process. Therefore, there is no room for complacency on either side of the Atlantic.

Another important difference pertains to the issue of *rule-based versus principles-based approaches*, which is exemplified in the set-up of the accounting systems in the US and the EU. The Generally Accepted Accounting Principles (GAAP) applicable in the US are, in fact, rules rather than principles. On the other hand, the International Accounting Standards (IAS) which are due to be introduced in the EU (see above) can be more appropriately described as principles.

Addressing the differences between the two systems, EU officials[7] have argued that the rule structure of the US GAAP carries the risk of encouraging a 'box-ticking mentality', i.e. companies try to comply formally with a rule, regardless of whether the underlying principle is met. By contrast, by setting out a number of principles and laying responsibility for fulfilling these principles upon the company, the IAS would make it more difficult to resort to a simple 'box-ticking' exercise.

The Commission is currently engaged in a dialogue with the US authorities to foster convergence between the two systems. Incidentally, the SOA contains elements that move in the direction of a more principles-based approach in US accounting (Bratton, 2003) and may thus facilitate convergence between the US and EU systems.

Another example for rule-based versus principles-based approaches can be found in the definition of auditor independence. The SOA prescribes a list of activities that are considered incompatible with auditing, most importantly consulting services. By contrast, the aforementioned draft EU Directive on statutory audit sets forth the principle that auditors must abstain from any services that could infringe on their independence, but it does not include a list of such activities, as the Commission believes that such a list might quickly become outdated by market developments.

In assessing the merits of rules-based versus principles-based approaches, Langevoort (2002) concludes that rules fare best under conventional and routine types of circumstances, as may typically be found in traditional industry branches. However, in innovative, fast growing sectors characterized by companies using sophisticated business techniques principles may be superior in terms of transparency and reliability. This may be an element in explaining why Enron could happen.[8]

Another interesting difference between the US and the EU pertains to the question of *regulatory competition*. Some elements of the proposed EU company law reform, in particular, the European Company Statute and the Commission's intention of facilitating the transfer of company 'seats' in the context of the fourteenth company law Directive, are likely to foster regulatory competition within the EU, as it would become easier for companies to choose the location of their 'seat' across Member States. On the other hand, the approach adopted by the Commission in the Communication on company law and corporate governance mentioned above, namely, to aim at harmonization of the regulatory framework through secondary legislation for the essential part of its proposals, can be considered as a step in the other direction and was criticized by some industry representatives and academics for this reason (Lannoo and Khachaturyan, 2003; CEPS, 2004).

The experience of the US may provide some guidance in evaluating the effects of regulatory competition in corporate regulation. As is well-known, almost 60 per cent of listed US companies are registered in Delaware, not because these companies have any significant business interest in this state but because Delaware's corporate law is deemed to be attractive. US academics are debating the reasons for this development and investigating whether the Delaware example is to be considered as a regulatory race to the top, or to the bottom, or whether no race has taken place at all.

- Data from the US suggest that Tobin's Q for companies registered in Delaware is, on average, higher than those of other companies. Moreover, companies that changed their corporate seat from elsewhere to Delaware experienced higher-than-average gains in shareholder wealth. This is considered as an indication that regulatory competition is in the interest of shareholders, as it fosters corporate wealth.[9] By the way, for those who wonder, Enron was registered in Oregon.
- By contrast, it has been argued that the causality could be inverse, i.e. firms with upward perspectives might be attracted by Delaware Corporate Law. Bebchuk and Cohen (2003) noted that US states could be roughly divided into two groups, those with regimes that are hostile to takeovers and others that are neutral or friendly towards takeovers. Apparently, the first group, which comprises a number of smaller states (including Delaware) tend to attract company registration, which is a decision taken by executive management.[10] As it is generally acknowledged that shareholders benefit from takeover-friendly regimes, this conclusion is at odds with the above mentioned assertion that regulatory competition in the US led to increase in shareholder wealth. Bar-Gill *et al.* (2002: 27) have thus concluded that in cases where the interests of shareholders and managers might conflict (such as in the case of takeover regimes), regulatory competition incites authorities to offer rules that benefit managers, not shareholders (such as allowing 'poison pills' for management to fend off hostile takeovers). This line of reasoning, if correct, would lend support to

the Commission's approach on corporate governance (which, as explained above, is considered as favouring harmonization of rules over regulatory competition).

• For completeness, it should be added that, according to Roe (2003), ultimately no regulatory competition at all is taking place in the US. In his view, regulatory competition among states would only be possible in the total absence of a federal regime. However, since the US federal authorities may legislate on corporate law (see, for example, the SOA), states always need to take into account the possibility of federal intervention when passing legislation. Thus, 'that which persists in Delaware is that which the federal authorities tolerate' (Roe, 2003: 588).

Conclusion

Unlike the SOA – which was adopted in a record six months in the US – there is no single act overhauling the entire corporate governance framework in the EU. Rather, the EU is adopting a sequenced response, which incorporates a variety of legislative acts. Under this more cautious approach, which includes consultation of a variety of stakeholders, the adoption of some 18 legislative proposals is foreseen, requiring agreement by the European Parliament and the 25 Member States. This, obviously, will take time. Once accomplished, the EU's corporate governance regime will, unlike the US, rely more on legally enforceable rules than on self-regulation. At the same time, as witnessed by the ongoing transatlantic dialogue on accounting systems, there is an interest in the US and the EU in fostering convergence of key features in corporate regulation, with a view to minimizing regulatory spillover effects for companies operating in both markets and facilitating transatlantic capital flows.

Notes

1 The views expressed are those of the author and not necessarily those of the ECB.
2 In line with OECD (2004), corporate governance is defined as 'the rules and practices that govern the relationship between the managers and shareholders of corporations, as well as stakeholders like employees and creditors'.
3 Gatekeepers are defined as 'reputational intermediaries who provide verification and certification services to investors' (Coffee, 2003: 13).
4 The following explanations are largely based on Bratton (2003), Coffee (2003) and Langevoort (2002).
5 In some important sectors, there was in fact a duopoly: in 2002, 86 per cent of companies in the US air transportation sector and 95 per cent of companies in the US petroleum and coal sector were audited by only two firms (Walkner, 2004: 27)
6 Attempting to explain these differences through path-dependence, Bebchuk and Roe (1999: S. 37) have argued that 'countries in which social democratic ideologies are dominant may empower employees more than do countries with

other types of governments, putting more pressure on managers to side with employees instead of owners. As a consequence, owners may prefer their next best means of control (to resist such pressure), and the next best means may be concentrated ownership.' At the same time, a trend towards more dispersed ownership has been identified in the EU over recent years (Coffee, 2001).

7 For example, Frits Bolkestein, Member of the European Commission responsible for the Internal Market, Taxation and Customs Union, in a hearing at the European Parliament's Committee on Economic and Monetary Affairs on 19 March 2002.

8 By contrast, others (e.g. Bratton, 2003) pointed out that the GAAP include a substantial amount of rule-orientation, and that the Enron collapse was the result of audit failures rather than failures in the US accounting system.

9 An overview on literature supporting this argument is provided in Bainbridge (2003).

10 According to this line of reasoning, regulatory competition in the US is distorted since only smaller states try to attract company incorporations (which is associated with some, albeit limited, corporate tax revenues). By contrast, larger states (such as New York) do not take part in the competition as these states have a large population of shareholders that would not approve of hostile takeover rules.

References

Bainbridge, S.M. (2003) 'The creeping federalization of corporate law', *Regulation* Spring: 26.

Bar-Gill, O. and Bebchuck, L.A. (2003)'Misreporting corporate performance', Harvard Law School, John M. Olin Center for Law, Economics and Business, Discussion Paper, no. 400.

Bar-Gill, O., Barzuza, M. and Bebchuck, L.A. (2002) 'The market for corporate law', NBER Working Paper, no. W9156.

Bebchuk, L.A. and Cohen, A. (2003) 'Firms' decisions where to incorporate', *Journal of Law and Economics* 46: 383–425.

Bebchuck, L.A. and Roe, M.J. (1999) 'A theory of path dependence in corporate governance and ownership', Columbia Law School, Center for Law and Economic Studies, Working Paper, no. 131.

Bratton, W.W. (2003) 'Enron, Sarbanes–Oxley and accounting: rules versus principles versus rents', the George Washington University Law School, Public Law and Legal Theory Working Paper, no. 64.

Centre for European Policy Studies (CEPS) (2004) 'Corporate governance reform in the EU – First Meeting of the Task Force, 17 June 2004', Brussels.

Coffee, J. (2001) 'The rise of dispersed ownership: the role of law in the separation of ownership and control', Columbia Law School, the Center for Law and Economic Studies, Working Paper, no. 182.

Coffee, J. (2003) 'What caused Enron?: a capsule social and economic history of the 1990s', Columbia Law School, the Center for Law and Economic Studies, Working Paper, no. 214.

Commission (2002) 'A first EU response to Enron related policy issues, *Note for the Informal ECOFIN Council in Oviedo*, 12 and 13 April.

Commission (2003) 'Communication from the Commission to the Council and the European Parliament: modernising company law and enhancing corporate governance in the European Union – a plan to move forward' (COM (2003) 284 final).

Commission (2004a) 'Proposal for a directive of the European Parliament and of the Council on statutory audit of annual accounts and consolidated accounts and amending council directives 78/660/EEC and 83/349/EEC' (COM (2004) 177 final).

Commission (2004b) 'Commission Recommendation of 14 December 2004 fostering an appropriate regime for the remuneration of directors of listed companies' (2004/913/EC).

Commission (2005) 'Commission Recommendation of 15 February 2005 on the role of non-executive or supervisory directors of listed companies and on the committees of the (supervisory) board' (2005/162/EC).

Commission (2006) 'Proposal for a Directive of the European Parliament and of the Council on the exercise of voting rights by shareholders of companies having their registered office in a Member State and whose shares are admitted to trading on a regulated market and amending Directive 2004/109/EC' (COM(2005)685 final).

Commission (2006) 'Directive 2006/46/EC of the European Parliament and of the Council of 14 June 2006 amending Council Directives 78/660/EEC on the annual accounts of certain types of companies, 83/349/EEC on consolidated accounts, 86/635/EEC on the annual accounts and consolidated accounts of banks and other financial institutions and 91/674/EEC on the annual accounts and consolidated accounts of insurance undertakings'.

Langevoort, D. (2002) 'Managing the "expectations gap" in investor protection: the SEC and the post-Enron reform agenda', Georgetown University Law Center, Working Paper Series in Business, Economics and Regulatory Law, Working Paper, no. 328080.

Lannoo, K. and Khachaturyan, A. (2003) 'Reform of corporate governance in the EU', Centre for European Policy Studies (CEPS), Policy Brief, no. 38.

OECD (2004) 'The OECD Principles of Corporate Governance', Paris.

Roe, M.J. (2003) 'Delaware's competition', *Harvard Law Review* 117: 588.

Walkner, C. (2004) 'Issues in corporate governance', European Commission, Directorate General for Economic and Financial Affairs, Economic Paper, no. 200.

6 Multiple regulators and insolvency regimes

Obstacles to efficient supervision and resolution[1]

Robert R. Bliss

Financial markets and the large complex financial institutions that dominate them span borders and traditional lines of business with seeming ease. The regulators who supervise these markets and the institutions that resolve failures when they occur, do not. This gives rise to two sets of direct problems: *ex ante*, the multiplicity of regulators and regulatory regimes weakens supervision and may compromise early intervention; *ex post*, conflict and competition among resolution authorities heightens legal uncertainty and undermines the efficient resolution of financially distressed institutions. Markets and firms respond to these problems constructively by devising mechanisms for reducing legal uncertainties and strengthening the enforceability of their claims. They lobby for widespread adoption of consistent laws governing certain types of contract, make increased use of secured transactions, and structure their contracts defensively. Some firms, however, may find in these problems an opportunity for malfeasance.

These problems are inherent in the national and sometimes narrow, functional character of regulatory institutions and laws. They are exacerbated by the inconsistent objectives and philosophies underlying these institutions and laws, the tendency for historically based structures to become entrenched, and the disincentives for cooperation across groups. None of these factors is unique to the regulatory and legal environment of financial markets.

This chapter will explore the legal and regulatory environment in which large complex financial institutions operate today, the historical antecedents that have produced this structure, and through examples, show how this environment has led to undesirable outcomes. Much of the discussion will focus on the US. This is not simply due to the importance of large US financial firms in international markets, but rather because the US presents a uniquely complex legal and regulatory environment that may directly effect countries that host branches and subsidiaries of US financial institutions and foreign institutions that operate branches and subsidiaries in the US. Ongoing developments in the European Union provide examples of both recognition of and concrete efforts to ameliorate the problems inherent in multinational financial conglomerates.

Structure of large US bank holding companies

Today virtually all major US 'banks' are organized as bank or financial holding companies. Table 6.1 provides summary statistics for the five largest bank holding companies. The first point to note is their legal complexity as indicated by the number of distinct entities falling under the holding company structure. Many of these are trusts and other bankruptcy-remote special purpose entities. Nonetheless, a large number of operating subsidiaries in different countries are also represented. Some of these involve multiple layers of ownership – holding company/bank/foreign subsidiary/trust – up to eight layers deep.

These bank holding companies and the major banks within them are not solely or invariably even primarily lending institutions (Table 6.2).

Table 6.1 Summary information on the five largest US bank holding companies

	CitiCorp	Bank of America	J P Morgan Chase	Wells Fargo	Wachovia
Assets (US$, millions)	1,396,568	1,039,764	817,763	420,305	418,441
Loans (% of assets)	37.0	47.0	24.8	63.2	42.4
Total deposits (% of liabilities)	40.5	61.0	49.9	69.7	64.1
Domestic deposits (% of liabilities)	14.2	55.4	29.7	66.0	62.0
Number of distinct entities	1,616	1,891	992	672	972

Note
This information is taken from the 30 June 2004 'Consolidate Financial Statements for Bank Holding Companies', FR-Y-9C, available on the Federal Reserve Board's website.

Table 6.2 Summary information on the five largest US banks

	Bank of America	J P Morgan Chase	Citibank	Wachovia	Wells Fargo
Assets (US$, millions)	706,888	654,641	648,243	368,871	364,698
Loans (% of assets)	48.3	25.3	54.0	45.4	64.2
Total deposits (% of liabilities)	73.3	55.4	71.4	74.3	82.9
Domestic deposits (% of liabilities)	60.9	35.4	20.0	70.2	77.1

Note
This information is taken from the 'Consolidate Report of Condition for Insured Commercial and State-Chartered Savings Banks for 30 June 2004', Schedule RC, available on the Federal Reserve Board's website.

Loans and leases count for less than one half the assets of three of the largest five banks and four of the largest five bank holding companies. While deposits fund a majority of liabilities at all five lead banks and at three of the bank holding companies, the liability structure contains significant amounts of non-depository debts. CitiCorp and J P Morgan/ Chase derive less than half their liabilities from deposits and only a small fraction of their funding is derived from domestic deposits.[2] Bank of America also has significant foreign deposits.

The implicit assumption underlying US bank resolution procedures, that non-deposit liabilities are not material, is not tenable for LCFOs and some specialized smaller banks. This may have important consequences for creditor and regulatory incentives. On the one hand, if the non-depository creditors run, these banks will quickly become illiquid and the ability of the regulators to conduct an orderly resolution will be compromised. On the other hand, the large buffer of non-depository creditors may create incentives for the primary bank regulator (focusing on protecting the deposit insurance fund) and the FDIC to delay closure and once closed to delay resolution. For banks such as J P Morgan Chase and Citibank, it would be extraordinary if the FDIC did not obtain full recovery for domestic depositors (and itself) even if prompt corrective action fails to achieve early intervention. If prompt corrective action works as intended, the general creditors (non-deposit creditors, foreign depositors, etc.) will have major claims on the banks' assets and no effective representation in the process for discharging their claims (see below).

In cases where the failed banks' assets do not cover the domestic deposits, the FDIC acting with the Federal Reserve would likely seek to become a creditor of the holding company through a source of strength claim (as happened with MCorp), effectively nullifying limited liability for equity positions in subsidiary banks and setting up litigation between the holding company's creditors and the FDIC.[3]

Financial regulation in the US and EU

The US regulatory environment

The regulation of financial institutions in the US is uniquely complex. This complexity is the result of historical developments and the asymmetric evolution of markets and governmental institutions. Furthermore, the US political system has, at least in the last several decades, exhibited considerable difficulty in responding to changes in financial markets.[4]

There has always been a historical tension between state and federal governments in the US as to the scope of their legal and regulatory powers. This derives from the original limited definition of federal government powers under the constitution and subsequent evolution of those powers, generally increasing the role of the central government. Initially the central government was not involved in the regulation of financial institutions. Instead, banks were chartered and supervised, to varying degrees, by the states in which they were located. These state bank charters imposed various restrictions on banking activities. It was not until the National Banking Act of 1864 that a national banking charter was created to compete with state banks. This act also created the Comptroller of the Currency to supervise those banks that chose to take a national charter. However, since the national charter was neither required nor initially attractive, the result was that state chartered and supervised banks coexisted with federally chartered and supervised ones. Throughout the later nineteenth and early twentieth centuries, banking and financial markets in the US evolved in scope and complexity. While most banks remained what we now call community banks – that is small, local institutions – a few major banks, mostly located in New York, became powerful domestic and international institutions, engaged in a wide variety of 'universal' banking activities.

The Federal Reserve Act of 1913 created the Federal Reserve in large part to ensure 'an elastic currency', that is to provide liquidity in times of crisis. For banks to have access to this liquidity they had to become members of the Federal Reserve System. Membership was mandatory for nationally-chartered banks and open to state-chartered banks. *Inter alia*, the Federal Reserve Act granted both the OCC and the Federal Reserve authority to supervise member banks. This overlap of authority was resolved in 1917 with the OCC supervising national banks and the Federal Reserve supervising state member banks. However, state banks remained simultaneously subject to state supervision.[5]

The banking crises of the early 1930s that accompanied the Great Depression led to the enactment of a series of laws which laid the foundation of today's US regulatory environment. The Banking Act of 1933 (a.k.a. Glass–Steagall) required separation of commercial and investment banking. Since that time, the term 'bank' has had a narrower meaning in the US than elsewhere. The Securities Exchange Act (1934) created the Securities and Exchange Commission to set and enforce standards for securities markets and broker/dealers, i.e. investment banks. Thus, universal banks in the US were divided into commercial banks (depository institutions) and investment banks, each with their own regulatory regime.

The Glass–Steagall Act also created the FDIC with the authority to resolve failed banks, but left the authority to close banks with their respective regulators – state, Federal Reserve, OCC – or the bank's directors. This had the effect of creating a resolution process for banks that was entirely separate from the bankruptcy process that applied to other corporations (and individuals).

So long as banks confined themselves to the traditional banking activities of deposit taking, lending and payments processing, and maintained simple organizational structures, the potential effects of this arrangement were improved supervision and efficiency of the closure process. However, pressures developed for expansion of banks across state lines (and, within unit-banking states, outside their local market) and for expansion of banks into non-traditional activities prohibited under banking laws. Bank holding companies provided a means of realizing these goals. To rationalize this development, which had previously proceeded by means of individually-negotiated arrangements with regulators and state authorities, Congress passed the Bank Holding Company Act in 1956 permitting formation of multi-bank holding companies (subject to state/interstate laws) and allowing some non-banking activities to take place under the holding company, though, outside the subsidiary banks. The Bank Holding Company Act gave the Federal Reserve supervisory authority for bank holding companies, but not for the constituent banks unless they were already subject to Federal Reserve oversight as state member banks. The Bank Holding Company Act was amended in 1970 to permit one-bank holding companies; that is, holding companies that control a single bank along with one or more non-bank subsidiaries.

Throughout this development, insurance company regulation and insolvency resolution remained a state matter. Insurance companies are state chartered and regulated. They are resolved under state law when they fail (rather than under the Federal Bankruptcy Code). No national charter exists for insurance companies and attempts to create one have consistently failed. Thus, the three major financial services industries – commercial banking, investment banking and insurance – are, in the US, subject to different regulators and different legal processes for handling failures.

The Financial Modernization Act of 1999 (Gramm–Leach–Bliley) removed a number of restrictions on banking activity that had been imposed under Glass–Steagall. Gramm–Leach–Bliley also permitted combining banking, securities and insurance subsidiaries under a single newly-defined financial holding company structure. The Act gave the Federal Reserve the power to authorize formation of financial holding companies, and to serve as 'umbrella regulator'. However, Gramm–Leach–Bliley further entrenched the separate functional regulators who regulate insurance, securities broker/dealers and commercial banks within the financial holding company. The Federal Reserve's powers as umbrella regulator are mitigated by requirements to defer to functional regulators in numerous ways.[6] The Federal Reserve has considerable powers once a threat to the deposit insurance fund or more broadly a systemic concern has developed, but considerably less power to coordinate processes aimed at early detection and distress avoidance.

European unified regulators

While the US financial regulatory structure remains firmly rooted in the functional regulation model, members of the EU have moved away from functional regulation and towards unified regulators. In 1997, the incoming Labour government in the UK announced the merging of banking and securities regulation into a single Financial Services Authority (FSA), with enabling legislation being passed in 2001. Subsequent regulatory mergers rolled the remaining functional regulators into the FSA, creating a single regulator responsible for all aspects of financial institutions and markets. Though much of the internal regulatory framework remains functional, the role of single regulator has allowed the FSA to provide 'a coherent and integrated approach to supervising' large complex financial groups.[7] In 2002, German financial regulation was unified under the Bundesanstalt für Finanzdienstleistungsaufsicht (BaFin). While, these and a number of other EU countries have moved towards a unified regulator, the 2002 EU Financial Groups Directive legislation has mandated consolidated supervision of large complex financial groups operating in the EU for purposes of safety and soundness and systemic risk.[8] This requirement extends to non-EU firms operating in the EU. Where the non-EU parent's country does not meet the requirements of the directive, the firm's EU operations must be placed in a separate subsidiary subject to EU supervision. This has caused considerable concern for large US firms and US regulators since it is not immediately obvious that the US umbrella regulator model meets the requirements. Accommodations within the US functional regulatory framework have been recently negotiated.

Multiple regulators

Multiple regulators arise for a number of reasons and in a number of forms. Alternative regulators arise where firms have an alternative regulator to choose from. In US banking, this choice is exercised through the charter that the bank chooses. Functional regulators arise where a firm is simultaneously regulated by multiple regulators. These functional regulators may regulate different parts of the same firm or they may regulate different aspects of the firm's behaviour.

Excepting for regulators with completely distinct regulatory objectives (safety and soundness, work place safety, equal opportunity) it is difficult to identify multiple regulators that have arisen by design. Multiple financial regulators have usually developed to serve distinct, minimally-overlapping industry segments, which later merged either through business extension into common areas or through holding company formation.

For more-or-less distinct sectors and specialized firms, multiple regulators have certain advantages, though not without possible disadvantages. Alternative regulators also present potential advantages and disadvantages. However, when structural changes in the industry result in different regulators simultaneously regulating different parts of the same firm, a wholly new set of issues is created.

Alternative regulators

US bank regulation has a multiplicity of bank supervisory authorities, all serving the same basic function – ensuring the safety and soundness of individual banks.[9] Some observers view this 'regulatory competition' as beneficial, providing a market test for optimal regulation and supervision. The presence of alternative regulators provides banks with the ability to escape ill-advised or onerous regulation on the part of any one regulator, by changing their charters. The alternative view is that competition for clients will lead to a regulatory 'race for the bottom', providing lax supervision and permitting inappropriate risk taking in order to attract fee-paying banks[10] and/or to justify regulatory staffing levels. In fact, regulators have little flexibility to compete in a dynamic sense. While different supervisory structures impose different costs, and may have some differences in policies or examination practices, the differences tend to be static. Rosen (2003) explored the two alternative hypotheses and found some evidence for beneficial competition, though on a local level. Banks that wanted to change their strategy, but found their local supervisors resistant, sometimes changed charters to obtain the desired approval. However, there was no consistent direction of change of charter, say from OCC regulated national bank to Federal Reserve state member bank. Changes occurred in all directions suggesting that the motivation was tied to local supervisors rather than to agencies' policies. Rosen found no evidence supporting the 'race to the bottom' hypothesis, at least in US banking. Further evidence of successful regulatory competition is evident in international financial markets: the Eurobond market and the London swaps market both developed (at least in part) in response to US regulatory burdens. The widespread adoption, through the efforts of the International Swaps and Derivatives Association, of enforceable master agreements has been motivated by the desire of countries to keep their financial institutions 'in the game'. If derivatives markets were not international and fluid, many countries could have forgone adopting this important mechanism for mitigating risk.[11]

LCFOs with multiple bank subsidiaries can and do maintain portfolios of charters with more than one supervisory agency, each examining and supervising a different group of subsidiaries. This may be for reasons of strategic flexibility. If a proposed activity is not approved by one regulator, another regulator may be more accommodating. However, since the regulatory policies are similar, and idiosyncratic variation in individual supervisory decisions unpredictable, the effect on approved risk taking is probably marginal. However, one effect is to divide the constituent parts of the holding company into distinct parts each with its own regulator, further deepening the compartmentalization produced by functional regulation.

Functional regulators

Functional regulation is not unique to the US. Countries with unified regulators may still organize their supervision along functional lines. Functional regulation is a natural consequence of historical distinctions between different financial services – traditional banking, insurance, securities brokers/dealers. These financial sectors present different issues for regulators to address. Where financial firms specialize in single sectors and the activities are distinct, functionally-separate regulators are more likely to address the interest of their constituencies, including lobbying for sufficient resources to carrying out their responsibilities. Indirect evidence of regulatory champions is provided by the persistence of niche regulators – e.g. Office of Thrift Supervision – and the strong resistance by client industry groups to changes in the regulatory structure that would absorb 'their' regulator into another agency, even though their market overlaps with those of other groups (e.g. community banks and savings and loans). A risk of regulatory specialization is an increased chance of 'regulatory capture' as the interests of the regulator (staffing, resources) become aligned with the interests of the regulated (market share, profits, barriers to entry). Since regulation is generally intended to benefit the public and not the regulated firms, such identification of interest can have adverse consequences.

As financial markets became more sophisticated and the interests of firms in different sectors came into conflict,[12] the presence of separate regulators may make these conflicts and the resulting policy debates more transparent and provide each constituency with representation in the formulation of policy. Unitary regulators responsible for functionally different industry sectors may internalize conflicts between the sectors, making the policy discussions less transparent. Furthermore, allocation of scarce resources within an organization may leave some sectors less well served than would be the case if each sector had its own regulator.[13]

Multiple regulators of LCFOs

Functional regulators usually have differing, sometimes overlapping, objectives. These objectives are rooted in the problems the underlying, historically separate, regulatory institutions were designed to address.

Bank regulators have always been concerned with safety and soundness of both individual banks, and the financial system as a whole. This concern derives from the 'banks are special' view that banking functions – deposit taking, payments processing, liquidity provision – are particularly important to the functioning of the economy, so that failure of banks, particularly if they are large or widespread, are likely to generate negative externalities that are best avoided. The existence of deposit insurance, explicit or implicit, raises concerns about taxpayer liability, reinforcing the desire of bank regulators to avoid or limit bank failures. Banking regulators, particularly when they are also monetary authorities, are also concerned with the functioning of the financial system as a whole. Concerns about systemic risk are more likely to be discussed in the context of banking and payments than in security dealing and insurance.[14] A number of other objectives have been added to bank regulators function over the years – consumer protection (e.g. fair lending), ensuring consumer access to credit (e.g. Community Reinvestment Act requirements), criminal law enforcement (e.g. money laundering) – but these ancillary functions, though important, are not at the core of banking regulation.

In contrast, securities regulation has its origins in investor protection and law enforcement. The policing of various criminal activities – fraud, money laundering, market manipulation, insider trading – remains a primary focus of securities regulation. Considerable less attention has been traditionally paid to the safety and soundness of securities firms. Securities regulators have also been involved in market structure – ensuring a level playing field. Recently they have become more assertive in areas of corporate governance and accounting.

Insurance regulators appear to focus on consumer protection. Because insurance policies are not usually insured by the state, insurance regulators do have an interest in safety and soundness. Nonetheless, the focus is on consumer protection rather than financial system protection. Frequently insurance regulators will also become involved in consumer access and pricing issues, particularly where insurance commissioners are elected as they are in some US states. Where insurance regulators are geographically fragmented, as they are in the US, their interests are inevitably focused on their own constituents (citizens) rather than on broader questions of widespread impacts of potential failure.[15]

Differences in core regulatory objectives lead to a number of important differences that make cross-function cooperation difficult. Information collected by regulators is tailored to their own purposes and thus is likely to be incompatible across functional areas. Where different information is being collected (likely using incompatible data systems) it becomes difficult if not impossible to aggregate information for consolidated supervisory purposes.[16]

A more subtle potential friction arises from the intellectual and cultural backgrounds of the persons staffing and dominating different regulators. Regulatory agencies employ lawyers, economists and accountants in varying degrees, but the internal power structure and hence culture is apt to favour one group or another. Central banks are frequently dominated by economists. Bank examination is largely an accounting function. Securities regulation tends to focus on legal issues. These groups – lawyers, economists, accountants – may approach (even) common objectives with different implicit intellectual frameworks. This intellectual diversity is a potentially powerful source of improved regulation and supervision. But the lack of common intellectual framework and modes of addressing issues can also have adverse effects if no (or weak) mechanisms exist for coordinating across organizations. Where different groups dominate each organization and each sets their own organization's agenda, then cross-organizational cultural differences may impede rather than aid over-arching regulatory goals, even where the different groups can articulate broad collective goals.

The mere existence of different groups can impede the pursuit of common goals. It is a basic instinct of humans to identify with their own group and subgroup and to differentiate their group from other groups. Even where 'outside' groups are clearly working towards the same objec-tive, there is a tendency to perceive differences; to perceive others as less trustworthy, competent, or well motivated; and for cooperation within organizations to be stronger than across organizations.[17] These social-psychological influences are inherent in human nature and cannot easily be ameliorated as long as group separateness is preserved. Combining functional regulators into a single unified regulator does not necessarily solve the problem if functional separateness is preserved in different departments of the new organization. The formation of special cross-func-tional groups within the organization and separate from the functional departments, for instance to deal with complex financial groups as has been done in the UK FSA, may be expected to break down these barriers by creating a new group identity, and incorporating within that group most of the persons needed to achieve the overall organization goal.

Finally, multiple regulators may have different objectives and be answerable to different constituencies. Goodhart (2005) analyses the potential problems inherent in failure resolution when decision making is spread across multiple agencies: the central bank, which is able to provide emergency liquidity, the bank supervisor, who has detailed knowledge of the bank's situation, and the Treasury, representing political and taxpayer interests. Goodhart's analysis is in terms of the UK regulatory structure, but similar multi-agency decision-making structure exists in other coun-tries: for instance, in the US, invoking the 'systemic risk exemption' to least cost resolution requires approval by a committee representing a similar span of interests. Committees representing diverse interests can serve an important role in balancing those interests. But as Goodhart (2005) points out, they can also impede decision making when their agendas, information and competencies differ, particularly when decision making is taking place in a crisis.

EU regulation of LCFOs

The problems of cross-border supervision and regulation are particularly acute in the EU where financial liberalization is leading to within-EU, cross-border expansion of banking.[18] The EU has solved the potential problem of multiple regulators by mandating home-country supervision. This achieves clarity, but leaves open a number of issues. Countries within the EU differ as to their banking laws, the rigour of their financial supervision, and their deposit insurance. Potential exists for banks to locate where supervision is lax, and this may be exacerbated by locating most business outside of the country in which the bank is technically domiciled so as to further reduce incentives of home country supervisors to supervise.[19]

Home country supervision also does little to solve incentive problems that may arise in crisis management of failed banks, particularly when combined with deposit insurance issues.[20] Indeed where there is separation of place of business (and the concomitant stakeholders) and the locus of regulatory control, an agency problem is created with all the attendant problems.

The adoption of home country supervision is essentially a political rather than economic decision. It serves to clarify who will supervise without asking who is best able to supervise or who will suffer from regulatory failure. Not all supervisory agencies enjoy the same resources, trained staffs or political independence. Home country rules may theoretically permit host countries to take action (deny access or insist on host country supervision), but such action would be so politically costly that it is unlikely to be undertaken, certainly not before a major failure had occurred. Thus, without convergence of legal, regulatory and supervisory standards, home country supervision remains a problematic solution to the problem of multiple regulators. And even with convergence, asymmetries in potential loss sharing may bedevil its application.

Failure resolution and LCFOs

Function of bankruptcy proceedings

All developed legal systems provide legal processes for resolving the claims of insolvent firms. The central purpose of these processes is to coordinate the claims of multiple creditors and, in some cases, the interests of other stake holders (including management). Some legal systems favour creditors over management and shareholders, while others favour debtors.[21] Regardless of orientation the role of the bankruptcy court is to provide a coordination mechanism for resolving the collective interests of the parties concerned. Without such coordination, creditors would seek to seize and liquidate assets to satisfy their own claims. The seizure of assets would necessarily result in the destruction of any going-concern value (if there was any).

The liquidation of assets by individual creditors sets up perverse incentives that encourage runs on an insolvent firm. If the law requires creditors to pay excess recoveries (realized liquidation values in excess of the amounts of their claims) into a common pool, then creditors in possession of assets would have little of no incentive to maximize the recovery values once their claims are satisfied. If creditors get to keep any excess recoveries, then they have incentives to maximize recoveries, but this is of little benefit to creditors as a group.

For this reason, bankruptcy courts (and alternative insolvency administrators) seek to first gain control of the firm's assets and to collect and validate creditor claims. The court then, in principle, attempts to determine how best to protect the collective interests of creditors.[22] Central to this deliberative (and usually very slow) process is the ability of courts to stay execution of contracts (in effect to call a 'time out') so that assets are not dissipated while the court carries out its tasks.[23]

While stays are explicitly provided for in most legal frameworks, the neutrality of adjudicator is an implicit component. Conflicts of interest among creditors (and between creditors and shareholders and management) are inherent in the bankruptcy process. With few exceptions, bankruptcies are ultimately administered and overseen by judges (or administrative officers), who have no direct financial interest at stake. The neutrality of the controlling authority is important to lend credibility to the process. Where the neutrality and fairness of the bankruptcy process is lacking, creditors may adapt in ways that are not in the interests of financial markets and society. Creditors may seek to gain control of assets prior to the bankruptcy filing, thus precipitating the 'rush to the exits' that bankruptcy attempts to avoid. They may demand collateral, raising the effect costs of borrowing and limiting credit to firms that have good (liquid) collateral to pledge. Creditors may seek to conduct business in jurisdictions that are more creditor friendly, forcing companies to follow them, setting up potential conflicts of law should the firm fail in multiple jurisdictions. Or creditors may simply price the risks they face in bankruptcy into their contracts, raising the price of credit.

In some jurisdictions, for instance in the US under Chapter 11 reorganizations, immediate control of the firm and the resolution planning is at least initially vested in management which does have strong personal and financial interests that may not be aligned with those of creditors. Nonetheless, the management's actions are usually subject to court oversight and the resolution process is itself designed to protect the interests of all (or most) creditor classes. In particular, creditors usually have standing to appeal decisions of the bankruptcy trustee/administrator and in some instances to vote on final plans for liquidation or reorganization.

A major exception to the general practice of having a neutral authority oversee the administration of a bankruptcy and to provide all creditors with standing to participate in the process, is the treatment of bank insolvencies in the US. When a US bank fails the insolvency is solely administered by the FDIC which is also a major creditor.[24] While depositor preference laws align the interests of other depositors with those of the FDIC, these laws leave other creditors (including foreign depositors) with

residual claims. 'Least cost resolution' requires the FDIC to conduct resolutions to minimize its own losses rather than the collective losses of all
creditors. This combination of a residual class and a mandate to minimize
own losses, creates little incentive for the FDIC to maximize recoveries of
liquidated assets once its own claims are covered.[25] The process of US
bank resolution provides creditors with only extremely circumscribed
means of appealing the actions of the FDIC.

Handling international insolvencies

The failure of an LCFO will inevitably present multiple challenges to this
paradigm of coordinated resolution of creditor claims supervised by a
neutral authority. A failed LCFO, like any major international firm will
have assets and creditors in multiple legal jurisdictions. In the US, the situation is complicated by the existence of multiple domestic venues to
handle different parts of a failed LCFO. There are two methods for
dealing with international insolvencies: the universal or single entity
approach and the territorial approach. The universal approach seeks to
achieve a coordinated resolution of insolvency by having the courts in the
relevant jurisdictions act in concert with one court taking the lead role
and other courts conducting ancillary proceedings to support the activities of the lead court: gaining control of local assets, collecting local creditor claims, enforcing judgments of the lead court etc. The territorial
approach, on the other hand seeks to conduct simultaneous independent
proceedings in each relevant jurisdiction, with each court seeking to gain
control of assets under its jurisdiction in order to satisfy the claims of its
own creditors.

The universal approach can, in principal, achieve a coordinated resolution, however the actions of ancillary courts are often subject to local laws.
Where courts attempt to enforce differing local laws within the context of
ancillary proceedings, creditors recoveries can differ.[26] These potential
disparities may undermine the incentives of courts to fully cooperate. It is
unclear whether it would be possible to conduct a multinational reorganization through the courts in different countries operating under materially different laws. The incentives of courts to take actions that would
potentially undermine their own domestic creditors' potential positions –
whether by allowing asset transfers or reducing creditors' claims – may
make collectively optimal solutions difficult to achieve. On the other
hand, the territorial approach offers no hope of reorganization as each
jurisdiction operates independently and in the interests of its domestic
creditors. The territorial approach also suffers from the problem that
incentives for courts to maximize recoveries of liquidated assets are much
diminished once their own domestic creditors' claims have been satisfied.

Thus, any cross-border bank insolvency is apt to fall far short of the
ideal of coordinate and cooperative resolution of collective creditor

claims. Some creditors may be advantaged, while others would necessarily be disadvantaged. Moreover the impediments to cooperation and coordination must necessarily mean that going concern value will be sacrificed and total recoveries (other than by lawyers) diminished. Fortunately, complex cross-border insolvencies are rare, but this means that great uncertainty exists as to how they might play out. Such uncertainty may itself create incentives for regulators to intervene prior to insolvency to prevent triggering legal processes. Such intervention may take the form of facilitating a market solution (recapitalization) as was done in the case of Long Term Capital Management. The alternatives, regulatory recapitalization (bail-out) or refusing to close a bank, raise both coordination (across regulators) and moral hazard problems.

Recent revisions to the US bankruptcy laws (Bankruptcy Abuse Prevention and Consumer Protection Act of 2005) have adopted many of the provisions of the United Nations Commission on International Trade Law (UNCITRAL) model law for governing international insolvencies. These provisions may come into play in the insolvency of a US bank holding company. However, both the model law itself and US law specifically exempt banks from the UNCITRAL framework.

US failure resolution regimes[27]

The US has specialized insolvency regimes for depository institutions ('banks' in the US sense), broker/dealers, insurance companies and housing-related agencies.[28] Individuals and most other corporations fall under the federal Bankruptcy Code.[29] The Bankruptcy Code has two major forms: Chapter 11 is intended to preserve the company as a viable entity, and Chapter 7 is intended to liquidate the company. Chapter 11 initially gives management the sole right to propose a workout. This right is limited in time and if the proposal is not adopted a trustee can be appointed to carry on the negotiations. The plan however must be approved by the creditors and stockholders. This gives junior claims considerable leverage, resulting in frequent violations of apparent legal and contractual priority of claims. In Chapter 7, the creditors elect or the court appoints a trustee to oversee the settlement of claims, subject to approval of the court. Both Chapters 7 and 11 provide creditors with the right to be represented, to vote on proposed settlements, and to appeal bankruptcy court rulings. Importantly, no interested creditor has absolute control of the process.

US bank resolution is complex, indeed Byzantine. First, closure authority lies with the primary regulator. There is no mechanism for a bank's depositors or other creditors to petition for an insolvency proceeding to be initiated.[30] While prompt corrective action (PCA) legislation specifies seemingly precise rules for when the primary regulator must close a bank, these rules are tied to financial statements. Financial statements are subject to considerable judgment (and occasional misrepresentation), and examiners have some discretion as to when to require restatement of disputed values. The result is that the closure rules under PCA are less useful than they should be.[31] Once closed, resolution of virtually all banks is handled by the FDIC. The FDIC acts as conservator (though rarely) or receiver, taking immediate control of the bank's assets. It is able to act expeditiously; its powers are sweeping and its actions are not subject to judicial review.[32] The FDIC pays off the insured depositors and assumes their claim, thus becoming itself the major creditor in the proceeding it is administering. Depositor preference legislation (see Kaufman, 1997) effectively aligns the interests of the FDIC with those of the uninsured domestic depositors as any recoveries must be shared pro rata by the FDIC and domestic depositors. Claims of foreign depositors (depositors in foreign branches), and other creditors are subordinated to those of the domestic depositor and the FDIC.

In carrying out its resolution duties, the FDIC is required by law to maximize recoveries for all creditors and simultaneously minimize losses to the deposit insurance fund. However, the focus of both legislation and regulatory practice is on the latter goal. The FDIC is required to choose the resolution option that is expected to minimize losses to the FDIC as deposit insurer ('least cost resolution'), rather than to all creditors. This goal is met when the FDIC's losses are zero, though the uninsured, non-domestic depositors and general creditors may be wiped out.[33] There is no requirement in law or policy to choose among those options that minimize losses to the FDIC that option which minimizes losses to other creditors.

The Federal Reserve is the supervisor of bank and financial holding companies. However, Federal Reserve policy explicitly seeks to protect the bank subsidiaries, rather than the holding company's creditors. Under the Fed's source of strength doctrine, holding companies must do everything possible to ensure that the bank subsidiaries are well capitalized and are required to recapitalize them if they fall short. The statutory and legal support for this doctrine is weak, except in the case of approving mergers.[34] The regulatory perspective that the primary function of the holding company is to protect bank subsidiaries aligns the interests of Federal Reserve with those of the FDIC rather than the holding company and its creditors.

This depositor-focused resolution procedure is well suited to banks whose only liabilities are deposits. This liability structure is apt to be substantially true for the multitude of small US banks, either because they have few non-deposit liabilities or because by the time they fail those uninsured creditors that they did have already run. For these banks, the efficiency of the FDIC resolution process may be superior to the uncertainties of the bankruptcy process, though it does ignore the interests of non-financial market claimants such as suppliers and employees.[35]

Tensions in US law between insolvency regimes for holding companies and their constituent bank, securities and insurance subsidiaries, and a strong tendency for US banking law to disadvantage foreign interests (see the Appendix) are all apt to undermine cooperation with foreign courts in any major LCFO insolvency involving US firms. Similarly, cooperation between US insolvency venues is uncertain.

EU approach to LCFO resolution

The EU has adopted a universalist approach to cross-border, intra-EU insolvencies. Paralleling home country regulation and supervision, in an insolvency home country courts would take the lead and host country courts would conduct ancillary proceedings. This structural cooperation is however mitigated by fundamental differences in bankruptcy law across countries. Host country courts may either apply home country laws that conflict with their own laws resulting in creditors being treated differently in the same court from case to case, or they may apply host country laws resulting in different creditors being treated differently from venue to venue in the same case. The former outcome is likely to be viewed as unfair and lead to political pressures, while the latter outcome will cause differential recoveries by otherwise identical creditors, leading to disincentives to cooperate if own-country creditors are to be adversely affected.

Significant differences in pro-creditor and pro-debtor orientation across EU jurisdictions raise the possibility of strategic home country selection. As in the US where managers sometimes preemptively file for Chapter 11 because it serves their interests, managers might be tempted to position their headquarters where the laws give them greatest leverage against creditors. This possibility seems remote however. To the degree that home country positioning is an active business decision, as apposed to an artifact of the company's history, the choice is more likely to be determined by factors that affect the firm as a going concern, such as taxes and corporate governance laws.[36]

Conflicts between resolution agents

In the event of an LCFO failure, the ideal cooperative resolution of the insolvency is likely to be undermined by failure of resolution authorities to cooperate in pursuit of collective solutions. Adversarial conflicts between resolution authorities or agents may even arise, particularly if US financial institutions are involved. The failure of BCCI produced a ring-fenced proceeding in the US that resulted in all US creditors being paid in full, while coordinated proceedings in Europe were subject to different, host country laws so that different European creditors were treated differently. Each venue simply pursued their own solution, in the light of their own laws and legal standards. However, information sharing between venues appears to have been cooperative, even if common solutions were not the primary goal. On the other hand, the failure of two US bank holding companies – MCorp in 1989 and Bank of New England Corp (BNEC) in 1991 – resulted in extensive litigation between regulators and trustees of the holding company. Both cases are informative of the potential for multiple resolution authorities pursuing their own interests to lead to a total break down of the cooperative/collective ideal of insolvency administration.

When a number of MCorp's subsidiary banks were closed in 1989 and taken over by the FDIC, the holding company filed for Chapter 11 protection. The Federal Reserve as supervisor for the holding company sought to compel the bankruptcy court (and trustee) to downstream assets from the holding company to the banks, in effect transferring assets from the holding company creditors to the FDIC (as creditors of the failed banks). The Federal Reserve asserted its claim under its 'source of strength' doctrine. The matter was litigated all the way to the US Supreme Court. The substantive issue (the claim that the FDIC stands ahead of other holding company creditors) was never resolved and the matter was finally settled.

Prior to the failure of BNEC in 1991, the holding company transferred substantial assets to its distressed Bank of New England subsidiary with the full knowledge of the regulators (Federal Reserve and OCC).[37] Following the asset transfers, the subsidiary banks were declared insolvent and closed, thus precipitating the bankruptcy filing of the parent holding company. Resulting litigation between the FDIC and the bankruptcy court trustee concerned, among other issues, the pre-closure asset transfers. The bankruptcy trustee sought to void the transfers (claw back the assets) on the theory that the managers and regulators knew that the subsidiary bank was insolvent and thus the transfers were fraudulent conveyances. Resulting litigation continued for years and again was finally settled without reaching an adjudicated decision (the FDIC transferred substantial sums to the holding company bankruptcy estate).

Without judging the merits of the MCorp and BNEC cases, they both point out the potential for conflicts of interest between regulators – who tended to act on behalf of the deposit insurer rather than creditors as a whole – and bankruptcy courts and their trustees – who act on behalf of the holding company creditors. These conflicts of interest resulted in costly and protracted adversarial proceedings, rather than orderly collective resolution of claims. The BCCI presents a less extreme case, but nonetheless illustrates the limits of cooperation between jurisdictions that see their primary duty in local terms (local laws, local creditors).

Recommendations

The foregoing analysis strongly suggests that the insolvency of an internationally active LCFO is likely to be costly and inefficient. Rather than providing a forum for the coordinated resolution of claims, the multiplicity of insolvency regimes that will be involved and their natural tendency to favour local interests, reinforced by positive legal requirements to do so in many cases, is likely to exacerbate the problems that bankruptcy is intended to solve. Given the potential systemic importance of such an institution, the inability of the legal framework to mitigate the costs of failure, suggests that recourse to legal closure is to be avoided if at all possible.

This does not mean that bail out is inevitable. Indeed, it may be difficult for multiple regulators, wary of committing resources to benefit other countries' creditors, to agree on a bail-out. Rather it suggests that early, pre-insolvency intervention to close or arrange recapitalization of a distressed, though still solvent firm is essential.

Early intervention however presumes both early detection and the legal and moral authority to compel remedial action. As argued above, multiple supervisors set up dynamics that undermine the oversight necessary to reliably detect distress before it is too late. Therefore, it appears to be preferable, for systemically important LCFOs at least, that a single agency conduct safety and soundness supervision of the entire firm on a consolidated worldwide basis. Such oversight is not currently provided for US financial and bank holding companies. This also means that home country supervisors must be able to examine foreign incorporated subsidiaries with the same rigour that they can examine subsidiaries in the home country. This requires cooperation between regulators to allow supervisors access and to compel foreign-parented firms to cooperate with home country supervisors.

Laws and practices that discriminate between domestic and foreign firms and creditors undermine the international supervisory cooperation necessary to ensure effective early intervention. They also make post-insolvency cooperation across jurisdictions difficult, if not impossible. Attempts by regulators to position assets in advance of insolvency necessarily rely on asymmetric information between different regulators. Such non-cooperative behaviour undermines early intervention. A narrow view by regulators that their role is to protect one potential creditor group at the expense of another undermines the purpose of consolidated supervision: to detect and minimize the costs of distress, rather than to detect distress for the purpose of minimizing losses to one group of creditors.

Finally, early intervention requires the legal means for intervening. In the US a solvent bank can be closed if it is undercapitalized or even if the regulators deem it in danger of becoming so. No such power exists to close a holding company that has not actually defaulted on its obligations. And while regulators have considerable means of influencing holding companies to take actions they desire, their legal means of forcing action should moral suasion fail, may be limited. For early intervention to work it is necessary that regulators be able to back up their moral suasion with the legal authority to close a troubled institution in an orderly manner while the institution still has positive net worth. Only then can the adversarial and destructive scramble for assets across creditors and jurisdictions be averted.

Appendix: domestic/foreign distinctions under US law

US law and regulatory practice, as it applies to financial institutions, distinguishes between foreign and domestic institutions and individuals in important ways.

- Under US law, deposits are given priority in settlement of creditors' claims of a failed bank.[38] However, the definition of a deposit effectively limits the scope of that term to domestic deposits.[39] Foreign deposits – those held at foreign branches – are not 'deposits' under the law and thus become general credits, subordinated to domestic deposits, unless payable in the US. The same is true for deposits held in US banks in International Business Facilities.
- At US branches of foreign banks, only deposits of US citizens, residents and businesses are insured.[40]
- Where a branch or agency of a foreign bank becomes insolvent, the receiver can attach (seize) all of the foreign parent's assets and property in the US even if they are part of a different non-bank subsidiary.[41] When a domestic bank becomes insolvent, the FDIC cannot seize the assets of the non-bank affiliates, it can however hold affiliated bank subsidiaries of the same holding company liable for any losses.
- In contrast to its ring-fenced or territorial approach to the failure of a foreign bank with US branches, in resolving a failed US bank, the FDIC will attempt to gain control of all the bank's worldwide assets – in effect taking a universalist stance.[42] These worldwide assets will then be used to payoff domestic depositors first, thus affording domestic creditors preferential treatment over foreign creditors.
- While Gramm–Leach–Bliley reaffirms functional regulation for Financial Holding Companies, the Federal Reserve in approving FHC applications for foreign financial institutions strongly favours them to have comprehensive consolidated supervision of the foreign parent lead bank.[43]

Notes

1 The author thanks Kern Alexander, Harald Benink, George Kaufman and participants at the conference on *The Structure of Financial Regulation* Helsinki, September 2004, for helpful comments. Any remaining errors are solely the author's. The views expressed herein are those of the author and do not necessarily reflect those of the Federal Reserve Bank of Chicago or the Federal Reserve System.

2 As explained below only 'domestic deposits' are insured (up to $100,000) and protected under depositor preference legislation.

3 A claim on the holding company would arise if the Federal Reserve induced the holding company management to 'agree' to recapitalize the bank (the Federal Reserve has considerable powers of persuasion), failing which it may issue an administrative order to do so. Such agreement, if it predated the insolvency, would have priority over the holding company's general creditors. In MCorp, the Federal Reserve attempted to impose such an administrative order after the subsidiary banks had failed and the holding company was in bankruptcy. Resulting litigation failed to clarify the Federal Reserve's right to do so, the case being settled years later with the recapitalization of the remaining solvent subsidiaries.

4 Contrast the overnight creation of the Financial Services Authority in the UK with the decades' long efforts leading up to the much less sweeping Financial Modernization Act of 1999 in the US.

5 Spong (2000).

6 The Federal Reserve must 'to the fullest extent possible' accept functional regulators reports, forego examination of functionally regulated subsidiaries, and cannot impose capital requirements on functionally regulated subsidiaries or require non-bank subsidiary assets be used to recapitalize bank subsidiaries (under the 'Source of Strength' doctrine) without the permission of the functional regulator.

7 www.fsa.gov.uk/supervision/.

8 Consolidated supervision, in contrast to functional regulation by multiple regulators, requires only that a single regulator examine and supervise a given firm in its entirety for safety and soundness. Consolidated supervision does not necessarily imply a single regulator for all financial firms – domestically or globally – nor does it mean that multiple regulators could not address different unrelated issues, for instance work place safety, fair lending or equal employment opportunities.

9 Different regulators may have additional, non-overlapping objectives: The Federal Reserve is concerned with systemic risk, the FDIC with managing deposit insurance.

10 The OCC and the state bank examiners rely, at least in part, on examination fees for their budgets. The Federal Reserve and FDIC do not.

11 See Bergman *et al.* (2003) for a discussion of whose risks are being mitigated. Cogent arguments can be made for both sides of the proposition that this is an example of beneficial competition. Bliss and Kaufman (2005a) discuss the interdependence between the special legal treatment derivatives contracts and the structure of derivatives markets.

12 Banks desiring to sell insurance, banks underwriting securities, lending (and loan syndications) by investment banks, and banks and securities firm competing in derivatives markets are just a few areas where changes in financial market practices have blurred the lines separating institutional types.

13 The assumption made here is that resources are more easily reallocated within institutions than across institutions.

14 It is noteworthy that while systemic risk is most frequently discussed in terms of the banking system, a number of real or perceived systemic crises have arisen in non-bank securities markets – the US silver crisis of 1980, the stock market crash(es) of 1987, and Long Term Capital Management in 1998 – all prompting central bank intervention.

15 This problem has important parallels in the EU with home-country/host-country issues of bank supervision, deposit insurance provision, and economic impact of bank failure. See Mayes (2005) and Eisenbeis and Kaufman (2005).

16 Even firms with similar lines of business and information needs frequently face enormous problems following mergers in linking or replacing their legacy accounting and risk management systems.

17 A striking example of this phenomenon was the failure of US intelligence agencies to cooperate prior to 9/11 and even within agencies for headquarters to cooperate with field offices.

18 Progress has been uneven at best, and cultural, political and structural barriers continue to impede cross-border expansion and consolidation. However, EU financial liberalization legislation is decidedly aimed at achieving a unified financial services market and progress has been made in the Nordic countries and the new members states which did not have entrenched domestic banking institutions prior to 1990.

19 Economic reasons are more likely to determine strategic home country decisions than deliberate efforts to elude supervision. However, home country regulatory deference has in the past been a contributing factor to outright fraud. BCCI was domiciled in Luxembourg, but carried out no significant business in that country. As a result Luxembourg regulators had little interest in supervising it (and limited resources in any case), leaving it effectively unsupervised on a global basis.

20 Mayes (2005) discusses these issues with particular reference to in Nordic countries and deposit insurance, while Eisenbeis and Kaufman (2005) look at countries that effectively outsource there banking systems to foreign parented banks (e.g. New Zealand).

21 See Bliss (2003) for a discussion.

22 There is a tension between the protection of the collective interests of creditors (and other stakeholders) on the one hand, and the contractual and legal priority of claims and treatment of security interests on the other. The discussion of this problem is beyond the scope of this chapter.

23 Derivatives and some other financial market contracts are noteworthy exceptions to the ability of courts to prevent creditors from acting outside of the bankruptcy proceeding. See Bergman *et al.* (2003).

24 The FDIC becomes a creditor by paying off insured deposits and then taking over (subrogating) their claims. The FDIC may also become a creditor through pre-insolvency extension of credit, though this is increasingly rare.

25 While US banking law provides for conservatorship of a distressed bank, in practice, US bank insolvency inevitably results in the sale or liquidation of an insolvent bank.

26 For instance, in the case of BCCI, the main European proceeding was in Luxembourg with UK courts acting in an ancillary role. However, the UK courts applied UK netting rules, which differed from those used by the Luxembourg court. Since most of BCCI's European assets were located in the UK this ruling lead to many UK creditors realizing higher recoveries than creditors whose claims were settled in Luxembourg.

27 See Bliss and Kaufman (2005b), for a detailed discussion.

28 These include the Federal Home Loan Banks, and mortgage agencies Fannie Mae and Freddie Mac.

29 The federally-chartered housing agencies – Federal Home Loan Banks, Fannie Mae and Freddie Mac – are exempted from the Bankruptcy Code, though no alternative venue is provided for liquidating them or resolving their creditors claims.

30 However, since the parent bank holding company falls under the Bankruptcy Code, the holding company's creditors can initiate proceedings if a holding company event of default occurs. This is usually the result of prior or imminent closure of the lead bank subsidiary. It is unclear whether initiation of a bank-

ruptcy proceeding against a bank or financial holding company would force bank regulators to move against the subsidiary banks. It seems likely that this might happen if only to shield the bank's assets from the bankruptcy court and holding company creditors.

31 Under PCA rules banks should be closed when their equity is still marginally positive, leaving uninsured depositors and general creditors protected. In fact, it is rarely the case that general creditors receive payment and frequently the case that uninsured depositors suffer losses.

32 It is possible in some cases to sue the FDIC for actual, though not punitive, damages, after the fact, but not usually possible to stay the FDIC's actions.

33 The FDIC itself expects that this will usually be the case. '[i]nasmuch as most liabilities of a failed institution are deposit liabilities, the practical effect of depositor preference in most situations is to eliminate any recovery for unsecured general creditors.' FDIC Resolution Handbook, 2003: 72; available online.

34 No explicit affirmative granting of powers asserted under the doctrine appears in legislation. Several courts have ruled that the Federal Reserve may impose source for strength requirements of limited duration as a condition for approving regulatory actions. Broader claims of unlimited duration or unrelated to a regulatory approval process have not been supported by courts. The source of strength doctrine is mentioned in Gramm–Leach–Bliley only for purposes of prohibiting its application to subsidiaries regulated by other agencies without their approval (while remaining silent on whether it can be applied to the holding company and unregulated subsidiaries).

35 Bliss and Kaufman (2005b) provides a more detailed comparative analysis of US bankruptcy and bank insolvency law.

36 In the US the state of Delaware developed a reputation for having manager-friendly courts, and over time developed a body of case law that favoured the interests of managers over those of stockholders and other parties. As a result, a large fraction of businesses were incorporated in Delaware. More recently, other states have adopted similar laws to attract incorporations. Thus, strategic incorporation was an impetus for legal harmonization, though advocates of stockholder rights may decry the legal philosophy on which harmonization converged – an example of race to the bottom.

37 It is unclear to what degree regulators encouraged the asset transfers.

38 12 U.S.C. 1821(d)(11)(A).

39 12 U.S.C. 1813(l)(5)(A). See Curtis, 2000 for a full discussion.

40 12 U.S.C. 1813(m)(2)(A).

41 12 U.S.C. 3102(j)(1).

42 Mattingly *et al.*, 1999: 270.

43 Federal Reserve Reg. Y §225.92(e)(2).

References

Bergman, W.J., Bliss, R.R., Johnson, C.A. and Kaufman, G.G. (2003) 'Netting, financial contracts, and banks: the economic implications', in Kaufman, G. (ed.) *Market Discipline in Banking: Theory and Evidence*, Vol. 15: *Research in Financial Services*, Amsterdam: Elsevier Press, pp. 303–4.

Bliss, R.R. (2003) 'Bankruptcy law and large complex financial organizations: a primer', Federal Reserve Bank of Chicago *Economic Perspectives* First Quarter: 48–58.

Bliss, R.R. and Kaufman, G.G. (2005a) 'Derivatives and systemic risk: netting, collateral, and closeout', Wake Forest University, Working Paper.

Bliss, R.R. and Kaufman, G.G. (2005b), 'US corporate and bank insolvency regimes: an economic comparison and evaluation', Wake Forest University, Working Paper.

Curtis, C.T. (2000) 'The status of foreign deposits under the federal depositor-preference law', *University of Pennsylvania Journal of International Economic Law* 21(Summer): 237–71.

Goodhart, C.A.E. (2005) 'Multiple regulators and resolutions', in Evanoff, D. and Kaufman, G. (eds) *Systemic Financial Crises: Resolving Large Bank Insolvencies*, forthcoming.

Kaufman, G.G. (1997) 'The New Depositor Preference Act: time inconsistency in action', *Managerial Finance* 23(11): 56–63.

Eisenbeis, R.E. and Kaufman, G.G. (2005) 'Bank crisis resolution and foreign owned banks', Loyola University Chicago, Working Paper.

Mattingly, J.V., Misback, A., Milenkovich, M., Hansen, J.M. and Sommer, J.H. (1999) 'Country report: United States', in Giovanoli, M. and Heinrich, G. (eds) *International Bank Insolvencies: A Central Bank Perspective*, Vol. 12: *The International Banking, Finance and Economic Law Series*, J.J. Norton (ed.), The Hague: Kluwer Law International.

Mayes, D.G. (2005) 'The role of the safety net in resolving large financial institutions', in Evanoff, D. and Kaufman, G. (eds) *Systemic Financial Crises: Resolving Large Bank Insolvencies*, forthcoming.

Rosen, R.J. (2003) 'Is three a crowd? Competition among regulators in banking', *Journal of Money Credit and Banking* 35(6): 967–98.

Spong, K. (2000) *Banking Regulation: Its Purposes, Implementation, and Effects* 5th edn, Federal Reserve Bank of Kansas City.

**COMMENT: THE INSTITUTIONAL FRAMEWORK OF US
PRUDENTIAL REGULATION – SOME UNRESOLVED
PROBLEMS**

Kern Alexander

My remarks focus on the legal framework of US banking regulation and
the economic rationale it serves in promoting safe and sound banking
systems. Robert Bliss's paper addresses the institutional complexities and
policy dilemmas that have confronted US bank regulators in promoting
an efficient supervisory and insolvency regime for banking institutions.
The chapter raises a number of important issues regarding the US
approach for protecting depositors in US financial institutions and resolving bank failures. US banking law requires US regulators to wind-up an
insolvent US bank by placing the interests of US depositors first at the
expense of the claims of foreign depositors and foreign non-deposit creditors. Professor Bliss argues that this framework creates an incentive for
foreign depositors and non-deposit creditors to make a run on a US bank
in times of financial distress. Moreover, the focus of the Federal Deposit
Insurance Corporation (FDIC) on protecting depositors might lead it to
delay closure and resolution of a failed bank in order to protect US depositors. He also suggests that the Federal Reserve Board of Governors and
the FDIC 'do not recognize the concept of limited liability for equity positions in banks' and therefore can act to protect the interests of depositors
in a US bank by going after the bank/financial holding company that
owns or controls the failed bank by imposing source of strength charges
on the holding company. This is an important and complex area of US
banking regulation and what I do in my comments is to set forth some of
the basic principles of US bank prudential regulation and the law of
depositor protection. I then analyse some of the case law that applies to
the regulation of bank/financial holding companies and show, in a more
precise way, how the source of strength requirements apply to bank/finan-
cial holding companies. I conclude with the implications of this under the
Gramm–Leach–Bliley Act (Financial Services Modernisation Act of 1999)
and discuss the risks to financial stability.

The rationale of US banking regulation

The United States has traditionally had a federal-state structure for
banking regulation. Federal and state regulators share responsibility for
overseeing the prudential soundness of US banks and foreign banks operating in the US. Before the 1980s, a foreign bank could obtain a state
bank charter without seeking approval from a federal regulator.[1] This
fragmented institutional structure of regulation was not well-equipped to
deal with the challenges of globalized and deregulated banking markets.

For instance, liberalized foreign exchange markets in the 1970s led US banks to become more exposed to forex risk and volatility in the whole-sale banking market. This led to increased systemic risk in the payment system, resulting in several major bank failures. Deregulation of banking activities in the 1980s led to more bank failures and to a collapse of the savings and loan industry requiring a government bailout (Mishkin, 2004). Although US regulators had broad powers to deal with these problems, the various federal and state regulators with responsibility for banking supervision often had different and conflicting objectives, thus undermining effective supervision.

An important objective of US banking regulation has been to address the wide range of potential agency problems within financial institutions. The banking literature has examined these principal–agent problems from a number of perspectives, including the major stakeholder groups, such as shareholders, creditors, depositors/customers and supervisory bodies (Allen and Gale, 2000; Stiglitz, 1989). Agency problems arise because responsibility for decision-making is directly or indirectly delegated from one stakeholder group to another in situations where objectives differ between stakeholder groups and where complete information which would allow further control to be exerted over the decision maker is not readily available. In the case of financial institutions, some of the most studied agency problems involve depositors and management/shareholders, and supervisors and management. While that perspective underpins the major features of the design of regulatory structures – deposit insurance and capital adequacy requirements, etc. – incentive problems that arise because of the conflicts between management and owners have become a focus of recent attention; Biais and Pagano (2002) discuss conflicts between shareholders and management.

US bank regulators have sought to address the agency problems inherent in financial institutions as part of the broader statutory objective of promoting the safety and soundness of the financial system. Indeed, the concept of prudential regulation in US banking law grew out of the vague statutory requirement that banks should be managed and operated in a safe and sound manner (Holzman, 2000). The 'safety and soundness' principle has been the driving force in US banking regulation. This has involved a number of regulatory techniques, including capital adequacy and fit and proper standards for bank managers.[2] US regulation has also set strict standards for the auditors and accountants of banking institutions with the potential for civil and criminal liability for failing to report accurately the financial condition of banks and other regulated financial institutions. In the US and UK, the soundness principle and prudential regulatory standards provide the basis for the development of standards and principles of corporate governance for banking institutions. US and UK regulators have therefore adopted specific standards to regulate the management practices of banks in order to reduce conflicts of interest and self-dealing. These efforts to address agency problems within financial institutions are essential to protect the interests of not only bank depositors and shareholders, but also the broader public, which is exposed to the social costs of bank failure.

In addition, US bank regulators have always had broad authority to take civil enforcement actions and to impose administrative penalties and civil sanctions on banks or their directors and employees for taking actions that threaten financial safety and soundness. This type of discretion, however, can be criticized on the grounds that it places too much power in the hands of the regulator to act in a way that some might view to be arbitrary and capricious. Indeed, the discretionary power of the regulator may result in discriminatory treatment between banks or individuals that might violate human rights legislation. Moreover, it might violate a person's right to have civil penalties or sanctions reviewed by a fair and impartial tribunal.[3]

Regulatory discretion and US case law

Regulatory discretion has been an important element of US banking regulation. One reason for this is that US banking law has never defined the phrase 'unsafe and unsound practices', nor does it provide any examples of practices that might be classified as unsafe or unsound. Congress, however, observed in committee hearings in 1966 that the phrase 'unsafe and unsound' has the following meaning:

> [U]nsafe or unsound practices' has a central meaning which can and must be applied to constantly changing factual circumstances. Generally speaking, an 'unsafe or unsound practice' embraces any action, or lack of action, which is contrary to generally accepted standards of prudent operation, the possible consequences of which, if continued, would be abnormal risk or loss or damage to an institution, its shareholders, or the agencies administering the insurance fund.[4]

Based on this broad meaning, US banking law has implied a discretionary power for US banking supervisory agencies to establish and apply standards of prudential supervision for banking institutions.[5] In the 1970s the US courts had recognized this regulatory discretion to establish prudential standards so long as the standards adopted were rationally related to legislative objectives set by Congress.[6]

However, critics viewed regulatory authority in this area to be too broad, and based on subjective factors that were not defined in regulation or statute (Harrell, 1995). The Fifth Circuit Court of Appeal in 1983 addressed this issue in the *Bellaire* case[7] when it overturned a US court's affirmation of a regulator's decision to impose higher capital standards on one bank, viewed by the regulator to be weak, as compared to the capital standards imposed by the regulator on other banks with a similar risk profile. The regulator had grounded its decision to impose higher capital charges on its statutory authority to promote 'safety and soundness' of the banking system. But the federal banking statute and regulation had not provided any specific criteria to serve as a basis to justify the regulator in treating one bank differently from the others. In the absence of any published statutory or regulatory criteria that demonstrated a rational reason to treat one bank differently from another, the court found the regulator's decision to impose higher capital charges on one bank in relation to others to be a violation of equal protection under the law and due process of law. The court essentially held that the regulator had acted arbitrarily and capriciously by treating the bank in a discriminatory manner on the basis of standards and criteria that were not apparent in statute or regulation. The implication of the holding was, that if Congress had expressly provided criteria in statute or had delegated power to the regulator to set criteria in regulations to justify the discriminatory treatment of banks that were a threat to the safety and soundness of the banking system, then such regulatory decisions would not have been arbitrary or capricious and therefore not in violation of US law.

International Lending Supervision Act of 1983

In the aftermath of the *Bellaire* decision and the Latin American sovereign debt crisis, Congress was concerned that the authority of the bank regulatory agencies 'to exercise independent discretion' in imposing prudential requirements on banks had been unnecessarily restricted.[8] Congress responded by enacting the International Lending Supervision Act (ILSA), which provides that each federal banking agency shall require, by regulation, banking institutions to disclose to the public, information regarding material foreign country exposure in relation to assets and capital.[9] The ILSA also requires each appropriate federal banking agency to cause banking institutions to achieve and maintain adequate capital by establishing minimum levels of capital for such banking institutions and by using such other methods that the relevant agency deems appropriate.[10] Each federal banking regulator shall have the authority to establish minimum capital levels and management standards for a banking institution according to discretionary authority exercised in the particular circumstances of the banking institution.[11] ILSA also conferred express enforcement powers on US federal bank regulators through the use of capital directives.[12] In other words, the federal banking regulator had the discretionary authority to take remedial action against banks or the management of banks who had failed to manage the bank in a safe and sound manner, for instance, if the bank had failed to maintain capital at or above the minimum level or to have committed 'an unsafe or unsound practice' within the meaning of the federal banking statutes.[13] The broad authority granted in the ILSA to federal banking regulators effectively overruled the *Bellaire* decision. The courts now interpreted the phrase 'unsafe or unsound practice', as set forth in ILSA, to be a deliberately flexible concept designed to give the regulators 'the ability to adapt to changing business problems and practices'.[14]

Deposit insurance – the Federal Deposit Insurance Corporation and FDICIA 1991

The Federal Deposit Insurance Corporation (FDIC) was established by statute during the Great Depression in 1931 to provide deposit insurance to the depositors of failed US banking institutions. The FDIC is charged with the difficult task of administering the deposit insurance fund. Its funding depends on risk premium payments (and the interest those payments earn) made into the fund by covered depository institutions. During its first 60 years, it assessed the insured institutions at the same flat rate for deposit–insurance coverage. Although the FDIC was crucial for restoring depositor confidence in the US banking system following the 1940s and undoubtedly played a key role in the recapitalization of US banks, it has been criticized for creating moral hazard among bank managers and depositors who perceive, respectively, that they can be bailed out for making poor lending decisions with depositor's money.

In 1991, as a response to savings and loan crisis of the 1980s, Congress sought to mitigate the moral hazard problem by enacting the Federal Deposit Insurance Corporation Improvement Act of 1991 (FDICIA). The risk premium charged on each deposit was made more risk sensitive based on the risk weightings of each depository institution. An institution, for example, that has low levels of capital as a percentage of its assets and liabilities will be given a higher risk weighting and thus be required to pay higher insurance premiums into the insurance fund. The assessments that produce revenue for the deposit insurance fund enable the FDIC to absorb losses arising from a crisis caused by financial institution failure.

Under FDICIA, the FDIC has been vested with discretion to make determinations of unsafe and unsound banking practices in violation of the FDICIA that would place the insurance fund at risk. Indeed, US courts have adopted a standard of review under federal banking law for determining the lawfulness of agency action in regulating prudential standards of banking institutions. Indeed, in *Doolin Security Savings Bank* v. *F.D.I.C.*, the Fourth Circuit Court of Appeals ruled that the applicable standard of review under 12 U.S.C. §1818(h)(2) for determining whether the FDIC abused its discretion in establishing a particular risk-based capital adequacy scheme for federally-insured depository institutions was that a Court:

> [C]annot reverse the FDIC Board action unless the findings upon which it is based are not supported by substantial evidence on the record as a whole, or unless the remedies formulated by the Board constitute an abuse of discretion or are otherwise arbitrary and capricious.[15]

In exercising its authority, the FDIC has discretion to adopt a risk-based capital assessment scheme and procedure structure under which the FDIC may terminate an institution's insured status and terminate its banking licence if it determines that the depository institution's practices are unsafe and unsound.[16] Before analysing this statutory scheme, it is important to provide a general background of the FDIC deposit insurance statute.

FDICIA established a risk-based assessment system under which the premiums paid by federally insured financial institutions are based on risks the institutions pose to the insurance fund. Specifically, Section 302(a) of the FDICIA requires the FDIC to establish final risk-based assessment regulations, and section 302(f) authorizes the FDIC to promulgate transitional regulations governing the time period between the flat-rate assessment system and the risk-based assessment system required under section 302(a). The FDIC adopted the transitional regulations on 15 September 1992,[17] and subsequently adopted the final regulations on 17 June, 1993.[18] Both regulations were codified under Title 12 of the Code of Federal Regulations §327.[19]

In section 302(a) of the FDICIA, Congress defined a 'risk-based assessment system' as:

> a system for calculating a depository institution's semiannual assessment based on:
>
> i the probability that the deposit insurance fund will incur a loss with respect to the institution, taking into consideration the risks attributable to:
>
>> I different categories and concentrations of assets;
>> II different categories and concentrations of liabilities, both insured and uninsured, contingent and non-contingent; and
>> III any other factors the [FDIC] determines are relevant to assessing such probability;
>
> ii the likely amount of any such loss; and
> iii the revenue needs of the deposit fund.[20]

The FDIC has responded by using a risk-based classification system based on detailed reports and expert evaluations of the financial condition of an institution. The FDIC's regulations require the agency to analyse objective 'capital' factors as well as subjective 'supervisory' factors.[21] The capital factors determine the institution's 'capital group', signified as a 1, 2 or 3 in the risk classification. The supervisory risk factors determine the institution's 'supervisory sub-group', signified as an A, B or C in the risk classification.[22] Further, the regulations provide that the FDIC will assign an institution a supervisory sub-group based on the FDIC's 'consideration of supervisory evaluations provided by the institution's primary federal regulator'.[23]

Issues of constitutional due process

In determining whether FDIC procedures for issuing capital directives satisfied due process requirements of the US Constitution, the Fifth Circuit Court Appeals held in *FDIC* v. *Coushatta*,[24] that the FDIC must adhere to a three-factor inquiry that courts are required to use in determining what type of procedures satisfy due process before the government may deprive an entity of a property interest protected by the Due Process Clause of the Fifth or Fourteenth Amendments.[25] The three factors are: (1) the private interest that will be affected by the official action; (2) the risk of an erroneous deprivation of such interest through the procedures used, and the probable value, if any, of additional or substitute procedural safeguards; and (3) the Government's interest, including the function involved and the fiscal and administrative burdens that the additional or substitute requirement would entail.[26] Essentially, due process is flexible and calls for such procedural protections as the particular situation demands.

In assessing prudential supervisory practices, the Fifth Circuit in *Coushatta* concluded that procedures for determining capital adequacy and risk-based supervisory ratings satisfied due process. The court reasoned that the private interest of accurate capital directives is significant but that the risk of an erroneous deprivation of property because of the application of a directive is marginal. The court noted that a pre-deprivation evidentiary hearing (as opposed to an informal hearing) was not warranted because a bank has adequate opportunity to respond to the notice through written procedures. Also, the court found that the government's interests is substantial because delay would considerably weaken the benefits from a prompt directive, which seeks to rectify a bank's troublesome undercapitalization. Similarly, in *Doolin,* the Fourth Circuit reviewed the procedures allowing a bank to challenge a FDIC determination of risk-based capital ratings, and found the procedure to be in compliance with constitutional standards of due process.[27]

The FDIC procedure allowing banks to contest their risk-based capital ratings meets the due process test because it provides banks with notice of its risk classification and an opportunity to challenge the classification through the review procedures established in the regulations.[28] Accordingly, the Courts have held that the due process clause does not require a pre-deprivation evidentiary hearing before a particular risk-based weighting is applied to banks' capital position.[29]

Similarly, the Office of Thrift Supervision[30] has discretion to determine whether the business activities of savings banks are 'unsafe or unsound practices' and thus, are in violation of prudential supervisory standards of federal banking law. Such determinations may only be overruled by a court if it concludes that the agency action was arbitrary, capricious or an abuse of discretion, nor is there sufficient evidence to overcome the presumption of regularity and correctness afforded to the appointment.

The Courts have generally upheld the discretionary authority of the OTS to apply prudential supervisory standards to federal savings banks that rely on a combination of objective and subjective standards for determining whether the bank was acting in a prudential manner.[31] These prudential assessments produce specific composite ratings of each savings bank. Banks may challenge the risk-based assessments that are applied to their activities by the OTS. The review procedure involves a three-tier administrative review whereby an institution may challenge its risk-based ratings at the district level of the OTS, and then may appeal the decision to the OTS Director. Once administrative review with the OTS is exhausted, an institution may seek review before an administrative law judge pursuant to the Administrative Procedure Act.[32]

Under the above legislation and regulations, federal banking regulators are thus given the authority to establish required minimum capital levels and to deny particular transactions or activities by banking institutions if they constituted 'unsafe and unsound' banking practice and to have general statutory enforcement powers to effect these standards.[33]

The challenge posed by bank holding companies

According to Akhgbe and Whyte (2004), bank holding companies and financial conglomerates pose a special type of agency problem for regulators because these financial companies often own separate subsidiaries and divisions that perform various financial functions, often in multiple jurisdictions. The complex structure of conglomerates and financial holding companies poses a particular type of agency problem which is not necessarily the same as within the individual bank or financial institution. This is an important question because most banks and financial institutions operate within holding companies and multi-national financial conglomerates that are composed of hundreds of subsidiaries and affiliate companies that operate in multiple jurisdictions. What is the nature of the principal–agent problem within these banking groups or conglomerates? It may depend on the structure of the management within the conglomerate. For instance, does the holding company have a centralized management structure controlled by the board of directors and managers of one company, or is it more diffuse with management authority shared among several or more subsidiaries and affiliates within the group? Identifying the exact nature of the principal–agent problem will likely depend upon which company or individual(s) exercise, or have the ability to exercise, control over the group's operations. Saunders *et al.* (1990) argue that this will depend on whether there is alignment of interests and incentives between managers and the block shareholders. This view is based on the notion that there are two main factors affecting risk taking within the financial holding company: managers' incentive and block ownership.

The goal of regulating bank and financial holding companies should be to align the incentives of the managers and directors of the holding company with those of the managers and directors of the subsidiaries which they control. The regulator has a further responsibility to ensure that the incentives of the holding company and its subsidiaries are socially optimal in so far as the social costs of financial risk-taking should be minimized throughout the conglomerate. The evidence from block ownership in bank holding companies shows that the presence of safety nets (e.g. lender of last resort) increases the incentive for risk-taking in holding company structures, and these incentives can be difficult to estimate because most financial holding companies in G10 countries operate in multiple jurisdictions, which have different levels of safety net protection.

US regulation of bank holding companies: the case law

Since 1956, US banking law has sought to address the risks posed by managerial incentives and block shareholder interests within bank holding companies by adopting legislation that governs the structure and activities of these financial entities. Bank holding companies are a type of financial conglomerate. In modern financial markets, most banks operate in holding companies. In these corporate groups, banks may exercise control, or be controlled, or simply be affiliated to other banks and companies within the holding company structure. The holding company structure of banks creates particular principal–agent tensions that require a different approach than what would be the case for individual banks.[34] The Bank Holding Act of 1956 and the Financial Services Modernisation Act of 1999 attempt to address the principal–agent problem within the group structure of banks and financial firms. To do so, the Board of Governors of the Federal Reserve System (Federal Reserve) have been granted broad authority to adopt regulations to govern the management of banking and financial holding companies. These broad supervisory powers extend to considering and approving any proposal or transaction by a banking institution, or its affiliate, or the holding company which controls such a banking institution, that would divert earnings, diminish capital or otherwise impede such banking institution's progress in achieving its minimum capital level.[35] The Federal Reserve may deny such approval for particular transactions where it determines that certain management practices or transactions would adversely affect the ability of the banking institution to comply with such a plan. These powers to regulate the management of bank and financial holding companies have been influenced by judicial decisions that have developed two important doctrines of prudential regulation: *the source of strength requirement* and *change of bank control.*

Supervisory authority for bank holding companies: the institutional gap

Statutory regulation of US bank holding companies began when Congress enacted the Bank Holding Company Act of 1956 (BHCA).[36] The congressional intent behind the BHCA was to prevent the concentration of ownership and control of banking facilities, and to prevent the combination of both banking and non-banking enterprises so that banks would not engage in business wholly-unrelated to banking.[37] The BHCA also addressed a concern regarding monopolistic control of credit and directed the Federal Reserve to review bank acquisitions under several standards, including financial and managerial soundness, and access to capital.[38]

Specifically, the BHCA grants the Board supervisory control over the formation, structure and operation of bank holding companies and their non-bank subsidiaries. Section 3(a) of the Act[39] provides that no company may acquire control of a bank without prior approval by the Board. In determining whether to approve an application, section 3(c) of the Act[40] directs the Board to consider 'the financial and managerial resources and future prospects of the company or companies and the banks concerned'.

The Board has argued that the Act has provided its broad authority to oversee the safety and soundness of bank holding companies and the financial institutions that operate within them. The Board has also argued that section 3(c) grants it statutory authority to impose source of strength charges on bank holding companies. The alternative view has been that the Board has authority to review the safety and soundness of bank holding companies and their banks and to impose source of strength charges *only* when the bank holding company has applied to acquire or merge with a bank.

The former view is supported by Board's regulations adopted pursuant to its authority under the BHCA. The Board adopted Regulation Y in 1984 which provides:

§225.4 Corporate Practices

  a *Bank holding company policy and operations.*
      (1) A bank holding company shall serve as a source of financial and managerial strength to its subsidiary banks and shall not contuct [sic] its operations in an unsafe or sound manner.[41]

In April 1987, the Board reinforced this view by publishing a policy statement that provided:

It is the policy of the Board that in serving as a source of strength to its subsidiary banks, a *bank holding company should stand ready to use available resources to provide adequate capital funds to its subsidiary banks* during periods of financial stress or adversity and should maintain the financial flexibility and capital-raising capacity to obtain additional resources for assisting its subsidiary banks...

A bank holding company's failure to meet its obligation to serve as a source of strength to its subsidiary bank(s), including an unwillingness to provide appropriate assistance to a troubled or failing bank, will generally be considered an unsafe or unsound banking practice in violation of Regulation Y, or both...[42]

The Board also asserts broad authority to adopt whatever regulatory measures are necessary in this area by relying on section 5(b) of the BHCA[43] that states:

The Board is authorised to issue such regulations and orders as may be necessary to enable it to administer and carry out the purposes of this chapter and prevent evasions thereof.

The case law has generally supported the Board's authority in this area. In *Board of Governors* v. *First Lincolnwood Corp.*,[44] the Supreme Court upheld the Board's authority to impose source of strength requirements on a bank holding company as part of its application to acquire a bank. The issue was whether the Board could deny the application based *solely* on the financial unsoundness of a bank within the holding company, or was the Board also required to show that the application would have had an uncompetitive effect on the banking industry. The Supreme Court held that it was permissible for the Board to rely *solely* on a showing of financial unsoundness as grounds to reject the holding company's application. The Supreme Court stated in relevant part:

The language of the statute supports the Board's interpretation of section 3(c) as an authorisation to deny applications on grounds of financial and managerial unsoundness even in the absence of any anti-competitive impact. Section 3(c) directs the Board to consider the financial and managerial resources and future prospects of the applicants and banks concerned '[i]n every case,' not just in cases in which the Board finds that the transaction will have an anti-competitive effect...[45]

The Court, however, was careful to state that its holding was not intended to extend the Board's authority to day-to-day supervision of banks, but allowed the Board to disapprove an application to prevent the formation of an unsound holding company.

In the dissent's view, the Board, by looking beyond the transaction before it, attempted to exercise day-to-day regulatory authority over banks which Congress denied to it and conferred on the Comptroller.

> We disagree with the basic premise of the dissent's argument. As the Board found, the *effect* of this transaction would have been the formation of a financially unsound bank holding company. Thus, the Board's attempt to prevent this effect and to induce the respondent to form an enterprise that met the Board's standards of financial soundness was entirely consistent with the language [of the statute].[46]

In *First Lincolnwood*, the Supreme Court relied on the express provisions of section 3(c) that required the Board to consider the financial soundness of the subsidiary bank in determining whether to approve a holding company's application; however, the Court made it clear that it did not interpret the BHCA as granting the Board authority to regulate the day-to-day financial soundness of the subsidiary banks.

In a similar case, the Supreme Court in *Board of Governors v. Dimension Financial Corp.*,[47] considered whether the Board exceeded its authority in expanding its regulatory authority to impose source of strength charges on non-bank firms within bank holding company structures. Under Regulation Y, the Board had defined non-bank institutions or non-bank financial firms as being subject to source of strength requirements. The Court rejected this position by holding that the Board had exceeded its statutory authority in attempting to include non-bank financial firms within its regulatory authority.

First Lincolnwood and *Dimension Financial Corp.* are narrowly written and expressly limit the Board's authority, in respect to granting or denying a holding company application, to consider the financial and managerial soundness of bank holding companies and their subsidiary banks. Section 3(c) of the BHCA expressly grants this authority to the Board. The courts, however, have rejected authority for the Board to review the financial and managerial soundness of subsidiary banks and the holding company and to impose source of strength charges following the approval of a holding company's application. And *First Lincolnwood* finds this regulatory authority lacking in the day-to-day operations of a subsidiary bank.

The Fifth Circuit Court of Appeal further supported this view in *MCorp Financial Inc.* v. *Board of Governors of the Federal Reserve System.*[48] *MCorp* presented the legal issue of whether the Federal Reserve Board had the authority to order a bank holding company to transfer funds to its ailing subsidiary when the order was not part of the holding company's application to acquire a bank. The Board had argued that MCorp's failure to transfer its assets to a weak banking subsidiary was an unsafe and unsound practice in violation of sections 1818(b)(1) and (3).[49] The Board argued that MCorp had failed to act as a source of strength for its bank subsidiaries in violation of Board regulation and policies, and that this failure constituted an unsafe or unsound practice. The Board therefore imposed source of strength charges on MCorp requiring it to inject funds into its banking subsidiaries. MCorp sought judicial review of the Board's order by arguing that the Board did not have supervisory authority to issue source of strength capital directives to a bank holding company or to its banks unless the order was part of the Board's review of the company's proposed acquisition or takeover of a bank.

The *MCorp* case stands for the proposition that the Board does not have the authority to compel a solvent bank holding company to transfer its funds to its troubled subsidiaries, even for the purpose of maintaining the subsidiaries' financial soundness.[50] The enforcement of such a source of strength regulation would require a holding company to transfer funds to its troubled subsidiary banks. The Fifth Circuit held that such a prudential requirement 'can hardly be considered a generally accepted international standard of prudential operation'.[51] The court observed that such a transfer of funds would require the holding company to disregard its own corporation's separate legal status and would amount to a wasting of the holding company's assets in violation of its duty to its shareholders. Further, the court noted that one of the main purposes of the BHCA was to separate banking from commercial enterprises, and that purpose would not be served if the Board is permitted to treat a holding company as merely an extension of its subsidiary bank.[52] On appeal, the US Supreme Court essentially left intact the Court's ruling regarding the Board's authority to impose source of strength requirements *only* in situations when the holding company has applied to acquire or merge with a bank.[53]

The regulation of financial holding companies: the case of the Financial Services Modernisation Act 1999

In 2000, Congress enacted the Financial Services Modernisation Act of 1999 (otherwise known as the Gramm–Leach–Bliley Act)[54] which is the most significant US banking legislation since the Glass–Steagall Act of 1933. The statute authorized the Federal Reserve Board to adopt regulations that allow bank holding companies or foreign banks to apply for a universal bank structure at the holding company level. The new universal holding companies are known as 'Financial Holding Companies' (FHC) and would be able to establish wholly-owned subsidiaries that can provide an array of financial services that were previously restricted under previous banking law. For our purposes, the prudential supervision provisions are most important. Section 103 of the Act requires that for a banking holding company to make an election to become an FHC, it must show that its subsidiaries are 'well capitalized' and that affiliated or subsidiary institutions are 'well-managed'.

A well-capitalized bank essentially means that a bank has and maintains at least the capital levels required to be well-capitalized under the capital adequacy regulations or guidelines applicable to the bank under the 'prompt corrective action' standards of section 38 of the Federal Deposit Insurance Act.[55] The Act does not require that an FHC meets specific consolidated capital standards to operate as a holding company as a condition for engaging in expanded financial activities through non-bank subsidiaries. However, because an FHC is also a bank holding company (BHC), the Federal Reserve Board's Regulation Y[56] requiring financial and managerial soundness for a BHC and its bank subsidiaries when it applies to acquire a bank will also apply to FHCs when they apply to acquire banks. These source of strength requirements will also apply to BHCs and foreign banks when they apply to the Board for FHC status.

Conclusion

Professor Bliss provides an interesting critique of the institutional framework US banking regulation and the incentives of bank regulators, especially in the areas of deposit insurance and insolvency. My comment builds on this critique by examining the legal framework of deposit insurance and the existing institutional and legal gaps for the regulation of US bank/financial holding companies. Although the US Congress has enacted banking legislation that delegates broad discretion to bank regulators, the US courts exert active oversight in key areas of US bank prudential regulation. The Bank Holding Company Act is a case in point, where Congress authorized the Board to exercise supervisory control over the formation, structure and operation of bank holding companies and their non-bank subsidiaries. No company can acquire control or ownership of a bank without prior approval of the Board. In reviewing an application, the statute directs the Board to consider 'the financial and managerial resources and future prospects of the company or companies and the banks concerned'.[57] US court cases, however, have narrowly construed the Board's powers in this area.

In *First Lincolnwood* and *MCorp.*, the US courts restricted the Board's efforts to exercise supervisory oversight of bank holding companies and their banking institutions to periods when holding companies have applied to acquire or merge with banks. These decisions have exacerbated existing institutional gaps in the US federal bank regulatory regime and pose a risk to systemic stability. Moreover, Congress did not address these problems when it enacted the Gramm–Leach–Bliley Act of 1999 with the result that the Federal Reserve Board can only impose source of strength charges when a bank or bank holding company is applying to become a financial holding company, or when a financial holding company applies to acquire or merge with a bank. Outside these situations, the only regulator who can act is the relevant functional regulator. These cases suggest that, when regulators attempt to fill the institutional gaps in prudential oversight that exist in a federal-state system of government, US courts will be quick to strike down their actions as exceeding statutory authority. Such narrow legal interpretations of statutory authority may not be conducive for building an efficient prudential regulatory regime in today's rapidly changing global financial markets.

Notes

1 This allowed the Bank of Credit and Commerce International SA (a Luxembourg holding company) to purchase control over a US state-chartered bank in Georgia without obtaining approval from federal regulators. *United States* v. *Bank of Credit and Commerce International SA* No 88-330-CR-T (MD Fla. Jan 16, 1990).

2 It should not be forgotten that the 'soundness' principle was derived from the supervisory practices of the Bank of England which emphasized the need for fit and proper standards for senior managers and directors of banks. See discussion in Alexander (2004).

3 See art 6(1) of the European Convention on Human Rights. See also, *R (on the application of Fleurose)* v. *Securities and Futures Authority Ltd* [2001] EWHC Admin 292, [2001] 2 All ER (Comm 481).

4 Financial Institutions Supervisory Act of 1966, Hearings on S. 3158 before the House Committee on banking and Currency, 89th Congress, 2d Sess., at 49–50 (1966).

5 It should also be mentioned that Congress has expressly delegated enforcement authority to the relevant federal bank regulator to issue 'Cease and Desist' orders against an insured depository institution or against an institution-affiliated party who has, is or is about to engage in unsafe or unsound banking practices or who has violated, is violating or is about to violate a law, rule or regulation. 12 USC sec. 1818 (b)(1).

6 *First National Bank of Eden* v. *Department of Treasury* 568 F.2d 610, 611 (8th Cir. 1978) ('upholding Comptroller of the Currency's power to decide that certain conduct deemed contrary to accepted standards of banking operations which might result in abnormal risk or loss to a banking institution or shareholder').

7 *First Nat'l Bank of Bellaire* v. *Comptroller of Currency* 697 F.2d 674, 684–7 (5th Cir. 1983) (where the regulator's cease and desist order requiring a capital ratio was set aside as not being supported by substantial evidence and as violative of equal protection and due process under US constitution).

8 See Senate Rep. No. 98–122, 98th Cong., 1st Sess. 16.

9 12 U.S.C. §3906 (b) (2002). The appropriate federal banking agencies are thus required to 'promulgate regulations or orders necessary to implement this section. See 12 U.S.C. §3906 (c). The foreign exposure requirement was important because US banks lost substantial amounts on loans to Latin American sovereign debtors, which threatened the stability of the US banking system. The US government orchestrated an intervention that bailed out the US banks by providing guarantee on the repayment of private loans to the banks through the issuance of Brady Bonds.

10 12 U.S.C. §3907 (a)(1) (2002).

11 12 U.S.C. §3907 (b)(1).

12 12 U.S.C. §3907 (b)(2)(B)(ii).

13 12 U.S.C. §3907 (b)(1). For instance, the federal banking regulator may issue a directive to a banking institution that fails to maintain capital at or above its required level that may require it to submit and adhere to a plan acceptable to the appropriate federal banking agency describing the means and timing by which the banking institution shall achieve its required capital level. 12 U.S.C. §3907 (a) and (b)(1).

14 In *re Seidman*, 37 F.3d 911, 927 (3rd Cir. 1994).

15 *Sunshine State Bank* v. *FDIC*, 783 F. 2d 1580, 1584 (11th Cir. 1986); see also, *Bullion* v. *FDIC*, 881 F. 2d 1368, 1372–3 (5th Cir. 1989) (adopting the same standard of review under §1818(h)(2) for civil penalty hearings regarding violations of 12 U.S.C. §1828(j)(4)(D).

16 See Federal Deposit Insurance Corporation Improvement Act of 1991, (FDICIA), Pub. L. No. 102–242, 105 Stat. 2236 (1991).

17 57 Fed. Reg. 45263 (Oct 1, 1992).

18 58 Fed. Reg. 34357 (June 25, 1993).

19 See 12 C.F.R. §327. The transition regulations were in effect from January 1, 1993 to January 1, 1994.

20 12 U.S.C. §1817(b)(1)(C).

21 *FDIC* v. *Coushatta,* 930 F. 2d 122 (5th Cir.), *cert. denied,* 502 U.S. 857 (1991).

22 12 C.F.R. §327.3(e)(1).

23 12 C.F.R. §327.3(e)(1)(ii).

24 930 F. 2d 122 (5th Cir.), *cert. denied,* 502 U.S. 857 (1991).

25 The fundamental requirement of due process is the opportunity to be heard 'at a meaningful time and in a meaningful manner'. *Matthews* v. *Eldridge,* 424 U.S. 319, 333 (1976).

26 *FDIC* v. *Coushatta.* at 335.

27 The FDIC procedures allow the bank to submit the request and supporting documentation to the FDIC Division of Supervision. The procedures also provide for an opportunity to request an informal oral hearing, which the FDIC may grant, in its discretion, 'when the Division of Supervision determines that an informal oral presentation would be productive under the applicable circumstances. 58 Fed. Reg. 34357, 34359 (June 25, 1993).

28 12 C.F.R. §327.3.

29 *Doolin,* 53 F.3d at 1403.

30 The Office of Thrift Supervision regulates and applies prudential supervisory standards to the operations of federal savings banks that are not regulated by the Comptroller (Treasury) nor by the Federal Reserve Board.

31 See *Doolin,* 53 F.3d at 1405.

32 5 U.S.C. 702 (1998) provides general right to judicial review of agency action.

33 12 U.S.C. §1818(ii).

34 I am indebted to Michael Blair QC for this observation.

35 See Board of Governors of the Federal Reserve System, Division of Banking Supervision and Regulation, SR 00-13 (SUP), (Aug. 15, 2000) pp. 3–5.

36 12 U.S.C. §1841 *et seq.*

37 Senate Rep. No. 1095, 84th Cong. At p. 5 (1955). In the 1956 legislation, bank holding companies were exempt from the legislation if they owned or controlled only one bank, the so-called one-bank exemption. H.R. Rep. No. 91–387, at p. 2 (1969). Congress eliminated this exemption when it adopted amendments to the 1970 Bank Holding Company Act.

38 H.R. Rep. No. 609, 84th Cong. p. 2 (1955).

39 12 U.S.C. §1842(a).

40 12 U.S.C. §1842(c).

41 Regulation Y, 49 Fed. Reg. 820 (1984) (codified at 12 C.F.R. §225.4(a)(1).

42 Policy Statement, 52 Fed. Reg. 15707, 15708 (1987) (emphasis added). This policy statement became effective on 24 April 1987. The Board solicited comments on the policy, with a view to revising the statement in light of such comments. No subsequent revision has been published.

43 12 U.S.C. §1844(b).

44 439 U.S. 234 (1978).

45 Ibid at 243.

46 Ibid at 250.

47 474 U.S. 361 (1986).

48 900 F.2d 852 (5th Cir., 1990).

49 Sections 1818(b)(1) and (3) authorize the Board to file charges against a bank holding company which the Board believes has violated or is about to

violate a 'law, rule or regulation', or is engaging in 'unsafe and unsound' practices.
50 *MCorp. Financial v Board of Governors*, 900 F.2d 852, 862 (5th Cir. 1990).
51 Ibid at 863.
52 Since Congress enacted a new financial services act to replace the Glass–Stea-gall Act in November of 1999, which took effect in March 2000, it will be inter-esting to see how the courts interpret its provisions that allow Financial Service Holding Companies to own unlimited interests in commercial non-bank enter-prises.
53 Board of Governors of the Federal Reserve System of the United States v. MCorp., Fin., Inc., 111 S. Ct. 1991 (1991). See also discussion in Bierman and Fraser (1993)
54 Pub. L. 106-102, 113 Stat. 1338.
55 12 U.S.C. §1831o.
56 12 C.F.R. §225.
57 Sec. 1842(c).

References

Akhigbe, A. and Whyte, A.M. (2004) 'The Gramm–Leach–Bliley Act of 1999: risk implications for the financial services industry', *The Journal of Financial Research* 27(3): 435–46.
Alexander, K. (2004) 'UK corporate governance and banking regulation: the regu-lator's role as stakeholder', *Stetson Law Review* 33(3): 991–1034.
Allen, F. and Gale, D. (2000) *Comparing Financial Systems*, Cambridge, MA: MIT Press, pp. 93–7.
Biais, B. and Pagano, M. (2002) *New Research in Corporate Finance and Banking*, Oxford: Oxford University Press, pp. 190–202.
Bierman, L. and Fraser, D.R. (1993) 'MCorp and the future of the source of strength doctrine', *Banking Law Journal* 110(2): 145.
Harrell, A.C. (1995) 'Deposit insurance reform issues and the implications for the structure of the American financial system', in Norton, J.J. (ed.) *International Banking Regulation and Supervision in the 1990s: Change and Transformation*, London: Kluwer Law, pp. 310–14.
Holzman, T.L. (2000) 'Unsafe or unsound practices: is the current judicial inter-pretation of the term unsafe or unsound?', *Annual Review of Banking Law* 19: 425–54.
Mishkin, F.S. (2004) *The Economics of Money, Banking and Financial Markets*, 7th edn, Addison-Wesley: Pearson, pp. 271–4.
Saunders, A., Strock, E. and Travlos, N. (1990) 'Ownership structure, deregulation and bank risk taking', *Journal of Finance* 45(2): 643–54.
Stiglitz, J.E. (1989) 'Principal and agent', in Eatwell, J., Milgate, M. and Newman, P. (eds) *The New Palgrave: Allocation, Information, and Markets*, Basingstoke: Macmillan, p. 60.

COMMENT: THE IMPLEMENTATION OF BASEL 2[1]

Harald Benink

Background of Basel 2

On 26 June 2004 the Basel Committee on Banking Supervision achieved consensus on the proposals for a new capital adequacy framework for banks to respond to deficiencies in the 1988 Capital Accord on credit risk (Basel Committee, 1988). The proposed framework, commonly referred to as 'The New Basel Capital Accord' or 'Basel 2', contains a number of new aspects to regulation and supervision of banks, structured with three 'pillars'. The first pillar deals with the minimum regulatory capital requirement and contains new rules for calculating more refined risk weights for different kinds of loans. Moreover, it suggests that capital should be held against so-called operational risk. The second pillar is the supervisory review process, which requires supervisors to ensure that each bank has sound internal processes in place to assess the adequacy of its capital based on a thorough evaluation of its risks. The third pillar aims to bolster market discipline through enhanced disclosure by banks. Although the new framework's focus is primarily on internationally active banks, its underlying principles are intended to be suitable for application to banks of varying levels of complexity and sophistication.

The Basel 2 Accord (Basel Committee, 2004) is the result of a dialogue between the international banking community and leading bank supervisors working together in the Basel Committee. This dialogue, which started around 1997, resulted in three consultative papers (Basel Committee, 1999, 2001, 2003a). The consultative papers generated many responses from the international banks, contributing to the final shape of the Basel 2 Accord.

There is general agreement that the risk classification determining capital requirements in the 1988 Basel Accord was too broad, making it possible for banks to shift assets to relatively high-risk categories. In June 1999 when the Basel Committee published its first consultative paper, it stated:

> The current risk weighting of asset results, at best, is a crude measure of economic risk, primarily because degrees of credit risk exposure are not sufficiently calibrated as to adequately differentiate between borrowers' differing default risks. Another related and increasing problem with the existing Accord is the ability of banks to arbitrage their regulatory capital requirement and exploit differences between true economic risk and risk measured under the Accord. Regulatory capital arbitrage can occur in several ways, for example, through some forms of securitization, and can lead to a shift in banks' portfolio concentrations to lower quality assets.

The June 1999 consultative paper intended to replace the existing system of credit risk weightings by a system that would use external rating agencies' credit assessment for determining risk weights. The Committee mentioned very briefly the possibility that 'sophisticated banks' could be allowed to use their internal ratings as a basis for setting regulatory capital charges. The debate triggered by the 1999 proposal quickly led to greater emphasis on internal ratings. The banking community as well as the European Commission (1999) paid increased attention to internal ratings, and in a survey on the range of practices in banks' internal ratings systems the Basel Committee shifted its focus in the same direction (Basel Committee, 2000).

Under the 2004 Basel 2 Accord, the Basel Committee tries to address the problem of regulatory capital arbitrage by refining the risk weighting process, in particular with respect to loans to the private sector. The risk weights are to be refined by reference to a rating either provided by an external credit assessment institution ('standardized approach') or produced by a bank's internal ratings based (IRB) system. In the IRB approach, which will only be allowed for banks having 'sophisticated' risk management systems, there are two options, namely the 'foundation approach' and the 'advanced approach'. In the foundation methodology, banks estimate the probability of default (PD) associated with each borrower, and the supervisor will supply the other inputs, notably the loss-given-default (LGD) estimates. In the advanced methodology, a bank with a sufficiently developed internal capital allocation process will be permitted to supply other inputs as well. Under both IRB approaches, the range of risk weights will be far more diverse than those in the standardized approach, resulting in greater risk sensitivity. However, all proposed approaches (standardized as well as IRB) are still additive, i.e. individual credit risks are summed up without consideration of portfolio effects. Incentives and scope for regulatory capital arbitrage remain, although to a lesser extent.

The Basel Committee aims at implementing Basel 2 for the standardized approach (using external ratings for calculating risk weights) and the foundation approach (using banks' internal ratings for calculating probabilities of default and related risk weights) by the end of 2006. For the advanced approach (using banks' internal ratings for calculating both probabilities of default and loss given default and related risk weights) the envisaged date of implementation is the end of 2007.

The role of capital and capital requirements

Shareholder's capital in banks as in other firms serves three important functions. First, capital is a buffer against unexpected losses causing bankruptcy. Second, equity capital creates incentives for management to manage risk appropriately from the point of view of shareholders. Third, equity capital of sufficient magnitude signals that lenders to the bank will not be taken advantage of. Under limited liability for shareholders the third function is particularly important from the lenders' point of view. Without sufficient capital, shareholders have the incentive to invest in excessively risky projects, because the project risk will be borne primarily by lenders.

Banking and, to some extent, other financial institutions are special because most of their creditors are explicitly or implicitly insured. The rationale for this insurance is the bank's role in the payment system, the risk the bank runs and the potential contagion among banks caused by one bank's failure. Without going into the economic validity of the risk of the bank runs and the contagion, it is a fact that supervisory authorities in all countries offer a degree of insurance of banks' creditors. There is explicit deposit insurance in many countries, and expected bailouts imply a degree of implicit insurance. This implicit insurance may be extended to shareholders as well.

The insurance of the banks' creditors implies that the latter will not monitor risks. If, in addition, the insurance is not priced, then banks have incentives to deliberately take too much risk, since relatively risky assets are likely to offer high returns.[2] Furthermore, under any system wherein banks do not compete by risk evaluation skills there is a high likelihood that these skills will be 'underdeveloped'. Thereby, the banking system as a whole may non-deliberately fail to take important risks into consideration. Capital requirements in excess of the willingly held equity capital are intended to ensure that shareholders have a stake in all projects, and to reduce incentives for risk taking.

The capital requirement for a particular asset determines its cost of capital. Thus, if assets with different risk-return characteristics have the same capital requirement, banks favour those assets that offer a relatively high expected rate of return. They can, as mentioned, engage in regulatory arbitrage and choose relatively risky assets offering the highest expected return among those with a certain cost of capital.

To avoid regulatory arbitrage it would seem that the 'optimal' risk-weighting system should be detailed and based on the 'true' or 'best available' measure of the risk of each particular asset. This reasoning presumes that there exists a generally agreed upon 'best' measure of risk for each loan. If such a 'best' measure could be identified, then most economists' view of banking, and the role of competition among banks, must be false. Economic theory emphasizes that an important role of banks is to assess risk. Banks are expected to develop risk assessment expertise in competition, and individual banks are able to gain competitive advantages in different loan markets wherein they are relatively good at evaluating and pricing its risks. Unlike in equity markets, there is, in credit markets, no one observable price reflecting market participants' aggregate risk assessment for an asset. This view implies that different banks may evaluate the same loan differently. A detailed, externally imposed, binding risk-weighting scheme renders each bank's internal risk-evaluation expertise irrelevant for the costs of capital for different bank loans. Thus, banks cannot gain competitive advantages by developing particular kinds of risk-evaluation expertise.

The regulatory dilemma that the Basel Committee has had to struggle with is therefore that if supervisors specify risk buckets that are too broad, then a bank's expertise can be used for regulatory arbitrage, while if they specify risk buckets that are too narrow, then the incentives for banks to develop expertise in risk assessment – their presumed comparative advantage – are removed.

The internal ratings proposal

The proposed solution to the regulatory dilemma of either allowing regulatory arbitrage with broad risk buckets or removing incentives for banks to develop risk-assessment expertise is to allow internal ratings as the basis for risk weighting.

The New Basel Capital Accord allows two approaches to internal ratings of loans. In the first one – the foundation approach – the ratings are based on banks' estimates of PD on various loans. The second approach – the advanced approach – would take LGD into account as well. Any approach taken by a bank must be evaluated and accepted by the bank's supervisory authority. If a bank is able to apply only the foundation approach, then supervisors will provide the bank with a standardized method for arriving at LGD estimates. Neither the foundations, nor the advanced approach, incorporate portfolio considerations.

The Basel Committee's own survey on banks' practices in credit-risk assessment (Basel Committee, 2000) shows that banks' practices vary from the highly intuitive placement of credits into risk categories to the use of fairly sophisticated risk-assessment models. However, all banks seem to allow room for intuitive or non-quantifiable elements to affect risk assessment.

A substantial challenge facing banks and supervisors of the internal ratings approach is to map an internal ratings method into risk weightings that are consistent across banks. Only if clear quantitative ratings are produced will it be possible to compare internal ratings across banks easily. To achieve comparability banks must, at a minimum, translate their ratings into estimates of PD. A number of proposals for implementation of internal ratings approaches exist, however, and much work is on-going (see, for example, Krahnen and Weber, 2000). More refined approaches may be adopted in the future within the framework of the new Accord.

Gaming and manipulation – the role of supervision and market discipline

Under an internal ratings standard, the Basel 2 Accord encourages the development of sound internal systems for risk evaluation since only banks complying with strict methodological and disclosure standards will be allowed to use these ratings as a basis for determining the regulatory capital requirement. Notwithstanding this very positive incentive effect associated with the new Accord, one could argue that at the same time it provides potentially perverse incentives for banks to develop new ways to evade the intended consequences of the proposed regulation.

Additional opportunities for risk arbitrage exist under an internal ratings standard, because risk weights are based on banks' private information rather than on external, verifiable variables. A major problem facing the supervisors is to check the truthfulness of even estimates of probabilities of default. There are great difficulties already for the banks themselves to translate their own ratings into probabilities of default. Essentially, each bank must develop data similar to 'mortality rate tables' that are applied in the corporate bond markets for bonds with different ratings. Input data for many years are needed to obtain estimates of mortality rates for all rating-categories over the lifetime of loans. Thus innovation to rating systems – and one would hope that innovations occur – make it more difficult both for banks and supervisors to gather the required data.

The additional opportunities for risk arbitrage under an internal ratings standard are created by the scope for 'gaming and manipulation' of ratings. Banks generally have access to private credit risk-relevant information that can be excluded from the system for risk-weighting presented to the supervisory authority.

One type of 'gaming and manipulation' would occur if a bank uses its private information to place relatively high-risk and high-return credits in a lower risk bucket. For example, if the foundation approach is used, then the probability of default reported to the supervisory authority can be made to differ from the bank's true estimate. The latter probability may have been updated by the bank based on information that is not available to supervisors. If the probabilities of default are based on a more refined credit scoring system that has been deemed acceptable by regulators, then private information within the bank would make manipulation of the credit scores prior to translation into probabilities of default possible. The quantitative importance of 'gaming and manipulation' has been estimated by Carey and Hrycay (2000). They conclude that officially reported default rates for a given rating can be made as low as half the bank's private estimates.

There is some discussion of penalties to be imposed on banks that systematically and deliberately 'miss-judge' risks, thereby placing the bank's liabilities at risk. The difficulties of implementing a penalty system are great, however. One reason is that the required data to prove deliberate, as opposed to non-deliberate, misjudgment is hard to come by even if a bank's errors are systematic. A second reason is that the penalty-system may lack credibility if penalties primarily have to be imposed on banks in distress.

Both the European Commission and the Basel Committee recognize the potential scope for gaming and manipulation. Two pillars of the capital adequacy framework, supervision and market discipline, carry the weight of having to limit this scope. Supervision and market discipline should also limit the scope for non-deliberate underestimation of risk by raising the consciousness and quality of risk assessment.

Under the new Accord most of the burden of controlling banks' internal risk assessment is placed on expanded and active supervision. Supervisory authorities are expected to build up their expertise substantially in both quantitative and qualitative terms. In fact, supervisors are expected to work closely with the banks, when they develop and upgrade their internal risk-scoring models. This envisioned very close cooperation between banks and supervisors is naturally intended to reduce the information and knowledge asymmetry between banks and supervisors. However, banks will always be able to make decisions based on private information. The intensified involvement of supervisors could instead lead to greater 'regulatory capture' in the sense that supervisors identify themselves more strongly with the banks they supervise.

The implication of the discussion so far is that the need for market discipline as an instrument to induce banks to hold sufficient capital is stronger under the new Accord. By market discipline, we mean that banks are given incentives by market participants' evaluation of banks' activities to assign costs of capital to credits reflecting the banks' best evaluation of credit risk from the point of view of shareholders and debt holders including depositors. To a particular cost of capital for a loan corresponds a choice of debt and equity financing, including a certain amount of equity held against a loan. If debt holders are insured, the bank's risk-taking will not be reflected in its cost of debt. Therefore, shareholders have an incentive to use too much low cost debt financing to finance relatively risky loans.

Market discipline should also enhance incentives to compete by means of credit-evaluation skills for loans. Non-deliberate underestimation of risk seems to have been an important element of banking crises in, for example, the Nordic countries and Japan. Regulators have generally been unable to detect this kind of underestimation. There is obviously no guarantee that market discipline resolves this problem, but it increases the likelihood that underestimation will be detected by some market participants. One advantage of market discipline is that credit risk and bank procedures for assessing credit would come under the scrutiny of a larger number of observers with stakes in the banks.

178   H. Benink

The European Commission and the Basel Committee rely on information disclosure to enforce market discipline. However, effective market discipline requires not only that information be available to some observers but also that the observers value the information and are able to impose a cost on the bank that releases negative information (or abstains from releasing positive information). As long as depositors and other creditors of banks are insured, or implicitly expect to be bailed out, information about potential credit losses is not going to be a major concern to creditors. Another aspect is that the disclosed information is going to be more relevant and effective, if the choice of disclosed information is based on demand for information in the market place.

By putting their faith in rules for information disclosure alone, to create market discipline, the European Commission and the Basel Committee neglect that the amount and truthfulness of information available in the market place depend on incentives on the demand as well as supply side for information.

Subordinated debt as an information and discipline device

Market discipline inducing a bank to serve the objectives of debt holders as well as shareholders requires that debt is priced according to the riskiness of the bank's asset. Such pricing could be achieved if most creditors of the bank were 'credibly uninsured'. An indirect method for imposing market discipline is for regulators to use information in the market risk premium on an uninsured portion of the bank's debt to assess a risk premium on debt to insured creditors. Given the prevalence of explicit and implicit guarantees regulators must be involved in the process of assigning a risk premium to the bank's insured debt. Currently, regulators try to impose costs for risk-taking only by means of binding capital requirements. The difficult, not to say the impossible, task facing regulators relying entirely on capital requirements has been described. By requiring banks to issue a minimum amount of 'credibly uninsured' subordinated debt regulators may obtain not only a discipline device, but also an information device for imposing costs on banks in proportion to asset risk.[3] In principle the yield spread on subordinated debt could be used to determine a deposit insurance premium for the bank. The effective pricing of deposit insurance would essentially make capital requirements unnecessary even for banks that are 'too big to fail'. An alternative route for the regulator is to use the information in the yield spread to adjust capital requirements and to intervene in the activities of banks approaching distress ('structured early intervention and resolution' or 'prompt corrective action').

In a recent paper Benink and Wihlborg (2002) propose a first phase of a mandatory subordinated debt requirement as part of the regulatory capital requirement, where the minimum percentage of subordinated debt to be issued is set in line with current levels of subordinated debt. The requirement should be limited to relatively large banks and the subordinated debt would have to be held by professional investors on financial markets such as pension funds and insurance companies. A similar proposal was made during an international meeting in June 2001 of the Shadow Financial Regulatory Committees of Europe, Japan, Latin America and the US. Many large American and European banks already issue large amounts of subordinated debt. On the average for the US this debt amounts to more than 2 per cent of total assets for the large banks according to a study by the Federal Reserve Board in 1999. Moreover, recent research by Sironi (2001, 2003) and by the Basel Committee (2003b) presents evidence that many large banks in Europe also have a ratio of about 1.5 to 2 per cent. Other important aspects of the requirement would consist of:

- Attempts to signal strongly, and to ensure international agreement that subordinated debt is credibly uninsured. Even in the case of a bail-out of other stakeholders, the holders of this debt must not be compensated for losses.
- Close monitoring of the risk premium on subordinated debt of each individual bank in order to establish whether the market's perception of increased riskiness is consistent with a bank's internal ratings system. This information should be integrated into the supervisory review process.

In this first phase of the subordinated debt proposal there would not yet be a system of automatic sanctions (such as prompt corrective action) when the risk premium goes up for a longer period of time. However, as part of the supervisory review process a supervisor might decide to increase the capital requirement of a particular bank. Since banks know that their supervisor is watching the yield spread on subordinated debt and might act on it, this will mitigate their incentives to underestimate the credit risk.

The idea that internal ratings might be generating incentives for gaming and manipulation and that the risk premium on subordinated debt could be a valuable indicator of the overall riskiness of a bank, are not only concepts put forward by academics and some researchers at the US Federal Reserve Board. In a lecture which Tommaso Padoa-Schioppa, Member of the Executive Board of the European Central Bank, delivered at the Financial Markets Group of the London School of Economics in 2002, he stated that:

> The regulations based on firms' internal practices impose a heavy verification burden on supervisory authorities and may leave room for 'gaming incentives' by those being disciplined. In concrete terms, this

means that when its financial condition deteriorates, an institution may have incentives to hide problems and manipulate results.... There is positive empirical evidence, gathered for European banks, that the prices of bank securities do constitute an indicator of their soundness. Similar evidence also exists for the United States. Hence, market discipline can apparently play a useful role in complementing supervisors' monitoring activities and would be further supported by developments in the disclosure regime.

Basel 2 and supervisory discretion

The Basel 2 Accord seems to mirror a subtle, but important, emphasis with respect to the potential use of pillar 2 (supervisory review or qualitative supervision) as a counterbalancing mechanism to the quantitative assessment based on banks' internal ratings systems (pillar 1 of the Accord). Much more than the 1999, 2001 and 2003 consultative papers, the Accord seems to express supervisory concern about the reliability of the internal ratings systems which are designed by the banks in order to determine the regulatory capital requirement. This heightened concern is discernible at several points in the text of the Accord.

For instance, in point 9 of the introduction the Basel Committee explicitly states that 'national authorities may use a *supplementary* capital measure as a way to address, for example, the potential uncertainties in the accuracy of the measure of risk exposures inherent in any capital rule or to constrain the extent to which an organization may fund itself with debt'. Moreover, in point 10 the Committee says that 'even in the case of the internal ratings-based (IRB) approach, the risk of major loss events may be higher than allowed for in this Framework'. As we know, these major loss events, usually having a low probability but being hard to capture in terms of probability distributions and IRB systems, are key in terms of stability of the banking and financial system. Apparently, the Basel Committee is concerned that the IRB approaches are not able to capture low-risk, high-severity events and, therefore, raises the question of requiring additional capital above the minimum based on IRB models.

The issue is emphasized in Part 2 of the Basel 2 Accord. In point 45 the Basel Committee discusses transitional arrangements and so-called *floors* with respect to implementation of the Accord. For instance, with respect to the advanced IRB approach, banks will be allowed to use their IRB models in order to calculate the regulatory capital requirement from year-end 2007 but the reduction in regulatory capital is limited to 90 per cent of in 2008 and to 80 per cent in 2009. So even if a bank's IRB model indicates that a reduction to 60 per cent of the current 1988 Basel 1 requirement would be justified, the floors of 90 per cent and 80 per cent will prevent this from happening. Interestingly, the Basel Committee is keeping open the option of maintaining the floors after 2009, preventing banks to grasp the full benefit of lower regulatory capital. In point 48 it says that 'should problems emerge during this period, the Committee will seek to take appropriate measures to address them, and, in particular, will be prepared to keep the floors in place beyond 2009 if necessary'. In point 49 the Committee elaborates on this issue and says that 'the Committee believes it is appropriate for supervisors to apply prudential floors to banks that adopt the IRB approach for credit risk and/or the Advanced Measurement Approach (AMA) for operational risk following year-end 2008'. Naturally, this supervisory discretion in defining floors is rather inconsistent with the current exercise of supervisors validating the reliability of banks' IRB systems.

Moreover, there is a huge scope for an unlevel playing field based on this regulatory discretion when the Committee reasons in point 49 that 'supervisors should have the flexibility to develop appropriate *bank-by-bank* floors that are consistent with the principles outlined in this paragraph, subject to full disclosure of the nature of the floors adopted'.

In point 14 the Basel Committee reiterates that it wishes to keep the aggregate level of capital in the banking system stable. In this respect, the Committee will further review the calibration of the Accord prior to its implementation. Based on the last Quantitative Impact Study (QIS-3) published in May 2003, overall banking capital in the G-10 and EU countries fell, which was 'repaired' by using a single scaling factor of 1.06 to the IRB capital requirement. This scaling factor changed because of the QIS-4 exercises, which was conducted in late 2004 and early 2005 in the US and several other Basel Committee member countries. The question remains to what extent national supervisors will be willing to have overall regulatory capital fall for the whole group of banks operating under their jurisdiction. For instance, if the Basel Committee sets the scaling factor in such a way that overall banking capital in the EU and the G-10 remains more or less the same, it could still be the case that, based on the risk characteristics of their portfolios, most banks in a particular country could be entitled to lower regulatory capital. What is unclear is whether national supervisors would be willing to allow this to happen in their national market (e.g. regulatory capital in the British banking system falls by 40 per cent).

Conclusion

Although the Basel 2 Accord provides sound incentives for banks to professionalize their risk measurement and risk management, it creates all types of problems with respect to the risk measurement from the supervisory point of view, which may have to be addressed by the application of a potentially substantial degree of supervisory discretion based on pillar 2 of the Accord.

Market discipline (pillar 3 of the Accord) could play a counterbalancing role since the risk assessment by professional investors on financial markets (such as pension funds and insurance companies) would prevent banks from lowering their capital too much and, hence, would reduce the need for supervisory discretion. The Basel 2 Accord contains many information disclosure requirements. At the same time, however, it fails to create incentives for professional investors to use this information in an optimal way. The reason for this is, as long as professional investors in a bank's liabilities have the perception that large banks are too big too fail, they will start developing the idea that their money is not really at stake, mitigating their incentives to use the information disclosed on the basis of pillar 3.

An interesting aspect of the sub debt proposal is that increased risk taking and/or increased leverage is likely to be translated rapidly into a higher risk premium, penalizing the bank and creating a potentially valuable information signal to bank supervisors. Supervisors could use this signal as a complement to the risk assessment of a bank's internal ratings model. An increase in the risk premium of subordinated debt accompanied by no change in the risk assessment of a bank's internal ratings system could be the start of a dialogue between supervisor and bank, eventually leading to a higher regulatory capital requirement.

The advantage of this new approach aimed at generating a more credible form of market discipline is that there will be less risk of arbitrary supervisory discretion since the supervisory assessment of the reliability of a bank's internal ratings system will be assisted and objectified by the assessment of professional investors on financial markets. Unfortunately, we will have to wait for Basel 3 before such a mechanism can be introduced in the regulatory capital adequacy framework.

Notes

1 These comments are an extension of Benink and Wihlborg (2002), Benink (2003, 2004a, b).
2 See, for example, Dewatripont and Tirole (1994) and Freixas and Rochet (1997) for expanded treatments of the economics of bank regulation.
3 The idea of using subordinated debt as an instrument of disciplining banks goes back to the 1980s, in particular to proposals made in the US by the Federal Deposit Insurance Corporation (1983) and by Benston *et al.* (1986). Recently, the literature analysing the proposals has been growing rapidly. Examples are Federal Reserve Board (1999, 2000), Federal Reserve Board and Department of the Treasury (2000), Calomiris (1999), Evanoff and Wall (2000 , 2001), Sironi (2001, 2003), and Benink and Benston (2004).

Bibliography

Basel Committee on Banking Supervision (1988) *International Convergence of Capital Measurement and Capital Standards*, Basel.
Basel Committee on Banking Supervision (1999) *A New Capital Adequacy Framework*, First Consultative Paper, Basel.

Basel Committee on Banking Supervision (2000) *Range of Practice in Banks' Internal Ratings Systems*, Basel.

Basel Committee on Banking Supervision (2001) *The New Basel Capital Accord*, Second Consultative Paper, Basel.

Basel Committee on Banking Supervision (2003a) *The New Basel Capital Accord*, Third Consultative Paper, Basel.

Basel Committee on Banking Supervision (2003b) *Markets for Subordinated Debt and Equity in Basel Committee Member Countries*, Working Paper, no. 12, Basel.

Basel Committee on Banking Supervision (2004) *International Convergence of Capital Measurement and Capital Standards – A Revised Framework*, Basel.

Benink, H.A. (2003) Toughening up Basel II, *Financial Regulator* 8(3): 33–7.

Benink, H.A. (2004a) 'Are Basel II's pillars strong enough?', *The Banker*, July: 162–4.

Benink, H.A. (2004b) 'Will supervisors have too much discretion under the new regime?', *Global Risk Regulator*, July/August.

Benink, H.A. and Benston, G.J. (2004) 'The future of banking regulation in developed countries: lessons from and for Europe', mimeo, Erasmus University, Rotterdam and Emory University, Atlanta, the paper was discussed in *The Economist* of 3–9 May 2003.

Benink, H.A. and Wihlborg, C. (2002) 'The New Basel Capital Accord: making it effective with stronger market discipline', *European Financial Management* 8(1): 103–15. The paper was discussed in *The Economist* of 23 February–1 March 2002.

Benston, G.J., Eisenbeis, R.A., Horvitz, P.M., Kane, E.J. and Kaufman, G.G. (1986) *Perspectives on Safe and Sound Banking*, Cambridge, MA: MIT Press.

Calomiris, C.W. (1999) 'Building an incentive-compatible safety net', *Journal of Banking and Finance* 23: 1499–520.

Carey, M. and Hrycay, M. (2000) 'Parameterizing credit risk models with rating data', Symposium on Credit Ratings and the Proposed New BIS Guidelines on Capital Adequacy for Bank Credit Assets, New York University, Salomon Center.

Dewatripont, M. and Tirole, J. (1994) *The Prudential Regulation of Banks*, Cambridge, MA: MIT Press.

European Commission (1999) *A Review of Regulatory Capital Requirements for EU Credit Institutions and Investment Firms – Consultation Document*, Brussels.

European Commission (2001) *Commission Services' Second Consultation Document on Review of Regulatory Capital for Credit Institutions and Investment Firms*, Brussels.

European Commission (2003) *Review of Capital Requirements for Banks and Investment Firms – Commission Services Third Consultation Paper*, Brussels.

European Commission (2004) *Proposal for New Capital Requirements Regime for Credit Institutions and Investment Firms*, Brussels.

Evanoff, D.D. and Wall, L.D. (2000) 'Subordinated debt and bank capital reform', in Kaufman, G.G. (ed.) *Research in Financial Services: Private and Public Policy*, Vol. 12, Greenwich, CN: JAI Press, pp. 53–119.

Evanoff, D.D. and Wall, L.D. (2001) 'Measures of the riskiness of banking organizations: subordinated debt yields, risk-based capital and examination ratings', mimeo, Federal Reserve Banks of Chicago and Atlanta.

Federal Deposit Insurance Corporation (1983) *Deposit Insurance in a Changing Environment: A Study of the Current System of Deposit Insurance Pursuant to Section 712 of the Garn–St Germain Depository Institution Act of 1982*, Washington, DC.

Federal Reserve Board (1999) *Using Subordinated Debt as an Instrument of Market Discipline*, Staff Study No. 172, Washington, DC.

Federal Reserve Board (2000) *Improving Public Disclosure in Banking*, Staff Study No. 173, Washington, DC.

Federal Reserve Board and Department of the Treasury (2000) *The Feasibility and Desirability of Mandatory Subordinated Debt*, Washington, DC.

Freixas, X. and Rochet, J.-C. (1997) *Microeconomics of Banking*, Cambridge, MA: MIT Press.

Krahnen, J.P. and Weber, M. (2000) 'Generally accepted rating principles: a primer', Symposium on Credit Ratings and the Proposed New BIS Guidelines on Capital Adequacy for Bank Credit Assets, New York University, Salomon Center.

Padoa-Schioppa, T. (2002) *Self vs. Public Discipline in the Financial Field*, LSE Financial Markets Group, Special Paper No. 142.

Shadow Financial Regulatory Committees of Europe, Japan, Latin America and the US (2001) *Reforming Bank Capital Regulation*, Joint Statement, Amsterdam, 18 June.

Sironi, A. (2001) 'An analysis of European banks' SND issues and its implications for the design of a mandatory subordinated debt policy', *Journal of Financial Services Research* 20: 233–66.

Sironi, A. (2003) 'Testing for market discipline in the European banking industry: evidence from subordinated debt issues', *Journal of Money, Credit and Banking* 35(3): 443–72.

US Shadow Financial Regulatory Committee (2000) *Reforming Bank Capital Regulation: A Proposal by the US Shadow Financial Regulatory Committee*, Statement No. 160, Washington, DC.

7 Institutional allocation of bank regulation

A review

Charles M. Kahn and João A.C. Santos[1]

The presence of multiple, overlapping regulations, policed by separate regulatory authorities, is a common feature of modern economies. The potential conflicts that may arise between the objectives and requirements of the various authorities pose a difficult problem for the designers of regulatory institutions. For example, while moving certain powers out of a given authority might be necessary to avert the concentration of power, this can at the same time lead to other distortions. A reason is that even if the objectives of each authority could be specified so completely as to render them perfectly consonant, the incentive difficulties arising from the agency problem and imperfections in monitoring the behaviour of the authorities will still lead to conflicts between the authorities' objectives.

The potential for these conflicts appears to be particularly important in banking regulation because of the strong interdependencies that exist between the various regulatory functions that form a bank regulatory arrangement. Bank regulation in most countries encompasses a lender of last resort, deposit insurance and supervision. These functions, though interrelated, are often the responsibility of different authorities, thus requiring them to coordinate their efforts. It is usually assumed that these authorities act in perfect synchrony. However, they are often established with different mandates, some of which are likely to be in conflict.

The potential conflicts of interest between the agencies entrusted with the authority to regulate and supervise banks has led some countries to introduce regulations targeting the agency responsible for these conflicts of interest. They have also led in other cases to the introduction of regulations this time protecting an agency from the costs that may arise with the policies of another agency.

The debate that followed the decisions in Australia and the United Kingdom in the late 1990s to move banking supervision from the central bank to a separate agency and that which followed the repeal of the Glass–Steagall Act in the United States have brought a great deal of attention to the issues of the potential conflict of interest and synergies between bank regulatory authorities.[2] They have also increased awareness of an alternative way of dealing with these potential conflicts of interest:

by changing the institutional allocation of the responsibility for a certain regulation. The issue of the institutional allocation of bank regulation in turn gained further prominence with the decision in the euro area to entrust the European Central Bank with powers to maintain price stability while leaving the responsibility for financial stability in the hands of national authorities.[3]

These debates, however, focused almost exclusively on the conflicts of interest and synergies of supervision for the conduct of monetary policy, and gave, for example, far less attention to the implications of the allocation of supervision to supervisors' incentives to monitor banks. In addition, they focused on supervision, and to a lesser extent on the lending of last resort function, and disregarded the other components that usually form the bank regulatory apparatus, most notably deposit insurance. This is somewhat surprising given that, as we will see below, deposit insurance is rarely managed by supervisory authorities or by central banks.

Our understanding of the implications of different institutional allocations of regulations is also limited because until recently this issue was in general absent from the literature on banking regulation. This literature has focused on the study of each regulation separately or when it considered the interplay between different regulations it implicitly assumed that these were managed by a single agency or by different agencies acting in perfect synchrony, thus disregarding the incentives of the regulatory agencies as defined by their mandates. On the other hand, the research that accounts for the incentives of regulators usually assumes a single regulatory agency.

The objective of this chapter is to contribute to the ongoing debate on the institutional allocation of bank regulation by putting together various relevant strands of the banking literature. The chapter reviews the main components of a bank regulatory arrangement and presents examples of the problems that may arise with the coexistence of these components. It then discusses how some countries have dealt with these problems through regulations. The chapter ends with a discussion of how the institutional allocation of regulation could be used to deal with such problems and with a review of the literature on the institutional allocation of bank regulation.

The chapter is organized as follows. The next section reviews the bank regulatory arrangements that most countries have adopted and the following section presents the institutional allocation of bank regulation in several countries. Next follows a discussion of the potential implications of various allocations of bank regulations among different authorities and then a review of the literature on the institutional allocation of bank regulation before concluding with some final remarks.

Banking regulatory arrangements

Why are banks regulated?

In modern theories of financial intermediation, the two most prominent explanations for the existence of intermediaries like depository institutions are the provision of liquidity and monitoring services, respectively.[4] Banks are valuable as providers of liquidity services because they provide depositors with liquidity insurance (Diamond and Dybvig, 1983). By issuing demand deposits, banks can improve on a competitive market because these deposits allow for better risk sharing among households that face idiosyncratic shocks to their consumption needs over time. The importance of banks in this framework arises from an information asymmetry: the shock that affects a household's consumption needs is not publicly observable.

Banks are valuable as providers of monitoring services because they act as delegated monitors to investors and thus avoid the duplication of monitoring costs (Diamond, 1984). As with the liquidity insurance explanation, the key to the existence of banks in this setup is also an informational problem. It is assumed that firms have more information about their investment projects than investors do. Investors can learn this information but only after incurring a monitoring cost. They may choose, however, to delegate monitoring to a bank, through which they all provide funding to the firm. By acting as delegated monitors of investors, banks save on monitoring costs and make funding available to firms at a lower cost than direct lending.

Banks' simultaneous performance of these roles leaves them with balance sheets combining a large portion of liabilities in the form of demand deposits, with a large portion of assets in the form of illiquid loans.[5] In the event of a liquidity shock, the same information asymmetries that lead banks to adopt this asset and liability structure make it difficult for them to borrow the necessary funds in the market. Thus a liquidity problem may generate an insolvency problem and force the bank into bankruptcy. The premature liquidation of bank assets is costly. It ends valuable relationships, it may lead to a knock-on effect on other banks through exposures in the interbank market and it may develop into a bank panic that culminates in a system failure.[6] This risk of a system failure forms the support of the classical argument proposing mechanisms to protect banks from liquidity shocks.

Regulatory arrangements

Bagehot (1873) is usually credited with the first analysis of one of the mechanisms that could be adopted to protect banks from liquidity shocks: the central bank's role as lender of last resort. He argues that the central bank should make clear in advance its readiness to lend any amount to a bank with liquidity problems, provided the bank is solvent. Lending should be done at a penalty rate (to reduce banks' incentives to use these loans to fund normal business) and only against good collateral (valued at pre-panic prices). Given that the inability of market mechanisms to insure banks against liquidity shocks usually stems from a problem of asymmetry of information on the bank's solvency, it appears that the conditions set out by Bagehot to operate the lending of last resort function impede the central bank from attaining its key objective. A solvent bank with good collateral will be able to borrow from the market. It is when there is some uncertainty about the value of the bank's collateral and its financial condition that the problems will arise.[7] In Bagehot's own words: 'Every Banker knows that if he has to prove that he is worthy of credit, however may be his argument, in fact his credit is gone' (1873: 68).

The central bank could avoid that problem by committing to extend liquidity support to all the banks seeking it. This, however, would come at a cost, as it would lead to moral hazard. This problem, in conjunction with the nature of the interbank market failure described above, provides a rationale for giving the agency responsible for the lending of last resort authority to supervise banks. This gives the lender of last resort access to private information and consequently an advantage over the other banks vis-à-vis the financial condition of a bank. Nonetheless, it is conceivable there will still be some residual information asymmetry between the lender of last resort and banks, and thus lead to cases where it will not be possible to distinguish with certainty between insolvency and illiquidity, particularly given the short period of time usually available for the lender of last resort to make a lending decision. As a result, some solvent banks may be denied liquidity support, and fail. Therefore, a lender of last resort that provides liquidity support to banks it considers to be solvent (and only against good collateral) will not be able to completely insure them against liquidity shocks and fully eliminate the risk of a system failure.

Because bank runs are believed to be one of the liquidity shocks that may lead to a system failure, there has been a great deal of interest in the mechanisms that protect banks from these shocks. Diamond and Dybvig (1983) show that a government backed deposit insurance scheme which guarantees full coverage eliminates bank runs.[8] This system, however, can lead to a deadweight cost as the government may have to tax other sectors if it has to compensate depositors, thereby leading to moral hazard. By offering a full guarantee, the deposit insurance provider bears the risk that would be placed on depositors and it eliminates their incentive to demand an interest payment commensurate with the bank's risk.[9] Furthermore, because it charges the bank a flat premium, it does not make the bank internalize the cost of risk, thus giving it an incentive to increase risk.[10] These distortions render a rationale for giving the deposit insurance provider authority to supervise banks in order to insure their solvency and to control for risk-shifting policies.

Deposit insurance can protect banks from runs driven by depositors but it does not insulate them from other liquidity shocks. For example, a bank may face liquidity problems if its interbank lenders refuse to rollover their loans or if it is unable to rollover maturing commercial paper. Hence, despite the presence of deposit insurance, the justification presented above for a lender of last resort still applies. The coexistence of these forms of regulation together with the monitoring they require, however, raises a number of issues concerning both their design and their assignment to authorities.

Despite the potential importance of these issues, as we will see below, only a few studies have examined them. Researchers have devoted a great deal of attention to the design of some of these regulations, but they have devoted less attention to the way they interact with each other and to the importance of their institutional allocation.

Institutional allocation of regulation

A bit of history

Most of the early-established central banks were founded as commercial banks rather than the public institutions into which they later developed. These banks were, however, special because they received a charter from the government. In addition, they were often the government's banker and in many instances received the monopoly of note issuance.

As the practice of central banking developed during the nineteenth century, central banks took on the responsibility for protecting the stability of the financial system and the external value of the currency. Following the Great Depression and the Keynesian revolution, the mandates assigned to central banks typically included both monetary stability and full employment objectives. With the inflationary forces that destroyed the Bretton Woods system and with the rational expectations revolution, the focus of monetary policy became the control of inflation, to the detriment of the level of output.

Though, historically, central banks have had some responsibility for safeguarding financial stability, this responsibility has varied across countries, partly because of country-specific factors such as the size and complexity of the financial sector, and partly because countries have chosen different institutional arrangements to protect financial stability. Many of the early-established central banks became the bank that financial institutions would turn to when all other channels were closed for lending because they were the largest banks in their respective countries. By some accounts, central banks started performing this lending of last resort function only in the second half of the nineteenth century. The Belgian National Bank started conducting lender of last resort operations in the 1850s, while the Bank of England, the Nederlandsche Bank, the Austrian

National Bank and the Banco de Portugal started doing so in the 1870s. This timing coincides with the publication in 1873 of *Lombard Street* by Walter Bagehot, who is most often credited with establishing the principles of the lender of last resort function. Following the financial turmoil that erupted in connection with the failure of a discount house, the Overend Gurney in 1866, Bagehot suggested that under certain conditions a central bank should make clear its readiness to lend any amount to a bank that is solvent but is facing liquidity problems.

Central banks' involvement in crisis management was, however, limited at the time, both in scale and scope. These institutions were often private entities, with the amount of funds they could apply in rescue operations limited to a large extent to their shareholders' funds. Moreover, they were not formally entrusted with prudential regulation and supervision powers, and tended to view themselves primarily as banks rather than the public institutions they evolved into. Because of their role, central banks had the finest credit standing in the country and they became the institution that banks would turn to for help when all other channels were closed. Their most common role was to orchestrate and lead a joint rescue party of a group of banks. This role was facilitated by banks' self-interest to participate in the rescue plans in order to be in good standing with their peers and thus, reasonably confident of a concerted rescue by them if the need arose. It was, therefore, largely a system of self-regulation through banking clubs under the leadership of the central bank. Deregulation and international competition in the 1960s led to the collapse of this system of clubs. It also led to a reduction in the willingness and the ability of the system to apply mutual surveillance and to a reluctance by banks to use their funds for the rescue of competitors.[11]

Not all central banks, however, played an active role in crisis management. In contrast to central banks like the Bank of England, which played an active role in organizing and leading bank rescues, the German Reichsbank and its forerunner the Prussian Bank were far less involved in similar micro-management of the financial system. Although the Reichsbank stood ready to provide liquidity to the banking system as a whole, it managed to avoid direct contact with individual banks. When the stability of the banking system was at stake during the Great Depression of the 1930s, the power of the Reichsbank to intervene in the management of this crisis was constrained by high levels of foreign debt and a system of fixed exchange rates. Consequently, the government had to intervene, acquiring substantial shareholdings in the problem banks. In 1961, the government founded the Federal Banking Supervisory Office as an independent institution responsible to the Minister of Finance, establishing the separation of monetary and banking supervision functions.

This difference between the UK and Germany contributed to the development of two trends. On the one hand, central banks in countries with close links to the UK, for example Australia, New Zealand, Hong Kong and Ireland, tended to be quite involved in the supervision and crisis management of banks. In contrast, central banks in countries with closer links to Germany, for example Austria, Switzerland and Scandinavia, tended to be less involved in these bank regulatory functions.[12]

The institutional allocation of the lender of last resort function

As we saw above, historically most central banks have had the responsibility for the lending of last resort function in their country. This is still valid today. The most prominent exception to it is Germany, where the central bank does not provide liquidity support to individual financial institutions, at least not directly. This support is provided by the Liquidity Consortium Bank, the Liko-Bank, which is a bank jointly owned by the central bank and the banking industry. Besides own funds, the Liko-Bank may have recourse to supplementary funds for which its owners are obliged if necessary and it has access to a rediscount line setup by the central bank.

Another exception to that pattern has emerged more recently in connection with the introduction of the euro. The Maastricht Treaty, besides setting up the conditions for the introduction of the euro, also reorganized Europe's multitude of central banks into the European System of Central Banks (ESCB), created a new institution, the European Central Bank, to head this system, and entrusted this institution with the full responsibility for formulating monetary policy. It also transferred the responsibility for promoting the smooth functioning of the payment system to the ESCB. However, neither the Maastricht Treaty nor the ESCB Statute give the European Central Bank an explicit mandate for providing emergency liquidity support directly to individual financial institutions. This remains the responsibility of national central banks.

The institutional allocation of deposit insurance

In contrast to the lending of last resort function, which by some accounts dates back to the 1850s, explicit deposit insurance schemes covering the entire banking system of a country are a more recent regulatory device.[13] Also in contrast with that function, central banks have been far less involved in the management of these schemes. Traditionally, they have been managed by a public agency, the industry itself or jointly by both of them.

There are, however, exceptions to the latter pattern. As Table 7.1 indicates, for example, in countries like Ireland, the Netherlands and Spain deposit insurance is managed by the central bank, and in Greece and Portugal the central bank shares the management of the scheme with another public institution. Though not evident from that table, in other countries, even though the central bank is not involved with the management of the

Table 7.1 Deposit insurance agencies

Country	Administration of deposit insurance	Type[a]
Australia	No scheme	
Austria	Austrian Banking Association	PR
Belgium	Rediscount and Guarantee Institute	J
Canada	Canada Deposit Insurance Corporation	PU
Denmark	Danish Insurance Agency	PR
Finland	Governing Board	PR
France	French Banking Association	PR
Germany	Federal German Banking Association	PR
Greece	Bank of Greece and Greek Banking Association	J
Hong Kong	No scheme	–
India	Deposit Insurance and Credit Guarantee Corporation	PU
Ireland	Central Bank of Ireland	PU
Italy	Interbank Deposit Protection Fund Council	J
Japan	Deposit Insurance Corporation	J
Luxembourg	Association for the Guarantee of Deposits	PR
The Netherlands	De Nederlandsche Bank	J
New Zealand	No scheme	–
Norway	Commercial Banks Contingency Fund Board	J
Philippines	Philippines Deposit Insurance Corporation	PU
Portugal	Banco de Portugal and Ministry of Finance	PU
Spain	Banco de España	PU
Switzerland	Swiss Bankers Association	PR
The United Kingdom	Deposit Protection Board	J
The United States	Federal Deposit Insurance Corporation	PU

Source: Goodhart and Schoenmaker (1998) and National Central Banks.

Note

a CB stands for central bank. PR, J and PU stand for private industry arrangements, managed jointly by public authorities and participating banks, and managed by public authorities, respectively.

scheme, it has some direct links with it. For example, in Canada, the governor of the central bank sits on the Board of Directors of the Canada Deposit Insurance Corporation, which is the entity responsible for managing deposit insurance in that country.

The institutional allocation of supervision

In contrast to the two functions already reviewed, there is more diversity in the institutional allocation of bank supervision. In many countries it is performed by institutions other than the central bank, but often with important links to the central bank. In addition, it is often mixed with the supervision of other financial institutions. Finally, it is the bank regulatory function that has been subject to several changes, in recent years, to its institutional allocation.

Traditionally, three institutions have been the subject of prudential supervision in most countries. They are banks, securities firms and insurance companies. Historically, countries have chosen different ways to supervise these institutions. As Table 7.2 shows, these differences are still evident despite the changes that have occurred in the 1980s and 1990s with regard to the prudential supervision of some institutions, most notably banks. The most common regulatory arrangement still includes a separate agency for each of the three institutions.

Whenever prudential supervision of these institutions is concentrated in a single agency, this function is usually performed by an agency other than the central bank.

The changes that occurred in the last two decades to the institutional allocation of supervision contributed to a reduction in the central banks' influence on bank supervision. During that time period several countries opted to move bank supervision out of their central banks. For example, Norway made this decision in 1986, Canada in 1987, Denmark in 1988, Sweden in 1991, Australia, Japan, Korea and the UK in 1998. Despite this trend, Table 7.3 indicates that as of 1999, central banks continued to have a prominent role among the prudential supervisors of financial institutions. This influential role is particularly strong in those countries that supervise banks separately from the other financial institutions that are usually subject to some form of supervision.

Table 7.2 Prudential supervision of banks, securities firms and insurance companies[a]

Arrangements	Percentage
Single agency: central bank	4
Other	14
Separate agencies for each financial institution	48
Banks alone: securities firms and insurance companies combined	4
Banks and securities firms combined: insurance companies alone	12
Banks and insurance companies combined: securities firms alone	18

Source: Llewellyn (1999).

Note
a As of 1999, based on a sample of 73 countries.

Table 7.3 Central banks' supervisory role (percentages)

Arrangements	Central bank	Non-central bank
Banks alone	51	6
Banks and securities	6	5
Banks and insurance	13	11
Banks, securities and insurance	2	6
Total	72	28

Source: Llewellyn (1999).

Note
a As of 1999, based on a sample of 123 countries.

Most of the statistics available, including those presented here, are based on an allocation of bank supervision to the regulatory authority that has the primary responsibility for this function. As we just saw, based on these statistics central banks continue to have a key role in the supervision of banks. When we consider the relationship between central banks and supervisory authorities in some of the countries where supervision is the responsibility of an agency other than the central bank, the influential role of central banks in the supervision of banks becomes even more pronounced.

Table 7.4 indicates the supervisory agency responsible for bank supervision in several countries and shows various examples where the central bank is not the sole agency responsible for bank supervision. In the US, the Federal Reserve System supervises only a portion of the banking industry, state member banks and bank holding companies. The remaining banks are supervised by the Federal Deposit Insurance Corporation, the Office of the Comptroller of the Currency and State Governments. In other countries central banks share bank supervision with another agency.

Table 7.4 Bank supervisory agencies

Country	Supervisory agencies
Australia	Australian Prudential Regulation Authority
Austria	Ministry of Finance
Belgium	Banking and Finance Commission
Canada	Office of Superintendent of Financial Institutions
Denmark	Finance Inspectorate
Finland	Bank Inspectorate and Bank of Finland
France	Commission Bancaire and Banque de France
Germany	Federal Banking Supervisory Office and Deutsche Bundesbank
Greece	Bank of Greece
Hong Kong	Hong Kong Monetary Authority
India	Reserve Bank of India
Ireland	Central Bank of Ireland
Italy	Banca d'Italia
Japan	Financial Supervisory Agency and Bank of Japan
Luxembourg	Luxembourg Monetary Authority
The Netherlands	De Nederlandsche Bank
New Zealand	Reserve Bank of New Zealand
Norway	Banking, Insurance and Securities Commission
Philippines	Central Bank of the Philippines
Portugal	Banco de Portugal
Spain	Banco de España
Switzerland	Federal Banking Commission
The United Kingdom	Financial Services Authority
The United States	Federal Reserve System, Office of the Comptroller of the Currency, Federal Deposit Insurance Corporation and State Governments

Source: Goodhart and Schoenmaker (1998) and National Central Banks.

A closer look at the latter set of countries reveals that the degree of central bank involvement in supervision is sometimes rather complex, depending on the extent to which the central bank shares the prudential tasks with other authorities and the precise linkages it has with them. For example, in France, the Commission Bancaire, the supervisory agency, is an independent authority but the Governor of the Banque de France is ex officio, Chairman of the Commission Bancaire, and the budget and staff of the Commission's General Secretariat come from the central bank. In Germany, the Bundesbank carries out off-site supervision and in certain areas, on-site inspection on behalf of the Federal Banking Supervisory Office, the country's primary bank supervisor. In Japan, the central bank conducts on-site examinations of institutions that hold accounts with it, independent of inspections by the Financial Supervisory Authority. Finally, in Canada the central bank interacts with the Office of the Superintendent of Financial Institutions, the country's bank supervisor, through its membership in the Financial Institutions Supervisory Committee, which is an interagency committee established to ensure consultation and information exchange on supervisory matters.[12]

Does the institutional allocation of regulation matter?

The incentive structure confronting a regulator is in general extremely complex. His utility depends on measures of performance by which his work is evaluated and the effort he expends on his work. He does not generally care directly about the performance measures; instead they affect his compensation and prospects for retention and advancement within the regulatory authority. However, government oversight of a regulator takes into account only a limited set of criteria, and in many instances there is only a fairly general link between the performance criteria and the regulator's utility.

For instance, a regulator may have budgetary responsibilities, such that, he is rewarded or punished for surpluses or cost overruns. In addition, he may be held accountable for bank failures and thus incur political costs whenever a bank goes bankrupt. In both cases, the performance criterion is easily observed but it is only partially linked to the regulator's utility. One reason is that when banks appear sound, the careful monitoring of their operations, in addition to being costly, may be tedious and apparently unnecessary. Whether the regulator exerted the appropriate effort monitoring the bank is not likely to be observable at the time by parties outside the regulatory authority.

Overseeing a regulator based on a limited set of criteria, which also happens to be only partially linked to the regulator's utility, makes it difficult to perfectly align the incentives of the regulator with those of the government. Note though that even if the objectives of each regulator could be defined so completely as to render them perfectly consonant, agency problems and imperfections in monitoring the behaviour of the regulators would still lead to conflicts between their objectives. The strong interdependencies that exist between the various components of a bank regulatory arrangement further contribute to the development of conflicts of interest between the regulators and for varying implications of different institutional allocations of bank regulatory powers and consequently makes it more likely for the arrival of conflicts of interest with other overlapping regulators.

For example, the assignment of the authority to close banks, which is usually attributed to the agency in charge of supervision, to an agency other than the deposit insurance provider, may result in a looser closure policy because that institution does not bear the full costs of delaying closure. Instead, these costs will fall on the bank's residual claimants, often the deposit insurance fund. Similarly, the allocation of the lender of last resort function to an institution other than the deposit insurance provider can lead to a more liberal policy of liquidity support to banks. By extending only short term or fully collateralized loans, the lender of last resort makes itself the most senior claimant vis-à-vis the other creditors and therefore avoids some of the costs induced by its liquidity support.

Policymakers have addressed some of the potential conflicts of interest between different authorities through the introduction of regulations protecting certain authorities from the policies of the other. For example, the regulation which assigns the deposit insurance provider the right to withdraw insurance coverage to a bank and that which gives legal priority to insured depositors, has the effect of protecting the insurance fund from the policies of the authority in charge of closing banks.[15] The authority to withdraw insurance coverage is a close substitute to the authority to close a bank because banks that do not offer this coverage on their deposits will find it difficult to stay in business. An example of a country where the deposit insurance provider has this authority is the US. In other countries, such as Canada and Italy, the deposit insurance provider has authority to intervene in a bank closure (Barth *et al.*, 2001).

In other cases, policymakers have introduced regulations targeting the authority whose policy may give rise to a potential conflict of interest. Some countries have adopted prompt corrective action schemes in order to reduce the discretion of the regulator charged with the authority to close banks. In 1991, the United States introduced a prompt corrective action scheme, which defines several trigger points based on a bank's capitalization and a set of mandatory actions for supervisors to implement at each point.[16]

Other countries have implemented regulations aimed at increasing the lender of last resort's incentive to extend liquidity support only to solvent banks, by making it potentially liable for the losses of its policy. For example, in the United States, since the enactment of the Federal Deposit Insurance and Recovery Act in 1992, the central bank can incur a liability to the agency in charge of deposit insurance, the Federal Deposit Insurance Corporation, if its liquidity support to a bank leads to an increase in that agency's costs.[17]

The debate in the 1990s on whether supervision should be performed by central banks, and the recent debate that followed the decision to entrust the European Central Bank with powers to maintain price stability while leaving responsibility for financial stability and prudential control in the hands of national authorities, has brought a great deal of attention to the issue of the institutional allocation of bank regulation. These debates, however, have been dominated by the issues arising from placing supervision in the central bank or in an independent agency and by the question of whether there is a need for a lender of last resort and banking supervisor at European level.

Institutional allocation of regulation: a literature review

Despite the growing interest among academics and policymakers, with the interplay between different regulations and the institutional allocation of bank regulation, there is still a reduced number of formal models on these issues, in particular the latter one.

On the one hand, research on the design of bank regulation has focused on the study of each regulation separately. For example, in the case of the lender of last resort, the focus has been on the issue of whether the central bank should retain discretion or pre-commit to a set of rules under which it will lend to banks (Goodfriend and Lacker, 1999; Freixas, 1999). In the case of deposit insurance, most of the research has focused on issues such as the moral hazard it causes (Kareken and Wallace, 1978; Merton, 1977), the feasibility of fair premia (Chan *et al.*, 1992; Freixas and Rochet, 1995) and the cost effects of depositor-preference laws (Osterberg and Thomson, 1999; Birchler, 2000). Finally, in the case of supervision the focus has been on bank closure, in particular the moral hazard resulting from different closure rules (Davis and McManus, 1991).

On the other hand, most of the literature that has studied the interplay between bank regulations has not taken into account the potential conflicts of interest between regulatory authorities, because it often assumes both regulations are administered by a single regulator or different regulators acting in perfect synchrony.[18] A strand of this literature analyses the interplay between deposit insurance pricing and bank closure policies. Pennacchi (1987) studies the impact of different failure resolution policies, Allen and Saunders (1993) study the impact of the deposit insurer's option to forbear on bank closure and Acharya and Dreyfus (1989) show the importance of endogenizing closure rules by jointly determining the optimal insurance premium and bank closure policy for a purely cost-minimizing deposit insurer. Another strand of this literature analyses the interplay between deposit insurance and lending of last resort.

Kanatas (1986) focuses on the pricing of government's exposure to bank risk-taking resulting from its provision of deposit insurance and lending of last resort. Sleet and Smith (2000) focus instead on the rationale for the simultaneous existence of deposit insurance and lending of last resort, and show that the choices made with respect to the lending of last resort policy are of more significant to the characteristics of equilibrium than those made with respect to deposit insurance pricing.

Finally, research which accounts for the incentives of regulators usually assumes a single regulator and therefore does not consider the interplay between regulatory authorities. For example, studies on the issues arising from the incentives of supervisors to monitor banks (Campbell *et al.*, 1992) or on the incentives of the deposit insurer to close banks (Mailath and Mester, 1994) assume a single regulatory authority. Pagès and Santos (2001) analyse the potential distortionary effects of depositor-preference laws on supervisors' incentives to monitor banks and to close them, but they assume the other regulatory agencies take on a passive role.[19]

Participants in the debate on the institutional allocation of bank supervision have put forward several arguments that build on the incentives of some regulatory authorities and on the potential conflicts of interest and synergies between supervision and other functions of these authorities, but they have not formalized these arguments. In addition, they have focused on the question of whether supervision should come under the jurisdiction of the central bank.[20] For example, proponents of keeping it in the central bank point to the importance of supervisory information for the conduct of monetary policy and for central bank's responsibility for financial stability. Supervision, it is argued, is particularly needed in times of financial crisis, when only direct contact can deliver the essential information on time, making it easier to ascertain if a bank asking for liquidity support is illiquid or insolvent, and to evaluate the implications of Proponents of moving supervision out of the central bank point to the potential conflicts of interest between this function and monetary policy. There may be times, the argument follows, when monetary authorities wish to increase interest rates (to bring down inflation) while the supervisory authorities oppose such a policy because of its adverse effect on the profitability and solvency of the banking system. Others point out that in cases where there are problems with banks, central bank supervision might have negative implications on its credibility and consequently affect its ability to achieve its monetary policy goal.

Repullo (2000) has made an important contribution to our understanding of the issues that arise through the interaction of bank regulators with different mandates not acting in perfect synchrony. He studies the optimal allocation of the lending of last resort function between the central bank and the deposit insurance provider in an incomplete contracting framework. In his model, a bank is subject to liquidity shocks that require borrowing from a lender of last resort because asymmetry of information makes private lending infeasible. The central bank and the insurance provider can act as lender of last resort. The selected agency is given supervision authority in order to get information on the bank's financial condition. Both agencies care about its financial wealth net of the costs of a bank failure. They both incur only a fraction of the social cost of a bank failure, but only the insurance provider considers the obligations to depositors.

Repullo's main conclusion is that the central bank should act as the lender of last resort when banks' liquidity problems are small, but delegate to the deposit insurance provider when they are large. This is explained by the following two results. A regulator that does not internalize the full cost of default is always too strict. A regulator that only internalizes the costs of liquidity provision will be less strict if these costs are small and stricter if they are large. Repullo then argues that if small liquidity problems are more frequent, to avoid duplication costs that allocation of lending of last resort suggests giving supervision to the central bank with the understanding that it will transfer the supervisory information to the insurance provider in case this agency has to deal with a large liquidity problem.

Kahn and Santos (2001) extend Repullo's analysis in several key directions. They examine the effects of competition in provision of the lender of last resort function – both the competition between regulators and private lenders, and the competition among the regulators themselves. They consider some aspects of the design of the deposit insurance scheme, most notably the legal priority of the deposit insurer's claims on the bank's assets, and the effect of the insurance provider's authority to withdraw a bank's insurance coverage and thus force it into bankruptcy even when the lender of last resort is willing to extend liquidity support to this bank. In addition, they consider an issue which has been absent thus far from the debates on the institutional allocation of banking supervision: authorities' incentives to collect information about banks and their incentives to transmit this information to the other regulatory agencies.

When regulatory authorities are reluctant to close failing banks because they incur political costs, the analysis of Kahn and Santos suggests two alternative regulatory structures to reduce regulatory forbearance. If it is feasible to pre-specify lending of last resort interest rates, then one can make the lending of last resort function the exclusive province of one regulator. The other regulator, the deposit insurance provider, should insure lending of last resort loans and be empowered to close banks. In this structure, the deposit insurance provider has a strong incentive against forbearance, while the lender of last resort can concern itself exclusively with liquidity.

If such pre-specification is not feasible, then a possible institutional structure is to have both the central bank and deposit insurance provider ready to act as lender of last resort, the competition between them making the pre-specification of interest rates unnecessary. In this structure it is important for the lender of last resort to be junior to the deposit insurer in order to reduce temptation to over-lend, although this somewhat increases the latter's temptation to forbear. In this structure, we found, like Repullo, a tendency for small liquidity shortfalls to be handled by the central bank and large liquidity shortfalls to be handled by the deposit insurer, because of the differences in the costs of a bank failure to the two regulators. However, these results stem from quite different mechanisms; in our analysis it is a matter of competition between regulators, while for Repullo it is a matter of voluntary delegation of the job by one regulator to the other. The significance of this distinction becomes apparent when there is asymmetry of information between the regulatory agencies because in this case, as Kahn and Santos show, regulators' incentives distort their decisions to share information. This suggests that conclusions on the institutional allocation of regulation that are intensive in information gathering should not be based on the assumption that agencies have perfect incentives to delegate activities based on the information they collect.

Final remarks

By implicitly assuming that regulation is managed by a single authority, most of the literature on bank regulation has ignored the question of the institutional allocation of regulatory powers. In practice, banks are regulated by overlapping authorities, often established with different mandates, some of which are likely to be in conflict. Thus, different institutional allocations of bank regulations are likely to heighten different conflicting goals.

Until recently only a minority of countries seem to have addressed the potential conflicts of interest between regulatory authorities, in general through regulations either protecting one agency from another's potential actions or targeting the agency whose actions may be costly to other agencies. The recent debate on whether bank supervision should be housed in the central bank or moved to an independent authority, though focused on supervision, has increased policymakers' awareness of the importance of the institutional allocation of the various components that form a bank regulatory arrangement.

This debate has also called researchers' attention to this issue. Research on the institutional allocation of bank regulatory powers is still in its early stages, but it has already produced some important insights and it has hinted at a host of several other related issues in need of further investigation. These include, for example, the role of the design of the deposit insurance and lender of last resort schemes on the institutional allocation of regulatory powers, and the role of certain authorities' informational advantage on this allocation of powers.

Notes

1 This chapter builds on the materials Santos prepared for two seminar presentations at the SEACEN (South East Asian Central Banks) in Taipei, Taiwan on 29–31 March 2000. We thank seminar participants for helpful comments and Nid Quah and Yun Yee for transcribing their presentations. The views stated herein are those of the authors and are not necessarily those of the Federal Reserve Bank of New York or the Federal Reserve.

2 The institutional allocation of supervision emerged in the debate on the repeal of the Glass–Steagall Act because the proposals to repeal the Act that would not require investment banking activities to be offered in a subsidiary of a bank holding company could influence the Fed's role in supervision. A reason is that the Fed has the sole authority to supervise these companies but not all the stand-alone banks in the country. See Santos (1998) for the arguments presented in this debate.

3 See Prati and Schinasi (1999), Vives (1999) and Lannoo (2000) for the debate on the institutional allocation of banking regulation in the European Monetary Union.

4 See Bhattacharya and Thakor (1993) and Freixas and Rochet (1997) for a review of modern banking theory. For a review of the earlier theories of financial intermediation, see Santomero (1984).

5 See Calomiris and Kahn (1991), Flannery (1994), Qi (1998) and Diamond and Rajan (1998) for explanations as to why it is advantageous for intermediaries to offer deposit-taking and lending services simultaneously.

6 Diamond and Dybvig (1983), Jacklin and Bhattacharya (1988) and Chari and Jagannathan (1988) developed models explaining one of the liquidity shocks that banks are susceptible to (runs on their deposits).

7 Flannery (1996) and Freixas *et al.* (2000) provide a rationale for the lender of last resort based on interbank market failures arising from asymmetry of information.

8 Other mechanisms proposed to deal with these problems are narrow banking and funding banks with equity instead of demand deposits. See Diamond and Dybvig (1986), Gorton and Pennacchi (1992) and Wallace (1996) for a discussion on narrow banks and Jacklin (1987) for a discussion on banks' funding sources.

9 Dewatripont and Tirole (1994) argue that, even without deposit insurance, depositors would not monitor banks because they lack the expertise and the incentive, as they hold small deposits and monitoring is costly.

10 Asymmetry of information makes it impossible or undesirable, from a welfare viewpoint, to charge banks fairly priced premiums. See Chan *et al.* (1992) and Freixas and Rochet (1995), respectively.

11 See Goodhart (1988) for a discussion of early-established central banks' involvement in crisis management.

12 See Goodhart *et al.* (1994) for a history of central banking.

13 There is evidence of several deposit insurance arrangements in the United States in the nineteenth century. However, these arrangements generally provided insurance coverage to only a small portion of the banking industry. See Calomiris (1989) for a detailed characterization of these deposit insurance schemes.

14 See Santos (2001a) for a further discussion of central banks' involvement in bank supervision.

15 Under a depositor-preference law, depositors have a senior claim over the other claimants of the bank. Thus, in the event of bankruptcy, they have to be fully paid back before the other claims can be honoured. The US, Switzerland, Hong Kong, Malaysia and Argentina are examples of countries that have some

202 *C.M. Kahn and J.A.C. Santos*

form of depositor-preference laws. See Garcia (1999) for information on regulations on depositors' legal priority in several countries.
16 See Benston and Kaufman (1998) for a detailed presentation of the US prompt corrective action scheme.
17 Following the US House of Representatives (1991) study claiming that Fed loans to troubled banks in the 1980s increased the losses to the Federal Deposit Insurance Corporation, Congress introduced restrictions on Fed loans and defined a penalty for lending to banks that subsequently failed (loss of the interest income received from such banks). See Gilbert (1994) for the Federal Deposit Insurance Corporation Improvement Act restrictions on Fed loans and a dispute of the congressional report claim.
18 An important strand of the literature on the interplay between regulations has focused on the relationship between bank capital regulation and deposit insurance. See Santos (2001b) for a review of the literature on capital regulation.
19 See Kane (1990) and Goodhart *et al.* (1998: Chapter 3) for a discussion of the principal–agent problems that can arise between a regulator and the banks he regulates.
20 See Haubrich (1996), Goodhart and Schoenmaker (1998) and Briault (1999) for the debate on the allocation of supervision.

References

Acharya, S. and Dreyfus, J.F. (1989) 'Optimal bank reorganization policies and the pricing of federal deposit insurance', *Journal of Finance* 44(5): 1313–33.
Allen, L. and Saunders, A. (1993) 'Forbearance and valuation of deposit insurance as a callable put', *Journal of Banking and Finance* 17: 629–43.
Bagehot, W. (1873) *Lombard Street: A Description of the Money Market*, London: H.S. King.
Barth, J.R., Caprio, J. and Levine, R. (2001) 'The regulation and supervision of banks around the world: a new database', mimeo, World Bank, Washington, DC.
Benston, G.J. and Kaufman, G.G. (1998) 'Deposit insurance reform in the FDIC Improvement Act: the experience to date', *Federal Reserve Bank of Chicago Economic Perspectives* 22(2): 2–20.
Bhattacharya, S. and Thakor, A.V. (1993) 'Contemporary banking theory', *Journal of Financial Intermediation* 3: 2–50.
Birchler, U.W. (2000) 'Bankruptcy priority for bank deposits: a contract theoretic explanation', *Review of Financial Studies* 13: 813–39.
Briault, C. (1999) 'The rationale for a single financial services regulator', Financial Services Authority Occasional Paper Series, no. 2.
Calomiris, C.W. (1989) 'Deposit insurance: lessons from the record', *Federal Reserve Bank of Chicago Economic Perspectives* 13(3): 10–30.
Calomiris, C.W. and Kahn, C.M. (1991) 'The role of demandable debt in structuring optimal banking arrangements', *American Economic Review* 81(3): 497–513.
Campbell, T.S., Chan, Y.S. and Marino, A.M. (1992) 'An incentive-based theory of bank regulation', *Journal of Financial Intermediation* 2: 255–76.
Chan, Y.S., Greenbaum, S.I. and Thakor, A.V. (1992) 'Is fairly priced deposit insurance possible?', *Journal of Finance* 47: 227–45.
Chari, V.V. and Jagannathan, R. (1988) 'Banking panics, information, and rational expectations equilibrium', *Journal of Finance* 43: 749–61.
Davis, S.M. and McManus, D.A. (1991) 'The effects of closure policies on bank risk-taking', *Journal of Banking and Finance* 15(4–5): 917–38.

Dewatripont, M. and Tirole, J. (1994) *The Prudential Regulation of Banks*, Cambridge, MA: MIT Press.

Diamond, D.W. (1984) 'Financial intermediation and delegated monitoring', *Review of Economic Studies* 51: 393–414.

Diamond, D.W. and Dybvig, P.H. (1983) 'Bank runs, deposit insurance and liquidity', *Journal of Political Economy* 91: 401–19.

Diamond, D.W. and Dybvig, P.H. (1986) 'Banking theory, deposit insurance, and bank regulation', *Journal of Business* 59: 53–68.

Diamond, D.W. and Rajan, R.G. (1998) 'Liquidity risk, liquidity creation and financial fragility: a theory of banking', mimeo, University of Chicago, Chicago, IL.

Flannery, M.J. (1994) 'Debt maturity and the deadweight cost of leverage: optimally financing banking firms', *American Economic Review* 84: 320–31.

Flannery, M.J. (1996) 'Financial crises, payment systems problems, and discount window lending', *Journal of Money, Credit and Banking* 28(4): 804–24.

Freixas, X. (1999) 'Optimal bail out policy, conditional and creative ambiguity', mimeo Universitat Pompeu Fabra, Barcelona.

Freixas, X., Parigi, B. and Rochet, J.C. (2000) 'Systemic risk, interbank relations and liquidity provision by the central bank', *Journal of Money Credit and Banking* 32(3): 611–38.

Freixas, X. and Rochet, J.C. (1995) 'Fair pricing of deposit insurance. Is it possible? Yes. Is it desirable? No', mimeo, University Pompeu Fabra, Barcelona.

Freixas, X. and Rochet, J.C. (1997) *Microeconomics of Banking*, Cambridge, MA: MIT Press.

Garcia, G.G.H. (1999) 'Deposit insurance: a survey of actual and best practices', IMF Working Paper, no. 54.

Gilbert, R.A. (1994) 'Federal Reserve lending to banks that failed: implications for the Bank Insurance Fund', *Federal Reserve Bank of St. Louis Review* 76(1): 3–18.

Goodfriend, M. and Lacker, J.M. (1999) 'Limited commitment and central bank lending', mimeo, Federal Reserve Bank of Richmond, Richmond, VA.

Goodhart, C. (1988) *The Evolution of Central Banks*, Cambridge, MA: MIT Press.

Goodhart, C., Capie, F. and Schnadt, N. (1994) 'The development of central banking', in Capie, F., Goodhart, C., Fisher, S. and Schnadt, N. (eds) *The Future of Central Banking*, Cambridge: Cambridge University Press, pp. 1–231.

Goodhart, C., Hartmann, P., Llewellyn, D., Rojas-Suárez, L. and Weisbrod, S. (1998) *Financial Regulation: Why, how, and where now?* New York: Routledge.

Goodhart, C. and Schoenmaker, D. (1998) 'Institutional separation between supervisory and monetary agencies', in Goodhart, C. (ed.) *The Emerging Framework of Financial Regulation*, London: Central Banking Publications Ltd.

Gorton, G. and Pennacchi, G. (1992) 'Money market funds and finance companies: Are they the banks of the future?', in Klausner, M. and White, L. (eds) *Structural Change in Banking*, Homewood, Illinois: Irwin, pp. 173–214.

Haubrich, J.G. (1996) 'Combining banking supervision and monetary policy', *Federal Reserve Bank of Cleveland Economic Commentary*, November.

Jacklin, C. (1987) 'Demand deposits, trading restrictions, and risk-sharing', in Prescott, E.C. and Wallace, N. (eds) *Contractual Arrangements for Intertemporal Trade*, Minneapolis. MN: University of Minnesota Press, pp. 26–47.

Jacklin, C. and Bhattacharya, S. (1988) 'Distinguishing panics and information-based bank runs: welfare and policy implications', *Journal of Political Economy* 96: 568–92.

Kahn, C.M. and Santos, J.A.C. (2001) 'Allocating bank regulatory powers: lender of last resort, deposit insurance and supervision', forthcoming in *European Economic Review.*

Kane, E.J. (1990) 'Principal–agent problems in S&L Salvage', *Journal of Finance* 45(3): 755–64.

Kanatas, G. (1986) 'Deposit insurance and the discount window: pricing under asymmetric information', *Journal of Finance* 41(2): 437–50.

Kareken, J.H. and Wallace, N. (1978) 'Deposit insurance and bank regulation: a partial-equilibrium exposition', *Journal of Business* 51: 413–38.

Lannoo, K. (2000) 'Challenges to the structure of financial supervision in the EU', Centre for European Policy Studies, Brussels.

Llewellyn, D. (1999) 'The institutional structure of regulatory agencies', in Courtis, N. (ed.) *How Countries Supervise their Banks, Issuers and Securities Markets,* London: Central Banking Publications.

Mailath, G.J. and Mester, L.J. (1994) 'A positive analysis of bank closure', *Journal of Financial Intermediation* 3(3): 272–99.

Merton, R.C. (1977) 'An analytic derivation of the cost of deposit insurance and loan guarantees', *Journal of Banking and Finance* 1: 512–20.

Osterberg, W.P. and Thomson, J.B. (1999) 'Depositor-preference laws and the cost of debt capital', *Federal Reserve Bank of Cleveland Economic Review* 35(3): 10–20.

Pagès, H. and Santos, J.A.C. (2001) 'Optimal supervisory policies and depositor-preference laws', mimeo, Federal Reserve Bank of New York, New York.

Pennacchi, G.G. (1987) 'Alternative forms of deposit insurance: pricing and bank incentive issues', *Journal of Banking and Finance* 11: 291–312.

Prati, A. and Schinasi, G.J. (1999) 'Financial stability in European Economic and Monetary Union', mimeo, IMF, Washington, DC.

Qi, J. (1998) 'Deposit liquidity and bank monitoring', *Journal of Financial Intermediation* 7(2): 198–218.

Repullo, R. (2000) 'Who should act as a lender of last resort? An incomplete contracts model', *Journal of Money Credit and Banking* 32(3): 580–605.

Santomero, A.M. (1984) 'Modeling the banking firm: a survey', *Journal of Money, Credit and Banking* 16: 576–602.

Santos, J.A.C. (1998) 'Securities activities in banking conglomerates: should their location be regulated?', *Cato Journal* 18(1): 93–117.

Santos, J.A.C. (2001a) 'Bank of England in central banking theory', forthcoming in Warner, M. (ed.) *The International Encyclopedia of Business and Management,* 2nd edn, London: Thomson Learning.

Santos, J.A.C. (2001b) 'Bank capital regulation in contemporary banking theory: a review of the literature', *Financial Markets, Institutions and Instruments* 10(2): 41–84.

Sleet, C. and Smith, B.D. (2000) 'Deposit insurance and lender of last resort functions', *Journal of Money Credit and Banking* 32(3): 518–75.

US House of Representatives (1991) 'An analysis of Federal Reserve discount window loans to failed institutions', by the staff of the Committee on Banking, Finance and Urban Affairs, Washington, DC.

Vives, X. (1999) 'Banking supervision in the European Monetary Union', mimeo Institut d'Anàlisi Econòmica, CSIC, Barcelona.

Wallace, N. (1996) 'Narrow banking meets the Diamond–Dybvig model', *Federal Reserve Bank of Minneapolis Quarterly Review* Winter, 3–13.

COMMENT: THE DEBATE ON THE EMU INSTITUTIONAL FRAMEWORK FOR DEALING WITH BANKING CRISES

María J. Nieto[1]

The launching of European Monetary Union (EMU) brought about a double separation, geographic and functional, of prudential supervision, deposit insurance and monetary policy activities for the euro area countries. In this context, the institutional framework for dealing with banking crises has become decentralized. Freixas (2003) describes the present framework as 'improvised cooperation' conveying the view of an efficient although adaptative exchange of information and decision making. The existence of an established network of contacts among supervisors; among central bankers and supervisors; and among central bankers is expected to help the efficiency of this exchange.

Deposit insurance

The role of deposit insurance (DI) has been largely ignored in the debate on the optimal allocation of regulators' responsibilities on managing banking crises in EMU, as pointed out by Kahn and Santos (2002, 2004). This can be explained by the role of 'pay-box' played by this regulator in Europe with little or no involvement in resolving bank failures.

The regulation of DI is only partially harmonized in the European Union (EU) by the 1994 Directive on deposit insurance schemes.[2] The Directive provided a missing link in the establishment of the single European banking market, insuring its depositors throughout the EU by requiring each national DI to cover depositors of Member States' banks as well as their branches in other Member States. This principle was inspired by the existing home-country regime for banking supervision embodied in the Second Directive. The coverage of international branches by the home country DI would thus provide a strong incentive for countries to maintain or improve their banking supervision. The reality is, however, that the largest part of EU banks' cross-border activities measured in terms of percentage of assets has been developed via subsidiaries.

The Directive discourages the use of government financing for DI schemes and exempts the Member States from any obligation to support one financially, even in the context of a banking crisis (Garcia and Prast, 2004). At the same time, the Directive pays little attention to avoiding bank rescues and bail outs, which are relevant issues considering the high concentration of the banking systems in the EU (Dale, 2000). Moreover, the DI schemes in the EU face the important limitation posed by the absence of a single tax authority in the EU as well as the limitations imposed by the EC Treaty on the ECB and national central banks' (NCBs) lending to governments or institutions (Article 101) and to the EU's capability to 'bail out' governments and public entities (Article 103), which limit *de facto* the effectiveness of the guarantee.

In sum, the present institutional arrangement relies heavily on the cooperation of home and host supervisors and between these and the NCBs, DI and eventually on the taxpayers' willingness to support international banks. Non-cooperative behaviour between authorities (supervisors, DI and NCBs) may delay dealing with individual crises which, in turn, may convert what might be a problem in one institution into a systemic crisis in another.

Against this background, the current debate on the optimal allocation of regulators' responsibilities on preventing and managing banking crises in the EU has mainly focused on the other two regulatory institutions: lender of last resort (LOLR) and prudential supervision

The LOLR

The LOLR role has always been seen as the domain of the creator of monetary base in a currency system (Goodhart, 2000). However, in EMU both the European Central Bank (ECB) and NCBs, the European System of Central Banks (ESCB), have the ability and the right to create base money by direct loans to credit institutions in addition to open market operations (ESCB Statute, Article 18.1, second indent). These loans are collateralized and can be either via regular or special ad hoc arrangements. Overnight lending facilities at interest rates that are normally substantially higher than the corresponding market rate are available without limit. Before discussing the ESCB's functions as LOLR, I would like to briefly comment on the economic literature on this regulatory institution.

The economic literature on LOLR has disagreed on whether the aim of 'staying the panic' may be achieved by open market operations (Goodfriend and King, 1988) or whether it demands lending to individual banks (Flannery, 1996). However, both sides seem to agree on the proposition that liquidity assistance can become an overused palliative that encourages moral hazard and excessive risk-taking that weakens the financial system. Along this line, Solow (1982) maintained that 'the existence of a credible LOLR must reduce the private cost of risk taking. It can hardly be doubted that, in consequence, more risk will be taken.' However, Goodhart (1999) claims that moral hazard is not 'at all times a major consideration' when considering whether a central bank should act as an LOLR. Repullo (2004) shows that the LOLR does not induce more risk taking by the banks when the decision to lend is based on supervisory information on the bank's financial condition. Moreover, it provides a new rationale for 'constructive ambiguity' (Goodfriend and Lacker, 1999), in that outside observers without access to the supervisory data cannot tell whether LOLR will be exercised in any particular circumstance.

The recent literature is based on the assumption that the regulator's, and in particular the LOLR's, utility function reflects any costs for its actions (Repullo, 2004; Kahn and Santos, 2002, 2004). This assumption implies that the regulator is democratically accountable and, hence, has a clear mandate with explicit and measurable objectives. While most central banks can take decisions on LOLR operations and that this task has been formalized in a substantial number of countries, its impact is difficult to measure, making the accountability process even more difficult. In this context, it is more realistic to assume that, for small or isolated bank failures, the regulatory structure places no responsibility, while these costs may be important in case of a large banking crisis that requires significant amounts of taxpayers' money.

Turning back to the basic functions of the ESCB, the EC Treaty refers to the task of promoting the good functioning of payment systems [Article 105(2)], but does not mention explicitly the function of promoting financial stability. However, a broad reference is included in Article 105.5 of the EC Treaty: 'the ESCB shall contribute to the smooth conduct of policies pursued by the competent authorities relating to the prudential supervision of credit institutions and the stability of the financial system.' Such a broad reference implicitly considers 'financial stability' as a non basic function of the ESCB. Consistent with Article 105(2) of the EC Treaty, the ECB could be expected to act as LOLR via the existing monetary policy operational framework, in the case of a general liquidity freeze. However, it is in the traditional role of LOLR envisaged by Bagehot that the ECB role of LOLR has been less clear and, implicitly, decentralized to the NCBs (Lastra, 2000a). In practice, the necessary coordination of NCBs' LOLR functions and monetary policy led to an agreement by which the ECB's Governing Council is always informed and consulted on those LOLR operations that may have implications for monetary policy in the euro area. Folkerts-Landau and Garber (1992), Pratti and Schinasi (1999) and Lastra (2000a) and Freixas (2003) are among the many authors who argue that an immediate response to a cross-border banking crisis would require further centralization of the LOLR decisions.

Furthermore, a general consensus exists that an integrated banking market in Europe requires greater coordination among regulatory institutions, particularly between the LOLR and prudential supervision.

Prudential supervision

The ECB considers that the attribution of prudential supervisory responsibility even beyond banking to NCBs (vs agencies) in the euro area is desirable from two points of view (Duisenberg, 2000). It allows central banks first, to understand the financial condition of financial intermediaries better, and second, to make possible a closer implicit coordination with the monetary policy function. Thygesen (2003) shares the ECB argument for 'not marginalizing central banks in bank supervision with the arrival of the euro and particularly in the absence of well-developed supervision coordinated at the level of the euro area'. The underlying assumptions of this approach are that asymmetries of information between banks and regulators do exist and that information has a cost.

However, at the national level, the regulatory arrangements for prudential supervision of financial intermediaries have focused more on efficiency of controls than on coordination with the central banks. As a result, diverse institutional structures for the supervision of financial intermediaries co-exist at the national level in the euro area. In recent years, various countries have embarked on institutional reforms of their models for the supervision of financial intermediaries (Nieto and Peñalosa, 2004) and those models are consistent with different levels of involvement by central banks, e.g. in Ireland; where this centralization of supervisory activities has taken place under the umbrella of the central bank. However, this has not always been the approach followed in the EU and the centralization of supervision of financial intermediaries has often involved the separation of central bank, prudential supervision and deposit insurance. The latter approach implies that the incentives of these agencies to gather information on banks are not perfectly aligned: the central bank as an LOLR would gather information on banks' liquidity and prudential supervisors on banks' financial condition. Moreover, to the extent that information has a cost, neither regulator will engage in information sharing. In order to reduce these adverse effects, the ECB, the NCBs and the supervisory agencies have signed a Memorandum of Understanding (MoU) with respect to the exchange of information among central banks and the prudential supervisors on the financial condition of distressed banks.[3] Nonetheless, this approach has limitations: first, it lacks legal enforceability (hence, no penalties are envisaged if the contract is breached); second, the lack of full regulatory harmonization (i.e. accounting rules) leaves room for interpretation about the financial condition of a bank; and third, the MoU is confidential, which seriously limits the accountability of the institutions involved. Moreover, this MoU neglects the role of deposit insurance and, more generally that of the ministries of finance, as well as prudential supervisors the securities and insurance markets.

During the first years of EMU, the existing coordination arrangements between regulators have been deemed sufficient to ensure adequate ECB access to supervisory information. However, the euro is encouraging the development of pan-European markets and financial institutions and, when more of these institutions emerge, the existing arrangements based on MoUs and Committees may prove complex to manage. Furthermore, they may not allow for a rapid assessment of the systemic implications of a banking crisis (Prati and Schinasi, 1999; Bini Smaghi, 2000; Schoenmaker and Oosterloo, 2004). Khan and Santos (2002) analyse the consequences of the allocation of the LOLR and supervisory functions in the euro area for the degree of forbearance in closing distressed banks and for the level of diligence in prudential supervision as well as the consequences for the order of centralization of LOLR and prudential supervision. The authors conclude that the lack of centralization of LOLR and supervision in an integrated banking market increases forbearance and reduces the diligence of supervision. At the same time, centralizing these regulatory functions will tend to reverse these effects. Moreover, they show that the centralization of supervision (and not LOLR) presents the advantage of increasing supervisors' incentives to invest in monitoring and reduces the financing cost of the LOLR. Policy makers do not share this view; they claim that centralizing some regulatory institutions and not others in a piecemeal approach may create adverse incentives (Schoenmaker, 2003).

Although there is no consensus among academics and policy makers on the assumption of responsibilities of prudential supervision by the ECB, the EC Treaty (Article 105(6)) and the ESCB Statute (Article 25.2) leave open the possibility that the ECB might gain responsibility for the prudential supervision of credit institutions and other financial entities, with the exception of insurance companies. In order to assign these responsibilities, a qualified majority of the EU Council must decide in favour.[4] In any event, in a hypothetical case in which the ECB would assume these responsibilities, the principle of subsidiarity contained in Article 5 of the EC Treaty would have to be taken into consideration (Lastra, 2000b).

The Lamfalussy process and the setting up of the Committee of European Banking Supervisors has provided for an EU supervisors' coordination forum (Committee of European Banking Supervisors) (Roldán, 2004). Implicit coordination with the euro area monetary policy is guaranteed by the presence of the ECB in each of the three levels of the Lamfalussy architecture.

Conclusions

The regulators' responsibilities on preventing and managing banking crisis (LOLR, supervision and DI) are fully decentralized at the national level in the EU (except for those NCB's LOLR operations that may have implications for monetary policy). This institutional framework allows for the accountability process at the national level. However, in the case of cross-border banking crises, it relies entirely on the existence of an established network of contacts among supervisors (Group de Contact); central bankers and supervisors (Banking Supervision Committee of the ECB; Committee of European Banking Supervisors); and central bankers (Governing Council of the ECB); as well as the MoU between central banks and supervisors. These arrangements contribute to attenuating the 'improvisatory' character of the cooperation among regulators, although they may prove difficult to manage and may not allow for a rapid assessment of the systemic implications of a banking crisis (Freixas, 2003).

Since the inception of EMU, the debate on the optimal allocation of regulators' responsibilities on preventing and managing banking crisis in the EU has mainly focused on the role of LOLR and supervision. Both the EU and the national debates have neglected the role of the DI and more importantly that of the Ministers of Finance. National authorities to the extent that they are exempted from any obligation to financially support a DI scheme even in the context of a banking crisis may have the incentive to delay and not cooperate with other Member State authorities.

Finally, I would like to highlight that national authorities are aware of the limitations of the existing institutional framework for bank crisis management in EMU. The Council of Economic and Financial Affairs (ECOFIN), which is comprised of the ministers responsible for economic affairs and finance in the EU, has recently echoed this concern:[5]

> [It] stresses the need for Supervisors, Central Banks and Finance Ministers to work together to ensure that appropriate plans and mechanisms are in place to respond to any developing financial crisis which threatens the stability of the financial system. It also [...] stresses the importance of promoting financial stability and market integrity, through both legislative and practical initiatives.

Notes

1 The opinions stated herein are those of the author and do not necessarily reflect those of Banco de España.
2 Directive 94/19/EC of the European Parliament and of the Council of 30 May 1994 on deposit insurance.
3 The MoU consists of a set of principles and procedures that deal specifically with the identification of the authorities responsible with the crisis and the required flows of information between all authorities and the practical conditions for sharing information at the cross-border level.
4 According to the new Constitutional Treaty (2004).
5 Draft Council conclusions on the Financial Services Committee's report on financial integration. Council of the European Union 9799/04. ECOFIN 186 EF 25, 26 May 2004.

References

Bini Smaghi, L. (2000) 'Who takes care of financial stability in Europe?', in Goodhart, C.A.E. (ed.) *Which Lender of Last Resort for Europe*, London: Central Banking Publications, pp. 225–50.

Dale, R.S. (2000) 'Deposit insurance in theory and practice', *Journal of Financial Regulation and Compliance* 8(1): 36–56.

Duisenberg, W. (2000) 'The future of banking supervision and the integration of financial markets', conference organized by the Euro Group on improving integration of financial markets in Europe, 22 May.

Flannery, M. (1996) 'Financial crises, payment system problems, and discount window lending', *Journal of Money, Credit and Banking* 28: 804–24.

Folkerts-Landau, D. and Garber, P.M. (1992) 'The ECB: a bank or a monetary policy rule', Cambridge, MA: NBER.

Freixas, X. (2003) 'Crisis management in Europe', in Kremers, J.J.M., Schoenmaker, D. and Wierts, P.J. (eds) *Financial Supervision in Europe*, Cheltenham: Edward Elgar, pp. 102–19.

Garcia, G. and Prast, H. (2004) 'Depositor and investor protection in the Netherlands: past, present and future', De Nederlandsche Bank Occasional Study Number 119.

Goodfriend, M. and King, R.G. (1988) 'Financial deregulation, monetary policy, and central banking', *Federal Reserve Bank of Richmond Economic Review* 74: 3–22.

Goodfriend, M. and Lacker, J.M. (1999) 'Limited Commitment and Central Bank Lending', *Federal Reserve Bank of Richmond Economic Quarterly* 85: 1–27.

Goodhart, C.A.E. (1999) 'Myths about the lender of last resort', LSE Financial Markets Group Special Paper, no. 120.

Goodhart, C.A.E. (2000) 'Introduction', in Goodhart, C.A.E. (ed.) *Which Lender of Last Resort for Europe*, London: Central Banking Publications, pp. 1–13.

Khan, C.M. and Santos, J.A.C. (2002) 'Allocating lending of last resort and supervision in the euro area', in Alexander, V., Melitz, J. and von Furstenberg, G.M. (eds) *Monetary Union: Why, How, and What Follows?*, London: Oxford University Press, chapter 19.

Khan, C.M. and Santos, J.A.C. (2004) 'Allocating bank regulatory powers: lender of last resort, deposit insurance and supervision', forthcoming in the *European Economic Review*.

Lastra, R. (2000a) 'The role of the European Central Bank with regard to financial stability and lender of last resort operations', in Goodhart, C.A.E. (ed.) *Which Lender of Last Resort for Europe*, London: Central Banking Publications, pp. 197–212.

Lastra, R. (2000b) 'The division of responsibilities between the European Central Bank and the national central bank within the European system of central banks', *Columbia Journal of European Law* 6(2): 167–74.

Nieto, M.J. and Peñalosa, J.M. (2004) 'The European architecture of regulation, supervision and financial stability: a central bank perspective', *Journal of International Banking Regulation* 5(3): 228–42.

Prati, A. and Schinasi, G.J. (1999) 'Financial stability in the European economic and monetary union', in Goodhart, C.A.E. (ed.) *Which Lender of Last Resort for Europe*, London: Central Banking Publications, pp. 69–117.

Repullo, R. (2004) 'Liquidity, risk-taking, and the lender of last resort', forthcoming in CEMFI Working Papers.

Roldán, J.M. (2004) 'Establishment of the committee and future challenges', 26 April, www.c-ebs.org/SP2.htm.

Schoenmaker, D. (2003) 'Comments on A. Ernia and J. Vesala', in Kremers, J.J.M., Schoenmaker, D. and Wierts, P.J. (eds) *Financial Supervision in Europe*, Cheltenham: Edward Elgar, pp. 94–9.

Schoenmaker, D. and Oosterloo, S. (2004). 'Financial supervision in an integrating Europe: measuring cross-border externalities', Financial and Monetary Studies 22-01, The Netherlands Ministry of Finance.

Solow, R.M. (1982) 'On the lender of last resort', in Kindleberger, C.P. and Laffar-

gue, J.-P. (eds) *Financial Crisis: Theory, History, and Policy*, Cambridge: Cambridge University Press.
Thygesen, N. (2003) 'Comments', on Goodhart, C. 'The political economy of financial harmonization in Europe', in Kremers, J.J.M., Schoenmaker, D. and Wierts, P.J. (eds) *Financial Supervision in Europe*, Cheltenham: Edward Elgar, pp. 142–50.

COMMENT: ALLOCATING FINANCIAL REGULATORY POWERS: THE TWIN VIEWS

Donato Masciandaro

The intense evolution undergone by the financial system in recent years has gradually lowered many of the barriers between the component sectors of financial intermediation. Distinctions among traditional sectors of activity have become blurred as part of a process tending to unify the financial markets, caused by the gradual attenuation of functional specialization within the intermediaries operating in those markets.

This increasing complexity of markets has required a drastic rethinking of the procedures by which supervisory powers are exercised over the financial system as a whole. In particular, the problem of dividing the powers among the various financial authorities has become increasingly critical.

What approaches can be used to analyse the allocation of regulatory and supervisory responsibility? The question can be explored both from the economic efficiency point of view and from the positive point of view of what lawmakers or policymakers would choose.

In other words, we can ask what the socially optimal allocation of tasks is, that is, the allocation that would be chosen by a social planner (*economic approach*). Usually the normative benchmark is the Benthamite utilitarian optimum, i.e. the policy maximizing the sum of individual utilities. But we can also discuss the positive issue of whether and how the public representatives choose the supervisory architecture[1] (*political economic approach*).

To understand the features and the evolution of these institutions, economic analysis should be integrated with a political economy approach. Both approaches are potentially useful and complementary for the analysis.

This comment discusses the two approaches to a key issue in financial supervision design: the definition of the optimal degree of unification of financial supervision.

The financial blurring process poses at least three choices in the debate on financial supervisory structure:

1   sectoral (institutional) approach versus functional approach;
2   single supervisory model versus multi-authorities model, and
3   in the EU, centralized setting versus decentralized setting.

From the perspective of increasing financial integration, the relevance of the first question has been rapidly declining. Theoretically, the institutional approach is based on the possibility of separating the banking, securities and insurance markets. The progressive erosion of market separation is likely to cause the breakdown of the institutional approach. That the 'financial blurring' trend favours the alternative functional

supervisory approach is confirmed by the fact that various models ('pure'
or 'mixed') of such an approach have been adopted recently or are currently under discussion in several countries.

From the other standpoint, in the European context the centralized
versus decentralized question seems to be a second-order problem given
that alternative solutions are likely to be strictly dependent on the various
European national answers or positions on the optimal design of the
financial supervisory framework. Furthermore it is closely linked to the
answer to the single supervisory approach versus multi-authorities
approach dilemma. Today, therefore, given the dominance of the
functional approach and the 'deferred' nature of the centralized–
decentralized questions, the choice between the single financial authority
model and the multi-financial authorities model seems to be the more relevant one.

In what follows we present the economic approach to the optimal allocation of supervisory responsibilities, followed by the political economy
approach. The political economy approach is then used to explore the
determinants of the unifications process, before concluding.

The economic approach

The problem of assigning power to the financial sector authorities is
linked first to the differences among the three principal sectors of financial activity (banking systems, securities markets and insurance). The
sectors in question differ in many respects and, precisely because of their
diversity, the solution of assigning control over each sector to a different
authority has long been viewed as the natural one within many legal
systems. This solution continues to be practised in many countries in spite
of the lowering of barriers between the sectors.

The problem is complicated by a second circumstance. Action of the
controlling authorities is intended to serve a number of objectives. The
purposes that can be assigned to financial supervision are numerous and
do not lend themselves to schematic representation. The regulatory
objectives are vastly different in nature and achieving them may require
procedures so different as to justify the assignment of each of the purposes to a separate authority.

The distribution of tasks among the authorities is much more complicated when the separation between markets, we have considered thus far,
disappears. *Prima facie* the single supervisor model seems to be the
'natural' and best answer to the challenges posed by the market blurring.
If, in the long run, the expected financial structure is a perfectly integrated, single market, the best design for the supervisory architecture
would seem to be the single authority. But the answer is not so simple.

While the principal advantage of a single authority lies precisely in the
fact that it avoids the complex issues associated with the allocation of

tasks, it can bring other benefits. The use of a single authority may result in economies of scale and scope. The economies of scale and scope may derive from the fact that the single authority can benefit from a centralized operating unit, with benefits from the standpoint of human resources, information systems etc. Furthermore, it avoids the multiplication of costs associated with the existence of multiple supervisory authorities. The presence of a single authority may also lead to a reduction in costs of information coordination and sharing of information, because cooperation and interchange can be better ensured among the various supervisory sectors. The costs associated with supervision can generally be reduced.

There can be significant benefit (in terms of efficiency) for the supervised parties, who need deal with only a single interlocutor, especially regarding authorization procedures. Also for the supervised parties, avoiding the multiplication of costs and obligations towards a number of authorities may result in benefits in terms of efficiency and reduction of supervision-associated costs. All ambiguities regarding tasks – who exercises supervision and is responsible for each procedure – are eliminated.

Another advantage of the single authority is that it may reduce the risks of arbitrage in supervision and the risks of competition among the various sectors of the financial system, ensuring greater neutrality of regulation through the harmonization (or even unification) of the sector regulations.

But the single authority model also presents problems and potential risks. According to some authors, the cost advantages associated with a single authority are not necessarily present, since the single authority comprises specialized divisions that may themselves be affected by problems of coordination, information interchange etc. It seems unlikely, however, that the costs of information coordination and sharing sustained by the various divisions of a centrally managed authority could exceed the costs associated with cooperation between different authorities.

One possible argument against the single authority is its potentially higher profile. This model of supervision could be associated with the idea, not necessarily true, of a totally secure financial system, an idea that would reduce the incentives for the supervised parties to have operating systems based on prudence and would relax the caution of consumers toward the financial services offered.

A further argument against having a single authority refers to the fact that the 'institutional failure' of such an authority, since it is active in several sectors, would generate broader negative effects.

In other words, one can say that, given a single authority, it is possible to increase the efficiency in the relationship between supervisor and regulated firms, because the cost of supervision and the possibility of supervisory arbitrage decrease.[2] But one can also say that, given the single supervisor model, efficiency in the supervisor-regulated firm relationships decreases because, with a single authority, risks of capture could increase[3] and the innovations incentive in the regulated industry could decrease,[4] Therefore, the sign and the magnitude of the single supervisor model effects, with respect to the regulated firm relationship issues, seem ambiguous.

One can reach the same kind of conclusion by analysing the relationship between the single authority and the political system (independence and accountability,[5] discretionality[6] or capture[7]), the effects in terms of supervisory organization and resource allocation (economies[8] or diseconomies of scale,[9] benefits or costs of goal conflicts' internalization[10]), and the consequences on the financial services consumers' behaviour (confidence[11] or over-confidence[12]).

The preceding considerations made it manifest that the quest for an optimal degree of concentration of powers in financial supervision cannot be pursued through a classic analysis of the costs and benefits expected from the possible alternative structures.

If, in fact, one proposes to compare the two alternative models – a single authority versus a system with multiple agencies – one realizes that each of them offers expected benefits, but also expected risks. So a theoretical analysis of the potential effects of alternative supervisory structures does not take us very far.

The first natural response to this problem would therefore be to estimate the effects the two alternative supervisory models have on key economic variables. But this leads to at least three difficulties.

First, the emergence of a single authority is only the most striking aspect of a more general and gradual phenomenon: diversification, from country to country, in the degree of centralization of financial supervisory power. What has occurred is that, compared to the traditional model of control by sectors, some countries have confirmed that model, others have radically changed it by adopting a single authority, while yet others have taken or confirmed intermediate choices. This raises the problem of measuring the degree of concentration of powers, country by country, in order to attempt the quantitative description of a qualitative phenomenon.

Second, the issue of the optimal degree of concentration of financial supervisory powers has emerged only recently, with the reforms adopted in various countries, so considering the type of supervisory regime as an explanatory or *exogenous* (though not unique) variable of any other economic phenomenon means undertaking an analysis of extremely short historical series, with all the related problems of interpretation.

Third, completely and satisfactorily identifying what the key economic variables are, and the most possible object of an estimate on which a supervisory structure makes its effect felt, is not a simple problem. Alternative supervisory structures may, for example, affect the level of efficiency of the public resources invested in monitoring the financial markets. Indicators need to be found for efficiency, so that empirical analysis can proceed.

The point is that alternative structures may also (perhaps especially) affect other variables that are important but less easily expressed in numerical indicators. Examples are reputation risk, or the risk that the authority will be captured by the policymakers or by the controlled intermediaries.

Thus a quantitative search for the effects of alternative supervisory structures is probably premature. It might be more interesting to ask: are there any common determinants in the decision each country makes to maintain or reform its control structure? Finding a response would help us not only to interpret what has happened in the past but also to project scenarios for the future, with particular focus on prospects within the EU.

Thus the second objective of the research agenda is to attempt to concentrate on an analysis of the causes that have helped bring about a given supervisory structure in different countries.

The political economic approach

Using the economic approach we pointed out that, given different institutional settings, it is possible to highlight the corresponding gains and losses, and then to perform a rational cost–benefit analysis to choose between alternative models.

We stressed the importance of the traditional cost–benefit analysis, but the conclusion on the possibility of using this approach alone to find an optimal supervisory regime was ultimately somewhat negative.

The preceding section showed that the quest for the optimal supervision architecture cannot be pursued through a simple analysis of the costs and benefits expected from the possible alternative structures, so a theoretical analysis of the potential effects of alternative supervisory structures does not represent the end of the story. The gains and losses from a supervisory model are *expected* variables, calculated by the agents (i.e. the lawmakers) that maintain or reform the supervisory regime. But lawmakers' choices are likely to be influenced by structural variables, which may vary from country to country. Therefore the supervisory regime is *not* a given. In the same way that financial institutions respond to the current and expected regulatory framework, so that framework will itself be changed in the light of revealed and expected responses. Optimal outcomes thus have to be viewed in a dynamic context and will be path dependent.

From a methodological point of view, we are indebted to the intuitions of the new political economy[13] for leading us to three hypotheses:

1 the definition of regulatory architecture is not independent, as in the traditional economics, but endogenous;
2 regulation design is not always determined by maximizing a social welfare function;
3 lawmaker maximization is constrained and influenced by the structural framework.

This research programme can be developed in different ways.

In the economics literature there are no theoretical studies that consider the lawmaker objective function for financial supervisory design.[14] A step forward in research will be to model the lawmaker decision framework, in order to highlight better the features of the institutional and political process that lead a supervisory regime to assume given characteristics. The problem could be analysed as a model of political delegation.[15] Using the principal–agent approach for addressing the architecture of financial supervision seems a very promising avenue for future research.[16]

From the institutional standpoint, in-depth studies on the individual countries could be very interesting, reconstructing the underlying reasons and the decision-making process that have driven the individual lawmakers to select a given architecture of financial supervision. In other words the case-study approach could be useful in the financial supervision architecture field. Historical and institutional analysis might also provide indications very useful for empirical developments.

The key question from the empirical standpoint, is: are there any common determinants in the decision each country makes to maintain or reform its regulatory structure? Finding a response would help us not only to interpret what has happened in the past but also to project scenarios for the future.

Thus, the complementary approach we intend to propose here is to consider the supervisory structure as dependent variable, determined in turn by the dynamics of other structural variables.

The methodological analogy with the abundant, consolidated literature on the independence of central banks[17] may be of some interest and clarify the approach better. In this literature, the theoretical models produced no general result regarding the desirability of a structure with an independent central bank versus one with a dependant monetary authority. In the industrialized countries, while the relationship between independence and control over inflation seemed sufficiently robust and convincing,[18] the relationship between independence, on the one hand, and fiscal and real variables,[19] on the other, was far from certain. Thus the theoretical cost–benefit analysis of alternative monetary regimes could not be considered conclusive.

Economists then went on to verify the theoretical conjectures with comparative, institutional and empirical analysis. After constructing indices of independence of the central banks,[20] and having historical alternative models of independent and dependent monetary authorities,[21] studies attempted to determine whether the degree of legal independence could be considered an independent variable in explaining important macroeconomic phenomena: inflation, deficits and public debt, income and growth.[22]

But above all, still on the methodological plane, an alternative research programme was to consider the degree of central bank independence as a dependent variable,[23] in order to identify what economic and/or institutional structures could explain the decision of one or more countries to maintain or reform their monetary regimes, i.e. the degree of independence of their central banks.

Studies of this type acquire great importance in periods when there is a desire to reform or at least to question the design of the rules. And while in the past this was the case with analyses of central bank independence, it now applies for the first time to the debate on authorities in the financial field.

Exploring the determinants of financial regulatory architectures

Financial supervision regimes vary significantly from country to country. A review of the financial supervision architectures[24] indicates a trend towards a gradual concentration of supervisory powers. A possible application of the political economy approach can therefore be to explore the dynamics in financial supervisory regimes, discovering their determinants, if any, in a worldwide cross-border perspective.

In order to apply the proposed approach, we have to consider actual lawmaker choices in determining the level of financial supervision consolidation. At each point, we observe the lawmaker decision to maintain or reform the financial supervision architecture, choosing the level of consolidation. In other words we consider lawmakers faced with discrete choices.

Building in a cross country perspective an empirical analysis consistent with this discrete choice process involves claiming, at least conceptually, the existence of unobservable lawmaker utilities Uij, where each Uij is the utility received by the ith national lawmaker from the jth level of financial consolidation. Since the utility Uij is unobservable, we represent it as a random quantity, assuming that it is composed of a systematic part, U, and a random error term, ϵ. Furthermore, we claim that the utilities Uij are a function of the attributes of the alternative institutional level of financial consolidation and of the structural characteristics of the lawmaker country. Combining the two hypotheses, we have a random utility framework for the unobservable financial consolidation variable. As usual, we assume that the errors ϵij are independent for each national lawmaker and institutional alternative, normally distributed. The independence assumption implies that the utility derived by one national lawmaker is not related to the utility derived by any other national lawmaker, and that the utility that a lawmaker derives from the choice of a given level of financial consolidation is not related to the utility provided by the other alternative.[25]

In this approach the first crucial issue is the measurement of lawmaker choices, that is, the definition of the dependent variable. To this end we propose a financial authorities concentration index (FAC Index).[26]

Regulatory regimes can be viewed as resulting from a continuous, unobserved variable: the optimal degree of financial supervision concentration consistent with the lawmaker utility. Each regime corresponds to a specific range of the optimal financial supervision concentration, with higher discrete FAC Index values corresponding to a higher range of financial concentration values. Since the FAC Index is a qualitative ordinal variable, the estimation of a model for such a dependent variable necessitates the use of a specific technique.

Our qualitative dependent variable can be classified into more than two categories, given that the FAC Index is a multinomial variable. But the FAC Index is also an ordinal variable, given that it reflects a ranking. Then an ordered model is an appropriate estimator, given the ordered nature of the lawmaker alternative.[27]

The latent variable y^* is unobserved. What is observed is the choice of each national lawmaker to maintain or to reform the financial supervisory architecture: this choice is summarized by the value of the FAC Index, which represents the threshold values. For our dependent variable there are seven threshold values. Estimation proceeds by maximum likelihood, assuming that ϵ is normally distributed across country observations, and the mean and variance of ϵ are normalized to zero and one. This model can be estimated with an ordered Logit or with an ordered Probit model.

Which economic model can be tested? To the best of our knowledge, there is no general theory of the determinants of the lawmaker's decision on the degree of supervision concentration.

Descriptive analysis[28] suggests an interesting result: the national choices on how many agencies must be involved in supervision are strictly linked to the role of the central bank: the degree of supervision unification seems to be inversely correlated with central bank involvement. The choice of the level of financial supervision concentration could depend on the role of the central bank in the supervision architecture.

The central bank effect can be explained as a special case of 'rule-driven path dependence'. Rule-driven path dependence[29] exists when, other conditions being equal, the choice of a given design of rules depends on characteristics already existing or already determined by the rules themselves. In this case, a given lawmaker's choice of supervision concentration level will depend on the role the central bank plays in the supervision, or that the lawmaker has decided to have the central bank play. In other words, the lawmaker's choice can be viewed as a sequential process in which the *institutional status quo* counts: the supervision concentration level is decided based on the position of the central bank (Figure 7.1). If the role of the central bank is limited, the supervision concentration level will probably be high and vice versa.

The central bank effect can be explained as follows. Let us assume that the lawmaker in a given country must decide whether to increase the supervision concentration level. In the most extreme case, he must decide

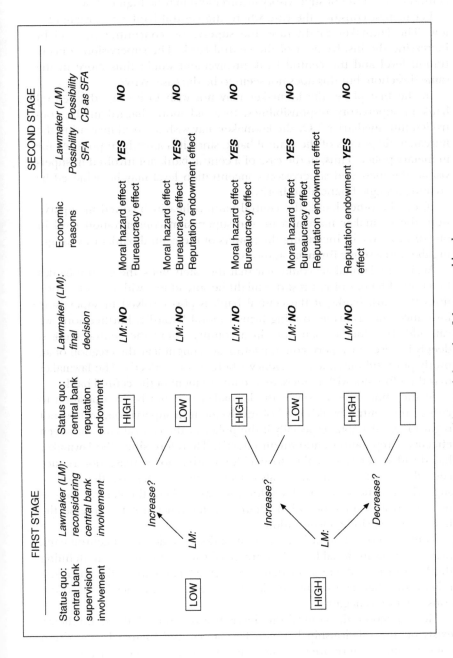

Figure 7.1 Supervision unification lawmaking and the role of the central bank.

whether or not to create a single financial authority. In that country, the central bank's level of supervisory involvement may be high or low.

Let us first consider the case where the central bank's involvement is low. The lawmaker might raise the supervision concentration level by increasing the involvement of the central bank. The supervision concentration level and the central bank involvement would thus move in the same direction, but this does not seem to be the case. Why?

In the first place, the lawmaker may not wish to involve the central bank in supervisory responsibilities, to avoid moral hazard in the controlled intermediaries.[30] Or the lawmaker may wish to avoid increasing the bureaucratic powers of the central bank, since it is already responsible for monetary policy. Thus, in the case of a central bank not involved in supervision, the increased supervision concentration level may be achieved by creating a single financial authority.

If, on the other hand, the central bank is heavily involved in supervision, the lawmaker may increase the supervision concentration level in one of two ways: by increasing the powers of the central bank or by assigning them to a single financial authority.

Again, the lawmakers could fear that the safety net – the central bank's function of lender of last resort – might be spread to a wider set of institutions than just banks, if the central bank is also involved in supervising insurance and securities trading firms ('moral hazard'). Furthermore, we can add the other explanation: in a country where the central bank is deeply involved in supervision, the lawmakers might fear the creation of an overly powerful bureaucratic agency ('bureaucracy effect'). The lawmaker may therefore not wish to increase the involvement of the central bank.

At the same time, however, the lawmaker may not be in a position to reduce the central bank's level of involvement in supervision, or may not regard it as advisable, especially if the policy of the central bank has been effective ('reputation endowment effect'). Therefore since the lawmaker has decided (or was unable to decide) neither to increase nor reduce central bank involvement, he also decides not to increase the level of supervision concentration. Therefore, in cases where the central bank is heavily involved in supervision, there is a tendency not to increase the level of supervision concentration.

Then the crucial empirical question is: does the degree of central bank presence ('institutional factor') in financial supervision matter in defining the level of consolidation in that supervision? The expected sign of the relationship between central bank involvement and financial supervision consolidation is negative.

How to choose the control variables? As was observed above, no theory exists on the relationship between lawmaking and financial supervision concentration. Therefore we shall try to test the more general hypotheses.

(a) The lawmaker chooses to maintain or reform the degree of supervisory concentration in response to the structure of the financial system. In the modern debate on financial structure, it is usual to confront the equity dominance model (or 'market-based regime') with the bank dominance model (or 'bank-based regime'). Furthermore, recent literature pointed out the close relationship in every country between the financial structure model and the corporate governance model, with particular attention to the relative political determinants.[31] Therefore, the control variables must capture the following effect: does the financial structure model ('financial factor') matter in defining the lawmaker's choices in the area of supervisory consolidation?

The expected sign of the relationship between the degree of supervision unification and the financial factor is undetermined (i.e. it can be either positive or negative). We earlier stressed the importance of the blurring process for banking and financial markets worldwide. The blurring process means potential changes in the nature and dimension of intermediaries ('the financial conglomerates effect'). In a bank-based regime, if we think that the lawmakers' choices depend on the features of their own regime, we can suppose a positive relationship between the kind of regime and the degree of financial supervision consolidation. The rationale for the creation of a single financial supervisory authority is the blurring of boundaries between banks, insurers and financial service providers. The increasing importance of financial conglomerates requires the unification of supervisory functions.

At the same time, however, the blurring effect also means potential changes in the nature and dimension of the financial markets ('the securitization effect'). Therefore, in a market-based regime we can also expect a positive relationship between the kind of regime and the degree of financial supervision consolidation. Therefore the relationship between the financial factor and the degree of supervision concentration remains an empirical question.

(b) The political and institutional environment can determine the ability of lawmakers to implement their choices. Furthermore, we pointed out in (a) that the financial structure itself could be influenced by political factors. Then the control variables must capture a possible second relevant effect: does the quality of public governance ('political factor') matter in defining the lawmaker's choices on the level of supervisory concentration?

The expected sign of the relationship between the degree of supervision unification and the political factor is also undetermined. We noted that, whatever the financial regime of his country, a lawmaker may choose a higher degree of supervision in order to improve the capacity to face the challenges of the blurring process. Then we can suppose a positive relationship between good governance indicators and supervision unification. But a lawmaker may prefer a single authority in order to increase the probability of capturing the financial supervisory structure. Therefore, at the same time we might expect a positive relationship between bad governance indicators and supervision consolidation. Again, the relationship between the political factor and the degree of supervision concentration remains an empirical question.

(c) But the relationship between the degree of supervision consolidation and the characteristics of the banking and financial markets, pointed out in (a), might 'obscure' the importance of other variables, which are themselves determinants in explaining the characteristics of the banking and financial markets.[32] Recently, the structure of the financial markets was explained with three different institutional approaches ('legal factors'):[33] the legal–financial view, in the static and dynamic versions; the political–financial view; and the endowment view. Then we have to insert control variables related to the legal–financial view and the endowment view, while the political–financial view was already represented by the indicator of governance.

(d) Finally, as the above descriptive analyses pointed out, the concentration of powers seems more particular to developed countries, particularly Europe. Then we asked whether the choices of lawmakers to increase the degree of consolidation of supervisory powers might depend on the level of development in their respective countries ('economic factor'). Furthermore, the 'geographical factor' might also be important, in terms of location in Europe. Then we could expect a positive relationship between European location and OECD membership, as well as the levels of economic growth, on the one hand, and financial supervision concentration, on the other.

The results of the estimates[34] show the robustness of the role of central bank involvement in explaining the degree of supervision concentration. In fact, the probability of a single financial authority is always inversely and significantly related to the involvement of the central bank.[35] The institutional factor seems to matter.

Furthermore, looking at the control variables, the probability that a country will move towards a Single Authority model is higher:

the more equity-dominated the financial system, and the smaller the financial system itself;[36]
the higher the quality of public governance;
when the concentration of powers is linked to the legal framework, especially to the Germanic and Scandinavian roots of the legal institutions.

Thus, the lawmaker's decision to raise the level of financial supervision consolidation seems to depend on the institutional factor, the financial factor, the political factor and the legal factor, while the effects of the economic and geographical factors seem negligible.

To test the robustness of the results, we modify the dependent variable, eliminating the weights attributed to the banking and financial markets respect to the insurance sector.[37] All the results are confirmed.

Second, we tested a more radical hypothesis. We assumed that the lawmaker does not select the supervision concentration level but more simply decides between the two extreme models of supervision: single authority versus 'pure' multi-supervisory authorities. The dependant variable becomes a binary variable,[38] to be estimated with simple Logit and Probit. The results confirm the relevance of the institutional factor, as well as the financial factor and the political factor.

We then tested the robustness of the hypothesis that the institutional factor could be considered an independent variable. In other words, we had to reject the hypothesis that central bank involvement is endogenous, i.e. that the lawmaker jointly determines the financial supervision level and the central bank involvement, based on the same explanatory model. We then considered central bank involvement as a dependant variable. Our conclusion is that the variables that could explain the degree of central bank involvement in financial supervision do not coincide with those that we use to analyse the degree of consolidation. In fact, if you perform Logit and Probit regressions using CBFA as a dependent variable and the same vector of financial and institutional variables, the results are not significant at all.

Furthermore, to test the robustness of the institutional factor, we tried changing the index of central bank involvement, making it perfectly symmetrical with the index of financial supervision level.[39] As expected, all the results are confirmed.

Lastly, we tried modifying the sample of countries analysed. First, we considered the group of 30 industrialized countries. The results confirm the role of the institutional factor, the financial factor, especially regarding the role of market dimension, and the legal factor. The political factor remains significant, but less systematically. Second, we considered the group of 41 European countries. The results confirm the role of the institutional factor, the financial factor, limited to the role of market dimensions, and the political factor. The legal factor we found to be insignificant.

How should the results be interpreted? First of all, the analysis seems to confirm the rule-driven path dependence hypothesis. The prior choice of the lawmaker regarding 'whom' to delegate supervisory policy seems to have consequences on the choice of 'how many' institutions to delegate, according to an inverse relationship. The central bank fragmentation effect holds true: the more the central bank is involved in financial supervisory powers, the lower the degree of concentration of those powers is likely to be. The econometric analysis confirms the descriptive trade-off between supervision consolidation and central bank involvement. The institutional factor seems to matter.

Second, the choice of the degree of supervisory unification seems to be influenced by the characteristics of the financial markets. More specifically, given a market-oriented model, the smaller these markets and the lower the level of economic development, the more likely it seems that consolidation will increase, perhaps confirming the hypothesis of lawmakers conditioned by the 'small country' situation. The financial factor seems to matter.

Furthermore, a positive relationship between the market-based regime and the degree of supervision consolidation seems to hold true. This could be explained by the focus of lawmakers on the securitization effect. In the face of changes in the nature and dimension of the financial markets, policymakers prefer to increase the degree of consolidation in the supervision structure. Alternatively, this fact could also be explained by the role of financial conglomerates, if there were robust evidence of a positive relationship between the degree of financial deepening and development of cross-sector intermediaries.

Third, the decision of lawmakers on the concentration of supervisory powers seems to be facilitated by an institutional environment characterized by good governance. The relationship between good governance and the supervision concentration process can be explained, if we suppose that a lawmaker who cares about soundness and efficiency would prefer the single financial authority as the optimal one in the face of the blurring challenges. Finally, the German and Scandinavian roots of the law seem to matter, signalling the possibility of a legal neighbour effect.

Conclusions

We discussed the economic and political economy approaches to the key issue in the overall design of financial supervision: the definition of the optimal degree of financial supervision unification.

To apply the political economy approach we analyse the tendency to consolidate the powers of financial supervision so as to determine its possible causes. The approach was to consider the supervisory structure with one or more authorities as a dependent variable, determined in turn by the dynamics of other structural factors. Looking for common determinants in the decision each country takes to maintain or reform its supervisory architecture, we reported the results of an empirical analysis, and highlighted that the level of financial supervision consolidation seems to depend on the institutional factor, the financial factor, the political factor and the legal factor, while the effect of the economic and geographical factors seems negligible.

The results seem particularly interesting for future research developments. They may prompt increases in the availability of institutional information, so as to expand the sample of countries that can be analysed. It will be necessary to study the role of various structural factors in determining the decision-making process of institutional, financial, political and legal lawmakers.

Notes

1 Kahn and Santos (2001) consider the problem of optimal institutional allocation, focusing on banking supervision only. From the methodological standpoint, their work represents a well thought out example of the economic
approach.
2 Briault (1999), Llewellyn (1999), Goodhart (2002).
3 Taylor (1995).
4 Barth *et al.* (2002).
5 Briault (1999), Llewellyn (1999), Lannoo (2000), Abrams and Taylor (2000).
On the meaning of regulatory and supervisory independence see Quintyn and
Taylor (2002). Beck *et al.* (2003) examine the impact of bank supervision
independence on the corporate financing obstacles.
6 Goodhart *et al.* (1998). See also Laslett and Taylor (1998), Quintyn and Taylor
(2002). On the risks of excessive power of a single regulator see also Taylor
(1995), Briault (1999), Llewellyn (1999).
7 Fender and Von Hagen (1998).
8 Briault (1999, 2002), Llewellyn (1999), Lannoo (2000). Abrams and Taylor
(2000) and Goodhart (2002) claim that the economies of scale argument is
most applicable in small countries or those with small financial systems.
Abrams and Taylor (2001) argue that the shortage of supervisory resources is a
serious problem particularly in emerging market economies.
9 Goodhart *et al.* (1998).
10 Briault (1999), Llewellyn (1999), Lannoo (2000), Wall and Eisenbeis (2000).
11 Llewellyn (1999).
12 Lannoo (2000).
13 For the new political economy see Drazen (2000) and Persson and Tabellini
(2000).
14 There are two theoretical models on banking supervision architecture –
Repullo (2000) and Kahn and Santos (2001) – but without any explicit identification and discussion of the policymaker (lawmaker) objective function. In
general, there are few recent examples of studies on politics and banking; for a
survey see Pagano and Volpin (2001).
15 A general framework for political delegation problems has been proposed in
Alesina and Tabellini (2003).
16 The delegation approach has been recently used to debate financial supervisory issues, see Eisenbeis in Chapter 8 of this book.
17 For a recent and complete survey see Berger *et al.* (2000).
18 See Cukierman (1994) and Berger *et al.* (2000). See also Alesina and Gatti (1995).
19 See Cukierman (1992).
20 After the seminal central bank independence indices published by Grilli *et al.*
(1991) and revised in Masciandaro and Spinelli (1994), followed by Cukierman
(1992), different indicators were proposed; for a discussion see Berger *et al.*
(2000).
21 See Toniolo (1988).
22 See Alesina and Summer (1993), Cukierman (1994) and Berger *et al.* (2000).
23 See Masciandaro (1995) and Berger *et al.* (2000); note the difference between
institutional setting endogeneity and inflationary bias endogeneity.
24 The review is performed in Masciandaro (2004).
25 See Maddala (1983), Greene (1997) and Wooldridge (2002) for in-depth discussion of the random utility models that generate discrete dependent variables.
26 See Masciandaro (2004). The original FAC index is built on the following
scale: 7 = single authority for all three sectors (total number of supervisors = 1); 5 = single authority for the banking sector and securities markets

(total number of supervisors = 2); 3 = single authority for the insurance sector and the securities markets, or for the insurance sector and the banking sector (total number of supervisors = 2) 1 = specialized authority for each sector (total number of supervisors = 3). We assign a value of 5 to the single supervisor for the banking sector and securities markets because of the predominant importance of banking intermediation and securities markets over insurance in every national financial industry. The index is created by analysing which and how many authorities in 68 countries are empowered to supervise the three traditional sectors of financial activity: banking, securities markets and insurance. The index building is described in detail in Masciandaro (2004).

27 See Maddala (1983), Greene (1997) and Wooldridge (2002) for ordered models. See also Cramer (2003).

28 Masciandaro (2004).

29 The concept of rules driven path dependence has been recently used in the corporate governance literature: see among others, Bebchuk and Roe (1999) and Clark and Wojcik (2003).

30 Llewellyn (2001).

31 Pagano and Volpin (2001) and Perotti and von Thadden (2003).

32 For example, in Demirgüç-Kunt *et al.* (2003) regulation becomes insignificant in explaining banking performance when checking for institutional indicators.

33 Different approaches have been proposed to explain the country choice between a bank-based model and a market-based model: the 'legal approach' (La Porta *et al.*, 1997, 1998); the 'economic approach' (Rajan and Zingales, 2000); the 'political economy approach' (Pagano and Volpin, 2001); Verdier (2001); Rosenbluth and Schaap (2001); Carney (2002); Perotti and von Thadden (2003).

34 The estimation has been performed in Masciandaro (2005).

35 In this regard, we contrast the qualitative statement of Nolle (2003), who claimed that there is no systematic pattern to the division between single and multiple supervisory regimes.

36 If we consider the sample of the countries (14) with a Single Supervisor only, the UK seems to be the classic case of 'outlier', i.e. the exception in the inverse relationship between the degree of financial supervision consolidation and the financial market dimension. In fact, if the same regressions are performed without the UK (Table 13) all the results are confirmed.

37 We use an index (FAC Two) according to the following scale: 5 = single authority for all three sectors (total number of supervisors = 1); 3 = single authority for two sectors (total number of supervisors = 2); 1 = independent specialized authority for each sector (total number of supervisors = 3).

38 We use an index (FAC Binary) according to the following scale: 1 = single authority for all three sectors; 0 = otherwise.

39 The different levels of central bank involvement can be measured using the identical scale of the FAU Index (labelled CBFA Two Index): 1 = the central bank has responsibility in no sector; 3 = the central bank has responsibility in one sector; 5 = the central bank has responsibility in two sectors; 7 = the central bank has responsibility in all three sectors.

References

Abrams, R., and Taylor, M. (2000) 'Issues in the unification of financial sector supervision', IMF Working Paper, no. 213.

Alesina, A. and Gatti, R. (1995) 'Independent central banks: low inflation at no cost?', *American Economic Review* 85: 196–200.

Alesina, A. and Summer, L.H. (1993) 'Central bank independence and macroeconomic performances: some comparative evidence', *Journal of Money, Credit and Banking* 25: 151–62.

Alesina, A. and Tabellini, G. (2003) *Bureaucrats or Politicians?*, Harvard Institute of Economic Research, Discussion Paper, no. 2009.

Bagehot, W. (1873) *Lombard Street: A Description of the Money Market*, London: H.S. King.

Barth, J.R., Nolle, D.E., Phumiwasana, T. and Yago, G. (2002) 'A cross-country analysis of the bank supervisory framework and bank performance', mimeo. Auburn University, Auburn, AL.

Bebchuk, L.A. and Roe, M.J. (1999) 'A theory of path dependence in corporate ownership and governance', *Stanford Law Review* 52: 127–70.

Beck, T., Demirgüç-Kunt, A. and Levine, R. (2003) 'Bank supervision and corporate finance', NBER Working Paper, no. W9620.

Berger, H., de Haan, J. and Eijffinger, S.C.W. (2000) 'Central bank independence: an update of theory and evidence', CEPR Discussion Papers, no. 2353, London.

Briault, C. (1999) 'The rationale for a single national financial services regulator', FSA Occasional Paper.

Briault, C. (2002) 'Revisiting the rationale for a single national financial services regulator', FMG Special Paper, no. 135, London, LSE.

Carney, R. (2002) 'The political economy of financial systems', mimeo, International Studies Association Conference, New Orleans.

Clark, G.L. and Wójcik, D. (2003) 'An economic geography of global finance: ownership concentration and stock-price volatility in German firms and regions', *Annals of the Association of American Geographers* 93(4): 909–24.

Cramer, J.S. (2003) *Logit Models from Economics and Other Fields*, Cambridge: Cambridge University Press.

Cukierman, A. (1992) *Central Bank Strategy, Credibility, and Independence*, Cambridge MA: MIT Press.

Cukierman, A. (1994) 'Central bank independence and monetary control', *Economic Journal* 104: 1437–48.

Demirgüç-Kunt, A., Laeven, L. and Levine, R. (2003) 'Regulations, market structure, institutions, and the cost of financial intermediation', NBER Working Paper, no. W9620.

Drazen, A. (2000) *Political Economy in Macroeconomics*, Princeton, NJ: Princeton University Press.

Fender, I. and von Hagen, J. (1998) 'Central bank policy in a more perfect financial system', ZEI policy paper.

Goodhart, C. (2002) 'The organizational structure of banking supervision', mimeo, Financial Market Group, LSE.

Goodhart, C., Hartmann, P., Llewellyn, D., Rojas-Suarez, L. and Weisbroad, S. (1998) *Financial Regulation. Why, How and Where Now?*, London and New York: Routledge.

Greene, W. (1997) *Econometric Analysis*, Upper Saddle River, New Jersey: Prentice Hall.

Grilli, V., Masciandaro, D. and Tabellini, G. (1991) 'Political and monetary institutions and public financial policies in the industrialized countries', *Economic Policy* 13: 341–76.

Kahn, C.M. and Santos, J.A.C. (2001) 'Allocating bank regulatory powers: lender of last resort, deposit insurance and supervision', Monetary and Economic Department, BIS Working Papers, no. 102.

Lannoo, K. (2000) 'Challenges to the structure of financial supervision in the EU', 22nd SUERF Colloquium, Wien.

La Porta, R., Lopez-de-Silanes, F., Shleifer, A. and Vishny, R.W. (1998) 'Law and finance', *Journal of Political Economy* 106: 1113–55.

La Porta, R., Lopez-de-Silanes, F., Shleifer, A. and Vishny, R.W. (1997) 'Legal determinants of external finance', *Journal of Finance* 52: 1131–50.

Laslett, R. and Taylor, M. (1998) 'Independence and accountability: tweaking the Financial Services Authority', Centre for the Study of Financial Innovation, London, Working Group on Regulation Paper, no. 3.

Llewellyn, D. (1999) 'Introduction: the institutional structure of regulatory agencies', in Courtis, N. (ed.) *How Countries Supervise Their Banks, Insurers and Securities Markets*, London: Central Bank Publication.

Llewellyn, D. (2001) 'Unified financial supervision: some key issues and perspectives', mimeo, Loughborough University, Leicester.

Maddala, G.S. (1983) *Limited Dependent and Qualitative Variables in Econometrics*, New York: Cambridge University Press.

Masciandaro, D. (1995) 'Designing a central bank: social player, monetary agent or banking agent?', *Open Economies Review* 6: 399–410.

Masciandaro, D. (2004) 'Unification in financial sector supervision: the trade off between central bank and single authority', *Journal of Financial Regulation and Compliance* 12(2): pp. 151–9.

Masciandaro, D. (2005) 'Central banks or single financial authorities? A political economy approach', in Masciandaro, D. (eds) *Central Banks and Single Financial Authorities*, Cheltenham: Edward Elgar.

Masciandaro, D. and Spinelli, F. (1994) 'Central banks' independence: institutional determinants, rankings and central bankers' views', *Scottish Journal of Political Economy* 41: 434–43.

Nolle, D.E. (2003) 'The structure, scope, and independence of bank supervision: an international comparison', *Quarterly Journal, Office of the Comptroller of the Currency* 22(3): 21–33.

Pagano, M. and Volpin, P. (2001) 'The political economy of finance', CEPR Discussion Paper, no. 3231.

Persson, T. and Tabellini, G. (2000) *Political Economics: Explaining Economic Policy*, Cambridge, MA: MIT University Press.

Perotti, E. and von Thadden, E.L. (2003) 'The political economy of bank and equity dominance', CEPR Discussion Paper, no. 3914.

Quintyn, M. and Taylor, M. (2002) 'Regulatory and supervisory independence and financial stability', IMF Working Paper.

Rajan, R. and Zingales, L. (2000) 'The great reversals: the politics of financial developments in the 20th century', mimeo, University of Chicago, Chicago, IL.

Repullo, R. (2000) 'Who should act as lender of last resort? An incomplete contracts model', *Journal of Money, Credit and Banking* 32 (August): 580–605.

Rosenbluth, F. and Schaap, R. (2001) 'The domestic politics of banking regulation', *Industrial Organization* 57: 307–36.

Taylor, M. (1995) 'Twin peaks: a regulatory structure for the new century', Centre for the Study of Financial Innovation, London.

Toniolo, G. (ed.) (1988) *Central Bank Independence in Historical Perspective*, Berlin and New York: de Gruyter.

Verdier, D. (2001) 'Financial capital mobility and the origin of stock markets', *International Organization* 55: 327–56.

Wall, L.D. and Eisenbeis, R.A. (2000) 'Financial regulatory structure and the resolution of conflicting goals', *Journal of Financial Services Research* 17(1): 223–45.

Wooldridge, J.M. (2002) *Econometric Analysis of Cross Section and Panel Data*, Cambridge, MA: MIT Press.

8 Agency problems and goal conflicts in achieving financial stability

The case of the EMU

Robert A. Eisenbeis[1]

The importance of establishing goals for financial regulators is recognized by the Basel Committee on Banking Supervision (1997). The first sentence of the Committee's first principle states:

> An effective system of banking supervision will have clear responsibilities and objectives for each agency involved in the supervision of banking organizations.

The core principle goes on to state the following:

> Each such agency should possess operational independence and adequate resources. A suitable legal framework for banking supervision is also necessary, including provisions relating to authorization of banking organizations and their ongoing supervision; powers to address compliance with laws as well as safety and soundness concerns; and legal protection for supervisors. Arrangements for sharing information between supervisors and protecting the confidentiality of such information should be in place.

Effective design of a regulatory system to ensure financial stability typically includes specification of a set of regulations to ensure that institutions operate in a safe and sound manner, a system of prudential supervision of depository institutions either vested in the central bank or some other regulator, and a system of safety nets in the form of a lender of last resort function coupled with either an explicit or implicit deposit insurance scheme. However, the regulatory systems can often be plagued by agency problems and potential goal conflicts, especially since regulations and financial structures dynamically evolve over time, which may interfere with the objectives of ensuring safety and soundness.[2] Clearly, regulatory design and agency problems have been important contributors to financial crises in the US, such as the collapse of the Ohio State Deposit Insurance Fund, and more recently the collapse of the Rhode Island Credit Union Insurance Fund, not to mention the problems that contributed to the collapse of the Federal Savings and Loan Insurance Corporation (FSLIC). Similar issues have been equally important in the rest of the world as well.[3] Witness the many incidents of financial crises that have occurred in even the last few years – often at great cost to taxpayers. Because of the importance of a sound, well-functioning financial system to achieving economic growth and improving societal welfare through the promotion of efficient allocation of resources, the potential for goal conflicts and agency problems to arise should be considered in designing a financial regulatory and supervisory system. Moreover, an effective design would consider not only current issues but also be incentive compatible and time-consistent to address new problems as they arise.

The Economic and Financial Committee (2001) of the European Union (EU) concluded that 'the existing regulatory and supervisory arrangements in Europe provide a coherent and flexible basis for safeguarding financial stability, but recommended that their practical functioning needs enhancement'. Furthermore, the Committee put forward the general principle that 'private institutions should be involved as much as possible in both crisis prevention and, if this fails, in crisis management. Each financial institution is responsible for its own safety and soundness. If financial losses occur, the firm's shareholders should bear the costs and its management should suffer the consequences.'[4] While such pronouncements sound good, without also providing explicit mechanisms detailing how the private sector will be involved, little has been accomplished, especially if the loss control incentives of the regulators and financial institutions are misaligned.

It has been widely recognized both in the US and elsewhere that goal conflicts and agency problems exist which may frustrate the effective functioning of these loss control arrangements. Without more explicit consideration of these issues in designing a financial regulatory structure, it may be difficult to assure that, should a crisis arise, it will be handled efficiently or that the public (taxpayers) will be adequately protected from losses.

This chapter, employing the framework in Wall and Eisenbeis (1999), first discusses the nature of these conflicts and then considers whether the structure being put in place for the European Monetary Union (EMU)[5] raises special considerations that have not yet been addressed and may impact the ability to achieve the objectives put forth by the Basel Committee. In particular, there is an attempt to isolate key features of the 'new' system that may be vulnerable to conflicts or problems. In the process, the experience of the US is relied upon to the extent that there are relevant parallels that may provide useful insights as to the potential vulnerabilities in the European design.

Subsequent sections first define and discuss the nature of the goal and agency conflicts. The chapter then turns to ways that they typically are resolved in a democratic system. Finally, sections turn to design features that would help mitigate the problems and their application to the EMU. The last section is a summary and conclusion.

Agency problems and goal conflicts

The issues surrounding the appropriate way to structure financial regulatory agencies and how to apportion their responsibilities are long standing but are seldom dealt with in a systematic way before a crisis arises. In the US, Congress tends to address financial regulatory problems in a sequential and evolving way. It usually responds to weakness or design flaws exposed by financial crises or emerging competitive inequities spawned by innovations of financial institutions designed to take advantage of regulatory arbitrage.[6] When problems appear, Congress often puts regulatory solutions in place in a piecemeal fashion without regard to secondary consequences of subsequent market responses. But more important for this discussion, while at least temporarily solving one problem, the solutions may result in conflicts and imprecise or overlapping mandates to different regulatory bodies that carry with them another set of problems. For example, a staff report of the US Senate Committee on Governmental Affairs (1977) notes that 'Where several agencies are involved in a particular regulatory function there is the possibility of omissions, inconsistencies and conflicting policy.'

Horvitz (1983) stresses the importance of this problem to financial services by pointing out that Congress has assigned multiple goals to the financial service regulators. Each of the three major federal banking agencies – the Office of the Comptroller of the Currency (OCC), the Federal Reserve System and Federal Deposit Insurance Corporation (FDIC) has a different mix of goals. The OCC, for example, charters and regulates national banks. The FDIC provides federal deposit insurance and supervises state chartered banks that are not members of the Federal Reserve System and certain thrift institutions. The Federal Reserve not only conducts monetary policy but also serves as the lender-of-last-resort (LOLR) and the supervisor of both state chartered member banks and bank holding companies. Because of this differing mix of responsibilities and goals, policies may be applied or implemented differently, and jurisdictional conflicts arise between the regulatory agencies over the form, substance and implementation of regulations.

One clear example of such a goal conflict existed many years ago between the US banking agencies' safety and soundness responsibilities and their requirement to enforce the securities laws when applied to banks. The banking agencies long perceived that providing disclosures to investors of the financial condition of a bank might in some instances trigger a run on the bank to the detriment of depositors and result in potential losses to the deposit insurance fund. This problem was particularly critical to the FDIC, that perceived its primary mission to protect the deposit insurance fund, even if it came at the expense of shareholders. For this reason, for many years the FDIC resisted the disclosure of financial information – even a basic income statement – out of fear that accurate information might trigger a run on financial institutions it was responsible for, even if the information was relevant to investors. It was not until the bank holding company form of organization became the dominant form of banking organization, whose disclosure requirements were administered by the SEC, New York Stock Exchange and other securities exchanges, and not the banking agencies, that financial institutions were required to expand their financial disclosures. Of course now, we would regard such information as not only relevant to investors, but also important to achieving market discipline, which was an anathema in earlier regulatory regimes.

An additional layer of potential conflicts among the regulators exists beyond just those at the federal level because each of the 51 states not only charter banks and thrift institutions but also promulgate rules and regulations governing their operations and activities within their home states. They also provide overlapping supervision of these institutions. State and federal regulations are not necessarily harmonized and can be conflicting. For example, there is currently a dispute brewing between many state regulators and the OCC who has pre-empted state banking agency enforcement actions for national banks as well as the application of state laws pertaining to mortgage lender/broker licensing laws, escrow account laws, credit score disclosure laws and anti-predatory lending laws by national banks.[7] As a result, many larger institutions, especially those with significant multi-state operations are now opting for national over state charters. The resulting loss of constituents – that is, institutions to supervise and regulate by state banking regulators not only threatens the agencies' raison d'être but also depletes their financial base. State regulators typically rely upon examination fees for their funding, a feature of regulatory design that is also fraught with potential conflicts of interest. This trend away from state charters is clearly an example of regulatory arbitrage.

More generally, in the financial regulatory arena, there are several affected parties with stakes in the outcome. These include the Congress and other legislative bodies, the public, regulated and non-regulated financial institutions, shareholders and financial institution customers, and the regulatory agencies themselves. Each of these different parties interact with each other in a dynamically evolving economy in a dialectical process described by Kane (1977). As has been already illustrated, there are many examples where conflicts arise from agency problems, such as the case where the FSLIC used the provision of tax benefits to induce acquirers to take over failed S&Ls. These inducements may have helped protect the FSLIC fund, but shifted risk to the US taxpayer who ultimately ended up paying over 150 billion dollars to resolve the thrift crisis in the late 1970s and early 1980s. It has also been illustrated how the assignment of different and possibly conflicting goals to regulatory agencies may lead to problems. In many cases the conflicts can be resolved in a consistent fashion in the public arena only by congressional action or compromise between the agencies. When goal conflicts are resolved external to the agencies, this is termed 'external conflict resolution'.[8]

In some cases, these conflicts could be reduced or eliminated by assigning jurisdiction for the conflicting goals to a single agency. However, in most important instances, assigning jurisdiction to a single agency does not eliminate the conflict, rather, it merely transforms the way that the conflicts are resolved, as was the case with the conflict described earlier for the FDIC between the interest of the insurance fund and the interests of investors. Resolving goal conflicts administratively means that the decision will be conditioned by agency's perception and interpretation of the primacy of its responsibilities and mandates. And the resulting outcomes may not necessarily reflect those that would arise if the conflicts were resolved in the political arena. When the resolution process is de facto delegated to a single agency to solve, this process is called 'internal conflict resolution'.

While the concerns about financial regulatory structure noted by Horvitz have long existed, the problem has become more acute in recent years. Financial firms have used advances in information processing and financial technology to exploit legal loopholes and to offer ever more products that are functionally equivalent to those offered by differently regulated financial services firms. The result has been that competing institutions offering essentially identical products are subject to different rules, regulations and regulatory burdens that differentially impact firms' profits and competitiveness in markets. To exploit these differences, institutions now routinely seek the most favourable regulatory climate in which to operate for the products they offer. As a consequence, policies adopted by one regulator intended to achieve a specific public policy goal often have the unintended consequence of shifting market shares either to financial services firms regulated by another agency with different goals or to unregulated firms who perceive a competitive advantage and enter the market. The range of policy areas with possible goals that may be subject to possible conflicts includes: consumer protection (for both retail and wholesale customers), monetary policy, community development, investor protection, market transparency, safety and soundness, ensuring the safety net, reducing systemic risk and antitrust. The potential problems associated with conflicting regulatory goals are almost certain to increase whenever financial innovations arise to arbitrage regulations or financial modernization legislation is passed to modify the legal barriers separating different types of financial services firms. The question is to how best resolve the conflicts, and this issue is considered conceptually in the next section.

A framework for optimal resolution of agency and goal conflicts

At the highest level, design of optimal policies to resolve conflicting policy goals requires policymakers to have information on the trade-offs (costs and benefits) among the available alternatives to achieve their policy goals. Selection of the best combination of policies and methods for their implementation depends on social preferences and requires knowledge of, and the ability to, measure utility that is aggregated across all of the individuals in society. Because the aggregate social welfare function depends on preferences of the members of society, its parameters are surely not known, nor are they directly observable. In the absence of knowledge of the social welfare function, revealed preference exercised through the political process can be used as an indirect mechanism to infer the appropriate goal tradeoffs. To this end a presumption of a representative democracy is that the elected members of the legislature are a microcosm of society whose views and preferences reflect those of society at large. But since voters cannot directly control their legislator's actions, the elected official is essentially the voters' agent.[9] Moreover, these representatives are able to listen to and balance competing special interests. This process reveals preferences for different policy outcomes. For this reason, legislators are better suited to make policy judgements than is a bureaucratic agency, for example, which often has a narrower set of goals and priorities. Because the legislature is explicitly structured so as to reflect society's views and preferences, it could be argued that all goal conflicts should be resolved by the legislature.

But the myriad of issues and lack of time makes reliance upon the legislature to essentially micromanage disputes among competing interests in a timely fashion in financial markets infeasible. One option would be for parties with special interests in particular regulatory outcomes to appeal to the legislature each time there is need for a new regulatory policy or a change in regulation. The legislature would then be faced with two costly choices. One would be to attempt *ex ante* to gather information and write legislation that covers all contingencies – a task that would generally be prohibitively costly and difficult, and another would be to plan regularly to write new legislation to cover changing circumstances. The alternative would be to legislate a general framework for regulatory decision making and delegate, subject to judicial oversight, to regulatory agencies the responsibility to make case by case decisions and to write specific regulations to achieve specified policy objectives. This, of course, is the option most often selected by the US Congress. For example, in passing the Bank Holding Company Amendments of 1970, there was great debate over what activities would and would not be permitted to banking organizations through the holding company form. In the end, instead of putting forth a laundry list of permissible activities, it listed several activities that presumptively would be permissible, and then delegated to the Board of Governors of the Federal Reserve System (Board), the authority to decide what activities would be permissible. Congress also specified the criteria that the Board would use – that permissible activities would be 'so closely related to banking or managing or controlling banks as to be a proper incident thereto'.[10] This delegation to the Board has resulted in new activities being authorized over time and illustrates how delegation to an agency can work. There has been little need for the US Congress to intervene in the authorization of new banking activities. Having said this, some criticism has been levied that the Board has not been pro-active enough in authorizing new activities in a timely fashion.

Agency problems also arise within legislative bodies because of the need to conserve members' time, which is the scarce resource. The committee system, with oversight responsibility over related sets of issues, not only economizes on time through specialization but also creates the potential for members of the oversight and funding committees to obtain control rents from regulatory agencies and their constituencies. Members who are particularly interested in a set of economic goals may be able to exercise substantial influence over an agency's choice of priorities. Indeed, these members may be able to induce the agency to establish priorities among the goals in cases where there is almost no chance the full legislature would agree to such priorities. This ability to influence agencies provides a further incentive for the committee writing legislation to delegate goal conflicts to a regulatory agency especially when that agency will be subject to the committee's jurisdiction in the future. Blinder (1997) offers another reason for delegation of more decisions to government agencies, related to the fact that agencies tend to have longer time horizons than legislators.[11] US congressmen for example, must stand for election every two years, and thus need to demonstrate to their constituents that they have been productive on their behalf before the next election. By definition, this means that they prefer solutions to problems that generate immediately perceivable results or that avoid imposing short-term costs on their constituents. In contrast, those regulators who serve at the pleasure of the President are likely to have the option of staying in their positions for at least four years, while other regulatory appointees, such as the Comptroller of the Currency serve six-year terms and members of the Board of Governors of the Federal Reserve serve 14-year terms. These longer-term serving regulators can afford to take a longer view when assessing regulatory alternatives and this might result in more socially desirable decision making.

Regulatory agencies play two important roles in setting public policy: (1) they provide legislative bodies with information about the set of efficient policies, and (2) they implement the resolution of conflicting goals delegated to them. One consideration is the relative efficiency of different agency structures in producing information. If economies of scope exist in gathering information across different types of financial services, especially when institutions are headquartered in one locality but operate across borders, then internalizing goal conflicts may enhance the efficiency of information production. Alternatively, there may be diseconomies of scope such that information is more efficiently produced by agencies that specialize in particular problems or industries. This issue may be especially important in situations where regulation is decentralized, as in the EMU, but there is great need for information sharing across jurisdictions when institutions operate across borders.

Potential agency problems and goal conflicts within the EMU

There are many areas where the potential for agency problems and goal conflicts may arise within the structure of the regulation of financial institutions within the EMU. Faced with these conflicts, authorities can:[12,13]

1   rely upon legislation to hardwire the choices and tradeoffs;
2   assign the resolution of conflicts to a single agency and rely upon *internal resolution of conflicts* by the agency itself; or
3   assign conflicting goals to different regulatory agencies so that conflict resolution is externalized and ultimately left to the political process.

As a practical matter, the EU did not have the luxury of a clean slate as far as banking supervisory structure is concerned. While the EU did create a central bank, existing financial systems and legal/regulatory structures have been too different to permit the creation of a single banking regulatory agency. Thus, in practice, the choice of goal conflict resolution had to rely upon quasi-legislative solutions. In this case the European Commission, which is the body formally charged with originating and drafting legislative proposals to the Council and the European Parliament, delegated through directives to individual member countries and their respective regulatory and supervisory agencies (external resolution) the responsibility to design their own regimes.

The intent of the EU was to create a single market for goods and services, including financial services to foster economic growth and to enhance consumer welfare through increased competition. Under the agreements, a so-called 'single passport' was agreed to which allowed any financial institution chartered in one member country to operate freely in other member countries. However, having established this principle, the question then was how to shape the regulatory structure?[14] Historical practice had been to rely upon the host country to regulate how firms doing business within its borders would conduct their business. The problem with this in the EU was the concern that the host country would potentially structure regulation in ways that would disadvantage the foreign firms in competing with domestic institutions.[15] But this would be inconsistent with the single market objective, and this was made more imperative with the introduction of the euro. The alternative selected was to rely upon the home country to provide regulation, supervision and deposit insurance for the depository institutions that they chartered.[16] Furthermore, over the longer run, regulatory competition would likely come into play facilitating the evolution of a single market. Individual country self interest in promoting their institutions would also be an inducement to compete via deregulation of financial services. Countries offering more attractive charter options or accommodative regulatory regimes would expect to see their institutions gain market share in the EU. The logical consequence of allowing home country regulation would, as the result of regulatory competition, be a less regulated and homogeneous market place.

One consequence of leaving regulation and supervision to the home country is that the member countries in the EU have adopted different structures for financial institution supervision and regulation. Some have split supervision and regulation according to function while others have consolidated supervision and regulation into a single agency. In some instances the central bank is involved and in other countries it is not. Hence, if faced with the same supervisory or regulatory issue, agencies with different mix of functions will potentially choose different sets of policy tradeoffs depending upon their mix of responsibilities and their individual statutory mandates.[17] Some will face external resolution while others will be faced with internal resolution of conflicts. Policies will also differ across countries to the extent that internal goal conflict resolution is required as compared with external goal resolution. These differing tradeoffs will result in different policies and will set up many opportunities for individual institutions to pit the countries' agencies against each other and will foster regulatory arbitrage on the part of financial institutions to seek a competitive advantage.[18] Relying upon regulatory competition to level the playing field carries with it the risk of a race to the bottom and more lax supervision as far as safety and soundness is concerned. The EU has attempted to address this problem by setting minimum supervisory standards to be universally applicable through directives and agreements. In effect, the attempt is at least to set a lower boundary as far as safety and soundness risks are concerned.

One of the more important of these directives sets policy towards capital adequacy through the Capital Adequacy Directive, which led to the Basel 1 capital standards for EU supervisors to follow. Basel 1 has now been refined by the Basel Bank Supervisors Committee now known as Basel 2. Unfortunately, concentration of supervisory efforts on capital standards substitutes supervisory judgement for market-based risk weights to determine if an institution has sufficient capital. Wall and Eisenbeis (2002) argue that this focus is misplaced and misdirects supervisory attention from prompt corrective action and least cost resolution of troubled institutions.

While the EU has attempted to set minimum regulatory standards and promote cooperation and information sharing among the individual country supervisors, there is no EU-wide supervisor responsible for resolving the failures of institutions, and hence any goal conflicts that may arise should a major institution experience financial difficulty must rely upon *external resolution* of those conflicts. With no national supervisor to make the goal tradeoffs, it will likely be left to the European Commission or some similar body to resolve conflicts as they arise. The kinds of conflicts and implications for financial stability are significant and may become more so as the EU evolves. The financial system will become more integrated and more countries with different economic and financial systems at different stages of development are joining the EU. The remainder of this chapter will focus on three critical areas where the goal conflicts are likely to be most important: the design of deposit insurance system, the apportionment of supervisory responsibilities between home and host country regulators and the structure of bankruptcy resolution in the event that institutions get into financial difficulties.

The structure of deposit insurance within the EMU

The desired structure for deposit insurance in the EU was sketched out in the EU's Deposit Guarantee Directive (DGD) that went into effect in 1995. The DGD endorses a decentralized approach to deposit insurance, despite the fact that depository institutions are authorized to operate within any of the member countries, and delegates to the member countries the responsibility to provide coverage to the depositors in the banks headquartered within the country. Additionally, it is the responsibility of the home country's central bank to serve as the lender of last resort in cases that do not involve EU-wide systemic risk issues.[19] The broad-based systemic lender of last resort function is left to the European Central Bank. In effect, the system bifurcates the responsibilities for controlling banking risk between the micro-risk associated with the operation of single institutions from the macro-risk associated with contagion risk or risk that spreads from one institution to another regardless of where the institutions are headquartered.

The DGD specifies the general features that an acceptable deposit insurance system should have. The most specific features being that the system should provide deposit insurance coverage of 20,000 euros, should exclude coverage of inter-bank deposits, and may exclude other liabilities at the discretion of the national government.[20] Co-insurance of liabilities is permitted but not required. Coverage of depositors in branches in countries other than the home country is the responsibility of the home country. Interestingly, there is a provision that permits the branches of a multinational bank to opt to provide top coverage up to those branch depositors through the host country's deposit insurance scheme, when that coverage would be 'better' than that provided by the home country's plan.[21] Finally, it is also instructive in terms of what deposit insurance features are not prescribed. These include funding of the plans, pricing of coverage, who should operate the plan (the private sector or public sector), how troubled institutions should be handled, what too-big-to-fail policies might or might not be pursued, or how conflicts would be resolved where two deposit insurance funds might be affected by failure of an institution with top up coverage.[22]

In establishing the minimal requirements for deposit insurance schemes, the attempt was obviously to balance the fact that some EU members already had deposit insurance plans in place and generally, most of the key provisions and features of their programmes were different. There was no one obviously optimal structure for deposit insurance plans, and presumably the best that could be hoped for was that the schemes would be harmonized over time. The potential for cross-boarder conflicts appeared minimal since there were few truly multinational institutions in the EU. As might be expected, those plans that were put in place in order to comply with the DGD varied substantially from those already in place.[23] Finally, responsibility for supervision and risk monitoring is apportioned differently across the system and within the different countries.

Going forward, however, the patchwork set of deposit insurance schemes, when coupled with the bifurcated approach to controlling systemic risk, seems fraught with the potential for agency and conflicts of interest problems.[24] These arise from several sources including:

1   uncertainties about the funding of the deposit insurance plans;
2   differences in deposit insurance coverage and pricing of coverage;
3   reliance upon the home country, as opposed to host country responsibility, should institutions get into financial difficulties;
4   differences in treatment with respect to the LOLR function;
5   differences in approaches to bankruptcy and priority of claims in troubled institutions; and
6   differences in EMU versus non-EMU participants.

Based upon the long history within the US with multiple decentralized deposit insurance schemes and a fragmented bank regulatory and supervisory structure, there is a very great risk that the system being put in place in the EU will be fraught with conflicts and regulatory competition and that it will not be robust to financial crises. Much of the difficulty flows from a fundamental misunderstanding of the role of deposit insurance, the nature of the guarantees being given and the relationship between deposit insurance systems and the central bank's lender of last resort function in controlling systemic risk. These issues are covered in the next section

US experiments with deposit insurance that are relevant to assessing EU deposit insurance structure

The most transportable of experience between the US and the new EU architecture lies in the efficacy of systems that place reliance upon a decentralized approach to deposit insurance. The US has experimented extensively with decentralized deposit insurance systems that were not creatures of the federal government. These started with the New York State Safety Fund and culminated with the failure of the Rhode Island Share and Deposit Indemnity Corporation in 1991. Between 1908 and 1917 a total of eight states established deposit insurance systems.[25] Most of these systems failed within a few years. In every case, the insurance systems were unable to meet unusual demands for a payout when either a very large institution got into financial difficulty or many smaller institutions failed at the same time. However, this experience did not deter other states from establishing similar funds; Nebraska even re-established a fund, albeit on a much smaller scale, only to see it collapse again in 1983. The same fate befell funds in Ohio in 1985 and Rhode Island in 1991.[26]

There were several design flaws in these deposit insurance systems (Pulkkinen and Rosengren, 1993). First, the systems tended to be critically under funded. Second, they tended to be undiversified in one of two ways. Either they were undiversified because the institutions being insured were not geographically dispersed and hence were vulnerable to regional business cycles or economic shocks, or they were undiversified because the failure of one or two large institutions was sufficient to bankrupt the funds. Third, they often had poorly designed governance systems, and this was particularly the case in the privately sponsored plans. Finally, when threatened with collapse, there was no recognition that what provided the credibility to the plan was not so much the size of the fund, but the willingness of the sponsoring entity – the particular state legislature – to make good on the guarantees the fund offered.

Many of the same design flaws in these state-sponsored systems appear to be potentially inherent in many of the systems being put in place in the EMU. It seems clear that any fund whose insured base is not adequately diversified or that does not have the ability or willingness to use taxpayers resources, should fund resources be depleted, will not likely stand up to the costly failure of a few large banks. At a minimum, this means that reliance upon private deposit insurance systems, which the EU directive permits, seems extremely risky. In addition to insufficient funding, the lack of diversification, which was a major problem for the Rhode Island fund, means that the failure of one institution was likely to be accompanied by others.[27] One wonders about these diversification issues in another way when considering countries with only one or two major institutions, the failure of even one might endanger the entire fund.

What most architects of deposit insurance schemes seem to miss is that it is nearly impossible to determine *ex ante* whether or not a fund is fully funded. In the case of the US, the coverage ratio for the Federal Deposit Insurance Corporation of 1.25 per cent of insured deposits was a political compromise and not based upon any actuarial calculation. More importantly, what gives the fund credibility, especially when the financial problems in one institution threaten to spill over to others, is not the size of the fund *per se* but rather the willingness to make good on the guarantees should the fund run out of resources.[28,29] This uncertainty was also a problem in both Rhode Island and Ohio. The state legislatures procrastinated and ultimately failed to provide sufficient funds promptly to make up for losses. Because of this, the credibility of the conjectural deposit guarantees went to zero, resulting in a mass exodus of both depositors and institutions. In essence a dual run occurred on the insurance funds and the institutions they insured. Complicating the funding of the ODGF was that member institutions held a deposit with the fund amounting to 2 per cent of deposits, which they carried on their books as a reserve asset. In effect this requirement tied the health of each member institution to the solvency of the ODGF. When it became apparent that the losses to the fund from the institution whose financial difficulties triggered the crisis – Home State Savings – were large and threatened the solvency of the fund, depositors became concerned about the solvency of other ODGF members. In part, this was due to the perception that the value of the deposits members held as their reserve with the fund had declined in value and thus initiated runs on member institutions.[30]

Kane (1987) argues that waffling and legislative delay was partly a political ploy to embarrass the controlling political party in the Ohio State legislature and partly an attempt to shift the costs of the fund collapse from the taxpayers of Ohio to the federal government. But we have also seen the tendency to delay and avoid recognition of losses applies to federally sponsored programmes as well. The events surrounding the eventual collapse of the FSLIC in the US demonstrates the propensity of legislators to avoid facing up to the problem. Their dilemma is that if they appear responsible and vote to impose resolution costs on their constituents, then they may risk being re-elected.[31]

The circumstances surrounding the Ohio Deposit Guarantee Fund (ODGF) crisis also points to another problem related to the split of responsibilities for systemic risk between the member countries of the EU and the ECB. Specifically, the longer the delay in attempting to deal with the problem, the more likely it is that runs or systemic problems would develop that would convert what might be a problem in one institution into a problem for the deposit system itself. State authorities, to the extent that they are reluctant to impose costs on their own taxpayers, have incentives to delay and gamble that a broader authority would step in and assume the responsibilities for a crisis. This is clearly what happened in the ODGF situation. As Kane (1987) points out, the Ohio authorities responded to the initial withdrawal of funds from one institution – Home State Savings – whose ultimate failure triggered the deposit insurance crisis, as if it was an irrational run. They attempted to convince the public that all the other ODGF member institutions were sound, despite the lack of hard empirical evidence as to the solvency of Home State Savings. Interestingly, Kane (1987) argues that this was not an irrational run at all. He cites evidence that depositors knew fairly precisely which institutions were vulnerable and did not withdraw their funds from either federally insured or even solvent but uninsured institutions.

In Ohio, of the losses to the ODGF, approximately $134 million were attributed to the failure of Home State Savings. Initially, to make up for deficiencies in the fund, the state allocated another $50 million and surviving ODGF members contributed another $40 million. Ultimately, at least another $120 million was ultimately paid by Ohio taxpayers to facilitate the acquisitions of some of the troubled institutions that subsequently failed. The reluctance of the state legislature to appropriate somewhere in the vicinity of $170 million to make good on the guarantees implicit in its state sponsorship of the fund, illustrates two facts. First, it is the ability to tap into taxpayers' resources as needed rather than the size of the fund that provides the credibility of the deposit insurance guarantee. The initial reluctance of the state of Ohio to live up to its commitment which provides an interesting comparison to many of the countries currently in or entering the EU. Ohio's state gross domestic product (GDP) in 1985 was $176 billion. This is larger than eight of the original EU countries' GDP – Austria, Belgium, Finland, Greece, Luxembourg, the Netherlands, Portugal and Spain. It is also larger than the real GDP of all the newly admitted countries to the EU. It is not clear why countries with even smaller resources would be more willing than a relatively richer state like Ohio to honour its deposit insurance liabilities, especially, if payments were to be made to resident depositors in larger EU countries.[32] The temptation on the part of poorer countries and their politicians to gamble, just as Kane (1987) described the behaviour of the state officials in Ohio, that they will be bailed out by the ECB or member nations will likely prove to be very strong, should a major crisis arise. The chief difference, of course, between the ODGF crisis and a potential deposit insurance crisis in the EU is that there is no federal deposit insurance fund in the EU to which losses could be shifted.

In the case of the failure of the Rhode Island fund a poorly designed governance structure resulted in conflicts of interest and agency problems in its administration. The fund was owned and governed by the institutions that it insured. There is evidence that the fund board often traded off safety and soundness concerns of the fund for short-term profit interests of its members (Pulkkinen and Rosengren, 1993). In addition, since the fund's examiners were reporting to the management of the institutions they were evaluating, it was difficult for the examiners to be objective without facing either implicit or explicit resistance to some of their evaluations of member institutions. Competition with a competing fund (the FDIC) also played a role in weakening the insurance fund. Over time, larger insured institutions left the fund for federal deposit insurance whose credibility was greater.[33]

One can envisage many of these same problems potentially arising in the EU, especially as the larger institutions begin to take advantage of their ability to establish offices throughout the EU. This expansion will likely lead to deposit insurance arbitrage as institutions seek coverage from the larger, better diversified insurance funds. In the US experience, attempts by state-sponsored insurance plans to keep insured members, and hence maintain premium levels, led to increases in deposit insurance coverage limits. This would seem to be a natural response by EU country funds as they begin to lose insured institutions to other countries. Fund ownership may also prove to be a problem for several of the EU countries. Industry involvement, either exclusively or jointly with the government may give rise to the same kind of conflicting tradeoffs between profitability and safety and soundness that were manifest in Rhode Island. This may also prove to be a potential problem for EU countries that have privately administered funds. Barth *et al.* (1997) document that 15 EU countries had either industry administered deposit insurance funds or funds that were jointly administered by industry and the government at the time of their study.[34]

Another lesson from the US pertains to persistent design problems with the current deposit insurance structure that should be avoided by EU deposit insurance plans. This concerns perverse incentive and monitoring structures incorporated into the system by the Federal Deposit Insurance Corporation Improvement Act (FDICIA). FDICIA explicitly attempts to minimize the losses to the deposit insurance fund. But in addition, is designed to make failures isolated events, and to minimize the change for systemic crises. In the event that a failure occurs, FDICIA first requires depository institutions on an *ex post* basis to cover any losses that the insurance fund incurs, should those losses cause the coverage ratio of insured deposits to fall below 1.25 per cent.[35] In effect, FDICIA created a call on the equity of the banking industry in the event that a systemic or huge problem caused the FDIC coverage ratio to fall below 1.25 per cent or to bankrupt the fund. This provision made the FDIC the agent for the banking industry in terms of requiring it to protect the industry's capital. The chief risk to the banking industry and its capital is the failure of the FDIC and other regulators to close institutions before their net worth becomes negative. Yet the industry has no power to monitor the performance of the regulators.[36] The FDIC is answerable to Congress, and must report to Congress when failures result in significant losses to the insurance fund. But Congress' main constituent is the taxpayer and not the banking industry, who has the most to lose should the FDIC not perform.

This organizational design contains obviously miss-aligned incentives and inadequate monitoring of resolution performance, and should not be copied or modelled by other countries.[37] Unfortunately, this is what has happened in many of those EU countries with private or mixed private and public managed deposit insurance funds.

Home country versus host country conflicts in deposit insurance and banking supervision

The current deposit insurance and banking supervision structure in the EU relies upon 'the principle of home country control combined with minimum standards and mutual recognition.'[38] The idea was to permit duly chartered institutions to operate throughout Europe under the supervision of the home country supervisory authority, which was to be recognized by the host country supervisors. While apportioning clear supervisory responsibility for the institution, the structure is still exposed to problems for two reasons. First, many institutions not only operate a parent institution, but also have affiliates and subsidiaries whose financial health, like the situation with bank holding companies in the US, is intimately tied together. But under the EU supervisory model, when affiliates are chartered in other countries, the supervisory responsibility for overseeing those parts of the organization devolve to the supervisory agencies in those countries and not the home country of the parent organization.[39] As the experience in the US suggests, it becomes very difficult to separate an organization in this way, because in truly global financial institutions, their operational structures do not parallel their legal structures. They often will establish operational affiliates of subsidiaries to provide services and operational support, for example, across the entire organization, the health and viability of the entire entity can often hang on the viability of a given subsidiary or affiliate. Hence the home country supervisor cannot necessarily rely totally upon the supervisor of the home country or the affiliate. In many instances, US experience has suggested that institutions that become troubled will shift assets and liabilities as well as make payments upstream or downstream within an organization in order to prop up one or more affiliates or subsidiaries, but this might affect the perceived soundness of another entity. This also can shift risk from one country to another and perhaps to different country insurance funds within the EU. To hope that a financial crisis within a given entity can be managed cooperatively, given the complexities of financial institutions and their organizational structures, without clearly delineating primary and secondary roles *ex ante*, seems an especially risky strategy to use in designing a financial supervisory structure. The experience in managing the problems in Bank of Credit and Commerce International (BCCI), Daiwa and Barings tend to support this concern, and one can not rely on attempting to fix coordination and responsibility for crises in the middle of the crisis. In the US, while there is segmented regulation and supervision of depository institutions at the federal level, and even multiple regulators of multiple banking subsidiaries within a bank holding company, there is a single regulator – the Federal Reserve – of the entity, and it is viewed as a consolidated entity when inspected by Federal Reserve examiners.[40]

Banking organizations in Europe tend to operate more as universal banks rather than rely upon a holding company structure, and to date there are a limited number of institutions that could be considered truly pan-European in their operations. Schoenmaker and Oosterloo (2004a, b) indicate that as of 2001, there were only seven of Europe's 30 largest institutions that had significant cross-boarder operations. This should tend to mitigate some of the jurisdictional conflicts and coordination problems that may be associated with organizational complexities. However, should an EU institution experience financial difficulty, there is every reason to believe from the US experience, that as geographical and economic barriers to expansion decline, expansion and consolidation can take place very rapidly. Often the financial inter-relationships due to derivative transactions and syndicate lending will mean that institutions may be more closely tied together financially due to cross-border transactions, even if they do not have cross-border offices.[41] Furthermore, even though cross-border penetration is still not extensive, banking concentration within many European countries is quite high, as compared with the banking concentration within those US states whose state sponsored deposit insurance funds failed.[42] It should also be noted, however, that foreign bank penetration into accession countries is greater than in the original EU countries. Schoenmaker and Oosterloo (2004a or b) indicate that foreign bank share of total banking assets in countries like the Czech Republic, Poland and Slovakia as of 2001 was greater than 80 per cent. This suggests that problems in a 'foreign institution', should it experience financial difficulties, might have systemic spillover effects in these accession countries, even though it might not have similar repercussions in other countries or the home country. Hence the failure of even one significant institution may be more likely to precipitate a deposit insurance funding problem within the EU than was the case in the US.

Finally, as financial integration proceeds, differential deposit insurance coverage, terms and pricing will surely create a competition among the deposit insurance funds across the EU. In particular, presumably privately operated funds will be motivated and be able to respond to market forces more quickly and will likely begin to offer more favourable terms on insurance. Current EU policies allow institutions who operate across different countries to have their deposits insurance topped up by deposits insurance funds in host countries. If the terms are more favourable than deposits insurance offered by home country plans, then one would expect institutions would opt for the more favourable insurance coverage.

The growth of cross-border insurance where an institution might have its deposits insured under several different plans raises a number of potential problems should the institution get into financial difficulty. First, the moral hazard incentives would suggest that troubled institutions would seek to fund themselves in countries with the healthier plans, thereby shifting the risks to host rather than home country deposit insurance plans. But host countries would still bear primary supervisory responsibilities even though the risks were decreasing for the home country deposit insurance funds at the expense of the host country funds.

Second, there is the risk that a financial crisis in a host country that resulted in either repudiation of deposit insurance liabilities or a run on institutions insured by a vulnerable deposit insurance fund could have spillover effects to other countries through those institutions with cross-border operations. For example, should a problem in a host country result in depositors withdrawing funds from an institution insured by a troubled deposits insurance fund, then withdrawal of funds from a cross-border branch might trigger a liquidity crisis that could result in a bank failure. This increased risk would be transferred to the home country insurance fund, or require LOLR actions from the home country's central bank. Thus, there could be a systemic spillover from a deposit insurance crisis or financial crisis from one country's fund to another.[43]

Third, resolution of a problem institution might prove extremely difficult, since one would expect that the various affected deposit insurance funds would seek to grab assets to protect themselves against losses in the event of a failure. These incentives might be especially difficult if the host country were also providing LOLR support to a troubled institution, but were EU members who were not part of the EMU. This would expose both the LOLR and deposit insurance funds to exchange rate risks between the euro and non-euro currencies, and might be especially a problem for branches in EMU countries whose euro deposit liabilities might be dependent upon funding and support from funds raised in non-euro currencies.

Finally, there are the problems that differences in bankruptcy regimes may create, and difficulties that cross-border spillovers may have for deposit insurance funds, which are discussed in the next section.

Differences in bankruptcy policies and their implications for deposit insurance risks

Herring (2002) devotes considerable attention to potential conflicts that may arise should a major EU financial institution experience financial difficulties and be forced into bankruptcy.[44] Should European institutions operating branches across borders get into financial difficulties and actually fail, then the coordination of the resolution process will be especially complicated by the existence of different bankruptcy philosophies prevailing in home versus host countries. There are two different bankruptcy approaches that are common in the EU. First, some host countries have bankruptcy laws that require or enable them to 'ring fence' or segregate assets in branches of the failed entity within their jurisdiction. Their laws may permit them to seize branch assets located within their jurisdiction and use those assets to settle claims by their citizens against the failed entity. The aim is to protect the host country's deposit insurance liabilities and those of domestic depositors. This has proved to be a major problem in resolving the failure of BCCI.[45] Second, other countries, such as the UK, treat the failed institution as a consolidated entity and do not segment claims by the location of branches and subsidiaries or by the location of claimants.

When an institution fails that has operations in countries with different bankruptcy laws, then inherent goal and legal conflicts arise with competing and different claims on assets. While the Basel Committee may call for different countries to 'cooperate' and 'coordinate' their supervisory activities, these pleas are likely to have little effect or substance in actual cases, unless there are specific agreements and procedures for handling institutions in place *ex ante*.

Other conflicts may arise as well from the fact that different countries have different policies towards the application of bankruptcy laws to financial institutions and banks. In the US, for example, bank failures do not fall under the standard corporate bankruptcy laws applicable to non-financial corporations.[46] In many European countries, banking organizations are subject to standard corporate bankruptcy proceedings which are determined and controlled by the courts and are outside the control of banking supervisors. Bankruptcy proceedings may also give different priority to the claims of domestic versus non-domestic claimants.

Herring (2002) also notes important differences in country approaches on how claims are settled. For example, in many countries, debtors are permitted to evoke the right of offset to their liability claims.[47] Thus a large borrower, who is also a large depository or liability holder, may apply all deposits regardless of deposit insurance limits against its debts. That is, the institution is permitted to net its exposure. In effect, this gives large depositor/borrowers insurance against loss of their deposits, regardless of the legal limits on deposit insurance coverage. The consequence is that fewer assets may be available to cover the claims that the deposit insurance fund must then absorb. This constitutes a form of collateralization in which borrower/depositors have a priority position in bankruptcy when compared with depositors who are not also borrowers.[48] The Basel Committee (2001) specifically recognized the potential for this problem to complicate the resolution process and contribute to systemic risk by raising the uncertainty of how potential claims might be settled should an institution go into bankruptcy.

The EU has recognized the need to standardize the approach to bankruptcy of financial institutions across the EU by adopting the single entity model under the aegis of the home country as articulated in the EC Directive 2001/24/EC of 4 April 2001. As Krimminger (2004) notes, however, there is still an opt-out option from the Directive which suggests the possibility of a continuing conflict. Of course, given that the process has not been tested by a significant failure, it remains to be seen how the process will work in practice. Moreover, there does not appear to be a resolution yet as to how affiliates and subsidiaries will be treated in all cases.

Finally, there may be other issues that could frustrate the smooth liquidation or resolution of a large failing EU institution, such as the claims that potential legal actions or criminal actions may introduce, that would potentially reduce the pool of assets available to the deposits insurance funds to settle claims and cover losses.

Summary and conclusions and policy recommendations

Review of the potential for goal conflicts, agency problems and practical legal issues in dealing with failing or troubled institutions suggests that the structure being put in place within the EU, which relies upon country sponsored deposit insurance funds and home country responsibility for supervision and LOLR functions, is not likely to be robust to the failure of a large institution that threatens the solvency of the deposit insurance fund. The logical conclusion is that the EU needs a centralized and common approach for dealing with troubled institutions.

If the goal, and the position taken, in this chapter, is that it should be, to reduce failures of depository institutions to isolated events, then the best way to accomplish this is through a well-functioning and common early intervention and prompt corrective action scheme that closes troubled institutions before they actually become insolvent. Immediate resolution means that policies need to be put in place that let claimants know *ex ante* exactly where they will stand in the event of bankruptcy or closure of the institution. That is clearly not the case under current rules and policies within the EU.

At the same time, experience within the US with early intervention and prompt corrective action suggests that regardless of the provisions of the statute, there has been no noticeable reduction in losses that the insurance fund has incurred. This suggests that without attention and policies to control the incentive of regulators to engage in forbearance, losses to insurance funds are likely in certain instances to be very large, costly to taxpayers and may even cause state sponsored insurance funds to collapse and/or to trigger a financial crisis.

Notes

1 The views expressed in this chapter are the views of the author and do not necessarily reflect those of the Board of Governors of the Federal Reserve System or the Federal Reserve Bank of Atlanta. The author is indebted to Larry Wall, Scott Frame, Edward J. Kane and George G. Kaufman for helpful comments and suggestions.

2 See Kane (1988a or b).

3 See Honohan and Klingebiel (2003).

4 Economic and Financial Committee (2001: 11).

5 In EU parlance, EMU usually refers to economic and monetary union, but the discussion in this chapter is focused on the 'monetary' element.

6 See Kane (1988a or b).

7 The consumer protection regulations are not harmonized within the EU and this represents a similar set of challenges. See Nieto and Peñalosa (2004).

8 The most recent example of congressional involvement in resolving a conflict again involves the issue of OCC preemption of state enforcement actions and certain mortgage lender/broker licensing laws, escrow account laws, credit score disclosure laws and anti-predatory lending laws for national banks. Legislation has been introduced into both the US House and Senate which would overturn the OCC's preemption regulations.

9 However, in their role as agents, they not only are charged to act in the best interests of their constituents, similar to corporate executives, they also have incentives to expropriate wealth by engaging in perquisite consumption and attempting to keep their jobs (or in the case of Congress, to get re-elected). Elections are the mechanism to control, *ex post*, the agency problem posed by elected officials.

10 Bank Holding Company Act Amendments of 1970 (12 USC 1972).

11 Kroszner and Stratmann (1998) provide an additional reason why oversight committee members may want to exercise control over an agency. They argue that the Congressional Committee structure supports the development of a reputation equilibrium in which committee members gain a reputation for supporting the views of a particular special interest and the special interest group gains a reputation for providing campaign contributions to the member.

12 See Wall and Eisenbeis (1999).

13 The author is grateful to Larry Wall for insights and suggestions concerning this section.

14 Additionally, concern about being able to respond promptly to crises resulted in the European Commission elected to invoke comitology by creating special regulatory committees – the Banking Advisory Committee and the Committee of Banking Supervisors – to advise the Commission on banking and financial stability issues and to suggest policies and procedures for dealing with financial crises and supervisory issues (Nieto and Peñalosa, 2004).

15 Part of the motive for protectionism was to protect national champions from being takeover targets. Any number of central banks have actively intervened to thwart takeover attempts of a national champion by a foreign institution. The Bank of Italy, for example, intervened in an attempted takeover of Uni-Credito Italian by the Spanish institution Banco Bilbao Vizcaya Argentaria. Protectionism of champions has also led to government forbearance and bailouts. The French Government on three separate occasions intervened to prop up the economically insolvent Credit Lyonnais at great cost to the French taxpayer. Most recently, the European Commission ordered the French government to recover funds it had provided to an insolvent subsidiary before selling it back to Credit Lyonnais.

16 Schoenmaker (2003) has described the current supervisory structure within the EU in detail as well as focused on many of the issues surrounding choice of the optimal regulatory and supervisory structure.

17 Barth *et al.* (1997: Table 12) compare different supervisory and deposit insurance structures across EU and G-10 countries as of 1995. In the EU, the structures are far from uniform, and the powers and policies clearly differ.

18 Kremers *et al.* (2003) recognize the importance of the existence of certain of

Agency problems in financial stability 253

these conflicts involving systemic supervision (the lender-of-last resort) and prudential supervision in comparing the supervisory structure adopted in the Netherlands and the UK. While recognizing the issues, the consolidated option was adopted in the Netherlands for resolving the supervisory issues while conflicts between supervision and conduct of business are left to be resolved externally.

19 See Kane (2003a).

20 This represents a kind of depositor preference.

21 This raises the interesting question of what assets the host country may access in the branch should the institution fail, and it also sets up a conflict in terms of the status of claims in bankruptcy if the countries have different bankruptcy statutes.

22 See Dale (2000).

23 See Demirgüç-Kunt and Sobaci (2000).

24 See Kane (2003b).

25 These included Oklahoma, Kansas, Nebraska, Texas, Mississippi, South Dakota, North Dakota and Washington. See Thies and Gerlowski (1998).

26 For discussions of these failures see Kane (1987) and Pukkinen and Rosengren (1993).

27 Fraud was a major contributor to the failure, but the lack of diversification in terms of institutions insured was a key problem.

28 This problem plagued even the US FSLIC deposit insurance fund. See Kane (1985).

29 FDICIA changed the nature of the FDIC funding.

30 The funding of the ODGF in effect tied the health of all member institutions to the health of the fund in such a way that even the insolvency of one institution was easily turned into a systemic problem for all its members.

31 Kane (1985, 1987).

32 In the case of the Nordic countries, Sweden, Norway and Finland, government guarantees were both extended and honoured. But that was at a time when the banking systems were essentially domestic with little in the way of foreign activities or deposits and before the euro had been introduced in Finland and Sweden. See Moe et al. (2004).

33 See Schuler (1989) for a discussion of the Ohio Deposit Guarantee Fund and other state-sponsored deposit insurance systems and some of the governance incentive problems they experienced.

34 Industry administered funds included Austria, Finland, France, Germany and Italy, while those countries with jointly administered funds included Belgium, Greece, the Netherlands and Spain.

35 See Wall and Eisenbeis (1999).

36 An interesting example of this pricing occurred recently when the Office of Federal Housing Enterprise Oversight (OFHEO) forced Fannie Mae to increase its capital and review its accounting statements. The rating agencies downgraded Fannie Mae's subordinate debt but not its senior debt, which effectively was a recognition of the uncertainty of what actions OFHEO might take.

37 See Kane (2003b) for alternative views on deposit insurance system design in an international context.

38 Schoenmaker and Oosterloo (2004a or b).

39 Prati and Schinasi (1999) go so far as to argue, consistent with the view expressed in this chapter, that national authorities may have trouble dealing with cross-border financial crises or with those that have cross-border implications.

40 Even this structure required legislative action to indicate that when a bank within a holding company structure experiences financial difficulties, that

254   *R.A. Eisenbeis*

entity could not protect the assets and resources in other banking affiliates from being tapped by the authorities, if the institution got into trouble.
41 See Favero *et al.* (2000).
42 See Schoenmaker and Oosterloo (2004a, b).
43 Krimminger (2004) outlines the features that effective resolution policies have with an emphasis on speed in returning funds to insured depositors to which one should add that depositors should have certainty that they will receive their funds.
44 See also the discussion in Bliss (2003a) and Bliss (2003b).
45 Herring (2002) indicates that some countries have a single entity policy that effectively treats a foreign branch as a separate legal entity. Should a foreign institution fail, then the assets of its branches and agencies would be seized and the resource used to satisfy the claims of the liability holders in that branch. Any assets that remain would then be made available to other claimants, regardless of location.
46 Actually, the application of the bankruptcy status to a failed bank holding company is different from its application to a failed bank. The holding company would fall under the general corporate bankruptcy laws while banking affiliates and subsidiaries would fall under the banking laws governing failed banks.
47 Bergman *et al.* (2003) consider the specific problems of derivatives contracts in failure situations.
48 See Bliss (2003a) for an explicit treatment of the problems of dealing with derivatives and related issues in large complex banking organizations.

References

Basel Committee on Banking Supervision (1997) 'Core principles for effective banking supervision', Bank for International Settlements (September).
Basel Committee (2001) 'The insolvency liquidation of a large multinational bank', in 'Other supervisory issues', *BCBS Compendium of Documents, International Supervisory Issues*, Chapter III (May).
Barth, J.R., Nolle, D.E. and Rice, T.N. (1997) 'Commercial banking structure, regulation and performance: an international comparison', OCC Working Paper, 97(6) (March).
Bergman, W.J., Bliss, R.R., Johnson, C.A. and Kaufman, G.G. (2003) 'Netting, financial contracts, and banks: the economic implications', in Kaufman, G. (ed.) *Market Discipline in Banking: Theory and Evidence*, Vol. 15: *Research in Financial Services*, Amsterdam: Elsevier Press, pp. 303–34.
Blinder, A. (1997) 'Is government too political?', *Foreign Affairs* 76 (November/December): 115–26.
Bliss, R.R. (2003a) 'Resolving large complex financial organizations', in Kaufman, G.G. (ed.) *Market Discipline in Banking: Theory and Evidence*, Vol. 15: *Research in Financial Services*, Amsterdam: Elsevier Press, pp. 3–31.
Bliss, R.R. (2003b) 'Bankruptcy law and large complex financial organizations: a primer', Federal Reserve Bank of Chicago, *Economic Perspectives* (First Quarter): 48–58.
Dale, R. (2000) 'Deposit insurance in theory and practice', Société Universitaire Européenne de Recherches Financiéres, Amsterdam.
Demirgüç-Kunt, A. and Sobaci, T. (2000) 'Deposit insurance around the world: a data base', World Bank, Washington, DC (May).
Economic and Financial Committee (2001) 'Report on financial crisis management', *European Economic Papers*, no. 156, Brussels.

Favero, C., Freixas, X., Persson, T. and Wyplosz, C. (2000) *One Money, Many Countries – Monitoring the European Central Bank*, London: CEPR.

Herring, R. (2002) 'International financial conglomerates: implications for bank insolvency regimes', Wharton School, University of Pennsylvania Philadelphia, PA (July).

Honohan, P. and Klingebiel, D. (2003) 'The fiscal costs implications of an accommodating approach to banking crises', *Journal of Banking and Finance* 27(8): 1539–60.

Horvitz, P.M. (1983) 'Reorganization of the financial regulatory agencies', *Journal of Bank Research* (Winter): 245–63.

Kane, E.J. (1977) 'Good intentions and unintended evil: the case against selective credit allocation', *Journal of Money, Credit and Banking* 9(1): 55–69.

Kane, E.J. (1985) *The Gathering Crisis in Federal Deposit Insurance*, Cambridge, MA: MIT Press.

Kane, E.J. (1987) 'Who should learn what from the failure and delayed bailout of the ODGF?', NBER Working Paper (May).

Kane, E.J. (1988a) 'Changing incentives facing financial-services regulators', paper prepared for Perspective on Banking Regulation Conference, Federal Reserve Bank of Cleveland, Cleveland, OH.

Kane, E.J. (1988b) 'How market forces influence the structure of financial regulation', in Haraf, W. (ed.) *Restructuring the Financial System*, Washington, DC: American Enterprise Institute for Public Policy Research, pp. 343–82.

Kane, E.J. (with A. Hovakimian and L. Laeven) (2003a) 'How country and safety-net characteristics affect bank risk-shifting', *Journal of Financial Services Research*, (June): 21–30.

Kane, E.J. (2003b) 'What kind of multinational deposit-insurance arrangements might best enhance world welfare?', *Pacific-Basin Finance Journal* 11: 413–28.

Kremers, J.J.M., Schoenmaker, D. and Wierts, P.J. (2003) 'Cross-sector supervision: which model?', in Litan, R.E. and Herring, R. (eds) *Brookings-Wharton Papers on Financial Services*, Washington, DC: Brookings Institution.

Krimminger, M.H. (2004) 'Deposit insurance and bank insolvency in a changing world: synergies and challenges', International Monetary Fund Conference, Washington, DC (May).

Kroszner, R.S. and Stratmann, T. (1998) 'Interest group competition and the organization of congress: theory and evidence from financial services political action committees', *American Economic Review* 88 (December): 1163–87.

Moe, T.G., Solheim, J.A. and Vale, B. (2004) *The Norwegian Banking Crisis*, Norges Bank Occasional Papers, no. 33, Oslo.

Nieto, M.J. and Peñalosa, J.M. (2004) 'The European architecture of regulation, supervision and financial stability: a central bank perspective', *Journal of International Banking Regulation* 5(3): 228–42.

Prati, A. and Schinasi, G. (1999) 'Financial stability in European economic and monetary union', *Princeton Studies in International Finance*, no. 86.

Pulkkinen, T.E. and Rosengren, E.S. (1993) 'Lessons from the Rhode Island banking crisis', Federal Reserve Bank of Boston, *New England Economic Review*, (May/June).

Schoenmaker, D. (2003) 'Financial supervision: from national to European?', Financial and Monetary Studies, no. 22(1), Amsterdam: NIBE-SV.

Schoenmaker, D. and Oosterloo, S. (2004a) 'Financial supervision in the integrating Europe: measuring cross-boarder externalities', Financial Markets Group Special Papers, no. 156, London School of Economics, London (April).

Schoenmaker, D. and Oosterloo, S. (2004b) 'Cross-border issues in European financial supervision', prepared for the Bank of Finland Conference The Structure of Financial Regulation, Helsinki (September).

Schuler, K. (1989) 'Deposit insurance déjà vu', *The Freeman*, (July): 265–9.

Thies, C.F. and Gerlowski, D.A. (1998) 'Deposit insurance: a history of failure', *Cato Journal* 8(3) (Winter): 677–93.

US Senate Committee on Governmental Affairs (1977) *Study on Federal Regulation*, US Government Printing Office, Washington, DC, 5: 5.

Wall, L.D. and Eisenbeis, R.A. (1999) 'Financial regulatory structure and the resolution of conflicting goals', presented at a conference on Financial Modernization, FRB of Atlanta and FRB of San Francisco, September 1998, *Journal of Financial Services Research* 16(2/3) (September/December): 223–45.

Wall, L.D. and Eisenbeis, R.A. (2002) 'Reforming deposit insurance and FDICIA?', *Economic Review*, Federal Reserve Bank of Atlanta, (First Quarter): 1–16.

COMMENT

Jan Toporowski

Eisenbeis has made some wise and insightful remarks on the issue of supervisory fragmentation and I am aware that I cannot hope to rival this practical experience and knowledge of banking supervision. The best tribute I can give to them is to reflect upon some of his lucid and perceptive insights, and on how they may touch upon broader trends and issues in banking supervision. At the start of the twenty-first century, a number of circumstances have combined to make such supervision more complicated, perhaps, than ever before. Although Eisenbeis alludes to some of these circumstances in various parts of his chapter, it is worth identifying them, because they will be touched upon later in this comment.

First of all there is the issue of financial integration, and the ease with which balance sheet items, for banks and companies, can be shifted across regulatory boundaries. This has always been a feature of financial markets, but the markets today are perhaps distinctive in allowing such shifting on a larger scale than ever before. Obviously this is the outcome of modern technology, as well as arrangements, such as inter-bank borrowing or brokers' loans, designed to support the liquidity of financial markets. Support for liquidity in particular markets obviously eases transactions within that market. But it also eases entry and exit into particular markets, because entry (or exit) on a large scale may be expected to have lesser price effects if accommodating liquidity is provided.

Second, there has over the past 60 years been a fundamental and qualitative change in hedging behaviour by banks and financial institutions. Whereas, in the years that immediately followed the Second World War, financial markets and institutional portfolios were largely based on government paper, or government-guaranteed paper, this changed radically during the 1980s and the 1990s. After inflation had wiped out a large portion of public sector debt, relative to gross domestic product, much of the rest was effectively swapped for company liabilities through privatizations and the buy-back of Government debt. (It may be remarked here that this would have affected even a country such as the US, where there were few public enterprises available for sale to financial institutions: A public sector surplus correspondingly reduces the cash flow of business. Business is then obliged to borrow this money by borrowing from banks, or issuing liabilities into securities markets, effectively mopping up the liquidity placed into those markets by the government's repayment of its debt. However, in view of the fiscal policies of the present Administration in Washington, this is perhaps an academic point.)

The effect of this shift in financing, from a government finance base to a private sector finance base, has also changed hedging behaviour. In the old days, the portfolios of banks and investment funds were effectively hedged if they had a sufficient amount of government paper or central bank liabilities in them. Today, banks and investment funds hedge themselves à la Minsky, effectively buying or selling some instrument whose value, they hope or calculate, is positively correlated with the value of the commitment or liability into which they are entering. This in large part explains the huge increase in secondary market activity, as risk exposures are hedged and re-hedged.

A third feature of today's banking and financial markets associated with this activity is what in the early part of the twentieth century used to be called by German monetary theorists, 'credit inflation'. This is the increase in credit that does not arise from any increased income in the economy at large but is created autonomously in the financial system. The Basel Accord system of expanding bank capital in proportion to some calculated risk in bank asset portfolios, is an example of such credit inflation. Economists have a habit and tradition of confusing credit inflation (which *is not* derived from income) with 'saving' (which *is* derived from income). The practical effect of such confusion is to presume a greater stability of credit inflation, because incomes as a whole are generally stable, than is actually found in practice. It is this, I believe, that accounts for the apparent intractability of monetary aggregates that Charles Goodhart identified during the 1980s. Out of this arises the 'goal conflict' between monetary stability and financial stability.

The agency problems that Eisenbeis identifies, derive, in large part, from a historic legacy in the United States of overlapping and competing jurisdictions set up to guarantee deposits, as well as to ensure the prudent conduct of banking or financial business. Guaranteeing deposits is a matter of banking scale: the smaller the bank, in balance sheet terms, the smaller is the cost of refunding deposits in a given crisis. Much of the failure of deposit guarantee schemes arises not because such schemes are in principle unviable, but because mergers and acquisitions have created large banks, and hence large failures. Similarly, regulation to ensure the prudent conduct of banking and financial business has to contend with the practical need of banks and financial institutions to hedge their risks by diversifying their assets, whether through mergers and acquisitions, or purchase and sale of securities in spot and forward markets. If there is a case for laissez-faire banking and finance, it is that the desire for survival will tend to impel institutions to hedge their balance sheets. The case for regulation and supervision arises because such hedging creates balance sheets that are too large to be allowed to fail.

Obviously, one person's 'hedging' is another person's speculation. In a sense, it matters little what we call it, since the difference is a matter of motive rather than action and, contrary to what many economists believe, it is probably only novelists such as Conrad or Dostoevsky who have ever managed to come anywhere near unravelling the secrets of such human motivation. This creates difficulties for regulation, because obviously regulation should moderate speculation, but has at the same time to encourage proper hedging.

I concur strongly with Eisenbeis' conclusion that the scale of banking supervision has to be commensurate with the scale of possible loss, for such regulation to be effective. This, I believe, makes the case for centralized bank and financial regulation in Europe. However, such centralized regulation is justified not because *national* regulation offers too much scope for regulatory arbitrage, or because of the problems of effective cross-jurisdiction management of financial crisis. Rather, such regulation is needed because of the increasingly transnational scale of banking. Eastern Europe is a particular case in point: the figure quoted in the paper of up to 80 per cent of bank assets owned by foreign banks gives some idea of the enforcement problems that may arise within a national jurisdiction.

I will not enter into the question of whether elected legislators or specialist functionaries regulate best. Eisenbeis rightly expresses scepticism about the possibility of articulating a 'social welfare function'. The real problem seems to me to be again a matter of scale: in a small country, specialist functionaries may be much more subject to local preferences. On a larger scale, such as the Federal level in the US or EU institutions in Europe, legislative influence works less by articulating some US-wide, or Europe-wide, social preferences, and more by acting as a source of countervailing power against powers too great to be constrained by communities. But whether legislators can judge the best combination of policies and methods is debatable. Eisenbeis recommends the delegation of such powers. They need to be supported by residual powers of public enquiry, so that regulators can be made to explain themselves before well-briefed legislators, demonstrating to the public those regulators' coordination, or lack of it, with other agencies.

Finally, Eisenbeis recommends that 'the best way to reduce failures of depository institutions to isolated events is through a well-functioning and common early intervention and prompt corrective action scheme that closes troubled institutions before they actually become insolvent'. Such intervention, as we all know, is always going to be a matter of judgement in the face of uncertainty. The sanguine banker will always declare that, given more time and access to credit, solvency can be assured, and can always find the odd business school professor to confirm this. Moreover, the legal implications of such intervention remain complex and obscure. Even as we speak, the Bank of England is defending in the courts its decision to shut down the Bank of Credit and Commerce International. There is no litmus test for insolvency. On a fire-sale basis probably every bank is insolvent. With the rise of inter-bank markets, in which borrowing margins depend upon a reputation for solvency, any intervention that becomes known in the markets can immediately make a bank insolvent. The answer to financial crises may lie less in financial regulation than in the structure of financing in an economy, and the hedging behaviour that it induces.

COMMENT

Tuomas Takalo

In contrast to monetary policy, the supervision and crisis management of the financial services sector in the Economic and Monetary Union is a responsibility of national authorities. Over the past few years, however, pressure to reform financial market regulation and supervision has been mounting and, accordingly, a number of reforms are ongoing. In his clear and concise essay Robert A. Eisenbeis argues that because multiple financial supervisors worsen moral hazard problems in the banking sector, there is a need for a single European financial supervisory authority.

A key insight of Eisenbeis essay is to point out the multitude of moral hazard problems surrounding financial intermediation. The theory of financial intermediation (for a recent survey, see Gorton and Winton, 2003) traditionally emphasizes the moral hazard in the relationship between the intermediaries and their customers. The theory of political economy (extensively surveyed by Drazen (2000) and Persson and Tabellini (2000)) in turn emphasizes the moral hazard between voters and legislators. Eisenbeis fills the gap by considering the moral hazard, on the one hand, between legislators and supervisory agencies and, on the other hand, between supervisory agencies and banks. Eisenbeis shows how the fragmented structure of the European financial supervision and regulation is conducive for moral hazard, since it keeps the number of players unnecessarily high and can lead to the race to the bottom and regulatory arbitrage.

I have only two substantive critical remarks. Anyone writing on the reforms of financial market regulation in the EU faces the challenging task of improving on Vives (2001) which, at least to me, forms a landmark study among the non-technical evaluations of the European financial market regulation. Because Vives' (2001) article was made before the Economic and Financial Committee's (EFC) proposal for a new regulatory framework, there would be room for a careful evaluation of the proposal but, unfortunately, Eisenbeis remains a bit sketchy in his evaluation. My second concern is the question of whether the Eisenbeis' argument for the pan-European financial supervisory authority can be recovered from the first principles of banking regulation. A logical starting point for the quest of financial regulatory reform would be the very rationale for banking regulation. Even if picking up proper justification for the regulation were immaterial for the need of a reform, it should be relevant for the details of the reform agenda. In what follows, I will try to view Eisenbeis' essay against these backgrounds.

Prevailing financial market supervision in the EU and the EFC proposal for reform

As mentioned, the supervision and crisis management of financial markets in Europe are responsibilities of national authorities. Although there is some tendency towards a unified national authority that combines the supervision of banking, securities and insurance sectors, there is a wide variety of national arrangements among the EU countries. The national authorities cooperate to take care of the cross-border dimension of supervision and crisis management. The cooperation is based on home country and mutual recognition principles, taking place on multiple platforms, in particular, through the Basel Committee on Banking Supervision, Memoranda of Understanding, the Groupe de Contact, the Committee of European Banking Supervisors and the Banking Supervision Committee.

From Eisenbeis' essay it becomes quite clear that the current regulatory and supervisory framework is too convoluted to deal successfully with Europe-wide supervision and crisis management. The problems have been recognized at the highest level, and the EFC's proposal for reforming regulation and supervision in the EU is a result of these concerns. The EFC's recommendation is that the Lamfalussy model of securities market regulation and supervision should be extended to the banking and insurance markets. As a result, the new supervisory and regulatory framework will be a complicated multilevel arrangement based on cooperation of the national authorities in various committees (comitology). The proposed framework introduces a number of new committees without abolishing existing cooperative organizations.

Evaluation of the EFC's proposal

There are two main rationales for banking regulation, the existence of systemic risk and the need for protection of small investors (depositors). The latter rationale is associated with *the representation hypothesis for banking regulation* (Dewatripont and Tirole, 1994), which stems from the need to avoid duplication of monitoring costs.

If systemic risk is taken as the rationale for banking regulation, a Pandora's box will be opened: it is neither clear whether the on-going integration of European financial markets decreases or increases the systemic risk potential in banking in Europe nor whether the increased or decreased systemic risk potential requires more or less integrated supervisory framework. Putting these subtle issues aside, we can ask how the proposed new framework will cope with systemic risk. Given the laborious comitology structure of the new framework, the answer is not obvious. The new framework like its prototype, the Lamfalussy model of securities market regulation and supervision, mainly aims at governing legislative regulation. For this purpose, the new framework can be suitable: for example, the extensive cooperation of the national authorities will certainly promote the common implementation of regulation at the national level. However, the ability of the new framework to react to market developments is much in doubt, even if attention is restricted to preventive legislative actions, not to mention the actions needed in a crisis.

By contrast, if the protection of small depositors is assumed to be the rationale for banking regulation, the Lamfalussy model for securities market regulation and supervision will also be a natural candidate for banking and insurance regulation and supervision: the main rationale for securities market regulation has traditionally been investor protection, not systemic risk, as Allen and Herring (2001) argue. In that case it would be valuable to know how well the Lamfalussy model is working in securities markets.

To Eisenbeis, however, the need for the protection of small depositors suggests something other than the Lamfalussy model: a unified European deposit insurance is warranted because of the current decentralized approach nourishes the potential for agency and conflicts of interest problems. In particular, major cross-border banks such as Nordea also create problems in transferring funds between national deposit insurance schemes due to the home versus host country conflicts. Here Eisenbeis differs from Vives (2001), who thinks that the open issues concerning deposit insurance are minor compared with other areas of crisis management. For example, the lender-of-last-resort arrangement in the Monetary Union is essentially based on the delicate notion of 'constructive ambiguity'. It is inherent to the constructive ambiguity policy that it is neither transparent nor official. This ambiguity is ultimately reflected as ambiguity in deposit insurance schemes.

The EFC's proposal leaves monitoring of financial institutions at the national level. The current arrangement could be supported on the grounds of the informational advantage of the national authorities over the local supervised institutions. Degryse and Ongena (2004) show that national borders drastically increase the monitoring difficulties banks encounter with their customers. I see no reason why the relationship between supervisors and the banks should be different. This view is in contrast with Eisenbeis, who like Vives (2001), makes a political economy argument in favour of an independent and a centralized European financial services authority. One can, however, expect that technological and regulatory progress soon reaches a stage where monitoring information becomes sufficiently solid to be transposed to the cross-border level. Once we experience a rise of truly European banks, further centralization of monitoring of financial institutions from the national to European level will be warranted as argued by Eisenbeis. At this stage of the development, where the national borders still hinder the hardening of information, the representation hypothesis of bank regulation dictates further cuts in the branches of the National Central Banks.

The absence of specification of the underlying rationale for banking regulation hampers the use of Eisenbeis' study in the evaluation of the pending reforms of the European financial market regulation and supervision. The concerns about the workability of the Lamfalussy model in the case of systemic risk seems to support Eisenbeis' call for a centralized financial supervisory authority. However, Eisenbeis' emphasis on deposit insurance is in line with the representation hypothesis of bank regulation, which is more conducive for the Lamfalussy model. Recovering Eisenbeis' argument from this angle requires taking the representation hypothesis to the limit: a single regulator eliminates duplication of regulatory costs.

Summary

Designing a reform agenda for the European financial market regulation and supervision is an overwhelming task for a single scholar. The rather restricted focus of the Eisenbeis' study is therefore understandable. I would nonetheless urge a clarification of the underlying rationale for banking regulation, since this would provide a clear conceptual framework to guide the evaluation of the pending reforms. The urgency for such evaluation cannot be underestimated. In particular, more attention should be directed to the reform of regulation and supervision of financial conglomerates and the insurance sector. The eventual reforms of the pension systems in Europe will most likely involve at least partial privatization and deregulation of pension insurance schemes. Privatization and deregulation of the banking sector in the 1980s and the telecommunications sector in the 1990s revealed holes in the regulatory frameworks that destabilized economies worldwide. If financial conglomerate and insurance sector regulation and supervision are not updated before the reforms of European pension systems, a new boom-to-bust will be likely.

References

Allen, F. and Herring, R. (2001) 'Banking market versus securities market regulation', Wharton Financial Institutions Center Working Paper, no. 01-29.
Degryse, H. and Ongena, S. (2004) 'The impact of technology and regulation on the geographical scope of banking', *Oxford Review of Economic Policy* 20: 571–90.
Dewatripont, M. and Tirole, J. (1994) *The Prudential Regulation of Banks*, Cambridge, MA: MIT Press.
Drazen, A. (2000) *Political Economy in Macroeconomics*, Princeton, NJ: Princeton University Press.
Gorton, G. and Winton, A. (2003). 'Financial Intermediation', in Constantinides, G., Harris, M. and Stultz, R.M. (eds) *Handbook of The Economics of Finance*, Amsterdam: Elsevier, pp. 337–429.
Persson, T. and Tabellini, G. (2000) *Political Economics*, Cambridge, MA: MIT Press.
Vives, X. (2001) 'Restructuring financial regulation in the European Monetary Union', *Journal of Financial Services Research* 19: 57–82.

9 Cross-border issues in European financial supervision[1]

Dirk Schoenmaker and Sander Oosterloo

Over the last three decades, there has been a clear trend towards globalised finance. Large financial groups are run on a global basis, spreading their business – with almost no exception – over the three main regions of the developed world (the Americas, Europe and Asia). In response, regulations are also increasingly based on a global (Basel, International Organization of Securities Commissions (IOSCO), International Association of Insurance Supervisors (IAIS)) or regional (EU) footing to ensure their effectiveness as well as an international level playing field. However, supervisory authorities, who enforce these regulations, are still nationally rooted with some elements of international or regional coordination. The national base of supervisors is related to political sovereignty (Herring and Litan, 1994). In a more practical sense, it also related to the issue of jurisdiction. One needs a jurisdiction for enforcement of regulations, liquidation and winding-up procedures and taxation.

Two recent examples illustrate the challenges of cross-border cooperation for national supervisors. The first is the cross-border implementation of the new Basel Accord of 2004. Banks often run their internal risk management models on an integrated/centralised basis. Basel has therefore always put a strong emphasis on the consolidated supervisor in the home country. Nevertheless, Basel also envisages a role for host country supervisors, in particular where banks operate in subsidiary form, for the approval of banks' internal models (Basel Committee on Banking Supervision, 2003, 2004). This can lead to duplication, and, in the case of uncoordinated approval, diverging requirements for banks. There is thus a trade-off between ensuring effective supervision based on home–host cooperation and minimising the burden for banks. The second example is the recent reinforcement of local control by the New Zealand authorities. To maintain direct control over systemically important operations from overseas banks in their jurisdiction, the authorities will require these overseas banks to establish locally incorporated subsidiaries instead of branches (Reserve Bank of New Zealand, 2004). This will partly reverse the process of international financial integration.

The focus of this chapter is on cross-border issues in the European

Union (EU). As a European jurisdiction is (or can be made) available, policy makers have the choice to organise financial supervision on a national or a European basis. The basic argument in favour of moving to a European structure is that it might be difficult to achieve simultaneously a single financial market and stability in the financial system, while preserving a high degree of nationally based supervision with only decentralised efforts at harmonisation (Thygesen, 2003). This is an application of the classical trilemma in macro-economic policy. Policy makers are confronted with three desirable, yet contradictory, objectives: fixed exchange rates, capital mobility and independent monetary policy. Only two out of the three objectives are mutually consistent, leaving policy makers with the decision which one they wish to give up: the 'trilemma' (Rose, 1996). Figure 9.1 illustrates the three incompatible objectives in our case: (1) a stable financial system; (2) an integrated financial market; and (3) independent national financial supervision. An argument against moving to a European solution for financial supervision at the present time could be that the degree of integration in financial markets does not yet justify such a move.

The chapter is organised as follows. Starting with the first two elements of the trilemma, we first review the potential for cross-border contagion, given the level of financial integration within the EU. What are the channels for contagion? What is the intensity of cross-border externalities arising from the failure of financial institutions? Then we examine how financial institutions organise themselves. The country model in which financial institutions run their business according to geographical lines is rapidly fading. Instead, financial firms run their activities and in particular key management functions (including risk management) on an integrated and centralised basis. Turning to the third element of the trilemma, we next discuss the challenges posed by these trends for the predominantly national based supervisory framework. What are the policy options for the

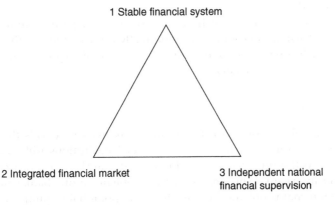

Figure 9.1 The trilemma in financial supervision.

structure of financial supervision? This raises the question of the appropriate division of responsibilities between home and host authorities and
their mandate (national or European). We argue that the supervisor
of the home country should act as consolidated supervisor, so as to stay
close to the operations of financial institutions, but with a European
mandate to incorporate cross-border effects. Taking an integrated
approach to financial supervision and stability (including crisis management), supervisory structures should involve supervisors, central banks as
well as ministries of finance. Finally we discuss the policy implications and
draw conclusions.

Cross-border contagion

Here we investigate how financial problems occurring in one member
state can affect the health of the financial system in other member states.
First, we discuss different channels through which shocks can be transmit-
ted from one institution or market to others and illustrate the importance
of the channels. Second, we present some evidence on the potential cross-
border externalities posed by financial institutions that come into existence as a result of integration of EU financial markets.

Contagion channels

According to De Bandt and Hartmann (2000), the mechanism through
which shocks propagate from one financial institution or market to the
other (contagion) is the very core of the systemic risk concept. They distinguish two main channels in banking markets through which contagion
can spread problems from one institution or market to others:

- the *real* or *exposure channel* which refers to 'domino effects' resulting
  from real exposures in the interbank markets and/or in payment
  systems, and
- the *information channel* which relates to the contagious withdrawals
  (*bank run*) when depositors are imperfectly informed about the type
  of shocks hitting banks and about their physical exposure to each
  other (*asymmetric information*).

Interbank market

The first channel for contagion is the interbank market. This is the risk
that a failure of one or a number of financial institutions will cause a
severe shock to the financial system due to high interbank exposures. As
cross-border interbank exposures increase, problems in one bank can not
only cause internal problems, but also have the potential to jump over to
banks in other member states.

With the move to Economic and Monetary Union (EMU), the national interbank markets in local currencies have shifted to an integrated and deep euro interbank market with multiple counterparties. The impact on financial stability at the European level is not clear cut. On the one hand, there is more scope for diversification as the number of counterparties is larger than in the previous national markets. On the other hand, there is more scope for cross-border contagion as the level of cross-border activity has increased. Table 9.1 shows that the importance of cross-border activities in the interbank market differs considerably across the euro-area countries. According to Cabral *et al.* (2002), this can be explained by the size of the local money market. In larger countries more local counterparties are available, which results in lower cross-border interbank activities. Interbank business is thus strongly oriented towards the domestic market in countries such as France, Germany, Italy and Spain. In smaller countries, such as the Benelux countries, Finland, Ireland and Portugal, cross-border activities (with euro-area as well as non-euro-area countries) account for at least 50 per cent of interbank assets. It should be noted that the figures in Table 9.1 can be somewhat misleading as Cabral *et al.* (2002) focus on euro-area countries rather than EU countries. For example, in 2002 the cross-border penetration from the euro area is rather low for Finland and the Netherlands, while domestic business is well below 50 per cent. This is due to the fact that EU countries like Sweden (an important trading partner for Finland) and the United Kingdom are not included in the euro-area figures.

Payment and settlement systems

Within payment and settlement systems there exists the risk that the failure of one or a number of financial institutions to settle their obligations causes other participants to fail as well. For an extensive overview of the literature on systemic risks in payment and settlement systems we refer to De Bandt and Hartmann (2000).

In the EU, the most significant payment system is the Trans-European Automated Real-time Gross settlement Express Transfer (TARGET) system, which started its operations in 1999. Currently TARGET is built on the 15 national payment systems of the former EU member states, complemented by the payment mechanism of the ECB (European payment Mechanism (EPM)) and an interlinking mechanism that enables the actual processing of cross-border payments.[2] TARGET has as its main objectives: (i) to provide a safe and reliable mechanism for the settlement of euro payments on a real-time gross settlement (RTGS) basis, (ii) to increase the efficiency of cross-border payments within the euro area, and perhaps most importantly (iii) to serve the needs of the monetary policy of the ECB. Table 9.2 shows that the use of TARGET has shown a sharp rise in payment flows since its establishment. Although the majority of

Table 9.1 Cross-border penetration of banks: interbank assets in the euro area (in percentages)

Country	1997		1998		1999		2000		2001		2002	
	h	*e*	*h*	*e*	*h*	*e*	*h*	*e*	*h*	*e*	*h*	*e*
Austria	56	18	63	16	65	14	61	18	61	18	61	18
Belgium	30	27	31	32	26	40	22	43	21	40	22	40
Finland	36	11	35	19	38	15	28	18	37	6	33	3
France	66	8	69	9	70	12	70	11	69	12	71	12
Germany	73	9	73	10	74	11	71	12	69	13	68	13
Greece	n.a.	n.a.	70	9	69	11	63	10	50	21	42	21
Ireland	41	17	46	23	36	29	35	29	36	25	34	26
Italy	57	16	53	24	59	22	63	20	67	17	64	19
Luxembourg	20	53	22	55	25	52	22	55	22	55	24	53
The Netherlands	39	23	37	24	41	21	48	17	38	17	39	17
Portugal	43	30	43	29	52	23	39	23	37	34	37	37
Spain	71	13	71	15	72	17	68	18	71	15	69	17
Euro area	60	15	61	17	62	18	61	18	59	18	59	19

Source: Cabral *et al.* (2002).

Notes
Interbank assets from the 'Home' country (denoted by *h*) and 'Rest of Europe' (denoted by *e*) are measured as a percentage of the total interbank assets of a country's banking system. 'Home' is defined as domestic institutions; 'Rest of Europe' is defined as branches and subsidiaries from euro area countries exclusive of the home country. Figures for 1997–2001 are measured in the fourth quarter, figures for 2002 are measured in the first quarter. The abbreviation n.a. means 'not available'.

Table 9.2 TARGET payment flows (euro billions)

	1999	*2000*	*2001*	*2002*	*2003*
TARGET overall	239,472	263,291	329,992	395,635	420,749
change %	–	*10%*	*25%*	*20%*	*6%*
Of which					
Domestic	146,236	153,253	201,390	271,914	283,871
	(69%)	(58%)	(61%)	(69%)	(67%)
Cross-border	93,236	110,038	128,602	123,721	136,878
	(31%)	(42%)	(39%)	(31%)	(33%)

Source: TARGET annual reports (2000–3).

payment flows is domestic, there is a sizeable cross-border component of over 30 per cent. TARGET business is mainly related to interbank business (about 95 per cent) and not so much to customer related business (only 5 per cent). In addition to the TARGET system run by the ECB and the national central banks (NCBs), there is a private EU-wide large value payment system, EURO 1, run by the European Banking Association.

Furthermore, there has recently been a trend towards consolidation of national security settlement systems within Europe. To give three examples (Bank of England, 2004), the Euroclear Group now comprises the national securities settlement systems in the UK, Ireland, France and the Netherlands, as well as Euroclear Bank, based in Belgium, which settles internationally-traded eurobonds. Similarly, LCH Clearnet Group – which began operating as a combined entity on 1 January 2004 – clears securities trades on exchanges located in the UK, France, Belgium, the Netherlands and Portugal. Finally, on a global basis the Continuous Linked Settlement (CLS) system operates as a settlement system for foreign exchange transactions in 11 currencies (including the euro), with average settled values of over US$1 trillion per day

Information channel

The information channel relates to contagious withdrawals when depositors are imperfectly informed about the type of shocks hitting banks (idiosyncratic or systematic) and about their physical exposures to each other (asymmetric information). De Bandt and Hartmann (2000) distinguish three potential causes of systemic events related to asymmetric information and expectations (see also Aharony and Swary, 1983). These are, first, the full revelation of new information about the health of financial institutions to the public; second, the release of a 'noisy signal' about the health of financial institutions to the public; and, finally, the occurrence of a signal which co-ordinates the expectations of the public without being actually related to the health of financial institutions. In this respect, the assessment of financial supervisors and central banks of potential threats to the financial system and their view on how to deal with them (for example through a Financial Stability Review) could influence the behaviour of depositors.

Cross-border externalities

Turning from the channels for contagion to the occurrence of a financial crisis, the literature on financial stability makes a distinction between general liquidity crises and institution-specific crises (Goodhart, 2000; Schoenmaker, 2003). General liquidity crises need to be resolved by the ECB by supplying liquidity to the market, without the specific need to obtain detailed supervisory information on individual institutions. This is to be contrasted with institution-specific crises, where national central banks need detailed information on the position of the respective institution (especially the availability of sufficient collateral) before granting any emergency liquidity assistance.

In this section, we focus on institution-specific crises. In an earlier paper (Schoenmaker and Oosterloo, 2005), we argue that the level of cross-border business of financial institutions is an appropriate measure for the cross-border impact of the (potential) failure of these institutions ('cross-border externalities'). There are different approaches to measuring the cross-border business of financial institutions. Sullivan (1994) reviews 17 studies estimating the degree of internationalisation based on a single item indicator. However, using just a single indicator increases the possibility for errors, as for example, the indicator could be abnormally susceptible to external shocks. Depending on the choice of indicators, this might provide a better approximation of the degree of internationalisation, but the choice of indicators may be restricted by data availability rather than by theoretical induction (see Sullivan, 1994; Slager, 2004).

Schoenmaker and Oosterloo (2005) collect a new data-set on cross-border penetration (as a proxy for cross-border externalities) of large banking groups, based on the Transnationality Index (Slager, 2004) calculated as an unweighted average of (i) foreign assets to total assets, (ii) foreign income to total income, and (iii) foreign employment to total employment. In order to determine whether the cross-border externalities are significant, Schoenmaker and Oosterloo (2005) develop a tool that enables them to make a distinction between the activities in the home market (h), the rest of Europe (e) and the rest of the world (w). Financial institutions (in particular banks) that have the potential to pose significant cross-border externalities in the European context are defined as follows:

1   50 per cent or more of their business is conducted abroad ($h \leq 0.5$), and
2   25 per cent or more of their business is conducted in other EU countries ($e \geq 0.25$).

The first criterion makes a distinction between domestic and international banks. Banks that conduct more than half of their business abroad are regarded to be 'international'. In the case of $h \ll 1$, there are significant cross-border externalities on a global scale. The second criterion identifies European banks among the international ones. International banks that conduct a quarter or more of their business in the rest of Europe are regarded to be 'European'. In the case of $e \geqslant 0$, a large part of the cross-border externalities are in the rest of Europe.

On the basis of these criteria Table 9.3 divides the 30 largest EU banking groups into three categories: (i) European banks, (ii) international banks

Table 9.3 Categories of banking groups (top 30 EU banks in 2003)

Category	Banking group	h (in %)	e (in %)
European	1 Deutsche Bank	25	41
	2 Nordea Group	28	71
	3 ABN AMRO	28	36
	4 KBC Bank	40	40
	5 Fortis Group	44	28
	6 BNP Paribas	47	25
	7 Westdeutsche Landesbank	48	43
	8 HypoVereinsbank	48	33
	9 Groupe Caisse d'Epargne	50	38
International	1 HSBC Holdings	24	6
	2 ING Group	29	24
	3 Banco Bilbao Vizcaya Argentaria	44	3
	4 Santander Central Hispano	45	16
Domestic	1 Dexia	54	37
	2 Société Générale	56	21
	3 Dresdner Bank	59	29
	4 Crédit Agricole Groupe	61	19
	5 UniCredit	71	13
	6 Bayerische Landesbank	72	14
	7 Commerzbank	75	15
	8 Rabobank	75	9
	9 Crédit Lyonnais	77	8
	10 Royal Bank of Scotland	77	5
	11 Banca Intesa	78	10
	12 Barclays	80	8
	13 HBOS	91	5
	14 Lloyds TSB Group	94	3
	15 Abbey National	97	3
	16 Crédit Mutuel	n.a.	n.a.
	17 Groupe Banques Populaires	n.a.	n.a.

Source: Schoenmaker and Oosterloo (2005).

Notes
'Home' is defined as a bank's business in its home country (denoted by *h*); 'Rest of Europe' is defined as a bank's business in other European countries (denoted by *e*); 'Rest of the world' is defined as a bank's business outside Europe (these figures are not shown). The three categories add up to 100 per cent. Banks in each category are ranked according to the share of their international business. The abbreviation n.a. means 'not available'.

and (iii) domestic banks. As these are figures from 2003, recent developments such as the takeover of Abbey National by Santander Central Hispano have not been included.

Nine banks out of the sample of 30 large EU banking groups are considered as 'European' banks that have the potential to pose significant cross-border externalities. Over a longer period, Schoenmaker and Oosterloo (2005) report a statistically significant upward trend of emerging European banking groups (rising from six European banks in 2000 to nine in 2003). Although the criteria for classifying banks into European, international and domestic banks are intuitive, they are also somewhat arbitrary as well. Therefore, a sensitivity analysis is conducted. To see whether more banks have the potential to pose 'significant' cross-border externalities in the European context, the criteria are lowered by 10 per cent and 20 per cent. An 'international' bank is then defined as a bank that conducts more than 45 (40) per cent of its business abroad ($h \leq 0.55$; $h \leq 0.6$). A 'European' bank is an international bank that conducts more than 22.5 (20) per cent of its business in the rest of Europe ($e \geq 22.5$; $e \geq 0.2$). In the case of a 10 per cent decrease (moving to the 45/22.5 per cent criteria), two more banks (ING Group and Dexia) would be regarded as 'European'. In the case of a 20 per cent decrease (moving further to the 40/20 per cent criteria), two more banks (Société Générale and Dresdner Bank) would become 'European'. Thus, a substantial relaxation of our criteria (to 40 and 20 per cent) would add four banks to the sample of nine 'European' banks. This would suggest that the results are somewhat, albeit not excessively, sensitive to the choice of the criteria.

In our empirical survey, we conclude that cross-border penetration within Europe is substantial and increasing (Schoenmaker and Oosterloo, 2005). These findings are different from a recent study by Berger et al. (2003), who focus on the global reach of banks' cash management services. Out of a sample of over 250 banks, they find that only eight banks have a broad coverage in Europe (defined as a presence in at least nine of the 20 European nations in their data-sample). Of these eight banks, five are headquartered in the EU and three in the US. Berger et al. (2003) conclude that the extent of future bank globalisation may be significantly limited as many corporations continue to prefer local or regional banks for at least some of their services (such as cash management). The conclusion that bank globalisation may be limited in the future should be treated with care, as the survey data of their study refer to one year (1996). Our data show that there is a clear upward trend in the Europe-wide coverage of banks.

Regional versus pan-European banks

Not all of the 'European' institutions in Table 9.3 are pan-European. There are some banks that focus on a specific region in Europe and can be regarded as 'regional' European banks. HypoVereinsbank has merged with Bank Austria in Austria and the predominant part of its business is conducted in Germany and Austria. Fortis primarily operates in Belgium and the Netherlands. Similarly, the Nordea Group primarily operates in the Nordic countries. Nordea holds 40 per cent of banking assets in Finland, 25 per cent in Denmark, 20 per cent in Sweden and 15 per cent in Norway. Therefore, Nordea also can be seen as a 'regional' European financial institution. With the acquisition of 60 per cent of the Italian bank Banque Sanpaolo, Groupe Caisse d'Epargne also became a regional European banking group.

The other banks can be regarded as 'pan-European' banks. ABN AMRO, BNP Paribas and Deutsche Bank have spread their activities throughout Europe. For example, they operate cash management services in 19, 12 and 10 European countries, respectively (Berger *et al.*, 2003). The KBC Group occupies a leading position in Belgium as well as in its second home market in Central and Eastern Europe. The Westdeutsche Landesbank also operates throughout Europe (including Eastern European countries and Turkey).

Foreign ownership

So far, we have looked at the European activities of individual EU banks. But how are banking systems in member states affected by the increasing cross-border activities of financial institutions? As can be seen in Table 9.4, a rather significant fraction of the banking system's assets in most new

Table 9.4 Fraction of banking system's assets in foreign owned banks (2001)

Country	%	Country	%
1 Austria	n.a.	14 Latvia	65
2 Belgium	n.a.	15 Lithuania	78
3 Cyprus	13	16 Luxembourg	95
4 Czech Republic	90	17 Malta	60
5 Denmark	0	18 The Netherlands	2
6 Estonia	99	19 Poland	69
7 Finland	6	20 Portugal	18
8 France	n.a.	21 Slovakia	86
9 Germany	4	22 Slovenia	21
10 Greece	11	23 Spain	9
11 Hungary	89	24 Sweden	n.a.
12 Ireland	n.a.	25 The United Kingdom	46
13 Italy	6		

Source: World Bank, Bank Regulation and Supervision Database 2003.

Notes
Foreign owned banks are defined as banks that are 50 per cent or more foreign owned. Data refer to year end 2001 with the exception of Slovenia (year end 2002). The abbreviation n.a. means 'not available'.

member states (as well as Luxembourg) is in banks that are foreign owned.

Although the presence of strong foreign participation can add to the stability of the financial system (diversification), it also poses challenges to the respective supervisory authorities. For example, in its Financial System Stability Assessment of the Czech Republic the International Monetary Fund (IMF) (2001) states that 'the predominant foreign control of the Czech banking system highlights the urgent need for strengthening supervision of foreign banks' establishments. Most importantly, it will require an efficient system of information sharing and formal Memoranda of Understanding (MoU) with supervisory counterparts.' With respect to Slovakia the IMF (2002) argues that the predominance of foreign banks 'will require the implementation of effective cross-border prudential supervision as well as consolidated supervision and close and effective working relations with foreign supervisors'. Before turning to the important issue of how to supervise foreign establishments we first review how financial institutions run these foreign establishments in practice.

How do financial institutions operate?

This section discusses two elements of the corporate structure of financial institutions that greatly affect the scope for control of supervisory authorities. The first element concerns the growing integration and centralisation of key management functions, such as risk management, internal controls, treasury operations (including liquidity management and funding), compliance and auditing. The second element concerns the legal structure of financial institutions and, in particular, the question whether a firms organises its cross-border operations through branches or subsidiaries.

Integration of risk management functions

One of the most notable advances in risk management is the growing emphasis on developing a firm-wide assessment of risk (Joint Forum, 2003). These integrated approaches to risk management aim to ensure a comprehensive and systematic approach to risk-related decisions throughout the financial firm. Although costly to realise, Flannery (1999) argues that once firms have a centralised risk management unit in place, they should expect to reap economies of scale in risk management. Moreover, the potential capital reductions that can be achieved by applying the advanced approaches of the new Basel 2 framework could encourage banking groups to organise their risk management more centrally. Nevertheless, these centralised systems still rely on local branches and subsidiaries for local market data.

Kuritzkes *et al.* (2003) point out that internationally active financial conglomerates are putting in place centralised risk and capital management units. According to these authors the dominant approach is to adopt a so-called 'hub and spoke' organisational model. The spokes are responsible for risk management within business lines, while the hub provides centralised oversight of risk and capital at the group level. Activities at the spoke include the credit function within a bank, or the actuarial function within an insurance subsidiary or group, each serves as the front-line managers for most trading decision making. Moreover, aggregation across risk factors within a business line also typically takes place in the spokes, often in a finance unit that is responsible for funding and business reporting for the subsidiary. While the hub is dependent on risk reporting from the spokes, in many cases it is also responsible for overseeing the methodology development of an integrated economic capital framework that is then implemented within the spokes. The specific roles of the hub vary, but tend to include assuming responsibility for group-level risk reporting; participating in decisions about group capital structure, funding practices and target debt rating; liaising with regulators and rating agencies; advising on major risk transfer transactions, such as collateralised loan obligations and securitisations; and in some institutions, actively managing the balance sheet.

On the basis of a survey of 31 financial institutions in 12 jurisdictions, the Joint Forum (2003) observes two important trends:

1   greater emphasis on the management of risk on an integrated firm-wide basis; and
2   related efforts to 'aggregate' risk through mathematical risk models.

These integrated risk management systems seek to have in place management policies and procedures that are designed to help ensure an awareness of, and accountability for, the risk taken throughout the financial firm, and also to develop tools needed to address those risks. A key objective of integrated risk management systems is to ensure that the firm does not ignore any material source of risk. The Joint Forum study shows that in order to accomplish this, many firms have increased the share of firms resources devoted to risk management activities and/or created a dedicated risk management function. However, in contrast to Kuritzkes *et al.* (2003), the Joint Forum (2003) finds that the organisational infrastructure of risk management decision making varies considerably across firms without any single approach becoming dominant.

Legal structure: branches versus subsidiaries

The second element concerns the legal structure that financial institutions adopt, in particular the whether a financial institution organises its cross-border operations through branches or subsidiaries. While subsidiaries have a legal status (own corporate charter and balance sheet), branches have no separate legal status but are part of another legal entity (parent company). As more fully discussed in the next section, subsidiaries are separately licensed and supervised within the EU (host country control), while branches are supervised through the parent company (home country control). In a recent survey, Freshfields Bruckhaus Deringer (2003) examined to what extent legal firewalls (separate legal personality and limited liability of subsidiaries) can help to reduce or prevent contagion risk within a group. They find that legal firewalls can help to protect from direct contagion (credit exposures arising from intragroup transactions or operational risk from sharing of services), but are less effective in limiting indirect contagion (reputation risk and funding risk). This is because indirect contagion arises from perceptions and behaviour of (potential) counterparties and other market participants.[3]

Although organising cross-border activities through branches lessens the number of supervisory authorities that a financial institution has to deal with (large banking groups like ABN AMRO and Deutsche Bank have to deal with at least 20 different supervisory authorities in the EU) many firms chose to operate through subsidiaries. According to Dermine (2003), the motivation to keep a subsidiary structure can be driven by eight different arguments:

1   protection of the original brand: at the time of a merger financial institutions will like to keep 'business as usual' and not to change the brand;
2   management trust: to reassure the local management that key-functions will not be transferred;
3   shareholder approval: to reassure shareholders so as to get their approval for a merger;
4   nationalistic feelings: to reassure member states that they keep (supervisory control over) their bank;
5   corporate tax: a subsidiary structure is often more flexible from an international corporate tax point of view;
6   deposit insurance: a financial institution would have to contribute extra deposit insurance premia to the home country insurance fund if it transfers a subsidiary into a branch;
7   ring-fencing: protection from risk-shifting and the ability to do a separate listing; and
8   flexibility: the ease of selling a business unit.

The first four arguments are of a temporary nature, the following two are due to the incompleteness of EU integration and the last two are permanent features of business. From this analysis, Dermine (2003) concludes that the corporate structure of European banks is very unlikely to meet the single entity with branches' textbook case, but will involve a web of branches and subsidiaries.

Since Dermine's analysis, there has been an interesting development. The European Company Statute (ECS) was introduced in October 2004, which gives companies operating in more than one member state the option of being established as a single company under community law. This enables firms to operate throughout the EU with one set of rules and a unified management and reporting system instead of operating through subsidiaries and being subject to the different national laws. The main advantages of the ECS is that it helps companies move their business across borders and the potential for significant reductions in administrative and legal costs ('synergies').

In the financial sector, the Nordic banking group Nordea has already indicated that it will adopt the ECS (Schütze, 2004). In practice this means that the entire banking group will convert into one legal body under Swedish law, while most of its activities are performed by foreign branches.[4] As Nordea is a systemic banking group in all Nordic countries, this transformation poses a significant challenge to the relevant authorities in these countries. For example, how should these countries design their deposit insurance funds, and what about crisis management decisions (e.g. emergency liquidity assistance and potential burden sharing)? These issues are addressed in the next section.

Diverging structures

We described the trend to centralise key management functions that previously belonged with the separate entities of a financial group. Centralisation implies that strategic decision making is transferred from the functional or sectoral entities of the group to the level of the group as a whole (that is, the holding level). The centralisation of activities (such as asset management) and key management functions results from the drive by financial groups to reap the benefits of synergy. The prospect of co-operation between different entities of a financial group is an important part of the rationale for the group. During this process, the difference between the legal structure and the operational structure of the group will increase. In consequence, it becomes harder to attribute activities to the legal entities on which the division of supervisory responsibilities is based. A large difference between the legal structure and organisational structure will complicate the execution of supervision, since supervision is based on statutory power to supervise legal entities and this may not correspond to where activities actually take place (Kremers *et al.*, 2003b). This tension between operationally integrated financial groups looking for synergies and legally constrained supervisors looking for an effective lever on key decision-makers of these financial groups poses a challenge for policy. We review the policy options in the next section.

Challenges for the supervisory framework

In this section, we focus on the prudential supervision of financial institutions.[5] As argued earlier, payments systems are also important for maintaining EU-wide financial stability. See Bank of England (2004) for an interesting discussion of the spectrum of models for cross-border supervision of systemically important providers of infrastructure. Before reviewing the policy options for the future, we briefly describe the present institutional set-up of financial supervision and stability. When looking at the supervisory framework, it is important to take an integrated approach from preventive actions (prudential supervision and monitoring financial stability) to curative actions (crisis management). The relevant players are supervisory authorities, central banks (monitoring financial stability as well as providing possible emergency liquidity assistance) and ministries of finance (bearing the ultimate cost of possible bail-out).

Present system of EU financial supervision

The current system of prudential supervision in the EU is based on the principle of home country control combined with minimum standards and mutual recognition. A financial institution is thus authorised and supervised in its home country and can expand throughout the EU (via offering cross-border services to other EU countries or establishing branches in these countries) without additional supervision. The host country has to recognise supervision from the home country authorities.

The arguments for home country control are twofold. First, it promotes the effectiveness of supervision, as the home supervisor is able to make a group-wide assessment of the risk profile and the required capital adequacy of financial institutions (i.e. the concept of consolidated supervision). The concept of consolidated supervision is well established in banking.[6] The recently adopted Directive on Financial Conglomerates introduces a single co-ordinator who is responsible for group-wide supervision of financial conglomerates.[7] However, the concept of solo-plus supervision is applied in insurance. The primary focus of supervision is on the separate legal entities (the solo-element) with some limited attention for group-wide supervision (the plus-element).[8]

Second, home country control promotes the efficiency of supervision, as financial institutions are not confronted with different supervisors possibly resulting in duplication of efforts and a higher regulatory burden. Home country control is applicable to financial institutions that offer cross-border services to other EU countries or establish branches in these countries. In practice, however, as we have noted, financial institutions also operate through subsidiaries (separate legal entities) in other countries for reasons of taxation and limited liability. These subsidiaries are separately licensed and supervised by the host country authorities (*de jure* control). The scope for control by host countries of these subsidiaries is limited in practice, as key-decisions are often taken at the parent company in the home country and the financial health of the subsidiary is closely linked (via intra-group transactions and/or joint branding) to the well-being of the financial group as a whole. The effective control of large financial groups is primarily in the hands of the consolidated supervisor in the home country (*de facto* control).

While home country control may be useful for the effectiveness and efficiency of prudential supervision, home country authorities are not responsible for financial stability in host countries (Mayes and Vesala, 2000). Stability of the financial system is the remit of the host country. Increasing integration within the EU gives rise to cross-border spill-over effects or externalities. A failure in one country may cause problems in other countries. The policy question is whether home country control for supervision and host country responsibility for financial stability is sustainable in an integrating market.

The present organisational structure of crisis management in the EU has been reviewed in the 'Report on Financial Crisis Management' (EFC, 2001). The guiding principles are that the instruments of crisis resolution are available at the national level and that the costs are born at the national level. As regards the instruments for crisis management, there is a strong preference for private sector solutions as opposed to public intervention tools (e.g. bail-out). In line with the allocation of supervisory responsibilities, the responsibility for decision making in crisis situations regarding an individual institution and its branches rests with the home country authorities. However, home country authorities are not responsible for the financial stability of host countries. Moreover, the home country taxpayer may not be prepared to pay for cross-border spill-over effects of a failure. The Report therefore calls for enhanced co-operation between home and host countries for crisis-management. To achieve such enhanced co-operation incentives to co-operate may need to be improved.

Policy options for the future

On a conceptual level, the main policy options for the structure of financial supervision are summarised in Table 9.5.[9] In practice, several hybrid forms are possible. In the current system (row A), the home supervisor is responsible for a bank and its EU-wide branch network and is the consolidated supervisor as well. The host country is responsible for a bank's EU subsidiaries and controls the stability of its financial system. As discussed above, the home and host authorities have to co-operate for financial supervision and stability.

The first alternative (row B) is to give the home supervisor full responsibility for the EU-wide operations, both branches and subsidiaries. The

Table 9.5 Structure of financial supervision: policy options

Supervisory structure	Criteria				
	1 *Effectiveness of supervision*	*2* *Efficiency of supervision*	*3* *Financial stability*	*4* *Competitiveness of financial firms*	*5* *Proximity to financial firms*
A Home and host (current system)	+	+/−	+/−	+/−	+
B Home on the basis of a national mandate	+	+	−	+	+
C Home on the basis of a European mandate	+	+	+	+	+
D Central body on the basis of a European mandate	+	+	+	+	−
E Host on the basis of a national mandate	+/−	+	−	−	+

home supervisor can act on a national or a European mandate. In option B, the home supervisor keeps its national mandate and is the consolidated supervisor as well. The home supervisor will therefore be predominantly responsive to the needs of domestic depositors and concerned with domestic financial stability.

The second alternative (row C) is again to give the home supervisor full responsibility for the EU-wide operations, both branches and subsidiaries. In option C, the home supervisor has a European mandate to ensure that the interests of all depositors/countries are taken into account. In some form of European System of Financial Supervisors, national supervisors can work together with a decision-making body or agency at the centre (see below). Within the System, the supervisor in the country where the bank is headquartered can then act as consolidated or lead supervisor. Accordingly for financial stability purposes, the home country authorities (supervisor and central bank) within the European System of Financial Supervisors and the European System of Central Banks (ESCB) can act within their respective systems.

The third alternative (row D) is to give the central body of some form of European System of Financial Supervisors full responsibility for the EU-wide operations, both branches and subsidiaries, of pan-European banks. Similar to option C, the central body has a European mandate to ensure that the interests of all depositors/countries are taken into account. Different from option C, the supervision is mainly conducted by the central body, which can work together with national supervisors. Breuer (2000) has advocated the approach of supervision of truly European banks by the central body. The central body acts as the consolidated or lead supervisor. The logical equivalent would be that the ECB is the focal point for financial stability within the ESCB. In a crisis, the central bodies of the European System of Financial Supervisors and the ESCB take the lead within their respective systems.

The remaining possibility (row E) is to give the host supervisor responsibility for operations in its country, both branches and subsidiaries. If a bank's operations become significant in a country, the host country can require that bank to conduct these operations in a separate subsidiary to have a stronger lever on these operations. New Zealand is, for example, taking this approach as described in the annex.[10] Supervisors work on a strict national mandate and are thus only responsible for financial supervision and stability in their own country. There is no consolidated supervision.

Summing up, three options assume a national mandate (A, B and E) with or without some form of co-operation. National supervisors keep their sovereignty. Two options (C and D) assume a European mandate (that is a European jurisdiction). Supervisors work on a supra-national basis.

Horizontally, Table 9.5 provides the criteria to judge the different policy options:

1 effectiveness of supervision: supervision of all parts of a financial group[11] and consolidated supervision of the group as a whole;
2 efficiency of supervision: no duplication or overlap of supervision;
3 financial stability: cross-border externalities of a failure of a financial institution are incorporated;
4 competitiveness of financial institutions: financial institutions can operate cross-border without additional burden (e.g. notification, regulatory reporting) and are allowed to realise synergies from centralised or integrated operations (e.g. risk management, asset management, back-office operations); and
5 proximity to financial institutions: supervisor is close to the (main) operations of financial firms.

Assessment

The different policy options are scored against the criteria in Table 9.5. We consider the current system (option A) to be adequate, but not optimal. Supervision is effective. Home and host authorities work together for financial stability. However, as mentioned, co-ordination failure is possible during a crisis, as resolving cross-border externalities relies on voluntary co-operation. Competitiveness is also half-way: cross-border expansion through branches can be done without extra supervision (only some minor notification procedures), but subsidiaries in the host country experience duplication in supervision from the supervisor in the host country and the consolidated supervisor in the home country.

According to the European Financial Services Round Table (EFR) (EFR, 2004) a clearly defined lead supervisor (usually the home supervisor) for prudential supervision of cross-border financial institutions would be an important step towards a more coherent and efficient supervisory framework in the EU. The EFR argues that the lead supervisor should in particular be the single point of contact for all reporting schemes, validate and authorise internal models, approve capital and liquidity allocation, approve cross-border set-up of specific functions and decide about on-site inspections. Furthermore, the lead supervisor should not only be responsible for supervision on a consolidated level, but also on the solo and subconsolidated level.

The EFR agrees that host countries should be involved in the supervisory process, as local supervisors have generally a better understanding of the local market conditions. The EFR suggests forming colleges of supervisors (one for each specific group) that advise the lead supervisor and discuss proposals of involved local supervisors, but would not have the power to delay decisions of the lead supervisor. As the role and the powers of the host supervisor in these colleges are non-committal,[12] the actual involvement of host authorities can be limited in practice. The EFR recommendation seems to get close to option B.

In our view the concept of a lead supervisor is ambiguous, and can be designed in different ways: the lead supervisor authority can either be the home supervisor, on the basis of a national or European mandate (option B or C), or a central EU body (option D). We would therefore like to take the analysis one step further and look at the pros and cons of these different options.

In comparison with option A, both the efficiency of supervision and the competitiveness of the financial sector are enhanced under option B. Nevertheless, option B does poorly with respect to financial stability, as the national mandate does not induce the lead supervisor to incorporate the cross-border externalities of a failure of a financial institution in its decision making.

Option C does well on all five criteria; by taking the mandate to the European level, cross-border externalities are taken into account and duplication in supervision is avoided. This European mandate can be created through some form of European System of Financial Supervisors, created by the national supervisors in tandem with a centralised body. Key supervisory decisions as well as the design of policy are done at the centre (in the same way as the ESCB takes decisions on monetary policy).[13] In this way, host country authorities are fully involved and the interests of their depositors are fully taken into account. Day-to-day supervision is conducted by the home country close to the financial firms.

Option D does well on the first four criteria. Like option C, it is operating within a European System of Financial Supervisors. But it could be placed too far away from the (main) operations of financial firms to execute its supervisory responsibilities properly, as the focal point for day-to-day supervision will be at the central body in option D. This is different from option C, where the focal point remains with the home supervisor. Option D has been promoted by Breuer (2000: 9) who proposes that 'it may also be sensible to have those banking groups that operate on a truly European scale supervised directly by the central agency'. The appropriate degree of (de)centralisation is discussed in more detail in the next section.

Finally, option E would reverse the process of financial integration promoted by the Single Market Programme and the Financial Services Action Plan. Significant cross-border activities have to be conducted through a subsidiary in the host country. Financial firms are then not able to realise synergies from centralisation or integration. There is, however, no duplication of supervision, as each supervisor is concerned with operations in its own national jurisdiction. Finally, financial stability cannot be effectively managed due to the lack of co-operation between home and host country authorities. Option E is basically the establishment of autarky.

Based on the five criteria to judge the available policy options, we conclude that option C (home on the basis of a European mandate) is the best supervisory structure to deal with the challenges posed by the growing interdependence of EU financial systems. Option C follows the 'decentralised' element of the lead supervisor concept promoted by the EFR, but adds the novel element of a European mandate to allow for adequate involvement of host country authorities.

Other aspects

When considering option C (home supervisor with a European mandate), there are some further aspects to be explored. These are (i) the appropriate level of (de)centralisation, (ii) the geographical reach (regional or EU-wide), (iii) degree of financial integration, (iv) deposit insurance and (v) the fiscal mechanism.

Level of (de)centralisation

Centralisation of supervision may become desirable to preserve financial stability in an integrating European financial system. The policy challenge is to deal effectively with cross-border externalities. If and when the intensity of cross-border externalities increases, supervisory as well as crisis management decisions may need to be taken at the European level to incorporate these externalities. One can think of a body at the centre working in tandem with the national supervisors: a 'European System of Financial Supervisors' (Schoenmaker, 2003; Vives, 2001). Such a system could evolve from the newly created supervisory committees at level 3, similar to the creation of the ESCB.

Would the establishment of a European System of Financial Supervisors necessarily result in a predominantly centralised system of supervision? There is a strong case for decentralisation. First, there are many small- and medium-sized financial institutions which operate mainly within national borders. There is no need for involvement at the European level for these institutions. Padoa-Schioppa (1999) draws an interesting picture citing from Italian experience:

1   small banks are supervised by the respective regional branch of Banca d'Italia;
2   national banks are supervised by the respective branches but key decisions are taken at the headquarters of Banca d'Italia in Rome;
3   pan-European banks are supervised by a group of national supervisors working collectively in a multilateral mode as a single consolidated supervisor.

Second, financial supervision should be executed at the local level where the financial institutions are based. The use of field inspections is an important tool of prudential supervision. By being close to the business, supervisors would get a feeling for what is going on at an institution and would also be more familiar with local market conditions in which an institution is operating. For pan-European financial institutions, the 'lead supervisor' should thus remain located near the head office of the financial institution.[14]

Policy rules (e.g. the rulebook and reporting requirements for institutions under supervision) and information pooling (e.g. reporting format and computer systems) may at some stage and in some form be made uniform. Such a uniform policy framework would very much be built on the unified regulatory regime established by EU Directives. Next, appropriate decision making and incentive mechanisms should be designed to ensure that local supervisors adhere to this policy framework. Furthermore, information pooling will allow effective market surveillance of systemic risks (including a peer group analysis of large pan-European financial institutions).[15]

Geographical reach

Of the top 30 EU banks, nine are found to pose significant cross-border externalities (Table 9.3). Some of these 'European' banks are regional:

Nordea, Fortis, HypoVereinsbank and Groupe Caisse d'Epargne. The remaining can be regarded as pan-European (ABN AMRO, Deutsche, BNP Paribas, KBC and Westdeutsche Landesbank) operating throughout the EU. While an EU-wide mandate is needed for the latter, regional mandates can be applied to the former. Arguably, Nordea is the most pressing case at the moment. Nordea will adopt a European charter and has a significant market share in all Scandinavian countries. Furthermore, Nordea's business in its home market is relatively low, compared to that of other EU banks: 28 per cent as illustrated in Table 9.3.

It may be tempting to start a regional solution among Nordic–Baltic authorities (supervisors, central banks and ministries of finance) to address the Nordea case. However, 'good' policy making suggests that one would first design (and negotiate) the preferred end-model with an EU-wide mandate. Next, further regional steps could be taken if and when needed within the confines of this end-model, before (full) implementation of the end-model. Otherwise, regional steps may need to be reversed when wider solutions are introduced.

Degree of financial integration

There is still some work to do on the Single Market front before a new system of home supervision with a European mandate can operate fully. Key areas are legal and taxation systems (Heinemann and Jopp, 2002; Dermine, 2003). Consumer protection and contract law are rooted in national legislation. Corporate tax and VAT are also nationally organised. As described earlier, firms tend to integrate their activities and management functions to achieve economies of scale. If shared services centres sell their services across countries, these services incur VAT charges (Schütze, 2004). These are important elements on the not yet fully complete Single Market agenda.

Deposit insurance

The move to a European mandate causes intractable problems for the currently nationally organised deposit insurance funds. There is a diversity of funds with differing set-ups: levying premium, or not; level of premium if one is levied; organisational structure (private or public). As a result, some funds are fully funded, others partly and the remaining not at all. Branches are covered by the fund from the home country and subsidiaries by the host country.[16] When a bank switches from subsidiaries to branches (or the other way round), there are no provisions for a possible transfer of funds. There can thus be (huge) swings in the premium for the bank, if it moves from a fully funded scheme to a less funded scheme. This seems to be the case for Nordea (Schütze, 2004). This is an area for further research and policy making.

Fiscal mechanism

Following financial supervision arrangements, crisis management would need to be organised with a European mandate. This implies that emergency liquidity assistance is provided at the European level. The key in the Statute of the ESCB and ECB to distribute monetary income could, for example, be applied to share the possible cost of lender of last resort (LOLR) operations. This key is based on an average of the share in total gross domestic product (GDP) and total population of the participating members.

European supervision also raises the thorny issue of who should bear the fiscal costs of a possible bail-out. The first-best solution is to keep decision making on supervision and fiscal bail-outs at the same level. Moving the supervisory function to the European level, while leaving the fiscal function at the national level, would cause problems. Following the principle 'he who pays the piper calls the tune', the national ministry of finance would like to control the supervisor if the national taxpayer is seen to be potentially liable (Goodhart and Schoenmaker, 1995).

In a recent lecture, Goodhart lucidly remarks that:

> Absent such a shift of the fiscal competence for crisis resolution to the EU level, calls for transfers of supervisory functions to a central, European body are, in my view, nugatory and little more than whistling in the wind. That brings us back to the question of how to share the burden of rescues when the relevant public authorities are national but the financial system is international
>
> (Goodhart, 2004: 8)

However, there is no meaningful European budget which can be drawn upon for such cases. Moreover, a fixed rule to share the costs (e.g. the above mentioned ESCB key) may give rise to moral hazard, as countries with a weak financial system may face reduced incentives to prevent potential bail-outs. A fixed rule may thus not be politically feasible (or desirable), as countries with a strong financial system may not be prepared to pay up each time.

Further research is needed to explore mechanisms for co-operation between a putative European system of financial supervisors and national tax-authorities to deal effectively with pan-European threats to financial stability. Crisis management would also include the ECB (and the relevant national central banks) and possibly the European Commission. Could such co-operation really be effective? There is a precedent in European history that contains many of the characteristics that are relevant in this case: speedy confidential decision making by many (inter)national players. In the former European Monetary System, confidential decision making on realignments took place over the weekend, involving ministers of Finance, Central Bankers and the European Commission. The rules of procedure of this committee could serve as a starting point for thinking about the development of a European structure for crisis management (Kremers *et al.*, 2003a). To simplify matters, only the ministers of finance and central bankers of the countries affected (in addition to a putative European System of Financial Supervisors, the ECB and possibly the European Commission) should be involved.[17]

Conclusions

Supervisory structures should, in our view, adapt to market developments and not the other way round. The chapter therefore starts with examining the current state of integration of EU financial markets. Ongoing financial integration fostered by the advance to EMU and the nearly full completion of the Financial Services Action Plan gives rise to increasing cross-border penetration of interbank markets and payment systems, which are important channels for cross-border contagion. Furthermore, emerging pan-European and regional banks give rise to cross-border externalities arising from the (potential) failure of these banks.

Due to these market trends, it is increasingly difficult to organise financial supervision and stability on a predominantly national basis. This raises the question of the appropriate division of responsibilities between home and host authorities and their mandate (national or European). To stay close to the operations of financial institutions, it is argued that the supervisor of the home country should act as lead supervisor, but with a European mandate to incorporate cross-border effects. The focal point would remain at the national level, as the home supervisor would conduct the day-to-day supervision. The European mandate can be created through some form of European System of Financial Supervisors, created by the national supervisors in tandem with a centralised body. Key supervisory decisions as well as the design of policy are done at the centre. In this way, host country authorities are fully involved and the interests of their depositors are fully taken into account. European structures raise the thorny issue of dividing the fiscal costs of possible bail-outs. The chapter explores some avenues for further research in this area.

Efficient supervisory structures are also important for the competitive position of EU financial institutions. A system with home country supervision and no duplication by host countries with (slightly) different requirements and reporting formats (as is currently the case for subsidiaries) would reduce the burden on financial institutions and foster cross-border expansion within the EU. This would put European banks at par with their counterparts from the US, where the remaining barriers to interstate banking and branching were lifted in 1994.[18]

Annex: the New Zealand example

How do countries deal with home/host issues in cross-border financial supervision? On the one hand, authorities can decide to maintain supervisory control over all systemic relevant banking entities within their jurisdiction. On the other hand, authorities can try to facilitate the market by providing less complicated and less costly rules for streamlining cross-border operations. In New Zealand the authorities chose for the first option, while the EU has introduced new legislation that makes it easier to organise cross-border activities through branches (the European Company Statute).

In order to maintain direct control over relevant entities within its jurisdiction, the authorities in New Zealand require some overseas banks to establish locally incorporated subsidiaries instead of operating as branches (Reserve Bank of New Zealand, 2004). Under this policy, banks in the following categories are required to establish a locally incorporated subsidiary for their New Zealand operations:

- systemically important banks – that is, banks large enough to materially affect the operation of the financial sector as a whole;
- banks that take a significant level of retail deposits and come from countries with legislation giving home country depositors a preferential claim in a winding up – currently both the United States and Australia have such legislation;
- banks that take a significant level of retail deposits and which, in their home countries fail to publish the full information depositors would need to assess financial soundness.

Banks that do not fall into one of those categories can continue to choose whether they operate a branch or a subsidiary in New Zealand.

Notes

1 The authors would like to thank the discussants at the conference, Peik Granlund and Philipp Hartmann, as well as Bernhard Speyer for valuable comments and suggestions. The views in this chapter are those of the authors and not necessarily those of the Ministry of Finance.
2 Central banks of the new member states have the possibility – but not the obligation – to connect to TARGET. Participation in TARGET is only compulsory when they join the EMU.
3 A good example of indirect contagion is the Drexel Burnham Lambert collapse in 1990. While the Drexel Burnham Lambert Group was experiencing difficulties, the London subsidiary was solvent. Nevertheless, the Bank of England had to intervene as facilitator because the counterparties did not want to deal directly with the London subsidiary (Committee on Payment and Settlement Systems, 1996).
4 As an indication, Nordea's Annual Report (2003) shows that 29.1 per cent of its lending activities takes place in Sweden, 26.3 per cent in Denmark, 21.3 per cent in Finland, 15.1 per cent in Norway and 8.3 per cent in other countries.

5 The focus of this chapter is on prudential supervision aimed at the safety and soundness of financial institutions. We do not discuss conduct of business supervision aimed at the relationships between financial institutions and their clients and, more broadly, the behaviour of financial institutions in financial markets. See Kremers *et al.* (2003b) for a discussion of the synergies and conflicts of interest between these two supervisory objectives.

6 The revised Basel Concordat on international banking supervision introduced the concept of consolidation in 1983. In Europe the concept was adopted in the Consolidated Banking Supervision Directive 92/30/EEC (replaced by the Codified Banking Directive 2000/12/EC).

7 Financial Conglomerates Directive 2002/87/EC.

8 Insurance Groups Directive 98/78/EC.

9 We would like to thank Philipp Hartmann, one of the discussants, for suggesting that we extend our original menu of three options (relabelled A, C and E) to five options.

10 Option E assumes that there is no consolidated supervision in the home country. Each supervisor confines itself to its national mandate. However, one could allow for consolidated supervision in the home country as New Zealand does. In that case there would be duplication between the work of the consolidated supervisor and the host supervisor.

11 Given the importance of financial conglomerates in the EU, we assume that national supervisors operate on a cross-sector basis. See Kremers *et al.* (2003a) on the different models of cross-sector financial supervision.

12 In cases of lasting differences of opinion, the EFR proposes to refer cases to the level 3 committees (Committee of European Banking Supervisors (CEBS), Committee of European Insurance and Occupational Pensions Supervisors (CEIOPS) or the Conglomerate Committee), which can either act in an appeal procedure or could organise a mediation process. However, this seems to us a rather bureaucratic process which does not enhance timely decision making.

13 To draw the parallel in more detail, option B (lead supervisor with national mandate) is similar to the European Monetary System (EMS) in the pre-EMU era. The leader, Germany, used to set interest rates that fitted the German economy. To maintain stable exchange rates in the EMS, other countries had to follow German interest rates. Options C and D are similar to stage 3 of the EMU. The decision on interest rates is taken collectively by the Governing Council that consists of the Executive Board of the ECB as well as the Governors of the participating National Central Banks. An important feature is that members of the Governing Council have to vote on interest rates with conditions of the euro area in mind and are not allowed to base their vote on national conditions.

14 If needed, the lead supervisor could engage local supervisors to visit branches and subsidiaries located in other EU countries, while keeping full responsibility. This would create a team that consists of the lead supervisor in the home country and the supervisors in the host countries.

15 An instructive example of decentralisation is presented by the organisational structure of the two federal banking regulators in the US, the OCC and the Fed (see Schoenmaker, 2003).

16 Deposit Guarantee-Schemes Directive 94/19/EC.

17 In the case of Fortis (a Belgian–Dutch financial institution), for example, the Dutch and Belgian authorities would take decisions on crisis resolution in conjunction with a putative European System of Financial Supervisors and the ECB.

18 See Barth *et al.* (2000) for a review of the liberalisation of the US financial system.

References

Aharony, J. and Swary, I. (1983) 'Contagion effects of bank failures: evidence from capital markets', *Journal of Business* 56: 305–22.

Bank of England (2004) 'Strengthening financial infrastructure', *Financial Stability Review*, no. 16, London.

Barth, J., Brumbaugh, D. and Wilcox, J. (2000) 'The repeal of Glass–Steagall and the advent of broad banking', *Journal of Economic Perspectives* 14: 191–204.

Basel Committee on Banking Supervision (2003) 'High-level principles for the cross-border implementation of the new accord', Basel: Bank for International Settlements.

Basel Committee on Banking Supervision (2004) 'Principles for the home–host recognition of AMA operational risk capital', Basel: Bank for International Settlements.

Berger, A., Dai, Q., Ongena, S. and Smith, D.C. (2003) 'To what extent with the banking industry be globalized? A study of nationality and reach in 20 European nations', *Journal of Banking and Finance* 27, 383–415.

Breuer, R. (2000) 'Convergence of supervisory practices – a banker's view', Speech at the Conference of European Banking Supervisors, Copenhagen.

Cabral, I., Dierick, F. and Vesala, J. (2002) 'Banking integration in the euro area', *ECB Occasional Paper Series*, no. 6, Frankfurt am Main: European Central Bank.

Committee on Payment and Settlement Systems (1996) 'Settlement risk in foreign exchange transactions', Basel: Bank for International Settlements.

De Bandt, O. and Hartmann, P. (2000) 'Systemic risk: a survey', ECB Working Paper, no. 35, Frankfurt am Main: European Central Bank.

Dermine, J. (2003) 'Banking in Europe: past, present and future', in Gaspar, V., Hartmann, P. and Sleijpen. O. (eds) *The Transformation of the European Financial System*, Frankfurt: European Central Bank.

Economic and Financial Committee (2001) 'Report on financial crisis management', *European Economy Economic Papers*, no. 156, Brussels.

European Financial Services Round Table (EFR) (2004) *Towards a Lead Supervisor for Cross Border Financial Institutions in the European Union*, Brussels.

Flannery, M. (1999) 'Modernising financial regulation: the relation between interbank transactions and supervisory reforms, *Journal of Financial Services Research* 16: 101–16.

Freshfields Bruckhaus Deringer (2003) 'Study on financial conglomerates and legal firewalls', London.

Goodhart, C. (ed.) (2000) *Which Lender of Last Resort for Europe?*, London: Central Banking Publications.

Goodhart, C. (2004) 'Some new directions for financial stability', Per Jacobsson Lecture, Basel: Bank for International Settlements.

Goodhart, C. and Schoenmaker, D. (1995) 'Should the functions of monetary policy and banking supervision be separated?', *Oxford Economic Papers* 47: 539–60.

Heinemann, F. and Jopp, M. (2002) 'The benefits of a working European retail market for financial services', Report to European Financial Services Round Table, Berlin: Institut für Europäische Politik.

Herring, R. and Litan, R. (1994) *Financial Regulation in a Global Economy*, Washington, DC: Brookings Institution.

International Monetary Fund (2001) 'Financial system stability assessment – Czech Republic', Washington, DC.

International Monetary Fund (2002) 'Financial system stability assessment – Slovak Republic', Washington, DC.

Joint Forum (2003) 'Trends in risk integration and aggregation', Basel: Bank for International Settlements.

Kremers, J., Schoenmaker, D. and Wierts, P. (eds) (2003a) *Financial Supervision in Europe*, Cheltenham: Edward Elgar.

Kremers, J., Schoenmaker, D. and Wierts, P. (2003b) 'Cross-sector supervision: which model?', in Herring, R. and Litan, R. (eds) *Brookings-Wharton Papers on Financial Services: 2003*, Washington, DC: Brookings Institution.

Kuritzkes, A., Schuermann, T. and Weiner, S. (2003) 'Risk measurement, risk management, and capital adequacy in financial conglomerates', in Herring, R. and Litan, R. (eds) *Brookings-Wharton Papers on Financial Services: 2003*, Washington, DC: Brookings Institution.

Mayes, D. and Vesala, J. (2000) 'On the problems of home country control', *Current Politics and Economics of Europe* 10: 1–26.

Padoa-Schioppa, T. (1999) 'EMU and banking supervision', lecture delivered at the London School of Economics.

Reserve Bank of New Zealand (2004) 'Proposed new policy on bank organisational form', Wellington.

Rose, A. (1996) 'Explaining exchange rate volatility: an empirical analysis of "The Holy Trinity" of monetary independence, fixed exchange rates, and capital mobility', *Journal of International Money and Finance* 15: 925–45.

Schoenmaker, D. (2003) 'Financial supervision: from national to European?', *Financial and Monetary Studies*, no. 22(1), Amsterdam: NIBE-SVV.

Schoenmaker, D. and Oosterloo, S. (2005) 'Financial supervision in an integrating Europe: measuring cross-border externalities', *International Finance* 8: forthcoming.

Schütze, P. (2004) 'Creating competitive size in a European integrated financial market – the Nordea experience', Speech at the EU Conference 'European Financial Integration: Progress and Prospects', Brussels: DG Internal Markt.

Slager, A. (2004) *Banking Across Borders*, Rotterdam: Erasmus Research Institute of Management.

Sullivan, D. (1994) 'Measuring the degree of internationalization of a firm', *Journal of International Business Studies* 25: 325–42.

Thygesen, N. (2003) 'Comments on the political economy of financial harmonisation in Europe', in Kremers, J., Schoenmaker, D. and Wierts, P. (eds) *Financial Supervision in Europe*, Cheltenham: Edward Elgar.

Vives, X. (2001) 'Restructuring financial regulation in the European Monetary Union', *Journal of Financial Services Research* 19: 57–82.

COMMENT

Peik Granlund

A theoretical scheme expressing the significant factors that could be considered in the assessment is needed to assess alternative ways for the future organisation of the supervision of the EU banking sector. Such a scheme may be created in various ways but should at least comprise three basic features:

> *relevant aspects of the existing market and legislative structure* (the starting point),
> *the parties involved* (the aims and features of the bank, home and host country), and
> *the environment* (the various forms of threats towards financial stability).

Once the theoretical concept is created, it illuminates the values and priorities that lie behind arguments, indicates the strength of conclusions made and supports alternatives to the organisation of supervision.

The existing market and legislative structure. The key stability question for EU banking supervision and crisis management is the fact that responsibility for supervision and responsibility for financial stability do not always go hand in hand. Overall, the supervisory problem has three dimensions, of which two are problematic. First, we have the non-problematic situation where a nationally based bank does significant business only in its own country, a constellation where there is less disparity between the responsibility of supervision and responsibility of financial stability. In this case both responsibilities belong to the bank's home authorities. In the second situation, a cross-border bank has established operations in other EU countries through subsidiaries. In this case, supervision of a unit in a given country is carried out independently by that country and in addition, consolidated supervision is carried out by the parent company's supervisor. Because of intra-group activities, the supervision of the units may be more challenging than otherwise. Eventual disparity between the responsibility for supervision and responsibility for financial stability is mostly generated by the fact that national supervisors may not have 'the whole picture'. Finally, there is the situation, where a cross-border bank has established itself in other countries through branches. In this situation, according to the current EU regime, the supervisor of the bank's home office is responsible for the supervision of the bank, including the branches. The supervisors in the countries, where the branches are situated, are responsible for the financial stability of those countries without having any supervisory powers towards the bank. The disparity between the responsibility of supervision and responsibility of financial stability is evident if branches have a significant market share in the host country.

The second feature of a theoretical concept for the assessment of alternatives for the organisation of the supervision of the EU banking sector comprises *the parties involved.* The interest is mainly in the aims and features of the primary parties, i.e. the bank, the home country and the host country. The question of parties' *aims* is important since it is the value-base that strongly directs the format of an optimal supervisory regime and also gives signals about the possibility to find backup for suggested alternatives. In addressing *the aims of the banks,* their interests are in improved business conditions. These business conditions may be described in terms of additional benefits and decreasing disadvantages. Various supervisory arrangements may affect benefits or limit disadvantages directly. Other supervisory arrangements may have indirect implications, enabling solutions that may increase benefits and cut disadvantages at a later date. Additional benefits include increased stability, better image among customers, liquidity and solvency support when needed. Decreasing disadvantages include less administrative complexity, less supervisory related work and less costs. *The aim of the home country and its supervisor* is financial stability. The promotion of financial stability in the home country is carried out through supervision and additional arrangements such as deposit insurance and schemes for eventual financial assistance. The responsibility for financial stability in the home country is to a large extent unproblematic. But the aims of the home country and its supervisor in the area of host country (both in the cases of subsidiaries and branches) stability are largely unknown, despite their responsibility for the supervision of the individual institution. In order to form a picture of these aims one may distinguish between three dimensions, i.e. the home country's obligation, opportunity and desire to take part in the promotion of financial stability in the host country. Finally, *the aims of the host country* should be considered. It is clear that ensuring financial stability in its own right is a number one priority for the host country. But opinions diverge over how this should be attained. Is there a need for 'own' supervision or can the responsibility for supervision be allocated elsewhere? Characterising supervision as, receiving a flow of data covering the institution, as, powers to intervene if problems arise in the institution, or as, a possibility to take part in crisis handling, provides a concept for the assessment of host country aims in the supervisory area.

A theoretical concept for the assessment of alternatives for the organisation of the supervision of the EU banking sector should also take certain *features* of the primary parties involved into consideration. In other words, which factors in the home country, host country or the bank itself should one address more closely when assessing supervisory structures? In principle, there are three kinds of such additional features to take account of. These are features that illuminate the need for supervisory arrangements on a general level or of specific types, affecting the implementation of alternative supervisory arrangements or otherwise have implications on the assessment of the supervisory alternatives. On these levels significant factors may be considered by distinguishing between public and private sector issues from a macro-perspective and micro-perspective issues. Features that *illuminate the need for supervisory arrangements* on a general level or of specific types are, for example, the number of cross-border banks or conglomerates, the regional dispersion of the banks and the existence of complementing arrangements promoting financial stability. Also micro-level issues such as unsatisfactory levels of capital adequacy or liquidity problems may, in the case they concern large cross-border banks, generate an interest for reformed supervisory arrangements. Features that *affect the implementation of alternative supervisory arrangements* are mainly aspects relating to the existing legal regimes in the home or host countries. Still, since regulatory powers in the area in question have been transferred to the EU, most features that shape the implementation of alternative supervisory arrangements are found at the EU level. On the other hand, all supervisory arrangements will require national contributions, for example, financing of supervision, an aspect that will have some implications on the choice of supervisory arrangements. Finally, one may identify factors that *otherwise will affect the assessment of supervisory alternatives.* These factors primarily comprise established values or cultures in the public or private sector in home or host countries. Consideration of these kinds of national features is important, especially from a political viewpoint, because the success of any new supervisory arrangement proposed for the EU requires political support.

The environment (here defined as the various forms of threats to financial stability in an EU cross-border context). The main focus is on crises with a systemic element. Though crises in specific institutions with EU cross-border activities may generate certain cross-border problems, the absence of systemic implications means that the influence of these crises on the structuring of EU banking sector supervision is minor. Given systemic relevance, one may schematise crises by focusing on the original cause of crises, their type and their further transmission. There are crises with a clear institution-specific origin and crises with more macro-oriented, banking sector specific or more general origins in macro-economic terms. Crises are either liquidity or solvency related and transmission is traditionally conceived as interbank dependencies, payment and settlement system issues and information channel matters.

Applying this theoretical concept for the assessment of alternatives for the organisation of the supervision of the EU banking sector to Schoenmaker's and Osterloo's chapter in an evaluative manner, reveals certain points. As for the chosen *starting point* (the stability problem) it is strongly restricted to stability issues. Other supervisory issues are not analysed, e.g. supervisory issues dealing with market confidence are not included in the chapter. The stability problem is conceived as a given, traditional liquidity or solvency deficit in a cross-border context. Moreover, the stability problems relating to consolidation are not clearly separated from the ones relating to branch activity. The search for solutions to an eventual banking crisis is straightforward and restricted to the structure of supervision (including crisis management) and the identification of the source of finance. In practice, this means that new and unconventional responses for dealing with banking crises are left out, i.e. various types of private sector arrangements, European bridge bank schemes, etc.

As for *the parties involved*, the chapter perceives the stability problem more as a European issue than a combination of conflicting national aims or interests. This may be problematic, since any supervisory arrangement proposed for European cross-border banks is in need of all available national political support. On the other hand, significant attention is given to the banks' aims and interests. Such an approach is naturally motivated on competitive grounds, since the development of the EU internal market corresponds with improved business conditions. Other features relating to the parties involved and affecting the assessment of supervisory arrangements are presented in a more scattered manner. On this point a more systematic approach would be more desirable. Reflecting the chapter's proposed concept of 'the home country acting as a consolidated supervisor, but with a European mandate to incorporate cross-border effects' towards *the anticipated threats against financial stability*, i.e. the various types of crises, there is some uncertainty what the concept actually comprises. To this extent, a more detailed description would be valuable. What are the exact elements in supervision and crisis management that would be the responsibility of the consolidated supervisor?

COMMENT

Philipp Hartmann

It is extremely timely to re-address cross-border issues in European banking supervision. In the past, cross-border penetration by banks – in Europe and elsewhere – was very limited. This has started to change. One expression of this development is that at the time of the present confer-ence, the Committee of European Banking Supervisors (CEBS) begins to operate in London.[1] Somewhat earlier, the finance ministers of Germany (Hans Eichel) and the United Kingdom (Gordon Brown) already raised the open issues surrounding the structure of banking supervision in Europe forcefully at an informal ECOFIN Council in Spain. It seems that the time is ripe to discuss cross-border issues in European banking more intensely.

In so doing, the views expressed by policy makers and market particip-ants from the BeNeLux and Nordic countries are extremely important. In both these regions of Europe, cross-border banking activities have existed for much longer. Groups like ABN AMRO, Dexia, Fortis, ING and Nordea had already established operations in neighbouring countries a long time ago. The regulators concerned have developed particular expertise in supervising such cross-border groups and in co-operating with foreign authorities. So, the present chapter, drafted by representatives from the Dutch finance ministry, has to be considered very carefully. Last but not least Dirk Schoenmaker is certainly one of Europe's greatest experts in the area of supervisory structures.

The authors and readers may forgive me, however, for also mentioning with a little bit of irony that in 1995 Dirk wrote an influential paper that forcefully argued for maintaining banking supervision at the national level. One of its main arguments was that the absence of a sizeable EU budget would make it impossible to manage a financial crisis effectively at the European level and agree on the sharing of costs it might cause. A decade of gradual banking integration may have made the issue pressing enough to look at such arguments from a different perspective. But, strictly speaking the budget situation has not changed since then.

I structure the remainder of my discussion of Schoenmaker and Oost-erloo in two parts: first, I provide complementary evidence on the risk of cross-border contagion in Europe and, second, I discuss the different options for supervisory structures. A last section briefly concludes.

Assessing cross-border bank contagion risk in Europe

According to ECB services there were 41 major banking groups in the EU-15 in 2004. Each was – on average – active in five to six member countries. These groups tend to have complex corporate structures, with – on average – seven subsidiaries and four branches in other member states. The figures in Table 9.3 show a similar picture. The fact that they indicate somewhat less cross-border penetration may be related to the fact that the ECB figures also include some groups below their thresholds. The general dominance of subsidiaries for cross-border activities as opposed to branches is often interpreted as showing that the single banking passport introduced by the Second Banking Directive is not working properly (see e.g. Dermine, 2003). In any case, the cross-border penetration of these major groups is significant enough to think carefully about the consequences for optimal supervisory structures and the scope of financial surveillance. The recent merger of UniCredito with HypoVereinsbank is another point in case.

We can juxtapose the situations in two different types of cross-border banking activities, retail banking and wholesale banking. Figure 9.2 shows the degree of cross-border penetration in the corporate loan market. The Figure suggests that bank-to-customer lending across borders is extremely limited. In particular, cross-border corporate lending among euro-area countries is only 3 to 4 per cent of domestic lending to corporations. It has increased somewhat after the introduction of the euro, as one would expect, but not much. Total cross-border loans to non-EU-15 countries is even larger than the aggregate of within-EU-15 cross-border loans.

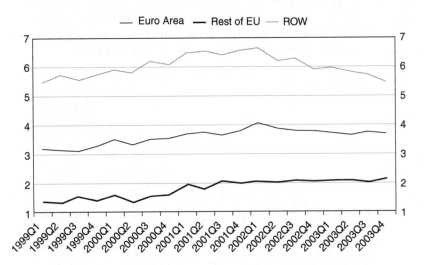

Figure 9.2 Cross-border loans of banks to non-banks in percentage of domestic loans, 1999 to 2003 (data sources: ECB).

Notes
Update of Hartmann *et al.* (2003: figure 11). EU refers to all member states during the sample period, i.e. EU-15. Therefore, rest of EU comprises Denmark, Sweden and the UK. ROW means rest of the world, i.e. all countries outside the EU-15.

The situation is quite different for interbank lending, which is shown in Figure 9.3. In particular, euro area cross-border interbank lending is a much larger share of domestic interbank lending than the case for corporate lending. Hartmann *et al.* (2003: figure 11) show that the share exceeds 25 per cent. Moreover, Figure 9.3 suggests that this share has increased with EMU in Europe. In the two to three years following the introduction of the euro, cross-border interbank claims within the euro area have increased from about 35 per cent of the world total of cross-border interbank claims reported to the Bank for International Settlements (BIS) to almost half of the world total.

From the difference between retail and wholesale activities across borders in Europe one would infer that contagion through the interbank market is more of a concern than adverse macroeconomic shocks abroad that deteriorate the quality of the corporate loan portfolio of domestic banks.

One way to examine the scope for bank contagion risk more directly is to look at spillovers between equity returns of individual banks. Since contagion should relate to crisis situations, only extreme negative returns are of interest. The advantage of this approach is that, as long as markets price banks correctly, co-movements in equity returns should reflect all channels of contagion discussed by Schoenmaker and Oosterloo in this chapter.[2] Moreover, they reflect effective spillovers instead of measuring positions and exposures. In principle the Schoenmaker–Oosterloo indicators of contagion risk may have two sources of bias. First, they may underestimate risk by neglecting contagion risks related to asymmetric information and multiple equilibria. Second, they may overestimate contagion risk, as collateralised cross-border assets are not deducted.

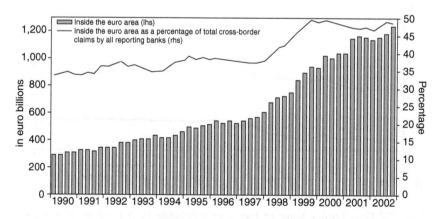

Figure 9.3 Euro-area cross-border interbank claims, in billion euro and in percentage of total cross-border interbank claims, 1990–2002 (data sources: BIS).

Notes
Reproduced from Gasper *et al.* (2003), building on Galati and Tsatsaronis (2001). Total cross-border interbank claims are covered for industrial countries and off-shore centres.

Hartmann *et al.* (2005a, 2005b) apply extreme-value theory to examine the issue of bank spillovers in Europe and compare it to the United States. One measure they look at is the following simple conditional probability.

$$P_{M|N} = P\{\cap_{i=1}^{M} X_i < Q_i \mid \cap_{j=1}^{N} X_j < Q_j\} \text{ for } X_i, X_j, Q_i, Q_j < 0 \text{ and } |Q_i|, |Q_j| \text{ large}$$ (1)

It measures the likelihood that $M=1$ (or more) bank(s) experiences a crash of its (their) stock price beyond the negative extreme quantile Q_i, given that N banks experience a similar stock price crash beyond the quantile Q_j. The data used are daily bank stock returns between 1992 and 2002. The extreme quantiles or crisis levels considered are about the largest (in absolute values) observed during the sample period.

As also pointed out in Schoenmaker and Oosterloo, for the European supervisory structures it is particularly important whether cross-border spillover risks are comparable or still much lower than domestic spillover risks. Greater cross-border risk increases the case in favour of bilateral or multilateral supervisory co-operation or even centralisation of supervisory structures.

A few examples of the risks found are quite instructive. The probability that Deutsche Bank faces a crash, given that HypoVereinsbank faces one is 22.4 per cent. In contrast, the probability that Banco Santander faces an extreme downturn of its stock market value, given that HypoVereinsbank experiences one is 11.2 per cent. In this example, the estimated cross-border spillover risk is only half of the domestic risk. Similarly, the probability that Banca Intesa's stock market value crashes, given that the ones of both UniCredito and IMI-San Paolo crash is 16.4 per cent. In contrast, the same probability for the Finnish bank Sampo Leonia is only 3.2 per cent. The estimated spillover risk between Italy and Finland seems to be very low. More generally, Hartmann *et al.* (2005a, 2005b) find that in most cases of the 25 largest banks from euro-area countries cross-border spillover risk is lower than domestic spillover risk. There are, however, also some interesting exceptions. For example, the conditional probability of ABN AMRO with respect to HypoVereinsbank is 26.5 per cent. In other words, for a country like the Netherlands – where a few large European and global banks (or financial conglomerates) dominate the domestic market – cross-border risks can be more pronounced than domestic risk in comparable countries. A similar phenomenon can be observed for Belgium, for example.

Hartmann *et al.* (2005a, 2005b) also test whether the differences in estimated domestic and cross-border spillover risks are statistically significant or not. It turns out that the differences tend to be insignificant between some large 'centre' countries of the euro area (Belgium, France, Germany, the Netherlands and Spain). The major banks of a few smaller countries – closer to the outside border of the euro area (Finland and

Greece, and perhaps Ireland and Portugal) – are, however, significantly less at risk from foreign problems. Moreover, we assess whether spillover risks have changed over time, using structural stability tests. In almost all cases we found that they have increased in Europe during the second half of the 1990s. In sum, the evidence from equity valuations presented so far suggests that cross-border contagion risks among euro area banks are not to be neglected. Moreover, more recently they have become more of a concern than they used to be.

Now, how high are these risks and how bad is the increase observed? To answer these questions, Hartmann *et al.* (2005a) estimate a parameter of extreme stock return dependence for all 25 euro-area banks and the comparable 25 top banks of the United States. In other words, this parameter η measures the overall systemic risk among the major banks of the euro area and the US, considering both bilateral and multilateral linkages. It can vary between 0 and 1, where unity describes the case of perfect dependence (maximum systemic risk) among all 25 banks. The case of independence is $\eta = 1/N = 0.04$.

It turns out that – according to this measure – there is some systemic risk among both the US and the euro-area top banks. For the whole sample, the amount of risk in the US ($\eta = 0.39$) is about twice as large as in the euro area ($\eta = 0.17$). It appears that most of the difference is explained by the relatively lower cross-border risks in the euro area. For example, the domestic ηs for France, Germany or Italy are comparable to the one for the US, or in the case of Italy even larger. The recursive calculation of η over time shows how systemic risk increases very gradually, in particular during the second half of the 1990s. This is consistent with a gradual integration process in European banking during this period. Interestingly enough, however, an even stronger increase of systemic risk is observed in the US. De Nicolo and Kwast (2002) associate the latter with the consolidation process between large and complex banking organisations. Structural break tests show significant upward breaks in the systemic risk parameter η for both economies during the second half of the 1990s.

To sum up, the considerations above come to quite similar conclusions as the ones presented by Schoenmaker and Oosterloo and their companion paper (2005). Cross-border spillover risks are gradually increasing in European banking, and – while still limited – they seem to have reached a dimension that cannot be ignored from a supervisory perspective. It is also reassuring that two papers primarily about national contagion risks in the euro area also provide support for such conclusions. Degryse and Nguyen (2004) and van Lelyveld and Liedorp (2004) simulate contagion risks from actual interbank exposures in Belgium and the Netherlands, respectively. Both sets of simulations suggest that contagion through interbank exposures is a relevant phenomenon in the presence of bank failures. In addition, both conclude that foreign risks are of great relevance to the Belgian and Dutch banking sectors.

Alternative supervisory structures for Europe

Where does that leave us in terms of supervisory structures? Clearly, discussions about their design need to take the financial stability implications of cross-border contagion risk into account. Schoenmaker and Oosterloo provide a lucid discussion of the different options in Table 9.5, taking also other relevant criteria for the effectiveness and efficiency of supervision into account. In addition, I very much welcome their decision to incorporate one of my earlier suggestions of extending the 'menu' of options and adding the information criterion related to physical proximity. However, I still have some comments on how they distinguish the cases of home supervision on the basis of a European mandate and the central body with a European mandate as well as on the issue whether markets or policy should lead.

In the earlier version of their chapter, option B was described as allocating all supervisory responsibilities at home and abroad to the home supervisor with a European mandate. This raised obvious legal and sovereignty issues about how effective a supervisor of one country could examine bank subsidiaries with their own legal character in another country. Moreover, it opened questions about whether the authorities would not have incentives to favour their own banks that compete with foreign banks abroad and at home. This option has now been replaced with a different scheme (option C) under which the home supervisor would in some form be part of a European System of Financial Supervisors. In that system, national authorities would conduct all the actual supervision and the federal body would take the general regulatory decisions.

The difference between option C and the new option D is that in the latter case the federal body at the centre of the system would also conduct actual supervision and on-site examinations. This option is quickly 'discredited' by the introduction of the new criterion of proximity. This can probably be agreed, in particular, when their own supervisory responsibility of the central body goes beyond a small number of truly pan-European banks. In any case, these fully pan-European banks are presently more a futuristic vision than a reality. For example, the only bank that comes close to a fully pan-European bank at present is probably Citigroup.

On the other hand, it is perhaps a little bit odd to denote option C as home supervision (with a European mandate). The only way this system could be made to work is that the central body casts a careful eye over the uniform application of area-wide regulations by each of the local supervisory bodies. One could imagine some tools to achieve this, apart from close monitoring of national teams by the central body. For example, a system of arbitration could be used in which a bank could complain to the centre about different standards being applied. An internal or at least a multi-national committee could then examine those cases. Another way how such a federal system, based on the principle of subsidiarity, could be made to work is to mix in non-nationals of the home country into examination teams. While probably not strictly comparable, maybe the example of IMF article IV or programme missions could provide some lessons. For example, as a rule the mission chief of an IMF mission does not come from the country to be examined. These thoughts suggest that more realistic and effective supervisory structures may actually lie more on the middle ground between options C and D. The main reason being that the risk of national biases has to be prevented through some rules *ex ante*. Actually, it might even be useful to add this as a sixth criterion for evaluating the different options. It may also be useful to provide a time dimension to the attractiveness of the various options. Some options may be good for now, others for the relatively near future, and again others may only make sense as a long-term end point.

An important question in the assessment of the speed with which more European or centralised structures should be established is whether markets should lead the policy institutions or policy institutions should lead the markets. Schoenmaker and Oosterloo take a position by providing a clear answer to this question: 'Supervisory structures should, in our view, adapt to market developments and not the other way round.' While this statement is placed in a prominent position at the start of the conclusions, it is not further discussed. So, it may be worthwhile to pause and look at the main arguments. On the one hand, politicians – who decide on supervisory structures – may not be very good in anticipating market developments. More specifically, they cannot be sure about the degree of integration various markets will achieve in the future and within which geographical perimeter. But the more integrated banking markets are, the greater the case in favour of common supervisory structures in the integrated area. This argument would support the authors' point of view. On the other hand, one requirement for markets to find the optimal degree of integration is that existing supervisory structures are relatively neutral. In other words, they neither prevent nor distort market integration. Only if this condition is fulfilled, could supervisory structures safely follow market integration. It is now anybody's guess whether national supervision, based on home country control with minimum standards and mutual recognition, can imply obstacles to or distortions of integration that are strong enough to overturn the first argument above.

It is clear that European financial integration to complete the single market for financial services is a policy priority under the Lisbon Agenda and the Financial Services Action Plan. Moreover, when the EU agreed on creating a single market for goods, services, capital and people the perimeter to which the single market rules would imply was very much a political decision. Sometimes policy and markets may successfully go in the same direction.

Conclusions

Let me conclude by re-emphasising that this is a very nice chapter by true experts in the areas of banking risks and supervisory structures. I very much agree with the authors that contagion risk is not massive and everywhere, even though by several measures it has gradually increased in the EU-15 in its cross-border variant. One should, however, keep in mind that the structure of systemic risk is influenced by more factors than cross-country asset exposures, even though they are particularly important. While cross-border banking penetration is advancing only slowly in Europe, in particular in retail markets, it seems to have now reached a dimension that justifies a serious debate about the optimal institutional structures in supervision. Schoenmaker and Oosterloo delivered an admirable intellectual re-opening for this debate by advancing important criteria and providing relevant options. An important issue in this discussion is to which extent supervisory structures are neutral relative to market integration. More research on this particular aspect will allow this debate to make further progress.

Notes

1 CEBS is the so-called level-3 Lamfalussy Committee, bringing together all the banking supervisors of the EU.
2 In principle, they should even reflect the degree of collateralisation of interbank lending.

References

Degryse, H. and Nguyen, G. (2004) 'Interbank exposures: an empirical examination of systemic risk in the Belgian banking system', paper presented at the Symposium of the ECB-CFS Research Network on 'Capital Markets and Financial Integration in Europe', Frankfurt, 10–11 May.

De Nicolo, G. and Kwast, M. (2002) 'Systemic risk and financial consolidation: are they related?', *Journal of Banking and Finance* 26(May): 861–80.

Dermine, J. (2003) 'European banking: past, present and future', in Gaspar, V.. Hartmann, P. and Sleijpen, O. (eds) *The Transformation of the European Financial System*, Frankfurt: European Central Bank.

Galati, G. and Tsatsaronis, K. (2001) 'The impact of the euro on Europe's financial markets', BIS Working Paper, no. 100, Basel, July.

Gaspar, V., Hartmann, P. and Sleijpen, O. (eds) (2003) *The Transformation of the European Financial System*, Frankfurt: European Central Bank.

Hartmann, P., Maddaloni, A. and Manganelli, S. (2003) 'The euro-area financial system: structure, integration and policy initiatives', *Oxford Review of Economic Policy* 19(1): 180–213.

Hartmann, P., Straetmans, S. and de Vries, C. (2005a) 'Banking system stability: a cross-Atlantic perspective', NBER Working Paper, no. 11698, October, forthcoming in Carey, M. and Stulz, R. (eds) *Risks of Financial Institutions*, Chicago, IL: Chicago University Press and National Bureau of Economic Research.

Hartmann, P., Straetmans, S. and de Vries, C. (2005b). 'Europäische Bankenstabilität', in Franz, W., Ramser, H. and Stadler, J. (eds) *Funktionsweise und Stabilität von Finanzmarkten*, Tübingen: Mohr Siebeck.

Schoenmaker, D. (1995) 'Banking supervision in stage three of EMU', FMG Special Paper, no. 72, London, October.

Schoenmaker, D. and Oosterloo, S. (2005) 'Financial supervision in an integrating Europe: measuring cross-border externalities', *International Finance* 8(1): 1–27.

van Lelyveld, I. and Liedorp, F. (2004) 'Interbank contagion in the Dutch banking sector', De Nederlandsche Bank Working Paper, no. 005, Amsterdam, July.

10 Regulating cross-border retail payment systems – a network industry problem

Kari Kemppainen[1]

The smooth operation of payment systems is often taken for granted both in the academic literature on financial integration and in practical policy considerations. However, recent developments in the European integration process have shown very clearly the critical role of payment systems in the financial integration process. In this context, the smooth and efficient functioning of payment systems, especially at the cross-border level, has been emphasised. When analysing payment system efficiency issues, the interaction between competition, cooperation and regulation also plays a key role. While *competition* among payment service providers has commonly been seen as an important contributor to efficiency, the need for *cooperation* in building infrastructures as well as in defining and implementing standards has also been raised, due to the specific characteristics of the payment industry. In this context, the appropriate role of *regulation* has also been debated. In essence, the focal point in the debate on payment systems efficiency has been the trade-off between competition and cooperation, and the potential impact of regulatory intervention.

This debate has been going on also in the context of cross-border retail payments in the European Union (EU), and in recent years much of the discussion has been provoked by their high prices and costs. Dissatisfied with the development efforts by the banking sector to improve the situation, the European Parliament and the Council adopted Regulation (EC) No. 2560/2001 on Cross-border Payments in Euro (RPE) in December 2001.[2] The RPE obliges banks to reduce charges for cross-border payments of up to €12,500 (€50,000 as of January 2006) to the level of those of corresponding domestic payments. The RPE has been applied to card payments and ATM (Automated Teller Machine) withdrawals as from 1 July 2002 and to cross-border credit transfers as from 1 July 2003. This regulatory intervention was strongly criticised by the banking sector that argued for a market-driven solution.

Dispute on proper regulatory tools in payment systems at the EU-level is, however, not an extraordinary phenomenon. At the national levels, regulation and competition issues have also been raised by authorities. For example, in the card payments area the role of interchange fees has been surveyed by regulatory authorities (e.g. in Australia, the EU and the US). Moreover, general competition issues in financial markets were studied in Australia and the US in the late 1990s. In Australia, the Wallis Committee (1997) proposed a regulatory structure to ensure a competitive, efficient and flexible financial system consistent with financial stability, integrity and fairness. The most visible outcome of the report in the payment systems area was the establishment of the Payment Systems Board within the Reserve Bank of Australia. The Payment Systems Board has concentrated on payment systems regulation and has initiated studies and provided reports on payment systems competition and efficiency. In the US, the Rivlin Committee (1998) examined the role of the Federal Reserve as a payment service provider dealing also with the competition issues in the area.

More recently competition issues have been analysed in the UK. The Cruickshank review (HM Treasury, 2000a) investigated UK banking services and concluded that there was a profound lack of competition in the payment systems. According to the review, this was caused by 'the underlying economic characteristics of the industry, where network effects place a natural limit on the level of competition'. HM Treasury subsequently issued a consultation document (HM Treasury, 2000b) on competition in payment systems, where it announced its intention to give the Office of Fair Trading (OFT) responsibility for regulation of payment systems and new powers to promote competition in payment systems. Also in the Netherlands, the so-called 'working group Wellink' has recently signalled some shortcomings of the Dutch market for retail payments with respect to the organisation of debit card payments, pricing of consumer payments, infrastructure and accessibility.[3] Finally, many national central banks have dealt with competition issues as part of their payment system oversight duties, and the BIS has published three special reports on retail payment issues (BIS, 1999, 2000, 2003), where the role of central banks in facilitating competition and efficiency has also been discussed.

Along with the public interest, the interest of academic circles and central banks in the payment systems issues has also increased since the beginning of the 1990s. In the area of large-value payment systems, the focus has mainly been on the risk and efficiency issues in net and gross settlement systems.[4] Research in the area of retail payment systems has also activated.[5] However, less attention has been paid to the general assessment of regulation and public policy intervention in retail payment systems given 'the network nature' of the business. The present study aims to contribute to this area by analysing retail payment systems as networks.[6]

The main aim of this chapter is to provide a comprehensive discussion of regulation and competition issues in retail payment systems by first introducing and then applying the key findings of network economics literature. In addition to general policy analysis, the chapter also surveys developments in the European retail payment system field and discusses the roles and aims of the key parties involved in the development process.

The chapter begins by presenting the institutional framework of retail payment systems in the EU, emphasising the fragmented structure. The roles and policy goals of the key parties involved in the development process of retail payment systems are also analysed. It then moves on to define retail payments briefly and describes the special characteristics of retail payment services. Thereafter, network effects in retail payment systems are analysed from the viewpoint of the network economics theory. This is followed by an examination of market structure issues and the role of joint ventures in retail payment systems. General implications for competition policy and regulation are discussed. Moreover, antitrust issues, especially regarding network exclusivity, are briefly analysed, and the regulatory tools used in other network industries are described and their applicability in the context of retail payment systems is discussed. This takes us to an evaluation of the competition–cooperation nexus in retail payment systems, based on the main findings thus far. The potential roles of regulatory authorities in shaping the competitive environment are also discussed. Finally, some prognoses for the European retail payment markets are presented before reviewing the main findings and drawing general conclusions.

The general framework of the study is summarised in Figure 10.1, where the interaction of the competition, cooperation and regulation is also highlighted.

The general framework of the study can be summarised as follows. In retail payment systems, competition and cooperation issues are closely tied because of the network nature of the industry. On the one hand, competition between systems is needed in order to have contestable

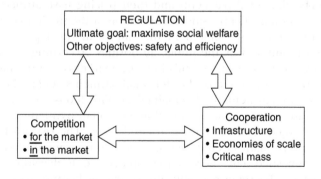

Figure 10.1 General framework of the study.

markets where efficiency of systems is facilitated. On the other hand, a certain degree of cooperation among service providers is also needed so that critical mass of users can be achieved and potential economies of scale utilised. From a regulator's point of view, the critical question in this context is whether *competition for the market* (i.e. competition between systems) or *competition in the market* (i.e. service competition using same system or compatible systems) would lead to the most efficient outcome.

The ultimate goal in payment system regulation and in payment system oversight is to ensure smooth operation of financial markets so that social welfare can be maximised (or social cost minimised). In the payment systems field, this goal can be achieved by requiring and ensuring that the systems are both safe and efficient. The regulators' task is challenging because there is normally a trade-off between safety and efficiency requirements. In fact, it is the safety requirement that has to be fulfilled first, and only thereafter the efficiency requirement steps in. This is very clear in large-value payment systems where systemic risk and potential disruptive contagion effects are large. To a lesser extent, this also applies to retail payment systems where the potential of system risk is also present, although not in so pronounced a way as in large-value payment systems. Accordingly, the safety requirement for retail payment systems is well recognised. As the present study focuses on the competition and efficiency issues in retail payment systems, the following analysis assumes that the safety requirement is fulfilled and concentrates purely on efficiency and competition issues.

Institutional framework

Background for the debate on cross-border retail payments in the euro area

In the EU, cross-border retail payments and their pricing have attracted the attention of policy-makers ever since the creation of the single market in 1992. Since then the development in the European retail payment markets has been monitored by the public authorities. According to the pricing surveys by the European Commission, the market operators had made hardly any progress in the cross-border retail payments field and the prices of cross-border payments had remained at high levels, and their execution times a lot longer, compared to domestic retail payments even on the eve of introduction of the euro notes and coins. The reasons for this slow progress were many-faceted. On the one hand, payment service providers have emphasised that 'there is no business case' to develop and invest in new cross-border retail payment infrastructures because there is insufficient demand for these services. On the other hand, the authorities and consumer associations have maintained that the high prices are the principal obstacle to activating and expanding the demand for these services.

A variety of infrastructural factors may also have delayed the development of efficient cross-border retail payment systems in Europe. One of the main factors is the existence of different national payment systems, which have developed within different historical contexts, with different governance, access, pricing and transparency traditions as well as different legislative environments. As a result, the retail payment infrastructure in the EU is fragmented and is still largely based on traditional national payment habits and characteristics. Figures 10.2 and 10.3 provide two illustrative snapshots on the situation.

In Figures 10.2 and 10.3, the fragmented structure of retail payment methods in the EU countries can be clearly seen. In some countries, such as France, the cheque continues to be an important payment method even though its relative share has been declining in recent years. In other countries, such as Finland, credit transfers are dominant. Naturally, the differences in payment methods used in different countries are reflected in the structure and organisation of payment systems in these countries. Generally speaking, the development of payment system infrastructures in

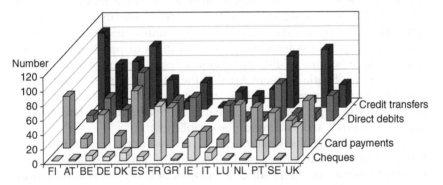

Figure 10.2 Number of cashless payments per inhabitant in EU countries, 2000 (source: European Central Bank).

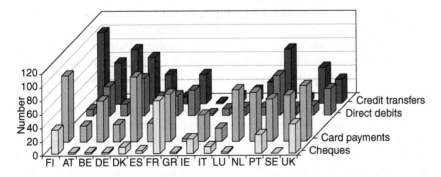

Figure 10.3 Number of cashless payments per inhabitant in EU countries, 2002 (source: European Central Bank).

different countries is likely to have been influenced by some sort of *path dependence*[7] ('history matters') where the key ingredients are the structure of service providing sector, national payment traditions and legislative environment. Consequently, each national payment system has its own membership criteria, standards and practices that have evolved over time. Another factor affecting the development of national payment systems is the observation that *payment habits are slow to change*. This applies especially to consumers, and, to a lesser extent, also to enterprises.[8] It is obvious that these factors have affected the development of payment systems, but only the coming years will tell if the development of payment transfer technology, accelerating financial integration process and deepening global financial linkages, will change the picture.

Figures 10.2 and 10.3 also support the argument that the retail payment infrastructure in the EU consists of 15 heterogeneous payment areas (and with the new member countries even more), even though some convergence has taken place. In this context, it has been claimed that the present heterogeneity in the retail payments field can potentially hinder the development of efficient cross-border retail payment systems. The idea behind this argument is that the heterogeneity in demand for different payment instruments in different countries makes it more difficult to develop truly compatible payment systems or one common cross-border system because of different national needs. On the other hand, the formation of a 'Single Payment Area' in the EU may not necessarily mean that the national payment habits and methods should be totally harmonised; more important, is that, reliable and efficient cross-border retail payment methods and systems can be established.

When examining the situation at the cross-country level further, the following observations can be made. The current national/domestic retail payment systems are the result of development processes that have been strongly guided by the national payment habits and, therefore, the organisation and operating procedures of national retail payment systems differ from each other. In some countries, the degree of 'electronification' in retail payments processing is high and the retail payment systems function efficiently. In this context, one important factor contributing to the efficiency in national payment systems has been standardisation. Standards in retail payment systems have traditionally been set domestically by national authorities and banking associations. Accordingly, the standardisation process at the national level has benefited from relatively small and homogeneous stakeholder groups. However, standardisation at the cross-border level has been more of a problem because of the greater number of different parties involved and strict adherence to heterogeneous domestic standards adopted in different payment methods. This has surely slowed down the development and implementation of international retail payment standards, which has, in turn, negatively affected the establishment of efficient cross-border retail payment systems.

Another factor affecting the slow development of cross-border retail payment systems in the EU is the low volume of cross-border retail payments. These payments currently account for 1–2 per cent of all retail payments in the EU. Whether this figure will increase in the future naturally depends on customers' needs, but also on the existence of efficient cross-border retail payment systems to execute payments reliably and cheaply. The establishment of such an infrastructure will require cooperative efforts by the service providers. However, the service providers may be unwilling to invest in such systems if it is not seen as a prospectively profitable business. Accordingly, a sort of 'chicken-and-egg' problem may further delay the establishment of efficient cross-border payment systems.

Key parties involved in the retail payment systems in the euro area

In principle, the key parties that are involved in the development process of retail payment systems can be grouped into three:

end-users;
payment service providers; and
regulators.

In the following paragraphs, their motives and roles are discussed. In addition, their main motives as well as their recent actions are presented in the European context.

End-users

In retail payments, customers (i.e. consumers and enterprises) are the end-users of the services. Accordingly, their adoption patterns of new payment instruments play an important role in shaping the future payment systems. As in many other network industries, end-users' expectations about the future usage of different instruments also affect the actual adoption of these instruments in retail payment systems. Often the need for 'coordination of expectations' is emphasised, because users need to form their expectations (and their respective decisions) of which technology will be widely used by other users. The practical problem is that very often the decision of which payment method is chosen depends on the present price and availability of usage points of the payment instruments. When the present users are few and the price is high, a new payment method has a lot of difficulties in achieving the critical mass needed to utilise potential economies of scale in its production and thereby validate its existence. In a practical context, the previous observation that payment habits are slow to change is also relevant when new payment methods are introduced to customers. Accordingly, the incentives of end-users[9] certainly play an important role in fostering efficiency of retail payment systems.

Payment service providers

The banking sector has traditionally been and still is the main payment service provider even though some new service providers are now emerging. As in any other industry, appropriate incentives for innovation ('need for the existence of a real business case', as many bankers have phrased it) are crucial when establishing payment infrastructure. Therefore, without sufficient innovation incentives, the development of efficient infrastructure is doomed to be slow. In the context of European cross-border retail payments, the banking sector has emphasised that the slow development of the systems was due to low demand for these payments and the consequent lack of a real business case. However, after the adoption of the RPE, the banking sector was forced to act. In the aftermath of the RPE, the banking sector commissioned and published a White Paper: *Euroland: Our Single Payment Area!*[10] In the White Paper, the banking sector emphasised the crucial need for a pan-European payment infrastructure in order to be able to respond to the dictates of the Regulation. In this context, the development of a pan-European Automated Clearing House (PEACH) with fair and open access has been advocated.

As a further reaction to the Regulation on cross-border payments in euro, European banks and banking associations established the European Payments Council (EPC) in June 2002 to represent the industry and to support the development of the Single Euro Payment Area (SEPA). Moreover, the European banking sector has signalled that they are prepared to move the necessary harmonisation of payment systems and instruments forward, as much as possible through self-regulation. In their opinion, legislation and regulation should only be used where harmonisation cannot be achieved by other means. The EPC has argued further that the fully integrated European payments infrastructure will be achieved in steps: first, for credit transfers, in combination with the existing clearing and settlement systems; then a pan-European infrastructure, that bridges current domestic and cross-border payments, will develop.

Regulators

In the EU/euro area, the European Commission and the European Central Bank (ECB)/the European System of Central Banks (ESCB) along with competition authorities are the main regulators in the payment service field. Their respective, partly overlapping, roles are discussed next.

THE EUROPEAN COMMISSION

In fulfilling its role in promoting the development of the Single Market, the European Commission has been active in facilitating financial market integration. Since the beginning of the 1990s, the Commission has been arguing that high costs for cross-border money transfers are inhibiting the

Single Market development and financial market integration. In this context, the Commission has formulated the following objectives for the single payment area:

- to make the Internal Market the domestic market;
- to promote efficient and secure payment means and systems;
- to enhance customer protection and strengthen consumer confidence relating to all payment means;
- to ensure competition on equal terms on a level playing field.

In pursuing these goals, the Commission has assumed a more active role in recent years. The fact that the charges for cross-border retail credit transfers had remained high over the years prompted the European Parliament and the Council to adopt RPE in December 2001. The Regulation aims at facilitating the expansion of the 'Single Market' concept to cover the money transfers and payment systems markets as well. The adoption of the Regulation was seen as the ultimate tool for fostering the development of the market where, according to the Commission, 'no substantial development efforts by market participants' were observed before that. The European Commission is also working to harmonise the legal framework for payment services in order to facilitate the development of the Single Payment Area in the Internal Market. The New Legal Framework for Payments in the Internal Market should establish a modern and comprehensive set of rules to all payment services in the EU.[11]

ECB/ESCB

The ECB/ESCB's interest in the efficiency of payment systems is based on Article 105(2) of the Treaty and Article 22 of the Statute. According to these, 'the ESCB shall promote the smooth operation of payment systems'. This also includes facilitating and ensuring the efficiency of payment systems. In the area of retail payment systems, the Eurosystem has focused on the importance of providing efficiency and safety standards for retail payment instruments and euro retail payment systems with the aim of fostering the achievement of a single euro payment area. In principle, both the safety and efficiency targets are important, and in many cases, as in the large-value payment systems where potential for systemic risk is bigger than in retail payments, the safety requirement is the first one to be achieved.

The ECB/ESCB has communicated its policy stance on retail payment issues by publishing various reports and studies. The ECB has published two reports *Improving Cross-Border Retail Payment Services – the Eurosystem's View* (September 1999) and *Improving Cross-Border Retail Payment Services – Progress Report* (September 2000) in which it highlighted inefficiencies and set objectives for cross-border retail payments. Moreover, the article

'Towards a uniform service level for retail payments in the euro area' (ECB, 2001a) examined the variety of issues in the retail payments area. In November 2001, the ECB prepared a report *Towards an Integrated Infrastructure for Credit Transfers in Euro* (ECB, 2001b), in which it reviewed ways to remove obstacles that are the origin of the high costs of retail cross-border credit transfers and provided an overview of measures to improve the payment infrastructures. The ECB report *Towards a Single Euro Payments Area – Progress Report* (June 2003) assessed developments achieved in the retail payment system field. In the report, the Eurosystem's strong support for the banking sector's SEPA project was emphasised. Moreover, the importance of the Eurosystem's own catalyst and overseer roles was emphasised.

In general, one of the essential future tasks for all the key parties, including both service providers and regulators, involved in the development of retail payment systems is to strengthen their cooperation so that efforts can be focused on the most relevant issues and overlapping development efforts can be avoided. On the regulatory side, the cooperation between the European Commission and the ECB/ESCB is crucial in order to avoid the situation where too extensive and overlapping regulation would act as an impediment to the development. Furthermore, the roles of competition authorities and other regulators (including central banks as overseers of the payment systems) in the quest for the market contestability and payment systems efficiency are not totally clear both at the national as well as at the European level. This is likely to require further cooperation efforts, at least at the European level.

Retail payment systems as a network industry

Special characteristics of retail payments

The BIS (2003) report defines retail payments as follows. First, retail payments are typically made in large numbers by large numbers of transactors and typically relate to purchases of goods and services in both the consumer and business sectors, rather than, for example to the settlement of transactions between financial institutions. Second, retail payments are made using a much wider range of payment instruments than large value payments and in more varied contexts, including, for example payments made in person at a point of sale as well as for remote consumer and commercial transactions. Third, retail payment markets are characterised by extensive use of private sector systems for the transaction process and for clearing. The above definition clearly reveals the complex and many-faceted nature of retail payments. Therefore, it is useful to examine the special characteristics of retail payments before moving into analysing retail payment systems as a network industry.

Strong linkage to other banking services

One fundamental characteristic of retail payment services is that they are strongly linked to other banking services, like deposits. In fact, one could argue that the payments are not themselves final products but, instead, essential services provided as part of a general banking service. In this context, it has also been claimed that payment services are often treated as loss leaders in the bundle of the whole banking service. This can be clearly seen in the pricing of retail payment services where indirect pricing through cross-subsidisation is commonly used. As a result, the pricing of payment services does not reflect their true marginal cost. Instead, payment services are often offered free or underpriced (i.e. the price of payment service is below the production cost) but they are implicitly charged through low interest on transaction account balances.[12] This may introduce a potential problem for payment market efficiency: when the price system does not function properly and charges do not adequately reflect production costs, the use of the most cost-efficient instrument is not sufficiently advocated. The pricing issue is very important because direct, cost-based pricing of payment services can be used to influence consumers' choice of payment instruments. In fact, direct pricing of payment services has been gaining popularity in recent years. The proponents of this direct pricing approach have welcomed this development and have stated that this has increased the efficiency of payment systems by guiding the customers to use the most efficient payment instruments.[13]

Retail payment instruments and systems also possess other inherent features that differentiate them from goods and services of traditional industries. In the following, some fundamental features are briefly discussed.[14]

The presence of two final customers

The payer making the payment and the payee receiving the payment are the two final customers involved in a payment transfer. The situation is similar to telecommunications services – again there are two customers.[15] The ability to make and receive payments or telecommunications requires that the sender and recipient have access to a compatible system or that the systems they are attached to are interconnected. This illustrates the importance of compatibility issues in payment networks that is analysed more in detail later. Furthermore, the presence of two final customers also affects the pricing conventions of retail payment services. In principle, it allows for three different charging options: the payment service can be charged to the payer (OUR), to the payee receiving the payment (BEN) or divided between them (SHARE). In addition to direct payments charges, charges are also levied indirectly through the practise of paying low interest on transaction account balances as discussed already.

Multiple payment service providers and cooperation

Retail payment services are normally provided by numerous different service providers; a typical account-based payment may involve five different parties. In addition to two final customers, there are two banks providing them with transaction facilities and an interbank payment system for effecting the settlement between the two banks. Accordingly, by its nature, the operation of an interbank payment system requires cooperation among banks. This cooperation can lead to anticompetitive concerns: there is a danger that collusive pricing may emerge or competition may be limited by exclusive access conditions to the cooperatively operated system.

Ownership of payment systems

The cooperative nature of payment services provision is reflected in the ownership of payment systems. Commonly retail payment systems are jointly owned by participating banks; if not, they are most commonly in public ownership (held by the central bank). The ownership structure can play an important role in the access conditions to the system especially if some sort of exclusivity restrictions is applied by the owners of systems. Accordingly, when aiming at 'a level playing field' in payment service provision, ownership and related governance issues are important.

Network effects in retail payment systems

A central feature of networks is that network goods or services exhibit *network externalities* (called *network effects* by some authors).[16] In a nutshell, this means that adding another customer adds value to the existing customers of the network. In this context, the telephone or fax system has often been used as a demonstrative example. Network effects and their implications have long been debated in many modern industries like transportation and communications industries among others. The development of a systematic framework for their analysis was started in the mid 1980s by Katz and Shapiro (1985) and Farrell and Saloner (1986).[17] Networks also play an integral part in financial markets and in payment systems. For example, McAndrews (1997) analyses network effects in payment systems and defines a network good or service as having two main characteristics:

i   the value a person gets from the product increases as more people consume it
ii the technique a firm chooses to produce the product will depend on the technique chosen by other firms.

Both these characteristics can be identified in the retail payment service provision. Concerning point (i), the more widely a payment instrument is accepted, the more benefits it brings to a consumer using it (*demand side externality*). Concerning point (ii), economies of scale in production of payment services foster industry's willingness for cooperation (common standards, joint network ownership) in providing these services (*supply side externality*). Naturally, both these characteristics cannot be observed in their pure forms in real life. However, in the adoption process of payment cards and in mergers of ATM-networks for example, they have clearly played a major role. In the following, some key concepts related to network industries are briefly discussed.

Complementarity and compatibility

In network markets, there are *complementarities* between users and/or products, which give rise to network externalities. These network externalities can be classified into two types: *direct and indirect externalities* (Katz and Shapiro, 1985; Economides, 1996). For direct network externalities, the complementarities exist between users of the same product or service. For indirect network externalities, the complementarities exist between products or services in different markets. In other words, direct network externalities are generated through the direct effects of the number of the agents consuming the same product, whereas indirect network externalities arise when the value of product increases as the number of the complementary goods or services increases (sometimes also referred to as the hardware–software paradigm). In retail payment systems complementarity plays an important role. For example, in credit card systems the complementarity is straightforward: as more people use credit cards, more merchants are induced to add terminals, since allowing customers a convenient means of payment will potentially increase their sales, and as more merchants permit card payment, the value to the customer of having a credit card increases too (McAndrews, 1997).

Along with complementarity, *compatibility* between products is also essential for the existence of network externalities. In essence, for complementarities to be exploited, interaction channels are needed: it is necessary that products, users or systems can interact. This means that complementary products or systems must operate on the same or compatible standard. According to Economides (1996), it is compatibility that makes complementarity actual and is thus crucial in network industries. In payment systems, compatibility can, in principle, be achieved by adherence to technical standards. However, it should be emphasised that *technical compatibility* does not necessarily mean that different systems or actors can truly interact. The interaction can be limited by exclusivity arrangements that hinder the interaction. What is also needed is *commercial compatibility* that ensures that technically compatible products or systems really can interact because it is possible to limit the potential interoperability by specific operating rules or entry requirements to systems.

In practice, compatibility at the system level is of crucial importance in enabling interoperability of systems, e.g. ATM systems.

Economies of scale in production

It is often argued that payment systems are subject to economies of scale because of the significant investment in infrastructure needed to start the operation (large fixed costs) and a relatively small marginal cost for services produced over the existing infrastructure. As in the case of traditional industries, this supports the existence of large production units. This argument is of relevance, for example, for electronic payment transfers processed by an automated clearing house where a sufficiently large volume of payments is a prerequisite for the establishment of such a system.

Consumption externalities

A consumption externality can be defined as the increasing utility that a user derives from consumption of a product as the number of other users who consume the same product increases. Some authors, e.g. Guibourg (1998), have labelled this as 'demand side economies of scale'. In this context, consumers' expectations about the future size of the network are a decisive factor in the actual size that the network achieves. This means that consumers' expectations are often self-fulfilling: the larger the network, the greater the number of customers who would like to join it; and conversely, the smaller the network, the less attractive it is to new customers. In retail payment services, these consumption externalities are clearly present. Any payment system, like a giro system, is of no value for a customer if no other customer is participating in the system. In establishing new payment systems or instruments, consumers' expectations of the future size of the payment network are also crucial. In practice, the difficulty of achieving a critical mass of users tends to limit the adoption of new payment instruments.

Switching costs

In network industries, consumers and firms often have to face costs if they are willing to switch from one network to another. If high enough, these switching costs may effectively lock users into the existing system and provide barriers that prevent them from entering another network. Switching costs may lead to inefficiency by preventing users from adopting a new and superior technology. Shy (2001) argues that switching costs affect price competition in two opposing ways. First, if consumers are already locked-in using specific products, firms may raise prices knowing that consumers will not switch unless the price difference exceeds the switching cost to a competing brand. Second, if consumers are not locked-in, brand-producing firms will compete intensively by offering discounts and free complementary products and services in order to attract consumers who later on will be locked in the technology.

According to Shy (2001), switching costs can be significant in many service industries, including banking. From the customers' point of view, the costs associated with switching between banks (i.e. closing an account in one bank, and opening an account and switching the activities to a different bank) could be significant. Accordingly, some sort of lock-in effect may prevent customers from switching frequently among banks and payment service providers. Also from the payment service providers' point of view, switching costs can also be significant: e.g. upgrading or changing to a new payment system may require large investments in computer systems and training.

Retail payment networks and public policy

Nowadays it is widely recognised that safe and efficient retail payment systems and instruments are in the public interest, because they contribute towards the broader effectiveness of the financial system, in particular to consumer confidence and to the smooth and efficient functioning of commerce.[18] Public authorities can influence the efficiency of retail payment systems by applying competition and regulatory measures. In this context, the challenge for public authorities is to take into account the fact that the network characteristics of the retail payment industry have very strong implications for the general performance of the market, and thereby also on the effectiveness of their regulatory measures and actions. Accordingly, this section first concentrates on the typical market structure issues in network industries – tipping, excess inertia/momentum, path-dependence and underproduction – and assesses them in the context of retail payment systems. The analysis then continues with a discussion of joint ventures and antitrust issues in retail payment systems. In the last section, regulatory tools used in network industries are analysed.

Market structure issues in payment networks

The vertical structure of industry is common in the retail payment markets. Accordingly, the basic framework of retail payment industry can be generalised as follows:

> Payment service providers compete directly in the provision of retail payments instruments and services to end-users but, at the same time, they also cooperate in shared payment networks.

In other words, it can also be said that there is *upstream cooperation combined with downstream competition.*[19] This poses several challenges to public authorities. On the one hand, viewed from the efficiency standpoint, it is desirable to facilitate the utilisation of economies of scale by means of allowing cooperation between market players. On the other hand, there is a risk that such cooperative arrangements may be anti-competitive. From a competition policy point of view, it is possible that cooperation on one level may lead to collusive behaviour also on another level. For payment system regulators, these are crucial points in assessing the trade-off between competition and cooperation. In this context, straightforward application of economic theory will need to be supplemented by taking into account all the industry-specific characteristics.

In general, it has been argued that market competition is the way to promote efficiency in many traditional industries. In retail payment markets, a particular characteristic is, however, that competition among market participants needs to coexist with the mutual cooperation in payment system infrastructure arrangements. In this context, a key issue is whether the service providers are able to achieve an adequate balance between competition and cooperation to benefit market users. Therefore, public authorities should consider whether the market structure supports innovation and new market entrants and whether existing access restrictions serve to promote or impede competition and contestability.

In retail payment systems, cooperation is required among market participants in the context of their participation in payment system infrastructure arrangements. The main issue for regulators is, then, whether this cooperation supports market efficiency. The BIS (2003) report argues that established payment networks are a typical context in which this issue will arise. They have the potential to provide a stepping stone for innovation but they are also in a position to create entry barriers that impede competition and innovation. In protecting their own interests members of established payment networks can create entry barriers either by imposing access restrictions or by more indirect means, for example, by a choice of standards and rules that are inappropriate, difficult or costly for other initiatives to adopt.

A related question is whether competition between different systems or competition within one system is better for overall market efficiency. If excluded entrants to a particular system decided to establish their own system that is more efficient, and they are also able to attract enough customers for the new system to survive, market efficiency will be fostered. However, the uncertainty in reaching the critical mass of users may make the establishment of the new system difficult. This clearly points out the importance of market dynamics in network industries that strongly affects the market structure. In the following, some further key market structure issues and their implications in network industries are discussed.

Tipping

In network markets, market dynamics may lead to extreme outcomes where one network good or service provider dominates the market. Besen and Farrell (1994) refer to this phenomenon as 'tipping'.[20] The existence of one dominant system can be explained by the economies of scale in production and positive demand side externalities. This 'tipping' phenomenon can also be seen in retail payment systems. At the national level, it is common that only one major retail payment system exists. In some cases, two or more systems may exist in parallel but they are often dedicated to different payment instruments (paper-based versus electronic). However, heterogeneity in demand for different payment instruments may facilitate the existence of more than one retail payment system.

Excess inertia/excess momentum

Network markets may tend to get locked-in to obsolete standards or technologies. This *excess inertia* means that users tend to stick with an established technology even when total surplus would be greater were they to adopt a new but incompatible technology (Katz and Shapiro, 1994). This can be explained, as pointed out by Farrell and Saloner (1986), by the fact that today's consumers may be reluctant to adopt a new technology if they must bear the cost of transition from one technology to the next, and if most of the benefits of switching will accrue to future users. On the other hand, Katz and Shapiro (1994) argue that network markets may also exhibit the opposite of excess inertia, which they call 'insufficient friction' (also referred to as *excess momentum*). The market may then be biased in favour of a new, superior, but incompatible technology. Katz and Shapiro call the phenomenon as 'stranding': today's buyers may ignore the costs they impose on yesterday's buyers by adopting a new and incompatible technology. Accordingly, those who previously bought the old technology are stranded. Both effects are also possible in retail payment service markets, but as in many network markets, excess inertia is normally the dominant characteristic. An example is the slow development of e-money adoption where the service providers have long waited for its start-up but customers have been reluctant to start to use it.

Path dependence

In network markets *history matters*: network market equilibria cannot be understood without knowing the pattern of technology adoption in earlier periods.[21] This means that the effects of decisions by early adopters on the decisions of later adopters are often significant in network markets. In payment systems, path dependence can be seen in the development of national payment systems and, especially, in the slow change of national payment habits. For example, the division of giro and cheque countries in the EU is still prevailing.

Critical mass and the chicken-and-egg problem

The *critical mass* or *installed base* of network facilities plays a crucial role in the start up and growth of a network. The start up problem is often referred to as the 'chicken-and-egg' problem: many consumers are not interested in purchasing the good because the installed base is too small, and the installed base is too small because an insufficiently small number of consumers have purchased the good. Accordingly, the potential problem for the payment system development is that a new, more efficient payment system may not attract enough customers to validate its existence.

Underproduction

Network effects may also lead to possible *underproduction* of network goods or services. According to McAndrews (1997), the market production of network services may often be inefficiently low because using a network imposes an external effect on other users of network, an effect these other users typically disregard in making their own production decisions. For example, when deciding whether to join a service network, consumers do not take into account the benefit to other users of that larger network. Accordingly, the equilibrium network size is smaller than the social optimum, when social benefits of joining a network exceed the private benefits. In the retail payment systems area, where economies of scale are also present at least in the electronic payments, some authors (e.g. Gowrisankaran and Stavins, 2002) have argued that the underproduction is a relevant problem and it should be influenced, for example, by actions of relevant authorities.

Role of joint ventures and shared networks

While competition between sellers of goods and services in many circumstances yields the most efficient outcome, markets with network externalities may benefit from cooperation between providers of the underlying service or good. In payment systems, cooperation often occurs in the establishment of infrastructures; joint ventures and shared networks have become common, for obvious reasons. In the first place, joint ventures make it easier to achieve the essential critical mass of users when a network is established. Second, joint ventures facilitate utilisation of the potential economies of scale in production. And third, joint ventures allow the investment costs for establishing the network to be shared.

However, joint ventures in payment networks may also pose certain threats that can negatively affect overall market efficiency. The potential danger of dominant networks abusing their market power is clear. Payment networks may be able to engage in collective actions, e.g. in the pricing of services, that allow their members to exercise market power. Furthermore, exclusive conditions of access to joint networks can also result in significant competitive problems, most notably in terms of fore-closure of new entrants. In this context, non-discriminatory and publicly disclosed participation criteria are essential to ensuring the contestability of the market.

Based on the above, it can be argued that regulation of joint ventures or shared payment networks is a challenging task for public authorities. When limiting this cooperation, the regulator should also take into account that unexploited positive network externalities also imply efficiency losses in the market. This could happen, for example, when the size of networks is limited by regulators to foster intersystem competition among different systems. Accordingly, the decision to allow joint ventures depends on whether the regulator prefers intersystem competition or intrasystem competition. When making the decision, the external business environment is of importance; does it hinder or favour competition and market contestability? This cannot be answered without taking all the external business factors, including market structure and competition legislation among others, into account.

Other aspects related to payment system joint ventures are also worth pointing out. It has been argued that joint ownership can have a positive effect on technological development. For example, Guibourg (1998) argues that, when strategic decisions on technological innovation must be made, consumers' expectations about the range of system are decisive. The situation is complicated because the old system already has an installed base, which is rarely compatible with the new technology. In principle, everyone would like to switch to superior technology but wants a sufficient number of others to switch first. Here, joint ownership or joint development projects may have a positive effect on market expectations, about the spread of new technology and thereby facilitate its establishment and adoption. Another important aspect in joint ventures is their governance and the decision-making procedures. It has been claimed that the decisions in joint ventures are often dictated by the largest shareholders protecting their interests. Finally, the antitrust issues may also become more pronounced in dominant joint ventures that have significant market power.

Antitrust issues in payment systems

The goal of antitrust legislation should be to maximise the benefits society obtains from competition. Carlton and Frankel (1995) argue that joint ventures, particularly those involving networks that contain many industry participants, pose the most difficult antitrust issues. This is also the case with payment networks. Along with many beneficial effects for customers, payment networks may also be able to engage in collective actions that allow their members to exercise market power. The competition problem may also be further aggravated: rival systems may simply not exist because the established networks exhibit significant economies of scale. In any case, economies of scale can make it hard for a relatively small network to compete and grow if the dominant network is significantly larger.

In principle, one way to promote competition in retail payment systems is to use antitrust intervention to ensure that multiple payment networks remain separate and compete with one another. Carlton and Frankel (1995) argue that this simple policy recommendation is inadequate. Instead, a thorough analysis of the competitive effects of any proposed antitrust intervention in these networks must be done before such intervention. This clearly points out the difficulty in judging whether competition between systems (competition for the market) or competition in one system (competition in the market) is better for society's welfare on the whole. As a consequence, before any antitrust intervention, the specific market environment should be studied and carefully taken into account.

In all network industries, access and exclusion considerations have received a lot of attention because of the nature of industry. For example, Balto (1999) argues that exclusivity arrangements have been an issue in some of the most important joint venture and network antitrust decisions. He categorises the anticompetitive and procompetitive effects of joint network exclusivity as follows.

a   *Anticompetitive effects of network exclusivity*

    1   foreclosure of new entrants;
    2   enhancement of the ability to exercise market power;
    3   enhancement of opportunity for cartel activity;
    4   deterrence of innovation.

b   *Procompetitive effects of network exclusivity*

    1   promoting network competition;
    2   encouraging promotional services by preventing free-riding;
    3   reducing supply and demand uncertainty;
    4   recovering network investments.

The most important task for the regulator is to define which of the above effects are stronger in the situation that is analysed. Even though originally not tailor-made for payment system issues, the above list can be used in determining the importance of network exclusivity in payment system field as well. However, the most difficult task is to evaluate each of the sub-items in quantitative terms and then strike the overall balance.

Balto (1999) further discusses procedure of how to apply antitrust analysis of network exclusivity. He sets out the procedure as follows:

a careful scrutiny of market power: defining relevant markets;
b analysis of market power;
c realistic assessment of de facto exclusivity;
d a structured analysis of free-riding.

In principle, this method can be applied to assessment of exclusivity in payment systems where the definition of relevant markets plays a crucial role. This is especially important when considering cross-border payment markets, like the euro area, where national borders should not play a role any more. Furthermore, as in any network exclusivity assessment, the quantitative analysis of market power as well as assessment of de facto exclusivity, remains ultimately, somewhat a subjective decision even though economic theory can provide some guidance in the assessment.

Regulatory tools in network industries

Regulatory tools in network industries rely on the regulation theory developed for the regulation of natural monopolies and oligopolies. In network industries, firms having economies of scale in production and facing consumption externalities can obtain substantial market power in the absence of regulation. In essence, the aim of regulation is to provide a fair framework, or a 'level playing field' as it is commonly called in the context of payment system competition, under which efficiency and safety is safeguarded, and innovation incentives to develop new products and services are not hindered.

The tools to regulate network industries have been developed over time. In many countries the bottleneck problem in natural monopolies was handled by government/public ownership of that facility, and, in some cases, direct consumer price regulation was also used.[22] In recent years, regulatory attention has focused more on the design of an appropriate market structure and the behaviour of the bottleneck owner. New regulatory methods have also been introduced for regulating network industries. For example, *access price regulation* (regulation of the price of the infrastructure service) has been adopted to regulate bottleneck type industries. The underlying problem in most bottleneck industries is that when the bottleneck owner/incumbent is allowed to compete against other firms, it can set sufficiently high access charges making entry difficult. On the one hand, this would suggest that the regulated access price should be set low, in order to counteract the potential anti-competitive behaviour of the bottleneck owner. On the other hand, if the regulated access price is set too low, inefficient entry may occur and market efficiency deteriorate even further.

Another important issue in the economics of regulation is how to encourage firms to invest in infrastructure. It has been pointed out by many authors; including Mason and Valletti (2001), that there is a trade-off between optimal access regulation in static and dynamic frameworks. If static regulation reduces the use of monopoly power over the infrastructure, then it also reduces profits that can be earned by the owner of the facility. Accordingly, access regulation based on simple cost-recovery rules can discourage investment and even result in underprovision of the service concerned. Moreover, there is also a potential free-riding problem if market participants know beforehand that that the regulator will grant access to everybody to any new system that has been developed.

In regulating access and entry conditions in bottleneck infrastructures, the regulator should aim at the downstream market. There the 'playing field' should be level, to use a well-worn phrase. At the same time the regulator can ensure that the incumbent can recover its upstream fixed costs. This is also relevant in payment systems where a desire or sometimes even a claim by market participants to have a level playing field is often emphasised. Mason and Valletti (2001) argue that, in principle, the regulator may want to promote particular entry modes, where the typical dilemma is between (1) *facility-based* and (2) *service-based* competition. The first case refers to the *competition for market* situation where competition between different systems is emphasised. In this case, innovation incentives are clearly supported as incompatible systems compete for the market. The danger is that it may involve unnecessary duplication of infrastructure. The second case refers to the *competition in the market* situation, where competition takes place in a single network. In this case, the economies of scale in production can be better utilised and the critical mass of users more easily achieved, but dynamic efficiency may be reduced as innovation incentives are lowered because of a potential free-riding problem. According to Mason and Valletti (2001), there are also differences in the regulators' attitude towards the mode of competition in the two situations (i) and (ii). In the first case, the regulator can rely more on direct competition between systems than on regulatory intervention. In the second case, more regulatory intervention is needed in order to provide fair access and a level playing field.

Regulation and competition in retail payment systems

The competition–cooperation nexus in retail payment systems

As discussed above, competition and cooperation are both important in retail payment systems. For example, regarding the development in the euro area retail payment systems, the ECB[23] has argued that *the lack of competition* among banks explains the lack of progress with regard to the price level of cross-border credit transfers, whereas *the lack of cooperation* on standards and infrastructures explains the lack of progress in reducing the cost of processing cross-border transfers.

This quotation nicely reveals the network nature of payment systems that has strong effects on the competition and innovation incentives of the area. On the one hand, cooperation among service providers is needed on establishing standards and infrastructures in order to have a large enough customer base for their services (*network effect*). On the other hand, agreement on common standards (compatibility) increases competition and may thus reduce service providers' incentives for the increased compatibility (*competition effect*). Accordingly, the crucial question for policy-makers and regulators is to find measures that maximise social welfare in this type of environment.

Economic theory does not provide any clear answer to the question of whether competition in services in a single network (the *competition in the market* case), or competition between several networks (the *competition for the market* case) is better for efficiency. In practice, regulatory choices can be geared towards either services competition or infrastructure competition. The basic question for the regulatory authorities is which form of competition should be promoted. When taking a position on the question, the industry characteristics requirements need to be critically evaluated.

Certain characteristics of payment systems indicate that competition rules of traditional industries cannot be directly applied to the payment service industry. In payment systems, the main factor to be considered is that a certain degree of cooperation among operators in the provision of payment services is highly desirable, or even a prerequisite for the systems to function efficiently. By cooperation among payment service providers, it is possible to avoid overlapping investments and unnecessary and inefficient duplication of networks, as well as extend services to a larger population. While in many other markets it is evident that competition between service providers leads both to benefits for consumer, and to increased efficiency of the market as a whole, in the provision of payment services the customers themselves may require providers of the service to reach certain degrees of cooperation, because this normally provides more access and destination points in the payment systems. Therefore, the competition–cooperation nexus is of special importance in retail payment systems where cooperation among service providers needs to exist in order to achieve viable and efficient payment systems. In a broader context, the compatibility of competing systems, or at least the existence of common standards, can also contribute to the efficiency in retail payment markets.

In conclusion, it can be argued that joint ventures in the payment systems area should be more easily tolerated by authorities because of the network nature of the industry. However, at the same time, 'fair and open' access to systems by other potential participants is a prerequisite to that tolerance. The principal problem for the relevant authorities is related to the question of how to define 'fair and open' access. On the one hand, access requirements should not limit competition in the market by making potential competitors' entry impossible. On the other hand, too low access fees may bring in the free-riding problem and thus reduce investment incentives to improve payment systems.

Potential roles of regulators in the retail payment systems

The authorities have several general options for regulating the retail payments market. They can leave the development to the market and aim simply to foster a competitive environment and provide investment incentives in the field, for example, by assuming a tolerant attitude towards payment system joint ventures. They can also act as catalysts or facilitators for development, for example, by participating in the development of payment standards and supporting the work of cooperative groups within the industry. As a stronger measure, they can resort to specific regulation to influence market development, e.g. enforcement of standards or even regulation of prices. Finally, as the ultimate measure, the authorities can become 'operationally active' by establishing their own systems for providing payment services. This option should be used only when the authorities judge that reliable and efficient payment systems cannot be provided by the market.

The following roles of public authorities have recently been put forward in international fora:[24]

i   *to address legal and regulatory impediments to market development and innovation;*

ii   *to foster competitive market conditions and behaviours;*

iii *to support the development of effective standards and infrastructure arrangements.*

All these points suggest that the development in the retail payment markets should be primarily market-led, and that public authorities' main role should be that of assisting and supporting it. Public action is required only when market or coordination failure occurs. Accordingly, one of the main tasks for public authorities is to review the legal framework to identify barriers to improvements in cooperation with the private sector.

Future developments in European retail payment markets

The landscape of European retail payment markets is today still fragmented even after the introduction of euro notes and coins as the ultimate manifestation of the monetary integration process. In general, it can be argued that the EU still consists of 25 heterogeneous payment areas instead of one single payment market. However, the development of the Single Market in the retail payment system area cannot take place overnight, and the development of systems is characterised by path dependence and slow change of payment habits. Many national payment systems are already functioning efficiently but what have been lacking are the well-functioning and efficient cross-border retail payment systems to contribute to the financial integration process in Europe.

The slow development efforts by the banking sector to develop more efficient cross-border retail payment methods finally triggered the European Parliament and the Council to adopt RPE in December 2001. The RPE obliged banks to reduce charges for cross-border payments of up to €12,500 (€50,000 as of January 2006) to the level of those of corresponding domestic payments. This policy intervention was strongly criticised by the payment service provider sector that argued for a market-driven solution. Undoubtedly, price regulation is a regulatory method that should be used in a cautious way. However, it should be noted that the RPE has already had some positive development effects in the European retail payment systems field. In fact, it was only after the usage of the regulatory power by the European authorities that the payment service providers were forced out. Accordingly, in the aftermath of the RPE, the banking sector activated itself and formed a new cooperation body, the European Payments Council (EPC).[25] In principle, the EPC should be able to address the potential difficulty of reaching consensus among wide and divergent participant groups and thereby accelerate the development efforts considerably.

The EPC was established by the European banks and banking associations in June 2002 to support the development of SEPA. The final aim of the EPC is to achieve 'a real domestic market for euro payments' by 2010. The EPC has established different working groups and approved market conventions in order to facilitate the development. The EPC members have also approved PEACH as the preferred model of the industry for credit and debit transfers. In practice, the Euro Banking Association's STEP 2 – retail payment system, established in summer 2003, acts as a PEACH and provides a pan-European system for processing bulk payments. In the light of network economics theory, the crucial question for the viability of this new system is whether it attracts a sufficient number of payments processed through it in order to facilitate cost-recovery. Accordingly, the volumes of pure European cross-border credit transfers may not be sufficient to ensure the critical mass of payments and, therefore, also parts of the national retail payments may need to be directed through it as well.

Another factor that can have an effect on the future European retail payment landscape is the emergence of new payment initiatives. For example, card payment providers are expanding their traditional field of business and entering credit transfer markets currently dominated by the banks and their joint ventures as primary service providers. For example, Visa EU has launched its Visa Direct initiative that has been developed to enable payment service providers to comply with the RPE. Competition may also be intensifying by alternative new, non-bank payment service providers as well as mobile payment operators. In general, it can be concluded that competition from other payment service providers, besides the traditional banks, is likely to increase. This development is going to foster competition and strengthen innovation incentives among service providers, and, thereby, contribute to improvements in efficiency in retail payment markets.

The authorities also have an important role to play in promoting efficiency in European retail payment systems. In essence, they should provide a regulatory and legal framework that supports a level playing field and safeguards innovation incentives. The European Commission is currently working to harmonise the legal framework for payment services in order to facilitate the development of the Single Payment Area. The ECB/ESCB, in turn, has been emphasising its role as a catalyst for development and cooperating closely with the banking sector in a number of fora. Accordingly, it can be concluded that the authorities and regulators have recognised their role in facilitating the development towards the Single Payment Area. This reflects the findings here on the interaction between the competition–cooperation nexus and regulation, where industry-specific network effects do play an important role and need to be taken into account by the regulatory authorities. In an ideal situation, market players would provide the most efficient solutions and regulatory authorities would only be in charge of their oversight.

Conclusion

As in any other network industry, the crucial question for regulators in retail payment systems is whether competition in services in a single network (*competition in the market*) or competition between several networks (*competition for the market*) is best for the market efficiency. There is no universal answer to that question because industry-specific factors play a decisive role in practical applications of regulatory policy. In the payment system area, the main industry-specific factor to be considered is that a certain degree of cooperation among payment service providers is needed for payment systems to function efficiently. The reason for this is that there are several parties involved in money transfers: sender, service provider, receiver, and their respective institutions. The essential requirement from the efficiency standpoint is that all these can be connected to the same system or compatible systems. An additional prerequisite is that a viable system needs to achieve a *critical mass of users* so that the existence of the system can be established and potential economies of scale in payment production realised. Therefore, it is no wonder that the payment system industry is dominated by joint ventures and shared networks. In the same vein, the chicken-and-egg problem has also proved hard to overcome for many new payment initiatives as witnessed, for example, by the slow development of e-money schemes in many countries.

The network nature of the payment system industry poses several challenges to regulators. In essence, regulatory policy has to face the fact that payment service providers often cooperate in shared networks while at the same time they compete directly in the provision of retail payment services (upstream cooperation combined with competition). This can yield socially optimal outcomes in industries where network effects are present. Therefore, regulators should tolerate this upstream cooperation by payment service providers in order to exploit positive network externalities. However, cooperation in operation and development of payment systems (i.e. in the upstream market) can lead to collusive behaviour in the downstream market for providing payment services, especially when access to the shared payment networks is restricted. To mitigate this problem, regulators should monitor market conditions frequently and require that criteria for participation in systems are not too restrictive. In this context, non-discriminatory and publicly disclosed participation criteria are essential for ensuring the contestability of the market.

To advance European financial integration, one of the most important future tasks for all the key parties involved in the development of retail payment systems is to strengthen their cooperation, so that efforts can be focused on the most relevant issues and overlapping development efforts can be avoided. In this context, the following roles of regulators have been advocated:

1 *fostering a competitive environment and innovation incentives* (using regulatory tools in providing a level playing field and investment incentives in payment systems);
2 *supporting the development of effective standards and infrastructure arrangements* (catalyst and facilitator role of public authorities, resort to stronger regulatory intervention if seen appropriate); and
3 *influencing customers' payment habits* (promotion of direct, cost-based pricing of payments to guide customers to use the most efficient payment methods).

Accordingly, financial market integration and payment system development should be primarily market-led and public action is required only when market failure occurs. In the European regulatory field, cooperation between the European Commission and the ECB/ESCB is also essential to avoid a situation where too extensive and overlapping regulation acts as an impediment to the development.

Notes

1 The views expressed are those of the author and do not necessarily reflect the views of the Bank of Finland.
2 See the Official Journal of the European Communities (2001).
3 A summary discussion of the main conclusions of the report can be found in Wellink (2002).
4 For early studies, see, e.g. Angelini and Giannini (1993), Schoenmaker (1995), Calomiris and Kahn (1996), Berger *et al.* (1996), and Folkerts-Landau (1997).
5 Studies on retail payment systems include *inter alia* Carlton and Frankel (1995), Saloner and Shephard (1995), McAndrews (1996, 1997), McAndrews and Rob (1996), Guibourg (1998, 2001), Gowrisankaran and Stavins (2002), Gangulny and Milne (2002a, b) and Weinberg (2002).
6 For a broader analysis of network and competition issues in retail payment systems, see e.g. Gangulny and Milne (2002a) and Kemppainen (2003).
7 The most well-known (but nowadays also disputed) example in the context of efficiency and path dependence is the QWERTY-keyboard system.
8 This can be clearly seen in some European countries (Figures 10.2 and 10.3) and especially in the US, where the cheque continues to be an important payment method.
9 In fact, the behaviour of end-users finally determines which payment systems survive. Therefore, along with investment incentives for payment service providers, the usage incentives for customers are also essential when fostering efficiency in payment systems. This is an important aspect in deciding on the pricing conventions of different services because pricing can be used to guide customers to adopt the most efficient payment methods.
10 European Payments Council (2002).
11 European Commission (2003).
12 For theoretical analyses on the determination of deposit interest and bank service charges, see, e.g. Tarkka (1995). For issues on cost recovery and pricing in payment services, see, e.g. Humphrey *et al.* (1997).
13 See for example, Norges Bank (2002 and 2004), Gresvick and Øwre (2002), as well as Humphrey *et al.* (2001).
14 The following part is an adapted list of features provided by Gangulny and Milne (2002a).
15 Even though similar in many aspects, the payment service and telecommunication industries do have some fundamental differences. In principle, information is exchanged in both (telephone call and payment information in payment message need have a compatible system through which messages are transferred), but in payment services the settlement of money transfer also needs to take place through a safe and reliable settlement system.
16 This study uses both terms (network externality and network effect) in interchangeable ways.
17 For an analysis of the basic structures of networks see, e.g. Economides (1996).
18 See, e.g. BIS (2003).
19 McAndrews and Rob (1996).
20 According to Besen and Farrell (1994), network markets are often 'tippy'. This means that the coexistence of incompatible products may be unstable, with a single winning standard dominating the market (*tipping*). The dominance of the VHS videocassette recorder technology and the virtual elimination of its Betamax rival is often used as an example.
21 See, e.g. Liebowitz and Margolis (1995).
22 The rest of this section relies strongly on the discussion in Mason and Valletti (2001).

23 ECB (2001b).
24 For an extensive discussion on the policies relating to the efficiency and safety of retail payments, especially from the viewpoint of central banks, see BIS (2003).
25 For more information, see the web page of the EPC: www.europeanpaymentscouncil.org.

References

Angelini, P. and Giannini, C. (1993) 'On the economics of interbank payment systems', Banca D'Italia Discussion Paper, no. 193, May.

Balto, D. (1999) 'Networks and exclusivity: antitrust analysis to promote network competition', *George Mason Law Review* 7(3) (Spring): 523–76.

Berger, A., Hancock, D. and Marquardt, J. (1996) 'A framework for analysing efficiency, risks, costs, and innovations in the payment system', *Journal of Money Credit and Banking* 28(4), Part 2 (November): 696–732.

Besen, M. and Farrell, J. (1994) 'Choosing how to compete: strategies and tactics in standardisation', *Journal of Economic Perspectives* 8(2) (Spring): 117–31.

BIS (1999) *Retail Payments in Selected Countries: A Comparative Study*, Report of the Working Group on Retail Payment Systems, Committee on Payment and Settlement Systems, CPSS Publication, no. 33, BIS, Basel, September.

BIS (2000) *Clearing and Settlement Arrangements for Retail Payments in Selected Countries*, Report of the Working Group on Retail Payment Systems, Committee on Payment and Settlement Systems, CPSS Publication, no. 40, BIS, Basel, September.

BIS (2003) *Policy Issues for Central Banks in Retail Payments*, Report of the Working Group on Retail Payment Systems, Committee on Payment and Settlement Systems, CPSS Publication, no. 52, BIS, Basel, March.

Calomiris, C. and Kahn, C. (1996) 'The efficiency of self-regulated payment systems. Learning from the Suffolk system', *Journal of Money, Credit and Banking* 28(4), Part 2 (November): 766–97.

Carlton, D. and Frankel, A. (1995) 'Antitrust and payment technologies', *Federal Reserve Bank of St. Louis Review*, November/December: 41–54.

ECB (1999) *Improving Cross-border Retail Payments: The Eurosystem's View*, September

ECB (2000) *Improving Cross-border Retail Payments Services: Progress Report*, September.

ECB (2001a) 'Towards a uniform service level for retail payments in the euro area', *Monthly Bulletin*, February.

ECB (2001b) *Towards an Integrated Infrastructure for Credit Transfers in Euro*, November.

ECB (2003) *Towards Single Euro Payment Area – Progress Report*, June.

ECB (2004) *Payment and Securities Settlement Systems in the European Union – Addendum Incorporating 2002 Figures*, April.

Economides, N. (1996) 'The economics of networks', *International Journal of Industrial Organisation* 14(6) (October): 673–99.

European Commission (2003) *A New Legal Framework for Payments in the Internal Market*, europa.eu.int/comm/internal_market/en/finances/payment/area/index.htm.

European Payments Council (2002) *Euroland: Our Single Payment Area!*, White Paper, May, www.europeanpaymentscouncil.org.

Farrell, J. and Saloner, G. (1986) 'Installed base and compatibility: innovation, product preannouncements, and predation', *American Economic Review* 76(4): 940–55.

Folkerts-Landau, D. (1997) 'Wholesale payments and financial discipline, efficiency, and liquidity', IMF Working Paper, no. WP/97/154, International Monetary Fund.

Gangulny, B. and Milne, A. (2002a) 'Do we need public policy intervention in UK retail payment systems and if so how?', mimeo, Version 1.4, May, City University Business School, London.

Gangulny, B. and Milne, A. (2002b) 'UK retail payments: competition, regulation, and returns to innovation', mimeo, version 1.1, May, City University Business School, London.

Gowrisankaran, G. and Stavins, J. (2002) 'Network externalities and technology adoption: lessons from electronic payments', NBER Working Paper, no. 8943, May.

Gresvik, O. and Øwre, G. (2002) 'Banks' costs and income in the payment system in 2001', *Norges Bank Economic Bulletin* Q4, 125–33.

Guibourg, G. (1998) 'Efficiency in the payment system – a network perspective', *Quarterly Review*, 3, Sveriges Riksbank, pp. 5–24.

Guibourg (2001) 'Interoperability and network externalities in electronic payments', Sveriges Riksbank Working Paper Series, no. 126.

HM Treasury (2000a) *Competition in UK Banking: A Report to the Chancellor of Exchequer*, Cruickshank Review.

HM Treasury (2000b) *Competition in Payment Systems: A Consultation Document.*

Humphrey, D., Keppler, R. and Montes-Negret, F. (1997) 'Cost recovery and pricing of payment services: theory', Methods and Experience, mimeo, World Bank, Washington, DC.

Humphrey, D., Moshe, K. and Vale, B. (2001) 'Realizing the gains from electronic payments: costs, pricing and payment choice', *Journal of Money Credit and Banking* 33(2), Part 1 (May): 216–34.

Katz, M. and Shapiro, C. (1985) 'Network externalities, competition and compatibility', *American Economic Review* 75(3): 424–44.

Katz, M. and Shapiro, C. (1994) 'Systems competition and network effects', *Journal of Economic Perspectives* 8(2): 93–115.

Kemppainen, K. (2003) 'Competition and regulation in European retail payment systems', Bank of Finland Discussion Papers, no. 16/2003.

Liebowitz, S. and Margolis, S. (1995) 'Path dependence, lock-in and history', *Journal of Law, Economics and Organization* 11: 205–26.

Mason, R. and Valletti, T. (2001) 'Competition in communication networks: pricing and regulation', *Oxford Review of Economic Policy* 17(3): 389–415.

McAndrews, J. (1996) 'Pricing in vertically integrated network switches', Federal Reserve Bank of Philadelphia, Working Paper, no. 96-19.

McAndrews, J. (1997) 'Network issues and payment systems', *Federal Reserve Bank of Philadelphia Business Review*, November/December: 15–25.

McAndrews, J. and Rob, R. (1996) 'Shared ownership and pricing in a network switch', *International Journal of Industrial Organisation* 14(6): 727–45.

Norges Bank (2002) *Payment Services Have Become More Efficient*, Press release, 6 November.

Norges Bank (2004) *Annual Report on Payment Systems*, Norges Bank, June.

Official Journal of the European Communities (2001) *Regulation (EC) No. 2560/2001 of the European Parliament and of the Council of 19 December 2001 on Cross-border Payments in Euro*, L 344/13, 28.12.2001.

Rivlin Committee (1998) 'The Federal Reserve in the payment mechanism', Committee on the Federal Reserve in the Payments Mechanism, Federal Reserve System, January.

Saloner, G. and Shephard, A. (1995) 'Adoption of technologies with network effects: an empirical examination of the adoption of automated teller machines', *Rand Journal of Economics* 26(3)(Autumn): 479–501.

Schoenmaker, D. (1995) 'A comparison of alternative interbank settlement systems', LSE Financial Markets Group Discussion Paper, no. 204, ESRC Research Centre, London.

Shy, O. (2001) *The Economics of Network Industries*, Cambridge: Cambridge University Press.

Tarkka, J. (1995) *Approaches to Deposit Pricing: A Study in the Determination of Deposits Interest and Bank Service Charges*, Bank of Finland Studies, E:2.

Wallis Committee (1997) *Final Report: Financial Systems Inquiry*, Canberra: AGPS.

Weinberg, J. (2002) 'Pricing of Interbank Payment Services', *Federal Reserve Bank of Richmond, Economic Quarterly* 88(1)(Winter): 51–66.

Wellink Report (2002) 'Tariff structure and infrastuctures in Dutch retail payments', *De Nederlandsche Bank's Quarterly Bulletin*, June: 37–43.

11 Payment system developments – their dependence on competition, cooperation, incentives and authority actions[1]

Harry Leinonen

Payment systems have changed considerably since the dawn of computerised processing at the end of the 1960s and beginning of the 1970s. The development has been continuous, towards more efficient and electronic versions. Still, a frequently asked question is why the development speed is so slow. Why are old paper-based conventions widely used? Why are the development paths nationally so different?[2]

In this chapter we analyse the development objectives and development patterns in payment systems. How are cooperation and competition enhancing developments and what kinds of roles could authorities have? We analyse the different issues on a general level and present a list of hypotheses regarding the factors affecting development speed. We focus especially on the lack of development incentives. The idea is, as the next step, to make a cross-country study to verify these hypotheses.

Payment systems are defined very broadly to include service providers' internal systems, any inter-providers systems, but also the systems and processes of the end-users. The development objective is seen from the end-users' perspective and/or the whole community's perspective. Payment systems constitute a basic infrastructure.

Payment systems

The glossaries of the ECB (2001b) Blue Book and BIS (2004) Red Book define payments as:

> The payer's transfer of a monetary claim on a party acceptable to the payee. Typically, claims take the form of banknotes or deposit balances held at a financial institution or at a central bank.

Payment systems are defined as:

> A payment system consists of a set of instruments, banking procedures and, typically, interbank funds transfer systems which facilitate the circulation of money.

In this chapter we follow the Blue/Red Book definition of payment quite closely. We also include credit balances at different kinds of financial institutions including credit card companies.

Payment systems are seen as the infrastructure built by payment service providers for receiving the payment order from customers, processing and transporting them within and among service providers and notifying the customers of sent/received payments.

Payment system developments

Overall development objectives

Processing payments is a form of transportation industry. A given amount of funds should be transferred from the payer (payer's account) to the payee (the payee's account) as efficiently as possible. This general objective can be broken down into the following sub-objectives from the end-users' perspective

- high speed of processing;
- low cost of processing;
- efficient and convenient user interfaces;
- high security;
- low amount of foregone interest or paid extra interest;
- system stability.

These sub-objectives are partly interdependent so in order to reach overall efficiency a 'balanced basket' needs to be chosen. For example, security can always be improved but after a given point the marginal costs will exceed marginal benefits. Higher speed may increase costs to such an extent that the end-users are more content with a slower processing speed. Efficient and convenient user interfaces make it possible for the end-customers to send and receive payments easily from the payment systems of the banks. Today it means standardised electronic interfaces with sufficient data for automatic pre/post-processing in, especially corporate, customers' systems. The hardware and telecommunication solutions should be such that they are generally available at low cost to the end-users and preferably usable for other purposes at the same time. In addition to pure processing costs, a considerable amount of payment system costs consists of criminal abuse of payment systems (e.g. counterfeits and thefts) and the costs of preventive measures against criminality. The foregone interest on savings/money account depends on interest paid on payment funds and on the float time, which is dependent on processing speed and value dates. On credit accounts the customers prefer low interest rates and immediate crediting. The change-over from cash payments to bank-account payments has partly been due to the interest received on bank accounts. The payment systems need to be stable and trustworthy. Users avoid unstable systems and will not invest in necessary interfaces if the future of a system is unclear. Stability and safety is essential in payment systems. If there are stability concerns in one system, there may also be a contagion affecting other similar systems and service providers.

A maximum service level can be foreseen for some of these objectives, while others can show a continuous improvement process. The maximum processing speed, i.e. immediate real-time transfers, has already been achieved in some typically large value or internet-based systems. Foregone interest will be zero when payments can be made in real-time using investment assets, e.g. the payer sends a payment from assets in his investment portfolio (e.g. of mutual funds type-a), which are converted in the process and through the market to assets required by the payee (e.g. of mutual funds type-b). Because of the bulk service character of payment processing, one can also foresee that at some stage a common international palette of technical user standards with data fields, syntax definitions, communication alternatives, etc. will be available and which will suit most of the end-users. The remaining development and competition areas would then be processing costs and security features.

The overall objective should be to maximise the total benefits of payment services to the payers and payees and therefore their payment-related costs have to be included in the calculations. Improving the payment system services can therefore increase the costs in the payment systems of the service providers, but overall benefits will be created via cost reductions in the internal payment processes of the payers and payees. The reference code[3] for updating receivables files is a typical example, where adding a code to the payment data will increase costs somewhat in payment providers' systems but reduce costs considerably in payees' receivables systems.

Historic developments

The development patterns and speed have varied nationally resulting in different payment customs and development levels in various countries. For example, cheque truncation was introduced in Finnish cheque clearing in the early 1970s, while it is currently part of the cheque 21 bill in the USA. The differences in national payment habits in the EU-area can be seen from Figure 11.1.

The overall usage of cashless payment methods varies considerably in the EU. Low usage countries are Spain, Greece, Ireland and Italy. In some countries cheques are still common, i.e. France, Ireland, Portugal and the UK. Credit transfers are popular in Finland, Austria, Germany, Denmark and the Netherlands. Direct debits are used considerably in Germany, the Netherlands and Sweden. Card payments are popular in many countries, i.e. Finland, Belgium, Denmark, France, Luxembourg, the Netherlands, Sweden and the UK.

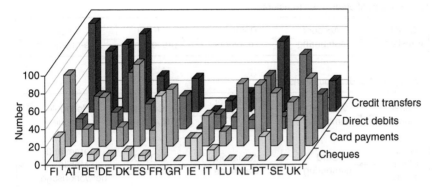

Figure 11.1 Number of cashless payments per inhabitant in EU countries in 2001 (source: E:uropean Central Bank).

The development of payment systems and payment patterns has been based on national evolutions. National standards have been created in all countries for credit transfers and direct debits, and these vary considerably. The only exception from this rule is in credit/debit card developments, where international standards have emerged.

The payment service developments seem to follow a given general pattern, which is described in Figure 11.2.

The general development trends are sketched roughly in Figure 11.2. The payment system developments are described separately for credit push and debit pull services. Some of the developments have clearly been technology driven. New card features and transmission possibilities have been implemented in all service types.

The credit push service has only one major form for sending a payment directly from the payer to the payee. In some markets a separation into urgent and normal transfers can be found but the basic service design is the same. Standardising the account number has most often been the first development step on the national level after the general establishment of an interbank credit transfer service. The next step, introduction of reference numbers, has been implemented in order to make updating of receivables easier for large payees. The electronic interface for sending and receiving payments as well as invoices (e.g. complete e-bill presentment) has been achieved by using modern ICT. However, the e-bill presentment is in a start-up phase and it will still take some years before it becomes a major service form. A 'true' e-payment refers to the emerging Internet-based credit transfer services, where a payment can be made end-to-end in real-time as a dialogue between payer, payee, payer's bank and payee's bank (e.g. the payee sends the e-bill for a software product, the payer accepts it and sends it to his/her bank, which debits the payer's account and sends the payment to the payee's bank, which credits the

Development of credit push transfers

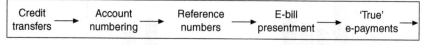

Development of debit pull transfers

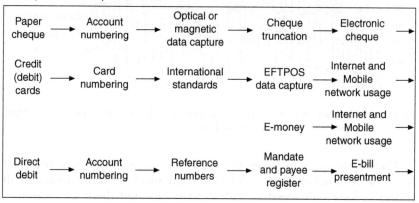

Development of card technology

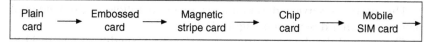

Development of transaction transmission technology

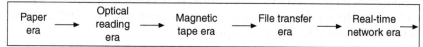

Development of customer identification

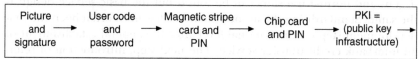

Figure 11.2 The general development patterns on payment technology.

account and notifies the payee about the received amount including the necessary references in the payment data). The implementation of real-time end-to-end service is still modest and can be found only on limited markets. However, PayPal, an originally non-bank real-time payment system, has been able to grow exceptionally fast in the US and is currently also expanding rapidly in Europe.

The debit pull service type shows a number of variations. In the debit pull case the payer gives the payee a mandate to debit the payer's account with a given amount. Because of the right to debit another person's account, the debit pull services contain more risks than the more straight forward credit transfer services. Is the payer referring to the right account? Is there enough liquidity on that account? Is the payee debiting the right amount and from the right account?

The oldest debit instrument is the cheque, which is still used in many countries. It has been partly or completely replaced by debit cards in several countries (Finland and Norway were among the first).

Debit and credit cards are technically identical. The major difference can be found in the issuer status. Debit cards are generally bank issued cards, which most often are connected to some type of savings or current account. Credit cards are mainly issued by separate credit card companies and use an account with a credit line and with a pay back scheme. Credit cards can be of the charge card type in which the card customer settles the total credit for example once a month or a long-term credit, 'revolving' credit, in which the customer settles only a given part of the outstanding credit. Credit cards can also be issued by banks especially within the Visa and MasterCard schemes, but even then they sometimes provide the service via special subsidiaries of card services. International standards have helped credit and debit card processing towards large scale automation. Debit and credit card transactions can be routed and settled in the same or different systems depending on the national developments.

E-money can be seen as a modern chip-based card service. However, the definitions of e-money vary and in some definitions all account-based schemes relying on completely electronic access are seen as e-money (e.g. the PayPal type of modern payment systems). The e-money market has seen many newcomers leaving the market rapidly. Some schemes have been bank schemes but the majority have been non-bank schemes. Up till now e-money has only been able to capture a small part of the payment market.

Direct debit is a debit transaction based on the payer's account number. In order to reduce risks payees have been required to present mandates stating the right for debiting. Technically it is close to debit/credit card schemes but it does not use cards for identification and card numbers for routing. Direct debit is a major payment method in some countries especially for recurrent payments from known creditors.

The many variations of debit pull schemes are the results of different payer/payee needs and security issues as well as competing service providers, e.g. banks versus credit card companies.

Card technology developments have made it possible to identify the payer more efficiently and with higher security, together with a more secure mandate for the payee to debit the account. The development of encryption techniques has been essential for the new identification possibilities. The transmission technology developments have made payment transportation faster, more cost efficient and secure both between different banks and between banks and their customers.

The development of electronic user interfaces for payments has been rapid. More and more customers use the Internet for sending payment instructions to their banks. Modern interfaces are easy to install and use. Generally customers just need to click on the right point on the internet screen and a secure window to their e-banking service is opened. User identification, transaction content and liquidity can be checked online with an immediate confirmation to the payer. The electronic user interfaces and e-banking/payment services vary a lot from provider to provider and from country to country.

The development of cash has concentrated on security features. Increased forgery, with improved methods, has required new and better security features to be developed.

Competition among payment methods

Payments are perfect complementary goods. The market for payments is completely dependent on economic activity in general. Payments are needed only for transferring the funds connected to an economic transaction. The costs of making a payment are generally so low that it does not currently affect the decision regarding the underlying economic transaction except maybe for international payments.

The consumers and companies have fixed budgets out of which the payments are made. The total value of payments is therefore fixed. The number of payments can only increase if the amount is split into smaller payments. The overall size of the market can therefore be considered quite stable.

The different payment products compete to get their share. Cashless payments have continuously increased their share as cash looses ground. Figure 11.3 shows the number of cashless payments per capita in year 2001 and the difference from year 1994.

There has been a significant increase in most countries except for Greece, Ireland and Luxembourg where no increase, or even decreasing, transaction volumes are reported. The overall numbers show clear differences with France, the Netherlands, Finland and the UK as leading in volumes, all counting for more than 180 transactions per year per inhabitant.

Figures 11.4 and 11.5 show the development in EU countries in 1994 and 2001 for outstanding cash. All countries show a significant reduction in cash per GDP for that period except the UK.

The cash stock held per capita (see Figure 11.5) shows an increase in four countries (the UK, Ireland, Denmark and Sweden). The others show a clear reduction in cash stocks. The large difference in Germany is partly due to the euro-conversion, which reduced the DM cash holdings outside Germany. There was an exceptional decrease in all euro-countries during the change-over period. After that the amount of cash held by the public has increased to the same level as before the change-over. The difference can to a large

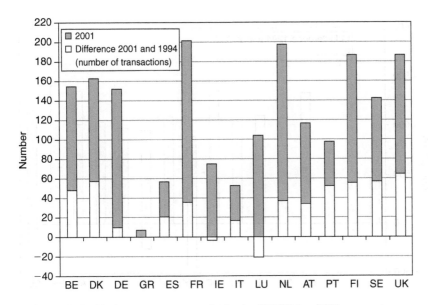

Figure 11.3 Cashless payments per capita in the EU 1994 to 2001.

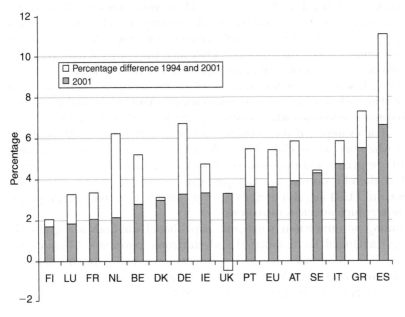

Figure 11.4 Cash stock as percentage of GDP in the EU 1994 and 2001.

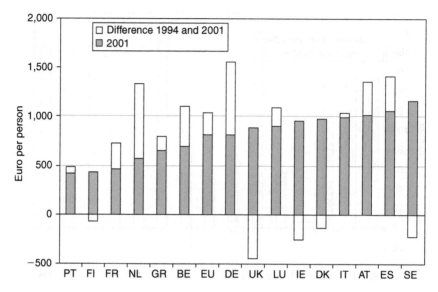

Figure 11.5 Cash stock by the general public per capita in the EU 1994 and 2001.

extent be interpreted as the amount held for non-transactional purposes. The amount of outstanding euro-cash will probably be higher in future than the prior amount of outstanding national currencies due to large amounts of euro holdings outside the euro-area. Over time the euro will most probably become an international currency comparable with the US dollar.

We lack statistics on the number of payments made using the cash stock. The cash stock can also remain quite constant although the number of payments decreases when customers maintain their replenishing patterns. For example, if the customer normally withdraws €200 from the ATM when his cash stock is close to €20, his cash stock will be on average €110 irrespectively of the turnaround time. Cash is also used for hoarding and is thereby outside normal payment circulation. Some currencies (USD and EUR) are also used extensively outside their own geographical territory, which affects comparisons.

Among account-based payments, paper-based methods are gradually being exchanged for automated and electronic payments. Cheques are mainly being converted to card payments and card payment slips are being converted to EFTPOS systems. Paper-based giros are being exchanged for e-banking credit transfers or direct debits.

Future developments

In processing speed a clear trend can be seen towards true end-to-end real-time processing. The development of telecommunication services has been rapid. Real-time processing will probably result in a reduced amount of the debit pull type of processing. The credit push type of payment will be as fast, but more secure. It is easier for the end-user's service provider to identify its own customers securely, than it is for a merchant or another service provider to do so. In a widely used debit-pull system the problem will be to standardise and to implement a common identification solution, which will allow flexible changes over time (e.g. a chip-card and its security features, which will be interoperable with any terminal). In a credit-push transaction, the liquidity in the account can be established at the same time. For the payee there will be no difference in reception time and processes, when everything is done in real-time. For example the online CEPS e-money standard has been developed based on a credit push process instead of the debit pull process generally used for card payments.

The account numbering/addressing code is one of the most import future developments. International Bank Account Number (IBAN) is proposed to be used for international bank account numbering and it has been implemented in Europe. However, the European implementation requires the Bank Identification Code (BIC) to be used together with IBAN although BIC information is redundant. For card payments the accounts are addressed based on the internationally standardised card number. One way to standardise the account address would be to start to use card numbers as the reference for all accounts. This would eliminate the addressing difference between credit push and debit pull transactions. This might happen when the major credit card companies (Visa and MasterCard) start to provide credit transfer services using card numbers.

There are several parallel debit pull products; this is partly due to different service providers. Some are seen as bank products while others are seen as credit card company products although they are basically identical. A consolidation of the offers can be seen as a result of international standardisation. A bank debit card transaction can be seen as a one-time direct debit and mandate to debit the account. The debit (credit) card transaction could be expanded to provide data for multiple mandates for a given time period. A secure direct debit product requires mandates to be limited per payee, for a time period and for the debit amount per time period. The mandate information could also be transferred via the payee, when it is encrypted using modern chip-card features.

Mobile telephone developments could provide possibilities for payment system developments. The mobile telephone will be a device giving telecommunication access to everybody. It can be used from almost any location. It provides a screen, a keyboard interface, processing capacity and new security features. There is also a trend for including (mobile) phones in different kinds of hardware, e.g. PCs and cameras, which will give the same opportunities. There are currently several mobile telephone schemes being tested; all are using different structures. The EU Commission's Mobile Payment Blue Print project[4] has tried to enhance standards for mobile payments. However, the advances towards common mobile payment standards have as yet been quite slow.

Large-scale e- and m-payments implementation requires strong and easy-to-use security features. Customers must be identified securely and payment messages must be protected against fraud, when transported in networks. Proper security will require hardware-protected solutions, because as the numerous Internet worms and viruses prove, the customers' current PC environments are too vulnerable against outside attack. This could easily breed a new kind of monopoly security provider and authority certifier in payment systems.

Future payment system developments will be dependent on many factors and after some years a new dominant global design for payment services will probably emerge. Payments have been, until recently, a very low tech product mainly based on manual processes. The new electronic design will require more software and hardware for all user groups. Starting up a new payment scheme will therefore be more difficult, as both the user end and the provider end has to be equipped with suitable ICT facilities. When a new product offering can penetrate the initial threshold it will probably expand rapidly. One interesting newcomer is, therefore, PayPal, which in a few years has been able to attract a large number of customers to use a very basic Internet-based credit transfer scheme.

Payment systems have been considered to be almost natural monopolies due to the fixed start-up costs and centralised processing facilities. The new network environment and new low cost ICT structures are changing the picture. In an open network infrastructure the necessary investment for newcomers will decrease drastically. The economies of scale may largely disappear.

Lack of development incentives

There are traditionally two general types of service providers in payment systems; those keeping the end-users' payment accounts and those providing inter-provider services. These can be both private and public companies. The end users' service providers can be specialised in servicing mainly one (or a few) types of customers, but in most cases, and especially banks, generally serve all types of customers (cardholders, consumers, merchants, corporate customers, etc.). Inter-provider services are provided to a limited number of service providers. In many cases the provision of these services is organised as non-profit companies owned by their direct users. The development objectives of these companies are derived from the general objectives of the company and can differ considerably from the overall development objectives of society. Service providers' interest in developing services can be limited due to market conditions and short-term profit preferences, as will be discussed more in detail later. Service providers generally have an interest in tying customers to their services and making it difficult for users to change their service provider. One of the issues for regulators is how to bring the incentives and objectives of service providers closer to that of end-users' and society's objectives.

In most markets the service providers have an interest in developing their products in order to improve their market position and the total demand. Competition improves services/products and reduces prices as production becomes more effective. Compared to other markets and services payment systems contain many factors and characteristics, which result in a general lack of development incentives.[5]

- *An almost fixed total demand* for payment services, as the budgets of the payers are fixed. The number of payments is also fixed as these are tied to the number of economic contracts as a complement good. Nobody is paying just out of fun, but always related to some agreement. Improving services or lowering tariffs will not increase the total market volume.

- A *'cannibalising' zero sum game among payment services* is generally the result of the fixed demand. When one type payment service is improved via new features its volume can only be increased by transactions moving from inferior services. Banks generally provide several types of payment services and the improvement and investments in one type of services will result in reduction of the sales of the other services. General service providers, such as banks, therefore, have less incentive to develop services, as these may reduce their own output of competing products.

- *Short-term secure benefits* are preferred in private companies compared to risky long-term investments. Investments in payment system developments are always long-term projects and the returns are received over many years in small streams. It is therefore difficult to gain management interest, when there are always competing investments in e.g. marketing which have more obvious and instant returns.

- *The sunk costs of legacy systems* need to be recovered, but not by new entrants. Generally a new technology level will have lower costs and thereby also lower margins, which makes it more difficult to recover costs and the payback period will be longer.

- *Network externalities* are large in payment services. Both payers and payees need to be interested in the payment products. Technically the services provided by different service providers need to be interoperable. New developments have to overcome the initial 'chicken-or-egg' problem and gather the critical mass. The initial hurdle seems to be very large for payment service developments.

- *Cooperation for unequal benefits is required among competitors* in order to create an inter-provider payment infrastructure. Payments need to be transferred among service-providers as a service provider is seldom in a so dominant market position that customers would be satisfied with just internal transfers within one service provider. Cooperation among competitors has proven to be difficult as the results of developments and/or the investments for developments will be unequally distributed. For example if payment processing is made more rapid some banks will lose more float benefits than others and if one particular technical solution is selected this may be a more preferred alternative for some banks due to implementation benefits.

- *Centralised monopolistic interbank processing structures* have emerged in many countries as the result of payment infrastructure cooperation. An automated clearing house (ACH) in a monopoly setup is the most common domestic interbank processing structure. In an ACH setup all banks send all transactions to a common ACH for clearing and routing to the receiving bank. Once created the ACH will have a monopoly position, which will be difficult to challenge. The users, generally the owners, will have little incentive to create a competing ACH as their internal costs will increase if multiple and non-standardised interfaces need to be maintained. The costs of the monopolistic ACH will be shared by the participants and covered by the tariff income from payers and payees. The large participants and owners often dominate the decision making in an ACH, which means that the participation rules tend to favour large participants and may imply an extra hurdle for newcomers.

- *The width of the monopolistic structure* can vary from very basic interbank clearing service to advanced end-customer related add-on functions. For example e-banking interfaces for payment services can be provided by each bank itself or by the common ACH. The larger the cooperative and non-competitive area is, the less incentives banks will have for payment system development. There is a fundamental conflict between cooperation and competition in payment systems. Cooperation via common resources will make it possible to share costs. However, competition benefits will be lost.

- *Participation rules to inter-institution payment infrastructures* may limit competition. Participation in payment infrastructures is necessary in order to provide transfers to a wider group of service users. Participation rules can be exceptionally demanding thereby limiting the access to only a small number of institutions. Generally, this results in a tiered payment structure with a small number of core banks, often called clearing banks, which own the interbank payment system infrastructure, generally an ACH, and provide correspondent banking services to smaller banks and other institutions, which need access to interbank payment facilities. Generally, the tighter the inner group the more competition will be restricted. The total cost will also be higher in a tiered and hierarchical processing structure, due to the higher number of processing phases and points. In an infrastructure based on manual paper-processing and physical logistics a hierarchical structure has been efficient, but in an automated data processing environment based on modern telecommunication the processing structure needs to be re-engineered towards a network-based structure (compare the difference between surface mail and e-mail transportation structures).

- *Non-transparent pricing conventions and cross-subsidising* hinder the normal pricing mechanism's functioning. Because the payment is a mandatory complement to any sales transaction, the cost of paying is often included in the price of the good or service. This convention was used when cash payments were dominant and was transferred to other types of payment. The credit card companies have previously maintained a surcharge prohibition, stating merchants were not allowed to add the merchant card fees to the bills of their card paying customers. This prohibition has recently been forbidden by many authorities. Especially in card payment systems common inter-change fees can be found which impose a cost factor agreed upon among the service providers.[6] The inter-change fee is often decided upon in a cartel type of agreement, which therefore, often requires special permission by competition authorities. Only in the last decade have banks started to price their payment services separately and in many cases these services are still heavily cross-subsidised by other bank products, e.g. via interest rate margins.[7] The float income has also been a non-transparent pricing method used by banks, which has led to banks' interest in maintaining a slow payment process and adding (non-)value days in order to increase float income. Float-based pricing should be avoided as the float income depends on the transferred amount, while most payments costs are not value dependent. Central banks have also in some cases (cross-) subsidised their cash handling services, which has made cash more competitive compared to modern payment methods. The customers cannot see the true cost difference between different payment methods and they cannot therefore make an efficient choice.[8] Especially as cash payments have had a customer fee of zero, more efficient payments methods have had little price competition possibilities, without providing some kind of discounts to customers.[9] Merchants want to avoid negative customer feed back, which the addition of special payment type-related billing add-ons would often imply and are therefore content with including a non-transparent average add-on on their prices. Compared to the overall price of the goods and services the payment fees tend to be quite low. The general conclusion can therefore only be that the pricing mechanisms do not function particularly well in the payment industry.

- *Authority regulations* can also reduce development incentives and competition. Providing payment services have been completely or partly limited by regulation to banks, because of stability concerns. But authorities have also reduced competition possibilities, e.g. via pricing regulations.[10] Authorities seem to have a bias towards avoiding payment system risks through regulations compared to promoting competition and development. The risks are often more concrete and obvious to the public in the form of service problems or high one-time extra costs, while the constant small but very frequent extra costs of less efficient payment conventions are not that obvious. The benefits of change can be large, but consist of small improvements in millions of transactions of many users. The authorities' interest to act on efficiency concerns is therefore often lower than out of stability concerns.[11]

The overall conclusion to be drawn is that there are more obstacles and disincentives for development in the payment industry compared to other industries. This will delay developments in the payment systems and methods. It will also mean that authority involvement in order to reduce the disincentives could be necessary when higher development speed is desired.

Cooperation dimensions

Payment services are clearly network products.[12] The more users can be reached within the same system, the more value will it have for the users. In order for competing providers to reach the whole user community cooperation is required to establish at least the minimum standards for interoperability. These interoperable standards have in most cases in the past specified the payment infrastructure just for a given country. The objective within the EU/euro-area is to define a common infrastructure for the common currency area.

The international credit card companies have taken a somewhat different route as they have not established one interoperable infrastructure but instead established different parallel infrastructures and defined for these, common standards for user interfaces. The international card schemes have their own processing networks but the card standards, message standards, etc., are common so that the users (acquirers, issuers, merchants, etc.) can use the same equipment and software.

The global cooperation within SWIFT has established the interbank standards and conventions for cross-border payments. It is largely based on a correspondent banking convention and is therefore quite different from the national clearing centre based solutions.

The service provider cooperation can encompass the following areas:

• *Account and entity addresses.* In order to route payments efficiently the accounts, cards, service providers, processing centres, etc. have to have clearly defined addresses, e.g. account numbers and card numbers.

- *Service content and rules.* Each interoperable service needs a common service content and rules, which all service providers follow. The elaboration level can vary, but over time these 'service manuals' tend to become quite detailed. The rules will define the obligations between service providers and towards their customers, but also between the payee and payer. One important area is the finality of payments and the possibility of revoking/cancelling payments. The larger the common area of service content and rules are, the narrower will the area of bank specific extra features become.
- *Message standards* are needed between providers and their customers and directly between the providers, and between the providers and any clearing centre.
- *Telecommunications standards and common services* to ensure connectivity and low-cost contracts with TELCOs.
- *Security standards* to reduce the risk of criminal abuse of the system.
- *Centralised administration and processing facilities* to provide the required centralised services in a payment network.
- *Address/account number switching facility* to give the end-customer an easy way to switch service providers.
- *Back-up and service and availability requirements* to ensure that the components in the system are able to provide the overall service and availability objectives.
- *Service provider licensing requirements,* e.g. institutional status, risk grading, guarantees/collateral, in order to ensure system stability.
- *Interchange fees* for inter-provider transactions and cost distribution between payer and payee.
- *End-user fee calculation rules or fee structures* to make price comparisons possible.

Provider cooperation is generally helpful to reduce costs via standardisation and common processes. However, inter-provider cooperation can be very slow and therefore lock up systems in old and inefficient standards.[13] The larger the provider/user community, the more difficult it is, generally, to make changes to existing systems. There are many recent examples of this, e.g. the process of changing SWIFT standards and moving from magnetic-stripe cards to chip cards in VISA and Mastercard systems. However, modern technology makes conversion between data standards easier and more efficient. There are ready-made conversion systems with cross-referencing facilities. Because payment data are digital they can in principle be converted as easily to different formats as we are accustomed in different mobile telephone or video-systems. The main interoperability problems in standardisation will therefore be found in hardware-based solutions such as card and hardware based security standards.

Centralised payment processing entities will in most cases have a monopoly, e.g. interbank transactions need to be routed through the common

clearing house. Cooperating providers will seldom invest in parallel infrastructures. Due to lack of competition, there is a risk that the processing
monopoly will be less efficient and prone to maintain its current services
and service levels. A change process implies project risks and change-over
costs, for which extra incomes are needed, which can generally only be
obtained through tariff increases.

Account/address number switching facilities are quite rare in payment
systems. One general example can be found in Norway and a limited one
in Finland. The interest in these has increased lately due to the positive
competition effects found in the mobile phone industry, when phone
number switching was introduced. Account number switching will require
provider cooperation so that the transactions can be routed to the new
account holder based on the old account number. In a system with a centralised switching centre, this centre has to reroute all transactions. In a
decentralised forwarding-based system all transactions have to be sent to
the original account manager, which reroutes it to the current account
managing service provider. In a system based on a decentralised rerouting
register all service providers keep rerouting registers for most frequently
rerouted accounts in order to reduce the number or reforwarded transactions. Switching account numbers automatically implies extra processing
costs over the direct addressing method, which should be compared to
the costs for ordinary account number changes and the benefits of
increased competition. The necessary switching processing will increase
with the size of the market, which may be a problem on the global level or
even a currency area level. However, based on the good experiences in
some countries of mobile phone number switching, this might be an
important way of increasing competition and thereby increasing incentives for development.

The licensing or membership requirements have been found important in order to ensure stability in the payment systems. However, if these
are too demanding or biased, they become competition hurdles and
reduce the interest for developments. It is clearly a demanding task to
strike the right balance in this issue.

Interchange fees between service providers can mainly be found in
international credit card schemes, with separated issuing and acquiring
functions. These are typically also single direction systems, i.e. the payers
are private customers paying merchants and consumer to consumer payments, for example, are not possible. It is easier to segregate the market in
these kinds of systems and thereby use the interchange fee to move
incomes from one part of the market to the other (e.g. merchant acquirers to cardholder issuers). The network 'pressure' can be used to increase
merchant tariffs via interchange fees and thereby increase card company
profits. In bi-directional markets the segregation is more difficult. Interchange fees are rarely implemented in domestic bi-directional payment
systems. In domestic markets especially, payment flows tend to be rather

balanced, i.e. service providers are sending and receiving almost the same amount of payments, which results in an interchange fee total close to zero for most of the service providers. There is an ongoing debate about the benefits and drawbacks of interchange fees, which has it roots in credit card companies defending their current pricing policies. It is difficult to find a logical connection between development incentives and interchange fees in a bidirectional system, because of the zero-sum situation.

It has been customary in international payments to specify who shall pay the transfer costs, the payer or payee, by stating three cost sharing options via the codes OUR (= payer pays), BEN (= payee pays) or SHA (= costs are shared, based on the idea that both parties pay the costs of its service provider). The payer can in this kind of system select, case by case, the preferable cost sharing option. OUR and BEN also require some kind of interchange fee transferring system between the service providers. The SHA option requires only the transaction data to be transferred. Generally there is only one option available in domestic systems, which is the share SHA option and this is due to efficiency considerations. OUR and BEN will require additional functions to transfer the tariffs between the service providers. It will also reduce competition as the payer cannot negotiate with his service provider regarding the payee's tariffs or the interchange fee and the payee is in the same situation regarding the payer's tariffs. A system with only one main option available is also more efficient than a system with parallel options. Even if the infrastructure is only providing the share option, the payer and payee can agree on paying more or less in order to cover the tariff costs of the other party, when this is necessary. However, the need for this must be very low, because this is seldom observed in domestic payment conventions.

Payment services can be priced using transparent and some non-transparent factors. The traditional way of pricing payments has been value dates generating float to the service providers. Payments have also been heavily cross-subsidised in the past by other services, mainly deposit and credit interest margins. In addition to the most transparent transaction fee-based pricing, service providers tend to introduce different kinds of package pricing. The basic idea of these packages is to try to get the customer to concentrate his transactions and businesses on the same service provider by granting different kinds of package benefits, and to keep them there. The more complex and varying the pricing structure is for payment services, the more difficult it is for the customers to find out which offer is the most favourable. Within a common and straight-forward pricing structure the price competition would function better.

Possible authority actions

General objectives and alternatives

The central bank objectives in the area of payment systems have been written in the Treaty establishing the European Community and in the ESCB's statue as 'to promote the smooth operations of payment systems'. This has been interpreted as promoting both efficiency and stability/safety.

The Committee on Payment and Settlement Systems (CPSS) of the G-10 central banks state in their report on policy issues for efficiency and safety in retail payments[14] the following:

a   address legal and regulatory impediments to market development and innovation;
b   foster competitive market conditions and behaviours;
c   support the development of effective standards and infrastructure arrangements;
d   provide central bank services in the manner most effective for the particular market.

The CPSS has also established Core Principles for systemically important payment systems.[15] These have been amended by the Eurosystem for important retail payment systems by removing those requirements, which are applicable to large value payment systems only. The Core Principles set out the public policy objectives for safety and efficiency in ten principles covering the legal basis, financial risks, settlement procedures, security and operational liability, efficiency for the economy and end-users, governance and participation rules.

These objectives and policies are in line with the general development objectives described earlier, although the development and efficiency requirements are in most cases more general than the requirement regarding stability.

Many authorities have an interest in payment systems. Central banks are traditionally heavily involved through oversight and operations. Laws governing payment systems are mainly prepared by ministries. Financial supervisors supervise the payment services of credit institutes and often also financial infrastructures like clearing houses, etc. Consumer protection authorities check consumer issues in payment services. Competition authorities control fair trading in the payment industry. Police and security forces are involved in reducing criminal activities in payments. Cooperation between authorities is necessary. International cooperation has to increase, because payment networks need to cover the whole world in the same way as telephone networks. Payment systems will only be efficient if we can create truly global standards and processing conventions.

Authorities have a variety of tools for advancing development in the desired direction. These can be categorised into the following groups:[16]

- operational involvement,
- subsidisation,
- research and studies,
- recommendations and moral suasion,
- regulations
- monitoring and control.

Action by the authorities is, in general, called for when there is a market failure. This is a situation when the market will not provide a sufficiently efficient or stable payment service. An authority intervention is needed in order to support developments. The cause for the market failure can vary. The general market conditions can be such that the private service providers do not have sufficient incentives to invest in developments. Abuse of monopoly or dominant market position can delay developments. Short-sighted security solutions can increase future risks. Cooperation problems can delay use of new technology. Outdated regulations can also hamper developments and authorities also have to review their own policies to support development. The system structures and regulations should preferably be such that they increase the incentives for development and keep development hurdles low.

Authorities will always face the problem of adjusting their interventions according to the need of the situation. This can in most cases only be an issue of judgement, which is easy to criticise up front and even easier after an unsuccessful intervention. In development issues, the costs of change are often imminent, while the benefits are often spread over many years, among many parties/users, and are less easy to quantify to their full extent.

Operational involvement

Central banks have a tradition of performing settlement services for retail payments and also in some cases clearing house functions. In some cases central banks also provide retail payment services to government agencies and the general public. Central banks generally constitute the highest level in the liquidity hierarchy. National central banks have a monopoly position in central bank money settlement. Central bank money has been seen as the safest way to conduct interbank settlement, which is supported by the liquidity provision for intra and inter-day purposes together with emergency liquidity assistance in special situations.

In clearing house service and payment processing central banks sometimes compete with private systems and sometimes they can even have a monopoly in interbank payment processing. However, in most cases central banks have a very minor role in retail payment processing and focus on providing settlement services for private retail payment systems and other ancillary payment systems.

In settlement operations central banks have a key role in deciding which institutions are eligible for central bank settlement. If there are unjustifiably strict requirements, it will deepen the liquidity hierarchy and decrease the competition among service providers by limiting the number of direct central bank counterparties.[17] In order to support competition, openness of systems and interoperability between systems, a large number of service providers should have access to central bank money for settlement. In order to be able to use the settlement facilities the service providers would also need liquidity facilities at least for intraday purposes, but preferably also for overnight purposes in order to square the daily payment positions. This leads to the question, which institutions are entitled to the lender-of-last-resort or emergency liquidity facilities of central banks? The overnight liquidity facilities have an impact on the implementation on the monetary policy and thereby on which institutions are monetary policy counterparties. Central banks have been restrictive regarding access to monetary policy instruments and emergency liquidity facilities and are generally allowing access only for credit institutions. Infrastructural institutions, e.g. clearing houses, can have settlement accounts with central banks but are seldom entitled to overnight services. If non-banks have no access to central banks settlement facilities, this will to some extent reduce their competitiveness with credit institutions. Opening the payment system market for non-bank competition is a political issue with several dimensions.

Central banks create an extra layer in clearing and payment processing. Central banks are independent from service providers, but the service providers have the good and direct contacts to the markets and a clearer view on development needs than the central banks with limited market contacts. The service providers also need to get central bank support for interbank system changes in central bank systems, while in a privately operated clearing house changes are decided upon among the owners/providers community. Compared to the bilateral processing structure, central bank processing will introduce an extra processing phase between the service providers in the same way as with a private clearing house. Central bank clearing therefore automatically introduces a centralised structure. In a bilateral structure with centralised functions the central bank could be the network administrator, if the service providers prefer a public instead of a private solution.

The central bank clearing and processing operations probably tend to have a bias towards safety and stability over efficiency. This is due to the public setup. If there were malfunctions and safety problems, private service providers, the newspapers and the general public would all blame the public authority for poorly managed services. This results in political pressures to avoid such problems and therefore easily in over-investment compared to a private competitive solution. The development speed would probably also be slower due to the same bias, because unsuccessful investments will be more heavily criticised than delayed investments. Public payment operations, especially in a monopoly situation, have a shortage of efficiency incentives as the costs, which are not subsidised, will have to be accepted by the other service providers and carried on to end-users, because there are no alternatives available and no possibility for the other service providers to affect the costs or development decisions of the central bank(s) directly.

When one compares a public monopoly and a private monopoly clearing house the differences are not that big. The private clearing houses have a closer relation to the providers and their objectives as private clearing houses are most often owned and governed by service providers. The public clearing house can have a closer relation to the objectives of the end-users based on its public tasks. Although clearing houses are in most cases in a monopoly position there are also countries (e.g. the USA) with public and private systems in competition with each other. There are also clearing houses that are jointly owned by private and public entities.

Subsidisation

Subsidisation of public payment systems will crowd out competing private systems and hence reduce the competition and efficiency in the market. Subsidisation could be used to promote developments in order to overcome the chicken-or-egg situation for new solutions. For example, a new security or identification solution could be government supported to acquire enough initial interest. However, subsidisation generally distorts the market so much, that it is not justified. By subsidising one security solution, the possibilities for other more efficient ones to be introduced will be reduced or delayed.

Subsidising cash operations will delay the change-over to account-based payments. This issue has recently got some more attention. The monetary income, i.e. seignorage for notes and coins, is sufficiently large that it covers the production and distribution costs. However, this is mostly due to the high-value notes, normally not used for payment purposes. The distribution costs for coins and small value notes are higher than their seignorage income to the central bank. In order to cover the distribution costs of low-value denominations and reduce cross-subsidisation from high-value notes some increase in central bank cash handling tariffs would be needed.

Research and studies

Payment systems are a neglected area of academic research. Central banks have a tradition of payment system studies and research. Basic studies and research are necessary to find out the current stability and efficiency situation and to analyse the improvement possibilities. It is also the basis for recommendations and regulations.

It would be important to study pricing and cost issues in payment systems and collect the necessary background information. Only a few central banks (e.g. Norway) are currently collecting detailed price and cost information of payment methods.[18]

Recommendations and moral suasion

Different kinds of recommendations and lists of best practices are used by authorities to guide the market towards preferred processes and practices.[19] These can, together with moral suasion, be a very practical way towards improved stability and efficiency. Recommendations are more easily changed and adapted to new situations than strict regulations. Recommendations can also be implemented in a more flexible way according to the needs in a given market or for a given service type. Recommendations are efficient in markets with good discipline and self-regulation among service providers. However, the flexible implementation of recommendations can also be a drawback in cases where strict interoperable standards are required.

Regulations

Payment systems will require basic laws and regulations as any other business areas with large economic impact. In Europe the EU Commission has taken, as a special task, to harmonise the legislation for payment systems via, e.g. the directive for cross-border payments, the directive for settlement finality, the directive for e-money institutions and the regulation for payments. Currently a special legal framework for payment services is under preparation.[20]

A large part of the payment services are provided by banks and other credit institutions, due to historical and regulatory reasons, and are thereby governed by the detailed banking regulation requirements. This limits the competition in payment services and the possibility for new entrants. However, this is often seen as a political necessity, in order to ensure high-enough stability in payment systems. Capital demands and service provision restrictions for credit institutions lead to higher fixed costs, which require high volumes in the low-margin payment services in order to reach profitability. In order to increase competition and thereby promote efficiency and development of innovative payment services, the EU Commission and some EU member states (especially the Nordic countries) have proposed and/or implemented relaxed regulations for small scale service providers, like e-money institutions and merchants interested in providing payment services along side other business areas. Currently the regulations regarding 'eligible' payment service providers seem to be somewhat unclear and under discussion. For example, the traditional traveller's cheque companies operate generally without licences, while chip card-based e-money schemes need special licences in the EU area. However, national waivers and national variation can exist. The definition of 'eligible' payment service providers needs to be clarified.

The general warnings concerning regulation are both the risk of over and under regulation together with the need to maintain a level playing field among providers and avoid regulatory arbitrage. Regulations need also to be updated overtime, when the market situation changes. For example most cheque regulations from the paper processing era need to be updated in order for the industry to be able to employ the new electronic possibilities.

Monitoring and control

Authorities need to monitor the market in all situations, but regulations require strict controls in order to check that the service providers follow the regulations. The controlling costs should be seen as part of the overall costs for payment services. A heavy regulatory framework and control organisation will increase the costs of the payment infrastructure and an 'optimal' balance should be found in order to reduce the overall costs.

Actions for enhancing developments

Due to the lack of development incentives authorities could use their different tools to enhance payment system developments. The use of these tools should always be carefully assessed, i.e. will positive developments be enhanced and can the negative effects be avoided or limited. In Table 11.1 some concrete authority actions are proposed and assessed in relation to their ability to enhance development incentives in payment systems.

The crucial question is to what extent authorities' regulatory interventions are needed or will the market developments by themselves go in the preferred direction. Is there a clear market failure, which could be bypassed via authority involvement?

Authorities have two general options: increase competition (by decreasing the hurdles for new entrants and/or establishing a level playing field among current providers) or direct interventions. Direct interventions need to be carefully planned and justified. In this area international authority cooperation would be needed, because the costs for payment service developments can increase considerably if authorities in major markets go first in different directions and a harmonisation process is started only after that.

Authority actions should be carefully considered because on most points there are hazards of overregulation. It is generally advisable

Table 11.1 Possible actions for enhancing payment system developments

Action	Positive effects	Negative effects to avoid
Common open account number standard and space	All accounts can be addressed using on numbering standard. National addressing barriers will disappear.	Too 'closed' numbering system, which does not allow for expansion over time.
Common payment reference (payment identification) number	Will make it possible for payees to reconcile their receivables file automatically.	
Common payment audit trail identifier among service providers and in ACHs	Makes it possible to identify payments through their processing path and different processing phases.	Too 'closed' numbering system, which does not allow for expansion over time.
Common clearly defined message standards for inter-provider messages	Same message formats and processing investments can be used for different connections.	Rigid standards, which are difficult to develop when needed.
Common clearly defined customer-to-provider message standards	Customers can more easily switch service providers. Software houses can build payment applications with automated provider interfaces for a wider market.	Rigid standards, which are difficult to develop when needed.
Portable account numbers/addresses	Makes it possible for customers to switch providers more easily. Increases competition.	Too expensive technical solutions. Too short a migration time.
Decrease the number of float and valuation days to zero	Banks will have less interest in delaying payments in a system without float income.	Possibility to circumvent the basic rules.
Generally same day delivery	Providing service speed according to technical possibilities. Due date, payment date and delivery date will coincide.	Too short a migration time.

continued

Table 11.1 Continued

Action	Positive effects	Negative effects to avoid
Payments transferred in full amount	Receiver can reconcile the accounting more easily, when all payments are recorded in full without service provider deductions. Service fees will be transparent in separate invoices (for a time period), which is also clearer as a separate booking entry.	Parallel conventions, which makes it difficult to recognise which have been and/or should have been used.
The shared (SHA) option for tariffs, i.e. no interchange fees between service providers	The customers negotiate with their service providers about their tariffs and service contents. Enhances competition.	Parallel conventions (OUR and/or BEN) as this will increase overall costs considerably.
Limitations on services to be included in payment service package fees	Less cross-subsidisation and more competition as customers can choose and compare prices per each service type and switch providers for separate service entities.	Too tight service definitions, which hinder establishing efficient packet pricing for services with direct relationships.
Common transparent and cost-based pricing conventions	Competition increases as customers can more easily compare offers of different providers and compare the costs of different payment methods/instruments.	Direct price regulations.
Free right to surcharge payment method costs	Payees will be able to state different prices depending on the payer's choice of payment method reflecting the costs associated with a given payment method.	An implementation which would discriminate against customer groups and/or make price comparisons, etc. difficult.
Open systems, i.e. free access possibility	Increases competition as all service providers are given access based on equal footing.	Access criteria, which on a general level are 'equal', but imply relatively higher costs for smaller providers or newcomers.

continued

Table 11.1 Continued

Action	Positive effects	Negative effects to avoid
Flat processing hierarchy	Utilise the possibility of modern technology to provide direct access to large communities, which increase competition, compared to tied structures.	
Universal service obligation (providers' obligation to process transactions to/from any other provider in the network)	Customers can send payments from their provider to anyone using another provider and receive payments from any payer using any sending provider.	
Open central bank settlement services	All payment service providers can use central bank account for interbank settlement, which increases competition.	
Standardised central bank settlement services	Multi-country providers can use the settlement services in many countries without extra investments.	Too rigid development of settlement services.
Common interoperable security standards	Interoperability among service providers, which enhance competition and software/hardware developments.	Too rigid development of security features.
Common interoperable customer identification standards	Interoperable card security standards and e-banking identification software/hardware solutions.	Too rigid development of security features.

to start with less powerful authority measures (e.g. public studies and recommendations) and escalate the measures step-by-step, if positive market reactions have not emerged as a result of the less powerful measures.

Conclusions

Compared with other network services, payment systems have not employed new technological solutions and have not introduced international standards and addressing elements to the same extent. The user of payment services would benefit considerably from rapid developments towards harmonised and standardised global payment conventions in the form of more rapid and low-cost processing with efficient user-interfaces in a secure and stable environment. Technically payments could be made as easy as sending an e-mail or mobile text message.

Market developments lack incentives for radical changes at the international level although efficient national solutions exist. This is partly due to special market conditions for payments in which the transaction volumes are given by payers' budgets and are due to the small cross-border volumes. However, standardised international solutions would bring benefits to all users.

Most authorities have only a national responsibility. International cooperation between authorities on payments has increased and there may be a possibility for reaching agreement on the major markets. This could trigger the necessary developments. Authority involvement seems to be needed to start the progress towards the next technology level of payment systems.

Notes

1 The views expressed are those of the author and do not necessarily reflect the views of the Bank of Finland.
2 This has been a special concern for the Eurosystem and the EU Commission when trying to improve and speed up cross-border payments in the EU area. ECB have published special reports (e.g. ECB, 1999, 2000, 2001a, 2002, 2003, 2004) and the EU Commission has issued communications (e.g. EU Commission, 2000, 2003b) and made cross-border payment delivery-time and cost studies (e.g. EU Commission, 2001). The same kind of concerns are also voiced in the UK especially after the Cruickshank report on competition in UK banking (HMSO, 2000) and in the OFT report on payment systems (OFT, 2003).
3 A more detailed analysis of the reference code and its benefits can be found in Leinonen (2000).
4 EU Commission (2003a).
5 See, for example, Ganguly and Milne (2001).
6 There is a literature defending and trying to establish an optimal inter-change fee to increase development incentives, see, e.g. Rochet and Tirole (2002), Schmalensee (2002) and Wright (2001). The basic assumption in these studies is that there is a two-sided market for the payment services, and card customer side and the merchant side. The merchant will not be able to pass on the interchange fee and the merchant fee to the card customers, but has to include the costs in the average price of the goods and services. However, this assumption distorts the price mechanism. If the paying card customers could see the total costs, which they anyhow have to pay, they would be able to make an efficient choice of payment method. In the interchange fee and surcharge prohibition case they cannot make an efficient choice.
7 The lack of competition in the UK payment systems have been pointed out by the Cruickshank Report (HMSO, 2000) and the payment area has been further studies by the OFT (OFT, 2003).

8 For example, one of the main reasons for the rapid change-over from cheques to debit cards, seen in some countries (e.g. Finland and Norway), has, in addition to establishing the new competing debit card service form, been a competitive pricing scheme, i.e. cheques have been priced clearly higher than debit card services.

9 At one time petrol stations favoured card-based self-service customers in order to increase card-based sales compared to cash sales.

10 Examples of this are the zero-discount rule on cheques in the US and the zero-interest rule on cheque accounts together with the zero-pricing rule on cheques in France.

11 See Biltoft (2001: 142).

12 See Kemppainen (2003) for analysis and overview of the network characteristics, cooperation requirements and competition in payment networks.

13 McAndrews (1995) and Hill (2000) discuss the benefits of common standards, open access and switching costs.

14 See BIS (2003a).

15 See BIS (2001, 2003b).

16 BIS (2001) defines following categories of oversight tools: collect information, analyse information and take action. Within the take action group are subcategories: publicise the objectives of oversight, persuade payment system operators to make changes to rules and procedures, make provision of central bank settlement dependent on relevant conditions and establish formal agreements with payment system operators.

17 For example, OFT has in its report 2003 highlighted the issue of indirect and direct participation in UK systems and the implications on competition among service providers. The Governor of Bank of England, Mervin King, announced that the need for a wider participation in CHAPS will be explored (King, 2004).

18 BIS (2003a) and van Hove (2004) are clearly supporting central bank studies on this topic.

19 See, for instance, BIS (2001) and ECB (1999, 2004).

20 The communication regarding the new legal framework (EU Commission, 2003b) covers a very wide area of possible regulatory issues, e.g. the right to provide payment services, information requirements, non-resident accounts in the EU area, value dates, portability (switching) of bank account numbers, evaluation of the security of payment instruments and components, alternative dispute resolution mechanisms, revocability of a payment order, non-execution or defective execution of a payment, obligations and liabilities related to unauthorised transactions, tariff sharing alternatives, execution times, harmonisation of direct debiting, removing barriers for cash circulation, data protection and security for payment networks. However, many of these issues will probably be outside the directive to be proposed and only the most important one will be included in the first phase.

References

Biltoft, K. (2001) 'The objectives of oversight – What are they?', *E-payment and Payment Systems Review*, London, Central Banking Publishing.

BIS (2001) *Core Principles for Systemically Important Payment Systems*, Basel, Committee on Payment and Settlement Systems, January.

BIS (2003a) *Policy Issues for Central Banks in Retail Payment Systems*, Basel, Committee on Payment and Settlement Systems, March.

BIS (2003b) *The Role of Central Bank Money in Payment Systems*, Basel, Committee on Payment and Settlement Systems, August.

BIS (2004) Red book, *Statistics on Payment and Settlement Systems in Selected Counties*, Basel, Committee on Payment and Settlement Systems, March.

ECB (1999) *Improving Cross-border Retail Payment Services – The Eurosystem's View*, Frankfurt, European Central Bank, September.

ECB (2000) *Improving Cross-border Retail Payment Services – Progress Report*, Frankfurt, European Central Bank, September.

ECB (2001a) *Towards an Integrated Infrastructure for Credit Transfers in Euro*, Frankfurt, European Central Bank, November.

ECB (2001b) Blue Book, *Payment and Securities Settlement Systems in the European Union*, Frankfurt, European Central Bank, June.

ECB (2002) Issues Paper *E-payments in Europe – The Eurosystem's Perspective*, Frankfurt, European Central Bank, September.

ECB (2003) *Towards a Single Euro Payments Area – Progress Report*, Frankfurt, European Central Bank, June.

ECB (2004) *Towards a Single Euro Payments Area – Third Progress Report*, Frankfurt, European Central Bank, December.

EU Commission (2000) Communication from the Commission to the Council and the European Parliament, *Retail Payments in the Internal Market*, Brussels, January.

EU Commission (2001) *Study on the Verification of a Common and Coherent Application of Directive 97/5/EC on Cross-Border Credit Transfers in the 15 Member States – Transfer Exercise*, (Price study), Brussels.

EU Commission (2003a) *EU Blueprint on Mobile Payments*, (draft)Brussels, May.

EU Commission (2003b) *Communication ... concerning a New Legal Framework for Payments in the Internal Market*, Brussels, December.

Ganguly, B. and Milne, A. (2001) 'Retail payment systems in the UK: is there a problem of lack of competition?', *E-payment and Payment Systems Review*, London, Central Banking Publishing.

Hill, B. (2000) 'Common message standards for electronic commerce in wholesale financial markets', *Bank of England Quarterly Bulletin*, August.

HMSO (2000) Cruickshank Report, *Competition in UK Banking*, March.

van Hove, L. (2004) 'Cost-based pricing of payment instruments: the state of the debate', *De Economist* 152(1) (March): 79–100.

Kemppainen, K. (2003) 'Competition and regulation in European retail payment systems', Bank of Finland Discussion Paper, no. 16/2003, June.

King, M. (2004) Speech at the Lord Mayor's Banquet for Bankers and Merchants of the City of London at the Mansion House, 16 June.

Leinonen, H. (2000) 'Re-engineering payment systems for the E-world', Bank of Finland Discussion Paper, no. 17/2000.

Leinonen, H., Lumiala, V.-M. and Sarlin, R. (2002) 'Settlement in modern network-based payment infrastructures – description and prototype of the E-settlement model', Bank of Finland Discussion Paper, no. 23/2002.

McAndrews, J. (1995) 'Antitrust issues in payment systems: bottlenecks, access and essential facilities', *Federal Reserve Bank of Philadelphia Business Review*, September/October.

Office of Fair Trading (OFT) (2003) *UK Payment Systems – An OFT Market Study on Clearing Systems and Review of Plastic Card Networks*, London, Office of Fair Trading, May.

Rochet, J.-C. and Tirole, J. (2002) 'Cooperation among competitors: some economics of payment card associations', *RAND Journal of Economics* 33(4) (Winter): 549–70.

Schmalensee, R. (2002) 'Payment systems and interchange fees', *Journal of Industrial Economics* 50: 103–22.

Wright, J. (2001) 'The determinants of optimal interchange fees in payment systems', mimeo University of Auckland, Auckland, NZ, December.

COMMENT

Thorvald Grung Moe

This is a far-reaching chapter dealing with many important payment policy issues:

- Which objectives and factors influence payment system developments today?
- What is the right balance between cooperation and competition in payment system developments?
- What is the 'optimal' payment system structure?
- Which role should the authorities take (especially central banks)?
- Is regulatory intervention needed?

The author is clearly impatient with the current state of affairs. The need for, and benefits of, international payment standards are obvious, but the development speed is slow (some would say 'standing still'). Why is it so difficult to make international payments when we can so easily use our mobile phones worldwide? Leinonen suggests 'the market developments lack incentives for radical changes on the international level' and 'authority involvement seems to be needed'.

In the following, I will limit my comments to three policy issues that are addressed in the paper:

- the need for standardisation;
- access to central banks' accounts;
- authorities' objective function.

The author argues that 'payments could be made as easily as sending an e-mail or mobile text message'. Payment networks should cover the whole world in the same way as telephone networks. One way of creating such a unified payment system could be to use the common account numbers already in place for credit card systems. This is clearly an attractive vision and I really look forward to the day it materialises. Why wait, let's just do it! However, there may be good reasons why the market has not already converged on this standard. And the case for market failure is to me not yet quite clear. In my view, these issues are far from just technical. We also need some input from the 'sociology of money' to understand the issues involved in the fight for market shares, market power, etc.

In order to enhance competition, openness of payment systems and interoperability between systems, the author would also like to see a large number of service providers with access to central bank money for settlement. There seems to be a case for a more level playing field among service providers, specifically by opening up the payment system field to non-bank providers. Leinonen is aware that this is not an altogether easy issue. He notes that 'opening the payment system market for non-bank competition is a political issue with several dimensions', for example 'which institutions are entitled to lender of last resort or emergency liquidity facilities of central banks'.

Without taking a firm stand on the issue, I would just like to sketch three different scenarios, all with costs and benefits. First, you could allow new payment system providers into the central bank system if they posted sufficient cash up-front. This would involve considerable 'deadweight cost' to society, but would eliminate the need for supervision of these new entrants. This would be a radical departure from today's system and probably not very realistic, consider the extensive discussion about e-money providers in the EU. Second, non-banks could be allowed into the central bank's settlement system, provided they were properly supervised, i.e. by extending the supervisory reach of the FSA. This would in a sense be similar to labelling the new service providers 'quasi-banks'. This would be a trivial solution if the number of providers remained small, but a costly one if the number became large. Finally, a completely different solution would be to avoid central bank settlement altogether and encourage competing payment systems based on local netting. Some have even argued that such local systems will proliferate in the future (Cohen, 2003). In my view, these are all interesting options which pose interesting and challenging policy issues for central bankers. But none of them are trivial and they all show that the question of opening up central bank accounts to non-bank payment system providers is not just a technical issue!

This leads me to a third issue that I wanted to address, the authorities' objective function. To me, it is not at all clear which role the key authorities want to play in the development of (retail) payment systems or what their objectives really are. Leinonen refers in the chapter to recent payment system publications by the BIS and the ECB, where their role in promoting efficiency and stability is stated. However, most of these publications are rather general in their recommendations and give little guidance concerning the required trade-offs between the key objectives. Leinonen notes that 'the development and efficiency requirements are in most cases more general than the requirement regarding stability'. I would add that none are treated very specifically, which leaves us in the dark as to what specifically the authorities are trying to achieve:

- Do they want to increase the role of 'bank account money' in payments?
- Do they want to promote their own currency (i.e. discourage 'dollarisation')?
- Do they want to promote the use of debit card payments (versus credit cards)?
- Do they prefer one centralised payment infrastructure (i.e. ACH)?
- Do they prefer to maintain a bank-based payment system (discussed above)?

If Leinonen's vision of a smooth, unified international payment system operating in real time is to materialise, I would suggest that we need to pay more attention to some of these concrete issues. We also need to recognise the complexities involved, especially the link between regulatory issues in other fields (e.g. banking regulation) and payment system issues. And finally, we need to recognise that these issues are not just technical or economic, but also political and sociological. That should encourage us to engage in discussions with other scholars dealing with these same, important issues. Then, perhaps the vision will come through.

Reference

Cohen, B.J. (2003) *The Future of Money*, Princeton: Princeton University Press.

12 Competition and the rationalization of European securities clearing and settlement

Alistair Milne[1]

Introduction: reducing the barriers to a single market in securities settlement

The European securities industry, national governments, the European Central Bank and the European Commission all seek to establish a single market for the issuance and trade of financial securities across the European Union (EU). This is a key part of the development of an effective single European-wide securities market. This chapter examines the industrial organization of securities clearing and settlement, arguing that competitive forces can achieve the desired rationalization and efficiency improvements in European securities clearing and settlement, provided that steps are taken to ensure fair access to the underlying 'book entry' function of the central securities depositories and competing custodian banks. It argues that fair access may require accounting separation and some form of access pricing.

The European Commission has recently released a second communication on the future development of clearing and settlement in the EU (EU Commission, 2004), following up an earlier policy document (EU Commission, 2002) and following extensive discussion with industry and other interested parties. This communication outlines the policy measures they propose taking to promote the efficiency and safety of cross-border securities clearing and settlement within the EU. These policy proposals reflect what is in some key respects a very similar view of the appropriate role for public policy in European Clearing and Settlement as those put forward in the present chapter.[2]

The plans of the Commission are as follows:

- As a priority, to set up an advisory group of practitioners from the industry and expert groups on tax and on legal issues.[3] These three groups will seek ways to overcome barriers to cross-border settlement, through convergence of industry practice, law and taxation.
- The introduction of a 'framework' directive (this is a framework directive in the sense of Lamfalussy, many specific aspects will subsequently

be introduced through comitology by the Committee of European Securities Regulators (CES-R)), ensuring the freedom to provide clearing and settlement services throughout the EU. This directive should, for example, lead to the removal of current rules in a number of European equities exchanges, requiring trades to be settled through affiliated local central securities depositories. The directive will also cover the governance of clearing and settlement infrastructure.

•   The Commission will (presumably this will involve both the Director-General (DG) single market and DG competition), together with national competition authorities, seek to ensure the effective application of competition law to clearing and settlement, in particular to deal with any barriers to access services, or any discriminatory pricing of settlement services.

These policies have been developed in response to issues identified in the two reports of The Giovannini Group (2001, 2003), and in particular the need to overcome several barriers to cross-border securities settlement. Adapting the analysis provided in the November 2001 report of The Giovannini Group, these barriers can be placed in five different categories:[4]

1   national and proprietary differences in technical standards and procedure for the interface between various security settlement and custodian systems;[5]
2   limitations on investors choice of preferred supplier of different aspects of clearing and settlement services;
3   national differences in the settlement periods, operating hours, and settlement deadlines;
4   differences in the arrangements for the collection of taxes (withholding taxes, capital gains taxes and stamp-duties) and the granting of tax relief;
5   differences in the legal treatment of securities pledges and bilateral netting.

These five types of barriers considerably increase the costs of cross-border securities transactions, requiring brokers, settlement service providers and custodians to maintain multiple interfaces for dealing with several national settlement systems, frustrate their desire to centralize and automate clearing and settlement or other security operations, and limit the potential to exploit economies of scale in both netting and settlement. This is one of the principal reasons why, even within the euro area, European security markets continue to be fragmented along national lines, reducing liquidity and increasing the margin between investor returns and cost of finance to issuers.

Even more costly barriers inhibit the development of a single European market in other financial services, such as corporate banking, insurance, pensions and retail savings and investment products. The Lamfalussy report (Lamfalussy *et al.*, 2001) established a new process for the creation and operation of European directives for securities markets, in order to facilitate the harmonization of standards, practices, regulation and taxation of financial services across the EU (the new framework directive on clearing and settlement will take advantage of these 'Lamfalussy procedures'), with the co-legislation (level 1) defining high level principles and details of rules and implementation at European and national levels, and enforcement of the directives applied by lower level committees (levels 2 to level 4).[6] While the Lamfalussy arrangements were originally designed for securities market regulation, they are now to be applied to regulation of all financial services. But even with the use of such fast track arrangements, the process of creating a single market in financial services through harmonization remains slow and may still potentially be halted entirely by political obstacles.

Debates about the reduction of these barriers to trade in financial services in the European marketplace pay scant attention to alternatives to harmonization – especially, to the direct use of competition as a means of breaking down barriers to trade. The view adopted in the present chapter is that competition can best play this role when 'authorization' allows cross-border supply of financial services without a preceding minimum harmonization of national tax and regulatory regimes. Such authorization creates competitive pressure for convergence of standards and market practice. It also creates opportunities for regulatory and tax 'arbitrage' that provide a powerful incentive for voluntary convergence of national regimes of tax and financial regulation, since without such convergence providers of financial services will shift their activities to nations with less costly regimes. Competition can therefore be used to complement harmonization and more swiftly establish cross-border markets. This chapter argues that many of the Giovannini barriers are best addressed by such a policy, allowing authorization for cross border competition in securities settlement, without necessarily requiring full harmonization of tax, legal or other arrangements.

The limits of authorization are reached, if there are natural or other monopolies that prevent the free delivery of financial services throughout the union. Merton (2001) has drawn an apt analogy, liking the creation of a single market for financial services in Europe to a dialogue between two tribes about creating a single system for the supply of water. One tribe insists that everyone harmonize via an agreement to use piping with a square cross-section, the other tribe insist that everyone harmonize by using piping with a round cross-section. But the harmonization is not needed. All that is required is an appropriate connection that allows square pipes to be joined to round to support the flow of water across the border between the two tribes. In this case of security settlement, this chapter will argue, a policy of authorization can be made effective by supplementing it with appropriate access and access price regulation, thus connecting the round and square pipes of different European national settlement systems.

The use of authorization as an alternative to harmonization for promoting cross-border trade in financial services is not an entirely new idea. It is exemplified by the 'passport' principle, allowing financial firms to branch freely across EU borders while governed by their own home national tax regime and financial regulations. This approach has been successful in some cases, for example offering European banks a straightforward mechanism for establishing branches in the major European centres for international banking (London and Luxembourg); but apart from these exceptions financial services firms have made relatively little use of the passporting principle to deliver financial services across the EU. This indicates that there are continuing barriers that prevent pan-European distribution of most financial services.

A preference for competition over harmonization is also sometimes expressed in recent reports. The November 2001 report of The Giovannini Group (2001: 50), for example, makes the suggestion that 'much of the difficulty associated with the taxation of cross-border securities holdings could be eliminated by allowing investors the freedom to choose the preferred location of their securities'. This particular suggestion faces legal and institutional problems that are not fully discussed by the report. But the general point remains, that competition may often be preferable to harmonization as a means of addressing the barriers to trade within the EU.

Historically (see Appendix) no major change in infrastructural arrangements for securities markets has taken place without a leading role from regulatory authorities, for example, the part played by the US Congress and the Securities and Exchange Commission (SEC) in the creation of the Depository Trust Clearing Corporation (DTCC) or the role of the Bank of England in supporting the creation of CREST. This might suggest that market forces are incapable of achieving significant structural change and that the authorities must impose some appropriate but achievable structure on European securities settlement. But the example of the telecommunications industry in Europe provides an example of an industry where structural change can be achieved by more targeted regulatory intervention. The rapid spread of mobile telephony and dramatic reductions in the charges levied by incumbent fixed line operators, have been supported by regulations targeted at access to key competitive bottlenecks such as the termination of mobile calls (only one network is able to locate and connect to a particular mobile phone) or the 'local fixed line loop' (the physical connection from the local exchange to individual dwelling or workplace).

This chapter argues that there is a similar and crucial competitive bottleneck in the book-entry function of central securities depositories and custodians (i.e. the recording and transfer of share-ownership). It is because of this bottleneck that cross-border competition in supply of these basic depository functions is ineffective. But there are no other market failures restricting the cross-border provision of any other securities and settlement services. The implication is that policy efforts to reduce the costs of cross-border clearing and settlement and promote structural change can be concentrated on the ensuring access and non-discriminatory pricing of this basic book transfer function. The job of removing all other barriers can be left largely to competitive forces. With access regulation of book-entry, the tortuous process of harmonizing differing national securities laws or taxation then requires relatively little attention. Competitive pressures will lead industry to rationalize both industry structure and industry practices and standards. It is unnecessary to have compulsory horizontal merger of settlement activities nor to prohibit vertical ownership of settlement providers by securities exchanges. Once the book entry function is opened to competition, then, aside from some other co-operative work on the establishment of common communication standards, competitive forces can be left alone to determine an appropriate structure and organization of the industry.

The argument is developed as follows. We begin by describing the operation and (in the Appendix) historical development of securities clearing and settlement. We go on to discuss the industrial organization of the industry, examining the extent to which there are network complementarities in clearing and settlement, drawing comparison with the regulation of utilities such as telecoms, and showing how access price regulation can be used to open the market to potential competition. We also consider a key difference between securities settlement and these other 'network monopolies', the fact that in the case of securities settlement the competitive advantage stems from a fundamental *liquidity externality*. As a result it is possible (where there is sufficient liquidity) for there to be two or more providers of book entry settlement; but even in this case there is still a need for access regulation to ensure an efficient market outcome.

The chapter then summarizes some of the current debates about rationalization of European securities settlement, especially studies of costs and debates between proponents of horizontal integration and those who would allow continued vertical links between trading platforms and clearing and settlement services, and considers the implications of introducing access regulation of book entry. We finally consider, briefly, some practical issues before concluding with a discussion of the implications for the securities industry and for other financial services.

The operation and historical development of securities clearing and settlement

This section describes the process of clearing and settlement, identifying the functions of the several different institutions involved at each stage of the process and the major sources of costs. An Appendix reviews the historical development of securities processing.

Clearing and settlement operations

Post-trade processing of domestic security trades

The outcome of post-trade clearing and settlement is a transfer of ownership of securities against a cash payment according to the terms of the original trade. But several steps are required to achieve this end, a number of different institutions are involved, and there are a variety of associated costs.

Six steps of a securities trade can be identified, as follows:

Order. The investor (typically an asset manager) instructs the broker to execute the trade.

Execution via some trading system. This could be through an exchange but nowadays a large number of trades are executed via alternative trading systems such as electronic networks.

Matching. The brokers on each side of the trade confirm the various details of the trade (security, quantity, price, arrangements for settlement etc.); and obtain positive confirmation from the investor (referred to as affirmation) that the trade complies with the original order.

Netting. A considerable reduction in the value and volume of securities trades for settlement can be achieved, by netting off-setting cash and security flows. The maximum potential for netting is when there is a single central counter-party so that all flows can be reduced to a single daily payment and single net amount due for each security.

Clearing. The positioning of securities and the arrangement of payment prior to settlement (the term clearing often also covers matching and netting, but this more restrictive usage is convenient).

Settlement. The final transfer of ownership of securities and corresponding cash payments.

These steps take place sequentially. In most major financial centres most trades are processed on a 'T + 3' basis, with matching and netting of trades completed by the end of T + 1, i.e. one day after the date of trade, clearing (preparation for settlement) during T + 2, and final settlement on T + 3.[7] We are concerned with the last four steps – matching, netting, clearing and settlement.

Figure 12.1 shows the various institutions involved in a domestic securities trade and the subsequent post-trade processing, together with the associated flows of information.

A number of points are illustrated by this figure.

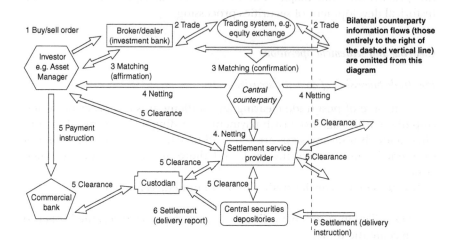

Figure 12.1 The six stages of a domestic securities trade and the information flows between institutions.

Several specialist institutions are involved in clearing and settlement. In addition to the investor and the broker conducting the trade, there are the custodian bank that holds securities on behalf of the investor, a settlement service provider that puts in place all arrangements for the trade to settle, a central securities depository where the security itself is lodged (often in a dematerialized form) and a payment system for the transfer of funds to or from the investor's bank. Finally, in addition, there may be a central counterparty that plays a key role in reducing credit risk and netting of trades.

A large number of information flows between these institutions are required in order to complete a trade. The institutions concerned must make considerable investment in processing systems in order to manage these information flows.

The four steps of post-trade processing can themselves be divided into two main stages: the immediate post-trade matching and netting, between investors, brokers and (where one exists) a central counterparty; and the subsequent process of clearing and eventual final settlement of the trade. Most information flows are within these two stages, not between them, indicating that they can be viewed as linked but are separate operations.

Figure 12.1 assumes that there is a central counterparty, as in US security trading, equity trades in the UK, and also in some other cases.[8] The central counterparty is the legal counterparty to all matched trades. But since it is on both the buy and sell side of all trades, the central counterparty is neither a net buyer nor a net seller of securities and does not have any involvement in subsequent clearing and settlement, other than routing information to settlement institutions.

The 'settlement service provider' – typically a national central securities depository, an international securities depository or a global custodian bank – plays a key role, arranging the settlement and helping investors manage both their cash flow and the flow of securities. This is done, first, by obtaining confirmation that the seller of a security has a security ready to deliver. If this is not the case then the loan of a security can be arranged to cover the settlement period. Second, by obtaining confirmation that the purchaser of a security has cash ready to make a payment. If not funds will need to be borrowed to complete the transaction. Finally. by setting up the simultaneous delivery versus payment (DvP) that is required for final settlement.

Underlying settlements are the parallel systems for transferring payment and ownership of securities. Title to securities is nowadays held in a centralized security depository. As illustrated in the Appendix, under most developed legal jurisdictions title may also be held in higher level custodian accounts that are themselves backed by accounts with the central securities depository; and several hierarchical layers of such ownership (multi-tiered securities accounts) are possible. Transfer of title requires only that an instruction to transfer ownership from one account to another is received from both sides of the trade. At the same time a payment must be arranged from one bank account to another (an account either with a central bank, i.e. settlement in central bank money or with a commercial bank).

The large number of information flows coming to and from the settlement service provider reflect its critical role in the final stage of clearing and settlement. Effective settlement service provision requires a combination of high quality systems to manage the flow of information and skilled staff who can provide investors with the necessary service support to deal with problems in cash and security flows. In practice much of 'value added' in securities settlement comes from the provision of additional services, such as security lending or cash management, not from the basic functions of handling instructions for transfer of ownership or the corresponding payment.

In many respects this is a highly efficient operation. Credit risk is kept very low. Especially with post-trade netting, both of the principal credit risks (the replacement risk of having to replace the trade on what may turn out to be unfavourable terms; the principal risk of delivering a security or making a payment for a security but not receiving anything in return) are kept under tight control. 'Pipeline costs' – the costs of having either securities or cash tied up in the settlement process are nowadays reduced to either an overnight or intra-day period – so the direct financial costs of the trade are only a small fraction of the outstanding principal. Trade failures – trades that are matched but do not then complete at due date – are minimized and moreover, with a central counterparty in place, the costs of trade failures can be further reduced through roll over of the settlement, on a net basis, to the subsequent day.

At the same time substantial costs can still be incurred. The staff and system costs of the settlement service provider and of the central securities depository must both be covered, increasing charges to the investor. Charges for settlement services can represent a significant component of post-trade processing costs, especially when transaction volumes are low and investment in standardized systems cannot be justified. Costs to the investor may be relatively large if the settlement service provider is a profit seeker and is not subject to effective competition. Finally there are considerable internal systems costs for all the participants in the trade.

The additional complications and costs of cross-border security trading

Greater complexity and additional trading costs arise when an investor buys or sells a security in another country from where they operate: there is considerable variation in the way in which cross-border settlements are handled. The Basel Committee on Payment and Settlement Systems (CPSS (1995)) identifies five different routes for cross-border access to a national central securities depository. These are:

i   direct membership;
ii   using a direct link between national central securities depositories;
iii access via a local agent;
iv   access via a global custodian who maintains their own network of local sub-custodians and agents – the major global custodians are the Bank of New York, Citibank, JP Morgan Chase and, among European institutions, BNP Paribas, ABN Amro and Deutsche Bank;
v   access via one of the international central securities depositories (ICSDs) Euroclear or Clearstream.

While all these different arrangements compete with each other most cross-border settlement takes place via (iii), (iv) or (v).[9] Dealers and asset managers do not find it cost-effective to maintain direct membership of the national central securities depositories (CSDs) in all countries where they do business (and local regulations can in any case prevent them becoming members). There are relatively few direct links between national CSDs. Most often dealers and asset managers prefer to use one or more global custodians or international CSDs to handle most of their cross-border settlements. To meet this demand these institutions in turn maintain an extensive but expensive network of relationships with local agents covering all developed world and all the principal emerging markets. Where they have sufficient volume dealers and asset managers may build their own relationships with local agents.

The necessity for indirect access, via a local sub-custodian or 'agent' or through a global custodian bank who in turn maintains links to the relevant central securities depository greatly increases costs. There are a number of reasons why the costs of these arrangements are so much higher than for domestic trades. Cross-border trades almost always involve system incompatibilities, requiring the expensive process of manual input of data and instructions to complete the trade; and increasing the proportion of trades that fail. The need for manual intervention is often increased by national differences in financial regulations and other local institutional factors, making it impossible for the investor to treat security settlement in a standard fashion across different countries. Also, most importantly, the local settlement service provider – whether a local agent or a global custodian – has market power and can substantially raise costs.

Reducing these additional costs of cross-border trading is the principal challenge facing the European securities industry if it is to reduce the costs of clearance and settlement in Europe relative to the US and create liquid European-wide securities markets.

The industrial organization of clearing and settlement

The objective of this section is to characterize a key barrier to competition in the provision of security settlement services.

Book entry and the liquidity externality

A major constraint on competition in security settlement arises because there has to be a consistent and definitive record identifying ownership of securities. Ownership can be recorded at any level of the multi-tiered ownership arrangements applied to securities, at the lowest level in security accounts maintained by the relevant national or international central securities depository; and in the higher level ownership account maintained by other depositories and custodians (see the previous section and Appendix for more description and discussion of multi-tiered ownership). All transfers of ownership have to be conducted by a transfer between accounts of these kinds: most commonly as an account transfer on the books of the central securities depository itself or as a transfer at a higher level on the books of custodian banks or other central securities depositories.

On receiving an acceptable settlement instruction from both sides to the trade, the security depository or custodian bank transfers a holding of the security from one security account to another.[10] This 'book entry function' is a relatively simple and low cost task (albeit it must be conducted with absolute security and no possibility of false transfer being made or of the record of ownership being lost or corrupted or a transfer being made without a corresponding payment having also been sent ('DvP')). But a competitive advantage in the provision of this book-entry function prevents competition in associated settlement services, such as advice and information on the positioning of cash and securities, collateral management, or securities lending.

One source of competitive advantage, arises from the kind of liquidity externality that frequently occurs in financial transactions, akin to the liquidity benefits of executing securities transactions on an exchange or other liquid marketplace. This aspect of competition in securities settlement has been described and analysed by Holthausen and Tapking (2004). As Figure 12.2 (adapted from Holthausen and Tapking, 2004: Figure 12.1) indicates, three possible settlement transactions are feasible:

1   An investor with a securities account at a CSD settling with another investor also holding a securities account at the same CSD (pure book entry settlement)
2   An investor with a securities account at a custodian bank, settling with another investor holding a securities account at the same custodian bank (pure book entry settlement)
3   An investor with a securities account at a CSD settling with an investor holding a securities account at a custodian bank (settlement involving two different books).

Settlement of this last kind, involving two different books, is inherently more expensive than a pure book entry settlement, requiring the utilization of links between the CSD and the custodian bank. The cost advantage of using a pure book entry means that most settlement takes place either through a pure book entry (mechanism 1 or 2). But this requires that *both* sides of the trade maintain ownership accounts with the same institution (CSD or custodian bank). This creates a 'virtuous circle' of liquidity – if most investor accounts in a particular security are held with one

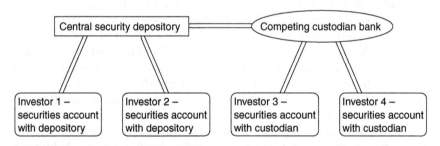

Three possible settlement arrangements
1 Book entry on the books of the central security depository (Investor 1 against investor 2)
2 Book entry on the books of the competing custodian bank (Investor 3 against investor 4)
3 Settlement with purchase or sale by the custodian bank (Investor 1 or 2 aganist investor 3 or 4)

Figure 12.2 Different possible arrangements for securities account transfer (source: Adapted from Holthausen and Tapking (2004: figure 1)).

settlement provider, then new investors will also wish to maintain accounts with the same settlement provider so as to minimize settlement costs.

There is thus a tendency for accounts and settlement to migrate to the lowest cost provider of book entry, i.e. the provider where most other investors maintain their ownership accounts. The outcome (in the terminology of network economics) is 'tipping' – a tendency for settlement volumes to shift to one provider of book entry transfer.[11]

Further points can be made about competition in book entry transfer:

- While book entry transfer is *not* a natural monopoly – it is possible to have competition from another provider – the liquidity externality gives the current incumbent a substantial competitive advantage.
- This competitive advantage may lead to inefficient pricing. Specifically the provider of book entry in a particular security is given a competitive advantage in the provision of associated 'value added' security settlement services – services such as the positioning of cash and securities for settlement, collateral management and securities lending. Other providers of these services will need to maintain accounts with the dominant provider of book entry transfer, and high charges on book transfer will increase their marginal costs and reduce their market share of these associated services.
- The competitive advantage derived from a liquidity externality may be re-enforced by national regulation or exchange rules, requiring settlement on the books of the national securities depository.

Book entry is only a small part of the services provided by central securities depositories and custodian banks. The greater part of their resources are devoted to other 'value added' activities such as providing settlement support for the whole range of settlement of their clients (including services such as security lending), custodian services for institutional investors, and in the case of the international central securities depositories banking and credit facilities. Depositories and custodian banks can earn substantial revenues from these other services, and as they are increasingly run on a for-profit basis will have strong incentives to use their natural monopoly over book entry to make it difficult for competitors to compete with them on the full range of these services. Competitors may simply be unable to make the necessary book transfer instructions to provide these value added services, or they may be charged relatively high fees that place them at a competitive disadvantage.

Because of the demand for these competitive value added services, it is *not* necessary to charge a high price for book entry transfer, and in fact providers of security settlement do not seek to discourage liquidity by making a high charge for this basic function (practitioners seem to indicate that taken on its own this is a loss making service). But *if* there are constraints that prevent competitors in the provision of the value added complementary services from accessing the basic book entry function, then there is a reduction in competition in these additional downstream services. The next subsection considers the application of a standard regulatory tool to promote competition in such downstream services.

Associated with the task of maintaining the record of ownership is the further job of communicating 'corporate actions'. There are a wide range of such actions. They include issuing instructions for payments of dividends and coupons; notification of rights issues and other capital restructurings; organizing shareholder voting in the event of a contested merger or acquisition; and execution of the various tasks involved in corporate governance, such as notification of shareholder meetings or issue of proxy voting rights. The handling of corporate actions is a further 'value added' service whose pricing may be affected by market power in book transfer.

These potential inefficiencies are, on the whole, fairly well controlled in domestic security settlement. It is usual for the charging of book transfer to be applied on equal terms to all members of the domestic central securities depository; and in this case there is effective competition between the national central security depository, local custodians and branches of global custodians in other related settlement services for domestic securities. Lack of volume may keep costs per transaction relatively high but the outcome is cost-efficient within the context of the domestic market. A potential exception is when the rules of an exchange require settlement to be undertaken through an affiliated settlement system, in this case competition may be ineffective even domestically.

These inefficiencies are a much greater concern in cross-border settlement, mainly because non-domestic institutions – whether investors, central securities depositories, or global custodian banks – are unable to effect direct book entry transfer on the accounts of the dominant (i.e. liquid) securities account provider or CSD on the same terms as domestic institutions. They depend instead on access via local agents, creating a competitive bottleneck. Local agents can then charge substantially for value added services such as securities lending. Moreover volumes are kept low, preventing international investors from benefiting from economies of scale in securities transactions and removing incentives to invest in standard systems that will minimize marginal per-transaction costs.

We now reach the central argument made in this chapter, that limitations on access are also a constraint on re-structuring of the European securities settlement industry. In principle the market should be allowed to determine the new structure of European securities settlement. There is a clear business case for major providers (ICSDs or those global banks actively providing securities settlement services) to develop single service platforms spanning a number of European countries, especially across different members of the euro zone but also possibly extending to 'out' countries such as the UK and Sweden. Doing so can both cut costs through economies of scale and, by increasing the range of services offered to clients, boost market share and revenues. Such market-led investment should be the main driver for the development of pan-European securities settlement, and achieve the same or better efficiency as current domestic arrangements, possibly first through regional 'affinity' areas such as the Nordic countries and the Netherlands, Belgium and France, and subsequently covering the entire EU.

But the key point is that the opportunity for market participants to develop platforms across several countries is severely limited by existing arrangements governing access to CSDs and on book entry on competitors securities accounts. One solution (exemplified for example by Euroclear's acquisitions such as CrestCo in the UK and Sicovam in France) is for a supplier to acquire a number of national CSDs; but this has two substantial problems as a route to the creation of effective pan-European supply of securities settlement services. First, this strategy links national securities settlement provision through a single provider. Without access regulation, ownership of a number of national CSDs can place other competitors at a competitive disadvantage in the provision of value added services.

This first problem is not fatal to achievement of the goal of pan-European provision of securities settlement service. With a single supplier, appropriate governance arrangements can still ensure that customers are given an efficient and fairly priced service. The second and crucial problem is that, for both political and business reasons, many national CSDs are and will not be available for acquisition (for example, the vertically integrated CSDs of Germany, Italy and Spain). Thus a policy of relying on market forces alone to achieve the restructuring of the European securities settlement industry will only ensure that provision remains for a long time divided between national markets. Access regulation is therefore also required so that different providers can build pan-European platforms without the necessity of acquiring domestic CSDs.

There is a further competitive benefit of access regulation, in a pan-European context. Security issuers can be given the choice of locating their securities wherever they wish. Thus different depositories can in principle compete for this business. In practice considerations such as language mean that most issuers have a strong preference for their own national depository. As a result of these frictions the overwhelming majority of domestic securities will continue to reside in only a single depository and this depository will nearly always be the national depository of the issuer concerned (or, where it is an international bond, one of the two international CSDs, Euroclear or Clearstream). But the ability to make book entry transfers on the accounts of these depositories will mean that issuers are not disadvantaged, by for example choosing to issue through a relatively small and illiquid national CSD. Different national CSDs will all be effective issuer access points to the EU wide securities market.

Access pricing of network monopolies and application to security settlement

This problem of access to book transfer has a parallel in the natural monopolies enjoyed by network utilities such as electricity and gas distribution, local fixed-link telecom networks and railway tracks. This suggests the possibility of designing a regulatory regime for securities settlement working analogously to the regulation of these natural network monopolies.

A standard diagrammatic analysis clarifies the issues involved. In these markets competitive and monopolistic activities co-exist.[12] The production of goods in the competitive market (the supply of household electricity, telephone calls or rail journeys) requires inputs from an 'upstream' network activity (mains cabling, local telephone lines or the network of rails and stations). If, as in most cases, the network operator is also present in the 'downstream' competitive sector, there is a danger that it will use the terms of access to thwart competition.

Figure 12.3 represents the structure of such an industry as well as the points of concern for the regulator. In this figure M is a monopolist controlling the supply of an upstream network. This network is used to supply directly to consumers in a monopoly Market 1 and is also used as input for the production of goods in a downstream sector. The downstream Market 2 is potentially competitive, i.e. there are sufficiently low fixed costs of operation that other providers can potentially supply to this market, provided they have access to the network.

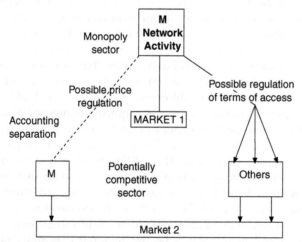

M is a monopolist controlling a network. Market 1, if it exists, is the upstream monopoly market supplied only by the monopolist. Market 2 is the downstream potentially competitive market, where competitors require access to the network.

Figure 12.3 Access price regulation (source: This figure is based on Armstrong *et al.* (1994)).

In the telecommunications example, Market 1 might be the market for local telephone links provided by a single operator and Market 2 the market for international calls where there is potential competition. Regulation of market structure may involve prohibiting the monopolist from competing in the downstream sector or requiring it to present separate accounts for its operations in the two sectors.[13] More commonly, price regulation is used in utilities to set both the price of the final product in the monopoly market M1 and the terms of access to the network for suppliers in the potentially competitive market M2.

In the case of securities settlement, M the 'monopoly' activity is the transfer of book entries and transmission of instructions for corporate actions. As discussed above, while this is not a natural monopoly, the liquidity externality in book entry transfer, means that the provider of book entry has a substantial competitive advantage.

The main point to take from this figure is that regulation of the terms and pricing of access can create effective competition in the second 'potentially competitive' market. This is now standard regulatory practice in many sectors and many countries. For example, in the UK household supply of gas and electricity is now openly competitive, despite the existence of incumbent network monopolists. Competitors input gas or electricity to the network and charge their own customers whatever they feel the market will bear. A regulated (cost-based) charge is imposed by the owner of the network to these potential competitors.

Application to the book entry function and the need for standardization of systems

Exactly this same approach can be taken to the book entry activities of custodians and securities depositories. European level regulation can be used to require them to:

- account for book entry functions separately from all other clearing and settlement services they provide;
- allow access to book entry to a wide range of users, with a requirement to charge all on a non-discriminatory basis, i.e. the same pricing tariffs and membership fees.

What practical impact would such arrangements have? This would provide a competitive discipline on local agents, who currently provide indirect access to national securities depositories. It would then be possible for example, for say Clearstream, or another settlement service provider, to offer a settlement service for any European security, for example an Italian corporate bond or Portuguese equity settled on the national CSD. Clearstream could do this by directly accessing the relevant Italian or Portuguese depository, effecting book entry changes on the same terms and conditions as any other member of the depository. As an alternative to direct depository membership, Clearstream could instead continue with an agency contract with another (local or international) settlement service provider who was a member of the Italian or Portuguese depository, and effect book entry changes indirectly via this agent. But the pricing of the local agent would be disciplined by the possibility that Clearstream could obtain direct access to the depository.

Opening up access to book-entry transfer (the competitive bottleneck) would thus encourage greater competition in the provision of settlement services (the potentially competitive sector). All institutions would be able to compete on a level playing field, supplying custody services in the Italian bond or Portuguese equity, either via direct membership or indirect agency access to the relevant depository.

There is one critical difference from access regulation in utilities, arising because there are many depositories and custodians, each with market power relating to the securities where they enjoy a liquidity externality. In order for competition to be effective, it will also be necessary for all European CSDs and custodian banks offering book transfer, to adopt harmonized communication standards concerning book entry changes, and related corporate actions. Without such harmonization it will still remain very costly for brokerages and asset managers to obtain direct access to securities depositories, even when charged on a 'non-discriminatory' basis. Occasional users will have much higher effective costs because of the need to treat such access in a non-standard fashion.

The need for harmonization of communication standards, to achieve effective interoperability of securities settlement systems across Europe, has been emphasized by the Group of Thirty (G30) (see G30, 2003), and it is generally accepted that such standardization (or 'interoperability') will greatly reduce the indirect internal costs of cross-border security settlement. The additional point made here is that such harmonization will also make it relatively easy for brokers and investors to access book entry directly; provided such book entry services are priced on a non-discriminatory basis this will reduce the market power of local agents and their ability to impose high levels of transaction charges for cross-border settlements.

The appropriate policies are then a combination of agreement on standards for the operation of a settlement system ('interoperability') – ultimately the responsibility of the industry – and regulation of access and of access pricing to ensure that all settlement service providers can compete fairly in the settlement of every security – the responsibility of the appropriate regulatory authorities. It is in the interests of investors, brokers and asset managers that communications be standardized, allowing 'straight through processing' (or STP) of securities transactions and corporate actions. The work of the G30 (G30, 2003) and of the Society for Worldwide Interbank Telecommunications (SWIFT, 2005) are already doing a great deal to promote such harmonization and support STP, although much remains to be done.

Note that access regulation of this form does not require regulators to impose a so-called 'spaghetti' solution to the restructuring of European securities settlement, in which all customers (brokers and dealers) are required to develop links with all suppliers of securities settlement services and all CSDs across the EU. Such regulatory requirements have no general business justification, only a minority of these interconnections would be used sufficiently to justify the associated investment and management cost. Where there is a business justification for these investments, then no regulatory requirement is necessary.

Such new bilateral links are likely to be most appropriately developed at the first stage between firms operating within certain national 'affinity groups' (e.g. Nordic, German–Austria–Luxembourg, Netherlands–Belgium–France, etc.) and a possible precursor to formal consolidation. The likely outcome are linkages in the form of a series of 'hub and spokes'. However, the key point is that there is no need, at a policy making level, to pay any attention to debates over whether 'hub and spoke' is more appropriate than 'spaghetti'. Access regulation of competitive bottlenecks is the necessary precursor to allowing the market to develop pan-European linkages on a commercial basis. The appropriate structure of linkages between securities settlement providers then becomes a purely commercial decision.

Further steps: free choice of issuer, settlement service provider and security 'location'

With such policies, many of the barriers to cross-border securities clearing and settlement identified in the Giovannini report will be addressed. The remaining barriers can be dealt with by allowing users (issuers, investors and intermediaries) free choice over the supply of three different aspects of securities processing.

These three critical areas where freedom of choice can be ensured are:

*   Choice of CSD for issuers
    At present national rules often prevent security issuers having any choice about the depository in which their security resides. For example sometimes the rules of an equity exchange require that shares traded on that exchange be deposited with the local CSD. There is no economic rationale for such a rule and it prevents competition between CSDs. All issuers must be allowed complete freedom to choose the CSD which offers them the best combination of service and financing costs.

    At the same time it has to be acknowledged that for reasons of language and culture many, possibly a large majority, of issuers will prefer to deal with there own national CSD for the foreseeable future. This preference is one good reason why an enforced horizontal integration is undesirable. Provided there is access regulation of book entry and transmission of corporate actions issuers can be allowed to continue to express a preference for their own national depository.

- Choice of settlement service provider for dealers and investors
  Similarly there should be no restriction on the choice of settlement service provider for brokers executing a trade. The regulation and accounting separation of book entry function means that there will be a very large number of institutions offering clearing and settlement services (the existing European national CSDs, the two international CSDs, overseas competitors such as the DTCC and the global custodian banks). Book entry access regulation will allow all these competitors to effect book entry changes to any specific security on the same pricing terms. This will allow open competition in all other aspects of clearing and settlement.
- Choice of security 'location' (custodian) by investors
  Finally, the location of the security holdings should be a free choice for the investor. Central securities depositories and custodian banks will be able to compete freely with each other for this business. Again, provided there is access regulation, then there is no need for any further restrictions. Any national requirements for investment funds to locate shares with preferred local custodians should be removed.

Implications for rationalization of European clearing and settlement

This section reviews some of the recent policy discussion of European clearing and settlement, argue that with effective access regulation, little further public sector intervention is required on issues such as settlement costs, horizontal versus vertical structure or the ownership form for European settlement service providers.

Costs of settlement

There has been considerable debate and attention paid to the costs of securities settlement in Europe. Several studies of costs have revealed wide discrepancies in the costs of domestic and cross-border settlements. While there is still uncertainty about the costs of clearing and settlement – both within Europe and when comparing Europe and the US – it is clear that costs are reduced dramatically when settlement takes place at high volumes on standardized systems. This does not however indicate any need for policy intervention, beyond achieving agreed system standards and ensuring open and non-discriminatory access to book entry transfer.

The most detailed examination of the costs of securities settlement in

Europe has been provided by National Economics Research Associates (NERA) (Linton and Starks, 2004). They use what they describe as a 'bottom up' procedure for assessing the costs of various types of securities settlement transaction, i.e. their estimates are based on a detailed examination of the tariffs for settlement by the various national and international central securities depositories. They also review the findings of previous cost studies and compare them with their own results.

Linton and Starks find that domestic securities trades in Europe range in cost from between €0.35–0.80, compared with €0.10 in the US, a difference that can be largely explained by the higher volume of securities settlements in the US. Domestic settlement in Europe appears fairly efficient. The costs of cross-border securities settlement in Europe however vary considerably; they find that cross-border trades settled internally within the systems of the two international CSDs cost on average only €0.57, similar to domestic settlements; but that standard cross-border trades settled via the two international CSDs cost around €37 per transaction, the dramatically higher figure reflecting the fact that these are bespoke rather than automated services.

Another detailed analysis of European settlement costs was conducted by the Centre for European Policy Studies (Lanoo and Levin, 2001), prepared as an input to the November 2001 Giovannini report (The Giovannini Report, 2001). Lanoo and Levin measure settlement costs, using data on operating income per transaction by different settlement service providers for different categories of transaction. All this data is obtained from annual reports and accounts. Even though this procedure may include some additional income for non-settlement related services, their results are broadly consistent with those of Linton and Starks. Again the cost of settlement in Europe varies considerably from one type of transaction and one system to another. As a broad figure, costs per trade can vary from 0.30 to 30 euro, with the highest costs arising for cross-border transactions.

The Centre for European Policy Studies' (CEPS) study argues that once allowance is made for netting, settlement costs per post-netted trade are often not so much higher in Europe than in the US, i.e. comparing per-settlement costs on a post-netted rather than pre-netted basis there is relatively little difference between the US and many domestic European settlement costs; but they also find that profit margins are higher in European settlement than in the US, suggesting that European settlement service providers price their services relatively aggressively. This may in turn be due to the profit incentives combined with a lack of competition in European settlement.[14]

The broad cost equivalent of the costs of European domestic securities settlement and US securities settlement on a post-netted basis can be interpreted in two ways. It supports the view that European (domestic) settlement is fairly efficient but also is consistent with the interpretation that pre-settlement transaction netting in the US is a highly effective means of achieving cost reductions. On a pre-netted basis the volumes of securities trading in the US are approximately ten times the volume of total securities trading in the EU. Given the substantial fixed systems costs, this means that on a pre-netted basis the US has much lower settlement costs than even domestic European trades, reflecting the much greater volume of trades going through their systems.

There are limitations to both the Linton and Starks (2004) and Lanoo and Levin (2001) comparisons. Linton and Starks were unable to obtain direct 'bottom up' measures of the cost of cross-border transactions conducted by local agents or global custodian banks, accounting for the bulk of cross-border settlement. This is because such transactions are not broken down on standard tariffs. Most importantly these estimates also exclude the indirect systems costs to brokers and asset managers of maintaining their own internal systems and interacting with fragmented cross-border settlement systems, estimated by Euroclear as accounting for some 60 per cent of the total costs of cross-border settlement (i.e. in addition to the €37 per trade reported by Linton and Starks).

This last observation shows that reducing the overall costs of settlement to the securities industry does depend to a large extent on the development of standardized processing conventions, such as Global Straight Through Processing (GSTP), and on consequent improved interoperability between systems. But this is not the full story. Open and non-discriminatory access will also be required, in order to place competitive pressure on local agents, and hence generate the pricing reductions and volume increases that will achieve the greatest possible cost reductions.

Provided there is effective competition in settlement, then policy makers need not be directly concerned with levels of costs. It is not the job of the authorities to play any direct role in reducing costs. Nor need the authorities devote much time and effort to measuring costs, outside the regulated domain of the basic depository functions of book entry and the transmission of corporate actions (these need to be measured as a basis for ensuring that access prices are set on an efficient and non-discriminatory basis). Once competition has been allowed across the entire range of settlement services, then competitive forces will bring effective downward pressure on other costs and settlement charges.

Proposals for integration

Proposals for horizontal integration

Is public policy intervention needed to create a single European settlement utility? A standard analogy here is with the US where a single dominant utility DTCC provides all securities settlement services. A leading promoter of this idea is Don Cruickshank, the chairman of the London Stock

Exchange. At a London conference in April 2001 (reported in the *Financial Times*, 27 April 2001) he argued for a European wide merger of the principal settlement service providers including Crest, Euroclear, Clearstream and others. But the costs of implementing such a merger might be high. And, unsurprisingly this suggestion is fiercely resisted by many individual settlement service providers, especially vertically integrated groups, such as Deutsche Borse – DBC – Clearstream who argue forcefully that organization structure is a decision to be left to the marketplace.

Opposition to such a forced rationalization will certainly remain strong. There are many existing examples of vertical integration, including Deutsche Borse's ownership of both Clearstream and of Eurex clearing, and Euronext's ownership of Clearnet, the Italian bourse ownership of the Italian settlement service provider Monte Titoli, and similar vertical integration in Spain.

Such a forced horizontal merger would be costly and have to overcome substantial political opposition. It is moreover quite unnecessary to achieve the benefits of horizontal economies of scale. With efficient and non-discriminatory access competition between settlement service providers will then establish whether one, few, or many, can survive as major suppliers of settlement services. These can co-exist with vertical silos. No regulatory intervention over organizational structure is required.

Take for example a share held in the German national CSD (part of Clearstream). If there is an unregulated monopoly over book transfer then the investor wishing to purchase this share has no choice but to pay the settlement fees set unilaterally by Clearstream. These fees can be set at a relatively high level, especially if (as is the case with Deutsche Borse) any trades are required to settle on the German national CSD.

But if access pricing regulation is imposed – through enforced accounting separation of the basic book transfer and regulation of the pricing requiring them to be set on a non-discriminatory basis, then the vertical silo is no longer able to assert market power from this depository monopoly. Transactors may still be willing to pay higher fees to Deutsche Borse, but this will reflect any premium valuation they place on the high level of service provided. Once again no further public policy intervention is required.

The other potential efficiency gain from horizontal integration is through the creation of a single central counterparty. The general case for a single central counterparty is a strong one since there are natural economies of scale in risk-management, especially in the netting of offsetting trades. There is a regulatory concern about systemic risk, since if a single counterparty was to somehow become fatally wounded, trading might conceivably become impossible on any trading platform. But this systemic concern can be dealt with, either by ensuring that bi-lateral trading by-passing the counterparty is still possible in the event of the absence of the Centralised Counter Party (CCP) or more directly through imposing extremely high standards of risk-management on the CCP. Concerns may also arise over the governance of a single central counterparty – Who is to own it and what influence will the owners have over its operation? Should it seek to make profits or merely cover costs? Will giving it a monopoly position not simply entrench operational inefficiencies? These are genuine concerns, but the potential for cost reduction from having a single CCP is generally thought to outweigh the possible costs of systemic risk or any inefficiencies due to weakness of governance.

Persuaded by these arguments the European Securities Foundation (ESF, an industry body) proposed in its December 2000 blueprint that a single central counterparty should be created for all the European exchanges. This has been characterized as an 'hourglass' proposal – reflecting the suggestion that competition should continue both between trading platforms and between settlement service providers, but that in between the trading platform and settlement all trades should pass through the hour-glass of the central counterparty. Based on US experience the ESF argued that this could lead to very significant reductions of post-trade costs. A sub-committee of ESF has held exploratory talks with various counterparties and exchanges in Europe to examine how such an integration might be carried out. But the outcome of these exchanges seems to be that, while many parties support in principle the development of a multimarket European CCP, few are enthusiastic about the immediate systems expenditure that this would require. The proposal for a single European CCP seems to have been putting the cart before the horse, in that only when there is a greater volume of cross-border trade will the cost advantages of such a CCP be evident.

A related point can be made about the harmonization of standards for settlement systems, allowing them to achieve effective 'interoperability'. All industry participants agree that this is a desirable goal, but implementing new standards sometimes requires substantial investment costs; and these investment costs are much easier to justify when settlement volumes are high and consequent costs savings are large. So while convergence of systems can be anticipated, convergence may be slow for those cross-border transactions currently characterized by high settlement costs and low volumes.

Organizational form and governance

For profit versus mutual organization

Another major issue of debate about the future of the European clearing and settlement industry focusses on the choice of organizational structure for the institutions that emerge after rationalization and especially the choice of 'for-profit' versus 'mutual' ownership.

Many variations of both of these organizational forms are found among financial exchanges and clearing and settlement service providers. Some are for-profit commercial organizations with owners largely separated from customers and suppliers. The company seeks to benefit its owners through the creation and distribution of current and future profits. This is, of course, the standard corporate organizational structure in most fields of business. The alternative to the for-profit commercial organization is the mutual, owned by the principal customers or users of its services, that seeks to benefit its customers, as well as, or instead of, making profits.

Among mutual commercial organizations a further distinction can be drawn between the consumer co-operatives and the non-profit mutual (see Lee (1998: 10–11) for more detailed discussion). A consumer co-operative is owned by a defined membership. Generally only these members may benefit fully from the services provided by the co-operative. In this case profits may be earned and can be redistributed back to the members. A non-profit mutual, by contrast, is not allowed to earn surpluses and must reduce the prices close to the cost of provision. But there is usually no restriction on who can benefit from the services of a non-profit mutual. While ownership claims on the assets of a consumer co-operative are defined by each member's shareholding, claims on the assets of a non-profit mutual are often legally unclear.

Mutual ownership by member broker–dealers has been the traditional organizational structure for securities and derivatives exchanges. There are a number of major reasons for this. Exchanges have long enjoyed a monopoly position in relation to the trading of particular securities or contracts. Under a for-profit organizational structure exchanges would then be able to exploit broker–dealers by setting high levels of membership and operational fees. Mutual ownership is therefore a protection against monopoly pricing. At the same time broker–dealers have often used mutual organization of financial exchanges to protect their own monopoly position vis-à-vis final investors. Adopting the rule that only members of the exchange are allowed to process trades can act as a barrier to entry, that allows them to charge higher fees to final investors. Profits can be further raised if, as in the UK before the 1986 big-bang, members can impose commission pricing arrangements that inhibit competition between them.

A second major justification for mutuality is that an exchange has access to a great deal of privileged information about its members and customers, especially if the exchange takes responsibility for their credit standing through the provision of counterparty services. Members and customers face the risk that a 'for-profit' exchange owned by outside shareholders might seek to use such information for its own private advantage. Mutual ownership, especially if as has often been historically the case accompanied by rotation of management staff between the member firms and the exchange, helps guard against the exploitation of informational privilege.

A final reason for the adoption of a mutual instead of for-profit structure is that customers of financial exchanges and securities processing companies make substantial relationship specific investments and could potentially be forced to bear undesirably high costs or even be put at a competitive disadvantage, if an exchange or securities settlement service provider were to make changes in its services that required substantial upgrading of customer systems. For this reason the major customers, at least in the situation where they would find it difficult to transfer their business to a competing supplier, are likely to wish to exert control over operation and strategy through direct equity ownership.

These are the advantages of a mutual rather than for-profit structure. At the same time a mutual organization operates under certain disadvantages relative to the for-profit organization. First it can be subject to constraints on the external funding of investment. This is especially true of the non-profit mutual that is restricted in its ability to generate surpluses and can offer no future dividend payments to outside equity investors. Second, the absence of the discipline of profit-creation, may encourage operational inefficiencies. This is most likely to occur when there are a wide range of customer–owners who find it difficult to co-ordinate their control over management. Third, a mutual may find it difficult to innovate, if most of the benefits of innovation accrue to a minority of customers while all customers bear the costs.

Over recent years, competition between different financial trading platforms has markedly increased. Exchanges now compete for order flows against each other. Moreover they also compete against broker dealers who are in a position to directly match buyers and sellers, and against a number of new 'alternative trading systems'. This increase in competition has lowered the exposure of broker-dealers to exploitation by monopoly trading systems, and lessened their technological dependence on exchanges. Thus, a direct consequence of this increased competition, has been a reduction in the principal advantages to customers of the mutual organization of financial exchanges.

This decline in the relative advantages of mutual organization explains the recent trend of demutualization among both securities and derivative exchanges. With access regulation of depository functions the decision about ownership structure is no longer of great concern even for settlement service providers. It can be expected that, over time, as market developments lead to rationalization of depository institutions then the usual ownership form for settlement service providers will become 'for profit' rather than 'mutual'. While mutual ownership may place barriers on direct merger of settlement service providers, inefficient providers protected by mutuality can be expected to gradually lose market share.

At the same time the argument in favour of mutual organization from the technological dependence of users on clearing and settlement providers is also much less important today than it was a few years previously. Technological standards in the security industry are increasingly open and in the public domain rather than closed and proprietary. For both security settlement and custodianship, communication conventions play an important role. As described in the previous section, the industry is already taking several steps for the standardization of messaging standards and communication protocols.

Practical implementation of access regulation

This chapter does not intend, and this author is not equipped, to give a full discussion of the legal or practical problems that will arise with implementing a regime of access pricing for European securities depositories. What this section does is to address some practical questions briefly, in order to persuade practitioners that this simple idea of introducing access pricing regulation of basic depository functions need not be immediately dismissed. The discussion is arranged through some simple 'frequently asked questions'.

Can the basic 'book entry function' be distinguished from other activities?

Most IT resources and staffing in the leading depositories and custodian banks are devoted to value added services, including reporting to clients on the positioning and status of settlement, providing securities lending, and a range of other services. These 'value added' services are where depositories generate the bulk of revenues and (if they are 'for profit') make their money.

What practical implementation of access pricing regulation requires is an accounting separation of the basic functions, accounting for a relatively small part of total resources. The setting of access prices will have to be based on these accounting statements.

This point is not addressed in the recent European Commission communication. This calls for the application of current tools of competition policy to ensure free access and non-discriminatory pricing. But without accounting separation it is possible for a settlement service provider to charge all 'outsiders' a high (non-discriminatory) charge for book entry transfer, hence supporting its own value-added settlement services.

The internal systems of the depositories have been developed in a way which makes it difficult to distinguish costs associated with these basic functions from those associated with value-added products. With present systems only a very approximate split will be possible.

This problem can be dealt with by initially introducing an access pricing regime for European depositories with a single EU wide tariff for book transfer and communication of corporate actions, based on the accounting statements of some of the leading European providers. Individual cost-based tariffs tailored to the cost structure of the individual depository could subsequently be available to all depositories who can develop effective accounting separation.

Under this regime depositories with relatively high cost structures, that are unable to provide an effective separate accounting for their basic depository structures, will lose money on their basic depository services and be forced to subsidize these out of their other activities. This will provide them with the incentive to develop accounting separation. By reducing the level of charges allowable in the EU-wide tariff over time, then the majority of depositories will eventually be persuaded to opt for separation of accounts.

Cost-based tariffs remove incentives for efficiency improvements in the basic depository function.
This is a well known problem in the price regulation of utilities. This can be dealt with by introducing a 'CPI − x' formula for the access price, where the access price is increased each year by the general level of consumer price inflation (CPI) less some allowance for prospective efficiency gains (x). In any case the resources devoted to basic depository functions are relatively low, the welfare losses from inefficient operation are therefore relatively small.

How can a centralized regulator set standards for communication? This is the job of the industry, not government.
Agreed. The point being made here is that effective competition in settlement services requires two developments: access price regulation that prevents providers exploiting their monopoly in the basic book transfer functions *and* further access regulation to ensure that these providers grant competitors access to these functions via open industry standards such as those promoted by SWIFT. The regulator does not need to establish the standard, merely to ensure that where this is one (or a small number) of open industry standards that the monopoly provider adheres to these standards.

Providing access is not enough – a major settlement service provider that seeks to compete across the full range of European securities will also have to invest in possibly expensive linkages to many national and international depositories.
Yes, this is a possibility. But it is then a commercial decision as to what extent national and international depositories merge and to what extent competitors in the settlement service industry need to interact with all remaining depositories. Appropriate linkages (whether in the form of a 'spaghetti' or more likely a series of 'hubs and spokes') will emerge as a consequence. Issuers in some of the smaller depositories may still find they simply do not get sufficient liquidity for their securities, and they will

have an incentive to switch to a major depositors. Settlement service providers will build the links if doing so earns them an adequate return on their investment.

Some industry discussion suggests that 'hub and spoke' arrangements with the majority of small depositories connected to a few leading depositories, is an efficient form of organization. Is a single regulatory tariff consistent with such a development?

The setting of access pricing tariffs may require further attention in the light of this point. One possibility would be to have an alternative (and higher) level of tariffs when there is indirect access to book transfer of this kind. The higher tariff level should be large enough to cover the costs of the 'spoke' linking the small depository to the major hub. In practice the resource costs involved may be sufficiently low that this is not a major issue.

Will competition in settlement of the kind proposed here not undermine the base for levying withholding taxes and stamp duties?

Under current national systems central securities depositories play a key tax gathering role. Thus for example a UK share settled through the UK depository CREST, now part of EuroClear, is subject to the UK stamp duty. Similarly, custodial institutions serve as collectors of a variety of withholding taxes. Access regulation, opening up settlement services to competition and allowing issuers free choice of where their security is deposited, will, over time lead to some degree of tax arbitrage, investors and issuers favouring the custodial arrangement and depository that give them the most favourable tax treatment. This in turn will lead to pressure for harmonization of these taxes across Europe. As already emphasized in the introduction above, a consequence of an 'authorization' approach to the creation of the single market in securities settlement is indeed that pressure for tax harmonization follows rather than precedes the removal of barriers to trade.

What will the legal basis be for defining basic depository functions subject to access pricing regulation?

Further work, involving commercial and regulatory lawyers, is now needed to specify the access pricing regime precisely. A legally watertight definition is required that will ensure that the ability to transmit instructions for the purchase or sale of securities is offered to any member of any European depository, that the charges for effecting such a transfer are the same for all members and subject to regulatory price control (as discussed above based either on cost-based accounts for the basic depository functions of the depository concerned or compliant with a European wide regulatory statement of permissible charges). It will also be necessary to apply regulations that ensure that depository membership is open to all applicants subject only to satisfying appropriate standards of risk management and internal control. The author is not aware of insuperable legal barriers to writing such a regulation, but clearly this question has to be fully explored by legal experts.

Access regulation can be assured through the application of existing competition law, with no requirement for a specific European wide regime of access price regulation of securities book entry transfer.

It will certainly be better if the appropriate pricing regulation can be enforced through existing competition law. In order for this to take place, the initial framework directive may have to require securities depositories and custodian banks to provide separate accounting of their book entry transfer function; an accounting exercise that will involve some unavoidably arbitrary allocations of fixed system costs. Such separated accounts need not be published as part of annual reports, but would have to be provided to regulatory authorities, in order to allow them to check whether pricing for settlement services are indeed non-discriminatory.

Summary and conclusions

This chapter has developed an analogy between securities settlement and household utilities such as telecoms or electricity supply, arguing that the core depository functions of book entry is a competitive bottleneck but that all other settlement services are potentially competitive, i.e. can be supplied by many producers.

The argument made here, on the basis of this analogy, is that an effective single market in European securities settlement can be achieved through a permissive 'authorization', applying access pricing regulation to the functions of book entry transfer of security ownership and authorizing the provision of settlement services in any European securities by any competing firm. Relatively little effort needs to be put into the time consuming process of harmonizing settlement arrangements.

Such access pricing regulation is a relatively simple policy intervention. All that is needed is EU level legislation requiring that securities depositories:

- account separately for their basic depository functions, namely book entry changes, distinguishing this function from all other clearing and settlement services they provide;
- offering access to book entry to a wide range of market participants, and adhering to widely accepted industry standards so that none of these market participant faces huge problems of access;
- imposing a requirement to charge all the same prices and membership fee, on a basis that can be justified as cost recovery, or cost recovery plus reasonable profit margin, on their separated book entry costs.

Where accounting separation has not yet been achieved, so costs of the individual depository cannot be measured, then standardized depository tariffs applicable across the EU may be imposed instead. Setting this tariff at an appropriately low level will provide an incentive to develop the necessary separate accounting.

At the same time, following the analysis of the November 2001 Govannini report (The Govannini Group, 2001), all limitations on investors choice of preferred supplier of different aspects of clearing and settlement services should be removed, and issuers should have complete freedom of choice over where there securities are deposited.

Finally policy makers can support industry initiatives that are promoting standardized communication within the settlement industry, requiring, for example, all regulated depositories to be fully compliant with industry arrangements such as those currently being developed by SWIFT.

The impact of such regulation would be to allow, for example, any nationally or globally based settlement service provider (e.g. Euroclear in Brussels, Monte Titoli in Italy, or the international settlement banks such as Citigroup or BNP-Paribas), to provide settlement in any European issued security (e.g. a Spanish equity or a Scandinavian corporate bond) on level terms with any other competing supplier of settlement services. Free competition in settlement would in turn provide the basis for a competitive single European wide market in securities trading, with direct competition between a variety of securities trading platforms (exchanges and alternative trading systems, both European and international).

With such a policy in place, many current concerns about European securities settlement are resolved:

- Authorities need not be concerned about vertical integration of settlement, since access regulation will prevent such 'silos' exploiting their natural monopoly.
- Equally there is no need for regulatory intervention of any kind to require rationalization of the industry. All decisions over rationalization, whether a horizontal or vertical merger, can be left to the market.
- There is no longer a policy concern over organizational structure – the choice between 'for profit' or 'mutual' ownership matters far less once there is effective competition. The market can be left to decide which organizational arrangement it prefers.
- Public debates over the relative efficiency of one national depository versus another are not required. Having created a competitive market it is up to the purchaser of clearing and settlement services to choose the lowest cost supplier.
- Political concerns about 'defending' the position of national depositories are no longer a problem – in the short to medium run there will (for reasons of language and culture) continue to be a strong demand for local issuance. National depositories will survive. But the market pressures for rationalization will force them to form cross border alliances or mergers and over time a simplified structure will emerge.

This access regulation approach to the rationalization of the European securities settlement industry is much more attractive than any 'big bang' approach, such as the creation of a European DTCC or the imposition (regardless of commercial criteria) of linkages between providers. Political objections to enforced cross-border rationalization do not have to be overcome. Horizontal merger will take place only if this leads to genuine cost savings. There is no need to require an unbundling of existing vertical integration such as that of Deutsche Borse and Clearstream. The creation of a single European market in securities settlement does not have to await the outcome of lengthy and difficult negotiations over harmonization of tax, regulation and trading arrangements. Pressure to harmonize these arrangements will arise as a consequence of the creation of the single settlement market with demand for settlement services migrating to the most effective providers.

This policy proposal, if it proves to be practical (practical objections have been briefly discussed) will be of significance well beyond the European securities industry. At least three reasons why those with a general concern with creation of a European market in financial services should pay attention to securities settlement.

The creation of effective competition in European securities settlement, could prove to be a precursor to a globally competitive market for settlement services. Working through the auspices of the World Trade Organization (WTO), one supposes that the EU might pressure for similar access regulation in other countries including the US. Open global competition will then determine which settlement services providers are the most effective.

The creation of a competitive European wide single market in trading and settlement will in turn lead to very substantial changes in other aspects of European financial services. Corporates will turn increasingly, as they have done in the US, to markets rather than banks for raising finance. It will become much easier to securitize traditional bank assets, such as mortgages and credit cards. Banks in turn will have to focus their efforts on the finance of small business and personal lending, in order to create profit for shareholders.

The 'authorization' approach to the creation of a competitive single European in securities trading and settlement, exemplified by the proposals of this chapter, is potentially applicable to many other financial services. To date the substantial micro-economic benefits predicted from the creation of the euro by the Cechini report have not yet been realized. The reason for this is that the principal financial services (securities, corporate banking, insurance, pensions and savings products etc.) continue to be traded within national markets. Authorization, rather than harmonization, may prove to be the only practical road to European monetary and economic union.

For those who wish to encourage the development of competitive

European wide markets in financial services, the road of competition and permissive authorization appears the most attractive route to follow.

Historical appendix: the development of securities settlement

An understanding of how costs of both domestic and cross-border European securities trading may be reduced is facilitated by some knowledge of the historical development of current systems of clearing and settlement. Major changes in these systems over the past 30 years have reduced both costs and risks. But the inheritance of varied national arrangements and the difficulties of introducing supra-national solutions makes it difficult for a policy maker to find obvious beneficial intervention in existing arrangements.

From an historical perspective, four related developments are relevant:

- the introduction of CSDs;
- the development of multi-tiered ownership (and associated legal issues);
- achievement of DvP and effective removal of principal risk;
- the horizontal and vertical integration of US clearance and settlement.

The development of CSDs

Until the late 1960s the standard practice in securities markets was for paper certificates to be lodged for safe-keeping with competing custodian institutions. Custodian banks took responsibility for the safe-keeping of certificates and for settling customer transactions (delivering the security in exchange for a cash payment). A central depository is an arrangement to 'immobilize' all certificates within a single institution.

While CSDs have existed for more than a century (an early example was the Wiener Giro und Cassen-Verein established by the Vienna stock exchange in 1872) it was not until trading volumes rose and this paper-based system became unacceptably costly and inefficient that central depository systems came into general use. This happened first in the US where the paper work crisis of the 1960s led to the establishment of the Central Certificate Service of the New York Stock Exchange (NYSE) in 1968, subsequently forming the core of the national Depository Trust Company.

Subsequently, typically with either central bank or exchange sponsorship, national CSDs have been established in all major countries, the hindmost being the UK where a CSD for equities was not created until the formation of CREST plc in the aftermath of the Taurus debacle. In some cases (e.g. France, Denmark, Norway, and more recently Italy) the CSD is dematerialized, i.e. securities are represented purely as entries on a computer database. Where local law allows it, dematerialization is a useful tidying up of the arrangements for the holding of securities; but makes relatively little practical difference. Even if securities are deposited in physical form, fungibility (see below) allows custodians and others to exchange claims on these securities against each other purely electronically.

It is a natural further step for a national CSD, working alongside the system for national large value payments, to use its processing systems to offer post trade settlement services, i.e. managing the settlement cycle through the stages clearing, i.e. indicating to each party of the trade, their obligations, whether delivery of security or in order for the trade to be settled and the point in time at which that obligation must be met; positioning, i.e. obtaining confirmation from participants that they are ready to meet these obligations; guaranteeing services; and finally completing, i.e. initiating the appropriate payment and delivery instructions so that delivery with finality is achieved. But conceptually, settlement and depository services are distinct functions and indeed, with appropriate links, a CSD can provide a settlement service for a security that is in fact held with another depository.

More recently, as volumes of cross-border trading have increased, a number of bilateral links have been developed between national CSDs to facilitate cross-border trading. Recent examples include links between CREST and the Swiss depository SIGA and between the Italian CSD Monte-Titoli and the Scandinavian CSDs.

Similar difficulties with the settlement of securities held in paper form led to the establishment of the two European-based ICSDs, Euroclear and Cedel, both created to provide settlement services for the international bond market that developed in Europe in the 1960s. Euroclear was founded in 1968 as an international bond settlement system by the Brussels office of Morgan Guaranty. Cedel was founded in 1971 as an alternative bond settlement system to compete with Euroclear. Overtime they also developed equity settlement services, but this was always a small part of total activity. In the 1990s the market for international securities settlement was split roughly 2:1, Euroclear:Cedel.

Both Euroclear and Cedel work through a network of depository banks, national depositories, and central banks. Cedel and Euroclear maintain links with each other (the bridge) in addition to their links with custodians and a number of national CSDs. This bridge allows DvP where the two sides of the trade choose to settle through the two different systems.

For both institutions, pre-settlement trade comparison/matching (since 1987) has been based on so-called ACE system. After successful matching, settlement takes place. The only netting arrangement is that Cedel offers an automated 'chaining' of trades, eliminates purchase sale of the same security by a market participant during a single settlement cycle. However, this netting has no risk-management function.

Cedel operated (1993) a daily settlement cycle with both overnight and daytime processing cycles (daytime allows same day T settlement). Euroclear operated only overnight. After matching, instructions to deliver securities are received and validated. During settlement processing, those instructions where the counterparties have both securities (for delivery) and cash (for payment) are then settled.

ICSD settlement is in commercial rather than central bank money, reflecting both customer preference for multi-currency settlement and the fact that, since they are international financial institutions, there is relatively less concern in the financial authorities of their home countries, Belgium and Luxembourg, that settlement should be in central bank money in order to reduce systemic risk. Participants maintain cash accounts, with JP Morgan Brussels or Cedelbank, respectively, for finance settlement. Settlement is DvP and multi-currency in these accounts. As of the early 1990s, securities lending facilities were provided by both Euroclear and Cedel in bonds but not equities.

An important consequence of the development of CSDs and ICSDs has been a shift in the business of custodian banking. As safe-holding and settlement functions have transferred to central securities depositories, custodian banks have compensated for the loss of this business by developing a range of basic custodian services including collection of income due, claims for repayment of withholding tax and response to corporate actions such as rights issues or take-overs.

Multi-tiered ownership

Another major development, closely associated with the shift to CSDs, has been the emergence of 'multi-tiered' ownership of shares and other securities, supported by the development of relevant legal conventions and the passage of relevant legislation. In modern securities markets only a relatively small proportion of shares are held directly by final investors. In the majority of cases ownership rights are exercised through a hierarchy of the following kind:

• final investor (typically an institution such as a pension fund);
• assets manager;
• custodian;
• sub-custodian;
• central securities depository.

The law of the major financial centres recognizes holdings of securities at each level as fungible, i.e. not a direct claim on a specific security, but a general claim on all the securities of that particular kind held at the next lower level in the hierarchy. For example here the final investor has a claim on a share of the securities held by a custodian, not a claim on an identifiable share certificate held at the central securities depository.

Fungibility facilitates trading in a number of ways. For example it makes it possible for custodians and for CSDs to lend securities to trading participants that they can use for settlement purposes; this is a key aspect of managing both cash and security flows. It also makes it feasible to establish links between CSDs that offer effective delivery against payment: the link is simply another level of the ownership hierarchy.

Fungibility plays a role where ownership or control of securities is contested, as may happen in a variety of contexts including corporate liquidation, personal bankruptcy or seizure of criminal assets. In all such cases it is the ownership claim at the highest level of the hierarchy that is disputed – and once that dispute is settled, no claim on ownership can be made at lower levels. An international drugs baron whose assets are frozen in a custodian cannot go to the CSD and ask to be given access to the securities, even if that CSD operated under a legal system that would not have allowed the assets to be frozen in the first place.

While fungibility is no longer an issue at national level, legal uncertainties over fungibility can sometimes arise in cross-border trading that fall under the jurisdiction of multiple legal codes. For example, effective links between CSDs have to be valid under the legislation under which both CSDs operate. Or the use of collateral to arrange a cross-border security loan might be called into question because of conflicts between national laws.

DvP and the effective removal of principal risk.

A further major development in securities settlement has been the effective removal of principal risk through the implementation of some form of DvP. Principal risk is the risk of the loss of an entire value of a security holding from the insolvency of a counterparty. Efforts by both the industry (as reflected in the 1989 report by G30) and by the regulators of payments and settlement systems (the Basel payments and settlement committee) led to the adoption of simultaneous delivery and payment during the working day.

The G30 report, developed under the chairmanship of John Reed, addressed a variety of problems of inconsistency in settlement arrangements between countries. Incompatible systems and procedures, different settlement arrangements and variation in the length of settlement cycle were a cause for concern, both because they hindered cross-border trade and were a source of systemic risk. The G30 recommendations were for: trade confirmation and affirmation on a compatible basis for both domestic and international markets by T + 1; settlement on a rolling basis by T + 3, DvP in all settlements preferably via electronic or book entry payments with 'same day funds'; use of a central securities depository; encouragement of securities lending; use of netting mechanisms where appropriate; and finally standard numbering systems. All were to be in place by 1992. The report also encouraged (in context of continuous rolling *net* settlement) the offer of complete trade guarantees.

The G30 report set, what are now, the basic standards for post-trade execution at the domestic level. Taken together with various reports of the Basel committee on payments and settlements it encouraged continued improvement in the speed and operation of payment and settlement cycles. A significant structural shift has been from batched settlement (e.g. the settlement at the end of a two-week account period, as was used in the London Stock Exchange) to rolling settlement, with settlement in a fixed period after the date of trade (e.g. $T + 3$ implying final settlement three days after the trading date). Trades that fail to settle on this day are deferred to the following day.

The G30 report recommended three models of DvP:

Model 1 – end of day delivery of security versus end of day payment;
Model 2 – middle of day delivery of security versus end of day payment;
Model 3 – simultaneous middle of day delivery and payment.

Speed of settlement has been facilitated, over the last decade or so, as the national large value payment systems used for all securities clearing and settlement passing through national CSDs have advanced from single end-day net settlement onto real time gross settlement. As a result Model 3 DvP is now the norm, minimizing principal risk during the final stage of settlement.

The horizontal and vertical integration of US clearing and settlement

US arrangements for clearing and settlement are of particular interest because of their complete horizontal integration, and more recently complete vertical, integration. It is necessary to examine both how this was achieved and the benefits it has offered, to see whether this model might be usefully applied in Europe.

The three major steps in the integration of US securities and clearing were:

The establishment in 1972 of the Depository Trust Corporation or DTC, the US central securities depository.

The creation in 1977 of a central counterparty for equities trading – the National Security Clearing Corporation; and the 1999 merger of the DTC (Depository Trust Corporation) and the NSCC within a single holding company, the DTCC. Since 1977 there have also been considerable and continuous technical developments in US clearing and settlement but we will not devote attention to these.

The DTC, like other central securities depositories, was a response to the paper work crisis of the 1960s. Its immediate forerunner was the Central Certificate Service (CCS) of the NYSE Stock Clearing Corporation, immobilizing certificates for stocks listed on the NYSE in 'nominee' names. An *ad hoc* industry group (the Banking and Securities Industry

Committee or BASIC) recommended that CCS be spun out of the NYSE to become an independent inter-exchange depository leading in 1972, to the creation of the DTC as a limited purpose trust company, owned by banks (42.3 per cent; 41 per cent through six exchanges on behalf of their broker-dealer members), with NYSE members owning 34.7 per cent, AMEX and NASD 4.6 per cent each, and finally 13.8 per cent directly by broker-dealers.

Originally an equity depository, DTC expanded its functions to include corporate debt, municipal debt and other securities. Other depositories continue to exist, e.g. Midwest Securities Trust Company (MSTC) and Philadelphia Depository Trust Company (PDTC) but these developed links with DTC allowing trade to take place through any of the depositories. The preferences of retail investors, who hold a fairly substantial proportion of US securities, have meant that the US has continued with physical immobilization of share certificates rather than dematerialization. Dematerialization has however been achieved for government bonds and for some corporate securities (the latter via so called 'book entry only' ownership at the DTC).

After 1972 industry, regulators and congress continued to look closely at the process of clearing and settlement. The 1975 'Securities Acts Amendments' mandated improvements and efficiencies in the US securities clearing process, requiring that netting of securities trading be performed by a single, industry-owned utility rather than by exchange-specific clearing arrangements. Thus, in 1977, NYSE, AMEX and NASDAQ merged their 'clearing arms', i.e. respective central counterparties, to form the NSCC.

Following the Bachmann Task Force Report of 1992, SEC instigated a further overhaul of settlement procedures, achieving by 1995 T + 3 settlement and introducing 'same day' funds. Attention is now being paid to the changes that would be needed to attain T + 1 settlement with the aim of implementing this by 2004.

In November 1999 ownership of the NSCC was reorganized. A single holding company, the DTCC, like the NSCC itself owned by the equity exchanges – became the holding company for both the DTC, the US central securities depository and the NSCC. As a result, there is in the US, vertically integrated clearance, settlement and custody for all US domestic cash-based securities trades.

The horizontal integration of US clearing and settlement seems to have yielded major benefits. First, as discussed earlier, in addition to its primary role in reducing risks, the presence of a CCP considerably reduces post-trade processing costs. Scale is important. As a consequence of netting some 94–97 per cent of US securities trades, in both value and volume, do not need to be settled. According to a SEC-led study of rationalization of US equity counterparties in 1977 offered cost savings of the order of 64 per cent of settlement costs. A single central counterparty has also facilitated the use of 'continuous net settlement' that reduces the costs of trades that fail to settle by carrying them over to the following day, as part of a single rolling net position for each participant.

Second, the DTC, operating as both central depository and single national settlement service provider, has also helped standardize the procedures for US settlement through its 'Institutional Delivery System' in which all information about the trade is received (confirmation of the deal from broker–dealer plus affirmation of the deal from investing institution).

Third, 'deliver–receive' instructions sent from DTC to broker–dealer and custodian to schedule both delivery and payment by guaranteed cheque and increasingly via electronic funds transfer.

Notes

1 I am grateful for comments from Harry Lahdenperä, Justin O'Brien, Diana Chan, Edouard de Lencquesaing, Salvatore Lo Giudice, and participants at the March 2002 business forum at Cass Business School and the September 2004 Bank of Finland conference on financial regulation. I am of course responsible for any remaining errors of fact or analysis.
2 Note that, among the policy papers reviewed by Linton and Starks (2004) and Milne (2002) – the original draft of the present chapter – comes closest to anticipating the Commission proposals and their emphasis on ensuring efficient and fair access to settlement services. The main difference is that the latest Commission communication (EU Commission, 2004) argues that, as far as possible, existing Treaty of Rome competition law should be used to remove barriers to competition in securities settlement. They do not envisage developing a scheme of access regulation in the forthcoming framework directive on securities clearing and settlement.
3 The expert advisory group is the Clearing and Settlement Advisory and Monitoring Expert (CESAME) group, details of which can be found on their web page at europa.eu.int.
4 The report identifies 15 separate barriers, ten relating to technical requirements and market practice, two relating to taxation and three relating to law. Categories 1, 2 and 3, proposed here are a finer classification of The Giovannini Group's 'technical requirements and market practice'.
5 Both industry and regulatory authorities have been addressing the harmonization of technical standards and procedures; the ECSB-CES-R have released their standards for securities clearing and settlement (ECSB-CESR, 2004), an implementation of the Basel CCPS/IOSCO recommendations on standards for securities clearing and settlement (CCPS, 2001a, b); while SWIFT, took up the responsibility given to it by the second Giovannini report, has produced proposals for the removal of the first Giovannini barrier (messaging standards and communications protocols), including the creation of a network of industry consultation groups (SWIFT, 2005).
6 The level 2 committee for securities markets is the CES-R, which will play a key role in the development of clearing and settlement regulation in the EU.
7 Germany achieves $T + 2$. In the US there has been active discussion of $T + 1$ but practical progress towards this goal has stalled.
8 The European Securities Foundation has proposed the creation of a central counterparty for all European securities trades as a means of facilitating the

integration of pan-European post-trade arrangements, see European Securities Forum (2000)

9 Euroclear (2003).

10 In practice, as noted, there is a substantial pre-settlement netting of most securities trades, so the transfer of ownership cannot be associated with a specific trade.

11 But not necessarily to the national central securities depository. One prominent example is the settlement of German government bonds. The German central securities depository is part of Clearstream but, for historical reasons, the bulk of settlement takes place on the account of the international securities depository Euroclear.

12 Often, there is an incumbent firm that is dominant and integrated, so that it is the regulator's job to encourage entry into the potentially competitive sector. See Armstrong *et al.* (1994) for more on vertically-related markets and case studies of the major UK utilities.

13 A well-known example of prohibition is the restriction on AT&T providing US long-distance telephony.

14 The US DTCC is customer owned and thus, despite being a monopoly, does not have an incentive to increase its charges aggressively.

References

Armstrong, M., Cowan, S. and Vickers, J. (1994) *Regulatory Reform: Economic Analysis and British Experience*, Cambridge, MA: MIT Press.

Committee on Payment and Settlement Systems (CPSS) (1995) *Cross-Border Securities Settlements*, Bank for International Settlements, March, available online at www.bis.org/publ/cpss12.pdf.

Committee on Payment and Settlement Systems (CPSS) (2001a) 'Core principles for systematically important payment systems', Report of the Task Force on Payment Systems, Bank for International Settlements, CPSS Publications, no. 43, available online at www.bis.org.

Committee on Payment and Settlement Systems (CPSS)/Technical Committee of the International Organisation of Securities Commissions (2001b) 'Recommendations for Security Settlement Systems' Report of the Task Force on Payment Systems, Bank for International Settlements, November, available online at www.bis.org.

ECSB/CESR (2004) *Standards for Securities Settlement in the European Union*, September, available online at www.ecb.int.

EU Commission (2002) 'Clearing and settlement in the European Union: main policy issues and future challenges', May, available online ateuropa.eu.int.

EU Commission (2004) 'Clearing and settlement in the European Union: the way forward', April, available online at europa.eu.int.

Euroclear (2003) 'Cross-border clearance, settlement, and custody: beyond the G30 recommendations', Morgan Guarantee Trust Company of New York, Brussels Office.

Euroclear (2003) see fn 8.

European Securities Forum (2000) *EuroCCP: ESF's Blueprint for a Single Pan-European Central Counter Party*, London, December.

Group of Thirty (G30) (1988a) *Clearance and Settlement Systems in the World's Securities Markets*, available for purchase from www.group30.org.

Group of Thirty (G30) (2003) *Global Clearing and Settlement: A Plan for Action*, January, available for purchase from www.group30.org.

Holthausen, C. and Tapking, J. (2004): 'Raising rival's costs in the securities settlement industry', European Central Bank Working Paper Series, no. 376, July, available online at www.ecb.de/pub/pdf/scpwps/ecbwp376.pdf.

IBC (1989) 'Global settlement standards', a research report co-published by Citibank, Societe Generale, SWIFT and Toronto Dominion Bank.

Ireland, J. and Ryan, T. (1993) 'Equity settlement in London: its importance to London as a financial centre', London Business School/Corporation of London City Research Project Discussion Paper.

Lamfalussy, ?., Herkströter, C., Rojo, L.A., Ryden, B., Spaventa, L., Walter, N. and Wicks, N. (2001) *Final Report of the Committee of Wise Men on the Regulation of Securities Markets*, February, available online at europa.eu.int.

Lanoo, K. and Levin, M. (2001) 'The securities settlement industry in the EU: structure, costs, and the way forward', Centre for European Policy Studies, Brussels.

Lannoo, K. and Levin, M. (2003), *Clearing and Settlement in the EU: Structures and Policy Issues*, Deutsche Bank Research, available online at www.dbresearch.com/ PROD/PROD0000000000048086.pdf.

Lee, R. (1998) *What is an Exchange?: The Automation, Management, and Regulation of Financial Markets*, Oxford: Oxford University Press.

Linton, E. and Starks, M. (2004), 'The direct costs of clearing and settlement: an EU–US comparison', Corporation of London City Research Series, no 1, June, available online at www.cityoflondon.gov.uk/NR/rdonlyres/0A6216E8-6153-44F3-B1EA-55FFA4CB19C2/0/CS_final.pdf.

Merton, R. (2001) 'Keynote Address', Annual Meeting of the European Finance Association, Barcelona, August.

Milne, A. (2002) 'Competition and the rationalisation of European securities clearing and settlement', mimeo, City University Business School, London, July.

SWIFT (2005) *The Proposal for the Removal of Barrier 1 of the Giovannini Report*, Consultation Paper, January, available online at www.swift.com.

The Giovannini Group (2001) 'Cross-border clearing and settlement arrangements in the European Union', Brussels, November, available online at europa.eu.int.

The Giovannini Group (2003), 'Second report on EU clearing and settlement arrangements', available online at europa.eu.int.

13 Links between securities settlement systems

An oligopoly theoretic approach

Karlo Kauko[1]

The key functions in secondary markets for securities are trading, clearing and settlement. In trading, agents simply agree on buying and selling securities. The deals are executed via clearing and settlement. Clearing entails the matching and verification of deals and computation of obligations. In the settlement process, monetary payments flow from buyers to sellers and securities are delivered from sellers to buyers.

Modern securities settlement systems (SSSs) are often highly centralised. The core of the system is a central institution that runs the system, e.g. the national central securities depository (CSD). A relatively small number of institutions participate directly in the process. These participants (members) are financial institutions, such as banks and investment firms (IFs). Government treasuries and central banks may also be members. A typical investor uses services provided by a member of the settlement system.

The European securities market infrastructure could undergo a historically exceptional upheaval in the near future. The existing structure appears to be outdated. There are many non-integrated national systems, and most of the securities traded are issued by domestic entities. Even though remote access from abroad to trading has become commonplace, remote participation in SSSs is still exceptional. The Giovannini report (Giovannini Group, 2001) discusses the practical problems related to cross-border clearing and settlement in the EU.

In recent years several mergers have taken place between securities market institutions. To a large extent consolidation has taken place at national level, although a few international mergers have occurred between EU member countries.

Links between CSDs are a relatively new arrangement, aimed at improving the possibilities for settling cross-border transactions. These links are established by bilateral agreements between SSSs. Customers of an SSS can hold securities in another system via the domestic service provider. The domestic service provider opens an omnibus account in a foreign book-entry system, and the holdings of its customers are pooled in this account. The domestic CSD keeps individual records on investors' holdings.

This chapter analyses the competition between two SSSs in a fragmented market. The focus is on pricing and inter-linking. The systems operate in a platform industry, as defined by Rochet and Tirole (2001), and must attract both issuers and investors. Even though there are earlier analyses on network effects and oligopolistic competition between stock exchanges (Di Noia, 1999; Shy and Tarkka, 2001), these focus on trading activities rather than SSSs.

The basic model is presented in the next two sections. Competition for issuers is fierce because trades must be settled in the CSD chosen by the issuer. The whole fee burden is borne by the investors. It is then assumed that the two CSDs are linked. Significant cost savings can be achieved in the use of liquidity and in operating costs. Moreover, competition for issuers is relaxed, and their relative fee burden increases. The following section demonstrates that it is not advisable to ban additional fees for using the link because this may simply lead to higher prices for domestic services. The main conclusions and a few suggestions for further research are presented at the end.

Assumptions of the basic model

There is a large number of bond issuers, each of whom issues I bonds in the primary market. The issuers are numbered 0, 1, 2,..., M. The bonds are in book-entry form. Issuers maximise the difference between value of bonds in the primary market and cost of registering and issuing them. The bonds are sold to investors at a price equal to the difference between a constant and the expected value of secondary market settlement costs paid by those who buy bonds in the primary market. The issuer pays all fees related to issuance.

Investors live in two countries, denoted 1 and 2. In each country these investors are divided into two groups, A and B. These groups might be households and institutional investors.

There is a profit maximising CSD in each country. Each CSD operates as a platform industry, because it needs two types of customers that need to interact – issuers and investors. The CSD is the registrar of the book-entry system, and it runs the SSS. Running the settlement process generates costs whereas registering new issues does not. The unit cost – per transaction, sale or purchase – of the centre for country j is denoted z_j.

Bonds are distributed in the primary market so that the proportion of issuer i's investors living in country 1 is $(M-i)/M$. Each issuer knows beforehand where its investors live.

All the original buyers of any issue belong to the same investor group. Half of the issues are subscribed by A investors, half by B investors. Issue number is not related to investor group. In most cases not all investors live in the same country, but the two groups exist in both countries.

There is a secondary market for bonds, in which trades are settled in systems operated by the CSDs. Investors must use investment firms (IFs) to settle transactions in the CSDs. In each country there are two IFs competing for A investors and two competing for B investors.

IFs cannot become members of the foreign SSS. Investors must use a foreign IF when they trade in foreign securities. Using a foreign IF is more complicated than using a domestic one, and entails an extra cost h.

The IFs achieve turnover via pricing of their services to investors. The price charged by an IF (v) is the same for a sale or a purchase. The IFs have simple cost functions. For any IF the cost of processing a transaction is y, which is an exogenous constant. One trade, consisting of a sale and corresponding purchase, is now defined as two transactions.

The IFs Bertrand-compete with identical services.

Only two of the randomly determined (equally likely) bond issues are traded. The two bonds are originally held by investors of each group. The two issuers' bondholders exchange securities. Each investor is simultaneously a seller and a buyer. Price formation and trading are ignored. The price of every security in the secondary market is the same, and does not depend on settlement costs. High settlement costs reduce both supply and demand, and the total impact on price would be unclear (see Barclay *et al.* (1998) for empirical analysis). Because each investor is simultaneously seller and buyer, his incoming and outgoing monetary payments sum to zero, except for the IF fees.

Monetary payments between SSSs and IFs are based on netting.[2] The IFs prefer situations where they intermediate both sales and purchases and need not make gross payments to the CSDs. If gross payments are made, the IFs may need large and costly cash balances. An IF might be unable to acquire liquidity to cover its net payment obligations, which could result in sanctions. Clearing parties with net obligations may have to post some assets as collateral, forcing the clearing parties to hold larger portfolios, e.g. of government securities, than they would otherwise prefer. Moreover, by pledging an important part of its assets a clearing party weakens its own creditworthiness in non-collateralised borrowing, because collateral assets cannot be freely liquidated to cover debts in case of bankruptcy. This probably affects the cost of external funding.

The expected total cost and disutility of being a clearing party with a gross payment obligation is α per security purchase to be intermediated. The analysis is restricted to cases where $2h > \alpha$. It will be shown that there is no meaningful equilibrium with two participating CSDs if this condition is not satisfied.

Events happen in the following order.

1   Profit maximising CSDs set their prices, including those to be paid by issuers (p_i for the CSD based in the country i), and a unit price per bond to be paid by clearing parties (b_i).

2   Issuers choose their CSDs, and bonds are issued.
3   Profit maximising IFs simultaneously set their fees (vs).
4   The two bond issues to be traded are determined.
5   Investors choose IFs and try to minimise settlement costs.
6   The trades are settled, net payments are made, and securities are transferred.

All the agents can immediately observe every decision and random outcome. All the agents are risk neutral.

Steps 4, 5 and 6 could describe a day. These three steps are repeated hundreds of times every year. The CSDs and IFs make no decisions at these stages. Expected values analysed in the following sections are simply multiplied by the number of repetitions and have no fundamental impact on optimal decisions by CSDs and IFs.

Solving the model

Competition between IFs

Because of Bertrand competition with identical services, the fee charged by an IF (v_i) must equal the marginal cost, which equals the sum of the unit fee charged by the CSD (b_j), the marginal processing cost for the IF (y), and the expected value of the per-transaction cost of gross payments (F_i).

$$v_i = F_i + b_j + y. \tag{1}$$

Gross payment costs are the only complicated component of the marginal cost. If two bond issues, i and j, are traded, the cost of gross payments (α) materialises as a part of country 1's IF cost in two possible cases. (Terms in parentheses are respective probabilities.)

Bond i is registered in the domestic country (Γ_1) and bond j in the foreign country (Γ_2). The IF represents half of the buyers.

Bond i is registered in the foreign country (Γ_2) and bond j in the domestic country (Γ_1). The IF represents half of the buyers.

Hence, the expected value of the total gross payment cost is

$$\alpha\left(\frac{\Gamma_1\Gamma_2}{2} + \frac{\Gamma_2\Gamma_1}{2}\right) = \alpha\Gamma_1\Gamma_2. \tag{2}$$

A part of the fee corresponds to this expected value. According to (1) the expected value of this cost factor must equal the expected value of the corresponding fee revenue.

The expected value of the number of transactions is the sum of two components.

- The IF collects fees if one of the two securities to be traded is registered in its home country. Each customer must pay the fee once to the IF. The probability of this equals $2\Gamma_1\Gamma_2$.
- The IF charges fees if both issues to be traded are registered domestically. The probability that both bond issues to be settled are registered in country 1 is $2\Gamma_1^2$. In this case each customer has to pay the same fee twice because he presents two settlement orders to the same IF.

The expected value of the part of the fee revenue that corresponds to gross payment costs is

$$F_1(2\Gamma_2\Gamma_1 + 2\Gamma_1^2). \qquad (3)$$

The expected value of fee revenue related to gross payment costs (3) must equal the expected cost of making gross payments (2)

$$\alpha\Gamma_j\Gamma_i = F(2\Gamma_j\Gamma_i + 2\Gamma_i^2) \Rightarrow F_i = \frac{\alpha\Gamma_j}{2}. \qquad (4)$$

This result is quite intuitive. If the market share of domestic CSD 1 is marginal ($\Gamma_1 \approx 0$), it is almost certain that if a domestically registered bond is traded, the other bond to be traded is registered abroad and netting cannot be used. The IF has a 50 per cent chance of representing a given buyer. The larger the domestic CSD's market share, the more likely it is that the IFs would benefit from netting. Therefore, (1) can be rewritten as

$$v_i = \frac{\alpha\Gamma_j}{2} + b_i + y. \qquad (5)$$

Pricing decisions by the CSDs

The CSDs maximise the expected value of profits. Their decision variables are the price paid by issuers (p_i) and the price per transaction paid by settlement counterparties (b_i). Issuers minimise the sum of fees paid by themselves and the settlement costs to their bondholders. Investors' costs are relevant because they affect securities prices in the primary market. If $100j$ per cent of the bondholders live in country 2, the cost of using CSD 1 is $p_1 + I(2/M)(v_1 + jh)$, where $2/M$ is the probability that the issuer will be one of the two issuers whose securities are traded and v_1 the price charged by all the IFs of country 1. The cost of using CSD 2 is $p_2 + I(2/M)[v_2 + (1-j)h]$.

Because $v_1 = \alpha\Gamma_2/2 + b_1 + y$ and $v_2 = \alpha\Gamma_1/2 + b_2 + y$, the condition for using CSD 1 can be written as

$$p_1 + \left(\frac{2I}{M}\right)\left(\frac{\alpha\Gamma_1}{2} + b_2 + y + jh\right) < p_2 + \left(\frac{2I}{M}\right)\left[\frac{\alpha(1-\Gamma_1)}{2} + b_2 + y + (1-j)h\right]$$

$$\Leftrightarrow j < \frac{2hI - \alpha I - 2Ib_1 + 2Ib_2 + 2\alpha \Gamma_1 I - Mp_1 + Mp2}{4hI}. \tag{6}$$

The condition implies a network externality. The market share of CSD 1 (Γ_1) has a direct impact on its competitiveness: if most companies are registered at CSD 1, it becomes more likely that IFs operating in country 1 need not make gross payments in the settlement system. This, in turn, has a direct impact on the fee paid by investors (v_1). This network externality implies that market forces are at least weakly inclined to integrate securities settlement by centralising the process in one centre.

In equilibrium, the relative share of issuers preferring CSD 1 must equal the market share Γ_1. Because issuers' bondholder structures are evenly distributed along the continuum from $j = 0$ to $j = 100$, it follows that (6) implies

$$\Gamma_1 = \frac{1}{2} + \frac{\left[2b_2 - 2b_1 + \left(\dfrac{M}{1}\right)(p_2 - p_1) \right]}{4h - 2\alpha}. \tag{7}$$

The CSD has two decision variables, b and p. As determinants of market shares, these two variables are perfect substitutes; any combination of p and b that satisfies the condition $2Ib_1 + Mp_1 = D$ (D being any constant) leads to the same market share. The CSD can decide these prices in the following way. CSD 1 decides first on a suitable value of D, then on the value of p_1. These decisions determine the value of b_1. Using this notation, the expected profit of CSD 1 can be written as

$$\Pi_1 = \Gamma_1 \left\{ Mp_1 + \left[\frac{4I(D - Mp_1)}{(2I)} \right] - z_1 \right\} = \Gamma_1(2D - Mp_1 - z_1)$$

$$\Rightarrow \frac{\partial \Pi_1}{\partial p_1} = -\Gamma_1 M < 0.$$

It follows that the optimal price paid by issuers is 0, so that the whole fee burden is borne by IFs and investors ($p_1 = p_2 = 0$, $b_1 = D/(2I)$). When choosing a CSD, an issuer pays no attention to the fees paid by future bondholders. However, these fees are a valuable source of revenue for CSDs.

There are two issues of I bonds to be traded. For each of them the probability of being registered in CSD 1 equals its market share (Γ_1), implying that the expected value of the number of processed securities equals $2I\Gamma_1$. Each traded issue registered in CSD 1 yields two service fees (b_1) per processed security, one for selling and another for buying. The cost per processed security equals $2z_1$. Therefore, the CSD i's expected profit is

$$\Pi_i = 2I(b_i - z_i)\left(\frac{-\alpha + 2b_j - 2b_i + 2h}{2h - \alpha}\right). \tag{8}$$

The first order optimisation condition of a CSD is

$$\frac{\partial \Pi_i}{\partial b_i} = -2I\left[\frac{\alpha + 4b_i - 2(b_j + h + z_i)}{2h - \alpha}\right] = 0. \tag{9}$$

This condition is satisfied for both CSDs iff (i = 1, 2).

$$b_i = \frac{-3\alpha + 6h + 4z_i + 2z_j}{6}. \tag{10}$$

The second order condition is $\partial^2 \Pi_1 / \partial b_1^2 = -8I/(2h - \alpha)$. This is negative and the extreme values are maxima iff $\alpha < 2h$. If this condition were not satisfied, (7) would imply that $\partial \Gamma_i / \partial p_i > 0$ and $\partial \Gamma_i / \partial b_i > 0$, which is not a meaningful result.

Result (10) is easy to understand intuitively. First, being cost inefficient means a high optimal price. A cost inefficient competitor improves the possibilities for charging high prices. If the cost of making cross-border transactions (h) is high, the CSD's pricing decisions are made in a less competitive environment because the issuer's decisions are determined by bondholders' home countries rather than the CSD's prices.

The most interesting finding might be the impact of netting possibilities on price competition. If almost nothing can be gained by netting ($\alpha \approx 0$), price competition is moderate. If the potential cost savings are substantial ($\alpha \gg 0$), price competition is fierce. By attracting an issuer with aggressive pricing, the CSD can easily attract another issuer, because its bondholders value the possibility to benefit from netting, should they exchange bond issues with the bondholders of the first issuer. This outcome is somewhat analogous with that of Katz and Shapiro (1986), but it differs in terms of the equilibrium price externality from the analysis of Economides and Siow (1988).

These pricing decisions imply the following market shares

$$\Gamma_i = \frac{-3\alpha + 6h - 2z_i + 2z_j}{12h - 6\alpha}. \tag{11}$$

The profits of the country i CSD can be calculated by combining (10) and (11)

$$\Pi_i = I\frac{(-3\alpha + 6h - 2z_i + 2z_j)^2}{9(2h - \alpha)}. \tag{12}$$

Because the cost of cross-border transactions is the CSD's only source of market power, it is not surprising that high costs increase the likelihood that both CSDs will earn positive profits. A high cost of gross payments (α), in contrast, intensifies price competition, making it increasingly difficult, especially for the smaller CSD, to charge prices that exceed costs.

The empirical prediction of this model is that the issuers are loss-leaders, as defined by Rochet and Tirole (2001), whereas investors are the profit-making segment for CSDs. It is surprisingly difficult to find suitable data on different sources of CSD revenue but casual observations indicate that revenue from secondary market trading has traditionally exceeded revenue from issuance.

Linking the two securities centres

Assumptions

Now, every IF can participate in the SSS of the neighbouring country via the domestic CSD and link between CSDs. The domestic CSD has an omnibus account with the foreign CSD, in which customers' securities are held. The operating costs of a transaction are borne by the CSD of the investor's home country. From the viewpoint of registration country processes, there is only one large net transaction on a particular customer account, whereas the CSD based in the investors' home country must administer thousands of small transactions on a large number of accounts.

CSD i sets three different prices.

1 a price paid by each issuer ($p_i \geq 0$);
2 a basic unit fee paid by IFs for each settlement transaction involving any security ($b_i \geq 0$);
3 an additional fee paid by IFs for each transaction with foreign securities ($r_i \geq 0$).

When trading in foreign securities, the investor can either use a domestic IF connected to the domestic CSD and the link, or he can participate via a foreign IF. If the investor uses a foreign IF, there is an extra cost, h, as in the basic model.

Events happen in the following order

- CSDs set prices for issuers (ps) and for IFs (bs and rs);
- IFs set their prices;
- Issuers choose CSDs;
- Investors choose IFs. Trades are agreed, cleared and settled.

Establishing the link is pointless unless the CSDs know that investors are going to use it. The following analysis can be restricted to cases where the link is in use. However, as we will see, investors' possibilities for using foreign IFs are not completely irrelevant when CSDs set prices.

Competition between IFs

If a cross-border transaction is processed via the link, every investor deals through one IF. Because no investor has to make a gross payment, the monetary payment between IF and investor is always zero. Consequently even the monetary payments between IF and CSD can always be netted. Interestingly, even the net payment between the two CSDs would always be zero because of complete netting at all the levels. If the CSDs offer no cross-border payment facilities, the IFs in different countries will use an existing international payment system in which payments can be netted. Hence, the cost component α vanishes. This reduced need for liquidity argues in favour of consolidation and linking in the securities settlement industry.

Equation (2) implies that the prices paid by customers in country i are

$$v_{id} = b_i + y \quad \text{and} \quad v_{if} = b_i + r_i + y \tag{13}$$

where v_{id} is the price paid by country i investors for domestic transactions and v_{if} the price paid for cross-border transactions.

Market shares

Issuer i, with $100(i/M)$ per cent of bondholders in country 2, prefers to use CSD 1 iff

$$p_1 + b_1 I\left(1 - \frac{i}{M}\right) + (b_2 + r_2) I \frac{i}{M} < p_2 + (b_1 + r_1) I\left(1 - \frac{i}{M}\right) + I \frac{i}{M} b_2$$

$$\Leftrightarrow i < M\left(\frac{Ir_1 - p_1 + p_2}{Ir_2 + Ir_2}\right)$$

The CSD's market share does not enter this expression. The network externality that prevailed in the previous version of the model no longer exists because all payments can be netted. The formulas for market shares can be derived easily from the above condition

$$\Gamma_i = \frac{Ir_i - p_i + p_j}{I(r_i + r_j)}. \tag{14}$$

Interestingly, the basic transaction fee (b_i) is irrelevant for market share. Possibly even more surprising is that high extra fees charged for cross-border transactions increase the market share because CSD 1 can make the rival CSD 2 unattractive for country 1 customers.

$$\frac{\partial \Gamma_1}{\partial r_1} = \frac{Ir_2 - p_2 + p_1}{I(r_1 + r_2)^2} > 0.$$

CSDs' profits

Now, the relative share of securities originally issued in a CSD has no direct impact on the number of secondary market transactions processed by it. Investors' home countries determine where the securities are settled irrespective of the original country of issuance.

CSD_1 can earn revenue in three different ways.

First, when securities are issued, the CSD collects fees related to securities registration and primary market transactions. This revenue equals the fee revenue from each issue (p) times the number of issuers (M) times the market share of the CSD (Γ).

$$p_1 M \Gamma_1. \tag{15}$$

Second, it earns revenue by selling services to buyers. The number of securities to be bought equals ($2I$). In expected value terms half of the buyers live in the home country of the CSD. A certain percentage of securities are registered abroad, implying that there is an extra fee revenue worth $I(1 - \Gamma_1)r_1$. Therefore the total net revenue from buyers equals

$$I(b_1 - z_1) + I(1 - \Gamma_1)r_1. \tag{16}$$

Calculating the fee revenue collected from investors that sell securities is more complicated. The country of registration covariates with original bondholders' home countries. The expected value of net revenue earned by providing services to sellers of domestically registered security i equals

$$\left(\frac{2}{M}\right) I(b_1 - z_1)\left(1 - \frac{i}{M}\right)$$

($2/M$) being the likelihood that the issue is traded, I the number of securities per issue, ($b_1 - z_1$) the net revenue per transaction and ($1 - i/M$) the relative share of bondholders living in country 1 and thus using the services of CSD 1.

As regards securities registered in the foreign country, the net revenue for selling is determined in a similar way, the difference being the extra fee, r_1

$$\left(\frac{2}{M}\right) I(b_1 + r_1 - z_1)\left(1 - \frac{i}{M}\right)$$

The number of domestically registered bond issues is $M\Gamma_1$ and the total number of issuers is M. It follows that the net income from providing services to sellers is

$$\int_0^{M\Gamma_1} \left(\frac{2}{M}\right) I(b_1 - z_1)\left(1 - \frac{i}{M}\right) di + \int_{M\Gamma_1}^M \left(\frac{2}{M}\right) I(b_1 + r_1 - z_1)\left(1 - \frac{i}{M}\right) di. \qquad (17)$$

The profit can be calculated as the sum of these three components, equations (15), (16) and (17):

$$\Pi_i = 2b_i I + \Gamma_i M p_i + 2Ir_i - 3Ir_i\Gamma_\iota + \Gamma_i^2 Ir_i - 2Iz_i. \qquad (18)$$

Prices and profits

When the expression (14) is substituted for market shares, optimal prices in the primary market are determined by the conditions

$$\frac{\partial \Pi_1}{\partial p_1} = 0, \quad \frac{\partial \Pi_2}{\partial p_2} = 0.$$

There is one combination of ps that satisfies both conditions, namely

$$p_i = I\left[\frac{-8r_ir_j + M^2(r_j^2 + 3r_ir_j + 2r_i^2) + M(r_j^2 + 5r_ir_j + 2r_i^2)}{M(3M - 2)(r_i + r_j)}\right]. \qquad (19)$$

The second order condition $(\partial^2\Pi_1/\partial p_1^2 = -2[(M-1)r_1 + Mr_2]/[I(r_1 + r_2)^2] < 0)$ is satisfied. Because $M \gg 0$, both $p_1 > 0$ and $p_2 > 0$ whenever $r_1 > 0$ or $r_2 > 0$ or both.

Differentiation of (18) yields

$$\frac{\partial \Pi_1}{\partial b_1} = 2I.0. \qquad (20)$$

It would always be optimal to charge a higher fee if pricing were not constrained. Therefore, the upper limit for this fee is determined by the condition that the total fee paid by cross-border investors cannot exceed the cost of using foreign IFs. It follows that if a CSD wants to intermediate settlement orders through the link, the highest feasible price satisfies the condition

$$b_i + r_i = b_j + h \Rightarrow b_i = b_j + h - r_i. \qquad (21)$$

Hence, both the fee paid by issuers (p_i) and the basic fee paid by investors (b_i) can be expressed as functions of r_i, b_j and h.

By substituting (21) for b_1, substituting the optimal price presented in (19) for p_1, and substituting (14) for market shares, and taking into account the assumption that $M \gg 0$, differentiation of (18) yields

$$\underset{M\to\infty}{Lim}\left[\frac{\partial\Pi_1}{\partial r_1}\right] = \underset{M\to\infty}{Lim}\ M\left[\frac{3p_2r_2 + 2Ir_1(r_1 + 2r_2)}{9(r_1 + r_2)^2}\right]. \tag{22}$$

Whenever $r_1 > 0$, $r_2 > 0$ or both, this equals $+\infty$. It follows that irrespective of rival prices, the additional fee for cross-border transactions (r_1) is the highest fee that still satisfies (21), and the optimal combination of b_1 and r_1 is

$$r_1 = h + b_2; \quad b_1 = 0. \tag{23}$$

Analogously $r_2 = h + b_1$ and $b_2 = 0$. It follows that $(r_1 = r_2 = h)$.

This outcome does not necessarily depend on the assumption of zero price elasticity of demand. The pricing decision of the CSD is constrained by the fact that domestic customers will use foreign IFs whenever the additional fee (r) is higher than investors' cost of using foreign IFs (h). If this condition is binding, it holds irrespective of whether there is a higher but finite optimal monopoly price. In real life, a CSD's fees for cross-border transactions are higher than its fees for domestic transactions (Lannoo and Levin, 2001).

Interestingly, the link does not promote integration of securities markets. In the absence of the link, the cost differential between domestic and cross-border transactions is an exogenous constant h, at least if both CSDs are equally cost efficient. Now, in the presence of the link, the difference still equals h, even though it consists of CSDs fees. This result has a clear policy implication. Even when the link has been established, governments could try to promote integration of financial markets by making it easier and cheaper for investors to use services offered by foreign IFs. This would limit CSD's possibilities for exploiting their monopoly position. Removing the causes of a high value of h would enhance integration more efficiently than pressing CSDs to establish mutual links.

When $r_1 = r_2 = h$ and $b_1 = b_2 = 0$, (19) implies that the fee paid by issuers equals

$$p_i = \frac{I(2 + M)h}{M}. \tag{24}$$

Applying (14), (18), (23) and (24) yields

$$\Pi_i = \frac{I[h(7 + 2M) - 8z_i]}{4}. \tag{25}$$

This model predicts that in the presence of the link, CSDs would charge issuers rather than investors. In the basic model issuers could make CSDs compete, whereas investors could not. If there is a link between the two CSDs, issuers no longer determine where the secondary market investors have to operate, which makes it less essential to attract them.

The empirical prediction is clear but it is surprisingly difficult to find reliable data on different sources of CSD revenue. Securities issuance is even more cyclical than secondary market trading, which would make meaningful comparisons difficult even if the data were readily available.

This outcome is somewhat analogous to a result of Laffont *et al.* (1998). They concluded that if telecommunications operators can charge additional fees for calls between nets, there can be positive network externalities between customers of the same operator, which might intensify price competition. However, because telecommunications networks are not two-sided markets, the fee burden cannot be shifted to another customer group.

Will the link be established?

Profit maximising CSDs establish the link if they can earn higher profits with than without it. The situation can be analysed by comparing the expressions for profits under the two alternative arrangements (12) and (25). CSD i would prefer to establish the link if

$$\frac{I(-3\alpha + 6h - 2z_i + 2z_j)^2}{9(2h-\alpha)} < \frac{I[h(7+2M) - 8z_i]}{4}. \tag{26}$$

If $z_1 = z_2 = z$, either both or neither of the CSDs will prefer to establish the link. Thus (26) can be rewritten as

$$M > \frac{1}{2} + \frac{4z - 2\alpha}{h}. \tag{27}$$

If there are no operating costs ($z = 0$), the CSDs always prefer to establish the link. Non-linked CSDs can pass this cost burden to investors, whereas linked CSDs cannot. Whether coincidental or not, ICT has improved SSS's efficiency while at the same time links between CSDs have become more commonplace. A large number of issuers (M) makes it more certain that the CSDs will want to establish the link because issuers become the profit-making sector, and if there is a large number of them, opening the link is a lucrative strategy. High costs of gross payments (α) encourage CSDs to establish the link; these costs intensify price competition in the absence of the link.

From the viewpoint of social welfare, the link is particularly useful if using foreign IFs is expensive for investors ($h \gg 0$). By opening the link, the two CSDs can transform investors' costs of making cross-border transactions into fee revenue. In this sense their incentives are 'correct'; they want to establish the link when the costs that can be avoided by using it are high.

Regulation of cross-border fees

Assumptions
The EU has issued a regulation saying that fees for cross-border retail payments are not to differ from those for domestic transactions. This section presents an analysis of the possible impact of a comparable regulation on SSSs. CSDs are obliged to form a link and not to charge additional fees for cross-border transactions ($r = 0$).

Investors trading in foreign securities can use domestic IFs and the link, or they can use foreign IFs. Exactly as in the previous sections, they incur a fixed cost (h) if they use foreign IFs. If issuers are indifferent between the two CSDs, they randomise between them. If there is no Nash equilibrium in the Bertrand game between CSDs, they end up in an undercut-proof equilibrium, as defined by Shy (2002).

The undercut-proof equilibrium

The situation presented in this section is highly analogous to the one presented by Shy (2002). Shy assumes two Bertrand competing firms. Every consumer has an established relationship with one of the two companies. Buying from the competitor would cause switching costs. Each consumer buys one unit of good. It turns out that there is no Nash equilibrium in pure strategies. The optimal price for each firm is that charged by the competitor plus the switching cost. It is obviously impossible to find any equilibrium where both companies would charge more than the competitor. A firm could also undercut by pricing low enough to get all the customers. The firm whose price is undercut would find it profitable to charge a fee that exceeds the price of the rival by the transaction cost. Firms might eventually end up in an undercut-proof equilibrium; both firms charge the highest price that the rival cannot profitably undercut, if the alternative is to charge the price that prevails in the undercut-proof equilibrium. This equilibrium is not a Nash equilibrium.

When $r_1 = r_2 = r$, (19) reduces to $p_i = I(2 + M)r/M$. When there are no additional fees for cross-border services ($r = 0$), the optimal fee to be paid by issuers equals zero. The CSDs end up in Bertrand competition with identical services and zero marginal costs, and the price (p) converges to zero. Therefore issuers randomise between the two CSDs, and there will be no correlation between country of registration of a security and investors' home country.

Because issuers pay no fees, and because there are no fees for cross-border transactions, both CSDs are completely dependent on the basic fees paid by domestic investors. The expression for profits reduces to

$$\Pi_i = 2I(b_i - z_i). \tag{28}$$

According to this expression it is always profitable to increase the price $(d\Pi_i/db_i > 0)$. However, investors have the option to use foreign IFs. The highest price the CSD i can charge and still get the transactions of domestic customers is

$$b_i = b_j + h - \epsilon \tag{29}$$

where ϵ is an arbitrarily small positive constant. The profit would equal $2I(b_j + h - z_i)$.

All payments can be netted, there are no costs related to gross payments, and the cost component α vanishes.

A CSD can also capture all the customers by undercutting. The highest price the CSD can charge and get all the customers is

$$b_i = b_j - h - \epsilon. \tag{30}$$

With this price CSD i would also get all the issuers because the undercutting CSD would be a cheaper alternative for all the investors. The expected value of its profit is

$$4I(b_j - h - \epsilon - z_i). \tag{31}$$

Undercutting, i.e. charging price (30) instead of price (29), is profitable for CSD i iff

$$4I(b_j - h - \epsilon - z_i) > 2I(b_j + h - z_i) \Leftrightarrow b_j > 3h + 2z_i + \epsilon. \tag{32}$$

With sufficiently high rival prices (b_j), (32) implies that it becomes profitable to undercut. When firms decide the basic fees (bs), the situation is analogous to Shy's model, and there is no Nash equilibrium in pure strategies.

If a customer living in country 2 deals with foreign securities, the cost of a transaction via a domestic IF and domestic CSD 2 equals $b_2 + y$. If the customer uses foreign IFs, the cost equals $b_1 + y + h$. If CSD 1 undercuts, the price (b_1') will satisfy the condition $b_2 + y - \epsilon = b_1' + y + h \Rightarrow b_1' = b_2 - h - \epsilon$, where b_1' is the price CSD 1 uses for undercutting if it decides to undercut.

The highest price that can be used for profitable undercutting (b_1') satisfies the condition

$$2I(b_1 - z_1) + \epsilon = 4I(b_1' z_1) \text{ and analagously } 2I(b_2 - z_2) + \epsilon = 4I(b_2' z_2).$$

Combining these conditions with (32) and letting $\epsilon = 0$ yields

$$b_1 = \frac{6h + z_1 + 2z_2}{3} \quad b_2 = \frac{6h + z_2 + 2z_1}{3}$$

$$b_1' = \frac{3h + z_1 + 2z_2}{3} \quad b_2' = \frac{3h + z_2 + 2z_1}{3}.$$

If there is no link between the CSDs, the cost of cross-border transactions for investors living in country 2 is determined by (5), (7) and (10) and the extra cost h:

$$h + v_1 = a\Gamma_2/2 + (-3\alpha + 6h + 4z_1 + 2z_2)/6 + y + h$$
$$= -(1 - \Gamma_2)\alpha/2 + (6h + z_2 + 2z_1)/3.$$

This is less than the transaction fee charged by CSD 2 (b_2) in the undercut-proof equilibrium. Hence, in the undercut-proof equilibrium, the fee for transactions is higher than the total cost of cross-border transactions that prevails without a link. Thus the regulation does not make it cheaper to trade in foreign securities. Instead, it becomes more expensive to process transactions with domestic bonds.

In the basic model the two CSDs had to compete for issuers by being attractive locations for investors. In the east where CSDs competed for issuers even more directly, the country of registration is no longer relevant to the costs for investors in the secondary market. Hence the main source of competitive pressure has been largely eliminated. It is not surprising that the average price for settlement services increases.

Somewhat similar results have been presented in the earlier literature. Banning price differentials between domestic and export prices may enhance tacit collusion between oligopolistic firms (see Martin, 2001: 203–4). If competing telecommunication operators are not allowed to charge different prices for calls between nets, they might increase the price for all the calls (Laffont *et al.* 1998).

Conclusions

Summary of the main results

This chapter has presented an oligopoly model on the securities settlement industry. The main focus has been on competition between two national CSDs, and the impact of a securities link on this competition.

It was assumed that the need for securities settlement services is exogenous. Each CSD runs both a book-entry register and a settlement system. Secondary market transactions must be settled in the system in which the security was issued. It follows that CSDs compete fiercely for issuers in the primary market because issuers' choices determine market shares. Consequently, CSDs collect all the revenue from IFs and investors, while issuers get services for nothing.

We analysed a situation where the two CSDs are linked. Investors can settle transactions with foreign securities via either domestic IFs and the domestic CSD, or they can use services offered by foreign IFs. Transactions do not have to be settled in the CSD chosen by the issuer, and it is no longer essential for CSDs to attract as many issuers as possible. Consequently, issuers become the profit-making segment, whereas investors can get domestic services free of charge and cross-border services at reasonable prices.

We also analysed what might happen if the CSDs of the two countries are obliged to establish the link and not to charge fees beyond the basic fee for domestic transactions for cross-border transactions through it. It may be unclear how the CSDs would price secondary market settlement orders but they might simply increase the price for all the transactions to a level that is higher than the costs of cross-border transactions in the absence of a link.

This chapter has one major policy implication. If policy makers want to enhance integration of financial markets, they must concentrate on eliminating the fundamental causes of obstacles to cross-border settlement. Encouraging the private sector to develop new ways to bypass barriers that remain basically unchanged may be much less useful. It is always possible that access to a detour is controlled by an institution with monopoly power. The institution could easily benefit from its monopoly position and capture all the benefits from the detour.

Concluding remarks and suggestions for further research

In real life many securities market infrastructure institutions are joint-venture undertakings of financial institutions. If the two CSDs maximised the sum of their own profits and the profits of the shareholder IFs, it might be possible that almost nothing would change. IFs' pure profits in their own operations are zero in any case, and it would be in their common interest to instruct the CSD to maximise its own profits (see Park and Ahn (1999) for a detailed analysis of jointly owned upstream suppliers).

Because this chapter contains pioneering work, much of the required analysis remains to be done. In the following, a few possible extensions are briefly mentioned.

Taking the price elasticity of demand into account would improve the possibility of analysing consumer surplus and issuer profits. Price elasticities could be highly important determinants of platform industries' pricing (Rochet and Tirole, 2001). Fortunately, the intuition behind the results is not greatly affected by the absence of price elasticity.

In real life there are many kinds of ownership connections and co-operative agreements between securities market institutions. The analysis could be expanded by taking into account several alternative structures. The settlement system and the book-entry register are often operated by different institutions. Moreover, the market place could also be explicitly modelled. In many cases stock exchanges operate their own settlement systems. One might also include international SSSs.

The impact of institutional problems that issuers might face in issuing securities in a foreign system could also be modelled. In the case of equities, there are largely unresolved legal problems.

And, last but not least, there are many more than two CSDs in the real world. Fortunately the intuition behind the main results is not dependent on the assumption of two CSDs. For instance, investors must use the CSD chosen by issuers irrespective of the number of CSDs. Establishing the link would weaken this effect, making it possible and necessary to compete for investors, irrespective of the number of CSDs.

Notes

1 Thanks are due to Juha Tarkka, Tuomas Takalo, Esa Jokivuolle, Kari Korhonen, Daniela Russo and seminar participants at the Bank of Finland research department for several insightful comments.
2 This is a satisfactory approximation for many gross settlement systems. In a typical gross settlement system no settlement counterparty is obliged to make all the outgoing payments during a day before receiving any incoming payments. Instead, automatic chaining procedures applied in many systems guarantee that incoming payments can be used efficiently as a source of funding for outgoing payments.

References

Barclay, M.J., Kandel, E. and Marx, L. (1998) 'The effects of transaction costs on stock prices and trading volume', *Journal of Financial Intermediation* 7: 130–50.
Di Noia, C. (1999) 'The stock-exchange industry: network effects, implicit mergers and corporate governance', Commissione Nazionale per le societa e la Borsa, Studi di Ricerche, Rome, p. 33.
Economides, N. and Siow, A. (1988) 'The division of markets is limited by the extent of liquidity', *American Economic Review* 78: 108–21.
Giovannini Group (2001) 'Cross-Border Clearing and Settlement Arrangements in the European Union', Brussels, November.
Katz, M.L. and Shapiro, C. (1986) 'Product compatibility in a market with technological progress', *Oxford Economic Papers* 38 (supplement): 146–65.
Laffont, J.-J., Rey, P. and Tirole, J. (1998) 'Network competition II. Price discrimination', *Rand Journal of Economics* 29: 38–56.
Lannoo, K. and Levin, M. (2001) 'The securities settlement industry in the EU', Centre for European Policy Studies Research Report, Brussels.
Martin, S. (2001) *Industrial Organization, a European Perspective*, Oxford: Oxford University Press.
Park, Y.-S. and Ahn, B.H. (1999) 'Joint ownership and interconnection pricing in network industries', *International Journal of Economics and Finance* 8: 183–98.

Rochet, J.-C. and Tirole, J. (2001) 'Platform competition in two-sided markets', Institut d'économie industrielle working papers, Université de Toulouse I.

Shy, O. (2002) 'A quick and easy method for estimating switching costs', *International Journal of Industrial Organization* 20: 71–87.

Shy, O. and Tarkka, J. (2001) 'Stock exchange alliances, access fees and competition', Bank of Finland Discussion Paper, no. 22/2001.

COMMENT

Evan Kraft

Karlo Kauko's chapter represents a brave foray into the unfamiliar (to many economists) world of securities settlement and the analytical relatively intractable and poorly understood world of network externalities. Since the chapter is rather abstract, I would like to attempt to put it into a bit of a broader perspective, and to reinforce a few caveats the author himself makes about the generality of the results and the policy implications.

To begin with the context. The question of cross-border securities settlement is closely linked to the formation of a single European financial market. Hartmann *et al.* (2003) offer a useful definition of financial integration. They argue that an economic area is financially integrated 'if there are no barriers that discriminate economic agents in their access to and investment of funds in that area, on the basis of their location'. They go on to suggest that, if such conditions are met, 'financial instruments with the same cash flows will command the same price and ... there should be no systematic differences in the portfolio allocations and sources of funding of economic agents within the area, after controlling for their individual characteristics' (2000: 17).

Clearly, widely varying costs of settlement due to the existence of incompatible national clearing systems or higher fees for cross-border settlements than domestic settlement would violate these conditions. Unfortunately, this is the prevailing situation in Europe. Costs of settlement are not easy to calculate, since they vary by the size and other characteristics of a transaction. Nonetheless, both the Giovannini reports (Giovannini Group, 2001, 2003) and Lanoo and Levin (2001) point to vastly higher costs of cross-border settlement as an important obstacle to European financial integration. And the 2001 Giovannini report suggests that fees are grossly out of line with costs (Giovannini Group, 2001: 66). Furthermore, settlement costs in Europe seem to be substantially higher than in the US, where the existence of a single securities clearing and depository system provides lower costs via its ability to net the vast majority of transactions.

High settlement costs would seem to be a brake on the development of pan-European securities markets, creating the very discrimination that Hartmann *et al.* (2003) warn about. In addition, high settlement costs would limit the liquidity of bond and equity markets. Certainly, there are plenty of other barriers to cross-border securities trading: differences in legal and accounting systems across EU countries that may make investors reluctant to purchase foreign securities, inadequate information about developments in foreign markets and the like. Still, decreasing or eliminating differences in settlement costs ought to make a difference.

How does cross-border settlement actually take place? There are three solutions at play: the first, involves bilateral links between CSDs in two different countries. The second involves investment banks (global custodians) that hold a broad range of securities for their clients, and often can settle trades on their own books. Just three banks, BNP Paribas, HSBC and Citigroup, represented 80 per cent of European securities settlement volumes as of 2003. The third involves International CSDs who provide indirect access to CSDs in about 120 countries. After a series of mergers, Eurostream, Clearstream and SIS-Sega are the ICSDs remaining on the European market.

Kauko models the interaction of two national CSDs. In his model, when the CSDs operate each in their own market and there is no link between them, the CSDs collect all the revenue from the investment service companies and issuers. With the link, the issuers actually become profitable, and investors get domestic services free of charge and pay a 'reasonable' fee for cross-border services. Finally, if financial integration were mandated, and CSDs were forced to link without charging any fees for cross-border transactions, prices rise on both the domestic and cross-border transactions to levels above the levels with a link but with a price differential allowed for cross-border transactions.

Thus, Kauko's analysis suggests it would not be wise to try to achieve financial integration by fiat. But one must emphasise the caveats. First, it is not clear that Kauko has modelled all three trading modalities in a general way. How would the global custodian modality, for example, fit into Kauko's model? To what extent can global custodians substitute for transactions between national CSDs or for the services of ICSDs? What would the pricing issues be in competition between global custodians and ICSDs? (For example, Hirata de Carvalho, 2004 raises this issue.)

Second, and perhaps even more important, Kauko has assumed away liquidity effects. To his credit he acknowledges this, and he acknowledges that this may invalidate the whole welfare analysis. From the pioneering analysis of Katz and Shapiro (1985), it is well-known that consumption externalities give rise to demand-side economies of scale. Guiborg (2001) argues that interoperability and the use of common standards is a crucial variable in the exploitation of network externalities in electronic payments systems. She also provides empirical evidence for this argument. Kauko's model, despite its ingenuity, really does not make room for such effects, and thus may miss the most important aspect of the problem.

Third, there may be an interesting extension involving cases where the two CSDs are of very different sizes. One of Katz and Shapiro's findings is that, in network industries where there are only two players, one large and the other small, market failure may occur. The large player may not want compatibility, because it would allow free riding, and the small firm may want it 'too much'. Given the relative size of Finland and some of the large EU states, this might be a particularly relevant case for researchers from the Bank of Finland to consider.

In the end, it is appropriate to note that, despite these caveats, Kauko's chapter is an important, rigorous analytical contribution to a very poorly understood area. I certainly hope that he will continue with such work in the future.

References

Giovannini Group (2001) 'Cross-border clearing and settlement arrangements in the European Union', Brussels, November, available online at europe.eu.int/economy_finance/publications/giovannini/clearing1101_en.pdf.

Giovannini Group (2003) 'Second report on EU clearing and settlement arrangements', available online at europe.eu.int/economy_finance/publications/giovannini/clearing_ settlement_arrangements140403.pdf.

Guiborg, G. (2001) 'Interoperability and network externalities in electronic payments', Sveriges Riskbank Working Paper Series, no. 126, September.

Hartman, P., Maddaloni, A. and Manganelli, S. (2003) 'The euro area financial system; structure, integration and policy initiatives', ECB Working Paper, no. 230.

Hirata de Carvalho, C. (2004) 'Cross-border securities clearing and settlement infrastructure in the European Union as prerequisite to financial markets integration: challenges and perspectives', HWWA Discussion Paper, no. 287.

Katz, M. and Shapiro, C. (1985) 'Network externalities, competition and compatibility', *American Economic Review* 75(3), 424–40.

Lanoo, K. and Levin, M. (2001) 'The securities settlement industries in the EU: structure, costs and the way forward', CEPS Research Report, Brussels.

Index

For Product Safety Concerns and Information please contact our
EU representative GPSR@taylorandfrancis.com Taylor & Francis
Verlag GmbH, Kaufingerstraße 24, 80331 München, Germany